Software Development in C:
A Practical Approach to
Programming and Design

David Conger

Prentice
Hall

Upper Saddle River, New Jersey
Columbus, Ohio

Editor in Chief: Stephen Helba
Assistant Vice President and Publisher: Charles E. Stewart, Jr.
Production Editor: Alexandrina Benedicto Wolf
Production Coordination: Custom Editorial Productions, Inc.
Design Coordinator: Diane Ernsberger
Cover Designer: Jeff Vanik
Cover image: Corbis Stock Market
Production Manager: Matthew Ottenweller
Marketing Manager: Adam Kloza

This book was set in Times Roman and Helvetica by Custom Editorial Productions, Inc. It was printed and bound by The Banta Company. The cover was printed by The Lehigh Press, Inc.

Pearson Education Ltd.
Pearson Education Australia Pty. Limited
Pearson Education Singapore Pte. Ltd.
Pearson Education North Asia Ltd.
Pearson Education Canada, Ltd.
Pearson Educación de Mexico, S.A. de C.V.
Pearson Education—Japan
Pearson Education Malaysia Pte. Ltd.
Pearson Education, *Upper Saddle River, New Jersey*

10 9 8 7 6 5 4 3 2 1
ISBN: 0-13-370172-7

**This book is dedicated to my wife, Susannah.
Eighteen years together is just the beginning.**

Preface

Software Development

There are many tools and skills needed to truly master the art of software development. When it was invented, C was a major step forward in the evolution of programming languages. To this day, it remains a powerful and popular tool for developing professional software. One of the best things that developers can do for their careers is to learn the C programming language.

This is true even with the advent of other languages such as C++ and Java. Both of these languages are based on C. A master programmer will likely need a reasonable proficiency in at least two of these popular languages. A familiarity with C is a tremendous aid in understanding the subtleties of C++ and Java.

However, having professional programming skills requires more than just familiarity with programming languages. We, as developers, must also know how to design software, how to test it, and how to fix it. Having these skills makes the difference between entry-level programmers and development team leaders.

Target Audience

If you are seeking to develop practical design and development skills using C, then this book is for you. It doesn't matter whether you're a student learning programming for the first time, a self-taught guru seeking C skills, or someone with a degree in Computer Science. The combination of C, design techniques, and hands-on experiences will make reading this book worthwhile.

Text Organization and Structure

In addition to C language skills, this book teaches top-down design skills. It also introduces debugging aids and demonstrates techniques for programming robust software. Because it is more than just a book on the C language, it is suited to readers pursuing professional programming careers.

Unlike other books, which present only small example programs, this book demonstrates the process of developing a completely working software system. Creating such a system is more than just writing code. It also involves the ability to organize that code into a form that is extensible, flexible, and maintainable. As you read this book and do the exercises, you'll design and develop a working text editor. In the process, you'll get hands-on experience in the essentials of how to design software, and learn how to implement the design. You'll see how C source code is arranged in files and why.

So that you can get the maximum value from the Hands-On Example programs, they all follow a common format: Objective, Experiment, Results, and Analysis. First, an experiment with a definite goal or set of goals is undertaken. This usually takes the form of writing some code to see what happens. We examine the output of the experiment for the results. Lastly, the experiment and results are analyzed to see what can be deduced about the C language, as well as designing and developing software in C.

Most of the examples are written in ANSI C. Therefore, you should be able to use them on nearly any computer that has an ANSI-compatible C compiler. The specific hardware and compiler you use should not make a difference.

Versions of the Gnu C/C++ compiler for the Microsoft Windows and Linux operating systems are found on the CD-ROM packaged with the text. Both versions run on IBM-compatible PCs. You'll find installation instructions in Appendix A.

Also, you'll find source codes for the text editor on the other CD. The text editor is designed to focus on C programming and avoid the complexities associated with programming under Windows or XWindows. Therefore, the Windows version of the text editor is a Windows console application. Likewise, the Linux version does not use XWindows.

In addition to an ANSI-compatible C compiler, you'll need a text editor in which to write your programs. It's also a good idea to obtain a debugger program. This will save you many hours of effort.

If you take the time to work through this book and gain as much hands-on experience as you can, you will go into professional programming situations already familiar with the process of developing software.

Chapter Overview

Chapters 1 and 2 discuss the evolution of the C programming language and demonstrate the most fundamental C programming concepts. Chapters 3 and 4 introduce the data types that are built into the C programming language. Chapters 5 through 9 provide a detailed examination of the essential C operators and control statements. A thorough discussion of arrays is presented in Chapters 10 and 11. The first eleven chapters of this book create a foundation of procedural programming for the student. We'll use this foundational knowledge to build the skills needed for designing robust and flexible software.

Chapter 12 presents the essentials of user input and output (I/O), as well as the basics of string handling. In Chapter 13, we examine basic design techniques as we build program components using functions. Chapters 14 and 15 expand that design knowledge into data and data types. These chapters help students to structure their programs around their data, keeping their data in a valid state at all times.

Chapters 16 and 17 extend the discussion of C program design. They examine the C preprocessor and how it can be used to organize programs. By this point, the reader has gone from designing individual program pieces (functions) and data types to designing program modules and entire programs.

The remaining chapters demonstrate some of the more powerful aspects of the C programming language and how they can be applied to common programming techniques. They also show how to use them in a robust way to design and implement the text editor.

Most of the chapters in this book contain extensive source code examples. Each line in the source code is numbered. Be aware, however, that you should not type in the line numbers when you type in these programs. Your C compiler will give you an error if you do.

There are 25 problems to solve in the Exercises section, found at the end of most chapters. Exercises 21–25 are provided for those majoring in building hardware or writing firmware. They enable the reader to use the C programming language to solve physics and math problems. In addition, they offer an opportunity to create data structures in C. Each data structure is a method of organizing information in a program.

The final chapter provides a look at the three most popular programming languages derived from C. They are C++, C# (pronounced "C sharp"), and Java.

Acknowledgments

I would like to thank the following reviewers for their useful comments and suggestions: Michaele Duncan, University of Southern Mississippi; Mohamad Haj-Mohamadi, North Carolina A&T State University; Eric Harrison, University of Southern Mississippi;

Bandula Jayatilaka, University of Houston; Dan Matthews, Tri-State University; Keith Quigley, Midlands Technical College; Philip Realbuto, Trident Technical College; and Anthony Zhou, DeVry Institute of Technology.

About the Author

David Conger, formerly a Professor of Computer Science and Business Computer Programming at the Albuquerque Technical-Vocational Institute, has developed software for a wide range of applications. These applications include military aircraft, games, a variety of specialized business applications, and programs for interactive TV. He currently produces custom software and technical documentation. His clients include Microsoft Corporation, for whom he has written developer documentation for the Windows Platform Software Development Kit (PSDK). The Windows subsystems he documented, in whole or in part, include DirectX, OpenGL, Extensible Scene Graph (XSG), Image Color Management (ICM), Still Image (STI), Windows Image Acquisition (WIA), Remote Procedure Calls (RPC), the Microsoft Interface Definition Language (MIDL) compiler, and the Mobile Internet Toolkit (MIT).

Contents

CHAPTER 12   USER I/O, STRINGS, AND STRING FUNCTIONS   182

CHAPTER 13   STRUCTURED DESIGN WITH FUNCTIONS   200

CHAPTER 14   PROGRAMMER-DEFINED DATA TYPES   230

CHAPTER 15   DESIGNING DATA TYPES   252

CHAPTER 16   PREPROCESSOR DIRECTIVES   264

CHAPTER 17   ORGANIZING PROGRAMS   284

CHAPTER 18   POINTERS   294

CHAPTER 19   DYNAMIC MEMORY ALLOCATION   346

CHAPTER 20   ENCAPSULATING DATA   374

CHAPTER 21   FILE INPUT AND OUTPUT   392

CHAPTER 22   FIDDLING WITH BITS   428

CHAPTER 23   DESIGNING THE TEXT EDITOR   448

1

A Brief History of C

OBJECTIVES

After reading this chapter, you should be able to:

- Explain the evolution of computer languages from binary to function oriented languages.

- Identify and explain the advantages of C.

- Identify and explain the disadvantages of C.

OUTLINE

PREVIEW

Like most computer languages, C evolved. It is the result of much thought and deliberation. Many talented people have had a hand in its creation. Knowing a bit about the history of the C language helps us understand its purpose. It also explains how C developed into the form that we know today.

1.1 Beginning with Binary

All data and programs that are entered into a computer are ultimately represented as **binary numbers**. Binary numbers are numbers in base 2. They are sequences of zeros and ones. For a detailed discussion of binary numbers, please see Appendix D.

When computers filled entire floors of buildings, almost all data was entered into them using switches. People flipped switches to input an instruction. They would then flip another switch to tell the computer they were going to input the next instruction. Each instruction would be entered into the computer in this manner. Eventually, even people who really enjoyed flipping switches decided that there had to be a better way.

1.2 Improving Things with Assembler

As time passed, some very perceptive people realized that we could write computer programs in a form more readable to humans. The computer could translate the programs into binary numbers. The first of these languages was called **Assembly Language**, or **Assembler**.

Assembly Language uses instructions that are abbreviations of actual words. For instance, MOV instructs the computer to move a value from one location in memory to another. ADD means add, INC means increment, and so on. When programming in Assembler, sequences of Assembly Language instructions are stored in files. A program called an assembler is used to translate the Assembly Language instructions into binary. Unless this translation is done, the program cannot be executed since the only "language" that computers understand is binary.

Assembly Language was easier than binary for people to read and write. It also enabled programmers to write portions of programs that could be reused. These chunks of program code were called **subroutines**. A program could jump to a subroutine, execute it, and come back to where it left off. Well-written subroutines could be used in many programs.

1.3 Function Oriented Languages

Over time, programs became larger and more complex. Repeatedly writing them from scratch was costly. Languages needed greater structure to simplify the task of organizing programs. They also needed to expand upon the utility of subroutines so that more and larger portions of programs could be reused.

The result of these trends was what we now call function oriented languages. Subroutines were expanded into **functions** and **procedures**. Functions and procedures are subroutines with formal parameter lists and return values. A parameter list is a way of getting information into a function. A return value is a way of getting information out of a function. The C programming language uses functions. These are discussed in detail in Chapter 13.

With functions and procedures, programmers could build libraries of program code. Rather than rewrite entire programs from scratch, successful software developers began to reuse existing functions and procedures.

The advent of functions and procedures spawned the development of a host of new programming languages. Hundreds, if not thousands, of programming languages were invented over the years to meet a variety of needs. Most of them are no longer used. Today we primarily use variations on a group of about 2 dozen computer languages. In fact, these days most programs are written either in Assembler, Basic, Pascal, Cobol, Fortran, C, C++, or Java. Other languages are in use (some of them are great to use, others are a nightmare); however, these few are the dominant ones.

1.4 C

The C programming language was invented by Brian Kernigan, Dennis Ritchie, and some of their colleagues at Bell Labs in the 1970's. Many of computing's great milestones came from this group at Bell Labs. C was based primarily on two programming languages: BCPL, invented by Dennis Ritchie, and B, developed by Brian Kernigan.

Together, Kernigan and Ritchie wrote *The C Programming Language*. This book defined the C standard for many years. Compilers that are compatible with the standard defined by this book are said to be compatible with K&R C.

In 1982, the American National Standards Institute (ANSI) created a subcommittee which defined the standard for the C programming language. The standard was formally adopted in 1989 with the name American National Standard X3.159-1989. Compilers that are compatible with this document are said to be compatible with ANSI C.

The inventors of C designed it to be as flexible and as powerful as Assembler, but more readable. For the most part, they achieved that goal. As a result, C became the favorite development language of many programmers. Even though other languages such as C++ and Java have replaced C in many development tasks, C remains a very popular language.

1.4.1 Advantages Of C

The following are the primary advantages of C:

- *C is an extremely efficient language.* C is powerful enough to be used to implement high-speed, hardware-intensive applications. Most versions of the Unix operating system are written in C. Many languages, such as Pascal or Cobol, can't access hardware devices directly (or they can't directly access it very easily). With C, you can program directly to the hardware in a straightforward manner.
- *C programs tend to be fast.* Usually, only Assembly Language programs are faster.
- *C stays out of the way.* The C language doesn't prevent you from doing things that are extremely unusual if you need to.
- *C can be portable.* Even though C provides many facilities for accessing hardware directly, it is an extremely portable language. A program is portable if it can be easily rewritten for different types of computers or different operating systems. C programs can be moved from computer to computer much more easily than programs in most other languages.

- *C is programmer-oriented.* C was written by programmers for programmers. Other languages were written for other groups or people. For example, Cobol was written for business people. Basic and Pascal originally were written primarily as teaching tools for students.

1.4.2   Disadvantages Of C

C does have some disadvantages as well. Some of these are:

- *C does not force programmers to structure their programs well.* In some languages, such as Pascal, it is much more difficult to write unstructured programs than in C. Structured programs are easier to read and maintain.
- *C can get cryptic.* In the past, programmers would often produce extremely efficient, but nearly unreadable, programs. With today's optimizing compilers, it is no longer necessary to write programs that are cryptic just to gain efficiency.
- *C is not strongly typed.* Unlike languages such as Pascal, C's data types are not strongly enforced. When writing programs, you can change from one type to another very fluidly. C was based on the idea that you as a programmer know what you're doing. This can be a very dangerous assumption. You are given enough rope in C to do pretty much whatever you want—even if this means you can hang yourself with great speed and efficiency.

1.5   A Word About C++

As time passed and programs continued to become more complex, programmers began to see the limitations of function oriented languages. One of the biggest drawbacks is that function oriented languages do not make it easy to structure programs the way the data is structured. Function oriented languages tend to be structured around actions that are performed on data.

In addition, function oriented languages don't force programmers to encapsulate or hide data. If the access to data is not strictly controlled, it is easy for data to become corrupted. When working on large projects with hundreds or even thousands of programmers, it is common for someone on the project to accidentally write a piece of a program that will alter data when it shouldn't.

Because function oriented languages often result in data that is less structured and exposed to all parts of a program, they often contain errors that are difficult to find.

Eventually the idea of **software objects** was born. A software object is a way of structuring software to encapsulate data. A software object also defines the operations that can be performed on the data. Objects can define those operations in a consistent way. Usually, they can easily be used as the building blocks of other objects.

The C++ programming language is an expression of C in object oriented forms. C was extended by Bjarne Stroustrup at Bell Labs into an object oriented language. Eventually, a committee from the American National Standards Institute (ANSI) took over the job of defining the standard for the C++ language.

The C++ language retains the power and flexibility of C. In addition, it adds the extensibility and reusability of object oriented programming. However, the added overhead of objects can result in programs that take slightly more memory than C programs. They also may execute more slowly.

Today, there is a wide market for both C and C++ programmers. Because C programs tend to be more efficient than C++ programs, C programmers tend to end up in more hardware-related jobs than C++ programmers. Most programs for end users are written in C++. However, most hardware drivers are still written in C.

TECHNICAL NOTE 1.2
A hardware driver is a piece of software that is shipped with computer hardware. The driver accesses the hardware directly and communicates with the operating system in a standard way. For example, every scanner ships with a hardware driver. To the computer's operating system, all scanner hardware drivers look very much the same. They all operate in a similar manner, even on widely different types of scanners.

SUMMARY

Computer programming has evolved over the years. It started with binary and progressed to function oriented languages like C. The C programming language offers many advantages for programmers. However, it is written with the assumption that programmers know what they're doing when they write the program. Therefore, it will not catch some of the programming mistakes that other languages would flag as an error.

TECHNICAL NOTES

1.1 Binary numbers are numbers in base 2. They are sequences of the digits 0 and 1.

1.2 A hardware driver is a piece of software that is shipped with computer hardware. The driver accesses the hardware directly and communicates with the operating system in a standard way. For example, every scanner ships with a hardware driver. To the computer's operating system, all scanner hardware drivers look very much the same. They all operate in a similar manner, even on widely different types of scanners.

REVIEW QUESTIONS

1. What "language" do computers understand?
2. In what way was Assembly Language an improvement over previous programming techniques?
3. What is a subroutine?
4. What are the advantages of using subroutines in a program?
5. What is a procedure?
6. What is a function?
7. How are functions and procedures different from Assembly Language subroutines?
8. What is the basic, underlying assumption of the C language?
9. What are some of the advantages of C?
10. What are some of the disadvantages of C?

EXERCISES

1. Explain why we don't program in binary today.
2. Give at least three reasons that using procedures and functions in a program might be helpful.
3. Name at least 5 computer publications that are dedicated to C programming or software design. You'll find this information at your local library or bookstore. You can also find it on the Internet.
4. Give at least three reasons why you think learning C might help you in your career.
5. Fill in the blanks.

   The C programming language was invented by _____ and _____, with contributions by some of their colleagues at Bell Labs.

6. Indicate which of the following are true.
   a. Humans cannot understand binary computer instructions.
   b. Subroutines provide programmers with reusable sections of program code.
   c. Procedures and functions are the same as subroutines.
   d. Now that C++ has been invented, there is no reason to learn C.

7. Fill in the blanks.

   _____ Language was invented because programming computers in binary was difficult and tedious. It uses a program called an _____ to translate instructions into binary.

8. Fill in the blanks.

   The C programming language is one of the most flexible and efficient languages ever invented. It generally results in faster programs than object oriented languages such as _____. However, it usually does not result in program code that is faster than _____ Language.

9. One of the underlying assumptions of the C programming language is that you know what you're doing when you write a program. Explain why this can be a problem for programmers who are new to the C language.

10. In the past, C programmers sometimes have had a reputation for producing code that is extremely fast and efficient but nearly unreadable to humans. Explain why this tendency might be a problem for companies that use and maintain large programs for many years.

11. The C language is said to be more programmer-oriented than other computer languages. Explain why this orientation might influence the popularity of C.

12. Cobol was created to enable business people to learn business programming tasks quickly. Basic and Pascal were invented primarily for teaching students to program. Compare the purposes of these languages with the purposes of C. Specifically, describe why you do or do not think that C might be more suitable than these languages for the types of jobs which graduates in technology majors seek.

13. Unlike many other computer languages, the C programming language enables programmers to access computer hardware directly without the aid of an operating system. Explain why this might be a problem. Explain why this might be a great advantage.

14. Describe the concept of program portability. Explain why the portability of C programs can be an advantage.

Exercises 15 through 20 require you to read Appendix D, which covers binary, decimal, and hexadecimal numbers.

15. Convert the binary number 10100101 to decimal and hexadecimal.
16. Convert the hexadecimal number 10 to binary and decimal.
17. Convert the decimal number 256 to binary and hexadecimal.

18. Convert the binary number 100011000 to hexadecimal and decimal.

19. Convert the hexadecimal number AE4F5 to binary and decimal.

20. Convert the decimal number 65,536 to binary and hexadecimal.

GLOSSARY

Assembler, Assembly Language An early programming language that used abbreviations of words as program instructions.

Binary Number A number in base 2.

Function A procedure that returns a value. It therefore has a declared return type.

Procedure A named subroutine with a declared parameter list. Each parameter in the parameter list must have a declared type.

Software Object A module of code that encapsulates data and the operations that can be performed on it. Software objects also support inheritance and polymorphism.

Subroutine A reusable block of source code that a program can jump to, execute, and return from.

2

A First Look at C Programming

OBJECTIVES

After reading this chapter, you should be able to:

- Explain the process of writing, compiling, and linking a computer program.
- Type the programs in this chapter into a text editor or an integrated development environment (IDE).
- Compile, link, and run the programs in this chapter.
- Use the `printf()` function for output.
- Use the `scanf()` function for input.
- Identify and explain the most essential parts of a C program.

OUTLINE

PREVIEW

This chapter presents the most fundamental aspects of developing computer programs. It also demonstrates how basic input and output is done in C.

Be aware that this chapter is intended to be an overview. Therefore, it presents many essential software development concepts but explains only the basics of them. You should not worry if some of the concepts presented in this chapter are not clear. All of the ideas and techniques presented in this chapter will be covered in greater detail in later chapters.

2.1   What Is a Computer Program?

Look in your pocket or purse. What do you find there? Keys? Credit cards? A comb? Each of these is a tool for getting along or getting around in our world. A computer is no different. *A computer is nothing more or less than a tool.*

Computers are smart tools. Most tools, such as hammers and saws, can do only one thing or one small group of things. A computer has a very simple type of "brain" called a **microprocessor**. This enables computers to be many different kind or tools. For instance, a computer can be used for word processing. The same computer can be used for accounting. It can also be used to play music. In each case, the computer is a different type of tool.

Of course, a computer has no actual brain, and it can't really think. However, the microprocessor of any computer can execute instructions. When we group these instructions together and store them in a file, we call the file a **program**, an **application**, or **software**. Programs tell the computer what type of tool to be. Companies sell programs as products. When they do, they're essentially selling tools.

A computer program, then, is:

- A set of instructions.
- A solution to a problem.
- A product.

2.1.1   A Set of Instructions

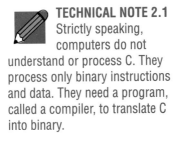

TECHNICAL NOTE 2.1
Strictly speaking, computers do not understand or process C. They process only binary instructions and data. They need a program, called a compiler, to translate C into binary.

From an internal point of view, a computer program is a set of instructions. When we write a program, what we are writing is a set of instructions that tells the computer how to be a particular type of tool. Since computers can't understand human languages such as English or Japanese, we must learn to communicate with them in a language they do understand, such as C.

2.1.2   A Solution to a Problem

A computer program is a solution to a problem. It is the answer to some sort of question. Whenever a program gets written, somewhere, someone said something like, "Is there an easier way to do this task?" The resulting program is the answer to that question.

Because a program is a solution to a problem, we as software developers must have good problem-solving skills. We also need organized ways to design and create our particular solution to the problem at hand.

We can solve problems using six basic steps.[1] These are:

1. *Identify the problem.* You can't solve a problem if you don't know what the problem is. My experience is that if I can't write the essence of the problem in one paragraph or less, then I probably don't know what it is.
2. *Understand the problem.* The solution to a problem usually depends on who the solution is for. As an example, let's say someone asks us to write them a word processing program. If that person intends to use the word processor for only one or two page letters, we'll write them a rather simple program. However, if he or she wants to use it to publish books and manuals, we'll write a much more complex program. Understanding the problem also involves familiarity with at least one set of tools that can be use to solve it. Programmers must know what computers are currently capable of. They must also know at least one programming language. The more languages programmers know, the better they can solve programming problems.
3. *Identify alternative ways to solve the problem.* As programmers, we tend to try to make problems we encounter fit solutions that we know. It's something we all do occasionally. It's good to recognize this tendency in ourselves. We need to be able to look at alternative technologies, computer languages, and even non-technical solutions to the problems our employers give us. There are always many ways to solve a problem.

---

[1]These steps are from Problem Solving and Programming Concepts, Fourth Edition by Maureen Sprankle (Upper Saddle River, NJ: Prentice Hall, Inc., 1992) pp. 3–4. I highly recommend this book to all beginning programmers.

4. *Select the best way to solve the problem from the list of alternative solutions.* Evaluate the strengths and weaknesses of all of the solutions you come up with in terms of the users' needs. You must also consider cost, time, and quality. There are always many ways to solve a problem. The needs of the people who will be using the software determine which solution is best.

5. *List instructions that enable you to solve the problem using the selected solution.* This list of instructions eventually becomes a computer program.

6. *Evaluate the solution.* This means we must test our solution to see how well it solved the problem. Sometimes our solution is just what the users need. Other times, we find we haven't done so well. We need to know when we succeed and when we fail, and find out why in both cases.

2.1.3   A Product

Typically, the program you write will be marketed as a product. Or it may be used to produce a product that your employer markets. As programmers, we must consider our users to be our customers. It doesn't matter if our users a people purchasing our software or people within our company who will be using our software to get their jobs done. Either way, they are our customers. Part of our job is keeping these customers happy. To do that, we need to communicate with them. The best programmers are good communicators.

When we begin program development, we should first identify everything that the user wants the program to do. This can involve interviews with users and user surveys. We must communicate well if we want to make the product fit the users' needs.

As we develop the product, we must communicate with other programmers, our managers, and our users. The program itself must communicate its functions to our customers.

TIP 2.1
Good communication skills are essential to developing a high quality product.

2.2   Designing Programs

Good programs are designed before they are developed. They are also designed as they are developed.

Before we start writing a program, we should always design it. Trying to write a program with no design to follow is like building a house with no house plans. We're never quite sure what we'll end up with.

When we build a house we first determine what our needs are. Do we want a roomy house with plenty of bedrooms for a large family? Or do we want a compact house for a retired couple? What's more important, energy efficiency or luxury? We consider all of these questions as we choose a floor plan. We give the floor plan to an architect who comes up with a design. The design then goes to a contractor who builds the house.

Writing computer programs follows a similar process. We determine the users' needs and then design a solution or product to meet those needs. This design can be given to a team of programmers. They write a program according to the design.

In many companies, the person who writes the program is the person who designs it. Therefore, we typically need to be good at both design and development. Even if we do not start our careers as software designers, design skills become increasingly important as we move up in a company.

There are many small design and development tips presented throughout this book. Detailed discussions of program design begin in Chapter 13. The intent in doing this is to present enough of the "building blocks" of the C programming language to enable you to start creating programs that are more than just small examples. After those "building blocks" have been presented, we discuss how to fit them together into something interesting.

2.3   Developing Programs

Once we have a design, we can develop a program. To develop programs in C, we must know the C language. We also need to know how to create a C program. So that's where we'll start.

We create C programs by:

1. Writing the source code.
2. Compiling the source code into object code.
3. Linking the object code into an executable program.

Figure 2.1 illustrates the process of creating a computer program. We must compile source code into object code. We then link it into executable code. These steps are explained in the next few sections of this chapter. The most important thing to understand at this point is that these three steps are required for writing C programs.

FIGURE 2.1 Creating a Computer Program

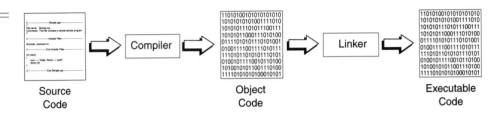

Source Code   Object Code   Executable Code

2.3.1 Source Code

Recall that a computer program is a group of instructions. We store program instructions, which is called **source code**, in files on a disk, CD-ROM, tape or other storage device. Computers store files in two different formats, text and binary.

Text files contain characters from the ASCII character set. The ASCII character set contains the letters of the alphabet in upper and lower case. It also contains the numbers 0 through 9 and some punctuation marks. We'll look at the ASCII character set in greater detail in Chapter 4.

Binary files contain binary numbers. All binary numbers are composed of ones and zeros. Each one or zero is called a **binary digit**, or a **bit**. In computing, we group eight bits together to make a **byte**. 1024 bytes are grouped together to form a **kilobyte**. A group of 1000 kilobytes is a **megabyte**. 1000 megabytes makes a **gigabyte**.

When we write C programs, we store the source code in text files. Programmers often build C programs from many text files of source code. Through the process of compiling and linking, which will be presented shortly, the source code in the text files is converted into binary instructions stored in binary files.

Because source code is stored in text files, we can use any text editor to create a C program. Many word processors will enable you to store files as plain text, so we can use them as well. However, programmers generally find that word processors are not well suited to their needs.

There are many reasons for this. Word processing programs tend to insert tabs in ways that are inconvenient for programmers. Typically, they store documents in a binary format rather than as text files. If you use a word processor to develop programs, you must often take extra steps to export your program as a text file.

Each line of a text file is terminated by a newline character. When you do export your program as a text file, you may find that the word processor added or removed newline characters in unexpected places.

Most software developers find that they get better usage out of a text editor that is written specifically for their needs. There are many excellent program editors available on the market today.

2.3.2 Compiling Source Code

Computers can't execute C source code. They understand only binary. We write programs called **compilers** and **interpreters** that translate programs from high-level computer languages, such as C, into binary.

There is a definite difference between a compiler and an interpreter. A compiler translates the entire program into binary at one time. An interpreter translates one line of code into a set of binary instructions and executes those instructions. It then translates another line of source code. Interpreted programs execute more slowly than compiled programs.

TECHNICAL NOTE 2.2
ASCII stands for American Standard Code for Information Interchange.

TECHNICAL NOTE 2.3
IBM mainframe computers do not use the ASCII character set. We'll only be using the ASCII character set in this book.

TECHNICAL NOTE 2.4
The ASCII set also contains characters other than those mentioned here.

TECHNICAL NOTE 2.5
Each line in a text file is terminated by a combination of a carriage return character and a line feed character. The carriage return character moves the cursor to the beginning of a line. The line feed character moves the cursor to the next line of output. In C these two characters are represented by a single character called a newline, which is written as the character '\n'.

C is a compiled language.

When we compile programs, the compiler reads the statements in our source files. It converts them into binary commands and stores the result in a binary file. However, the binary files that compilers produce are not executable programs. Compilers change programs into **object code**. Object code is an intermediate form between source code and an executable program. The next step is to link the program into an executable file with a linker.

2.3.3 Linking

When a **linker** links a program into an executable form, it links the object code together with libraries. A library is a collection of precompiled C functions that perform a task or a group of tasks.

In the case of a C program, there are a set of libraries that always come with a C compiler. These are called the C Standard Libraries. Programs use the C Standard Libraries for tasks such as input and output. We can link libraries that we create or that are created by commercial library publishers into C programs. This enables us to purchase libraries for special tasks, such as creating user interfaces or doing database operations. Because we buy the libraries, we don't have to write those portions of the program ourselves. Linking to libraries can save programmers many hours of work.

When the linker finishes, we have converted our source code into an **executable code**. Executable code is the final binary form of a program.

2.4 Debugging Programs

As software developers, we will make mistakes in nearly every single program that we ever write. This should not be discouraging. Part of our job is to find errors in our programs. This is a skill that all of us must acquire to be successful in the software industry.

One of the ways that we can avoid creating errors in our programs is by designing programs well. That is one of the primary reasons that this book stresses design skills.

Several different kinds of errors occur most frequently in our programs. They are syntax errors, logical errors, development errors, and runtime errors. All of these errors need to be prevented or removed from our programs. Although this overview introduces these types of errors, it will be left for later chapters to demonstrate how they are prevented, detected, and removed.

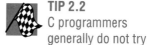
2.4.1 Syntax Errors

A syntax error occurs in our programs when we type C statements incorrectly. An example of a syntax error in English is, "Went they store to the." This sentence does not follow the rules for constructing statements in English. Similarly, all statements in a C program must follow the rules of C.

Because we're human, we can see that the English statement above should probably be "They went to the store." However, a compiler is unable to guess at the meaning of a C statement that uses incorrect syntax. Therefore, it prints an error message telling us what seems wrong with the statement. It is up to us to fix the error.

Syntax errors are found by the compiler whenever we compile a program.

2.4.2 Logical Errors

Our programs may compile and link without the compiler or linker reporting any errors. However, that doesn't mean our programs are correct. Computer programs are a set of step-by-step instructions for accomplishing a task. All of the individual statements can be correct, and yet they can still result in an incorrect sequence of steps.

For example, let's suppose we're making a cake for the first time. Let's say that each individual step in the recipe is correct. However, they are in the wrong order. Also suppose that the instruction to add the sugar is missing. In addition, imagine that there is an instruction to add curry powder to the cake. It is very unlikely that we'll be able to make a cake correctly if we follow these instructions.

Computer programs are the same. If they are missing instructions, if the instructions are in the wrong order, or if the instructions shouldn't be in the program, the program will not work correctly even if it compiles and links.

2.4.3 Development Errors

Many errors in a program are created in the development process. These include both syntax and logical errors. If we are creating a library for use in other developers' programs, we must write our software in such a way as to catch as many developer errors as possible. Specific techniques for doing this are introduced later in this book.

Generally, we write our software to be as "in your face" and obnoxious about development errors as possible. We do ourselves and other developers a favor when we make development errors impossible to ignore. Development errors should be found and fixed before the end user gets the software.

2.4.4 Run-time Errors

There are some errors that will occur when a program is running. The developer has no control over when they happen. For example, you and I are unable to tell when a computer running a program we write will run out of memory. When that happens, the program can't function properly.

Our programs must deal gracefully with runtime errors. We cannot ignore them. Dealing gracefully with a runtime error does not include crashing the program.

As a minimum, our programs should enable users to save their work when a runtime error occurs. They should also be able to shut down the program and restart it. Hopefully, that will resolve the runtime error. However, it is impossible to do this with large corporate systems. Huge companies can require days or weeks to get their system shut down gracefully and restarted. In that case, we'd better come up with a more efficient way of handling the problem.

2.5 Hello, World—Our First C Program

The first program that people write in a new programming languages is traditionally a Hello, World program. So let's be traditional.

Hands On 2.1

Objective

Write a program that prints the words "Hello, World" on the screen.

Experiment

Type the following program into your text editor or integrated development environment (IDE). Compile it and run it. Note that the line numbers are not part of the program. Do not type them into your text editor or IDE. If you do, you will get an error when you try to compile the program.

If you're using the Visual C++ compiler that comes with this book, create a new project as explained in Appendix A. Type your program into the IDE's editor window. Save it to the file hello.c. To compile and link the program, choose **Build** from the main menu. The **Build** menu appears. In the **Build** menu, select **Build**. Alternatively, you can press the F7 key. To run the program, press F5.

Note that Microsoft Visual C++ is a C++ compiler rather than a C compiler. However, it compiles C programs as well. You can use Visual C++ for all of your C programming needs. If you want to learn C++ later, you can continue using Visual C++.

If you are using another compiler, you will need to consult the documentation for your compiler. If you are using an IDE, it should come with a printed manual or an online help system. Since there are so many possible combinations of compilers and text editors, and so many IDEs available, it is impossible to present a set of instructions in this book that will walk you through the process of typing your program into a text file and compiling it.

```
1   //----------------------hello.c-----------------------
2   /*
3   File name:      hello.c
4   Comments:       This file contains a simple sample program.
5   */
6
7
8   //--------------------Include Files--------------------
9
10  #include <stdio.h>
11
12  //------------------end Include Files------------------
13
14  int main()
15  {
16          printf("Hello, World\n");
17          return (0);
18  }
19
20  //--------------------end hello.c----------------------
```

Results

```
Hello, World
```

Analysis

If you compiled this program using a Windows-based compiler such as Borland C++ or MS Visual C++, you may have had problems. The first, and easiest to solve, is that there is no `WinMain()` function. When you create a project for any of the programs in this book, create it either as an EasyWin program, a console application, or as a DOS program. See your compiler documentation for information on each of these topics.

TECHNICAL NOTE 2.8
Reminder: C++ compilers can compile C programs.

If you did create this as an EasyWin program or a console application, your compiler may have generated a warning stating you have no definition file. Most Windows-hosted C/C++ compilers will use a default definition file if none is provided. That will be perfectly acceptable for all of the programs in this book. Therefore, that particular warning is safe to ignore for these programs.

The Hello, World program demonstrates many of the fundamentals of C programming. In fact, this short program contains more concepts than we can cover in this overview. At this point, we'll have to be satisfied by discussing only the most important points that this program illustrates.

The first five lines of the Hello, World program consist of a file banner. This is a *minimal* example of how professional programmers document their programs. At the beginning of every program file that you create there should be a file banner describing what is in the file. This helps people who are maintaining your code. It also will help you. You might be surprised at how rapidly you'll forget what any one piece of a large program you write is doing. File banners are just one aspect of proper program documentation that will help you remember.

A file banner is contained in one or more **comments**. We type comments into our program strictly for the benefit of people reading our source code. The compiler completely ignores all comments. They are not compiled at all.

A comment in a C program is indicated with either the symbols // (two slashes) or /* (a slash and an asterisk) followed by */ (an asterisk and a slash).

The // symbol tells the compiler that the rest of the text on the line is a comment. Comments that begin with // can only be one line long.

On the other hand, comments that begin with /* may span as many lines of text as you like. When the compiler sees the /* symbol, it will treat all text in the file as comments until it sees a */ symbol. Be aware that forgetting the */ symbols at the end of a comment can cause many problems at compile time. The Troubleshooting Guide at the end of this chapter illustrates what can happen with unterminated comments.

Example 2.1 demonstrates the two types of comments in C.

EXAMPLE 2.1 Comments in C

```
// This is a one line comment.
/* This comment
can span multiple lines of text. */
```

On line 10, the program contains an #include directive. This is a symbol recognized by the preprocessor which the compiler automatically invokes when you compile a program. Using the #include directive essentially tells the compiler to read the text file that is specified in the angle brackets (<>) into the current file. In this case, it is the file stdio.h that comes with the Standard Libraries. You need to include stdio.h if your program is going to do input or output. For this overview, we do not have to worry about the preprocessor. A detailed discussion of the preprocessor and its role in the compilation process is presented in Chapters 16 and 17. For now, the only thing that is important is to remember to put the statement

```
#include <stdio.h>
```

at the beginning of all of our programs.

Every C program must have a main() function. The main() function is the **program entry point**. It is the point in the source code where the program starts execution. main() is a function and follows the format for functions. That is, it has a return type, which is int. It has a function name, main, and a parameter list, which in this case is empty. All of the commands within main() must be contained inside the braces, { and }. At this point in our overview, it is not necessary to understand return types and parameter lists. It is, however, important to remember that the main() function has them. We'll see when we discuss functions in more detail in Chapter 13 that all functions use this same format.

TIP 2.3
Indent statements inside braces.

All of the statements in the braces are indented. The compiler doesn't care about indentation. However, you should follow this practice in your own programs to make them more readable.

After the computer executes the last statement before the closing brace (which looks like this: }), it terminates the program because that symbol marks the end of main(). The program terminates at the end of main().

Line 17 shows the last statement in the main() function, which is

```
return (0);
```

We will discuss the purpose of this statement in Chapter 13. For now, the last statement in main() should always be return (0).

The only thing that the Hello, World program actually does is send "Hello, World" out to the screen. The string of characters "Hello, World" is enclosed in quotes. That is always the case with **literal strings** in C. A literal string is a sequence of characters that you actually type right into the source code, just like "Hello, World". Even though it is not a program instruction, literal strings are part of the program. They are data.

C programs send output to the display by calling the printf() function. The printf() function is provided in the C Standard Library. We call printf() by simply putting its name in our programs. When calling printf(), the string to be printed should appear in quotes inside the parentheses, as shown in the Hello, World program.

Notice that the quotes also contain the character '\n'. This signifies the newline character. It tells `printf()` to move the cursor to the beginning of the next line. A newline character can appear anywhere in a literal string. We'll look at newlines in more depth in later chapters.

Try This

Change the word **World** on line 16 of this program to your first name. Recompile the program and run it to see the result. Also, deliberately delete or alter the statements in the programs one at a time. Recompile and see what errors your compiler outputs.

TECHNICAL NOTE 2.10
All C statements that do not begin and end with braces should end with a semicolon. The only exception to this are statements that start with a # sign.

TIP 2.4
You should not put more than one C statement per line of code.

TIP 2.5
You will need to refer to the manuals that come with your editor and compiler. If you use a single integrated development environment, be sure to keep the manuals handy. Learning to use programming guides and reference manuals well and often is a big key to becoming a skilled programmer.

Notice that most of the statements in a C program end with a semicolon (;). In general, all statements in a C program that do not use the opening and closing braces (the symbols {and }) should end with a semicolon. The only exception to this is the statement

```
#include <stdio.h>
```

which will be discussed in detail in Chapter 16.

Although it is possible to put more than one C statement on a line of code, it is never a good idea. At times, you will encounter programmers who put more than one statement on a single line of code. For example, they will put a statement such as `printf()` on the same line as an opening brace, like this:

```
int main()
{ printf("Over the rainbow");
}
```

The C programming language allows this. However, it is widely considered poor programming practice.

2.6 Getting Input with `scanf()`

The Hello, World program demonstrated the basics of writing a C program. One thing that it doesn't show, however, is how to get input from the keyboard. For our next Hands On program, we'll modify Hello, World so that it reads data from the keyboard using the `scanf()` function.

Hands On 2.2

Objective

Write a program that:
Prints the string "Hello, World" to the screen.
Reads an integer from the keyboard.
Prints the integer to the screen.

Experiment

Modify the Hello, World program so that it is the same as the program below. The changes that you need to make are printed in bold type. They will not be in bold letters in your program.

```
1  //---------------------hello2.c---------------------
2  /*
3  File name: hello2.c
4  Comments:  This file contains a simple sample program.
```

```
 5   */
 6
 7
 8   //--------------------Include Files--------------------
 9
10   #include <stdio.h>
11
12   //----------------end Include Files------------------
13
14
15   int main()
16   {
17       int aNumber;
18
19       printf("Hello, World\n");
20       printf("Please type in a number and press Enter: ");
21       scanf("%d",&aNumber);
22       printf("\nThe number you entered was %d.\",aNumber);
23       return (0);
24   }
25
26   //----------------end hello2.c----------------
```

Results

Hello, World
Please type in a number and press Enter: **12**
The number you entered was 12

Analysis

This program prints the literal string `"Hello, World"` and then prompts the user to enter a number. In the Results section of this Hands On, I typed the number 12. It is shown in bold print to emphasize that it is user input and not something that the program is supposed to print. The number the user enters will not actually be in bold on the computer's screen.

After the user types in a number, the program prints it back to the screen. As you can see, all output in this program is done with the `scanf()` function from the C Standard Library.

The `scanf()` function requires at least two parameters. We put the parameters of functions we use in the parentheses after the function's name. If the function needs more than one parameter, they are separated by commas.

The first parameter to the `scanf()` function is a **format string**. In C programming, a format string is a string which specifies the types of the function's other parameters. The format string `"%d"` indicates that the next parameter is a decimal integer (an integer is a whole number).

The `scanf()` function's second parameter is an integer variable. Since this chapter is just an overview, we'll discuss integer variables in detail in Chapter 3. For now, it's only important is to know that the variable creates a space in memory to hold a number. When the user types in a number and presses the Enter key on the keyboard, the `scanf()` function stores the user's input in the variable.

The `printf()` statement on line 22 of this Hands On program also uses a format string. It tells the `printf()` function that the second parameter is a decimal (base 10) integer. Notice that the format string can also contain output for the user. In this case, it contains a '\n' character. As we can see from the Results section, the `printf()` outputs the words "The number you entered was" followed by the number, which is followed by a period. The `"%d"` in the format string tells the `printf()` function that it should print the value in the `aNumber` after the space following the word "was."

Since this chapter is intended to be an overview, don't worry if the details of this are not completely clear at this point. Later chapters will present much more information on the `printf()` and `scanf()` functions.

2.7   Using Pseudocode

Developers currently can choose from a variety of design methodologies. Many of them, at some point, have you write all or part of your program in **pseudocode**. When we write statements in pseudocode, we write generic, high-level statements of program actions. Example 2.2 shows the `main()` function from Hands On 2.2. One possible version of the pseudocode for this program is given in Example 2.3.

EXAMPLE 2.2   The `main()` Function from Hands On 2.2

```
 1   int main()
 2   {
 3           int aNumber;
 4
 5           printf("Hello, World\n");
 6           printf("Please type in a number and press Enter: ");
 7           scanf("%d.",&aNumber);
 8           printf("\nThe number you entered was %d.",aNumber);
 9           return (0);
10   }
```

EXAMPLE 2.3   Pseudocode Version of the Program in Example 2.2

Print "Hello, World" to the screen.
On the next line, print "Please type in a number and press Enter: "
Read an integer from the keyboard.
On the next line, print "The number you entered was ".
Print the integer to the screen.

Pseudocode provides a language-independent of describing what a program should do. In this case the term "language-independent" refers to computer languages such as Pascal or C, not human languages like English or Russian.

For the remainder of this book, most of the Objective sections of the Hands On examples will contain a pseudocode description of what the program does.

2.8   Troubleshooting Guide

After reading this section you should be able to:

- Recognize and fix problems caused by unterminated comments.
- Recognize and fix problems caused by missing semicolons.
- Recognize and fix problems caused by extra semicolons.
- Recognize and fix problems caused by unpaired braces.
- Recognize and fix problems caused by not using the & symbol with `scanf()`.

2.8.1   Problems with Unterminated Comments

One common mistake that even experienced programmers make is to forget to terminate comments. You'll remember that C uses two types of comments. One, marked by two slashes (//), ends at the end of the current line. The other can span multiple lines. It begins with /* and ends with */.

You can generally tell when you forget the */ mark when you compile your program. Most compilers will give you an error that says something like "Unexpected end of file." Some are even more helpful by saying something along the lines of, "Unexpected end of file in comment beginning on line 2."

Many modern integrated development environments and programmer's editors use color and style coding to indicate language features. For instance, keywords like int and return might be in bold. Comments might be in a particular color, say green or red. If you suddenly find that all the text in your program is in the color that indicates comments, you know that you've left off a */ somewhere.

2.8.2 Forgetting Semicolons

Forgetting a semicolon at the end of a C statement is one of the easiest mistakes to make. Even experienced programmers do it. However, it's also one of the easiest mistakes to detect. Often, your C compiler will tell you exactly what the problem is. It will print a message along the lines of "Semicolon missing before <statement>" where <statement> is the C statement that occurs right after the one missing the semicolon.

Unfortunately, some compilers are not so explicit. You may get error statements telling you that the compiler encountered something unexpected. For instance, it may say, "Unexpected variable declaration" or "Unexpected function declaration." When this occurs, it will typically point you to the statement right after the one missing the semicolon. So if your compiler tells you it ran into something unexpected, look in the lines above for one or more missing semicolons.

2.8.3 Adding Extra Semicolons

Another easy error to make is adding extra semicolons. Unfortunately, it can be *extremely* hard to detect.

In some cases, adding an extra semicolon on the end of a statement makes no difference at all. Example 2.4 shows the Hello, World program that we saw earlier in this chapter. Notice that there is an extra semicolon after the closing brace at the end of main() on line 6. Most C compilers will not complain about this even though it's unnecessary.

EXAMPLE 2.4   Hello, World with an Extra Semicolon

```
1    #include <stdio.h>
2    int main()
3    {
4        printf("Hello, World\n");
5        return (0);
6    };
```

In this case, it's okay to leave the extra semicolon. It's not needed, but it causes no problems.

Example 2.5, however, shows a misplaced semicolon that definitely does cause problems. It occurs right after the last parenthesis of main().

EXAMPLE 2.5   An Extra Semicolon After main()

```
1    #include <stdio.h>
2    int main();
3    {
4        printf("Hello, World\n");
5        return (0);
6    }
```

TECHNICAL NOTE 2.11 Your compiler might not see anything wrong with a semicolon after the) symbol in main(). The reason for this is that main() is a function, and functions generally have prototypes. A prototype looks exactly like the first line of the function except that it ends with a semicolon.

This little semicolon can cause you a world of problems. Your compiler may give you a very helpful warning such as, "Declaration terminated incorrectly" and indicate exactly where the extra semicolon is.

It may also not be able to figure out what's wrong at all. It could point you at a statement several lines from where the extra semicolon occurs. The problem is that the compiler may actually think that you are trying to do something valid.

The primary concept to understand here is that the compiler may think you're trying to make a valid statement by putting a semicolon at the end of the first line of main(). It will continue compiling statements. As it does, it encounters the rest of main() and gets extremely confused. So it basically asks you, "Why are you putting this stuff here?"

The most important thing you can take away from this explanation is that your compiler will detect that there's a problem with the extra semicolon on the first line of main(). However, it may not understand exactly what the problem is. The error message it gives you might be completely unrelated to the extra semicolon. Therefore, you're going to have to check for that mistake yourself.

Adding a semicolon to the end of a line when it should be left off can cause errors that are even harder to detect. In Chapters 8 and 9 we'll see that extra semicolons on the end of statements such as if and while can cause the program to function improperly even if it compiles without errors. As these C programming statements are presented, the Troubleshooting Guides of the chapters in which the statements are introduced will contain warnings about extra or misplaced semicolons.

2.8.4 Unpaired Braces

Another source of "Unexpected <statement>" errors is unpaired braces. This is a mistake that I remember making a lot when I was first beginning to program. The reason that I made this mistake so much was because I laid out my braces in the style shown in Example 2.6.

EXAMPLE 2.6 Unaligned Braces

```
1   #include <stdio.h>
2   int main() {
3         printf("Hello, World\n");
4         return (0);
5   }
```

As Example 2.6 illustrates, the opening brace of main() can appear on the first line of the function. The compiler doesn't care if you do this. It's not wrong and not harmful in any way. In fact, it's a common style that many experienced C programmers use. For experienced programmers, it's not a problem because they don't make this mistake very much. However my own experience as a novice programmer and as a teacher has led me to conclude that novice programmers will save themselves some time and frustration if they don't use this style.

For beginning C programers, an easy way to solve this problem is to always put closing braces under opening braces. Example 2.7 illustrates what I mean.

EXAMPLE 2.7 Aligned Braces

```
1   #include <stdio.h>
2   int main();
3   {
4         printf("Hello, World\n");
5         return (0);
6   }
```

Notice that the opening and closing braces for the block of code are aligned in the same column. If you print this program out, you can lay a ruler on the printout on the column where the opening brace occurs and draw a line straight down to the closing brace. If the closing brace is missing, it becomes immediately obvious.

We'll see the great value of this simple technique as we go along. As your programs become more complex, you'll use many opening and closing braces. If they're aligned in the same column, unpaired braces will be easier to find.

2.8.5 Forgetting the Ampersand in the scanf() Parameter List

Example 2.8 shows the program from Hands On 2.2. Take a close look at the scanf() function. Notice that the second parameter is a variable name. In front of the variable name is an ampersand (&). It is easy for even experienced C programmers to forget that ampersand. However, without it, the scanf() function will not be able to put the user's input into your variable. The program will run, but the output will not be right.

EXAMPLE 2.8 **A Missing Ampersand in the `scanf()` Function**

```
1   #include <stdio.h>
2
3   int main()
4   {
5       int aNumber;
6
7
8       printf("Hello, World\n");
9       printf("Please type in a number and press Enter: ");
10      scanf("%d",aNumber);
11      printf("\nThe number you entered was %d",aNumber);
12      return (0);
13  }
```

SUMMARY

Computer programs are groups of commands stored in text files. Computers don't execute text files, so the commands must be translated into binary. Compilers and interpreters perform the necessary translations.

An interpreter translates one line of source code into binary and then executes it. The next line of source code is then translated and executed. This continues until the end of the program.

A compiler translates an entire program into binary at once. The program can then be executed repeatedly without having to translate the code again. Compiled programs execute faster than interpreted programs.

A C program must have a `main()` function. The `main()` function is the program entry point. The program terminates when it finishes executing all of the statements in `main()`.

C programs send output to the display with the `printf()` function. They read input from the keyboard with the `scanf()` function. These functions are part of the C Standard Library.

TECHNICAL NOTES

2.1 Strictly speaking, computers do not understand or process C. They process only binary instructions and data. They need a program, called a compiler, to translate C into binary.

2.2 ASCII stands for American Standard Code for Information Interchange.

2.3 IBM mainframe computers do not use the ASCII character set. We'll only be using the ASCII character set in this book.

2.4 The ASCII set also contains characters other than those mentioned here.

2.5 Each line in a text file is terminated by a combination of a carriage return character and a line feed character. The carriage return character moves the cursor to the beginning of a line. The line feed character moves the cursor to the next line of output. In C these two characters are represented by a single character called a newline, which is written as the character `'\n'`.

2.6 In addition to linking object code modules and libraries, the linker also performs some additional tasks to convert your object code into an executable form. These details are not essential for this overview.

2.7 When libraries are produced, someone writes them as source code. They compile the source code into object code and distribute the object code. You link your object code to the object code in the libraries.

2.8 Reminder: C++ compilers can compile C programs.

2.9 Note that some older C compilers do not support the single-line style of comment. They require that all comments be enclosed in the `/*` and `*/` symbols.

2.10 All C statements that do not begin and end with braces should end with a semicolon. The only exception to this are statements that start with a # sign.

2.11 Your compiler might not see anything wrong with a semicolon after the) symbol in `main()`. The reason for this is that `main()` is a function, and functions generally have prototypes. A prototype looks exactly like the first line of the function except that it ends with a semicolon.

TIPS

2.1 Good communication skills are essential to developing a high quality product.

2.2 C programmers generally do not try to write their own versions of the functions in the C Standard Libraries. The C Standard Libraries are optimized to be as reusable and efficient as possible.

2.3 Indent statements inside braces.

2.4 You should not put more than one C statement per line of code.

2.5 You will need to refer to the manuals that come with your editor and compiler. If you use a single integrated development environment, be sure to keep the manuals handy. Learning to use programming guides and reference manuals well and often is a big key to becoming a skilled programmer.

REVIEW QUESTIONS

1. What does an interpreter do? What do you think the advantages or disadvantages might be in using an interpreter?
2. What does a compiler do? What do you think the advantages or disadvantages might be in using a compiler?
3. To what form does a compiler compile programs? Why?
4. What is a linker? Why are programs linked?
5. What is the purpose of the `main()` function in a C program?
6. What does the `printf()` function do?
7. What does the `scanf()` function do?
8. What is a literal string?
9. What is a format string?
10. What does '\n' stand for?

EXERCISES

1. Describe the process of writing source code and converting it into an executable program.
2. Explain the difference between source code and object code.
3. Explain the difference between object code and executable code.
4. Explain why using code libraries might be helpful. Describe how a library is incorporated into a C program.
5. Look in the directory \Examples\Chapt2 on the Examples CD included with this book. You will find a program called Ex_2_5.c. Load the program into your IDE or text editor and look at it. Compile and link it. Explain what errors you got and describe how you fixed them.
6. Look in the directory \Examples\Chapt2 on the Examples CD included with this book. You will find a program called Ex_2_6.c. Load the program into your IDE or text editor and look at it. Compile and link it. Explain what errors you got and describe how you fixed them.
7. Look in the directory \Examples\Chapt2 on the Examples CD included with this book. You will find a program called Ex_2_7.c. Load the program into your IDE or text editor and look at it. Compile and link it. Explain what errors you got and describe how you fixed them.
8. Look in the directory \Examples\Chapt2 on the Examples CD included with this book. You will find a program called Ex_2_8.c. Load the program into your IDE or text editor and look at it. Compile and link it. Explain what errors you got and describe how you fixed them.
9. Look in the directory \Examples\Chapt2 on the Examples CD included with this book. You will find a program called Ex_2_9.c. Load the program into your IDE or text editor and look at it. Compile and link it. Explain what errors you got and describe how you fixed them.
10. Look in the directory \Examples\Chapt2 on the Examples CD included with this book. You will find a program called Ex_2_10.c. Load the program into your IDE or text editor and look at it. Compile and link it. Explain what errors you got and describe how you fixed them.
11. Explain what a compiler does.
12. Explain what a linker does.
13. Explain the purpose of comments in a program.
14. Explain the difference between run-time errors and development errors.
15. Explain the difference between syntax errors and logical errors.
16. Show the output of the following C statement:

    ```
    printf("@\n@@\n@@@\n@@@@\n@@@@@\n");
    ```

17. Write a program that outputs the following pattern with the asterisk character:

18. Write a program that outputs the following pattern with the asterisk character:

19. Look back at the set of six instructions for solving problems given in section 2.2.2. Explain how you think these steps can be applied to writing a word processing program.
20. Computer programs often become products that companies sell. Describe how you think this might affect the design of a program.

GLOSSARY

Application   See **Program**.

Binary Digit   A one or a zero in a binary number.

Binary File   A file that contains information stored in binary format.

Bit   A binary digit.

Byte   A group of eight bits.

Comment   A statement in a C program that is there strictly for the benefit of people reading the program. The compiler completely ignores all comments.

Compiler   A program that translates source code into object code. It translates entire files, or entire groups of files, each time it compiles.

Executable Code   A binary file that a computer can execute. An executable program.

Format String   A string which specifies the types of the parameters to follow in a parameter list.

Gigabyte   A group of 1000 megabytes.

Interpreter   A program that translates source code into executable code. It translates a program line by line.

Kilobyte   A group of 1024 bytes.

Linker   A program that combines object code programs and libraries into an executable program.

Literal String   A string that is typed into the source code of a program. Literal strings are not program instructions. They are data that is embedded in the source code.

Megabyte   A group of 1000 kilobytes.

Microprocessor   A microchip that can carry out a set of instructions. This is the "brain" of the computer.

Object Code   An intermediate binary form between source code and an executable program.

Program   A collection of instructions that a microprocessor can execute. The collection of instructions carry out a particular task or group of tasks.

Program Entry Point   The point in the code where the program begins execution.

Pseudocode   Generic statements that describe program actions.

Source Code   Instructions in a C program that are stored in text files.

Software   See **Program**.

Text File   A file that contains data stored as text characters.

3

Atomic Data Types: Integer and Floating-Point Variables

OBJECTIVES

After reading this chapter, you should be able to:

- Explain what atomic data types are and how they are used.
- Name and utilize all of the integer and floating-point data types.
- Explain the differences between the various integer data types.
- Explain the differences between the floating-point data types.
- Explain and demonstrate overflow and underflow.
- Explain and demonstrate precision, rounding, and truncation errors.
- Understand the potential problems with mixed-type operations.

OUTLINE

PREVIEW

Computer programs aren't much good if they don't process data. This chapter presents some fundamental data types that we can use in our programs. Specifically, it explains some of the C atomic data types. It also discusses two potential problems with all data types, overflow and underflow.

3.1 What Are Atomic Data Types?

TECHNICAL NOTE 3.1
Logical data types are also called boolean data types.

Before we ask what an **atomic data type** is, it is reasonable to define the term **data type**. Every piece of data in a computer has a type. If we enter the amount of a bank deposit into an ATM, we're entering data. That data is a numeric type. If you type a customer's name into a database program, you enter a string of characters. The data you enter is of type character.

Many other data types are possible. For example, it is not unusual to want to store date and time information in a program. Some programming languages provide types for dates and times. Some languages, such as C++, contain a logical data type. It is used to store the values true and false. Each programming language comes with its own set of atomic data types.

The ancient Greeks defined an atom as the smallest possible particle of matter. Of course, we now have discovered subatomic particles (and sub-subatomic particles, and so on). However, the word atomic, in its original sense, suggests something that is as small as it can get. It indicates something that can't be divided into smaller pieces.

When we describe a piece of data as atomic, we mean that it is in the smallest possible unit of data. It can't be broken down any further. In C, the atomic data types are the data types that are built into the language. We use them as building blocks for other data types.

C comes with several numeric data types. It also has character data types which can be used to build strings. A string is just a group of characters. In addition, the C language lets you define your own data types. When we begin to talk about programmer-defined types, we'll see how all of the atomic data types can be used to build data types that reflect real-world programming situations.

3.2 Variables and Variable Names

TECHNICAL NOTE 3.2
When we create a variable, we allocate memory at a particular physical or logical memory address and assign that memory address a name and a type. The compiler then checks all attempts to access the variable against its assigned name and type.

TRAP 3.1
Compilers and their associated libraries often contain variables that begin with an underscore. It is best to avoid using an underscore at the beginning of a variable name so that your variables don't conflict with the ones that the compiler uses.

In C programs, data that changes is stored in **variables**. When we declare a variable in a program, we set aside a location in memory and give that location a name and a type.

Variable names can be any length that the compiler allows. Most compilers allow you to create variable names that are up to 256 characters in length. However, they usually only recognize the first 32 characters. This means that if two variable names are identical for the first 32 characters, the compiler will see them as the same variable. This is true even if characters 33 through 256 in the two variable names do not match. Only the first 32 are used to identify the variable.

Variable names must begin with a letter or an underscore. They cannot contain any spaces. The names of variables should describe the data they contain. This helps make the program more self-documenting.

Capitalization is also important in variable names. C is a case-sensitive language. So the names `thisInteger`, `ThisInteger`, and `THISINTEGER` are all seen by the compiler as different variables. In the past, variable names have used many different capitalization styes. However, lowercase has been preferred. More recently, the common practice seems to be to have the first word in a variable name be all lowercase. Other words in the variable name begin with a capital letter. It is not unusual to see names such as `inputData`, `voltageLevel`, or `currentVelocity` in programs. These each follow the style that is currently most common, and they provide some description of the data they hold.

The advantage of following the most common style of capitalization in your variable names comes when others read your programs. When another programmer looks at code you've written, he or she will immediately know that a name such as `positionVector` is a variable. If you use an uncommon capitalization style, it may be harder for other programmers to determine what your variables are.

Table 3.1 contains some good variable names and some that are not so good. It also explains why.

TABLE 3.1 Variable Names, Good and Otherwise

Variable Name	Is It a Good Name?	Why?
voltageLevel	Yes	The variable name describes the data it contains. It also follows the most common capitalization style.
XprGLfqq	No	The name does not describe the data. It uses an unusual capitalization style.
current Amperage	No	Spaces are not allowed in variable names.
fileDataRetrieved	Yes	The name follows the common format, it describes the data, and it describes variable's purpose.
x	Maybe	In most cases, the name does not describe the data it contains. However, in the context of a graphics program, this name is good.
output_data	Maybe	The name describes the data well. However, the name follows the old capitalization style.

3.3 Signed Integers

One of the most commonly used data types in C programming is an int, which stands for **integer**. An integer is a number that has no fractional part. The int data type is called a **signed integer** because it can contain either positive or negative numbers. Table 3.2 shows some numbers that are integers and some that are not.

TABLE 3.2 Examples of Integers and Non-Integers

Integers	Non-Integers
5	5.0
–23	0.888
56,345	75.75

TIP 3.1
All variable declarations in main() must come before any executable statements.

TIP 3.2
It's a good idea to leave at least one blank line after variable declarations to help them stand out from the executable statements.

Notice in the table that the number 5 is an integer. It is a whole number and has no fractional part. The number 5.0 is not an integer. It has a fractional part, even though the fractional part is zero. Any number that has a decimal point in it is not an integer.

To create an integer variable in a program, declare its name and type. All variable declarations in main() must occur before any executable statements. It is also a good idea to leave at least one blank line after variable declarations so that they stand out from the executable statements.

Hands On 3.1 demonstrates how programs declare variables.

Hands On 3.1

Objective

Write a program that declares and uses integer variables. The program should demonstrate proper and improper ways to use variables.

Experiment

Type the following program into your editor. Compile, link, and run it.

```
1   #include <stdio.h>
2
3   int main()
```

```
4   {
5          int i;
6          int j,k=5;
7
8          i=j+k;        // This is wrong!
9          j=7;
10         i=j+k;        // Now this is ok.
11         printf("i=%d j=%d k=%d",i,j,k);
12         return (0);
13  }
```

Results

`i=12 j=7 k=5`

Analysis

This short example demonstrates several important points about variables. First, notice how the program declares integers. It declares the variable i by itself on line 5. By stating the variable's name and type, the program allocates memory for one integer and names it i.

Programs can declare integers on a line by themselves, as i is. They can also declare them in groups, as the Hands On program does with j and k on line 6. When a program declares more than one variable on a line, it needs to separate the variable names with commas.

In addition to declaring the variable k, the program also initializes it. Using the assignment operator, which is an equal sign, the program gives k the value 5. A program can initialize any variable it declares.

The question then arises, what values do i and j have when the program declares them? The answer is, I don't know. No one does. There isn't any way to know in advance. Their values are undefined. Programmers must always remember this important characteristic of the C language. We must assume that any variables we declare in our programs contain random values if we do not explicitly initialize them.

Because the program does not initialize the variable j, line 8, which reads

```
i=j+k;          // This is wrong!
```

gives unpredictable results. There is actually nothing wrong with adding the value in j to the value in k and storing the results in i. However, we have no way of knowing what j contains. Therefore, we have no way of predicting what value will be stored in the variable i. This statement is wrong only because it will yield unpredictable results.

The Hands On program then assigns the value 7 to the variable j. That means j now contains a known value. Our program can try the addition again and it's okay. It will yield a predictable result.

Line 11 reads

```
printf("i=%d j=%d k=%d",i,j,k);
```

It uses the printf() function to send output to the screen. The format string tells printf() to output the characters "i= " and then print a decimal integer value. The printf() function replaces the "%d" with the first value in its parameter list that it finds after the format string.

The printf() function then sends the string "j=" to the screen. When it encounters the second "%d" in the format string, it gets the second value after the format string from its parameter list. It replaces the second "%d" with that value.

The printf() function will next output "k=", find the third "%d", and replace it with the third value in its parameter list that follows the format string.

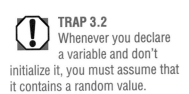

TRAP 3.2
Whenever you declare a variable and don't initialize it, you must assume that it contains a random value.

TIP 3.3
Many C compilers initialize all uninitialized data to zero. However, some don't. You must not depend on that happening. Many program errors occur because the programmer uses variables that are not yet initialized. Therefore, always initialize variables before you use them.

When our programs declare variables, they allocate the appropriate amount of memory for the variables. You may wonder about the size of an integer. The number of bytes that the C compiler allocates for an integer determines the largest value that an integer can hold. So how many bytes does the compiler allocate? The answer is, it depends. The ANSI definition of C leaves the size of an integer implementation-dependent. It is 16 bits on some operating systems and 32 bits on others. Still others use 64-bit integers.

Even if we do not know number of bytes in an integer, the C language provides us with qualifiers to modify its size. Integers can be declared as `short` or `long`. Example 3.1 shows some ways that the `short` and `long` keywords can be used.

EXAMPLE 3.1   Declarations of short and long Variable

```
short int aShort;
long int aLong;
short anotherShort;
long anotherLong;
```

Short integers can be declared using the keywords `short int`, or just `short`. In the same way, long integers can be declared using the keywords `long int`, or just `long`. The compiler knows that something declared as `short` or `long` is a `short int` or a `long int` respectively.

The ANSI definition of a `short` is that it can be no longer than an `int`. It can be the same size as an `int`. The definition of a `long` is that it can be no shorter than an `int`. Again, it can be the same size as an `int`.

Although it's confusing to possibly have the types `short`, `int`, and `long` be all the same size, there is a very good reason for this. By leaving the definition somewhat vague, the ANSI committee enables compiler writers decide how many bytes to allocate for each data type. They can create compilers with numeric types that best fit the particular computer on which the compiler will run. Companies writing compilers for computers on jet aircraft don't have to force their integer data to be the same size as integer data on a microcomputer. That kind of flexibility helps compiler manufacturers create efficient compilers. Because they can choose the best size of their data, the compilers can produce fast programs for the type of computer on which they run. It also helps to increase the portability of programs.

Usually, compiler manufacturers write their compilers so that a variable of type `short int` has half the width of an `int`. Since it has half the number of bytes in it, using `short` data types may mean that your program uses less memory.

Long integers generally are implemented as twice the number of bytes as an `int`. Because it has more memory space, larger numbers can be stored in a `long`.

On an MS DOS-based PC, the `int` data type is typically 16 bits, or 2 bytes. This means that an `int` can store 65,536 integers. About half of that range is given over to negative numbers, so the highest value these `int`s can store is 32,767. The lowest value is −32,768.

Some operating systems for microcomputers (Windows 95, Windows 98, Windows NT, Windows 2000, Mac OS, and Linux) support a 32 bit (4 byte) integer data type. Some support 64 bit integers. We can compile the same program on the same computer using different operating systems and get different-sized integers. Therefore, we should never depend on a data type being a particular size. It should not matter to us how many bytes a compiler allocates for an integer (or any other data type).

Hands On 3.2 illustrates the differences between short, int, and long.

Hands On 3.2

Objective

Write a program that:

Declares and initializes two short variables.
Declares two integer variables.
Declares a long variable.
Outputs the values in the short variables to the screen.
Multiplies the short variables and stores the results in the integer variable.
Outputs the result to the screen.
Initializes the second integer variable.
Outputs the value in the second integer variable to the screen.
Multiplies the two integer variables and stores the result in the long.
Outputs the result to the screen.

Experiment

Type the following program into your IDE or text editor. Compile, link, and run it.

```
1   #include <stdio.h>
2
3   int main()
4   {
5       short aShortVariable=127, anotherShortVariable=120;
6       int anIntegerVariable, anotherIntegerVariable;
7       long aLongVariable;
8
9       printf("The value of the first ");
10      printf("short variable is: %d\n",aShortVariable);
11      printf("The value of the second short ");
12      printf("variable is: %d\n",anotherShortVariable);
13
14      anIntegerVariable = aShortVariable * anotherShortVariable;
15
16      printf("When you multiply %d times %d you get %d\n",
17              aShortVariable,
18              anotherShortVariable,
19              anIntegerVariable);
20
21      anotherIntegerVariable = anIntegerVariable + aShortVariable;
22
23      printf("The value of the first integer ");
24      printf("variable is: %d\n",anIntegerVariable);;
25      printf("The value of the second ");
26      printf("integer variable is: %d\n",anotherIntegerVariable);
27
28      aLongVariable = anIntegerVariable * anotherIntegerVariable;
29
30      printf("When you multiply %d",anIntegerVariable);
31      printf(" times %d",anotherIntegerVariable);
32      printf(" you get %d",aLongVariable);
33
34      return (0);
35  }
```

Results

The value of the first short variable is: 127
The value of the second short variable is: 120
When you multiply 127 times 120 you get 15240
The value of the first integer variable is: 15240
The value of the second integer variable is: 15367
When you multiply 15240 times 15367 you get 234193080

Analysis

This program begins by declaring two variables of type `short` and initializing them. It also declares two integers and a long integer variable. As we saw in Hands On 3.1, your program can declare more than one variable at a time if the variable names are separated by commas.

Lines 6 and 7 declare two integers and a long integer. These are used later in the program.

On line 5, this example program initializes the two `short` variables to 127 and 120 respectively. On some operating systems, most notably MS DOS, the `short` data type is one byte (8 bits) in length. Therefore, the maximum value it can hold is 127. If the `short` data type on your system contains more than 8 bits, it can hold larger values.

TIP 3.4
Software developers often limit the number of characters per line in their programs to 80. This helps make the program more readable.

The program outputs the values in the `short` variables to the screen. Notice that it uses multiple `printf()` statements to output a single line of text. The primary reason that the line of text is broken into multiple `printf()` statements is to keep the lines of code short. The printed C source code must fit within the margins of this book. Therefore, I'm limiting the number of characters per line. This is a common technique in C programming. Usually, you want to limit each line of C source code to 80 characters. That's not a rule written in stone. It's just a guideline that you can use to help make your programs more readable.

After the program outputs the values in the two `short` variables (lines 9–12), it multiplies the two values and stores the answer in the integer variable (line 14).

One thing to notice in this example is that the variables into which the values are being stored are always on the left side of the equal sign. When we do math, we can write equations like this:

$$\pi r^2 = c$$

with the multiplication on the left and the destination of the assignment on the right. However, that is not allowed in C statements. The destination of the assignment must always be on the left side of the equal sign, as shown in Example 3.2.

EXAMPLE 3.2 An Assignment Statement

```
anIntegerVariable = aShortVariable * anotherShortVariable;
```

This Hands On program also demonstrates that C supports the multiplication operator. In math classes, we typically use an x for multiplication. However, in C it's the asterisk (*).

After the program in Hands On 3.2 multiplies the two `short` variables together and stores the result in the integer variable, it prints the result to the screen.

Next, the program initializes `anotherIntegerVariable` to a value by adding the variables `anIntegerVariable` and `aShortVariable`. It prints the values in the two integer variables and multiplies them together. The program stores the result in the `long`. Finally, it prints the value in the `long` variable to the screen.

Try This

Insert a blank line between lines 9 and 10 of this program. Move the statement on line 5 to the new blank line. Recompile the program and see what messages the compiler outputs.

3.4   Unsigned Integers

The three integer types that we have presented so far, `short`, `int`, and `long`, are all **signed data types**. A signed data type can be positive or negative. It can store numbers greater than zero or numbers less than zero.

The integer family also includes **unsigned data types**. The unsigned data types can hold only numbers that are greater than or equal to zero. No negative numbers are allowed. Because the data range is not split between positive and negative numbers, unsigned integers can store twice as many positive numbers as signed integers.

C provides three types of unsigned integers, `unsigned short`, `unsigned int`, and `unsigned long`. Unsigned integers are declared in a manner similar to signed integers. Example 3.3 illustrates their use.

EXAMPLE 3.3   Variable Declarations of Unsigned Integer Types

```
1   unsigned short int u = 0;
2   unsigned short int v = 127;
3   unsigned short w = 100;        // Same as unsigned short int
4   unsigned int x=5;
5   unsigned y=11;                 // Same as unsigned int
6   unsigned long int z=22;
7   unsigned long a=54567;         // Same as unsigned long int
8   unsigned b=-27;                // This is NOT allowed!
```

Notice that lines 3, 5, and 7 in this example omit the word `int` from the declarations of `unsigned short`, `unsigned`, and `unsigned long` variables. The rules of the C language allow this.

Programs use unsigned data in exactly the same way they use signed data. They just can't store negative numbers in unsigned variables, as shown on line 8 of Example 3.3.

An `unsigned int`, which is also just called an `unsigned`, is the same size as an `int`. Variables of type `unsigned short` are no longer than an `unsigned`. They typically contain half the number of bytes as an `unsigned`. An `unsigned long` can be no shorter than an `unsigned`. It usually contains twice the number of bits as an `unsigned`.

3.5   Floating-Point Numbers

In C, numbers that contain a decimal point are called **floating-point numbers**. Floating-point numbers are also called real numbers. Table 3.3 gives some examples of floating-point numbers.

TABLE 3.3   Examples of Floating-Point and Nonfloating-Point Numbers

Nonfloating Point	Floating Point
5	5.0
–23	0.888
56,345	75.75

As you might expect by now, programs declare floating-point numbers in essentially the same way as integers. Example 3.4 demonstrates the declaration of floating-point numbers.

EXAMPLE 3.4   Declarations of Floating-Point Variables

```
float f=7.2;
double aDouble;
long double d=.000005
```

The basic type in the floating-point group is `float`. C compilers usually implement a `double` as twice the number of bits as a `float`. However, the ANSI C standard defines a `double` as no shorter than a `float`.

The type `long double` is usually implemented as twice the width of a `double`. The ANSI C standard defines it as being no shorter than a `double`.

C compilers can implement a `float` as the same size as an `int`, but that doesn't have to be the case. In fact, many compilers promote variables of type `float` to type `double`. When a compiler promotes a data type, it substitutes a larger data type for the one you have stated. The types `float` and `short` are the ones that compilers most often promote to a larger type. They will do this without telling you and without changing your source code. So you generally don't need to worry about whether or not your compiler is promoting the data types in your programs.

When we use floating-point numbers with the `printf()` and `scanf()` statements, the format string must contain `"%f"` rather than `"%d"`. The `"%f"` can be used for variables of type `float` and `double`. The format string `"%Lf"` is used for variables of type `long double`.

3.6 Overflow and Underflow

Let's say we're working on a computer that uses a 16 bit (2 byte) integer. That gives us a data range of –32,768 to 32767 for integers. Example 3.5 shows an integer variable declared on this 16 bit system. Notice that the program initialized the variable to the maximum value it can hold. The next line adds 5 to that variable. The question is, what happens next?

EXAMPLE 3.5 Overflow

```
1   #include <stdio.h>
2
3   int main()
4       {
5       int anInteger=32767;
6
7       anInteger=anInteger+5;
8       printf("%d\n",anInteger);
9       return (0);
10  }
```

The answer is, no one knows by just looking at this code. When data in a variable exceeds the maximum value that the data type can hold, it **overflows**. The C standard does not define what happens when overflow occurs. Typically, the numbers wrap around. That is, the variable in Example 3.5 might contain 4. It might not. Only your compiler writer knows for sure.

Underflow is the opposite of overflow. In Example 3.6, the program tries to store a value that is too negative for the integer data type (we're still assuming we're working with 16-bit integers).

EXAMPLE 3.6 Underflow

```
1   #include <stdio.h>
2
3   int main()
4   {
5       int anInteger=-32768;
6       anInteger=anInteger-3;
7       printf("%d\n",anInteger);
8       return (0);
9   }
```

What happens when a data type underflows is also undefined. The moral is that you must be mindful of the data types that you use. Be sure to use types that are large enough for the data you want to store.

Students often ask, "How do you find overflow and underflow errors?" Generally speaking, overflow and underflow are indicated by large numbers that should be small, or small numbers that should be large. Unfortunately, it's sometimes difficult to look at output from a program and say, "Ah, that looks like an underflow error." If you have a good familiarity with the data that your program should be outputting, you might guess that overflow or underflow occurred. However, it has been my experience that most overflow and underflow errors are caught by testers, not by programmers.

Overflow and underflow also can occur on unsigned integer data types.

3.7 Troubleshooting Guide

After reading this section, you should be able to

- Understand problems with mixed-type operations.
- Understand and avoid precision errors.
- Understand and avoid rounding and truncation errors.
- Prevent overflow and underflow by using a larger data type.
- Prevent overflow and underflow by data validation.

3.7.1 Mixed-Type Operations

The C programming language allows us to do mixed-type operations. Hands On 3.3 shows some mixed-type operations.

Hand On 3.3

Objective

Write a program that uses mixed-type mathematical operations. It should:
Declare variables of type `short`, `int`, and `float`.
Initialize the `short` variable to 100.
Assign the value of the `short` to the `int`.
Print the contents of the `int`.
Assign 10000 to the `int`.
Assign the value of the `int` to the `short`.
Print the result.
Assign the value of the `int` to the `float`.
Print the contents of the `float`.
Assign the value 100.123 to the `float`.
Assign the value of the `float` to the `int`.
Print the result.

Experiment

Type the following program into your IDE or text editor. Compile, link, and run it.

```
1   #include <stdio.h>
2
3   int main()
4   {
5       short aShort = 100;
6       int anInt;
7       float aFloat;
8
9       // Shorts can be stored in ints.
10      anInt = aShort;
11      printf("%d",anInt);
12      printf("\n");
```

```
13
14          // This can be dangerous!
15          anInt = 10000;
16          aShort = anInt;
17          printf("%d\n", aShort);
18
19          // Ints can be stored in floating-point types.
20          aFloat = anInt;
21          printf("%f\n", aFloat);
22
23          // Be sure this is what you want.
24          aFloat = 100.123;
25          anInt = aFloat;
26          printf("%d\n",anInt);
27
28          return (0);
29   }
```

Results

Results given by the Gnu C compiler.

100
10000
10000.000000
100

Results given by the Borland C/C++ compiler.

100

10000.0

10000100

Analysis

The results that you get when you run this program may be different than what is shown in the Results section. I compiled this with two different compilers and got different outputs. You may also get warnings or errors from your compiler when you attempt to compile the program.

The program first declares its variables, one of type short, one of type int, and one of type float. It initializes the variable aShort to 100. Compilers implement short integer variables so that they contain at least one byte. Your compiler may allocate more than one byte. Because a short is never less than one byte long, the value 100 will fit nicely into a short on any computer.

An integer variable typically contains twice the number of bytes that a short does. If your compiler promotes short variables to type int, it may be the same size. Either way, anything you can store in a short can fit into an int. Therefore, the statement

    anInt = aShort;

on line 10 should be just fine on every computer, no matter which compiler you use. The same is not true, however, of the statement

    aShort = anInt;

which appears on line 16. This potentially can cause unexpected results. If your compiler promotes short variables to int variables, there will be no problem. Any value that you can store into an int can go into a short. If your compiler implements a short as half the number of bytes as an int, you can lose data by trying to assign the value of an int variable into a short. The short will only be able to hold half as much data as an int. For that reason, the program did not produce output for line 17 when compiled with Borland C++.

> **TRAP 3.5**
> Storing the value of a variable into a smaller data type can result in a loss of information.

TIP 3.5
Whenever you assign a value to a variable, avoid using data types smaller than the variables on the right side of the assignment operator (the equal sign).

Because the results of storing values from int variables into short variables is compiler-dependent, you should generally avoid doing it. Your compiler may warn you about possible data loss when doing this. I got such a warning when I compiled this program with Microsoft Visual C++.

Integer data types generally fit into floating-point types without a problem. Just be sure that the type of the variable on the left side of the equal sign is large enough to hold the value. The statement

```
aFloat = anInt;
```

on line 20 of the Hands On program is acceptable on *most* systems. However, there are systems where this assignment can cause problems. The trouble stems from how the compiler is implemented. Most compilers are fine with this statement because they convert the integer value to the same value with a zero after the decimal. In the Results section of this Hands On, results for the Gnu C compiler shows that the value in the variable anInt was 10000. When we assigned that value into the variable aFloat, the program converted it to 10000.000000. Borland C++ produced executable code that converted the 10000 to 10000.0 when this statement was executed.

TRAP 3.6
The results you get when you assign a floating-point value into an integer variable varies from compiler to compiler and from compiler version to compiler version.

Not all systems will do this. A C program allocates some of the bits in a floating-point variable for the significant digits of the value that it stores. The rest are for an exponent. When you assign a value in an integer variable to a floating-point variable, the compiler may interpret the pattern of the bits as a value and an exponent. The results will be very different than what is shown here.

The same is true when we assign floating-point values into integer variables. When this program executed the statement

```
anInt = aFloat;
```

TECHNICAL NOTE 3.4
Converting floats to ints or ints to floats can be made more reliable with a type cast. Type casts will be presented later.

the Borland C++ compiler interpreted the bit pattern as that of an integer. Gnu C converted the number to an integer by truncating (throwing away) the values to the right of the decimal point. Again, the results of this operation are dependant on what compiler you use (and often which version of the compiler).

As this Hands On program demonstrates, mixed-type operations are possible in C. However, they should be used with caution.

3.7.2   Precision Errors

Because each data type has a set number of bits in it, it is possible to get errors in your floating-point numbers if you don't use a large enough data type. The drawback to using a larger data type is that it is slower because there are more bits to manipulate. So you have to decide which is more important, speed or accuracy.

The errors you can get with floating-point numbers are particularly tricky to deal with. Numbers can lose small fractional parts. A number like 634721000000.0000005 is very likely to lose the fractional part if a large enough data type is not used. However, 0.000000005 is just fine.

The reason has to do with the way floating-point numbers are stored in memory. Some of the bits for a floating-point number are used to store the significant digits of the number. The rest of the bits are used to store an exponent.

If, for example, a program stores the number 12,300 in a floating-point variable, it may actually store 123 and 4. When this value is used it is treated as 1.23×10^4. The value 10^4 is the same thing as $10 \times 10 \times 10 \times 10$, or 10,000. As you can see, $1.23 \times 10,000$ is 12,300.

If we try to store a number like 634721000000.0000005 into a float, it may not fit. When using the float data type, the compiler allocates a limited number of bytes to store the **significant digits**. Usually, a float can contain only six or seven significant digits accurately.

In the number 634721000000.0000005, the most significant digits are 634721. The .0000005 will get lost. In order to store the entire number, including the .0000005, the compiler must allocate enough bytes to store every digit in the number as a significant digit. A float will probably not be large enough for that.

If we change the number to 634721000000.0, there is no problem. The significant digits are now 634721. There are only six of them, so it would probably fit into a `float`. A C program can store the number 634721000000.0 as 6.34721 and 11. To a C program, this means 6.34721×10^{11}, which is 634721000000.0.

3.7.3 Rounding Errors and Truncation

Two additional sources of problems that can happen when using floating-point numbers are **rounding errors** and **truncation**.

Rounding errors occur when the program approximates a value that it cannot store exactly. For example, suppose a program stores the value 0.0 into a `float` variable. Also suppose that the program contains 10 statements that increment the variable by 0.1. We would expect that the variable would contain 1.0 after all ten of the increments are executed. It doesn't. In floating-point binary numbers, the value 0.1 cannot be represented exactly. Therefore, the compiler generates code that approximates the value. After the ten increments, the variable will most likely contain the value 0.999999999 (or something very close to this value).

When the program uses `printf()` to output the contents of the variable, it is not unusual for the `printf()` function to round the output data. In this instance, the `printf()` function would probably print the value 1.0. The exact behavior of the program depends on the compiler used to create it.

Truncation errors are very similar to rounding errors. They occur when a program encounters a number with more digits than it can store. For instance, if a program contains the statements

```
double d;
d = 1.0/3.0;
```

what would you expect the variable d to contain? Of course, the answer to the division is 1/3. However, in decimal notation, the value 1/3 is 0.33333333, with an infinite series of 3's to the right of the decimal point. As yet, there are no computers that can store an infinite series of numbers. Therefore, the program must truncate the value so that it will fit in memory.

Developers of programs that use floating-point numbers must be aware that rounding and truncation errors occur. To maintain accuracy in your data, the easiest thing you can do is to use larger floating-point data types than you think you will need. The `float` type on most compilers is accurate to six or seven digits. If your data will only contain three or four digits, a `float` is fine. However, if you expect to use more than four digits in your floating-point numbers, it's best to use the type `double` instead. If you need more accuracy than 10 to 12 digits, use the `long double` type.

3.7.4 Preventing Overflow and Underflow

There are two basic methods of preventing overflow and underflow. You can use a larger data type than you think you will actually need, or you can perform validation on the data before you store it into an integer or floating-point variable.

Using a Larger Data Type   A simple way to solve overflow and underflow problems is to adjust the size of the variables your program is using. If it uses variables of type `int` and you think they might overflow or underflow, it can declare `int` variables as `long` instead.

Although this technique may prevent overflow and underflow, it is not without cost. Using larger data types is generally slower. Typically, the performance penalty is not severe.

Data Validation   Another way to prevent overflow and underflow is to check the data each time an operation is performed on it and ensure that it stays with acceptable limits. Although this requires extra code and more CPU time, it is usually necessary to ensure that your program produces accurate results.

To do this, your program must read in all user input as strings (which we will discuss later). The program can check the data to ensure it contains digits. It can also verify that the number that the digits form is within the acceptable range for the data type you want to use. It must then convert the digits in the string into a number.

SUMMARY

In C programs, the atomic data types are the fundamental units of data. The atomic data types are also called the built-in types because they are built into the C language.

The C standard specifies two groups of numeric types, the integer group and the floating-point group. Integers include the types `short`, `int`, `long`, `unsigned short`, `unsigned`, and `unsigned long`. The floating-point group includes `float`, `double`, and `long double`.

Integers are numbers that have no fractional or decimal part. Floating-point numbers have a fractional part to the number.

The data type `short` can be no longer than the type `int`. The ANSI standard defines data type `long` as no shorter than an `int`.

According to the standard, an `unsigned short` must not be longer than an `unsigned int`. An `unsigned long` can be no shorter than an `unsigned int`.

The C language specification does not allow a `double` to be smaller than a `float`. A `long double` can be no shorter than a `double`.

If a C program stores a value into a variable that is larger than the data type can hold, the variable overflows. The C standard does not define the result of overflow.

If a value is put into a variable is smaller than the data type of the variable can hold, the variable is said to underflow. The result of underflow is undefined.

Generally speaking, it's best not to mix types in an operation. That is, integers should be added to integers, floating-point values to floating-point values, etc. If a program performs an operation (+, -, *, or /) on an integer type and a floating-point type, it results in a floating-point value.

If a program stores a floating-point value into an integer type, the fractional part of the floating-point value will generally be truncated (thrown away).

Floating-point data types can lose information due to precision errors.

TECHNICAL NOTES

3.1 Logical data types are also called boolean data types.

3.2 When we create a variable, we allocate memory at a particular physical or logical memory address and assign that memory address a name and a type. The compiler then checks all attempts to access the variable against its assigned name and type.

3.3 Converting `float`s to `int`s or `int`s to `float`s can be made more reliable with a type cast. Type casts will be presented later.

TIPS

3.1 All variable declarations in `main()` must come before any executable statements.

3.2 It's a good idea to leave at least one blank line after variable declarations to help them stand out from the executable statements.

3.3 Many C compilers initialize all uninitialized data to zero. However, some don't. You must not depend on that happening. Many program errors occur because the pro-

grammer uses variables that are not yet initialized. Therefore, always initialize variables before you use them.

3.4 Software developers often limit the number of characters per line in their programs to 80. This helps make the program more readable.

3.5 Whenever you assign a value to a variable, avoid using data types smaller than the variables on the right side of the assignment operator (the equal sign).

TRAPS

3.1 Compilers and their associated libraries often contain variables that begin with an underscore. It is best to avoid using an underscore at the beginning of a variable name so that your variables don't conflict with the ones that the compiler uses.

3.2 Whenever you declare a variable and don't initialize it, you must assume that it contains a random value.

3.3 Not all compilers support the `long double` type.

3.4 When you try to store data in a variable and the data is too large for the type, the variable overflows. The result of an overflow is undefined.

3.5 Storing the value of a variable into a smaller data type can result in a loss of information.

3.6 The results you get when you assign a floating-point value into an integer variable varies from compiler to compiler and from compiler version to compiler version.

REVIEW QUESTIONS

1. What is a data type?
2. What is an atomic data type? What is a built-in data type?
3. How many bits are in an int?
4. How many bits are in a short?
5. How many bits are in a long double?
6. Which of these are integers? 6.0, –21, 764543, –111.1
7. What is the difference between an unsigned int and an int?
8. Why can data be lost from floating-point numbers?
9. What value does a variable contain when it is declared?
10. Why do variables need to be declared?

EXERCISES

1. Fill in the blank.

   An integer contains numbers with no _____ part.

2. Fill in the blank.

   A floating-point numbers are also called _____ numbers.

3. Indicate which of the following are floating-point values.
   a. 3.14159
   b. 3.00000
   c. 100
   d. –940322185
   e. –3.14159

4. Indicate which of the following are true.
   a. Unsigned integers can contain both positive and negative numbers.
   b. Programmers do not need to worry about overflow and underflow.
   c. An example of a mixed-type operation is adding an integer variable to a floating-point variable.
   d. Rounding and truncation errors can occur when using floating-point numbers.

5. Indicate which of the following are false.
   a. Atomic data types are only used in physics.
   b. A variable's data type specifies what kind of data it contains.
   c. A variable is a location in memory that a program assigns a name and a type.
   d. When using the printf() statement to output floating-point values, programs use the "%d" format string.
   e. A floating-point number is truncated when part of it is thrown away so that it will fit in memory.

6. Write a C program that declares a variable for each atomic data type that was discussed in this chapter. Initialize each variable to a value. Print the value in each variable to the screen. To print a long int variable with printf(), you must use the "%ld" format string. When printing an unsigned short or unsigned int, you must use "%u" as the format string. For an unsigned long, use "%lu" as the format string. Use the format string "%f" for variables of type float and double. Use "%Lf" to print variables of type long double.

7. Write a program that declares a variable of type int and prints out the value in that variable. Do not initialize the variable. Run the program at least 5 times. Explain what happened when you ran the program. Also explain why.

8. Write a program that declares a variable of type double. Set the variable to the value 430000.054. Print the value in the variable. Was it able to handle that number accurately? If the number was accurately printed, add a zeros to each side of the decimal point until you get 43000000000.0000000054. Compile and run the program again. If the number prints correctly, add five more zeros to each side of the decimal point and try again. Keep doing this until some of the information is lost. Explain what is happening when the program loses this information.

9. Write a program that initializes an unsigned int to 0. The program should then subtract 1 from the variable and print the result. Explain what happened and why.

10. Write a program that declares an integer variable called anInteger. It should also declare a long integer called aLongInt. Assign the value 2000000000 into the variable aLongInt with the statement

    aLongInt=2000000000;

    Next, add the statement

    anInteger=aLongInt;

    to your program. Compile your program and run it. Explain the results.

11. The ANSI C standard does not define the exact number of bytes for atomic data types. Describe how the standard defines the size of these data types. Explain why you think they are defined that way.

12. Explain what mixed-type operations are. Describe the potential problems with mixed-type operations. Suggest some strategies for handling those problems.

13. Explain why all floating-point data types are subject to precision errors. Describe what you can do to ensure they don't occur in your programs.

14. Explain what overflow is. Describe one way you can prevent overflow in your programs. List the advantages and disadvantages of this approach.

15. Explain what underflow is. Describe one way you can prevent underflow in your programs. List the advantages and disadvantages of this approach.

16. Write a program that demonstrates overflow using an integer variable.

17. Write a program that demonstrates underflow using an integer variable.

18. Write a program that declares an `int` variable called `thisInt` and a `float` variable called `thatFloat`. Initialize `thatFloat` to 123.45. Use the assignment operator (=) to assign the value in `thatFloat` into `thisInt`. Print the value in `thisInt` to the screen. Explain what happened and why.

19. Write a program that declares an `int` variable called `thisInt` and a `float` variable called `thatFloat`. Initialize `thisInt` to 12345. Use the assignment operator (=) to assign the value in `thisInt` into `thatFloat`. Print the value in `thatFloat` to the screen. Explain what happened and why.

20. On the Examples CD that comes with this book, you'll find a directory called Examples. It contains a subdirectory called Chapt3. In the Chapt3 directory is the file Ex_3_20.c. Compile, debug, link, and run Ex_3_20.c. Make a list of the error messages you got from your compiler. Explain what you did to resolve each of the errors.

21. Write a program that declares a floating-point variable called `result`. Put the following equation in the program:

```
result = 2.0 / 3.0;
```

The statement divides the number 2.0 by 3.0. Have your program print the value in `result`. Explain the output you got in terms of rounding and truncation.

22. Write a program that implements the following pseudocode. Explain the result. The program should:

Declare an integer variable and initialize it with the value 100.
Declare a short integer variable.
Store the value in the integer variable into the short integer.
Print the result.

23. Write a program that implements the following pseudocode. Explain the result. The program should:

Declare an integer variable and initialize it with the value 100000.
Declare a short integer variable.
Store the value in the integer variable into the short integer.
Print the result.

24. Write a program that implements the following pseudocode. Explain the result. The program should:

Declare an integer variable called `intVar` and initialize it with the value 1.
Declare a floating-point variable called `floatVar` and initialize it with the value 3.0.
Declare a floating-point variable called `floatResult`.
Perform the division operation specified by the statement:

```
floatResult = intVar / floatVar;
```

Print the result.

25. Write a program that implements the following pseudocode. Explain the result. The program should:

Declare a floating-point variable called `floatVar` and initialize it with the value 1.0.
Declare an integer variable called `intVar` and initialize it with the value 3.
Declare a floating-point variable called `floatResult`.
Perform the division operation specified by the statement:

```
floatResult = floatVar / intVar;
```

Print the result.

GLOSSARY

Atomic Data Type   The built-in data types. The data types that are part of the C programming language.

Data Type   Specifies the kind of information that can be stored in a variable. For instance, integers are stored in variables of type `int`. Floating point values are stored in `float` variables.

Floating-Point Number   A numeric value with a fractional part.

Integer   A numeric value that has no fractional part.

Overflow   Assigning a value to a variable that exceeds the upper range for that data type.

Rounding Error   An error introduced when a close approximation of a number is used, rather than the number itself.

Signed Data Type   A data type that can store both positive and negative values.

Significant Digits   The digits in a number with the highest, or most significant, numerical value.

Truncation   Throwing away part of a piece of data so that it will fit in memory.

Unsigned Data Type   A data type that can only store positive values.

Underflow   Assigning a value to a variable that exceeds the lower range for that data type.

Variable   A place in memory that is assigned a name and a type. It stores a value that can vary as the program executes.

Atomic Data Types in C: Characters

OBJECTIVES

After reading this chapter, you should be able to:

- Explain and use the `char` data type.
- Explain and use the `signed char` and `unsigned char` data types.
- Understand the potential problems with nonportable character assignments.
- Find and fix accidental escape sequences.

PREVIEW

This chapter presents two more atomic data types, `signed char` *and* `unsigned char`.

4.1 Characters

Someday computers will be able to talk to us and understand our speech. Until then, a primary means of communication with computers is the written word. As a result, all computers must be able to recognize **alphanumeric characters**. Alphanumeric characters include the characters in alphabet, both upper and lower case, and the numerals 0 through 9.

All computers use a specific set of built-in codes to represent alphanumeric characters. Most computers use a set of characters called the **ASCII character set**. ASCII stands for American Standard Code for Information Interchange. With the exception of mainframe computers made by IBM, all computers recognize this set. IBM mainframes use a different character set. In this book, we will discuss the ASCII character set.

In addition to the alphanumeric characters, the ASCII set also includes some punctuation marks and some other commonly used characters. The complete ASCII set of characters is shown in the chart in Appendix B.

C programs declare character variables by using the `char` keyword. Example 4.1 demonstrates how programs declare and initialize character variables.

EXAMPLE 4.1 Declaring and Initializing Character Variables

```
char aCharacter;
char anotherCharacter='C';
```

The first line of this example declares the variable `aCharacter` and leaves it uninitialized. Therefore we must assume it contains garbage until we put something in it. The second variable, `anotherCharacter`, is initialized to contain the character `'C'`. The `'C'` is a **literal character**. A literal character is character data that you type directly into a program's source code. Notice that in the C programing language, all literal characters have single quote marks (') around them.

Whenever a program uses `printf()` or `scanf()` with character variables, the format string should contain `"%c"`.

Because characters in C are surrounded by the single quote marks, you may wonder if C can store a single quote mark character in a character variable. The answer is yes, but you have to precede it with a backslash, like this `'\''`. The same is true for the backslash character, quote marks, and some other special characters. Collectively, we call these characters **escape sequences**. Table 4.1 shows a list of the C escape sequence characters. All of them must be preceded by a backslash.

TRAP 4.1

When you type a literal character into a C program, use the single quote mark before and after it. Only use this character '. Do not use this one `` ` ``. The second character (`` ` ``) is called the grave mark. Your C compiler will give you an error if you use it in your program to enclose a literal character.

Escape Sequence	Represents
\a	Bell (beep)
\b	Backspace
\f	Formfeed
\n	Newline
\r	Return
\t	Horizontal tab
\\	Backslash
\'	Single quotation mark
\"	Double quotation mark
\00	Octal representation
\xhh	Hexadecimal representation

**TABLE 4.1 C Character Constants that Require a **

In spite of the fact that an escape sequence contains a \ in between the single quote marks, an escape sequence is considered one single character, not two.

A character variable may contain only one character at a time. Characters are stored as numbers. The numeric value in a character variable is the character's ASCII value. The ASCII chart in Appendix B shows the ASCII set of characters and their numeric values. Each character in the ASCII set is in the column on the left of the table. The other columns contain the value that is stored in memory for that character, in both decimal and hexadecimal (base 16) numbers. This table shows that when we store an 'A' in memory, what we really store is the number 65.

Because programs store characters in char variables as numbers, it is possible to store a numeric quantity in a char variable. Most modern C compilers will complain about that though. They don't like you mixing numeric and character data types, but you can do it. Hands On 4.1 shows how this ability to treat characters as numbers can be useful.

Hands On 4.1

Objective

Write a program that demonstrates the equivalence of numbers and characters in C.

It should first prompt the user to enter a number between 0 and 9.

The program should then add the number to the character zero. The character zero should be type cast as an integer. The result of the addition should be stored in a character variable.

The program should print the character variable.

Using a type cast, have the program print the ASCII value of the resulting character.

Experiment

Type the following program into your text editor or IDE. Compile, link, and run it.

```
1   #include <stdio.h>
2
3   int main()
4   {
5       char aCharacter=' ';
6       int anInteger=0;
7
8
9       printf("Please input a number between 0-9 :");
10      scanf("%d",&anInteger);
11      aCharacter = (int)'0' + anInteger;
```

```
12          printf("I have converted your number to the character ");
13          printf("%c",aCharacter);
14          printf("\nThe ASCII value of that character is ");
15          anInteger=(int)aCharacter;
16          printf("%d\n",anInteger);
17          return 0;
18  }
```

Result

Please input a number between 0–9 :**1**
I have converted your number to the character 1
The ASCII value of that character is 49

Analysis

This program demonstrates the equivalence of numbers and characters. First, the program declares two variables, one of type `char` and another of type `int`. The character variable is initialized to the value of space. The ASCII character set includes a space in it. It is character number 32. A space character is generated every time you press the spacebar on your keyboard.

The program initializes the second variable, `anInteger`, to 0. It then asks the user to type in a number between 0 and 9, inclusive. The characters `'0'` through `'9'` are also in the ASCII set. They are not the same as the numbers 0 through 9. The numbers 0 through 9 are integers that have the values of 0 through 9. The characters `'0'` through `'9'` are of data type `char` and have the ASCII values of 48 through 57.

This program converts the numbers 0 through 9 to the characters `'0'` through `'9'`. It uses the fact that the ASCII values in memory are really numbers. The ASCII value of the character `'0'` is 48. If the user types the value 0 into `anInteger`, then 48+0 gives 48. If the user types in a number 1, then 48 + 1 is 49, which is the ASCII value of the character `'1'`. This works for all the numbers in the range of 0–9. We add them to the ASCII value of `'0'` to get the ASCII value of the number that the user entered on the keyboard.

There are several important points to recognize about the conversion from integers to characters. First, notice that line 11 reads

```
aCharacter=(int)'0'+anInteger;
```

The word `int` is in parentheses. This tells the C compiler that we are treating the character `'0'` as if it were an integer. It is called a **type cast**. For this one statement only, we are asking the compiler to treat `'0'` as an `int` instead of a `char`. The integer value that `'0'` evaluates to is its ASCII value.

Lines 12 and 13 of the program then tells the user that the conversion has been done. It also converts the character the user entered to its ASCII value with the statement

```
anInteger=(int)aCharacter;
```

on line 15. Here again, a type cast is used. For this statement only, the compiler will treat the `char` variable `aCharacter` as an `int`.

After it converts the character that the user typed to its ASCII value, the program prints the value on the screen.

Try This

Remove the type casts from lines 11 and 15 of this program. Recompile and link it. Observe what errors and warnings, if any, your compiler outputs. Run the program to see if it runs as it did before.

4.2   Signed and Unsigned Characters

We have seen that characters can be treated as numbers. We know that they are stored as their ASCII values in memory. By default, characters can be either signed nor unsigned. Remember that a signed number is one that can take on either positive or negative values. An unsigned number can only store positive values. It is left to implementor of the compiler to decide whether characters are signed or unsigned quantities.

In C programming, the `char` data type is often used to represent a byte because a `char` is usually implemented as a byte. In this case, the programmer must be able to state explicitly whether the byte is signed or unsigned. C allows this. Example 4.2 demonstrates the declaration of signed and unsigned character variables.

EXAMPLE 4.2   Declaring signed And unsigned `char` variables

```
signed char aSignedChar = -1;      // This is ok.
unsigned char anUnsignedChar = 'b';
anUnsignedChar = -5;               // Not allowed.
```

The drawback to defining a byte in this manner is that it is often not portable. Many C compilers promote all `char` variables to `int`.

4.3   Troubleshooting Guide

After reading this section you should be able to:

* Recognize and avoid nonportable character assignments.
* Find and fix accidental escape sequences in strings.

4.3.1   Nonportable Character Assignments

Some systems allocate one byte (8 bits) for character variables. A one-byte character variable can contain any value between 0 and 255. However, if you look at the ASCII chart in Table 4.2, you'll see that the characters in it range in value from 0 to 127. What about the values from 128 to 255?

Computers often use the values from 128 to 255 to form an **extended character set**. The extended character set is not standardized. You can use it in your programs, but it will not work the same way on every type of computer.

For instance, the statement

```
char aCharVariable = (char)248;
```

is a valid C statement on most computers. It declares a variable called `aCharVariable` and stores the character whose value is 248 in it. If your program executes this statement on a PC, it will store a different character than if it executes the same statement on a Macintosh. The result will be different on nearly every different type of computer. Therefore, we say that this statement is nonportable.

It is best to avoid using the extended character set. Both C and many graphical user interfaces (such as Windows or the Macintosh operating system) provide tools to display the same characters that you find in extended character sets. These tools are generally more portable than extended character sets.

4.3.2   Accidental Escape Sequences

If you are using MS DOS or some version of MS Windows (Windows 3.x, Windows 9x, Windows NT, or Windows 2000), it is possible to get accidental escape sequences in your programs. Example 4.3 shows a program fragment that demonstrates this.

EXAMPLE 4.3   Accidental Escape Sequences

```
printf("The file you're looking for is located ");
printf("at C:\adirectory\thisspot\bytes.txt");
```

TECHNICAL NOTE 4.1
One of the tools that C provides is a wide character data type that allows you to use a greater range of characters. It enables your program to use many of the same characters as those provided by extended character sets. This is an advanced topic that is beyond the scope of this book.

This string has three escape sequences in it. They are '\a', '\t', and '\b'. Any time any of the characters in Table 4.1 occurs in a string, the C compiler will treat it as an escape sequence. Does this mean that we can't put strings containing directory and file names in MS DOS or MS Windows programs?

The answer is quite the opposite. Any time we want the backslash character to occur in a string as a backslash and not as the beginning of an escape sequence, we must put '\\' in the string. This tells the compiler to treat it as a backslash character. Example 4.4 shows nearly the same string as Example 4.3. However, all of the backslash characters in Example 4.4 are doubled. The compiler will not treat them as escape sequences.

EXAMPLE 4.4 The Escape Sequences Removed

```
printf("The file you're looking for is located ");
printf("at C:\\adirectory\\thisspot\\bytes.txt");
```

Almost every C programmer using DOS or Windows occasionally puts accidental escape sequences in their programs. When we program on other operating systems, such as Unix, we are less prone to this mistake. Unix does not use the backslash character in path names. However, we must watch out for it any time we want to use a backslash in a string.

TECHNICAL NOTE

4.1   One of the tools that C provides is a wide character data type that allows you to use a greater range of characters. It enables your program to use many of the same characters as those provided by extended character sets. This is an advanced topic that is beyond the scope of this book.

TRAP

4.1   When you type a literal character into a C program, use the single quote mark before and after it. Only use this character '. Do not use this one `. The second character (`) is called the grave mark. Your C compiler will give you an error if you use it in your program to enclose a literal character.

SUMMARY

Character variables are declared as type char. A character variable can contain at most, one character. All computers except IBM mainframes use the ASCII set of characters.

There are some character values in C that are preceded by a backslash. These are called escape sequences.

The C standard does not specify by default whether the character data types are signed or unsigned. The implementor of the compiler can decide whether char variables should be signed or unsigned. If you absolutely need a character to be signed or unsigned, you can force it to whichever you want.

REVIEW QUESTIONS

1. What is the ASCII set?
2. What are alphanumeric characters?
3. How is a character variable declared in a C program?
4. What is a literal character? Give 10 examples of literal characters.
5. What is an escape sequence? How are escape sequences used?
6. In what way is a character really a number?
7. How can a character variable be treated temporarily as an integer in a program?
8. By default, are characters signed or unsigned?
9. How is a signed character variable declared in a program?
10. How is an unsigned character variable declared in a program?

EXERCISES

1. The ANSI C standard does not specify whether characters are signed or unsigned by default. Explain why you think the standard is written this way.

2. Fill in the blank.

   An escape sequence always begins with a _____ character.

3. Fill in the blank.

   A literal character in source code must have a _____ before and after the character.

4. In Chapter 17, we'll see that the C Standard Libraries define a marker called EOF. This is used to mark the end of text files. Text files contain characters from the ASCII set. The EOF marker has a value of −1. In light of this, explain why signed characters might be useful when reading characters from a text file.

5. Write a program that accepts a character as input from the user and prints its ASCII value.

6. Explain how to fix accidental escape sequences in a program.

7. Write a program that prints all of the escape sequences in Table 4.1.

8. Explain what it means when we say that program code is nonportable. Give at least three reasons why you think this might be important to companies for which you may work.

9. Explain what the extended character set is.

10. Explain why programs which use the extended character set are not portable.

11. Write a program the prints each character in your computer's extended character set to the screen.

12. Explain the difference between signed and unsigned characters.

13. Write a program that tries to store the value −1 in an unsigned character variable. Explain the results of this experiment.

14. To find out if your compiler uses signed or unsigned characters by default, declare a `char` variable in a C program. Assign the char variable the value of −1. Explain the results.

15. Write a program that accepts a number as input from the user. We will assume that the user will type in a number between 0 and 127, inclusive. Treat the number as an ASCII value and print the character that corresponds to that ASCII value.

16. Write a program that accepts a number as input from the user. We will assume that the user will type in a number between 128 and 255, inclusive. Treat the number as a character value and print the character that corresponds to it. Explain why this did or did not work on your computer system.

17. Find and fix the errors in the following program.

```
1   include <stdio.h>
2
3   int main()
4   {
5        char aChar = 'Q';
6
7        printf("The letter %c",aChar);
8        printf(" is a very nice letter.");
9        printf(Don't you think?\\n);
10       return (0);
11   }
```

18. Find and fix the errors in the following program.

```
1   #include <stdio.h>
2
3   int main()
4   {
5        char aChar = Q;
6        printf("The letter %d",aChar);
7        printf(" is a very nice letter.);
8        printf("Don't you think?\n");
10       return (0);
```

19. Explain what a type cast is and why it might be useful in C programming.

20. Type the following program into your text editor or IDE. Compile, link, and run it. Give a line-by-line description of what this program does.

```
1   #include <stdio.h>
2
```

```
 3   int main()
 4   {
 5          char aCharacter='A';
 6          char anotherCharacter;
 7
 8          printf("Programming in the C Language ");
 9          printf("is as easy as ");
10          printf("%c ",aCharacter);
11          anotherCharacter = (int)aCharacter + 1;
12          printf("%c ",anotherCharacter);
13          aCharacter = anotherCharacter + 1;
14          printf("%c.\n",aCharacter);
15          return 0;
16   }
```

21. Write a program that does the following:

Prompts the user to input a lowercase letter.

Reads the character from the keyboard and stores it in a character variable.

Uses type casting to subtract the value in the character variable from the letter 'a' and stores the result in another character variable.

Uses type casting to add the value in the second character variable to the letter 'A' and saves the result into the first character variable.

Outputs the result.

22. Write a program that does the following:

Prompts the user to input an uppercase letter.

Reads the character from the keyboard and stores it in a character variable.

Uses type casting to subtract the value in the character variable from the letter 'A' and stores the result in another character variable.

Uses type casting to add the value in the second character variable to the letter 'a' and saves the result into the first character variable.

Outputs the result.

23. When programming hardware directly, developers must often store, retrieve, and perform operations on individual bytes (8 bits). There is no byte type built into C. Many times, programmers use unsigned characters instead. Write a program that simulates sending values to a computer's input and output port. The program should:

Declare the unsigned character variables theByte and theAnswer.

Prompt the user for a byte value in hexadecimal. See Appendix D for a discussion of the hexadecimal number system if you are not familiar with it. It should use the string "Input a value to send to the i/o port:" as its user prompt.

Use scanf() to read the user's input into the variable theByte. The format string it will use to read in the byte is "%hu". Because a byte value has 8 bits, it can store a maximum value of 127.

Use type casting and subtract the value in theByte from 128 and store it in theAnswer.

Use these statements to output the result:

```
printf("The i/o port was sent the value %hu", theByte);
printf(" and it returned "%hu", theAnswer);
```

24. When programming hardware directly, developers must often store, retrieve, and perform operations on individual bytes (8 bits). There is no byte type built into C. Many times, programmers use unsigned characters instead. Some compilers convert all characters to integers. Explain why this could be a problem for programs that depend on 8-bit unsigned characters.

25. Write a program that uses signed characters. It should prompt the user for a value, either positive or negative. It should then print the value as a character. Explain the results.

GLOSSARY

Alphanumeric Characters   Characters that are either numbers or letters.

ASCII Character Set   American Standard Code for Information Interchange. Set of characters recognized by all computers except IBM mainframes.

Escape Sequence   A special character that is preceded by a backslash (\) character. See Table 4.1.

Extended Character Set   Nonstandard characters whose values fall between 128 and 255, inclusive.

Literal Character   Character data that is typed directly into a program's source code.

Type Cast   Casting one type into another temporarily.

5

Introduction to C Operators

OBJECTIVES

After reading this chapter, you should be able to:

- Use the addition (+), subtraction (−), multiplication (*), and division (/) operators in C programs.

- Explain what operator precedence is and how it can affect equations in programs.

OUTLINE

This chapter introduces C operators. Part of the richness of the C language is its powerful set of operators. Some of the most commonly used operators in C are the arithmetic operators: addition, subtraction, multiplication, and division.

5.1   Addition, Subtraction, Multiplication, and Division

As you would expect, the C programming language uses the plus sign (+) for addition and the minus sign (–) for subtraction. Multiplication is done with the asterisk (*), and division uses the forward slash (/). In most cases, their use is pretty straightforward. We've already used some of these operators in our sample programs. Hands On 5.1 demonstrates the use of the operators plus, minus, times, and divide.

Hands On 5.1

Objective

Write a program that demonstrates the use of the +, –, *, and / operators for integers.

Experiment

Type the following program into your text editor or IDE. Compile, link, and run it.

```
1    #include <stdio.h>
2
3    main()
4    {
5         int i=20;
6         int j;
7
8         // Print the value of i and j.
9         printf("i=%d\n",i);
10        printf("j=%d\n",j);
11        // Integer addition.
12        j = i+5;
13        printf("j=%d\n",j);
14
15        // Integer subtraction.
```

```
16        i = j-10;
17        printf("i=%d\n",i);
18
19        // Integer multiplication.
20        i = i * j * 2;
21        printf("i=%d\n",i);
22
23        // Integer division.
24        j = i/10;
25        printf("j=%d\n",j);
26
27        return (0);
28  }
```

Results

i=20
j=-1074004460
j=25
i=15
i=750
j=75

Analysis

When you compile this program, you will very likely get a warning about it. The compiler should tell you that you are trying to use the variable j before it has been initialized. However, the program should still compile and run.

On lines 9 and 10, the program prints the values of the variables i and j. We can see that j does in fact contain a random value. It will likely be different every time you run the program. Some compilers automatically initialize uninitialized data to zero. However, don't get in the habit of depending on that, because some compilers don't.

Next, the program performs an integer addition and prints the result to the screen. It shows that the variable j now equals 25.

On lines 16 and 17, the program performs a subtraction and assigns the result to the variable i. It then prints the value in i.

Next is a multiplication. Line 20 tells the computer to take the value in i, multiply it by the value in j, and then multiply that result by 2. The final result in this case is 25*15*2, or 750. It is stored back into the variable i by using the assignment operator. The program prints 750 to the screen on line 22.

It may seem funny to have the variable i on the right side of the statement

```
i=i*j*2;
```

Most programming languages allow this. When a variable appears on the right of an assignment operator, the program will read a value from it. When it appears on the left of the assignment operator, the program will write a value to the variable.

This Hands On program also performs an integer division. The value in i is divided by 10 and stored in j. The result is 75, which the program prints to the screen.

The four basic C mathematical operators can be used with other data types. Hands On 5.2 shows the use of +, -, *, and / with unsigned integers. Reminder: The format string for printf() and scanf() must contain "%lu" when you are using unsigned long integers.

Hands On 5.2

Objective

Write a program that demonstrates the use of the +, -, *, and / operators for unsigned integers.

Experiment

Type the following program into your IDE or text editor. Compile, link, and run it.

```
1   #include <stdio.h>
2
3   main()
4   {
5           unsigned i=20;
6           unsigned long j;
7           unsigned short k=50;
8
9           printf("i=%u\n", i);
10          printf("j=%lu\n",j);
11          printf("k=%u\n",k);
12
13          // This will cause underflow!
14          j = i-k;
15          printf("j=%lu\n",j);
16
17          j = i+k;
18          printf("j=%lu\n",j);
19
20          // This can cause overflow!
21          k=i * j * k;
22          printf("k=%u\n",k);
23
24          j = j/5;
25          printf("j=%lu\n",j);
26
27          return (0);
28  }
```

Results

i=20
j=3220962836
k=50
j=4294967266
j=70
k=4464
j=14

Analysis

When you compile this program, your compiler may give you a warning that indicates that you are trying to use the variable j before it is initialized, just like Hands On 5.1.

This sample program begins by declaring three variables, an unsigned integer, an unsigned short integer, and an unsigned long integer. It initializes the variables i and k. However, it does not initialize j to a known value. Therefore, we must assume that j contains garbage. The program prints the values in i, j, and k on lines 9–11. When it does, we see that j does, in fact, contain a random value.

The first mathematical operator that the program uses is a subtraction. Because the value in k is larger than the value in i, the subtraction will evaluate to a negative number. However, C doesn't allow us to store negative numbers in unsigned data types. Therefore, we are generating an underflow error through this subtraction. When the program prints the value of j, we can see clearly that it underflowed.

Next, the program does an addition on line 17. It assigns the result to the variable j. This assignment gives j a known value.

After performing the addition and printing the value of j on the screen, the program does a multiplication (line 21). It multiplies the value in i times the value in j and then multiplies that by the value in k. It assigns the result into k. Note that this may cause an overflow error. The Results section shows that, in this instance, overflow occurred. The values of i, j, and k at this point in the program are 20, 70, and 50, respectively. The result of multiplying these three values is 70,000. However, that number is too big to fit in an unsigned short variable on this example system. Some compilers will automatically promote the variable k to an unsigned. If yours does, this equation will not cause an overflow error.

The Hands On program finishes by performing a division and printing the resulting value.

Hands On 5.3 uses +, -, *, and / on floating-point data types.

Hands On 5.3

Objective

Write a program that demonstrates the use of the +, -, *, and / operators for floating point numbers.

Experiment

Type the following program into your IDE or text editor. Compile, link, and run it.

```
1    #include <stdio.h>
2
3    main()
4    {
5          float i=1000.1001;
6          double j=123.234567;
7          double k;
8
9          k = i+j;
10         printf("k=%10.10Lf\n",k);
11
12         k = i-j+500.951;
13         printf("k=%10.10Lf\n",k);
14
15         j = j*i;
16         printf("j=%Lf\n",j);
17
18         i = k/j;
19         printf("i=%f\n",i);
20
21         return (0);
22   }
```

Results

k=1123.3346646563
k=1377.8165306563
j=123246.902491
i=0.011179

Analysis

This short program first declares three floating-point variables and then uses them in an addition operation on line 9. It prints the result to the screen. It also performs a subtraction on line 12 and prints the resulting value.

The program prints the result of the addition and subtraction. You may wonder what the `"10.10"` portion of the `printf()` statement means. These are format modifiers that set the number of digits to the right and left of the decimal point in a floating-point number. In this case, the statement `"10.10"` sets the number of digits to the right of the decimal point to ten. It also specifies that the portion of the number to the left of the decimal point may have as many as ten digits. Although the details of `printf()` are not presented until Chapter 12, I used these format modifiers in this example to help ensure that this Hands On program produces the same output on as many different types of computers as possible.

Before ending, the program performs a multiplication and outputs the result. Finally, the program does a division and prints the answer to the screen.

As we saw in Chapter 3, it is possible to use different types in a single operation. For instance, variables of type `float` can be added to variables of type `int` or `unsigned`. It's important to note, however, that equations involving floating-point numbers result in answers that are floating-point numbers. Example 5.1 illustrates how a mixed-type equation can work.

EXAMPLE 5.1   A Mixed-Type Operation

```
int anInt = 10;
int anotherInt;
float aFloat = 56.78;
float anotherFloat;

anotherFloat = aFloat + anInt;
anotherInt = aFloat + anInt;
```

As Example 5.1 shows, integers and floating-point numbers can be used together in equations. The data types of the result of both of these additions are `float`. When the first addition is performed, the program fragment stores the answer into a floating-point variable.

The second addition stores the answer into a variable of type `int`. The results might surprise us. Older compilers might treat the bits being assigned as the bit pattern of an `int`. Integers are stored in completely different ways than floating-point numbers. Their bit patterns are not alike. Simply treating the bit pattern of a `float` as if it were the bit pattern of an `int` will not give us the answer we're looking for from this program fragment.

Most recent compilers will do what we would expect. They will truncate the fractional portion of the floating-point number when that floating-point number is assigned to an integer variable. However, because some older compilers will not, it is wise to create a small test program to see what your compiler does with mixed-type equations.

TIP 5.1
Either check your compiler documentation or write a test program to see how your compiler handles mixed-type equations.

5.2   The Process of Program Development

The ability to create programs that use variables and operators enables us to begin to write programs that actually do useful things. This is also a good opportunity to apply the problem solving steps we saw in Chapter 2 Section 2.1.2. As we go through this process, we'll use pseudocode to design our program.

Our goal is to start with a clear problem statement, develop an **algorithm** that solves the problem, and end with a program that implements the algorithm. An algorithm is step-by-step solution to a problem. It is similar to a recipe for cooking food. A recipe for strawberry cream pie is the algorithm that we can follow to turn raw ingredients into a great dessert.

The first step in developing a program is to identify the problem or task. We'll use the example of a program that finds the average of three numbers. The statement of purpose for the program is shown in Example 5.2

EXAMPLE 5.2   Statement of Purpose

Find and print the average of three numbers.

The second step is to understand the problem. To find the average of three numbers, we must add the numbers and divide the result by three. Example 5.3 is an initial pseudocode version of the program.

EXAMPLE 5.3   The Initial Pseudocode

Find the average of three numbers.
    Add the three numbers.
    Divide the sum by 3.
Print the resulting average.

The third and fourth steps for solving a problem are to identify alternative ways to solve the problem and to select the best way to solve the problem from the list of alternative solutions. Because this problem is so simple, we don't really need to perform these two steps. However, the ability to perform these two steps is crucial to being able to provide software that meets our users' needs.

The next steps in developing this program are to list instructions that will enable us to solve the problem and to evaluate the solution. This is exactly what pseudocode does for us. The initial versions of the pseudocode provide us with a detailed problem statement. As we repeatedly evaluate and refine our pseudocode, we get the actual instructions we can use to write the program from. Example 5.4 shows a refinement of our pseudocode.

EXAMPLE 5.4   Refining the Algoritm

Get three numbers from the user.
Find the average of the three numbers.
    Add the three numbers.
    Divide the sum by 3.
Print the resulting average.

This pseudocode algorithm is good, but it is still not specific enough to write a program from. The algorithm now states where the numbers come from, but to not say how they are obtained from the user. Example 5.5 fixes this.

EXAMPLE 5.5   Specifying the Input Process

Get three numbers from the user.
    Prompt the user for an integer.
    Read an integer from the keyboard.
    Prompt the user for an integer.
    Read an integer from the keyboard.
    Prompt the user for an integer.
    Read an integer from the keyboard.
Find the average of the three numbers.
    Add the three numbers.
    Divide the sum by 3.
Print the resulting average.

With this refined algorithm, we can now develop the final pseudocode for our program, as shown in Example 5.6.

EXAMPLE 5.6 **The Final Pseudocode Algorithm**

Declare the integer variables num1, num2, num3, sum, and average.
Get three numbers from the user.
> Prompt the user for an integer.
> Read an integer from the keyboard. Store it in num1.
> Prompt the user for an integer.
> Read an integer from the keyboard. Store it in num2.
> Prompt the user for an integer.
> Read an integer from the keyboard. Store it in num3.

Find the average of the three numbers.
> sum = num1 + num2 + num3.
> average = sum / 3.

Print average to the screen.

Using this algorithm, we can write a program. Hands On 5.4 implements the algorithm in Example 5.6.

Hands On 5.4

Objective

Write a program using the following algorithm:
> Declare the integer variables num1, num2, num3, sum, and average.
> Get three numbers from the user.
>> Prompt the user for an integer.
>> Read an integer from the keyboard. Store it in num1.
>> Prompt the user for an integer.
>> Read an integer from the keyboard. Store it in num2.
>> Prompt the user for an integer.
>> Read an integer from the keyboard. Store it in num3.
> Find the average of the three numbers.
>> sum = num1 + num2 + num3.
>> average = sum / 3.
> Print average to the screen.

Experiment

Type the following program into your text editor or IDE. Compile, link, and run it.

```
1   #include <stdio.h>
2
3   int main()
4   {
5        int num1, num2, num3, sum, average;
6
7        printf("\nPlease enter an integer: ");
8        scanf("%d",&num1);
9        printf("Please enter a second integer: ");
10       scanf("%d",&num2);
11       printf("Please enter a third integer: ");
12       scanf("%d",&num3);
13
14       sum = num1 + num2 + num3;
15       average = sum / 3;
16
17       printf("The average of those ");
18       printf("three numbers is %d.\n",average);
```

```
19
20          return (0);
21      }
```

Results

Please enter an integer: **1**
Please enter a second integer: **2**
Please enter a third integer: **3**
The average of those three numbers is 2.

Analysis

As in previous Hands On example programs, the user's input is shown in bold type in the Results section. This program exactly implements the algorithm developed in Examples 5.1 through 5.5. It demonstrates on a small scale how programs can be developed using pseudocode through successive refinement. With each pass over the pseudocode, the algorithm was refined until we were able to create a program from it. You'll use this same process throughout your programming career.

Try this

Delete the & character from inside the `scanf()` statements in this program. Recompile, link, and run it to see the result.

For the most part, the Hands On examples will not present the exact algorithm used to develop the programs. Instead, they give the initial problem statement and the final program code. It is left for you to derive the algorithm when necessary. You will also find exercises at the end of the various chapters of this book that help you practice the process of developing algorithms.

5.3 Precedence

Not all operators are created equal in C. Some operators have higher priority, or **precedence**, than others. Suppose, for example, that we want to type the equation in Example 5.7 into a program.

EXAMPLE 5.7   A Question of Precedence

$$i = \frac{j + k}{3}$$

A natural reaction would be to type the statement

```
i = j + k / 3;
```

into the program. However, that will not give us what we want. The reason is that the division operator has higher precedence than the addition operator. Therefore, a program containing this statement performs the division first. It then performs the addition. What we want is the addition done first and then the division. We can solve this problem using the parentheses operator, which has higher precedence than division. We would need to rewrite the equation above to the following:

```
i = (j + k) / 3;
```

Because the parentheses operator has very high precedence, everything inside the parentheses is evaluated first. Afterward, the program does the division. Appendix C shows a precedence chart. This chart lists all of the operators in C by order of precedence. Operators shown near the top of the chart have higher precedence than operators listed farther down.

Here's a Hands On example to demonstrate precedence.

Hands On 5.5

Objective

Write a program that demonstrates operator precedence.

Experiment

Type the following program into your IDE or text editor. Compile, link, and run it.

```
1   #include <stdio.h>
2
3   int main()
4   {
5         int i,j=60,k=30;
6
7         i=j+k/3;
8         printf("The answer to i=j+k/3 is %d\n",i);
9
10        i=(j+k)/3;
11        printf("The answer to i=(j+k)/3 is %d\n",i);
12
13        return (0);
14  }
```

Results

The answer to i=j+k/3 is 70
The answer to i=(j+k)/3 is 30

Analysis

The first equation, which appears on line 7 of the program, uses normal C precedence. The program performs the division first, then does the addition. The second equation contains parentheses that force the addition to be done first.

Try This

Change the division operator on lines 7 and 10 of this program to subtraction signs. Recompile, link, and run the program. What is the difference between the two answers that are printed out on lines 8 and 11? Why do you think you got the answers you did?

As we can see from the Hands On programs presented so far, operators with higher precedence are performed first. Table 5.1 provides more examples of equations whose precedence has been altered with parentheses. The left column contains several equations without parentheses. The second column shows how these equations will be evaluated. The third column gives an example of one way the precedence of the first equation can be altered with parentheses.

At this point you may be asking, "What if an equation includes two operators of equal precedence? Which one is done first?" The Associativity column of the precedence chart in Appendix C answers this question. The associativity of an operator tells us which operator to evaluate first if there are two operators of equal precedence.

Notice, for instance, that the multiplication (*) and division (/) operators are on the same level in the precedence chart. The rightmost column says that they have left to right associativity. That means in an equation like

```
a=b*c/d;
```

	Equation	Evaluation Order	Forced Precedence
TABLE 5.1 Altering Precedence	a=b+c*d	a=b+(c*d)	a=(b+c)*d
	a=b/c*d+e	a=((b/c)*d)+e	a=b/(c*(d+e))
	a=b–c/d*e	a=b–((c/d)*e)	a=(b–(c/d))*e

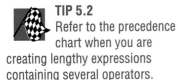

TIP 5.2
Refer to the precedence chart when you are creating lengthy expressions containing several operators.

the multiplication will be done first, then the division. Even though they are of equal precedence, the multiplication is done first because it's the leftmost of the two operators.

5.4 Troubleshooting Guide

After reading this section, you should be able to:

- Find precedence problems.
- Fix precedence problems.

5.4.1 Finding Precedence Problems

Tracking down precedence problems in a program is primarily a matter of knowing and validating your output data. You should thoroughly test the output of every program, and every piece of every program, before you release it.

Certain precedence mistakes tend to be made more than others. For instance, a programmer may write an equation in a program like this:

```
y=x/a+1;
```

when he really means this:

```
y=x/(a+1);
```

The first equation will divide the value in x by the value in a. Next, the statement adds 1 to the result. It stores the result in the variable y. The second equation first adds 1 to the value in the variable a and then divides x by the result of the addition. It stores the final value in the variable y.

Similar precedence mistakes are common with multiplication.

5.4.2 Fixing Precedence Problems

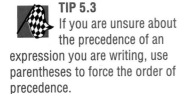

TIP 5.3
If you are unsure about the precedence of an expression you are writing, use parentheses to force the order of precedence.

Whenever you're unsure of what the precedence of an equation is, use parentheses to force it to what you want it to be. It's okay if you overuse parentheses a bit. That's better than spending large amounts of time tracking down a precedence bug in your program. Using parentheses to force precedence doesn't cause your program to run slower. There is no performance penalty for this technique.

SUMMARY

C supports arithmetic operations. This chapter presented the addition, subtraction, multiplication, and division operators.

Operator precedence controls the order that operations are performed. Operators with higher precedence will be done before operators with lower precedence. Operators with equal precedence are evaluated in the order specified in the precedence chart in Appendix C.

Programs can force precedence by using parentheses. They have very high precedence, so operations inside them are performed first.

TIPS

5.1 Either check your compiler documentation or write a test program to see how your compiler handles mixed-type equations.

5.2 Refer to the precedence chart when you are creating lengthy expressions containing several operators.

5.3 If you are unsure about the precedence of an expression you are writing, use parentheses to force the order of precedence.

REVIEW QUESTIONS

1. What is the order of evaluation for the following equation? It doesn't matter whether or not you know what the operators do. Only the order in which they are evaluated matters.

   ```
   a = b*c+d-e/f%d;
   ```

2. What data type is the result of the following equation?

   ```
   10/200.0;
   ```

3. What is stored in the variable i?

   ```
   int i,j=5;
   double d=7.6;
   i=j+d;
   ```

4. What is stored in the variable d?

   ```
   int i=5;
   double d,e=7.6;
   d=e+i;
   ```

5. What is precedence?

6. Why do operators have to have precedence?

7. What would be the result of the following equation if the addition and subtraction operators had higher precedence than multiplication and division?

   ```
   int i,j=5,k=9,m=1,n=21;
   i=j+k*m-n;
   ```

8. Why would you not want addition and subtraction to have higher precedence than multiplication and division? Use the equation in question 7 as an example.

9. When operators have equal precedence, in what order are they evaluated?

10. How can the precedence of an equation be forced into a particular order?

EXERCISES

1. Write a program that gets four integers from the user, adds them together, and prints the sum on the screen.

2. Write a program that finds the average of four numbers. Use the following algorithm:

   Prompt the user for four numbers.
   Get four numbers from the user.
   Add the numbers together.
   Divide the answer by four.
   Print the result on the screen.

3. Write a program that implements the following equation:

   ```
   a=(b-c)/(d*e);
   ```

   Declare the five integer variables a, b, c, d, and e in your program. When the program runs, it should prompt the user for the values of b, c, d, and e. After it executes the equation above, it should print the value of a.

4. Some of the equations from Table 5.1 are repeated below. Assume that b equals 7, c equals –3, d is 29, and e equals 114. Write a program that assigns values to the variables and calculates an answer for a for each equation.

   ```
   a=b+c*d          a=(b+c)*d
   a=b/c*d+e        a=b/(c*(d+e))
   a=b-c/d*e        a=(b-(c/d))*e
   ```

5. Write a program that gets an integer value and a floating-point value from the user. The program should multiply them together and store the result in an integer variable. It should then print the contents of the integer variable. Explain your result.

6. Write a program that gets an integer value and a floating point value from the user. The program should multiply them together and store the result in a floating-point variable. It should then print the contents of the floating-point variable. Explain the result.

7. Write a program that:
   Declares two unsigned integer variables.
   Assigns the values 10000 and 1000 into the unsigned integers.
   Multiplies them together and stores the answer into an unsigned short integer.
   Explain the result you get when you run this program.

8. Write a program that squares a value input by the user. The number that the user types in may be less than zero. The program should use the following algorithm:
   Get an integer from the user.
   Multiply the integer by itself (e.g., squares the number).
   Output the answer to the screen.

9. Write a program that gets a number from the user and divides it by 10. The program should then output the answer to the screen. Assume that the number that the user types is not less than zero.

10. Write a program that gets a number from the user and multiplies it by 10. It should then output the answer to the screen. Explain what happens when the number that the user types in gets very large.

11. Write a program that gets a number from the user and divides it by 100000.5. The program should then output the answer to the screen. Explain what potential problems can occur when the number the user inputs gets too small.

12. Write a program that prompts the user for the length and width of a rectangle. It should then calculate and print the area of the rectangle. The area of a rectangle can be found using the formula area = length * width.

13. Write a program that prompts the user for the length and width of a rectangle. It should then calculate and print the total combined length of the rectangle's edges. The

total combined length can be found using the formula combinedLength = 2 * length + 2 * width.

14. Write a program that prompts the user for the radius of a circle. The program should then calculate and print the circumference of the circle. The circumference of a circle can be found using the formula circumference = 3.14159 * radius * radius.

15. Write a program that prompts the user for the radius of a circle. The program should then calculate and print the area of the circle. The area of a circle can be found using the formula area = 2 * 3.14159 * radius.

16. Write a program that calculates the distance a car travels. Have the user input the rate of speed and the time the car travels. The distance that an object travels can be calculated using the formula distance = rate * time.

17. Write a program that converts a distance in miles to kilometers. Use the formula kilometers = miles * 1.61. Get the distance in miles from the user.

18. The rate of speed that an object travels can be calculated using the formula rate = distance / time. In your own words, write a problem statement for a program that calculates the rate a car travels. The program should have the user input the distance and the time the car is in motion. It will use these values to calculate the how fast the car moves. Demonstrate how you refine the problem statement into an algorithm.

19. Write a program for the algorithm you developed for Exercise 18.

20. In your own words, write a problem statement for a program that converts a distance in kilometers to miles. Use the formula miles = kilometers / 1.61. Get the distance in kilometers from the user. Demonstrate how you refine the problem statement into an algorithm.

21. Write a program for the algorithm you developed for Exercise 20.

22. In your own words, write a problem statement for a program that converts an angle measured in degrees to an angle measured in radians. Read the angle as input from the user. Use the formula radians = degrees * (180 / 3.14195). Demonstrate how you refine the problem statement into an algorithm.

23. Write a program for the algorithm you developed for Exercise 22. Are the parentheses shown in Exercise 22 necessary in your program? Why or why not?

24. In your own words, write a problem statement for a program that converts an angle measured in radians to an angle measured in degrees. Read the angle as input from the user. Use the formula degrees = radians * (3.14195 / 180). Demonstrate how you refine the problem statement into an algorithm.

25. Write a program for the algorithm you developed for Exercise 24. Are the parentheses shown in Exercise 24 necessary in your program? Why or why not?

GLOSSARY

Algorithm   A step-by-step solution to a problem.

Precedence   The order in which operators are evaluated. Operators with higher precedence are evaluated first.

6

Other Numeric Operators

OBJECTIVES

After reading this chapter, you should be able to:

- Explain and use the preincrement and postincrement operators.
- Explain and use the predecrement and postdecrement operators.
- Explain and use the modulus operator.
- Explain and use the `sizeof` operator.
- Explain and use the +=, -=, *=, and /= operators.

PREVIEW

In this chapter, we'll continue looking at C operators. In particular, we'll cover the use of the four increment and decrement operators, the modulus *operator, and the* sizeof *operators. This chapter also presents the use of the* +=, -=, *=, *and* /= *operators.*

6.1   Increment and Decrement

A common operation in C is to increment or decrement the value of a variable by 1. Because it is such a common operation, the C language provides us with operators for incrementing and decrementing. In fact, there are two operators for incrementing and two for decrementing. When we want to increase the value in a numeric variable by 1, we can use preincrement or postincrement.

The preincrement operator is shown in Example 6.1. The ++ sign occurs before the variable. As you look at the program, what do you think will be stored in the variable b?

EXAMPLE 6.1   Preincrementing a Variable

```
1   int main()
2   {
3        int a=10;
4        int b;
5
6        b=++a;
7        printf("a=%d\n",a);
8        printf("b=%d\n",b);
9        return (0);
10  }
```

The program in this example stores the value 11 in the variable b. A preincrement tells the compiler that you want to increment the variable before you use it for anything else. Therefore, the program in Example 6.1 incremented value in the variable a and then assigns its contents to b. When you run this program, it will print 11 for both a and b.

Example 6.2 shows nearly the same program as Example 6.1. In this case, however, it uses a postincrement.

EXAMPLE 6.2 Postincrementing a Variable

```
1   #include <stdio.h>
2
3   int main()
4   {
5           int a=10;
6           int b;
7
8           b=a++;
9           printf("a=%d\n",a);
10          printf("b=%d\n",b);
11          return (0);
12  }
```

TIP 6.1
The preincrement operator tells the compiler that a variable should be incremented before it is used for anything else. The postincrement operator tells the compiler that the variable should be used in an equation first and then incremented.

This program will print the number 10 for the variable b, and 11 for a. A postincrement tells the compiler to use the value in a variable and then increment it. Therefore, the program first assigns the value in the variable a into b. It then increments the value in a. At the end of the program, the variable a has the value of 11. However, b contains 10.

Predecrement and postdecrement work in a way that is similar to preincrement and postincrement. Hands On 6.1 shows a program that demonstrates the difference between predecrement and postdecrement.

Hands On 6.1

Objective

Write a program that illustrates the use of predecrement and postdecerement. It should:

Declare two integer variables, a and b.
Initialize a to 10.
Postdecrement a and assign its value to b.
Print the values in a and b.
Predecrement a and assign its value to b.
Print the values in a and b.

Experiment

Type the following program into your IDE or text editor. Compile, link, and run it.

```
1   #include <stdio.h>
2
3   int main()
4   {
5           int a=10;
6           int b;
7
8           b=a--;
9           printf("a=%d\n",a);
10          printf("b=%d\n",b);
11
12          b=--a;
```

```
13          printf("a=%d\n",a);
14          printf("b=%d\n",b);
15
16          return (0);
17   }
```

Results

a=9
b=10
a=8
b=8

Analysis

The program in this Hands On first uses a postdecrement to decrement the value in the variable a by one. The postdecrement made the program use the value in the variable a for the assignment first, then decrement it.

After outputting the values in a and b, the program again uses a predecrement to decrease the value in a by one. We can see from the Results section that it decremented the value in the variable a before it performed the assignment.

6.2 Modulus

The C language uses the percent sign (%) for the modulus operator. The modulus operator gives the remainder of an integer division. Example 6.3 shows an integer division in a program. The answer should be 2.5. However, because the example program uses integers, C truncates the fractional part of the answer. So the program prints the number 2 to the screen.

The fractional part that is truncated is called the **remainder**. The real answer to 5/2 is that 2 goes 2 times into 5 with a remainder of 1. In other words, 2*2+1=5.

EXAMPLE 6.3   An Integer Division

```
 1   #include <stdio.h>
 2
 3   int main()
 4   {
 5          int theAnswer=5/2;
 6
 7          printf("What is 5/2?\n");
 8          printf("The answer is %d\n",theAnswer);
 9          return (0);
10   }
```

If we ever want to know the remainder of an integer division, we use the modulus operator. Example 6.4 demonstrates this. Notice that it is almost the same program as Example 6.3. The primary difference is that the division sign has been removed and the modulus operator is used instead. If you type this program into your computer, compile it, and run it, you'll see that it prints the number 1.

EXAMPLE 6.4   Using the Modulus Operator

```
 1   #include <stdio.h>
 2
 3   int main()
 4   {
 5          int theAnswer=5%2;
```

```
 6
 7          printf("What is 5 modulus 2?\n");
 8          printf("The answer is %d\n",theAnswer);
 9          return (0);
10   }
```

6.3 sizeof

The `sizeof` operator evaluates to the number of bytes a piece of data requires when it is stored in memory. It can be used with any data type. You can also use it with a variable name, and it will evaluate to the number of bytes required to store the variable's data. However, this can lead to some answers that you may not expect. The Troubleshooting Guide for this chapter explains this potential problem.

Hands On 6.2

Objective

Write a program that demonstrates the use of the `sizeof` operator. The program should use the `sizeof` operator to tell the user the size of an `int`, `long`, `short`, `float`, and `double` on the computer on which the program executes.

Experiment

Type the following program into your text editor or IDE. Compile, link, and run it.

```
 1   #include <stdio.h>
 2
 3   int main()
 4   {
 5          printf("On this computer, ");
 6          printf("using this operating system,\n");
 7          printf("an integer is %d bytes.\n",
 8                  sizeof(int));
 9
10          printf("A long is %d bytes.\n",sizeof(long));
11          printf("A short is %d bytes.\n",sizeof(short));
12          printf("A float is %d bytes.\n",sizeof(float));
13          printf("A double is %d bytes.\n",sizeof(double));
14          return (0);
15   }
```

Results

On this computer, using this operating system,
an integer is 4 bytes.
A long is 4 bytes.
A short is 2 bytes.
A float is 4 bytes.
A double is 8 bytes.

Analysis

This program displays the number of bytes that are needed in memory to store an `int`, a `long`, a `short`, a `float`, and a `double`. Any type name can be used with the `sizeof` operator. The `sizeof` operator always evaluates to the size of a type in bytes.

When you run this program on your computer, you are likely to get a different answer for the size of the atomic data types than I did on mine. Unless you're using the same kind of computer with the same operating system and the same compiler that I used, you can't guarantee that you'll get the answers that I got.

This Hands On program demonstrates the flexibility of the C language specification. Notice that an integer and a long integer are the same size on my system. The implementors of my C compiler can do this because the `long` type is defined as being no shorter than an `int`.

6.4   +=, -=, *=, and /=

C provides some additional arithmetic operators that can be used as a kind of shorthand. For instance, the statement

```
anInteger += 5;
```

adds 5 to the value in the variable `anInteger`. It stores the result in `anInteger`. This notation is much more efficient than a statement like

```
anInteger=anInteger+5;
```

There are similar statements for subtraction, multiplication, and division. Their operators are `-=`, `*=`, and `/=`. They each take a value in a variable, perform an operation on it, and store it back in the variable.

6.5   Type Casting

Type casting is a technique that was mentioned and demonstrated in earlier chapters. Using a type cast, we can get the compiler to treat a variable as if it is a different type. Chapter 4 demonstrated how integers can be type cast to characters and characters can be type cast to integers. We can also type cast other numeric types. However, be aware that there are potential problems with type casts. Section 6.6.3 explains these pitfalls.

The following Hands On program illustrates the use of type casts.

Hands On 6.3

Objective

Write a program that uses type casts to convert various types of integers to floating point values and floating point values to integers.

Experiment

Type the following program into your text editor or IDE. Compile, link, and run it.

```
1    #include <stdio.h>
2
3    int main()
4    {
5         short aShort;
6         int anInt;
7         long aLong;
8         float aFloat;
9         double aDouble;
10
11        // Cast some integers to float.
12        aShort = 100;
13        aFloat = (float)aShort;
```

```
14          printf("aFloat = %f\n",aFloat);
15          anInt = 1000;
16          aFloat = (float)anInt;
17          printf("aFloat = %f\n",aFloat);
18
19          // Cast some floats to ints.
20          aFloat = 1234.567;
21          anInt = (int)aFloat;
22          printf("anInt = %d\n", anInt);
23
24          aDouble = 123456.789;
25          aLong = (int)aDouble;
26          printf("aLong = %d\n", aLong);
27
28          return (0);
29      }
```

Results

aFloat = 100.000000
aFloat = 1000.000000
anInt = 1234
aLong = 123456

Analysis

The program in this Hands On section shows that integer data types can be cast to floating-point types. The reverse is also true. However, be aware that, depending on your compiler, you may not get the results shown here. See Section 6.6.3 for more information.

Try This

Insert three blank lines between lines 27 and 28 of this program. On these three lines, add the statements

```
anInt = 12345;
aFloat = (float)(anInt / aShort);
printf("%f\n",aFloat);
```

Recompile, link, and run the program. What is the result? Is it what you expected? Now change the second statement to

```
aFloat = (float)anInt / (float)aShort;
```

Compile, link, and run the program again. How is the result different?

TRAP 6.1
Performing multiple increments or decrements of the same variable on a line of code often causes unpredictable results. Incrementing or decrementing a variable on the same line in which the variable is used with other arithmetic operators (such as +, −, * or /) can also cause problems.

6.6   Troubleshooting Guide

After reading this section, you should be able to:

- Find common problems with the pre- and postoperators.
- Be aware of possible mistakes that can be made with the `sizeof` operator.
- Avoid potential problems with type casting.
- Find and fix precedence problems with the +=, -=, *= and /= operators.

6.6.1   Confusion with Increments and Decrements

The most common problems that arise when using preincrement, postincrement, predecrement, and postdecrement arise when we try to get to fancy. C is a very flexible language.

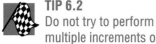

TIP 6.2
Do not try to perform multiple increments or decrements of the same variable on a single line of code.

TIP 6.3
Do not increment or decrement a variable on a line of code where that variable is used with another arithmetic operator.

As programmers, we all eventually make the mistake of being just a bit too clever and creative at times with our use of C. The result can be very surprising.

For instance, what do you think the following equation would evaluate to?

```
int i,j=5;
i=++j + j++ + --j - 1;
```

If you can predict what this will yield, you're borderline psychic. It is not always evaluated the way you think it should be. Experience with a variety of compilers has taught me that they all evaluate multiple increments and decrements on a single line of code differently. It's best to refrain from such tricky code and find simpler ways to express equations.

6.6.2 Surprises from `sizeof`

The `sizeof` operator is used to find the size of a data type. It can be used to find the size of other things, such as variables. However, I recommend against such uses. The code in Hands On 6.4 illustrates some of the other uses of `sizeof` and illustrates why there might be some confusion when `sizeof` is used in these ways.

Hands On 6.4

Objective

Write a program that demonstrates the uses of the `sizeof` operator.

Experiment

Type the following program into your text editor or IDE. Compile, link, and run it.

```
1    #include <stdio.h>
2
3    int main()
4    {
5         int anInteger;
6         long aLong;
7         double aDouble;
8         int anIntegerArray[10];
9         int *anIntegerPointer;
10
11        printf("%d\n",sizeof(anInteger));
12        printf("%d\n",sizeof(aLong));
13        printf("%d\n",sizeof(aDouble));
14        printf("%d\n",sizeof(anIntegerArray));
15        anIntegerPointer = anIntegerArray;
16        printf("%d\n",sizeof(anIntegerPointer));
17        return (0);
18   }
```

Results

```
4
4
8
40
4
```

Analysis

Notice that this example does not use the `sizeof` operator to find the size of data types. It uses `sizeof` to find the size of variables. Specifically, we're finding the size of an integer, a long integer, a double, an array of integers, and a pointer to an array of integers. We'll discuss arrays and pointers in later chapters.

Taking the size of the integer, long integer, double, and array gives the number of bytes that most programmers think they should. The problem comes in with pointers. Notice that even though the pointer is pointing at the array, the sizeof operator didn't give the size of the array. It gave the size of the pointer. Right now, we don't have to worry about what pointers or arrays are. We just have to understand that pointers and arrays can cause problems with the sizeof operator if we use variable names rather than types.

TRAP 6.2
The sizeof operator can yield results that may be confusing if it is used to find the size of a variable.

TIP 6.4
Your intention is communicated more clearly to maintenance programmers when you use type names with the sizeof operator rather than variable names.

In general, the safest way to use sizeof is with types. That way, you clearly state to the maintenance programmer that you know what you're finding the size of.

6.6.3 Surprises from Type Casts

The program in Hands On 6.3 demonstrates that floating-point types can be converted to integer types with type casts. Integer variables can also be converted to floating-point types by the same means.

However, there is a potential problem when performing these conversions, which were mentioned briefly in Chapters 3 and 5. Older compilers may not give the answers shown in the Results section of Hands On 6.3. This is especially true if the manufacturers of the compilers say that their compilers are K&R compatible rather than ANSI compatible.

When we assign floating-point values to integers, ANSI compatible compilers should truncate the part of the number to the right of the decimal point. When we assign integers to floating-point variables, ANSI compatible compilers should fill the places to the right of the decimal point with zeros. Older compilers or compilers for specialized hardware sometimes do not operate this way.

When assigning floating-point values to integer variables, these compilers might not truncate the fractional part of the number. They may just treat the pattern of bits in memory as if it were an integer data type. In that case, the program will store a value in the integer variable that appears to have no relation to the value in the floating-point number.

The same thing can happen when using a type cast to assign integer values into a floating-point number. Rather than fill the fractional part of the floating-point number with zeros, the compiler may treat the bit pattern of the integer value as if it were the bit pattern of a floating-point number.

If your compiler has this characteristic, it's best not to try to use type casts. Fortunately, most compilers these days don't act in this way.

TIP 6.5
If your program gives strange results when you use type casting, you may need to update your compiler.

6.6.4 Precedence with *= and /=

Now it's time for a pop quiz. The statement

```
thisInteger*=thatInteger-4;
```

is equivalent to which of the following?

a) thisInteger=(thisIteger*thatInteger)-4;
b) thisInteger=thisIteger*(thatInteger-4);
c) (thisInteger=thisIteger)*thatInteger-4;
d) thisInteger=((thisIteger*thatInteger)-4);

Ok, time's up. A quick glance through the list of answers will eliminate some possibilities right away. Answer c is illegal. It won't compile. In the C programming language, equations are divided into two parts—everything to the right of the = sign and everything to the left of it. Everything on the right of the = must evaluate to a value. Whatever is on the left must evaluate to a location in memory to store the answer. The formal name for these two parts of equations are **Lvalue** and **Rvalue**, for left value and right value. In answer c, the parentheses span both sides of the = sign. The compiler will not be able to separate that into an Lvalue and an Rvalue. So answer c is definitely wrong.

Answer a says exactly the same thing as answer d. The addition of the extra parentheses in d don't affect the results at all.

TRAP 6.3
The +=, -=, *=, and /= operators have much lower precedence than the +, -, *, and / operators.

By the process of elimination, we find that the answer is b. At first glance, you'd think it would be a and/or d. It looks like the multiplication should be done first because it has higher precedence. However, a glance back at the precedence chart in Appendix C will clear things up. The *= operator has much lower precedence than the subtraction operator. Therefore, C performs the subtraction first, not the multiplication. All of the operators in the group +=, -=, *=, and /= operate in the same way. Everything on the right side of the equation is done first because these four operators have very low precedence.

SUMMARY

To increment a variable means to increase its value by 1. To decrement it is to decrease its value by 1. C provides two increment and two decrement operators. They are preincrement, postincrement, predecrement, and postdecrement.

Preincrement increments the value in a variable before the program uses it for anything else.

Predecrement decrements the value in a variable before the program uses it for anything else.

Postincrement uses the value in a variable and then increments it.

Postdecrement uses the value in a variable and then decrements it.

It is best to do only one increment or one decrement per line in a C program.

The modulus operator evaluates to the remainder of an integer division.

The sizeof operator evaluates to the size of a data type. The answer is in bytes.

The += operator tells the C compiler to add the value on the right of the += to the value in the variable on the left. It stores the answer in the variable on the left of the += sign.

The -= operator works in the same fashion as the += operator. The only difference is that it performs a subtraction instead of an addition.

Likewise, the *= and the /= operators perform their operations similarly. The *= multiplies the Lvalue and the Rvalue and stores it in the Lvalue. The /= operator does the same with a division.

TIPS

6.1 The preincrement operator tells the compiler that a variable should be incremented before it is used for anything else. The postincrement operator tells the compiler that the variable should be used in an equation first, then incremented.

6.2 Do not try to perform multiple increments or decrements of the same variable on a single line of code.

6.3 Do not increment or decrement a variable on a line of code where that variable is used with another arithmetic operator.

6.4 Your intention is communicated more clearly to maintenance programmers when you use type names with the sizeof operator rather than variable names.

6.5 If your program gives strange results when you use type casting, you may need to update your compiler.

TRAPS

6.1 Performing multiple increments or decrements of the same variable on a line of code often causes unpredictable results. Incrementing or decrementing a variable on the same line in which the variable is used with other arithmetic operators (such as +, -, * or /), can also cause problems.

6.2 The sizeof operator can yield results that may be confusing if it is used to find the size of a variable.

6.3 The +=, -=, *=, and /= operators have much lower precedence than the +, -, *, and / operators.

REVIEW QUESTIONS

1. What does the preincrement operator do?
2. What does the postincrement operator do?
3. What does the predecrement operator do?
4. What does the postdecrement operator do?
5. What does the modulus operator do?
6. What does the sizeof operator do?
7. How might the sizeof operator be helpful in preventing overflow and underflow?
8. Why is incrementing or decrementing a variable more than once per line generally not desirable?
9. What do the +=, -=, *=, and /= operators do?
10. What potential confusion might occur with the precedence of the *= and /= operators?

1. Fill in the blanks.

   The modulus operator evaluates to the _____ of a _____ division.

2. Indicate which of the following statements are true.

   a. The += and *= operators have lower precedence than the + operator.

   b. The predecrement operator tells the compiler to use the value in the variable first, then decrement it.

   c. The postdecrement operator tells the compiler to use the value in the variable first, then decrement it.

   d. Incrementing and decrementing the same variable in the same expression is guaranteed not cause problems.

   e. You should avoid using variable names with the sizeof operator.

3. Fill in the blank.

   The sizeof operator evaluates to the number of _____ that are required to store the data type of its operand in memory.

4. Type the following program into your text editor. Compile, link, and run it. Explain the results you expected and the results you got. Explain how the answers were arrived at. Also explain why you think code like this might or might not be difficult for a maintenance programmer to understand.

```
1    #include <stdio.h>
2
3    int main()
4    {
5         int i,j=5;
6
7         i=j++ + ++j - --j;
8         printf("i=%d\n",i);
9         printf("j=%d\n",j);
10        return (0);
11   }
```

5. Write a program that uses the % operator to find even and odd numbers. The user should be able to type in any number. Your program will output a zero if the number is even. If not, it will output a one. Hint: The remainder of any even number that is divided by 2 is 0. The remainder of any odd number that is divided by 2 is 1.

6. Write a program that prompts the user for an integer and divides the integer by 3. The program should output the result of the division, as well as the remainder of the division.

7. Type the program in Hands On 6.2 into your text editor or IDE. Compile and run it. Print out your results and submit it with this assignment. Explain why the output of the program might be different if you run the program on a different computer with a different operating system.

8. Write a program that uses the *= operator to square any number that the user types in and then output the result to the screen.

9. Write a program that uses the += and / operators in the same equation. Explain why you think this usage might be confusing for maintenance programmers.

10. Write a program that uses the * and *= operators in the same equation. Tell whether you think a maintenance programmer would have trouble understanding this equation. Explain why.

11. Type the following program into your text editor or IDE. This program contains errors. Compile it, find the errors, and fix them. Describe the errors you found. Explain what the program does. Tell how the programming style did or did not help you understand the program.

```
1    #include stdio.h
2
3    int main(
4    {
5         int gasMilage, distanceTraveled;
6         int fuelConsumed,remainder;
7         float finalAnswer,
8
9         printf("Please enter the distance you traveled: ");
10        scanf("%d",&distanceTraveled).
11        printf("Please enter the amount of gas consumed ");
12        printf("(in gallons) on the trip: ");
```

```
13              scanf("%f",&fuelConsumed);
14              gasMilage = distanceTraveled / fuelConsumed;
15              remainder = distanceTraveled % fuelConsumed;
16              finalAnswer = (float)gasMilage;
17              finalAnswer += (float)remainder / (float)fuelConsumed;
18              printf("Your car got %f miles per gallon\n",
19                      finalAnswer);
20
21              return (0);
22      }
```

12. Explain what the following program does. Tell why you do or do not think that the programming style used here is easy to understand.

```
1   #include <stdio.h>
2   int main()
3   {
4           int aNumber;
5
6           printf("Please enter a number: ");
7           scanf("%d",&aNumber);
8           aNumber*=aNumber*aNumber;
9           printf("%d\n", aNumber);
10
11          return (0);
12  }
```

13. State the order of evaluation of the operators in each of the following C statements. Also, show the value of x for each statement. Assume that the initial value of x in statement b is 22. Assume these statements are being evaluated on a computer with a 32 bit integer.
    a. x = 4 + 5 / 9 * 3;
    b. x += 3 % 9 - 11 / (153 %12);
    c. x *= 3 + 5;
    d. x = 4 + sizeof(int);

14. Examine the following program. Is there a potential problem in it? Explain why or why not. If you feel that there might be a problem, describe how you would fix it.

```
1   #include <stdio.h>
2
3   int main()
4   {
5           float aNumber;
6
7           printf("Please enter a number: ");
8           scanf("%f",&aNumber);
9           aNumber+=1;
10          printf("%f\n", aNumber);
11          return (0);
12  }
```

15. Explain what the following program does. Describe any problems you might have with this coding style.

```
1   #include <stdio.h>
2
3   int main()
4   {
5           int i=6,j=7,k=8;
6
7           i += j *= k / 3;
8           printf ("i=%d\n",i);
```

```
 9        printf ("j=%d\n",j);
10        printf ("k=%d\n",k);
11        return (0);
12   }
```

16. Explain why the following is not a valid C statement:

    ```
    x + 5 = i + j;
    ```

17. Write a program that prompts the user for a temperature in degrees Celsius and converts it to a temperature in the Fahrenheit temperature scale. Use the formula

$$t_f = \frac{9}{5}t_c + 32$$

where t_f is the temperature in Fahrenheit, and t_c is the temperature in Celsius. Use the *= operator in this program.

18. Describe the output of the three printf() statements in the following program. Explain why they do not print the same value.

```
 1  #include <stdio.h>
 2
 3  int main()
 4  {
 5        float aFloat;
 6        int x = 6, y = 8;
 7
 8        aFloat = x/y;
 9        printf("%f\n",aFloat);
10        aFloat = (float)(x/y);
11        printf("%f\n",aFloat);
12        aFloat = (float)x / (float)y;
13        printf("%f\n",aFloat);
14
15        return (0);
16  }
```

19. Using any of the operators you have learned to this point, write a program containing the most confusing and unreadable expression you can create. Make it *really* nasty. Have another student in your class try to describe what your expression does. Explain in detail what the expression does and what makes it unreadable to other programmers.

20. Write a small program that uses the = and += operator in the same line of code. Describe in detail what this expression does. Explain why you think maintenance programmers may or may not have problems reading this expression.

21. In geometry, the sides of a triangle are labeled as shown in the figure. The label h stands for hypotenuse. The a stands for the side adjacent to the angle. The o represents the side that is opposite to the angle. The symbol θ represents the angle measured in radians.

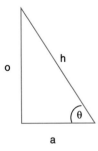

The relationships between the sides is defined by the following group of formulas:

$$\cos(\theta) = \frac{a}{h}$$

$$\sin(\theta) = \frac{o}{h}$$

$$\tan(\theta) = \frac{o}{a}$$

Therefore, the formula

```
o = h * sin(θ)
```

gives the length of the side opposite to the angle. Write the algorithm for a program that prompts the user for the length of the hypotenuse of a triangle and an angle measured in radians. The program should use these values to calculate the length of the side opposite to the angle. It should then print the result.

22. Write a program using the algorithm you developed in Exercise 21. The C Standard Library includes the `sin()` function. To use it, you must put the statement

```
#include <math.h>
```

on the line following

```
#include <stdio.h>
```

Find the value of the sine of an angle by using the statement `sin(varName)` in your program, where `varName` represents the name of the variable containing the value of the angle.

23. Using the formulas defined in Exercise 21, we can derive a formula to find the length of the hypotenuse of a triangle. Formula is

$$h = \frac{o}{\sin(\theta)}$$

Write the algorithm for a program that uses this formula to find the length of the hypotenuse of a triangle. It should prompt the user for the angle in radians and the length of the side opposite to the angle. It should then calculate the length of the hypotenuse and print the result.

24. Write a program using the algorithm you developed in Exercise 23. The C Standard Library includes the `sin()` function. To use it, you must put the statement

```
#include <math.h>
```

on the line following

```
#include <stdio.h>
```

Find the value of the sine of an angle by using the statement `sin(varName)` in your program, where `varName` represents the name of the variable containing the value of the angle.

25. Complex numbers are used in physics and electronics. Complex numbers have an imaginary part and a real part. We label the imaginary part `i` and the real part `j`. The number

```
5i-12j
```

has an imaginary part of `5i` and a real part of `12j`. To add two complex numbers together, add the imaginary parts together, then add the real parts together. For example, adding

$$\begin{array}{r} 5i - 12j \\ + \ 33i + 44j \\ \hline 38i + 32j \end{array}$$

Write a program that gets two complex numbers from the user, adds them together, and prints the result.

GLOSSARY

Lvalue   Any variable that can go on the left side of an assignment (=) operator. An Lvalue must be a location in memory where data can be stored.

Remainder   A number that is "left over" when an integer doesn't divide evenly into another integer.

Rvalue   Any value or variable that can go on the right side of an assignment (=) operator.

Logical Operators

OBJECTIVES

After reading this chapter, you should be able to:

- Explain what logical operators are.
- Explain truth and falsehood in C.
- Use the logical operators to create conditions.

OUTLINE

PREVIEW

One of the most powerful tools that programming languages give programs is the ability to make rudimentary decisions as they run. This capability enables computers to do more than repeat a sequence of simple instructions. The logical operators presented in this chapter help give computer programs the ability to react to changes in the conditions of data.

7.1   Logical Operators

To be useful, computer languages must provide programs with the ability to react to user input. They must be able to make decisions based on the current time. They have to be able to change their behavior based on input from a file or from data they retrieve over a network. Programs often select portions of code to execute based on values that they have calculated.

This description seems to attribute intelligence to machines. However, that is not the case. We currently have no computers or computer programs that can actually think. None of them have any real judgement. What actually occurs is that computer programs use **logical operators** to build and evaluate **conditions**. A logical operator is a C operator whose result evaluates to either true or false. A condition is an expression, usually involving a logical operator, that evaluates to true or false. Most conditions test the current state of a data item relative to another data item. For instance, a condition might use a logical operator to check if the value in a variable called `thisInteger` is greater than the value in a variable called `thatInteger`.

Another example of a condition is a program that is used to automatically perform a backup of a hard disk. At 1 A.M. every morning, the software would automatically copy the contents of the disk to a tape. The condition in this example consists of two pieces of data and one logical operator. The data items are the current time and the time of the scheduled backup (1 A.M.). The logical operator is the operator that tests for equality. If this condition evaluates to false, the backup is not performed. If it evaluates to true, the software starts the backup.

In C, conditions always evaluate to true or false. But what is truth or falsehood to a computer?

7.2 What Is Truth?

The C language defines truth with absolute certainty. Anything that is not zero is true. Everything that evaluates to zero is false. The logical operators usually evaluate to either 0 or 1, false or true. However, don't make the common mistake of assuming that 1 is the only value that is true. Table 7.1 demonstrates a few values that evaluate to true in C and some that evaluate to false.

TABLE 7.1 Some Truths and Falsehoods In C

Evaluates to True	Evaluates to False
5	0
–74	0.0
'Q'	'\0'
22.3	NULL

Table 7.1 illustrates the idea that all nonzero numbers evaluate to true in C. The type of the value does not matter. For instance, characters can evaluate to true or false. If the ASCII value of the particular character is nonzero, the character evaluates to true. There is only one character that has an ASCII value of 0. That is the null character '\0'.

Floating-point numbers can also evaluate to true or false. If a floating-point value *exactly* equals 0.0, it is false. Otherwise, it evaluates to true. However, be aware that the output of floating-point numbers is often truncated or rounded (see the Troubleshooting Guide in Chapter 3). Precision errors can also cause floating-point computations to result in values other than 0.0, even when we expect the result to be *exactly* 0.0. For this reason, it's usually not wise to expect floating-point values to evaluate to false.

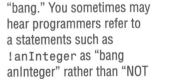

TRAP 7.1
Because of rounding, truncation, and precision errors, a floating-point value may not evaluate to exactly 0.0 after an expression is evaluated. When used in a condition, it may not be false when we think it should.

7.3 Arithmetic Values and Truth

Arithmetic expressions can also evaluate to true or false. The statement

```
anInteger+anotherInteger
```

can be used as a logical value. If the addition of these two variables results in a nonzero value, then the expression evaluates to true. If the addition results in a value of zero, the expression evaluates to false. We'll see how this can be used in the exercises for this chapter.

Using arithmetic expressions as logical values is generally not a good idea. People testing and maintaining your code often find it difficult to understand what you mean when you write that kind of condition. Also, it is not uncommon for tricky code like that to have unintended side effects. I'm not saying you should never use arithmetic expressions as logical values; there are times when they are appropriate. Just be careful, and try to make your code as clear as possible.

TRAP 7.2
Using arithmetic expressions as conditions can result in code that is unclear to maintenance programmers.

7.4 Logical Operators

Table 7.2 lists all of the logical operators in C. Each of these operators except one are used to compare two pieces of data. In other words, they are **binary operators**. The NOT operator, which is the exclamation point (!), is a **unary operator**. It performs its operation on one data item.

When a program uses these operators to evaluate data, the result of the condition is either zero or one. Example 7.1 demonstrates some conditions that use the logical operators.

TECHNICAL NOTE 7.1
An old term for the NOT operator is the "bang." You sometimes may hear programmers refer to a statements such as !anInteger as "bang anInteger" rather than "NOT anInteger."

EXAMPLE 7.1 Logical Conditions
```
i<j
color >= inputColor + currentColor
totalStudents != 0
errorStatus == 0
percentComplete <= 0.75
!doneReadingFile
```

Operator	Meaning
>	Greater than
>=	Greater than or equal to
==	Equal to
!=	Not equal to
!	Not
<=	Less than or equal to
<	Less than
&&	Logical AND
||	Logical OR

TABLE 7.2   Logical Operators

The conditions in this example show that conditional operators can be used to compare variables to variables. They can also be used to compare variables to literal values, such as 0 or 0.75. In addition, this example shows that programs can use logical operators with integer or floating-point types. Although this example only demonstrates their use with these two types, the conditional operators can be used with any of the C atomic data types.

The first condition in Example 7.1 evaluates to true when the variable i contains a value that is less than the value in the variable j.

The condition `color >= inputColor + currentColor` is true when the value in the variable `color` is greater than the result of adding the values in `inputColor` and `currentColor`. A quick look at the precedence chart in Appendix C shows that the logical operators have lower precedence than the mathematical operators. As a result, the addition in this condition is performed first, and then the comparison is performed.

The third condition in Example 7.1 is true when the variable `totalStudents` does not contain the number zero. The condition `errorStatus == 0` is true when the variable `errorStatus` contains zero.

The condition `percentComplete <= 0.75` demonstrates the use of a logical operator with a variable and a floating-point value.

Conditions such as `!doneReadingFile` are used often in computer programs. The NOT operator inverts the logical value of the variable. This condition evaluates to false while the variable `doneReadingFile` contains zero. Remember that truth in C is any value other than zero. As long as `doneReadingFile` contains zero, that variable *by itself* evaluates to false. When we add the NOT operator, it inverts the logical value in the variable. So the NOT operator will cause the condition `!doneReadingFile` to evaluate to true if the variable `doneReadingFile` evaluates to false. That is, NOT false is true.

When the variable `doneReadingFile` contains a nonzero value, the variable *by itself* evaluates to true. When we add the NOT operator, the condition `!doneReadingFile` evaluates to false when `doneReadingFile` evaluates to true. NOT true is false.

Programs use conditions like this one to control tasks that they do repeatedly. For instance, a program that reads data from a file one byte at a time will use the condition `!doneReadingFile` to tell itself when it to stop reading data. As long as the variable `doneReadingFile` contains false, the condition `!doneReadingFile` indicates that the program should read more data. When `doneReadingFile` contains true, the condition `!doneReadingFile` tells the program that it should not read any more data from the file.

The next few Hands On examples illustrate how programs can use the logical operators.

Hands On 7.1

Objective

Write a program that:

Gets a number from the user.

Outputs a 1 if the user enters a number greater than 0.

Outputs a 0 if the user enters a number that is less than or equal to 0.

Gets another number from the user.
Outputs a 1 if the user enters a number greater than or equal to 100.
Outputs a 0 if the user enters a number that is less than 100.

 Experiment

Type the following program into your text editor or IDE. Compile, link, and run it.

```
1   #include <stdio.h>
2
3   int main()
4   {
5         int aNumber;
6         int theResult;
7
8         printf("Please type in a number greater than 0. ");
9         scanf("%d",&aNumber);
10        printf("You will see a 1 on the line after this sentence\n");
11        printf("if the number you typed is greater than 0.\n");
12        theResult=(aNumber>0);
13        printf("%d\n",theResult);
14        printf("Please enter a number greater than or ");
15        printf("equal to 100. ");
16        scanf("%d",&aNumber);
17        printf("You will see a 1 on the line after this sentence\n");
18        printf("if the number you typed is greater than\n");
19        printf("or equal to 100.\n");
20        theResult=(aNumber>=100);
21        printf("%d\n",theResult);
22        return (0);
23  }
```

 Results

First Run

Please type in a number greater than 0. **5**
You will see a 1 on the line after this sentence
if the number you typed is greater than 0.
1

Please enter a number greater than or equal to 100. **200**
You will see a 1 on the line after this sentence
if the number you typed is greater than
or equal to 100.
1

Second Run

Please type in a number greater than 0. **–5**
You will see a 1 on the line after this sentence
if the number you typed is greater than 0.
0

Please enter a number greater than or equal to 100. **50**
You will see a 1 on the line after this sentence
if the number you typed is greater than
or equal to 100.
0

 Analysis

As you can see in the Results section, I ran this program twice.

The program asks the user to enter a number greater than 0. In the first run, I typed in 5, which is shown in boldface. The second time I ran the program, I entered –5. When the program reaches line 12, it stores the result of the comparison

    aNumber>0

in the variable `theResult`. The result of the comparison is a numeric value. It evaluates to 1 if the user types in a number greater than 0. If the user types in a number less than 0, as I did in the second run, the comparison evaluates to 0.

The program then asks the user for a number greater than or equal to 100. If the user enters a number greater than or equal to 100, the comparison

    aNumber>=100

evaluates to 1. If the user enters a number that is less than 100, the comparison evaluates to 0.

Hands On 7.2 demonstrates the use of the == and != operators.

Hands On 7.2

Objective

Write a program that:
Gets a number from the user.
Outputs a 1 if the number was 10 or outputs a 0 if the number was not 10.
Outputs a 1 if the number was not 10 or outputs a 0 if the number was 10.

Experiment

Type the following program into your text editor or IDE. Compile, link, and run it.

```
1    #include <stdio.h>
2
3    int main()
4    {
5         int aNumber;
6         int theResult;
7
8
9         printf("Please enter the number 10. ");
10        scanf("%d",&aNumber);
11        printf("\nYou will see a 1 on the line following\n");
12        printf("this sentence if you typed the number 10.\n");
13        theResult = (aNumber == 10);
14        printf("%d\n",theResult);
15        printf("You will see a 1 on the line following\n");
16        printf("this sentence if you typed wasn't 10.\n");
17        theResult = (aNumber != 10);
18        printf("%d\n",theResult);
19        return (0);
20   }
```

Results

Please enter the number 10. **10**
You will see a 1 on the line following
this sentence if you typed the number 10.
1

You will see a 1 on the line following
this sentence if you typed wasn't 10.
0

Analysis

This short example illustrates the use the == and != operators. If the user enters
the number 10, the comparison

```
aNumber==10
```

yields a result of true. Since the logical operators use 1 for true, the program
stores the value 1 in the variable theResult.
The comparison

```
aNumber!=10
```

evaluates to true if the user types anything other than 10. If the user enters 10, the
comparison evaluates to false. A false result causes the program to store a 0 in
theResult.

The logical NOT operator is used to turn true values to false and false values to true.
The reason for doing this may not be immediately apparent, but it will become clearer
when we discuss looping and branching. Hands On 7.3 demonstrates the use of the NOT
operator.

Hands On 7.3

Objective

Write a program that:
    Assigns a nonzero number to a variable.
    Uses the logical NOT operator on the value in the variable.
    Outputs the result.
    Assigns zero to a variable.
    Uses the logical NOT operator on the value in the variable.
    Outputs the result.
    Uses the logical NOT operator with the greater than operator.
    Outputs the result.

Experiment

Type the following program into your text editor or IDE. Compile, link, and run it.

```
1    #include <stdio.h>
2
3    int main()
4    {
5         int aNumber;
6
7         printf("In this example, we'll use the NOT operator.\n");
8         printf("It is the exclamation point !\n\n");
9         printf("If we assign a non-zero number to a variable,\n");
10        printf("and use the ! operator, this is what we get.\n");
11        printf("aNumber=5;");
12        printf("\n!aNumber is equal to ");
13        aNumber=5;
14        printf("%d\n",!aNumber);
15        printf("\nIf we assign aNumber=0, what will we get from\n");
```

```
16        printf("the statement !aNumber ?");
17            aNumber = 0;
18        printf("\n%d\n",!aNumber);
19        printf("\nNow here's an example of using ! with another\n");
20        printf("logical operator.\n");
21        printf("What do you think the result of these statements\n");
22        printf("will be?\n");
23        printf("aNumber = 1;\n");
24        printf("!(aNumber > 10)\n");
25        printf("The answer is ");
26        printf("%d\n",!(aNumber > 10));
27        return (0);
28    }
```

Results

In this example, we'll use the NOT operator.
It is the exclamation point !

If we assign a non-zero number to a variable,
and use the ! operator, this is what we get.
aNumber=5;
!aNumber is equal to 0

If we assign aNumber=0, what will we get from
the statement !aNumber ?
1

Now here's an example of using ! with another
logical operator.
What do you think the result of these statements
will be?
aNumber = 1;
!(aNumber > 10)
The answer is 1

Analysis

Whenever we use the NOT operator on a variable containing a nonzero number, we get zero. If we NOT zero, then we get one.

Here's a pop quiz. The statements in Example 7.2 use the NOT operator. What value will be printed to the screen?

EXAMPLE 7.2   Using The ! Operator

```
int aValue=7;
aValue=!(!aValue);
printf("%d\n",aValue);
```

I included parentheses to help clarify the meaning. However, they aren't required by C.

In the Example 7.2, the variable aValue is assigned the value of 7. The ! operator is used to NOT the value in aValue. Another ! is used to NOT it again. The result is stored back into aValue. What will be printed?

The answer is one. The statement

```
int aValue=7;
```

declares the variable aValue and stores the value 7 in it. The condition (!aValue) evaluates to true if the contents of aValue is false. It evaluates to false if the contents of aValue is true. Since aValue contains the nonzero value of seven, it evaluates to true.

NOT true evaluates to false. Remember that the C logical operators use the values 1 and 0 for false and true. Therefore, the condition (!aValue) in this example evaluates to false, or zero. The condition !(!aValue) evaluates to true if (!aValue) is false. It evaluates to false if (!aValue) is true. In this example (!aValue) evaluates to false, so !(!aValue) is true. The C logical operators use 1 for true. So the value that Example 7.2 prints is 1.

If we NOT any nonzero value we get zero. If we NOT zero, we get one.

The next Hands On will demonstrate the use of the < and <= operators.

Hands On 7.4

Objective

Write a program that:

Gets a number from the user.

Outputs a 1 if the number the user entered is less than 100 or outputs a 0 if not.

Outputs a 1 if the number is less than or equal to 100 or outputs a 0 if not.

Experiment

Type the following program into your text editor or IDE. Compile, link, and run it.

```
1   #include <stdio.h>
2
3   int main()
4   {
5           int aNumber;
6           int theResult;
7
8           printf("Please enter a number that is less than\n");
9           printf("or equal to 100. ");
10          scanf("%d",&aNumber);
11
12          printf("\nIf the number you entered is less than 100,\n");
13          printf("a 1 will be printed on the next line.\n");
14          theResult = (aNumber < 100);
15          printf("%d\n", theResult);
16
17          printf("\nIf the number you entered is less than or equal to\n");
18          printf("100, a 1 will be printed on the next line.\n");
19          theResult = (aNumber <= 100);
20          printf("%d\n", theResult);
21          return (0);
22  }
```

Results

Please enter a number that is less than
or equal to 100. **100**

If the number you entered is less than 100,
a 1 will be printed on the next line.
0

If the number you entered is less than or equal to
100, a 1 will be printed on the next line.
1

Analysis

In this Hands On example, the program highlights the difference between the less than (<) operator, and the less than or equal to operator (<=).

When I ran the program, it prompted me for a number that is less than or equal to 100. As you can see in the boldface type, I entered the value 100. The condition on line 14 of the program tested to determine whether the value I entered was less than 100. In this case, the test evaluated to false. Therefore, the program output a zero on line 15.

The condition on line 19, determines whether the input value is less than or equal to 100. As you can see, it evaluated to true.

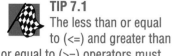

TIP 7.1
The less than or equal to (<=) and greater than or equal to (>=) operators must be typed in the order you see here. The symbols =< and => won't work.

Although not all of the logical operators are demonstrated in these Hands On programs, the remaining logical operators function in the same way as the operators in these programs.

It's important to know that switching the order of the symbols in logical operators will not work. C compilers require exact compliance with the syntax of the C language. This means that !=, <=, and >= cannot be changed to =!, =<, and =>. The C compiler will not recognize these symbols.

7.5   Logical AND

The logical AND operator enables programmers to concatenate more than one logical condition. Conditions combined in this way are said to be **compound conditions**. A compound condition using a logical AND operator is a way of saying, "This logical expression is only true if this condition AND that condition are true."

The logical AND operator is two ampersands, like this **&&**. Example 7.3 shows the use of the logical AND operator.

EXAMPLE 7.3   Using the Logical AND Operator

```
1    #include <stdio.h>
2
3    int main()
4    {
5         int anInteger=5, anotherInteger=10;
6         int result;
7
8         result = ((anInteger==5) && (anotherInteger<=10));
9         printf("%d\n",result);
10
11        return (0);
12   }
```

In this very contrived example, the condition will always evaluate to true. However, it demonstrates the use of the logical AND operator. The condition

```
((anInteger==5) && (anotherInteger<=10))
```

evaluates to true if the variable `anInteger` is equal to 5 and the variable `anotherInteger` is less than or equal to 10. Both conditions must be true for the entire expression to be true. If either one is false, the entire expression is false. Of course, if both conditions evaluate to false, then the entire expression also is false.

All compound conditions that use the AND operator are evaluated in the same way as Example 7.3. Table 7.3 contains a **truth table** for the logical AND operator. A truth table shows the conditions that are required for the logical AND operator to evaluate to true. In this table, the label *Condition 1* stands for the logical condition on the left of the **&&** operator. *Condition 2* stands for the logical condition on the right of the **&&** operator.

TABLE 7.3   A Truth Table for
Logical AND

Condition 1	Condition 2	Result
0	0	0
0	1	0
1	0	0
1	1	1

Since 0 evaluates to false in C and 1 evaluates to true, the false and true values in the table are indicated by 0's and 1's respectively.

The first line of this table tells us that the entire expression evaluates to false if the conditions on the left and right of a && operator both evaluate to false. The next line says that if the condition on the left of the && is false but the one on the right is true, the result is false. The third line of Table 7.3 says that if the condition on the left of the && is true but the one on the right is false, the complete expression is again false. In fact, the result is true only when both conditions evaluate to true.

7.6   Logical OR

Logical OR works similarly to logical AND. It allows programmers to combine two conditions into one expression. The difference is that both of the conditions in an expression with a logical AND must be true for the expression to be true. However, a logical OR requires that only one condition be true for the entire expression to evaluate to true.

The logical OR operator is two vertical lines together, like this ||. On many computers, the | character is on the same key on the keyboard as the \ character. That is, pressing Shift+\ often gets you a | character. Your keyboard may be different.

Table 7.4 contains the truth table for the logical OR operator.

TABLE 7.4   A Truth Table for
Logical OR

Condition 1	Condition 2	Result
0	0	0
0	1	1
1	0	1
1	1	1

When compilers generate binary instructions from a logical AND or a logical OR condition, they typically optimize the expression by not checking conditions unnecessarily. The truth table for the AND operator (Table 7.3) shows that it is not necessary to evaluate Condition 2 if Condition 1 is false because the entire condition cannot evaluate to true if Condition 1 is false.

A similar optimization is done with the logical OR operator. If Condition 1 in Table 7.4 evaluates to true, there is no reason to check Condition 2. The entire condition must evaluate to true if Condition 1 is true. Therefore, the compiler generates code that skips the evaluation of Condition 2 when Condition 1 in a logical OR condition is true.

TIP 7.2
Compilers optimize logical OR and logical AND conditions by not evaluating the right-hand operand when they don't need to. As a result, it's best to avoid using arithmetic expressions as logical conditions.

This is another reason to avoid using arithmetic expressions as logical conditions (see section 7.4). If you use an arithmetic expression as the right operand of a logical AND or logical OR condition, the arithmetic expression might never get evaluated. This can alter the results of your program.

The following Hands On example demonstrates the use of && and ||. It also illustrates how some of the other logical operators are used.

Hands On 7.5

Objective

Write a program that:

Gets a number from the user.

Outputs a 1 if the number is greater than or equal to 0 and less than or equal to 100, or outputs a 0 if not.

Outputs a 1 if the number is less than 0 or greater than 100, or outputs a 0 if not.

Experiment

Type the following program into your text editor or IDE. Compile, link, and run it.

```
1   #include <stdio.h>
2
3   int main()
4   {
5        int userResponse;
6        int theResult;
7
8        printf("Please type in a number that is in the\n");
9        printf("range of 0 - 100. ");
10       scanf("%d",&userResponse);
11       theResult=((userResponse >= 0) && (userResponse<=100));
12
13       printf("\nIf the number you typed was greater than or\n");
14       printf("equal to 0, and less than or equal to 100,\n");
15       printf("a 1 will be printed on the next line.\n");
16       printf("%d\n",theResult);
17
18       printf("\nIf the number you typed is less than 0, or\n");
19       printf("greater than 100, a 1 will be printed on\n");
20       printf("the next line.\n");
21       theResult = ((userResponse < 0) || (userResponse > 100));
22       printf("%d\n",theResult);
23
24       return (0);
25   }
```

Results

First Run

Please type in a number that is in the
range of 0 – 100. **50**

If the number you typed was greater than or
equal to 0, and less than or equal to 100,
a 1 will be printed on the next line.
1

If the number you typed is less than 0, or
greater than 100, a 1 will be printed on
the next line.
0

Second Run

Please type in a number that is in the
range of 0 – 100. **–10**

If the number you typed was greater than or
equal to 0, and less than or equal to 100,
a 1 will be printed on the next line.
0

If the number you typed is less than 0, or
greater than 100, a 1 will be printed on
the next line.
1

Third Run

Please type in a number that is in the
range of 0 – 100. **200**

If the number you typed was greater than or
equal to 0, and less than or equal to 100,
a 1 will be printed on the next line.
0

If the number you typed is less than 0, or
greater than 100, a 1 will be printed on
the next line.
1

Analysis

The program in this Hands On example asks the user to type in a number between
0 and 100. If the number the user enters is greater than or equal to 0 and less than
or equal to 100, the condition

```
((userResponse >= 0) && (userResponse<=100))
```

will evaluate to true. The program then uses the condition

```
((userResponse < 0) || (userResponse > 100))
```

to test to see if the number that the user typed in is less than 0 or greater than
100. Three runs were done on this program to demonstrate the different answers
that the logical expressions will give.

The input for the first run was 50. The first condition evaluated to true, so a 1
was printed. The second condition evaluated to false (0) because 50 is not less
than 0 and not greater than 100.

During the second run, I entered the number –10 from the keyboard. Since
–10 is less than 0, the first condition of the expression

```
((userResponse >= 0) && (userResponse<=100))
```

evaluated to false. The program doesn't even need to check the condition on the
right side of the && sign (and it usually doesn't) because only one side of a logical
AND expression has to be false for the entire expression to be false.

Because –10 is less than 0, the first condition in the logical expression

```
((userResponse < 0) || (userResponse > 100))
```

evaluated to true. In this case also, the second condition doesn't need to be
checked, and it probably won't be. If the left side of a logical OR is true, the right
side doesn't need to be checked. It only takes one true condition in a logical OR
expression to make the entire expression true.

The third run demonstrates the same ideas. The input was 200, which made
the expression

```
((userResponse >= 0) && (userResponse<=100))
```

false. The condition on the right side of the && was false, so the entire expression evaluated to false.

The expression

```
((userResponse >= 0) && (userResponse<=100))
```

evaluated to true. Because 200 is greater than 0, the condition on the right of the ‖ sign was true. One true condition in a logical OR expression makes the entire expression true.

Try This

Change line 11 of this program to read as follows:

```
theResult=!((userResponse >= 0) && (userResponse<=100));
```

Compile and link the program. Run it several times. Each time you do, enter different input and see how the program responds. After you have done so, change line 11 to this:

```
theResult=(!(userResponse >= 0) && !(userResponse<=100));
```

Once again, compile and link the program. Run it several times. How is the output different than it was when you used the previous conditions?

7.7 Troubleshooting Guide

After reading this section you should be able to:

• Prevent common problems with the assignment and equal to operators.
• Avoid confusion resulting from complex logical expressions.

7.7.1 The Pitfalls of == and =

The = and == operators look very much alike. It is extremely easy to use = for == accidentally. In fact, this is one of the most common errors in C programs. What makes it worse is that the compiler won't always catch the error. It will compile and run, but your program won't work correctly.

If we think about the definitions of true and false in C, we'll understand why the compiler can't always catch this type of error. Recall that in C, 0 is false and nonzero is true. That means that an assignment operation can be used as a logical condition.

For instance, let's suppose we have an integer variable in our program called anInteger. The statement

```
anInteger=5;
```

evaluates to a value. The value that it evaluates to is the value of the assignment. This statement assigns a 5 to anInteger. So the value of the assignment operation is 5. The number 5 is not 0, so it is true.

Although there are some instances in which you will want to use the assignment operator (=) as a logical condition, it is rare. If you see a single = in a logical condition, be extremely suspicious. It is probably incorrect.

To avoid this error, some people put the number in the condition first. That is they will use the condition

```
5==anInteger
```

instead of

```
anInteger==5
```

Although this may look funny, programmers often find it helpful. If you accidentally leave off one of the = signs, your condition is

```
5=anInteger
```

TRAP 7.3
It is easy to use the = instead of the == operator accidentally. They both can be used as logical conditions.

and the compiler will give an error. This is because you can't assign a value in a variable to a literal number like 5.

7.7.2 Problems with Complex Conditions

Because we can combine logical expressions, it is easy to make them overly complex. Conditions can become hard for people to read. They also tend to be prone to errors. Example 7.4 illustrates this.

EXAMPLE 7.4 An Overly Complex Condition

```
1   #include <stdio.h>
2
3   int main()
4   {
5        int result;
6        int intOne=20, intTwo=30, intThree=40,
7            intFour = 50, intFive=60;
8
9        result = intOne > intTwo &&
10               intThree <= intTwo || intOne <= intTwo &&
11               intThree >= intTwo || intFour == intFive;
12       printf("%d\n", result);
13
14       return (0);
15  }
```

 **TECHNICAL NOTE 7.2** White spaces are characters such as newlines, tabs, and space characters.

Note that the condition spans more than one line. That's fine with the compiler. It doesn't see the white space except in strings.

Although the compiler can evaluate this condition without a problem, many programmers will struggle with it. A C compiler would evaluate this expression in the order of its precedence. Example 7.5 shows the same condition in a slightly more readable style.

EXAMPLE 7.5 A More Readable Condition

```
1   #include <stdio.h>
2
3   int main()
4   {
5        int result;
6        int intOne=20, intTwo=30, intThree=40,
7            intFour = 50, intFive=60;
8
9        result = (intOne > intTwo) &&
10               (intThree <= intTwo) || (intOne <= intTwo) &&
11               (intThree >= intTwo) || (intFour == intFive);
12       printf("%d\n", result);
13
14       return (0);
15  }
```

This version of the condition uses parentheses to specify a particular order of evaluation. It makes the expression more readable. The expression is true if the variable intOne is greater than intTwo and intThree is less than intTwo. The condition will also evaluate to true if intOne is less that or equal to intTwo and intThree is greater than or equal to intTwo. In addition, the condition will evaluate to true if intFour is equal to intFive.

Another way to simplify this condition is to break it up into multiple conditions. Example 7.6 illustrates this.

EXAMPLE 7.6 **An Unmistakable Condition**

```
1    #include <stdio.h>
2
3    int main()
4    {
5        int result, result1, result2, result3;
6        int intOne=20, intTwo=30, intThree=40, intFour = 50, intFive=60;
7        result1 = (intOne > intTwo) && (intThree <= intTwo);
8        result2 = (intOne <= intTwo) && (intThree >= intTwo);
9        result3 = (intFour == intFive);
10
11       result = result1 || result2 || result3;
12       printf("%d\n", result);
13
14       return (0);
15   }
```

This example breaks the complex condition down into its component conditions. It is much easier to read. If you are writing a condition that you think the maintenance programmer might misinterpret, you can use this technique to help clarify it.

SUMMARY

In C, truth and falsehood are clearly defined. Expressions that evaluate to a nonzero number are true. Expressions that evaluate to zero are false.

The logical operators allow values to be compared. C programs use this ability to make decisions.

Compound conditions can be created with the AND and OR operators. For a compound condition using an AND operator to be true, the conditions on both the left and right of the AND operator must be true. For a compound condition using an OR operator to be true, the conditions on either the left or right of the OR operator must evaluate to true.

TECHNICAL NOTES

7.1 An old term for the NOT operator is the "bang." You sometimes may hear programmers refer to a statements such as !anInteger as "bang anInteger" rather than "NOT anInteger."

7.2 White spaces are characters such as newlines, tabs, and space characters.

TIPS

7.1 The less than or equal to (<=) and greater than or equal to (>=) operators must be typed in the order you see here. The symbols =< and => won't work.

7.2 Compilers optimize logical OR and logical AND conditions by not evaluating the right-hand operand when they don't need to. As a result, it's best to avoid using arithmetic expressions as logical conditions.

TRAPS

7.1 Because of rounding, truncation, and precision errors, a floating-point value may not evaluate to exactly 0.0 after an expression is evaluated. When used in a condition, it may not be false when we think it should be.

7.2 Using arithmetic expressions as conditions can result in code that is unclear to maintenance programmers.

7.3 It is easy to use the = instead of the == operator accidentally. They both can be used as logical conditions.

REVIEW QUESTIONS

1. What are logical operators?
2. What are logical operators used for?
3. What is truth in C?
4. What is falsehood in C?
5. What do the following logical operators mean? (Write them out in words.) > >= < <=
6. What do the following logical operators mean? (Write them out in words.) == != !
7. Which of these evaluates to true?
   a. 0.0
   b. −0.888
   c. 'b'
   d. 7
   e. 1
   f. '\0'
8. What is a truth table? What information does it convey?
9. Which of these evaluates to false?
   a. 0.0
   b. 0
   c. '\0'
   d. !7
10. Which of these is true if x is 10?
   a. (x>=0) && (x<10)
   b. (!(x>10)) || (x<=100)
   c. !(x>=0) && (x<10)
   d. !(!(x>10)) || !(x<=100)

EXERCISES

1. Fill in the blanks.

   A binary operator is an operator that has _____ _____.

2. Fill in the blanks.

   The == operator performs a test to see if its operands are _____. The = operator performs an _____.

3. Explain the conditions under which the following expression will evaluate to true.

   ```
   ((x>5) && (x<=y))
   ```

4. Fill in the blank.

   A _____ _____ is a logical condition composed of other logical conditions concatenated together using the logical AND or logical OR operators.

5. Explain the conditions under which the following expression will evaluate to false.
   ```
   ((x-y) || (x!=1000))
   ```

6. Explain why long compound conditions might be hard for a maintenance programmer to understand. Write an example of a compound condition that others might have difficulty reading.

7. Explain the purpose of a truth table.

8. Examine the table below. Given the inputs listed in the columns for the variables var1 and var2, fill in the truth table for the expression in the rightmost column. Use a 0 to indicate where the expression evaluates to false. Use a 1 to indicate where it evaluates to true.

var1	var2	(var1 < var2/10) || (var1 > var2)
−10.6	−8.001	
0.0001	0.0	
−3.03	99.6	
99.6	−3.03	
11.11	11.11	

9. Fill in the following truth table. Use a 0 to indicate where the expression evaluates to false. Use a 1 to indicate where it evaluates to true.

var1	var2	(var1 % var2) && (!(var1 <= var2))
0	53	
−5000	5000	
1	−44	
73	37	
53	0	

10. One way to write a truth table for a compound condition is to assign a letter variable to each of the parts of the condition. You can then write the truth table using zeros and ones for the input values. For example, we could write the expression

```
(x>y) && (y<=z) || (x==z)
```

as

```
a && b || c
```

where

```
a = (x>y)
b = (y<=z)
c = (x==z)
```

Using this form, the truth table for the expression is

a	b	c	a && b ‖ c
0	0	0	0
0	0	1	1
0	1	0	0
0	1	1	1
1	0	0	0
1	0	1	1
1	1	0	1
1	1	1	1

Wherever the columns labeled a, b, and c contain a one, their corresponding conditions evaluate to true. If those columns contain a zero, their corresponding conditions evaluate to false. In the second to the last row, conditions a and b evaluate to true, but c evaluates to false. In this circumstance, the compound condition evaluates to true.

Use this method to create a truth table for the expression

```
(!var1) || (var2>var1) && (var2<10000)
```

11. Describe the problems that can be encountered when using the = and the == operators. Explain how these problems can be prevented.

12. Write a program that gets a number from the user. If the number is greater than 1000 and less than or equal to 10000, your program should print a 1. If not, it should print a 0.

13. Write a program that gets a number from the user. If the number is equal to 1000 or equal to 10000, your program should print a 1. If not, it should print a 0.

14. Write a program that gets a number from the user. If the number is not greater than 1000 or not equal to 10000, your program should print a 1. If not, it should print a 0.

15. Write a program that gets a number from the user. If the number is not less than or equal to 1000 or not less than or equal to 10000, your program should print a 1. If not, it should print a 0.

16. Write a program that gets a number from the user. If the number is greater than 1000 and less than or equal to 10000 and not equal to 5000, your program should print a 1. Otherwise, it should print a 0.

17. Write a program that gets a number from the user. If the number is even your program should print a 1. If not, it should print a 0. Hint: Use the % operator.

18. Write a program that gets a number from the user. If the number is greater than 1000 and odd, your program should print a 1. If not, it should print a 0.

19. Examine the following statements and fix the errors they might contain:
    a. result = (inputValue =< 100);
    b. interest rate = inputValue < 100;
    c. result = 100 < currentTotal <= grandTotal;

20. Write a valid C statement to express each of the following conditions:
    a. x plus y is greater than y minus z.
    b. z is not greater than x plus y.
    c. salary is greater than 1000.00 and less than 10000.00.

21. Write a valid C statement to express each of the following conditions:
    a. x is greater than y or x is greater than or equal to z.
    b. b is equal to c and a is less than b or a is less than c.
    c. slope is less than deltaY divided by deltaX and slope is not equal to 1 and slope is not equal to −1.

22. Demonstrate other ways to write the following logical conditions:
    a. x < y
    b. a != b
    c. (r < s) != 1
23. Demonstrate other ways to write the following logical conditions:
    a. (velocity1 == velocity2) && (velocity1 <= 1000.00)
    b. !(voltageLevel > 1000) || !(voltageLevel < 0)
    c. !(!(dx!=y+dy) && (dy<x+dx))
24. When a computer executes a program that uses the logical AND or logical OR operators, the right-hand condition might not be evaluated. Explain why this is the case. Also tell why using an arithmetic expression as the right-hand operand with the logical AND or logical OR operators may cause problems.
25. Although we like to say that digital equipment such as computers operates using zeros and ones, it actually uses ranges of voltage levels. For example, a digital circuit may interpret a voltage level of 0.0 to 0.2 as a zero and a voltage level of 0.3 to 0.5 as a one. Write a program that:
    Prompts the user for a voltage level.
    Outputs a 0 if the voltage level is between 0.0 and 0.2 volts.
    Outputs a 1 if the voltage level is between 0.3 and 0.5 volts.

GLOSSARY

Binary Operator   An operator that performs its operations on two data items.

Compound Condition   A condition built with either the logical AND operator or the logical OR operator that is composed of other logical conditions.

Condition   An expression, usually involving a logical operator, that evaluates to true or false.

Logical Operator   An operator whose result evaluates to either true or false.

Truth Table   A table showing the conditions under which a logical operator evaluates to true.

Unary Operator   An operator that performs its operation on one data item.

8

Flow Control: Branching

OBJECTIVES

After reading this chapter, you should be able to:

- Explain what flow control statements are.
- Use the `if-else` statement in programs.
- Use the `switch` statement in programs.

OUTLINE

PREVIEW

In the last chapter, we saw how logical and arithmetic operators can be used to evaluate logical conditions. In this chapter, we'll begin to use logical operators to enable programs to make decisions. By making decisions based on logical conditions, programs can conditionally select which portions of program code to execute.

8.1 What Are Flow Control Statements?

Computers are able to make simple decisions and do tasks repeatedly. They do this by evaluating logical conditions, which we looked at in the last chapter. Whenever the flow of execution is altered by a C statement, we say that the **flow control** of the program has changed. A flow control statement is a C statement that controls or changes the flow of the program from one statement to the next.

There are two types of commands that enable computers to make decisions. One type, which we'll discuss in this chapter, is called a **branching statement**. The other, which is presented in the next chapter, is called a looping statement.

Flow control statements generally evaluate a logical condition as the program runs. They take action based on the value of the condition.

8.2 Branching

Most commands in a program execute sequentially, one after another. If the program encounters a conditional branching statement, it makes a decision based on a logical condition. If the condition is true, it does one thing. If it is false, it does something else.

C offers three conditional branching statements: the `if-else` statement, the `switch` statement, and the conditional operator.

8.2.1 The `if-else` Statement

Branching statements using `if-else` in a C program are very much like a person walking along and coming to a fork in the road. The traveler has to decide whether to go left or right. If she chooses the left fork, she will not see what's down the road to the right. The result of the decision will be different because of the choice she made.

In the same way, an `if-else` statement changes the execution flow of a program by providing it with two paths. The program makes a decision based on the condition of the `if-else` statement. If the condition evaluates to true, the program's flow control branches down one path. If the condition evaluates to false, it branches to the other path. Figure 8.1 illustrates the flow control for an `if-else` statement. Figure 8.2 shows its general form.

 TECHNICAL NOTE 8.1 Flow control statements that use a condition (most do) are generally referred to in the software industry as **conditional flow control statements**, or just **conditional jumps**. Flow control statements that do not evaluate a condition are called **unconditional flow control statements** or **unconditional jumps**.

FIGURE 8.1   **The Flow Control of an `if-else` Statement**

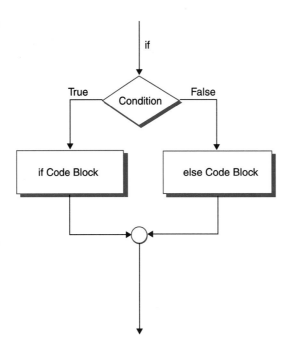

FIGURE 8.2   **The General Form of `if-else` Statements**

```
if (condition)
     statement; }Single-statement if body
else
     statement; }Single-statement else body



if (condition)
{
     statement;  ⎫
     statement;  ⎬ Multiple-statement if body
}               ⎭
else
{
     statement;  ⎫
     statement;  ⎬ Multiple-statement else body
}               ⎭
```

TECHNICAL NOTE 8.2
The branches of an `if-else` statement are said to be *mutually exclusive*. This means that they cannot both be executed. If one is executed, the other is not.

Figure 8.1 gives the flow control of an `if-else` statement. When a program encounters any `if-else` statement, it evaluates the condition. Both the `if` and the `else` portions of the `if-else` statement have blocks of code associated with them, as shown in Figure 8.2. The code blocks contain one or more C statements. If the condition evaluates to true, the program executes the code block for the `if` portion of the `if-else` statement. If the condition is false, it executes the code block for the `else` portion.

Hands On 8.1 demonstrates a simple `if-else` statement.

Hands On 8.1

Objective

Write a program that:
    Gets a number from the user.
    If the number is greater than 5,
        The program prints a message that tells the user they typed in a number greater than 5.

Else
> The program prints a message that tells the user they typed in a
> number less than or equal to 5.

Experiment

Type the following program into your IDE or text editor. Compile, link, and run it.

```
1   #include <stdio.h>
2
3   int main()
4   {
5       int inputValue;
6
7       printf("Please enter an integer: ");
8       scanf("%d",&inputValue);
9       if (inputValue>5)
10      {
11          // This is executed if the condition is true.
12          printf("Hold the phones, ");
13          printf("the input value is greater than 5.\n");
14      }
15      else
16      {
17          // This is executed if the condition is false.
18          printf("Don't worry, the input value is less than ");
19          printf("or equal to 5.\n");
20      }
21      return (0);
22  }
```

Results

First run

Please enter an integer: **3**
Don't worry, the input value is less than or equal to 5.

Second run

Please enter an integer: **10**
Hold the phones, the input value is greater than 5.

Analysis

In the `if-else` statement in this program, the `if` portion of the statement is executed if the contents of the variable `inputValue` is greater than 5. If the value in `inputValue` is less than or equal to 5, the program executes the `else` portion of the `if-else` statement.

The `if` portion of an `if-else` statement can contain more than one statement in its code block. When it does, the statements in the code block need to be between the opening and closing braces, { and }. If the code block contains only one C statement, you can omit the braces. Example 8.1 demonstrates an `if-else` statement with only one C statement in the `if` portion.

EXAMPLE 8.1 An `if` Without Braces

```
1   if (inputValue>5)
2       printf("The input value is greater than 5.\n");
3   else
```

```
4    {
5            // This is executed if the condition is false.
6            printf("Don't worry, the input value is less than ");
7            printf("or equal to 5.\n");
8    }
```

The else portion of the statement is not affected by the fact that the if portion does not use braces. The reverse is also true. If one has braces, it doesn't mean that the other has to have them. Example 8.2 shows an else without braces.

EXAMPLE 8.2 An else Without Braces

```
1    if (inputValue>5)
2    {
3            // This is executed if the condition is true.
4            printf("Hold the phones, ");
5            printf("the input value is greater than 5.\n");
6    }
7    else
8            printf("The input value is less than or equal to 5.\n");
```

There are some problems associated with omitting the braces from the if or else sections of an if-else statement. These are discussed in the Troubleshooting Guide for this chapter.

The else portion of an if-else statement is optional. If you leave the else portion off of the statement and the condition is false, the program simply continues execution with the next statement after the if.

TECHNICAL NOTE 8.3
Because the else portion of an if-else statement is optional, many programmers simply refer to if-else statements as if statements. However, that terminology can be confusing and is not used in this book.

EXAMPLE 8.3 An if Without an else

```
1    if ((anInteger>=0) && (anInteger<=100))
2    {
3            anotherInteger=100-anInteger;
4            anInteger=100;
5    }
```

An if-else statement may contain any valid C statement, even other if-else statements. Example 8.4 shows an if-else statement inside of an if-else statement.

EXAMPLE 8.4 Nested if Statements

```
1    if (x>0)
2    {
3            if (y>0)
4            {
5                    printf("%d\n",x+y);
6                    y++;
7            }
8            else
9                    printf("%d\n",x);
10           x++;
11   }
```

The outside if statement begins on line 1 of Example 8.4 and ends on line 11. It contains two C statements in its code block. The first is an if-else statement, and the second is a postincrement statement. The inner if-else statement spans lines 3–9. The entire inner if-else statement is seen as just one statement by the compiler.

Earlier chapters indicated that we indent to the right each time we enter a new block of code. By convention, we "unindent" (move text toward the left rather than the right) each time we end a block of code. Common programming practice does allow an exception to that rule. Example 8.5 shows an if-else statement with an if-else statement in its else section. That, in turn, has an if-else in its else, and so on. In a very real sense, these if-else statements are chained one onto the end of the other.

EXAMPLE 8.5   A Long `if-else` Statement

```
 1  if (x>0)
 2  {
 3        x++;
 4  }
 5  else
 6  {
 7        if (x<640)
 8        {
 9              x--;
10        }
11        else
12        {
13              if (y>0)
14              {
15                    y++;
16              }
17              else
18              {
19                    if (y<480)
20                    {
21                          y--;
22                    }
23                    else
24                    {
25                          x=0;
26                          y=0;
27                    }
28              }
29        }
30  }
```

This example shows how indentation can be both good and bad. By looking at the indentation, we can see which block of code each statement belongs in. However, as we indent, our code drifts to the right. In this case, it has shifted over quite a bit. That formatting can cramp the code and make it less readable.

Although the style in Example 8.5 is perfectly acceptable both to the compiler and to most people reading your code, the majority of C programmers don't use it. Example 8.6 demonstrates the more common format for chained `if-else` statements.

EXAMPLE 8.6   Chained `if-else` Statements

```
 1  if (x>0)
 2  {
 3        x++;
 4  }
 5  else if (x<640)
 6  {
 7        x--;
 8  }
 9  else if (y>0)
10  {
11        y++;
12  }
13  else if (y<480)
14  {
15        y--;
16  }
17  else
```

```
18   {
19          x=0;;
20          y=0;
21   }
```

The code in Examples 8.5 and 8.6 say the same thing. The compiler doesn't detect any difference. However, the formatting shown in Example 8.6 leaves more room for statements in each block of code. Which style you use is entirely up to you.

8.2.2 The `switch` Statement

The C language provides branching statement called the `switch` statement. A `switch` is used when there are many known values that a variable may take on. Figure 8.3 shows the flow control of a switch statement. Figure 8.4 gives its general form.

As Figure 8.3 illustrates, a `switch` statement compares a value to a constant value, also called a **literal constant**. A literal constant can be either a literal number or a literal character. The value being compared is contained in a variable.

If the value being compared equals the constant value, the statements associated with the constant value are executed. If the value being tested does not equal the constant

FIGURE 8.3   The Flow Control of a `switch` Statement

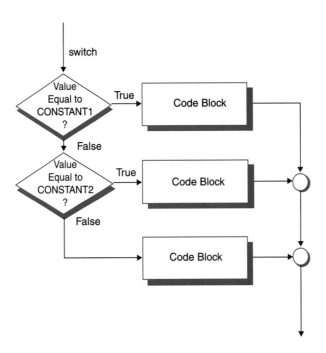

FIGURE 8.4   The General Form of a `switch` Statement

```
switch (value)
{
    case CONSTANT1:
        statement;
        statement;
    break;

    case CONSTANT2:
        statement;
    break;

    default:
        statement;
        statement;
        statement;
    break;
}
```

value, then the value is tested against the next constant value in the switch statement. If the value being tested does not equal any of the constant values, then the statements in the default section are executed.

Figure 8.4 shows that the switch statement begins with the keyword switch followed by a pair of parentheses containing the value to be tested. Inside the code block of the switch statement are literal constants and their associated code blocks. Before each literal constant is the keyword case. The constant is followed by a colon. As you can see from Figure 8.4, the code block associated with a literal constant can contain one or more C statements. Each literal constant and its associated code block is generally called a case by C programmers. A switch statement may contain many cases. The limit on the number of cases is set by your compiler.

The default statement works similarly to the else of an if-else statement. If none of the cases are executed, the computer will execute the statements in the default. Like an else statement, the default is optional. If you omit it and none of the cases are executed, the program continues with the statement follwing the switch statement's closing brace. A switch statement can contain only one default.

Hands On 8.2 illustrates how programs can use a switch statement.

Hands On 8.2

Objective

Write a program that:
Gets an integer from the user.
If the integer is 0,
The program increments the integer.
If the integer is 1,
The program decrements the integer and increments another integer.
If the integer is −100
The program increments the integer and decrements another integer.
In all other cases,
The program sets both integers to 0.
Outputs the result.

Experiment

Type the following program into your text editor or IDE. Compile, link, and run it.

```
1   #include <stdio.h>
2
3
4   int main()
5   {
6       int anInteger;
7       int anotherInteger = 1000;
8
9
10      printf("Please type in an integer: ");
11      scanf("%d",&anInteger);
12
13      switch (anInteger)
14      {
15          case 0:
16              anInteger++;
17          break;
18
19          case 1:
20              anInteger--;
```

```
21                        anotherInteger++;
22                break;
23                case -100:
24
25                        anInteger++;
26                        anotherInteger--;
27                break;
28
29                default:
30                        anInteger=0;
31                        anotherInteger=0;
32                break;
33            }
34
35        printf("\n%d\n",anInteger);
36        printf("%d\n",anotherInteger);
37
38        return (0);
39    }
```

Results

First run

Please type in an integer: **0**

1
1000

Second run

Please type in an integer: **1**

0
1001

Third run

Please type in an integer: **–100**

–99
999

Fourth run

Please type in an integer: **50**

0
0

Analysis

The switch statement in this Hands On example says the same thing as the code in Example 8.7. That is, if the variable anInteger equals 0, then increment anInteger. If it equals 1, decrement anInteger and increment the variable anotherInteger. If anInteger equals –100, increment it and decrement anotherInteger. If anInteger equals none of those values, the program selects the default case.

EXAMPLE 8.7 The Equivalence of the if-else and switch Statements

```
1   if (anInteger == 0)
2   {
3        anInteger++;
4   }
5   else if (anInteger == 1)
6   {
```

```
 7          anInteger--;
 8          anotherInteger++;
 9   }
10   else if (anInteger == -100)
11   {
12          anInteger++;
13          anotherInteger--;
14   }
15   else
16   {
17          anInteger=0;
18          anotherInteger=0;
19   }
```

I ran this program four times to demonstrate each case and the `default`.

TIP 8.2
If you put more than about three dozen cases in a `switch` statement, the maintenance programmers may have trouble reading it. Help them out by explaining what you're doing in comments.

In general, you should put as many cases as you need in a `switch` statement. However, if you put in more than about three dozen cases, other programmers will have difficulty reading and maintaining your program.

You may wonder what the `break` statements after the `case` and `default` statements do. The `break` statement marks the end of a case. It causes program execution to jump to the end of the `switch` statement. Hands On 8.3 shows what happens if the `break` statement is omitted.

Hands On 8.3

Objective

Write a program that:
Gets an integer from the user.
If the user types in the number 0,
    Output the string "Zero" to the screen.
If the user types in the number 1,
    Output the string "One" to the screen.
If the user types in the number 2,
    Output the string "Two" to the screen.
If the user types in the number 3,
    Output the string "Three" to the screen.
If the user types in the number 4,
    Output the string "Four" to the screen.
If the user types in the number 5,
    Output the string "Five" to the screen.
    Output the string "Six" to the screen.
    Output the string "Seven" to the screen.
If the user types in the number 6,
    Output the string "Six" to the screen.
    Output the string "Seven" to the screen.
If the user types in the number 7,
    Output the string "Seven" to the screen.
If the user types in the number 8,
    Output the string "Eight" to the screen.
If the user types in the number 9,
    Output the string "Nine" to the screen.
    Output the string "Ten" to the screen.
If the user types in the number 10,
    Output the string "Ten" to the screen.
If the user types in anything else,
    Output the string "That wasn't a number between 0–10." to the screen.

Experiment

Because this Hands On program is somewhat long, the code is provided for you on the Examples CD included with this book. The file, Ho8_3.c, is in the \Examples\Chapt8 directory. Load this program into your text editor or IDE. Compile it and run it.

```c
1   #include <stdio.h>
2
3
4   int main()
5   {
6       int userInput;
7
8       printf("This program contains a switch statement\n");
9       printf("Please enter a number between 0-10 ");
10      printf("inclusive :");
11      scanf("%d",&userInput);
12
13      switch (userInput)
14      {
15          case 0:
16                  printf("Zero\n");
17          break;
18          case 1:
19                  printf("One\n");
20          break;
21
22          case 2:
23                  printf("Two\n");
24          break;
25
26          case 3:
27                  printf("Three\n");
28          break;
29
30          case 4:
31                  printf("Four\n");
32          break;
33
34          case 5:
35                  printf("Five\n");
36
37          case 6:
38                  printf("Six\n");
39
40          case 7:
41                  printf("Seven\n");
42          break;
43
44          case 8:
45                  printf("Eight\n");
46          break;
47
48          case 9:
49                  printf("Nine\n");
50
51          case 10:
52                  printf("Ten\n");
```

```
53              break;
54
55          default:
56                  printf("That wasn't a number between 0-10.\n");
57              break;
58      }
59
60      return (0);
61  }
```

Result

First Run

This program contains a switch statement
Please enter a number between 0–10 inclusive :**2**
Two

Second Run

This program contains a switch statement
Please enter a number between 0–10 inclusive :**5**
Five
Six
Seven

Third Run

This program contains a switch statement
Please enter a number between 0–10 inclusive :**9**
Nine
Ten

Fourth Run

This program contains a switch statement
Please enter a number between 0–10 inclusive :**–100**
That wasn't a number between 0–10.

Analysis

This program has no break statements after cases 5, 6, and 9. In the first run, I typed in the number 2. The switch statement evaluated the variable userInput. Because the value of userInput was equal to the value for case 2, it jumped to case 2. When execution jumps to a case, the computer executes all statements between the case value and the break statement. In this instance, there is only one statement that the program can execute before the break. The statement tells the program to write the string "Two" to the screen.

On the second run, I entered the number 5. The computer found that the value of userInput was equal to case 5, so it jumped there. The program printed the string "Five" to the screen. So far so good. However, the program next encountered the label for case 6. C programs ignore this type of statement except when it's being used as the destination of a branching jump. Because the program already jumped to case 5, it won't jump again. The label for case 6 is the destination of a jump, not the start of a jump. It can't make program execution jump to another place. Therefore, the program ignored the label for case 6. Execution of statements in a case always continues until the computer encounters a break statement or until it reaches the end of the switch. Therefore, it printed the string "Six". There is no break statement after case 6, so case 7 was executed. The program printed the string "Seven" to the screen. Finally the program came to a break at the end of case 7. That caused execution to jump to the end of the switch statement.

The same type of situation occurred on the third run. When the program prompted me for input, I typed 9. Again, the `break` was left off the case. Both cases 9 and 10 were executed.

The fourth run demonstrates the use of the `default` statement.

Try This

Rearrange some of the cases in this Hands On program so that they are not in ascending numerical order. Recompile and link the program. Did you get any errors or warnings? Run the program and see if it performs any differently.

TIP 8.3
In general, it's best put a `break` after each `case` statement.

TIP 8.4
Always put your cases in order in a `switch` statement. Both you and other programmers will find your code more readable if you do.

Although Hands On 8.3 demonstrates that the `break` statement can be left off of a case, it is usually best not to do so.

The cases in a `switch` statement don't have to occur in any particular order. I presented them in ascending numerical order for readability. Most C programmers follow this practice.

8.2.3 The Conditional Operator

C provides a nice shorthand for simple `if-else` conditions. The conditional operator, which uses both the question mark and the colon, is a concise way of performing an `if-else`.

Figure 8.5 shows the general form of the conditional operator. If the condition in the parentheses evaluates to true, the whole conditional operator statement evaluates to the true result. The true result is the value between the question mark and the colon. If the condition is false, the conditional operator statement evaluates to the false result. The false result is value to the right of the colon.

FIGURE 8.5   The General Form of the Conditional Operator

```
value = (condition) ? true-result : false-result;
```

Example 8.8 demonstrates a conditional operator.

EXAMPLE 8.8   The Conditional Operator

```
finalValue = (currentValue < 1000) ? currentValue:1000;
```

The condition in this statement is enclosed in parentheses. If that condition evaluates to true, the whole conditional operator statement evaluates to the value in the variable `currentValue`. If it is false, the conditional operator statement evaluates to the literal number 1000.

The conditional operator is slightly more efficient than an equivalent `if-else` statement.

8.3   Troubleshooting Guide

After reading this section, you should be able to:

- Recognize and fix common problems with `if` statements.
- Prevent possible problems with `switch` statements.
- Avoid problems with the conditional operator.

8.3.1   Common Problems with `if-else` Statements

C compilers don't detect the indentation that we put into our programs. The indentation makes our programs easier for us to read. Normally, we indent to the right any time we begin a new block of code. The statements inside `if` and `else` portions of an `if-else` statement are in a new block of code, so we indent them.

Failing to indent can lead to unclear or misleading code. Example 8.8 demonstrates this.

EXAMPLE 8.9   Unindented Code

```
1   if (x>0)
2   if (y>0)
3   printf("%d\n",x+y);
4   else
5   printf("%d\n",x);
```

Just looking at this example, it's difficult to tell which of the `if` statements the `else` statement on line 4 goes with.

Even if our code is usually indented properly, it's easy to make a mistake. Take a look at Example 8.10.

EXAMPLE 8.10   An Indention Mistake

```
1   if (x>0)
2           if (y>0)
3                   printf("%d\n",x+y);
4   else
5           x++;
```

In this code fragment, the question is which `if` the `else` on line 4 goes with. The indentation indicates that the `else` statement is associated with the `if` statement on line 1. However, the rule the compiler follows is that the `else` is always associated with the closest `if`. So the `else` in Example 8.10 goes with the inner `if`, which begins on line 2. This may not be what the programmer intends. If it isn't, it can be changed by adding braces, as in Example 8.11.

EXAMPLE 8.11   Clearer Indentation

```
1   if (x>0)
2   {
3           if (y>0)
4                   printf("%d\n",x+y);
5   }
6   else
7   {
8           x++;
9   }
```

By placing the inner `if` inside braces, we've forced the compiler to see that the inner `if` and the `else` are in two different blocks of code. The compiler can't connect the `else` to the inner `if`.

Back in Example 8.4, it may not have been clear that the x++ was not in the code block of the `else` statement. We can clarify that by adding braces.

EXAMPLE 8.12   A Clarification of Example 8.4

```
1   if (x>0)
2   {
3           if (y>0)
4           {
5                   printf("%d\n",x+y);
6                   y++;
7           }
8           else
9           {
10                  printf("%d\n",x);
11          }
12          x++;
13  }
```

TIP 8.5
Always indent code to the right when you enter a new block of code. Indent to the left when you exit a block of code. This improves readability.

TIP 8.6
In general, it's a good idea to put the braces on an `if`-`else` statement even of there is only one statement in the `if` or `else` code blocks.

Using this formatting style, even inexperienced C programmers who might be maintaining your code should be able to tell that x++ is not part of the code block of the else statement which begins on line 8.

Another common problem with if-else statements is misplaced semicolons. In Example 8.13, there is a semicolon after the condition on the if statement on line 1. This code will actually compile and execute with no warnings or errors.

EXAMPLE 8.13   A Misplaced Semicolon

```
1    if (x<y);
2    {
3            x+=5;
4    }
```

The semicolon at the end of the if condition in Example 8.13 terminates the if statement. The compiler does not see the code block in the braces as connected to the if statement. It is just a block of code standing by itself. This is acceptable in C. Therefore, the compiler gives no errors. It often gives no warnings, depending on the complier.

When the program executes this if statement, it will do nothing if x is less than y because there are no statements in the body of the if statement. It will unconditionally execute the block of code after the if statement. This means that it will execute every time the program runs.

8.3.2   Avoiding Problems with switch Statements

The default statement can appear anywhere within the code block of the switch, which leads to a very interesting problem. I've been putting the default statements last in all of the switch statements presented so far. This is a common convention used by most C programmers. However, the C language doesn't force programmers to do this.

Because the default usually occurs last in a switch, programmers often omit the break statement from the end of the default. If the default occurs last, the missing break statement doesn't matter. After the default is executed, the program encounters the end of the switch statement.

However, if you do leave the break statement off the end of the default case, a maintenance programmer will invariably add another case after the default without noticing that there is no break between them. The maintenance programmer thinks, "Oh well, it doesn't matter because the statements in a switch can occur in any order." This is a potentially nasty problem because it's easy to overlook.

You may think, "Who would be stupid enough to add another case after the default without checking for a break?" Well I would, and so would you. In fact, I can honestly say that I have made this very dumb mistake and wasted a lot of time figuring it out. Many programmers have. For some reason, you can look at a switch statement over and over and not see that a break has been left off of the default. It's odd, but it's true.

Avoid the potential for problems. Always put a break after the default in a switch statement. Always put your defaults last. Never stick another case after the default.

Another simple mistake when writing a switch statement is to accidentally insert a semicolon after the condition. Just as with an if statement, adding that extra semicolon can be a difficult error to find. It is an extremely easy error to overlook.

8.3.3   Complex Conditional Operators

It is possible to combine conditional operators into complex operations, as illustrated in Example 8.14.

EXAMPLE 8.14   Nested Conditional Operators

```
1    maxValue = (value1 > value2) ?
2                    (value1>value3) ? value1:value3
3                    :
4                    (value2>value3) ? value2:value3;
```

TRAP 8.2
Be careful that you don't accidentally put a semicolon after a condition on an if statement. They are easily overlooked, which makes them a hard error to track down.

TECHNICAL NOTE 8.4
The cases and the default in a switch statement can occur in any order. By convention, programmers arrange the cases in ascending order and put the default last.

TIP 8.7
Always put a break statement at the end of the default in a switch statement.

TRAP 8.3
As with an if statement, a semicolon after the condition of a switch statement can be a hard error to track down. Be careful that you don't accidentally insert a semicolon there.

This complex use of the conditional operator is perfectly valid in C. Because the conditional operator evaluates to a value, you can use it anywhere you would use any value. That means you can use it in another conditional operator.

Example 8.14 finds the maximum of three numbers and assigns that value to the variable `maxValue`. The first conditional operator begins on line 1 and ends on line 4. I've isolated the parts of the conditional operator on separate lines to make it easier to read. The condition on line 1 asks if `value1` is greater than `value2`. If it is, then it evaluates everything in the true result section of the conditional operator statement.

The true result section, which is shown on line 2, contains another conditional operator statement. This conditional operator statement has its own condition. If `value1` is greater than `value3`, it is the maximum of the three variables. Therefore the conditional operator statement on line 2 evaluates to the contents of its own true section, which is `value1`.

If the condition on line 2 is false, the conditional operator on line 2 evaluates to `value3` because that is the value in its false section. Therefore, `value3` is the maximum of the three variables.

If the condition beginning on line 1 evaluates to false, the conditional operator in the false section is evaluated. This is the conditional operator on line 4. I've shown the colon of the outer conditional operator by itself on line 3 to improve readability.

The nested conditional operator statement on line 4 tests to see whether `value2` or `value3` contains the larger value. It evaluates to whichever is largest.

Confused? Most people are when confronted by multiple nested conditional operators. Experienced programmers try to live by the K.I.S.S. rule. K.I.S.S. stands for "Keep It Simple, Stupid." If there is a simpler way do doing something, it's generally best to use it. Therefore, it's a good idea to avoid multiple nested conditional operator statements.

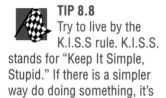

TIP 8.8
Try to live by the K.I.S.S rule. K.I.S.S. stands for "Keep It Simple, Stupid." If there is a simpler way do doing something, it's generally best to use it.

SUMMARY

C programs can conditionally execute blocks of code. When combined with the C branching statements `if-else`, `switch`, and the conditional operator, logical conditions enable a C program to decide whether or not to execute a block of code based on runtime information.

The `if-else` statement provides an alternative between two possibilities. If the condition of the `if-else` statement is true, it executes the block of code associated with the `if` portion of the statement. If it is false, the program executes the block of code associated with the `else` portion of the statement. The `else` block is optional.

A `switch` statement enables a program to choose one of many alternatives. Each alternative block of code is contained in a case. End each `case` with a `break` statement. The `default` is optional.

The conditional operator is an efficient shorthand which can be used instead of an `if-else` statement when the expression should evaluate to a value.

TECHNICAL NOTES

8.1 Flow control statements that use a condition (most do) are generally referred to in the software industry as conditional flow control statements, or just conditional jumps. Flow control statements that do not evaluate a condition are called unconditional flow control statements or unconditional jumps.

8.2 The branches of an `if-else` statement are said to be *mutually exclusive*. This means that they cannot both be executed. If one is executed, the other is not.

8.3 Because the `else` portion of an `if-else` statement is optional, many programmers simply refer to `if-else` statements as `if` statements. However, that terminology can be confusing and is not used in this book.

8.4 The cases and the `default` in a `switch` statement can occur in any order. By convention, programmers arrange the cases in ascending order and put the `default` last.

TIPS

8.1 Figure 8.1 contains a type of chart known as a flowchart. Flowcharts have been used by programmers for decades. It is a good idea to become familiar with them. For more information on flowcharts, as well as other types of charts used by software developers, see Maureen Sprankle, *Problem Solving and Programming Concepts* (Upper Saddle River, N.J.: Prentice Hall, Inc., 1992).

8.2 If you put more than about three dozen cases in a `switch` statement, the maintenance programmers may have trouble reading it. Help them out by explaining what you're doing in comments.

8.3 In general, it's best put a `break` after each `case` statement.

8.4 Always put your cases in order in a `switch` statement. Both you and other programmers will find your code more readable if you do.

8.5 Always indent code to the right when you enter a new block of code. Indent to the left when you exit a block of code. This improves readability.

8.6 In general, it's a good idea to put the braces on an `if`-`else` statement even of there is only one statement in the `if` or `else` code blocks.

8.7 Always put a `break` statement at the end of the `default` in a `switch` statement.

8.8 Try to live by the K.I.S.S rule. K.I.S.S. stands for "Keep It Simple, Stupid." If there is a simpler way do doing something, it's generally best to use it.

TRAPS

8.1 The common C style of indentation shown in Example 8.6 used is only for `if`-`else` statements. This is the exception to the rule. Programmers will usually find your code less readable if you apply this exception to other C statements.

8.2 Be careful that you don't accidentally put a semicolon after a condition on an `if` statement. They are easily overlooked, which makes them a hard error to track down.

8.3 As with an `if` statement, a semicolon after the condition of a `switch` statement can be a hard error to track down. Be careful that you don't accidentally insert a semicolon there.

REVIEW QUESTIONS

1. Why do programs use branching statements?
2. What is wrong with the following `if`-`else` statement?

```
if (x>100)
        x++;
        y++;
else
        x=0;
```

3. What happens when the condition of an `if` statement evaluates to false and there is no `else`?
4. Why do we indent to the right when we enter a block of code? Would the compiler generate errors or warnings if we didn't? Why or why not?
5. Why is it usually a good idea to put braces around the code blocks of an `if` and an `else`, even if there is only one statement in the block?
6. How many cases can be in a `switch` statement?
7. What happens if we leave off the `break` from a case in a `switch` statement?
8. What happens if we leave the `default` out of a `switch` statement?
9. In what order can the cases occur when using a `switch` statement?
10. According to the rules of C, where does the `default` of a `switch` have to be placed?

EXERCISES

1. Fill in the blanks.

   Branching statements enable C programs to _____ execute blocks of program code. After the _____ is evaluated, the branching statement will cause one block of code to be executed.

2. Even though the rules of C permit you to omit the braces from the `if` or `else` sections of an `if`-`else` statement, problems can arise when doing so. Identify and explain these problems.

3. Compilers ignore indentation. Explain why indentation is used in the source code of C programs.

4. Find the errors in the following source code.

```
1    switch (thisInteger);
2    {
3            case 10:
```

```
 4              printf("Ten")
 5      break:
 6
 7      case 20:
 8              printf("Twenty");
 9      break;
10
11      case 30:
12              printf("Thirty");
13
14      case 5:
15              printf('Five');
16      break;
17
18      default
19              Printf("That is not a valid entry");
20  }
```

5. Any `switch` statement can be replaced with a series of equivalent `if-else` statements. Explain why this substitution may or may not be desirable.

6. Fill in the blanks.

   K.I.S.S stands for _____ _____ _____, _____.

7. Tell what you think of the indentation style shown in Example 8.6. Explain why you think it is or is not good to use.

8. Throughout this book, you have read specific warnings that using particular techniques may be unclear to maintenance programmers. Sometimes, there are reasons why you must use these techniques. Describe what you can do in these instances to make it easier for a maintenance programmer to read your source code.

9. Write a program that demonstrates that the statements shown in Example 8.14 will actually work. Explain why using nested conditional operator statements can result in difficulties for the maintenance programmer.

10. Fill in the blanks.

    A literal constant can be a literal _____ or a literal _____.

11. Write a program that prints the word `"No"` on the screen if the user types in a number greater than or equal to 100. If the number is less than 100, your program should print the word `"No"` to the screen.

12. Write a program that will print the word `"Yes"` if the user enters a number that is in the range of 0–100, inclusive. If the number the user enters is greater than 100 or less than 0, your program should print the word `"No"` to the screen.

13. Write a program that gets two numbers from a user and prints the larger, or maximum, of the two.

14. Write a program that obtains a number from the user and uses a `switch` statement to convert it to a character. The numbers will be 0–9, inclusive. Your program should have two variables, one of type `int` and the other of type `char`. If the user enters a 0 into the `int`, your program should assign the character '0' into the `char`. If the user enters a 1, the `char` variable should be assigned a '1', and so on. After the number is converted to a character, print the character to the screen.

15. Write a program that will prompt the user to type in a character. It must print the word `"Yes"` if the user types in a 'y' or a 'Y'. It must print the word `"No"` if the user types in an 'n' or an 'N'. All other input should be ignored. Use a `switch` statement. Hint: This is an example of when it might be reasonable to leave the `break` statement off of the end of a `case`.

16. Write a program that determines whether a number that the user types in is even or odd. If it is even, your program should print the word `"Even"` on the screen. If it is odd, your program should print the word `"Odd"` on the screen.

17. Write a program that prompts the user for the radius of a circle. Use the radius to calculate the area of a circle. If you have a variable in your program named `radius`, the area is found by multiplying `3.14159*radius*radius`. If the user types in a radius that is less than or equal to zero, your program should print an error message and exit.

18. Write a program that calculates a customer discount. The user must enter the amount of a purchase. You'll probably want to use a `float`, `double`, or `long double` variable for this. If the purchase is greater than $100, the user gets a 2% discount. If it is greater than $500, the user gets a 5% discount. If it is greater than $1000, the user gets a 10% discount. Print the user's total with the discount subtracted. Make sure that the user types in a number greater than zero.

19. Write a program that prompts the user for the number of hours an employee has worked during the week and calculates that employee's gross and net pay. Assume that the employee is paid $10 per hour. Ask the user if he or she has worked overtime. If he or she has, the pay rate is time and a half ($15 per hour). Calculate the tax the employee owes and subtract it from the gross pay. Assume that an employee is taxed 10% if his or her pay is $300 or less. Tax the employee at 15% if his or her pay is greater than $300 and less than or equal to $1000. Earnings higher than $1000 are taxed at 25%. Output the employee's gross pay and net pay.

20. Modify the program in Exercise 19 so that it presents a menu to the user. The menu should allow the user to select from a set of standard pay rates which range from $5 per hour to $20 per hour in $5 increments. The program should calculate the user's gross pay and net pay based on the number of hours worked and the pay rate. Be sure to adjust the overtime pay according to the user's pay rate.

21. Write a program that calculates a user's income tax. The program should

    Prompt the user for his/her income.

    If the user's income is zero to $20,000, the user's income tax is zero. If the income is $20,001 to $30,000, the tax is 10%. If it is $30,001 to $40,000, the tax is 15%. If it is $40,001 to $50,000, the tax is 20%. If it is $50,001 to $60,000, the tax is 25%. If the income is above $60,000, the tax is 30%.

    Print the dollar amount of the tax the user must pay.

22. The potential difference in electrical current across a conducting material, such as a wire, can be calculated using Ohm's law for a steady electrical current. The formula is V = IR, where V is the potential difference across the conductor, I is the current, and R is the resistence. Write a program that prompts the user for the values for I and R, calculates the value of V, and outputs it to the screen. Note that there is no such thing as negative resistence. It is physically impossible. Also, there are no known materials that have a resistence value of zero. Therefore, your program must check the user's input to ensure that the value entered for R is greater than zero.

23. As a pendulum swings back and forth, the amount of time one swing takes is called its period. A pendulum's period can be calculated using the formula

$$T = 2\pi \sqrt{\frac{L}{g}}$$

where T is the time it takes for one period, L is the length of the pendulum, and g is gravitational acceleration. Gravitational acceleration equals 9.8 m/sec^2. Write a program that prompts the user for the value of L and calculates the period of a pendulum. If the user types a number that is less then or equal to zero, print an error message and end the program. Otherwise, calculate the value of T. Use the `sqrt()` function from the C Standard Library to find square roots. To use the `sqrt()` function, put the statement

    #include <math.h>

on the line following the statement

    #include <stdio.h>

near the beginning of your program.

24. The formula for finding points on lines is

$$y = mx + b$$

where m is the slope of the line, and b is the y intercept. When finding points on two lines, the equations are

$$y_1 = m_1 x_1 + b_1$$
$$y_2 = m_2 x_2 + b_2$$

If you are finding the (x,y) values of the point where the two lines intersect, then (x_1, y_1) and (x_2, y_2) are equal. Therefore, you can set these equations equal to one another and solve for x and y. In that case, the formulas become

$$x = \frac{b_2 - b_1}{m_1 - m_2}$$

and

$$y = m_1 x + b_1$$

Write a program that prompts the user for the m and b values of two lines. Calculate the intersection point. Warning: Computers are not able to divide values by zero. When solving for x, your program must test the value of $m_1 - m_2$ to ensure that it does not equal zero. If it does, the lines are parallel. In this case, your program should print a message stating that the lines to not intersect.

25. The quadratic equation takes the form

$$ax^2 + bx + c = 0$$

This equation has two solutions (two values for x) that can be found with the following formulas:

$$x_1 = \frac{-b + \sqrt{b^2 - 4ac}}{2a}$$

and

$$x_2 = \frac{-b - \sqrt{b^2 - 4ac}}{2a}$$

where x_1 and x_2 are the two values for x that solve the equation. If $\sqrt{b^2 - 4ac}$ is greater than zero, there are two solutions to this equation that are real numbers. If it is less than zero, the solution is a complex, or imaginary, number. Write a program that uses conditional branching to solve the quadratic equation. Use the `sqrt()` function from the C Standard Library to find square roots. To use the `sqrt()` function, put the statement

    #include <math.h>
on the line following the statement

    #include <stdio.h>
near the beginning of your program. Use the following algorithm for your program.

Declare the variables a, b, c, x1, x2, and result.
Prompt the user for the values of a, b, and c.
Get the values of a, b, and c from the user.
Set result equal to b*b − 4*a*c.
If result is greater than or equal to 0,
>   Set x1 equal to (−b + sqrt(result))/2*a.
>   Set x1 equal to (−b − sqrt(result))/2*a.
>   Print the real solutions.
Else if result is less than zero,
>   Set x1 equal to −b/(2*a).
>   Set x2 equal to sqrt(−result)/(2*a).
>   Print the complex number.

GLOSSARY

Branching Statement   A C statement that causes execution to branch to another location. Statements in the code block of the branching statement will be conditionally executed depending on whether or not its associated condition evaluates to true.

Conditional Flow Control Statement   A flow control statement that alters the flow of program execution based on the evaluation of a condition.

Conditional Jump   See **Conditional Flow Control Statement**.

Flowchart   A common type of chart used by programmers that shows the flow of execution of a program.

Flow control   The flow of execution from one C statement to the next.

Literal Constant   A constant value that is contained in the source code of a program. A literal constant can be a literal number or a literal character.

Unconditional Flow Control Statement   A flow control statement that does not use a logical condition to alters the flow of program execution.

Unconditional Jump   See **Unconditional Flow Control Statement**.

9

Flow Control: Looping

OBJECTIVES

After reading this chapter, you should be able to:

- Explain what looping statements are.
- Use `while` loops in programs.
- Use `do-while` loops in programs.
- Use `for` loops in programs.

OUTLINE

PREVIEW

Chapter 8 introduced flow control statements. It focused on the conditional branching statements that the C language provides. These are used to make decisions at runtime and conditionally execute blocks of code.

In addition to making decisions at runtime, a C program can use statements which evaluate conditions and decide whether to execute blocks of code repeatedly. This type of flow control statement is called a looping statement. This chapter will present the three basic loops used in C: while, do-while, *and* for.

9.1 Looping: You Can Say That Again

TECHNICAL NOTE 9.1
Because pre-test loops test their conditions first, they execute zero or more times. Because post-test loops evaluate their conditions at the end of the loop, they execute one or more times.

A loop is a block of code that a program executes repeatedly. All loops have a condition either at the beginning or end. Loops that evaluate the condition first are called **pre-test loops**. Looping statements that evaluate the condition at the end of the loop are called **post-test loops**.

We build a loop's condition using the logical operators we saw in previous chapters. If the condition evaluates to true, the program repeats the code block attached to the loop. If the condition evaluates to false, the loop terminates.

9.1.1 The while Loop

TECHNICAL NOTE 9.2
It is possible for a while loop to have no statements in its code block. This is usually not desirable, but it can be done.

The first looping statement that we'll look at is the while loop. It is a pre-test loop. Like all pre-test loops, it may execute zero or more times. If the condition at the beginning of the loop never evaluates to true, the code block for the loop never executes. Figure 9.1 shows the flow control of a while loop. Figure 9.2 illustrates its general form.

The while loop begins with the keyword while. It is followed by a condition in parentheses. The code block, or **body**, of the while loop may contain one or more statements.

FIGURE 9.1   The Flow control
of a while Loop

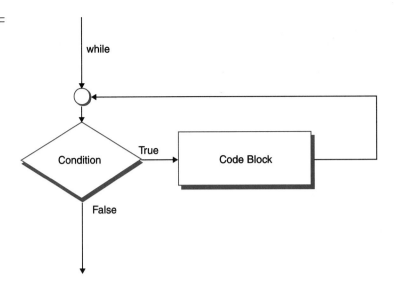

FIGURE 9.2   The General Form
of a while Loop

```
while (condition)
  statement;     } Single-statement body



while (condition)
{
  statement;     ⎫
  statement;     ⎬  Multiple-statement body
  statement;     ⎭
}
```

Hands On 9.1 illustrates the use of a while loop.

Hands On 9.1

Objective

Write a program that:
> Prompts the user for input.
> Gets a number from the user.
> Declares and initializes an integer counter variable.
> While the counter variable is less than the number the user typed in,
>> Output the value of the counter to the screen.
>> Increment the counter.

Experiment

Type the following program into your IDE or text editor. Compile it and run it.

```
1   #include <stdio.h>
2
3   int main()
4   {
5         int userInput;
6         int i=0;
7
8         printf("Please enter a number greater than 0:");
```

```
 9          scanf("%d",&userInput);
10          while (i < userInput)
11          {
12                  printf("i=%d\n",i++);
13          }
14
15          return (0);
16    }
```

Results

First Run

Please enter a number greater than 0:**10**
i=0
i=1
i=2
i=3
i=4
i=5
i=6
i=7
i=8
i=9

Second Run

Please enter a number greater than 0:**-9**

Analysis

I ran this program twice to demonstrate the pre-test nature of the while loop. In the first run, the program asked for user input. I entered the number 10. After the program got my input, it then encountered the while loop. Because the while loop is a pre-test loop, it first evaluated the condition. The variable i was initialized to 0 when it was declared on line 6. Because it contained 0, which is less than 10, the condition evaluated to true. Therefore, the program executed the loop's code block.

The code block attached to the while loop in this example contains only one statement. As a result, the braces were not required around the statements in the code block. Even so, I put them in. If there had been more than one statement in the code block, the braces would have been required.

Line 12 of this program does several things in one statement. First, it prints the string "i=" to the display. Next, the statement sends the value of the variable i to the display. Notice here that the program uses the value in i first, then increments it. That's because we used a postincrement statement. After the program increments the variable i, it prints the newline character to the display.

Try This

Change the postincrement on line 12 to a preincrement. Recompile, link, and run this program. How does the preincrement change the output of the program?

9.1.2 The do-while Loop

The do-while loop is a post-test loop. The test is performed at the end of the loop rather than the beginning. A do-while loop always executes at least once. Figure 9.3 presents the flow control of a do-while loop. Figure 9.4 shows its general form.

The do-while loop begins with the word do. The braces are required on a do-while loop. You cannot leave them off. They contain the body of the do-while loop. The

FIGURE 9.3 Flow Control of a
do-while Loop

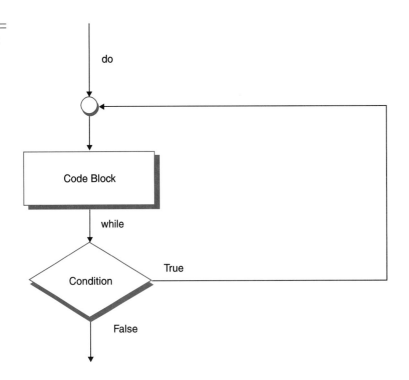

FIGURE 9.4 The General Form
of a do-while Loop

```
do
{
    statement;
    statement;
    statement;
} while (condition);
```

loop is ended with the word while, followed by the loop's condition. A semicolon appears immediately after the do-while loop's condition.

Hands On 9.2 demonstrates the use of a do-while loop.

Hands On 9.2

Objective

Write a program that:
    Prompts the user for input.
    Gets a number from the user.
    Declares an integer counter variable.
    Does the following repeatedly:
        Prints the current value of the counter.
        Increments the counter.
    Until the counter is greater than or equal to the number the user typed in.

Experiment

Type the following program into your text editor or IDE. Compile, link, and run it.

```
1   #include <stdio.h>
2
3   int main()
4   {
```

```
5          int maxLoopCount;
6          int i=0;
7
8          printf("Please enter a number greater than 0 :");
9          scanf("%d",&maxLoopCount);
10         do
11         {
12              printf("\nThe current value of i is %d",i++);
13         } while (i<maxLoopCount);
14
15         return (0);
16    }
```

Results

First Run

Please enter a number greater than 0 :**10**
The current value of i is 0
The current value of i is 1
The current value of i is 2
The current value of i is 3
The current value of i is 4
The current value of i is 5
The current value of i is 6
The current value of i is 7
The current value of i is 8
The current value of i is 9

Second Run

Please enter a number greater than 0 :**–10**
The current value of i is 0

Analysis

When this program runs, it prompts the user to enter a value. It stores the value the user enters into the variable maxLoopCount. Next, it enters the do-while loop, it prints out the current value of i. The variable i is initialized to 0 on line 6 when it is declared. Because this program uses a postincrement, it increments i after it sends the value in i to the display. The program then encounters the end of the loop, so it performs the loop's test. The test compares the value in i to the value in maxLoopCount. If i is less than maxLoopCount, the loop continues. If that is not the case, the loop terminates.

I ran this program twice to demonstrate the properties of the do-while loop. In the first run, I entered the number 10. As you can see, it made the loop execute 10 times. The values 0 through 9 were printed to the screen.

In the second run, I entered the value –10 into maxLoopCount. Note here that the loop did execute once. The program printed value of i, which was 0, to the screen. However, because i was found to be greater than maxLoopCount at the end of the loop, the loop terminated.

TIP 9.1
Be careful when using post-test loops. Always make sure that it is acceptable for the loop to execute at least once because that's what it will do.

Like C, most computer languages provide at least one type of post-test looping statement. However, because they will always execute at least once, post-test loops are not used as much as pre-test loops in computer programs.

The assumption with both while and do-while loops is that somewhere in the body of the loop, you will insert C statements that will eventually cause the condition to become false so that the loop will stop repeating. In Hands On 9.1 and Hands On 9.2, the statement i++ incremented the loop counter. When the loop counter became greater than or equal to the value input by the user, the loop condition evaluated to false and the loop stopped.

As developers, we need to ensure that we put this kind of code into our loops. If we forget to put it in, the loop will never terminate and our programs will lock up.

9.1.3 for Loops

The for loop is the most flexible and powerful looping statement in C. Consequently, it tends to be the most complex to use. Figure 9.5 shows the flow control of the for loop. Its general form is shown in Figure 9.6.

FIGURE 9.5 Flow Control of a for Loop

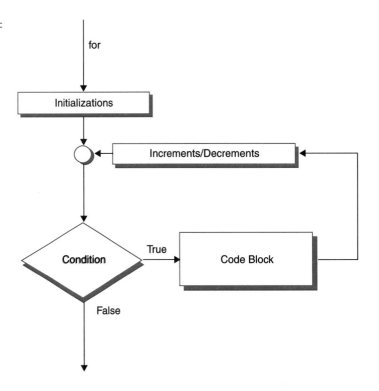

FIGURE 9.6 The General Form of a for Loop

```
for (initializations;condition;increments/decrements)
    statement;     }Single-statement body


for (initializations;condition;increments/decrements)
{
    statement;
    statement;     } Multiple-statement body
    statement;
}
```

The for loop, of course, begins with the keyword for. This is followed by the control portion of the loop, which is in parentheses. The control portion of the loop has three sections.

The initialization section comes first in the control portion of the loop. It is the first thing to be executed in the for statement. Typically, programmers use this section to initialize a loop counter variable. The initialization section of the loop is optional. You can leave it blank.

The second section of the control portion of a for loop contains the condition. Notice that the loop condition occurs before the loop's code block. That makes the for loop a pre-test loop. It will execute zero or more times. After the program executes the initialization section, it checks the condition. If the condition evaluates to true, the program performs the statements in the code block. If the condition does not evaluate to true, the code block is not executed and the loop terminates.

The third section in the control portion of a `for` loop is the increment/decrement section. It is executed only when the loop's code block is executed. If the loop condition is not true, neither the `for` loop's code block nor the increment/decrement section is executed. The increment/decrement section is always executed *after* the loop's code block is executed.

Hands On 9.3 demonstrates a typical `for` loop.

Hands On 9.3

Objective

Write a program that:
> Declares an integer counter variable and initializes it to 0.
> For each value between the range of 0 to 99 inclusive,
> > Output the value of the counter.
> > If the counter variable is divisible by 5,
> > > Output an endline.

Experiment

Type this program into your word processor or text editor. Compile, link, and run it.

```
1    #include <stdio.h>
2
3    int main()
4    {
5         int i;
6
7         for (i=0;i<100;i++)
8         {
9              printf("i=%d ",i);
10             if (i%5 == 0)
11             {
12                  printf("\n");
13             }
14        }
15
16        return (0);
17   }
```

Results

```
i=0
i=1 i=2 i=3 i=4 i=5
i=6 i=7 i=8 i=9 i=10
i=11 i=12 i=13 i=14 i=15
i=16 i=17 i=18 i=19 i=20
i=21 i=22 i=23 i=24 i=25
i=26 i=27 i=28 i=29 i=30
i=31 i=32 i=33 i=34 i=35
i=36 i=37 i=38 i=39 i=40
i=41 i=42 i=43 i=44 i=45
i=46 i=47 i=48 i=49 i=50
i=51 i=52 i=53 i=54 i=55
i=56 i=57 i=58 i=59 i=60
i=61 i=62 i=63 i=64 i=65
```

```
i=66 i=67 i=68 i=69 i=70
i=71 i=72 i=73 i=74 i=75
i=76 i=77 i=78 i=79 i=80
i=81 i=82 i=83 i=84 i=85
i=86 i=87 i=88 i=89 i=90
i=91 i=92 i=93 i=94 i=95
i=96 i=97 i=98 i=99
```

Analysis

This Hands On demonstrates how programs typically use `for` loops. It declares a counter variable of type `int`. The program uses the variable to control how many times the loop **iterates**, or repeats itself.

The `for` loop initializes the counter variable `i` to 0 in the initialization section of the control portion of the `for` loop. Next, it checks the condition section. In this program, the condition states that the loop should continue as long as `i` is less than 100. If that condition evaluates to true, the program performs the statements in the `for` loop's body, or code block.

The `for` loop's body contains two statements. The first sends some output to the screen. The second is an `if` statement. As you can see, the program doesn't print a newline character on line 9. The `if` statement beginning on line 10 sends a newline character to the output, but only if the condition (`i%5==0`) evaluates to true. This condition is true only when `i/5` leaves a remainder of 0. In other words, we are sending a newline to the screen when `i` is evenly divisible by 5. The output is shown in the Results section.

After the program executes everything in the `for` loop's body, it evaluates the increment/decrement statement, which contains `i++`. The program begins the loop again by checking the condition. If the condition evaluates to true, the loop continues. If not, neither the code block nor the increment is performed.

A C `for` loop also allows us to initialize multiple variables in the initialization section. The variables must be declared before the loop is encountered. The initializations must be separated by commas.

In addition, `for` loops may perform multiple increments and decrements. These too, must be separated by commas.

Example 9.1 illustrates both of these techniques.

EXAMPLE 9.1   A Slightly More Complex `for` Loop

```
1   int i,j;
2   for (i=0,j=100; i!=j; i++, j--)
3   {
4           printf("i=%d\n",i);
5           printf("j=%d\n",j);
6   }
```

TRAP 9.2
Do not try to separate multiple initializations with semicolons instead of commas. This will cause an error.

The loop in the example initializes `i` to 0 and `j` to 100. You can actually put more than two initializations in the initialization section. A common mistake that new C programmers make is to try and to separate multiple initializations with semicolons instead of commas. This will not work. The control portion of a `for` loop should contain exactly two semicolons, no more and no less.

Example 9.1 also demonstrates that a `for` loop may have multiple increments and decrements. Like multiple initializations, multiple increments and decrements must be separated by commas and not semicolons.

You may at this point be asking whether or not `for` loops can have multiple conditions. The answer is that you already know the answer. We saw in earlier chapters that logical conditions can be put together with the AND (`&&`) and the OR (`||`) operators. The condition on a `for` loop is no different than other logical conditions in C. Example 9.2 shows two `for` loops with multiple conditions.

EXAMPLE 9.2 for Loops with Multiple Conditions

```
1    int i,j,k;
2    char aChar = ' ';
3
4    for (i=0,j=100;(i<100) || (j>0);i++,j--)
5    {
6            printf("i=%d\n",i);
7            printf("j=%d\n",j);
8    }
9
10   for (k=0;(aChar!='q') && (aChar!='Q'); k++)
11   {
12           printf("k=%d\n",k);
13           printf("Type in Q to quit :");
14           scanf("%c",&aChar);
15   }
```

Compare the initialization sections of these two loops. The first loop initializes two integers, i and j. The second contains just one initialization, an integer variable called k. The program declares a character variable called aChar and initializes it in the declaration on line 2 of the Example 9.2. This demonstrates that variables can be initialized either when they are declared or at the beginning of a for loop.

TIP 9.2
Initialize loop control variables as close to the beginning of a loop as possible. When using while and do-while loops, initialize the variables that control the loop immediately before the loop begins. If you are using a for loop, try to initialize all loop control variables in the initialization section of the control portion of the for loop.

Most software companies insist that programmers initialize their loop control variables either just before the loop or (as in the case of a for loop) in the initialization section of the loop. This is extremely good programming practice. It helps other programmers find the starting values of your loop control variables.

All sections of the control portion of a for loop are optional. Any or all of them can be left out. The loop in Example 9.3 illustrates this.

EXAMPLE 9.3   A for Loop with No Increments or Decrements

```
1    char aChar;
2    for (aChar=' '; (aChar!='q') && (aChar!='Q'); )
3    {
4            printf("Type in Q to quit :");
5            scanf("%c",&aChar);
6    }
```

Notice that there is nothing between the second semicolon in the control portion of the loop and the closing parenthesis. The C compiler has no problem with this because all three sections are optional. If the program omits the initialization or increments and decrements, nothing is done for those sections of the loop. If it leaves the condition off, the program always assumes that the condition is true. Example 9.4 illustrates this.

EXAMPLE 9.4   An Endless Loop

```
1    for ( ; ; )
2    {
3            printf("This is a loop that never ends.\n");
4    }
```

Programmers have no real reason to create a loop like this. Doing so will only cause problems for yourself and whomever maintains your code. This type of loop is called an **endless loop**. Endless loops, which can be an endless source of program errors, are discussed in Section 9.2.1 of the Troubleshooting Guide for this chapter.

Here's another pop quiz. So far, all the for loops presented in this chapter have used a postincrement or postdecrement. If we changed them to preincrement or predecrement (as Example 9.5 shows), what would happen?

TRAP 9.3
Many beginning C programmers assume that if you change the postincrement in the increment/decrement section of a for loop to a preincrement, the loop will be incremented before the code block is executed. This is not the case. It doesn't matter whether you use a preincrement or a postincrement; the loop will always be incremented after the for loop's code block is executed. The same is true for predecrement and postdecrement.

Usually people assume that by changing the postincrement to preincrement, the program will increment the loop before it executes the loop's code block. Although this seems like a logical assumption, it is also an incorrect assumption.

Changing the postincrement in a for loop to a preincrement makes absolutely no difference. Your C program will always perform the increment after it executes the code block, no matter what. Whenever the code block is executed, any increments or decrements that you put into the increment/decrement section of the for loop will be performed after the code block.

9.2   Troubleshooting Guide

After reading this section you should be able to:

- Prevent common problems with while loops.
- Prevent common problems with for loops.

9.2.1   Preventing Problems with while Loops

Some of the most common problems with while loops are improper indentation, omitting braces when they are needed, endless loops, and misplaced semicolons.

Improper Indentation and Missing Braces   As with if statements, the indentation and use of braces in while loops can be confusing if not done properly. Example 9.6 illustrates this.

EXAMPLE 9.6   Confusing Indentation in a while Loop

```
1   #include <stdio.h>
2
3   int main()
4   {
5           int userInput;
6           int i=0;
7
8           printf("Please enter a number greater than 0:");
9           scanf("%d",&userInput);
10          while (i < userInput)
11                  printf("i=%d\n",i);
12                  i++;
13          return (0);
14  }
```

Notice that the program above is a slightly modified version of the program in Hands On 9.1. The program now increments the variable i on another line. But there's a problem here. If the braces are left off of a while loop, its code block can contain only one statement. The indentation indicates that we want two statements in the while loop's code block. Of course, the compiler will not see it that way. It doesn't care about indentation, so it will see the while loop as containing one statement in its body. Therefore, the only statement in the loop's body is the statement on line 11 that prints the value of i. The loop does not contain the increment on line 12. Because the loop does not contain the increment, the while loop will print out the number 0 for as long as you let the program run. This is another example of an endless loop.

By now you've probably anticipated the solution. We need to add braces to the while loop. Example 9.7 shows the resolution of this problem.

EXAMPLE 9.7 Proper Form for while Loops

```
1    #include <stdio.h>
2    int main()
3    {
4          int userInput;
5          int i=0;
6          printf("Please enter a number greater than 0:");
7          scanf("%d",&userInput);
8          while (i < userInput)
9          {
10                printf("i=%d\n",i);
11                i++;
12         }
13         return (0);
14   }
```

It's a good idea to put the braces around the block of code attached to a while loop, even if there is only one statement in the block.[1]

Endless Loops   Sometimes programmers will create endless loops intentionally, as illustrated in Example 9.8.

EXAMPLE 9.8 An Intentional Endless Loop

```
1    #include <stdio.h>
2
3    int main()
4    {
5          int userInput;
6          int i=0;
7
8          printf("Please enter a number greater than 0:");
9          scanf("%d",&userInput);
10         while (1)
11         {
12               if (i >= userInput)
13                     break;
14               printf("i=%d\n",i);
15               i++;
16         }
17         return (0);
18   }
```

This loop demonstrates a poor grasp of basic programming principles. There is no functional difference between the programs in Examples 9.7 and 9.8, except that the program in Example 9.8 is harder to read. When the program encounters the while loop in Example 9.8, it tests the condition. In this example, the condition is 1 so it always evaluates to true. It can never evaluate to false. A maintenance programmer will look at this and think it's an endless loop because, at first glance, it appears to be.

I inserted an if statement into the code block of the while loop. It checks to see whether the value in the variable i is greater than or equal to the value in the variable userInput. If it is, the program executes the break statement. This causes execution to break out of the loop. Program execution will continue with the next statement after the loop. This is an extremely bad way to use a break statement.

By using an intentional endless loop combined with break statements, programmers often make it easy for themselves to create the desired path through the code. However, the easy way is not always the best way. That's especially true in this case.

---

[1]This is a suggestion many long-time C and C++ practitioners offer. See also David M. Collopy, *Introduction To C Programming: A Modular Approach* (Upper Saddle River, NJ: Prentice Hall, Inc., 1997), pp 588–89.

Programmers who use this style of programming have no clear understanding of how to create high quality programs. They usually don't employ just one combination of an endless loop and a `break` statement. There are often dozens of constructs like this throughout their blocks of code.

What this means is that anyone reading their code has no clear idea of the conditions that will cause the loop to end. They must hunt through the entire code block to find the loop's termination conditions. If the loop is very long, the maintenance programmer will almost always miss one or more termination conditions.

Remember, the condition at the beginning of a loop is there for a reason. You shoot yourself (or someone else) in the foot if you short-circuit your loops by moving the termination condition anywhere else.

In addition, intentional endless loops make testing code a painful process. The paths through the code are no longer clearly defined. We must hunt for them. Using intentional endless loops and `break` statements together multiplies the number of possible paths through the code. You don't have to use very many of them before you create so many paths through the block of code that it is literally impossible to test them all.[2]

If you find that not all of your termination conditions can go in the condition portion of a loop, then at least use the technique shown in Example 9.9.

EXAMPLE 9.9 A Way to Avoid Endless Loops

```
1    int done=0;
2    while (!done)
3    {
4          if (condition 1)
5          {
6                do some processing
7                done=1;
8          }
9          else
10         {
11               do some more processing
12         }
13         if ((!done) && (condition 2))
14         {
15               done=1;
16         }
17         etc...
18   }
```

Example 9.9 does not show true C code, but it does give an approximation of what your C code would look like in a situation like this. The program sets the value of the variable `done` to 0, which is false. The test on the loop indicates that the loop should continue while it is not done (`!done`).

As soon as the variable `done` becomes true (indicating that the loop is finished), the test with the `!` operator will make the true value in `done` false. Because the condition on the loop now evaluates to false, the loop exits. Execution continues with the next statement after the loop.

What is the advantage of this method over using an `if` with a `break`? The primary difference is that it is more readable and maintainable. A maintenance programmer can search for the variable `done` to find all of the termination conditions of the loop. You might point out that they can just as easily search for the word `break`.

However, there are other ways to exit a loop that don't involve the word `break`. Programmers who use an endless loop with `break` statements scattered throughout the code will also use some of the other methods of exiting loops. Finding all possible combinations of exit conditions is a chore I don't wish on anyone. It's much much easier to use the technique shown in Example 9.9. It guarantees that a maintenance programmer who uses

---

[2]See also Michael Marcotty, *Software Implementation* (Upper Saddle River, N.J.: Prentice Hall, Inc., 1991), pp. 316–19.

his or her text editor's search function can find all of the exit conditions you put in your loops just by searching for the variable done.

Misplaced Semicolons Another common error that we programmers all occasionally make when we use `while` loops is to inadvertently insert a semicolon after the condition. Example 9.10 illustrates this.

EXAMPLE 9.10 A `while` Loop with a Misplaced Semicolon

```
1   int i=0;
2   while (i<100);
3   {
4           printf("i=%d\n",i);
5           i++;
6   }
```

The semicolon after the `while` loop's condition terminates the loop. This code will compile and run, usually with no errors or warnings. However, because the `while` loop ends at the semicolon, the statement on line 5 that increments the variable `i` is not in the loop. Therefore, the value of `i` will never change. The result is an endless loop. The program will hang.

9.2.2 Preventing Problems with `for` Loops

Let's do some variations on the theme we saw in Hands On 9.3. First, you probably already figured out that if there is only one statement in the `for` loop, we can leave out the open and closing braces. Example 9.11 illustrates this.

EXAMPLE 9.11 A `for` Loop with One Statement

```
1   #include <stdio.h>
2
3   int main()
4   {
5           int i;
6           for (i=0;i<100;i++)
7                   printf("i=%d\n",i);
8           return (0);
9   }
```

The loop in Example 9.12 shows the same sort of problem we've seen with all C statements that have a code block. The indentation indicates that the `for` loop's code block contains more than one statement. It indicates that the statements on lines 7 and 8 are both intended to be inside the `for` loop. However, the compiler doesn't see indentation because it ignores white space. Example 9.13 gives a corrected version of the loop.

EXAMPLE 9.12 A `for` Loop with an Indentation Error

```
1   #include <stdio.h>
2
3   int main()
4   {
5           int i;
6           for (i=0;i<100;i++)
7                   printf("i=%d",i);
8                   printf("\n");
9
10          return (0);
11  }
```

EXAMPLE 9.13 The Correction of Example 9.12

```
1   #include <stdio.h>
2
3   int main()
```

```
 4  {
 5          int i;
 6          for (i=0;i<100;i++)
 7          {
 8                  printf("i=%d",i);
 9                  printf("\n");
10          }
11
12          return (0);
13  }
```

TIP 9.3
It's wise to put the braces on a for loop even if there is only one statement in its code block.

TECHNICAL NOTE 9.3
It is possible for a for loop to have no statements in its code block. Such for loops perform their work in their conditions. This approach is sometimes used in professional programs. However, if you use this technique, be sure to put comments into your program that explain what the loop does and how it works.

As with while loops, it is easy to inadvertently insert a semicolon after the control portion of a for loop. The code in Example 9.14 shows how this might look in a program.

EXAMPLE 9.14   A Misplaced Semicolon in a for Loop

```
1  for (int i=0;i<1000;i++);
2  {
3          printf("i=%d",i);
4  }
```

The indentation and placement of the code block indicates we want the statement

```
printf("i=%d",i);
```

executed every time the loop executes. That's not what will happen. The semicolon after the for loop's control portion terminates the loop. The compiler determines that the code block is not attached to the for loop immediately before it. When the program runs, it faithfully executes the loop, doing nothing but incrementing the value of the variable i. Afterward, it unconditionally executes the statement in the code block after the for loop.

SUMMARY

C programs, like programs in most programming languages, are able to execute code blocks repetitively based on the evaluation of a condition.

Loops are either pre-test loops or post-test loops. A pre-test loop is one in which the condition is evaluated at the beginning of the loop. Therefore, programs execute pretest loops zero or more times, depending on the condition. A post-test loop evaluates its condition at the end of the loop.

Programs execute post-test loops one or more times. The C for and while loops are pre-test loops. The do-while loop is a post-test loop.

The while and do-while loops are the simplest to use. They execute their code blocks and evaluate their conditions. The for loop is more complex to use, but it is also more powerful and flexible.

TECHNICAL NOTES

9.1   Because pre-test loops test their conditions first, they execute zero or more times. Because post-test loops evaluate their conditions at the end of the loop, they execute one or more times.

9.2   It is possible for a while loop to have no statements in its code block. This is usually not desirable, but it can be done.

9.3   It is possible for a for loop to have no statements in its code block. Such for loops perform their work in their conditions. This approach is sometimes used in professional programs. However, if you use this technique, be sure to put comments into your program that explain what the loop does and how it works.

TIPS

9.1   Be careful when using post-test loops. Always make sure that it is acceptable for the loop to execute at least once because that's what it will do.

9.2   Initialize loop control variables as close to the beginning of a loop as possible. When using while and do-while loops, initialize the variables that control the loop im-

mediately before the loop begins. If you are using a for loop, try to initialize all loop control variables in the initialization section of the control portion of the for loop.

9.3   It's wise to put the braces on a for loop even if there is only one statement in its code block.

TRAPS

9.1 If the body of the loop doesn't eventually cause the loop's condition to become false, the loop will never stop repeating.

9.2 Do not try to separate multiple initializations with semicolons instead of commas. This will cause an error.

9.3 Many beginning C programmers assume that if you change the postincrement in the increment/decrement section of a `for` loop to a preincrement, the loop will be incremented before the code block is executed. This is not the

case. It doesn't matter whether you use a preincrement or a postincrement; the loop will always be incremented after the `for` loop's code block is executed. The same is true for predecrement and postdecrement.

9.4 Don't create intentional endless loops. They are a nightmare for maintenance programmers and testers.

9.5 Never insert the termination condition of a loop anywhere except in the condition section of the loop.

REVIEW QUESTIONS

1. What is a conditional loop in a C program?

2. What is a pretest loop? What is a post-test loop?

3. If a `while` loop has only one statement in it, the braces can be omitted. What is the main pitfall with leaving them off?

4. How are endless loops created? Why are endless loops a problem?

5. What can you do to avoid creating an endless loop when not all of your conditions will fit in the condition portion of the loop?

6. What happens if you leave the initialization section of the control portion of a `for` loop blank? What happens if you leave the condition blank? What happens if you leave the increment/decrement section blank?

7. How is a `for` loop affected if you use a preincrement in the increment/decrement section rather than a postincrement?

8. How can you use a loop to force the user of your software to enter a number in a specific range?

9. How many semicolons should there be in the control portion of a `for` loop? If multiple initializations are done, how many semicolons should you add?

10. What logical operators can you use to concatenate conditions together into a complex condition for a loop?

EXERCISES

1. Fill in the blanks.

   A _____ is a type of flow control statement that iterates over a block of code. The block of code is also called the _____ of the flow control statement.

2. Indicate which statements are true.
   a. To iterate means to do something repeatedly.
   b. Most programmers won't mind if you use endless loops in code they have to maintain.
   c. You don't have to worry about accidentally adding extra semicolons after the condition of a `while` loop. The compiler will report an error.
   d. Pre-test loops always execute at least once.
   e. Post-test loops always execute at least once.
   f. Because you can use the `break` statement in a loop, it is good programming practice to use them a lot.

3. Fill in the blanks.

   The _____ statement can be used to exit a loop. However, it is not considered good programming practice to use it for this purpose.

4. Scan this chapter to find all of the software design hints and the guidelines for good programming practices. Choose one and explain why you think that hint or guideline will help you as you write software.

5. Scan this chapter to find all of the software design hints and the guidelines for good programming practices. Choose one with which you disagree, and explain why. Describe how you think software should be written and why.

6. Find the errors in this program.

```
1   #include <stdio.h>;
2
3   int main()
4
5       int totalItems;
6       double currentTotal;
```

```
 7        double inputValue;
 8
 9        printf(""This program finds the average ");
10        printf("of all the numbers you type in.\n");
11        printf("Please enter a series of numbers ");
12        printf("that are greater than or equal to");
13        printf(" zero.\nAs long as you keep entering";
14        printf(" numbers greater than zero, it will ");
15        printf("continue\naccepting input from you. ");
16        printf("When you enter a number that is less ");
17        printf("than zero,\nit will calculate the ");
18        printf("average.\n\n");
19
20        for (totalItems=0,currentTotal=0,inputValue=0;
21                inputValue>=0;
22                totalItems++);
23      {
24                // Prompt the user for input.
25                printf("Please enter a number: ");
26
27                // Get the input from the user.
28                scanf("%lf",inputValue);
29
30                // If the user entered a value greater than
31                // or equal to zero...
32                if (inputValue >= 0)
33                {
34                        // Add the input value to the current total.
35                        currentTotal += inputValue;
36                }
37                // Else the user entered a value that is
38                // less than zero...
39                else
40                {
41                        /* The loop counter variable totalItems is
42                        used to keep track of the number of items
43                        the user types in. It will be incremented
44                        when this code block finishes. However, that
45                        total will be one more than the number of
46                        values the user typed in. Therefore, we need
47                        to decrement totalItems to compensate.*/
48                        totalItems--;
49                }
50      }
51
52        if (totalItems > 0)
53        {
54                printf("The average value of the numbers ");
55                printf("you typed in was %lf\n",
56                        currentTotal/(double)totalItems);
57        }
58        else
59        {
60                printf("The average value of the numbers ");
61                printf("you typed in was 0");
62        }
63        return (0);
64  }
```

7. Write a program that uses a `while` loop to start at 0 and count to a number that the user enters with the keyboard. Inside the `while` loop, use another `while` loop so that on each iteration of the outer loop, the program outputs a different set of 5 characters.

8. Write a program that uses a `do-while` loop to start at 0 and count to a number that the user enters with the keyboard. Inside the `while` loop, use another `do-while` loop so that on each iteration of the outer loop, the program outputs a different set of 5 characters.

9. Write a program that uses a `for` loop to start at 0 and count to a number that the user enters with the keyboard. Inside the while loop, use another `for` loop so that on each iteration of the outer loop, the program outputs a different set of 5 characters.

10. Write a program that uses a `for` loop. Inside the loop, create a statement asking the user to type in a character. If the character that the user types in is 'Q' or 'q', exit the loop. Otherwise, continue prompting the user.

11. Write the pseudocode for a program that prompts the user for a number greater than zero. It should use a pre-test loop, an `if` statement, and the modulus operator (%) to find all of the even numbers between 1 and the number that the user entered.

12. Write a program that implements the pseudocode you wrote in Exercise 11.

13. Write a program that uses a `while` loop to print all of the characters in the standard ASCII set. Hint: Using a type cast, character variables can be incremented and decremented. See Hands On 4.1 in Chapter 4. All of the characters in the standard ASCII set have a value of 0–127. When this program executes, don't be surprised if the computer beeps and there are some odd things printed to the screen. This is normal.

14. Write a program that uses a `for` loop and an `if` statement to print to the screen all of the characters in the ASCII set that are in the ranges 'A' to 'Z' and 'a' to 'z'.

15. Write a program that will repeatedly ask the user for the radius of a pizza. It should calculate the total square inches in a pizza using the formula πr^2 where π is 3.14159 and r^2 is the radius that the user typed in multiplied by itself (radius * radius). After the square inches of pizza are calculated, the program should ask the user if he or she wants to quit. If the user enters a 'Y' or a 'y', exit the loop. Otherwise ask the user for another pizza radius and perform the calculation again.

16. Write a program that uses a `for` loop. It should ask the user for a number. The condition of the `for` loop should be

        aDouble > 0

    where `aDouble` is a variable of type `double`. The number that the user types in should be stored in the variable `aDouble`. The increment/decrement section of the `for` loop should read

        aDouble/=2.0

    Run this program. Describe what happens. Explain why.

17. Write a program that gets an integer greater than 3 from the user. Use a loop to repeatedly ask the user for input until he/she enters a number greater than 3. When your program has valid input, it should calculate and output all of the prime numbers from 1 to the number that the user types in. A prime number is only divisible by 1 and itself. The first three prime numbers are 1, 2, and 3. Hint: The only way to tell if a number n is prime is to divide it by every number from 2 to $n-1$. Another hint: It's easier to test to see if a number is NOT prime than to test if it's prime.

18. Optimize the program you wrote for Exercise 17. Hint: All even numbers are divisible by 2, so they don't need to be checked. Another hint: If you're checking a number n to see if it's prime, you only need to divide it by the numbers in the range 2 to ($n/2$). Still another hint: This range can be optimized further.

19. Write a program that uses the following pseudocode algorithm to raise a number to a power.
    Do the following:
        Prompt the user for a number.
        Read the number from the keyboard.
    While the number is less than 0.

    Do the following:
        Prompt the user for a power.
        Read the power from the keyboard.
    While the power is less than 0.

    If the power is 0,
        Set the result to 1.
    If the power is 1,
        Set the result to the number.
    If neither of the above is true,

Initialize a loop counter variable to 0.

Initialize the result to 1.

While the loop counter is less than the power

Multiply the result by the number and store the answer in the result variable.

Increment the loop counter.

Print the result.

20. Write a program that uses a `for` loop inside a `for` loop to calculate and print a multiplication table for the numbers 0 through 12 inclusive.

21. According to Hooke's Law, the force F (in pounds) that is needed to stretch a certain spring x inches beyond its natural length is given by the equation

$$F = (4.5)x$$

Write a program that calculates and prints the values of F for each value of x in the range $20 <= x <= 40$.

22. The potential difference in electrical current across a conducting material, such as a wire, can be calculated using Ohm's law for a steady electrical current. The formula is

$$V = IR$$

where V is the potential difference across the conductor, I is the current, and R is the resistence. Write a program that prompts the user for the value of I. In addition, make it prompt the user for a range of R values from the user. To do this, have it prompt for starting and ending R values for the range. Have it ask the user for an R increment. Your program should begin at the starting R value, calculate V, and print it. It must use the R increment to increment to the next value for R and then calculate V for that value of R and print it. Make it continue to loop until it reaches the ending value for R.

23. As a pendulum swings back and forth, the time it takes for one swing is called its period. A pendulum's period can be calculated using the formula

$$T = 2\pi \sqrt{\frac{L}{g}}$$

where T is the time it takes for one period, L is the length of the pendulum, and g is gravitational acceleration. Gravitational acceleration equals 9.8 m/sec^2. Write a program that prompts the user for a range of values of L and calculates the period of a pendulum. Use a length increment of 1. If the user types a number that is less than or equal to zero, print an error message and end the program. Otherwise, calculate the value of T for each value in the range of lengths. For example, when prompted, the user may enter 2 as the start value of the range and 5 as the ending value. Your program would calculate T values for pendulums of length 2, 3, 4, and 5. Use the `sqrt()` function from the C Standard Library to find square roots. To use the `sqrt()` function, put the statement

        #include <math.h>

on the line following the statement

        #include <stdio.h>

near the beginning of your program.

24. The formula for finding points on lines is

$$y = mx + b$$

where m is the slope of the line, and b is the y intercept. Write a program that does the following:

Prompts the user for the values of m and b.

Gets the values of m and b from the user.

Prompts the user for a starting x value.

Gets the starting x value from the user.

Prompts the user for an ending x value.

Gets the ending x value from the user.

Prompts the user for an x increment.

Gets the x increment from the user.

For each value in the range of the starting and ending x values,

Calculate the y value that corresponds to the current x value.

Print the x and y values.

Increment to the next x value.

25. One example of a parabolic equation is the equation

$$y^2 = x$$

If solved for y, the equation becomes

$$y = \sqrt{x}$$

Given this equation, there are two solutions for *y*. For example, if *x* is 4, then the solutions for *y* are 2 and –2. Write a program that uses the following range of values for *x*.

Starting x Value	0
Ending x Value	1000
x Increment	1

Make your program calculate the values of *y* for each value of *x*. It should print the *y* values each time it loops.

GLOSSARY

Body   A code block associated with a C statement.

Endless Loop   A loop with no termination condition, or a termination condition that is never false.

Iterate   Do something repeatedly.

Post-test Loop   A loop that tests its condition after it executes its block of code.

Pre-test Loop   A loop that tests its condition before it executes its block of code.

10

Single-Dimensional Arrays

OBJECTIVES

After reading this chapter, you should be able to:

- Declare and initialize arrays in C programs.
- Access array elements.
- Initialize arrays.
- Define named constants to eliminate "magic numbers."

OUTLINE

PREVIEW

Previous chapters looked at how to declare variables that contain single items of data. They also examined some of the basic operations that can be performed on them. C, like most programming languages, also provides a way to declare variables that store collections of data. This type of variable is called an array.

The purpose of an array is to give a single variable name to a homogenous collection of data. A collection of data is homogenous if all of the items in the collection are the same type.

10.1   Declaring Arrays

C programs declare arrays in nearly the same way that they declare other variables. Applications must declare the name and type of an array variable, just as they would any other variable. The difference is that an array is a collection of data, so programs also must specify the size of the data collection.

Example 10.1 demonstrates how programs declare arrays.

EXAMPLE 10.1   Declaring Arrays

```
int anIntegerArray[10];
char aCharacterArray[15];
double aDoubleArray[1000];
```

TRAP 10.1
Sometimes new C programmers try to specify the size of an array in bytes. When we declare the size of the array, we specify the number of elements in the array, not the number of bytes of memory the array needs.

Example 10.1 shows that programs declare arrays by stating their type and name, followed by the number of array elements in square brackets ([]). An **element** is one item in an array. For example, in an array of integers, each integer in the array is one element.

The first line of code in Example 10.1 declares an array called `anIntegerArray`. The statement allocates space in memory for 10 integers. The second statement in the example declares `aCharacterArray`, which is an array of 15 characters. The array `aDoubleArray` can hold 1,000 elements of type `double`.

10.2   Accessing Array Elements

Each element in an array is numbered, starting with 0. Figure 10.1 illustrates the layout of the array `anIntegerArray`, which was declared in Example 10.1. Each element in the array is accessed by its number.

It's important to note that the **index numbers** of array elements of C arrays *always* begin with zero. Therefore, if an array has 10 elements in it, they are numbered 0 through 9.

FIGURE 10.1   Accessing Array Elements

anintegerArray

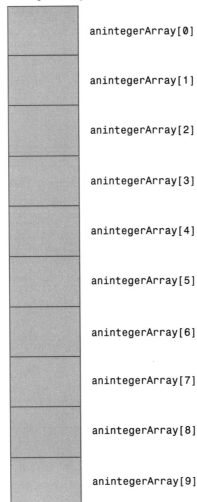

anintegerArray[0]

anintegerArray[1]

anintegerArray[2]

anintegerArray[3]

anintegerArray[4]

anintegerArray[5]

anintegerArray[6]

anintegerArray[7]

anintegerArray[8]

anintegerArray[9]

TIP 10.1
Each location in memory has an address. However, you do not need to worry about the addresses of individual elements in an array. Array elements can always be accessed by using the array name followed by an element number in square brackets.

TRAP 10.2
It is important to remember that array element numbering starts with 0. For instance, there is a difference between array element number 3 and the third element. Array element number 3 is the fourth element. The third array element is array element number 2.

TRAP 10.3
Never try to use an array index number that is smaller than 0 or larger than the last element number of the array.

An array element is accessed by stating the name of the array, followed by the element number in square brackets. The array element can be used anywhere a variable of that type can be used. For instance, the individual elements in an array of integers can be used in the same way you would use a single integer variable.

The array elements are said to be **contiguous**, which means that they are arranged one after the other in memory. Thus, an array is a homogenous collection of data stored in a contiguous block of memory.

It is vitally important that your program never try to access array elements outside the bounds of the array. Specifically, they must not use array index numbers that are less than zero or greater than the last element number in the array. The dangers of doing so are demonstrated in section 10.5.2 of the Troubleshooting Guide at the end of this chapter.

The following Hands On example demonstrates one way to use arrays in programs.

Hands On 10.1

Objective

Write a program that demonstrates the use of arrays.

Experiment

Type the following program into your text editor or IDE. Compile, link, and run it.

```
1   #include <stdio.h>
2
3   int main()
4   {
5       int i;
6       int anArray[100];
7
8       // Fill the array.
9       for (i=0;i<100;i++)
10      {
11          anArray[i]=i;
12      }
13
14      printf("\nPrinting the array.\n");
15      for (i=0;i<100;i++)
16      {
17          printf("%d ",anArray[i]);
18          if (i%10==0)
19          {
20              printf("\n");
21          }
22      }
23
24      printf("\n\nPrinting the array backwards.\n");
25      for (i=99;i>=0;i--)
26      {
27          printf("%d ",anArray[i]);
28          if (i%10==0)
29          {
30              printf("\n");
31          }
32      }
33
34      return (0);
35  }
```

Results

Printing the array.
0
1 2 3 4 5 6 7 8 9 10
11 12 13 14 15 16 17 18 19 20
21 22 23 24 25 26 27 28 29 30
31 32 33 34 35 36 37 38 39 40
41 42 43 44 45 46 47 48 49 50
51 52 53 54 55 56 57 58 59 60
61 62 63 64 65 66 67 68 69 70

```
71 72 73 74 75 76 77 78 79 80
81 82 83 84 85 86 87 88 89 90
91 92 93 94 95 96 97 98 99

Printing the array backwards.
99 98 97 96 95 94 93 92 91 90
89 88 87 86 85 84 83 82 81 80
79 78 77 76 75 74 73 72 71 70
69 68 67 66 65 64 63 62 61 60
59 58 57 56 55 54 53 52 51 50
49 48 47 46 45 44 43 42 41 40
39 38 37 36 35 34 33 32 31 30
29 28 27 26 25 24 23 22 21 20
19 18 17 16 15 14 13 12 11 10
9 8 7 6 5 4 3 2 1 0
```

Analysis

This program combines arrays, `for` loops, and `if` statements. The program declares an integer variable `i` for use as a loop counter. It also declares an array of 100 integers. Since array indexing begins at 0, the array elements are numbered 0 through 99.

The first `for` loop in the program stores the value in the variable `i` into the array. The program accesses each individual array element by its number. The first time through the loop, the variable `i` will contain the value 0. Therefore, the array element being accessed is `anArray[0]`. On the next iteration of the loop, the value in `i` will be 1, so `anArray[1]` will receive the value of `i`. When we read the statement `anArray[1]` aloud, we read it as, "anArray sub 1". The square brackets with a number in them are called the array's **subscript**.

This Hands On program executes its first loop 100 times. Each time it iterates, it increases the value of `i` by 1. So `i` will take on the values of 0 through 99. This corresponds exactly to the index numbers of the array elements. Therefore, these values can be used as array subscripts.

The program next prints a text label to make the output of the program more comprehensible. It enters a loop that prints the value in each array location, followed by a space character (character 32 in the ASCII set). The printing is done on line 17. This statement retrieves the value in `anArray[i]` and uses it as output to the screen.

The program then executes an `if` statement. The condition in the `if` statement tests to see whether the value of `i` is evenly divisible by 10. It uses the modulus operator to determine whether the remainder of `i` divided by 10 is 0. If it is 0, `i` divides evenly by 10. The code block of the `if` statement prints a newline character.

The last loop in the sample program iterates through the array in reverse, printing the values stored in it. Notice that it initializes `i` to 99, not 100. That is because the last element of the array has an index number of 99. The loop continues as long as the value in `i` is greater than or equal to 0.

In the next Hands On, we'll modify the program from Hands On 10.1 so that it uses characters. We'll also implement a simple type of document scrolling that we'll use in a text editor we'll be developing in the examples and exercises in this book.

Hands On 10.2

Objective

Write a program that:
    Fills an array with 100 characters.
    Declares and initializes the variable `top` to keep track of the first character to be printed.

While the user has not pressed 'Q' or 'q' to quit,
  Prompts the user for input.
  Gets input from the user.
  If the user types 'U' or 'u',
      Decrements top by 19 until it equals 0.
      If the user types 'D' or 'd',
      Increments top by 19 until it equals 100–20.
  Prints each character in the array beginning with top and ending with
      top+20.

Experiment

Because this program is somewhat lengthy, the source code for it is included on the Examples CD that is included with this book. Look in the Examples directory. You will find a directory called Chapt10. In the Chapt10 directory is the file called ho10_2.c, which contains the source code you see listed here. Compile, link, and run the program.

```c
1   #include <stdio.h>
2
3   int main()
4   {
5       int i;
6       int j;
7       char tempChar;
8       char anArray[100];
9       int top;
10
11      // Fill the array.
12      for (i=0,tempChar=' ';i<100;i++)
13      {
14          anArray[i]=tempChar++;
15      }
16
17      for (top=0,tempChar=' ';
18          (tempChar!='q') && (tempChar!='Q');
19          scanf("%c",&tempChar))
20      {
21          switch (tempChar)
22          {
23              case 'U':
24              case 'u':
25                  top -= 20-1;
26              break;
27
28              case 'D':
29              case 'd':
30                  top += 20-1;
31              break;
32          }
33
34          if (top<0)
35          {
36              top=0;
37          }
38          else if (top >= 100)
39          {
40              top=100-20;
41          }
```

```
42
43                     if (tempChar != '\n')
44                     {
45                         for (i=top,j=0;
46                             (i < top+20) && (i < 100);
47                             i++,j++)
48                         {
49                             printf("Display Line %d",j);
50                             printf(": Array element %d: %c\n",
51                                     i,
52                                     anArray[i]);
53                         }
54                         printf("\nCOMMAND:");
55                     }
56             }
57         return (0);
58     }
```

Results

The initial display will resemble Figure 10.2. After a 'd' or 'D' is entered at the keyboard, the display will look like Figure 10.3.

FIGURE 10.2   Initial Output of the Program in Hands On 10.2

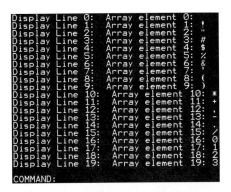

FIGURE 10.3   The Output After Scrolling Down

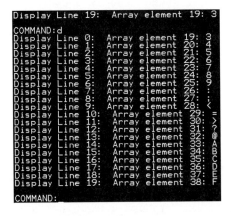

Analysis

This program declares an array of characters and fills the array using a `for` loop. When the program enters the loop on line 12, it assigns the variable `i` a value of 0. It also assigns the variable `tempChar` the value of space, which is ASCII character 32. The program then tests the variable `i` to see whether it is less than 100. The value 100 was used because that is the size of the array. During the course of the loop, `i` will take on the values 0–99. When the last iteration occurs, `i` will have a value of 100 and the loop will stop.

Each time through this loop, the program assigns the current value of `tempChar` into an array location. It also increments the variable `tempChar` to the next character.

The program enters another loop on line 17. I spread the control portion of this loop across three lines to make it easier to read. The initialization section is on line 17. The condition of the loop is on line 18, and the increment/decrement section is on line 19. If the control portion of a `for` loop gets too long, inserting a newline after each of the two semicolons is a good way to break it into multiple lines of text. Recall that this does not bother the C compiler. It just ignores the white space. Notice here that the three sections of the control portion of the `for` loop are aligned vertically. This helps other programmers read your code.

The initialization section sets the variable `top` to 0 and initializes `tempChar` back to space. The condition section says that the loop will continue for as long as `tempChar` is not equal to `'q'` and it is not equal to `'Q'`. As soon as `tempChar` is `'q'` or `'Q'`, the loop will end.

The increment/decrement section of this loop looks strange. It doesn't perform an increment or a decrement. Instead, it gets input from the keyboard at the end of each iteration of the loop and stores it in `tempChar`. Although this may look odd, it is perfectly valid C programming. If you use this technique, it is a good idea to put in a short comment explaining what you're doing.

When the program executes the body of the `for` loop, it enters a `switch` statement. In Chapter 8, I specifically advised you that you should put a `break` after each `case`. I've use this example to show a situation where it might be valid to break that rule. However this is an exception that validates the rule. In this case, we put two `case` labels for each block of code we want executed. The result is that if the user types in `'U'` or `'u'`, the line

```
top -= 20-1;
```

will be executed. If the user types in `'d'` or `'D'`, the line

```
top += 20-1;
```

will be executed.

We could have used an `if` statement to accomplish the same thing. It would look like Example 10.2

EXAMPLE 10.2   An Alternative to the `switch` Statement in Hands On 10.2

```
1    if ((tempChar=='u') || (tempChar=='U'))
2    {
3          top -= 20-1;
4    }
5    else if ((tempChar=='d') || (tempChar=='D'))
6    {
7          top += 20-1;
8    }
```

The difference between the two is that the `switch` statement is slightly more efficient. In addition, it is easier for the person writing the code to add cases to a `switch` than it is to add additional `if-else` clauses. For this reason, there are many C programmers who use this technique.

To me, these are not strong justifications for using this style of `switch` statement rather than a set of chained `if-else` statements. In my opinion, the set of chained `if-else` statements is safer because it's much harder to execute the wrong code block accidentally. Also, it's harder for the maintenance programmer to misinterpret. Your preference is something you'll have to decide for yourself.

TIP 10.2
If the control portion of your `for` loops get too long, a good place to insert a newline is after each of the two semicolons. It is also a good idea to vertically align the three sections of the control portion of the loop.

TECHNICAL NOTE 10.1
You must judge many stylistic issues for yourself when you take up C programming. In most cases, the overriding criterion should be whether or not the maintenance programmer will understand the code you've written. Modern compilers can optimize your code for you. Optimization isn't generally the highest priority these days; maintenance is. That's where much of the money is spent on a program. See Chapter 13 for details.

Many programmers would not agree. They would say that this is a perfect example of a situation where the `break` can be left off of cases. I don't feel that way. However, because this is a common technique you will see on the job, I have demonstrated it here and you will see it in other examples in this book.

The program in this Hands On uses the `switch` statement to increment or decrement a variable called `top`. This variable holds the array index number of the character that will be printed on the first line of the output. When the user presses a `'d'` or `'D'`, the program increments the variable `top` toward the end of the array. If we think of the array as a vertical collection of characters as in Figure 10.4, we are scrolling down toward the bottom of the array. If the user presses `'u'` or `'U'`, the program decrements the variable `top` upward toward the beginning. This tells the program to scroll its output toward the top of the array. We define a display area, which is the portion of the array that will be displayed on the screen. This is also indicated in Figure 10.4 by the blue box.

FIGURE 10.4 An Array of Characters Depicted Vertically

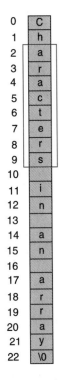

You may wonder why `top` is incremented and decremented by 20–1. Why don't we just write 19? This will become clearer later in this chapter when we cover named constants. However, the short explanation is that the portion of the array that we're displaying in this example is 20 lines long. When we scroll the display area up or down, we want to leave some overlap. By scrolling by the length of the display area minus one, the program will redisplay one of the lines that it displayed before scrolling. This helps users orient themselves within the context of our program's output.

After the program sets the variable `top`, it uses the `if-else` statement that begins on line 34 to check whether `top` has been decremented to a position before the beginning of the array or after the end of it. If it has, the program adjusts `top` so that it is within the bounds of the array.

Beginning on line 43, the program uses an `if` statement to check whether the character that was typed in was a newline. It is important to understand that every character you type on the keyboard is given to your program. When you type in a `'u'`, `'U'`, `'d'`, or `'D'` into this program, you must press the Enter key to terminate your input to `scanf()`. The operating system will send both the character *and* the newline to your program, one after the other. If the user types `'d'` and then presses the Enter key, this program will execute all of the code contained in the for loop that begins on line 17. It will react to the 'd' it gets from scanf(). It will then re-execute the loop using the newline ('\n') as input. That is not what we want. What we would like the program to do is get a single character from the keyboard, react to it, and then prompt the user for another character. However, that is not what scanf() does, even when we specify a "%c" in the format string. C does provide input functions in the Standard Library that will give us the behavior we want. These will be demonstrated in later chapters.

Because scanf() behaves in this way, the program uses the if statement on line 43 to check the current input character. If it is a '\n', it is ignored. If the input character is not a '\n', the Hands On program enters a for loop on line 45. The for loop starts at the array element indicated by top and prints each character on a single line. Before it outputs a character, it prints the display line number and the array index number.

If you scroll up and down, you'll see that it displays all characters in the array, 20 lines at a time. The program will not allow the user to scroll beyond the beginning or the end of the array. After it outputs each group of 20 lines to the screen, the program prints a prompt and waits for more user input.

Try This

Modify this program to use an array of 110 characters rather than an array of 100 characters. What other changes does this force you to make? This program can be written in a way that makes these changes easier. See section 10.4 for more information.

Hands On 10.1 and Hands On 10.2 demonstrated the power and flexibility of arrays. The program in Hands On 10.1 shows a simple method of using arrays to generate tables of information. Hands On 10.2 illustrates a technique for scrolling information in arrays. These are some of the basic tools we will eventually need to build the text editor.

10.3   Initializing Arrays

Like any other type of variable, an array can be initialized. Because an array is a collection of data, we initialize it with a collection of values.

The following Hands On demonstrates array initialization.

Hands On 10.3

Objective

Write a program that demonstrates array initialization and usage.

Experiment

Type the following program into your text editor or IDE. Compile, link, and run it.

```
1    #include <stdio.h>
2
3    int main()
4    {
5          int array1[10];
6          double array2[10]={1.2};
7          char array3[10]={'d'};
8          unsigned array4[]={1,2,5,6,7};
9          char aString[10]="A String.";
10         int i;
```

```
11
12          printf("Array 1\n");
13          for (i=0;i<10;i++)
14          {
15                  printf("%d\n",array1[i]);
16          }
17          printf("\n");
18
19          printf("Array 2\n");
20          for (i=0;i<10;i++)
21          {
22                  printf("%lf\n",array2[i]);
23          }
24          printf("\n");
25
26          printf("Array 3\n");
27          for (i=0;i<10;i++)
28          {
29                  printf("%c\n",array3[i]);
30          }
31          printf("\n");
32
33          printf("Array 4\n");
34          for (i=0;i<10;i++)
35          {
36                  printf("%u\n",array4[i]);
37          }
38
39          printf("\n%s\n",aString);
40
41          return (0);
42   }
```

Results

```
Array 1
-2124064700
44
2
39058936
2143490060
4198431
4202496
4202500
39058932
-1

Array 2
1.200000
0.000000
0.000000
0.000000
0.000000
0.000000
0.000000
0.000000
0.000000
0.000000
```

```
Array 3
d




Array 4
1
2
5
6
7
39058800
3220676862
3220677976
100
0

A String.
```

Analysis

In this example, we declare and initialize a variety of arrays. The first, array1, is declared but not initialized. What does it contain?

As the Results section of this Hands On shows, array1 contains random values. The statement on line 5 of the program allocates memory but does not initialize it. Therefore, it contains whatever bit patterns happen to be at those memory locations. Most C programmers use the term "garbage" to refer to random memory values such as this. You must assume that all data that you do not explicitly initialize contains garbage.

The second array, array2, is an array of 10 values of type double. The program initializes only the first location in the array. The Results section of this Hands On shows us that the first location in array2, which is location number 0, was initialized to 1.2. All other elements in the array were initialized to 0. Even though we initialized only the first location, the other elements in the array were initialized as well.

Most C compilers conform to this behavior. However, the old C standard was to leave all data that was not specifically initialized in an uninitialized state. If we were to compile this program with an older compiler, array2 would have contained 1.2, followed by garbage. Some C compilers still use this old style of initialization. This is particularly true when you are working on specialized hardware that is embedded into another product.

For instance, if you are writing the control program for jet fighter displays or the program that controls a microwave oven, you might very well use a C compiler that leaves garbage values in uninitialized variables and arrays. C compilers for any type of **embedded system** are much less likely to conform to the most recent C standard than the C compilers for desktop computers. C programmers who are technically inclined can often get jobs writing software for embedded systems. Programmers with this talent are always in high demand. Currently, most embedded software is still written in C. Because of this, it is helpful to understand where C compilers for embedded hardware are likely to deviate from the current C language standard.

TIP 10.4
Uninitialized memory must be assumed to contain garbage.

TRAP 10.5
Some C compilers will not initialize uninitialized data to 0 for you. You can't depend on it being done if you want your code to be portable. It is best to assume that data that you do not specifically initialize is garbage.

The array variable `array3` is declared on line 7 of this Hands On program. It allocates enough space to hold 10 characters. Like `array2`, element number 0 (the first element in the array) is initialized. The rest of the array is left uninitialized. When we print `array3`, the character `'d'` is printed on a line by itself. The other 10 lines are blank. That is because, like `array2`, the uninitialized portions of `array3` are set to 0. For characters, 0 is the `null character`. The null character means that there is no character there. It is the only character with the ASCII value of 0. When we represent the null character in source code, we use the character `'\0'`.

The next array, `array4`, has an unusual-looking declaration. We omitted the array size specifier in the square brackets. When the C compiler encounters an array declaration like this, it counts the number of array elements in the initialization. If the initialization is also missing, it will generate an error. In this case, we initialized five array locations, so the compiler will allocate memory for five unsigned integers.

The array declared on line 9 of the Hands On program, `aString`, demonstrates that character arrays can be used to store a string of characters. C compilers will allow character arrays to be initialized with a string in quote marks. When we do this, the C compiler will automatically put the null character (`'\0'`) after the last character in the string. So the contents of the array `aString` would be as shown in Figure 10.5.

TECHNICAL NOTE 10.3
If you leave the size specifier off an array, the compiler will count the number of items in the initialization. It will allocate memory for that number of elements.

TRAP 10.6
It is an error to leave both the size specifier and the initialization off of an array declaration.

FIGURE 10.5   The Contents of `aString`

TIP 10.5
In C, all strings must be terminated by the null character.

TIP 10.6
The null character, `'\0'` is one character even though it looks like two.

All strings in C must be terminated by the null character. When we declare an array of characters, we must be sure to allocate space for the null character at the end of the string. If we declare an array of 10 characters, it will hold a maximum of 9 printable characters and one null character.

The array `aString` could also have been initialized like this

```c
char anArray = {'A',' ','S','t','r','i','n','g','.','\0'};
```

But who wants to do that?

As the program in Hands On 10.3 demonstrates, there are a variety of techniques for initializing arrays. In general, most software designers recommend that you initialize all of the elements to a single value. While this is not a hard and fast rule, it is a good guideline. It is not unusual for the needs of your programming task to require you to use one of the other initialization methods presented in Hands On 10.3. However, you should do so only when you have a specific reason.

The most common advice on this subject that you will find in software development journals and periodicals states that if you initialize any portion of an array, you should initialize all of it. Even though the C language allows it, it is never a good idea to initialize some elements of an array and not others.

TIP 10.7
Unless you have a specific and compelling reason not to, it is a good idea to initialize all of the elements of an array to the same beginning value.

TIP 10.8

If you initialize any portion of an array, initialize all of it. Do not leave uninitialized data in your arrays.

10.4   Magic Numbers

Most of the programs we have written to this point contain what are commonly referred to in the software industry as **magic numbers**.[1] A magic number is a number that doesn't explain itself. Most numbers don't explain themselves. Unfortunately, many programmers use magic numbers with arrays.

---

[1]See Scott Meyers, *Effective C++* (Reading, Mass: Addison Wesley Longman, Inc., 1992), pp. 10–12, 31.

To illustrate the idea of magic numbers, let's take another look at the program we wrote for Hands On 10.2. It is repeated in Example 10.3 for convenience.

EXAMPLE 10.3   A Program with Magic Numbers

```
1    #include <stdio.h>
2
3    int main()
4    {
5         int i;
6         int j;
7         char tempChar;
8         char anArray[100];
9         int top;
10
11        // Fill the array.
12        for (i=0,tempChar=' ';i<100;i++)
13        {
14              anArray[i]=tempChar++;
15        }
16
17        for (top=0,tempChar=' ';
18              (tempChar!='q') && (tempChar!='Q');
19              scanf("%c",&tempChar))
20        {
21              switch (tempChar)
22              {
23                    case 'U':
24                    case 'u':
25                          top -= 20-1;
26                    break;
27
28                    case 'D':
29                    case 'd':
30                          top += 20-1;
31                    break;
32              }
33
34              if (top<0)
35              {
36                    top=0;
37              }
38              else if (top >= 100)
39              {
40                    top=100-20;
41              }
42
43              if (tempChar != '\n')
44              {
45                    for (i=top,j=0;
46                          (i < top+20) && (i < 100);
47                          i++,j++)
48                    {
49                          printf("Display Line %d",j);
50                          printf(": Array element %d: %c\n",
51                                i,
52                                anArray[i]);
53                    }
```

```
54                          printf("\nCOMMAND:");
55                  }
56          }
57          return (0);
58  }
```

The program in the example above uses numbers like 20 and 100. Twenty what? One hundred what? Why these numbers in particular? A person seeing this program for the first time would conclude that they must be important numbers because they are used repeatedly. However, he or she would not know that they mean.

C enables us to make these numbers more self-documenting by creating what are called **named constants**. A named constant is a name that we assign a constant value. Programs can use the name wherever the value would be used.

There are two advantages to replacing magic numbers with named constants. The first is that programs become more self-documenting. The name will hopefully explain the purpose of the number. Programs become easier to read.

The second advantage to using named constants is that they make a program easier to modify. Take Example 10.3 as a case in point. What if we decided to change the 20 to a 22? We would have to hunt through the program and find every 20 and replace it with a 22.

You may say, "That's okay, my text editor has a search and replace function. All I have to do is tell it to replace all 20's in the program with 22's." That's correct as far as it goes. The problems arise when we're working on large, professional programs. In that situation, the program will likely use the number 20 for things unrelated to the value we want to change. Globally changing all 20's to 22's would undoubtedly have a broader impact on the program than we intend. If we define a named constant, we can just change the value assigned to the name. That changes the value in all of the appropriate places throughout the program.

You might ask, "Are all numbers in programs magic numbers?" Strictly speaking, the answer is yes. However, most programmers will understand if you put the numbers –1, 0, or 1 in a program rather than a named constant. Those are just about the only magic numbers your program can safely use. If you do use them, use them sparingly. It is still better to use named constants, even for –1, 0, and 1.

A C program can create a named constant using the keyword const. When C programs declare named constants using the const keyword, they declare the constants very much like they declare variables. Example 10.4 illustrates this.

EXAMPLE 10.4   Declaring Constants with const

```
1   #include <stdio.h>
2
3   const int AN_INTEGER_CONSTANT = 20;
4
5   int main()
6   {
7           const double A_LOCAL_CONSTANT = 2.3;
8
9           printf("%d\n",AN_INTEGER_CONSTANT);
10          printf("%lf\n",A_LOCAL_CONSTANT);
11
12          return (0);
13  }
```

TECHNICAL NOTE 10.4 Programs can also define constants by using the #define directive. However, declaring named constants with the keyword const is the preferred method of declaring constants. The use of the #define directive is presented in Chapter 16.

The program in Example 10.4 declares two constants. The declarations look almost like the declarations of variables. The only difference is the keyword const at the beginning of each declaration.

By convention, programmers capitalize all named constants. C does not force you to do this. It does not prevent you from using lowercase letters if you want. However, other programmers will find your code more readable if you follow the convention of using all capital letters.

TECHNICAL NOTE 10.5
Variables can also be declared outside of main(). This is an *extremely* inadvisable practice. Companies will sometimes make you rewrite your software if you do. Declaring variables outside of main() in this way makes it a global variable. A global variable is one of the worst things you can put in your program. Using many global variables in a program demonstrates very clearly to other programmers that you don't know how to design professional programs. Technically speaking, global variables increase modular cohesion, which degrades program structure. See *Yourdon Systems Method* (Englewood Cliffs, NJ: Yourdon Press, 1993) pp. 4–5 and Maureen Sprankle *Problem Solving and Programming Concepts* (Upper Saddle River, NJ: Prentice Hall, Inc., 1998) pp. 64–65.

TECHNICAL NOTE 10.6
A constant declared outside of a function with the const keyword has what is called internal linkage. That means it can be seen only in the file in which it is declared. To make it truly global, it must be put in a header file. For more information on header files, see Chapter 16.

Notice also that constants can be declared outside of main(). In this example, the constant AN_INTEGER_CONSTANT is declared before main(). Declaring a constant outside of the function main() makes it a global constant. That is often exactly what you want. A global constant can be seen anywhere in the program. It is initialized when the program is loaded.

The program in Example 10.4 declares the constant A_LOCAL_CONSTANT inside of the function main(). It can be accessed only in the main() function. C programs usually contain many functions. Whenever programs declare constants inside a function, as A_LOCAL_CONSTANT is, only the function that declares the constant can access it. For more on functions, see Chapter 13.

Now that we have a way to declare named constants in a program, let's go back and fix the program from Hands On 10.2 so that it uses named constants.

EXAMPLE 10.5 A Program with Named Constants

```
1    #include <stdio.h>
2
3    //------------------------------------------------
4    // Constants
5    //------------------------------------------------
6
7    const int ARRAY_LENGTH        = 100;
8    hgconst int DISPLAY_AREA_SIZE = 20;
9
10   //----------------end Constants------------------
11
12
13
14   int main()
15   {
16        int i;
17        int j;
18        char tempChar;
19        char anArray[ARRAY_LENGTH];
20        int top;
21
22        // Fill the array.
23        for (i=0,tempChar=' ';i<ARRAY_LENGTH;i++)
24        {
25             anArray[i]=tempChar++;
26        }
27
28        for (top=0,tempChar=' ';
29             (tempChar!='q') && (tempChar!='Q');
30             scanf("%c",&tempChar))
31        {
32             switch (tempChar)
33             {
34                  case 'U':
35                  case 'u':
36                       top -= DISPLAY_AREA_SIZE-1;
37                  break;
38
39                  case 'D':
40                  case 'd':
41                       top += DISPLAY_AREA_SIZE-1;
42                  break;
43             }
44
```

```
45              if (top<0)
46              {
47                      top=0;
48              }
49              else if (top >= ARRAY_LENGTH)
50              {
51                      top=ARRAY_LENGTH-DISPLAY_AREA_SIZE;
52              }
53
54              if (tempChar != '\n')
55              {
56                      for (i=top,j=0;
57                          (i < top+DISPLAY_AREA_SIZE) &&
58                              (i < ARRAY_LENGTH);
59                          i++,j++)
60                      {
61                          printf("Display Line %d",j);
62                          printf(": Array element %d: %c\n",
63                              i,
64                              anArray[i]);
65                      }
66                      printf("\nCOMMAND:");
67              }
68      }
69      return (0);
70 }
```

It is important to note that there is another, older method of creating named constants. The older method is presented in Chapter 16. Some compilers will not let you use named constants created with the const keyword as the size specifier for arrays. They also will give an error if you use these kind of constants in the cases of a switch statement. If your compiler is one of these types, you must use the older method of creating named constants which is presented in Chapter 16.

This program demonstrates the use of named constants and program documentation. In a professional program, named constants are often put in labeled sections. That makes them easier to find. However, this practice leads to some differences of opinion.

Some say that the scope of constants should be strictly controlled. For example, since the constants in Example 10.5 were only used by the main() function, they should be declared in main(). As it is, other functions that we might add to this program would be able to access the constants ARRAY_LENGTH and DISPLAY_AREA_SIZE. Declaring these constants in main() declares them inside the code block that uses them. They should be only declared outside of a function if they are used by many functions in a program.

Others prefer to declare all constants outside of functions and make them global or nearly global. The advantage of this approach is that it is easier for the programmer developing the program. You don't have to worry about whether or not a constant will be available to a particular function. They are all available to all (or nearly all) functions. It is also easier to find a constant's value when you need it. They are always together in one place.

The style of organization you choose is up to you. Be aware, however, that different companies and organizations that you may work for may have different standards for where to put your constants.

One last note on the program in Example 10.5. Now that the number 20 is replaced in the program with the constant DISPLAY_AREA_SIZE, it is easier to see why we didn't put the number 19 in the program. It was always written as 20–1. That has now become DIS-PLAY_AREA_SIZE-1. Techniques such as this make the programmer's intentions clearer. In this case, the program uses the value DISPLAY_AREA_SIZE-1 to "scroll" the screen. By subtracting 1 from the DISPLAY_AREA_SIZE, we as the designers of the program indicate that we intend to repeat one line of the display. If the user scrolls the screen down, what used to be the bottom line of text is repeated as the top line. When the user scrolls the screen up, what used to be the top line is repeated as the bottom line.

TECHNICAL NOTE 10.7
We can make the code in Example 10.5 even more self-documenting by changing DISPLAY_AREA_SIZE-1 to DISPLAY_AREA_SIZE-DISPLAY_AREA_OVERLAP, where DISPLAY_AREA_OVERLAP is 1. This also gives the maintenance programmer the option of changing DISPLAY_AREA_OVERLAP to another value, such as 2.

10.5   Troubleshooting Guide

After reading this section you should be able to:

- Recognize and fix array boundary errors.
- Recognize and fix unternimated strings.

10.5.1   Going Beyond Array Boundaries

In the Hands On examples throughout this chapter, we very carefully avoided going beyond the bounds of the array. Some computer languages strictly enforce array boundaries. They absolutely won't let you access data before or after the array. C is not one of the those languages. There's actually a very good reason for this. We'll see the reason when we discuss pointers. For now, however, let's examine what can happen when we do go outside the allocated boundaries of an array.

EXAMPLE 10.6   A Quick Way to Crash a Program

```
1    #include <stdio.h>
2
3    int main()
4    {
5            int anIntegerArray[10];
6            int i;
7
8            for (i=-5; i<20; i++)
9            {
10                   anIntegerArray[i]=i;
11           }
12
13           for (i=-5; i<20; i++)
14           {
15                   printf("%d\n",anIntegerArray[i]);
16           }
17
18           return (0);
19   }
```

As the figure title suggests, this program is nothing but bad news. On my DOS PC I got the output shown in Figure 10.6. After displaying what you see in the figure, my computer locked up completely. I had to turn it off and back on again to get it going. When I ran this in a DOS box under Windows 98, Windows shut the program right down. It told me that the program had violated system integrity. Other operating systems (Windows 3.1, Windows 2000, and Linux) behaved similarly.

FIGURE 10.6   A Crashed Program and Garbage for Output

```
C:\fig10_6
-512340-972349811121131-582950
```

As these examples show, you should never try to access data beyond the boundaries of an array. Nothing in the C language prevents you from doing so. A program like this actually can work for awhile, depending on how your compiler lays out memory for programs. It can run perfectly well for a long time. That is, until you change something in the program that is completely unrelated to your array. Suddenly, after a perfectly reasonable modification, your program no longer works and there is apparently no reasonable explanation. This is a sure sign of a **memory overwrite**. That is what happened in the program in Example 10.6. By writing data outside the boundaries of the array, it overwrote other important data in memory.

When you declare an array, your program sets aside enough memory for all of the elements in the array. It does this when the program is loaded. When a program sets aside memory for data, we call it a **memory allocation**. In particular, it is a **static memory allocation** because the amount of memory that the program allocates for the array does not change as the program runs.

When a program declares a variable of an atomic data type, it statically allocates enough memory for that variable. When it declares an array, it statically allocates memory for every element in the array.

10.5.2 Unterminated Strings

As we have seen, C strings are created using arrays of characters. Every string should be terminated with a null character, which is represented by the symbol '\0'. The null character has the ASCII value of 0.

Failure to terminate strings can lead to strange output and crashed programs. Example 10.7 shows a small program that creates an unterminated string. The output of the program is given in Figure 10.7.

EXAMPLE 10.7   A Program That Outputs an Unterminated String

```
1    #include <stdio.h>
2
3    int main()
4    {
5         char aString[10];
6         int i;
7         char currentChar='A';
8
9         for (i=0;i<10;i++)
10        {
11             aString[i] = currentChar++;
12        }
13
14        printf("%s\n",aString);
15
16        return (0);
17   }
```

FIGURE 10.7   The Result of Printing an Unterminated String

```
D:\>a
ABCDEFGHIJ♪⌐ÿæ≈¬(•S●▌◄@
```

The for loop on lines 9–12 of Example 10.7 stores printable characters in every location in a string. It does not put a '\0' after the last printable character. The printf() function, which is used on line 14, uses the '\0' to determine when it has reached the end of the string. Because this string did not have a '\0' character, printf() cannot tell when to stop printing characters to the screen. It continues beyond the end of the array, reading values from memory. It treats each of these values as characters and prints them on the display. When it encounters a 0 in memory, it treats that as the '\0' and stops. Figure 10.7 demonstrates the kind of output you can get from a program like this.

The way to fix this is to adjust the for loop so that it does not store a printable character in the last position of the array. The program will then need to store the null character in that location. Example 10.8 shows the debugged program.

EXAMPLE 10.8   Terminating the String with a Null Character

```
1    #include <stdio.h>
2
3    int main()
```

```
 4  {
 5          char aString[10];
 6          int i;
 7          char currentChar='A';
 8
 9          for (i=0;i<9;i++)
10          {
11                  aString[i] = currentChar++;
12          }
13          aString[9]='\0';
14
15          printf("%s\n",aString);
16
17          return (0);
18  }
```

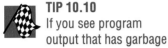

TIP 10.10

If you see program output that has garbage characters at the end of the string, it probably means that the program has created a string that is not terminated with a null character.

This version of the program alters the `for` loop beginning on line 9 so that it iterates 9 times. The variable `i` takes on the values 0 through 8. When `i` is equal to 9, the loop stops. Recall that the array locations in the character array `aString` are numbered 0–9. On line 13, the program in Example 10.8 explicitly stores the null character in location 9 of the array. This terminates the string so that the `printf()` function produces the proper output.

SUMMARY

An array is a homogenous collection of data. To declare an array in a program, you must declare its type, name, and the number of elements it holds.

If *n* represents the number of elements in the array, the individual elements are numbered 0 through *n–1*.

Array elements are accessed using the square brackets ([ ]). This is known as array notation or array subscripting.

Programs can use array elements anywhere they can use an atomic data variable.

Programs can set arrays to initial values when they declare them. It is best to assume that all uninitialized data in an array is garbage.

C programs use character arrays as strings.

Array declarations need a size specifier. That size specifier is a magic number. It does not document itself. Therefore, magic numbers like array size specifiers should be replaced with named constants. Create named constants with the keyword `const`.

TECHNICAL NOTES

10.1   You must judge many stylistic issues for yourself when you take up C programming. In most cases, the overriding criterion should be whether or not the maintenance programmer will understand the code you've written. Modern compilers can optimize your code for you. Optimization isn't generally the highest priority these days; maintenance is. That's where much of the money is spent on a program. See Chapter 13 for details.

10.2   It's important to remember that arrays in memory are neither horizontal nor vertical. They're just a collection of memory locations that are all together in a block. That is, they are contiguous. We just draw them vertically or horizontally so we can visualize them better. However, that is not how they are in the computer.

10.3   If you leave the size specifier off an array, the compiler will count the number of items in the initialization. It will allocate memory for that number of elements.

10.4   Programs can also define constants by using the `#define` directive. However, declaring named constants with the keyword `const` is the preferred method of declaring

constants. The use of the `#define` directive is presented in Chapter 16.

10.5   Variables can also be declared outside of `main()`. This is an *extremely* inadvisable practice. Companies sometimes will make you rewrite your software if you do. Declaring variables outside of `main()` in this way makes it a global variable. A global variable is one of the worst things you can put in your program. Using many global variables in a program demonstrates very clearly to other programmers that you don't know how to design professional programs. Technically speaking, global variables increase modular cohesion, which degrades program structure. See *Yourdon Systems Method* (Englewood Cliffs, NJ: Yourdon Press, 1993) pp. 4–5 and Maureen Sprankle *Problem Solving and Programming Concepts* (Upper Saddle River, NJ: Prentice Hall, Inc., 1998) pp. 64–65.

10.6   A constant declared outside of a function with the `const` keyword has what is called internal linkage. That means it can be seen only in the file in which it is declared. To make it truly global, it must be put in a header file. For more information on header files, see Chapter 16.

10.7   We can make the code in Example 10.5 even more self-documenting by changing `DISPLAY_AREA_SIZE-1` to `DISPLAY_AREA_SIZE-DISPLAY_AREA_OVERLAP`, where `DISPLAY_AREA_OVERLAP` is 1. This also gives the maintenance programmer the option of changing `DISPLAY_AREA_OVERLAP` to another value, such as 2.

10.8   Programs allocate memory from the stack when they encounter array or other variable declarations. When a C program loads, it sets aside a group of memory locations for the program's stack. The program then uses the stack whenever it needs to allocate space for variables.

TIPS

10.1   Each location in memory has an address. However, you do not need to worry about the addresses of individual elements in an array. Array elements can always be accessed by using the array name followed by an element number in square brackets.

10.2   If the control portion of your `for` loops get too long, a good place to insert a newline is after each of the two semicolons. It is also a good idea to vertically align the three sections of the control portion of the loop.

10.3   When your program scrolls output one screenful at a time, it is a good idea to repeat a line or two of the output from the previous screen. This helps the user understand where the current output is in the document in relation to the previous output.

10.4   Uninitialized memory must be assumed to contain garbage.

10.5   In C, all strings must be terminated by the null character.

10.6   The null character, `'\0'` is one character even though it looks like two.

10.7   Unless you have a specific and compelling reason not to, it is a good idea to initialize all of the elements of an array to the same beginning value.

10.8   If you initialize any portion of an array, initialize all of it. Do not leave uninitialized data in your arrays.

10.9   When your program is looping through the elements in an array, always check the beginning and ending condition of the loop to ensure that it does not try to access data outside the array.

10.10   If you see program output that has garbage characters at the end of the string, it probably means that the program has created a string that is not terminated with a null character.

TRAPS

10.1   Sometimes new C programmers try to specify the size of an array in bytes. When we declare the size of the array, we specify the number of elements in the array, not the number of bytes of memory the array needs.

10.2   It is important to remember that array element numbering starts with 0. For instance, there is a difference between array element number 3 and the third element. Array element number 3 is the fourth element. The third array element is array element number 2.

10.3   Never try to use an array index number that is smaller than 0 or larger than the last element number of the array.

10.4   Even if you specify `"%c"` as the format string for `scanf()`, every character the user types will be sent to your program. This includes such characters as the newline.

10.5   Some C compilers will not initialize uninitialized data to 0 for you. You can't depend on it being done if you want your code to be portable. It is best to assume that data that you do not specifically initialize is garbage.

10.6   It is an error to leave both the size specifier and the initialization off of an array declaration.

10.7   Writing data outside the memory allocated for the array will yield unpredictable results. It may crash the program, or it may work fine—for a while.

REVIEW QUESTIONS

1. What is an array?
2. How is an array declared?
3. How is an array initialized?
4. How are array elements numbered? In other words, what is the range of numbers used for the array elements?
5. What is an array subscript? What is it used for?
6. What happens if you try to store data outside the boundaries of an array? What warnings or errors will the C compiler produce when you do this?
7. What are two ways that an array of characters can be initialized?
8. What does uninitialized memory contain?
9. What is a magic number? How can we avoid using magic numbers in our C programs?
10. What is the purpose of the `const` statement?

EXERCISES

Note: Some of these exercises require the use of the `rand()` *function from the C Standard Libraries. You will find an explanation of this function in your compiler's documentation. It is also demonstrated in the programs for Exercises 9, 11, and 15.*

1. Explain what it means when we say that an array is a contiguous and homogenous collection of data that is accessed through subscripts.

2. Demonstrate how arrays are declared and initialized. Give examples. These should include a variety of data types, with initializations for each. Also, show at least one demonstration of an array in which not every element is initialized. Describe the contents of this array.

3. Explain what an array index number is. Demonstrate how array index numbers are used to access array elements.

4. Explain what a memory overwrite is. Describe how programs overwrite memory.

5. In your own words, define the terms *memory allocation* and *static memory allocation*.

6. Describe how to replace magic numbers with named constants in C programs.

7. Write a program that declares an array of 10 characters. Initialize the array to the string "This is a very, really, extremely, especially, truly long string that is definitely more than 10 characters". Compile your program and run it. Explain the results.

8. Write a program that contains an array of 100 integers. The integers can be any value. The program should print the contents of the array to the screen. Next, it should copy the array in reverse order into another array of 100 integers. It should then print the contents of the second array.

9. Load the following program into your text editor or IDE. You will find it on the Examples CD included with this book. It is in a file called Exr10_9.c in the Chapt10 directory. The Chapt10 directory is in the Examples directory. This program fills an array with 100 random integers. After you have loaded the program, finish it by writing a `for` loop which will search the array for the largest value. Use the comments as a guide.

```
1    //--------------------------------------------------
2    // Include Files
3    //--------------------------------------------------
4
5    #include <stdio.h>
6    #include <stdlib.h>
7
8    //End Include Files-----------------------------
9
10
11
12   //--------------------------------------------------
13   // Constants
14   //--------------------------------------------------
15
16   const int ARRAY_LENGTH = 100;
17
18   //End Constants---------------------------------
19
20
21
22   int main()
23   {
24        int i, integerArray[ARRAY_LENGTH];
25        int currentMax;
26
27        // Fill the array with random integers.
28        // For each array element...
29        for (i=0;i<ARRAY_LENGTH;i++)
30        {
31             /* Generate a random integer and store
32             it in the array. */
33             integerArray[i]=rand();
```

```
34                 }
35
36         currentMax=0;
37
38         // For each array element...
39                 /* If the array element is greater than
40                 the current maximum... */
41                         /* Set the current maximum to the
42                         value in the array element. */
43
44         return (0);
45  }
```

10. Write a program that fills an array with 100 characters. It should print the first 20 characters on a single line of the display. When the user presses 'r' or 'R', the display should scroll to the right 19 characters. That is, instead of displaying characters 0–19 in the array, it should display 19–39. The user should be able to scroll the screen to the last 20 characters in the array. If the user presses 'l' or 'L', the program should scroll the display of characters toward the beginning of the array. Do not use any magic numbers in your program.

11. Load the following program into your text editor or IDE. You will find it on the Examples CD included with this book. It is in a file called Exr10_11.c in the Chapt10 directory. The Chapt10 directory is in the Examples directory. This program generates simulated weekly rainfall data for a weather station. The program must calculate the total rainfall per year and the average rainfall per week. It must print these values, along with the weekly rainfall totals. Use the comments in the file as a guide for finishing the program.

```
1   //-------------------------------------------------
2   // Include Files
3   //-------------------------------------------------
4
5   #include <stdio.h>
6   #include <stdlib.h>
7
8   //End Include Files-----------------------------
9
10
11
12  //-------------------------------------------------
13  // Constants
14  //-------------------------------------------------
15
16  const int ARRAY_LENGTH = 52;
17  const float MAXIMUM_WEEKLY_RAINFALL = 5.0;
18  //End Constants---------------------------------
19
20
21
22  int main()
23  {
24          int i;
25          float weeklyRainfall[ARRAY_LENGTH];
26          float totalYearlyRainfall;
27          float averageYearlyRainfall;
28          float temp;
29
30          // Fill the array with random numbers.
31          // For each array element...
32          for (i=0;i<ARRAY_LENGTH;i++)
33          {
34                  /* Generate a random number that
35                  represents the monthly rainfall in
36                  inches. */
```

```
37                temp = rand();
38
39                /* While the number is greater than the
40                maximum number of inches of
41                rainfall possible ... */
42                while (temp > MAXIMUM_WEEKLY_RAINFALL)
43                {
44                        // Divide the number by 10.
45                        temp /= 10.0;
46                }
47                weeklyRainfall[i] = temp;
48        }
49
50
51        // For all weeks in the year...
52                /* Add the weekly rainfall to the
53                current total. */
54
55        // Calculate the average rainfall for the year.
56
57        // Print the weekly rainfall values.
58
59        // Print the total rainfall for the year.
60
61        // Print the average rainfall per week.
62
63        return (0);
64  }
```

12. Write a program that reads a maximum of 20 characters from the keyboard and stores the characters in an array. The program should not attempt to store more than 20 characters in the array. It must then print the contents of the array. Next, the program will copy the characters into a second array in reverse order. Finally, it should print the contents of the second array.

13. Write a program that reads a string that is entered by the user. The program should count the number of characters in the string and print the length.

14. Write a program that prompts the user for two strings and reads them into two arrays of characters. The program should use a loop to compare the each character in the first array to the corresponding character in the second array. If the arrays are named string1 and string2, the loop will compare string1[0] to string2[0], string1[1] to string2[1], and so on. If it finds that any characters are not the same in both strings, it should print the message, "These strings are not the same." If all characters in both arrays are identical, it should print, "These strings are the same."

15. Load the following program into your text editor or IDE. You will find it on the Examples CD included with this book. It is in a file called Exr10_15.c. in the Chapt10 directory. The Chapt10 directory is in the Examples directory. This program sorts a group of integers that are stored in an array. It uses a sorting technique called a Bubble Sort. Use the comments in the file as a guide for finishing the program.

```
1   //-------------------------------------------------------
2   // Include Files
3   //-------------------------------------------------------
4
5   #include <stdio.h>
6   #include <stdlib.h>
7
8   //End Include Files-------------------------------------
9
10
11
12  //-------------------------------------------------------
13  // Constants
14  //-------------------------------------------------------
15
```

```
16    const int ARRAY_LENGTH = 100;

17

18    //End Constants----------------------------------

19

20

21

22    int main()

23    {

24          int i, j, integerArray[ARRAY_LENGTH];

25          int temp;

26

27          // Fill the array with random integers.

28          // For each array element...

29          for (i=0;i<ARRAY_LENGTH;i++)

30          {

31                /* Generate a random integer and store

32                it in the array. */

33                integerArray[i]=rand();

34          }

35

36          printf("\nThe array in random order...\n");

37

38          // For each array element...

39                // Print the array element.

40          // For each array element...

41                // For each element less than the current element

42          for (j=0;j<i;j++)

43          {

44                if (integerArray[i]<integerArray[j])

45                {

46                      /* Swap the values in

47                      integerArray[i] and

48                      integerArray[j]. */

49                }

50          }

51    }

52

53          printf("\nThe array in sorted order...\n");

54          // For each array element...

55                // Print the array element.

56

57          return (0);

58    }
```

16. The program in Exercise 15 sorts integers into ascending order. Write a program that uses this sorting technique to sort an array of characters into descending order and prints the result.

17. Engineers are sometimes more concerned with the frequency of an event than with the data gathered by observing the event itself. To simulate this situation, write a program that fills an array with 100 integers. The program will scan the integers in the array and find the total number integers that are greater than or equal to 5,000. It should report that total.

18. At times, engineers are more interested in being alerted when data items do not fit within allowable ranges they have defined. To simulate this situation, write a program that fills an array with 100 random numbers. The program must print each value in the array, and also print a warning when any of the values are below 200 or above 20,000.

19. Write a program that accepts 10 integers from the user and stores them in an array. The integer values must be between 0 and 50. If the user enters incorrect input, the program should re-prompt the user until correct input is entered. When the user has typed in all 10 integers, the program should print a horizontal bar graph using the input values. It will do this by printing asterisks horizontally across the screen. The number of asterisks per line is specified by the number in each array location. For example, if the number 40 is stored in the first array location, the first line of the graph will have 40 asterisks. The bar graph will contain 10 horizontal lines of asterisks.

20. Using the technique for printing a bar graph specified in Exercise 19, write a program that fills an array with 100 random integers. The program must count the number of items that fall between the ranges of 0 to 999, 1,000 to 10,000, 10,001 to 19,999, and those that are greater than or equal to 20,000. It should print a bar graph with a horizontal bar of asterisks for each of these five ranges.

21. Write a program that declares an array of 100 integers. Fill the array with random integers by using the C Standard Library `rand()` function. Your program must search the array for the largest and smallest values it contains and then print them.

22. Write a program that declares an array of 100 integers. Fill the array with random integers by using the C Standard Library `rand()` function. Your program must calculate the sum of all of the integers in the array. Next, make it divide the sum by 100 to find the average value. Print the average.

23. The mode of a group of numbers is the number that occurs most often. Write a program that Write a program that declares an array of 100 integers. Fill the array with random integers by using the C Standard Library `rand()` function. For every integer the program generates with the `rand()` function, make the program check the array to ensure that the number being inserted is not already in the array. Your program must find and print the mode of the numbers in the array. Hint: You can keep the totals in another array.

24. The median value of a group of numbers is the value that has an equal number of values in the group greater than and less than the median value. For example, if the group of numbers is 2, 3, 10, 15, 20, the value 10 is the median because there are two numbers in the group that are greater than 10 and two numbers in the group that are less than 10. Write a program that declares an array of 100 integers. Fill the array with random integers by using the C Standard Library `rand()` function. Your program must find the median value of all of the numbers in the array. Use the following algorithm:

> Declare an array of integers called allNumbers.
> Use the rand() function to fill allNumbers with integers.
> For each value in the array,
> > Compare the current value with all other values.
> > Count the number of values that are greater than the current value.
> > Count the number of values that are less than the current value.
> > If both the number of values greater and less than the current value are greater than 50 (total array items/2), then the current value is the median. Otherwise, move to the next value in the array and try again.

25. The pressure of water at a given depth is calculated with the formula

$$P = h\gamma_w$$

where P is the pressure, h is the depth in meters, and γ_m is the weight density of water. The weight density of water is $9.8kN/m^2$. Write a program that prints the pressure of water over a range of depths. Start at 1 meter and end at 1000 meters.

GLOSSARY

Array   A homogenous collection of data that is given a single variable name and accessed using array subscript notation.

Contiguous   A group of items that are all together. Each one is immediately adjacent to the other.

Element   One data item in an array.

Embedded System   A computer that is embedded into another product. Products that have small embedded computers in them include microwave ovens, video cameras, car ignitions, VCRs, and airplanes.

Homogenous   A group of objects that are all of the same type.

Index Number   The number used to access an array element. The first element in array always has an index number of 0. The second has an index number of 1, etc.

Magic Number   A number in a program that doesn't explain itself. Most numbers in programs don't explain themselves.

Memory Allocation   Setting aside memory for use by a program.

Memory Overwrite   Writing data to an area of memory that hasn't been allocated, or has been allocated for something else. Writing data outside the boundaries of an array usually causes a memory overwrite.

Named Constant   A constant value that is given a name.

Null Character   The character `'\0'`. It has an ASCII value of 0, and is used to terminate strings.

Static Memory Allocation   A memory allocation that does not change size as the program runs.

Subscript   The array element index number in square brackets.

11

Multidimensional Arrays

OBJECTIVES

After reading this chapter, you should be able to:

- Declare multidimensional arrays.
- Initialize multidimensional arrays.
- Use multidimensional arrays.

OUTLINE

PREVIEW

Multidimensional arrays are a straightforward extension of the single-dimensional arrays we covered in Chapter 10. Normally, they would not warrant a complete chapter by themselves. However, we're going to take this opportunity to practice many of the other C statements we've learned. In fact, in this chapter we'll begin building what will become a text editor.

11.1   Extending Single-Dimensional Arrays

A single-dimensional array can be thought of as a row or a column of data. The elements in the single-dimensional arrays presented in Chapter 10 were atomic data. That is, they were arrays of integers, floating-point numbers, or characters.

A multidimensional array in C is also an array. Unlike a single-dimensional array, a multidimensional array is an array of arrays, as shown in Figure 11.1. The figure shows a two-dimensional array, often abbreviated as "2-D array." We can think of each element in the array as a row of data in a table. Because each row is a single array element, the figure shows them with bold borders. Each of these elements, or rows, is also an array. Each row array contains its own collection of elements. These elements can be thought of as columns in a table of data. In this example, each column contains an integer.

FIGURE 11.1   A Two-Dimensional Array of Integers

	0	1	2	3	4	5	6
0	5	-32	81	6	0	66	4
1	21	958	-568	12	-357	159	654
2	91	73	48	29	62	38	48

The 2-D array in the Figure 11.1 has three elements in it, which are shown as rows. They are numbered 0–2. Each row, which is also an array, has seven elements in it. They are numbered 0–6. Each element in a row array is an integer.

TECHNICAL NOTE 11.1
Programmers use 3-D and even 4-D arrays in computer graphics, engineering, and scientific computing.

It's important to remember, however, that a 2-D array does not actually have rows and columns in it. We just think of it that way for convenience. In reality, each "row" is allocated in contiguous memory one after the other.

It is possible to create 3-D arrays, 4-D arrays, and so on. However, these are not used as much as 2-D arrays because programmers often find them difficult to work with.

11.2   Declaring Multidimensional Arrays

When programs declare multidimensional arrays, they use nearly the same syntax as when they declare 1-D arrays. For each dimension you want to declare, add a size specifier in square brackets. Example 11.1 shows how this is done for 1-D, 2-D, and 3-D arrays.

TECHNICAL NOTE 11.2
The maximum number of dimensions you can declare on an array is set by the manufacturer of your compiler. Most compilers will allow you to declare up to seven dimensions.

EXAMPLE 11.1   Declaring Arrays of Various Dimensions

```
int aSingleDimensionalArray[10];
int a2DArray[3][7];
int a3DArray[5][10][15];
```

The first array in Example 11.1 is a 1-D array of ten integers. The second is a 2-D array containing three groups of seven integers. The third is a 3-D array containing five elements. Each element is a 2-D array containing ten groups of fifteen integers.

11.3   Accessing Array Elements

You access elements in multidimensional arrays in essentially the same way that you access them in single-dimensional arrays. The only difference is that you need to add a subscript for each dimension. Hands On 11.1 shows a small program that uses a 2-D array.

Hands On 11.1

Objective

Write a program that:
    Declares and initializes a 2-D array of integers.
    Displays the contents of each array location.

Experiment

Type the following program into your IDE or text editor. Compile, link, and run it.

```
1    #include <stdio.h>
2
3    int main()
4    {
5         int a2DArray[10][20];
6         int i,j;
7
8         printf("\n");
9         for (i=0;i<10;i++)
10        {
11             for (j=0;j<20;j++)
12             {
13                  a2DArray[i][j]=i+j;
14             }
15        }
16
17        for (i=0;i<10;i++)
```

```
18          {
19                  printf("Row %d:",i);
20                  for (j=0;j<20;j++)
21                  {
22                          printf("%d",a2DArray[i][j]);
23                          if (a2DArray[i][j] < 10)
24                          {
25                                  printf("  ");
26                          }
27                          else if (a2DArray[i][j] < 100)
28                          {
29                                  printf(" ");
30                          }
31                  }
32                  printf("\n");
33          }
34
35          return (0);
36  }
```

Results

The output of this program is shown in Figure 11.2.

FIGURE 11.2   The Output of Hands On 11.1

```
Row 0:0  1  2  3  4  5  6  7  8  9  10 11 12 13 14 15 16 17 18 19
Row 1:1  2  3  4  5  6  7  8  9  10 11 12 13 14 15 16 17 18 19 20
Row 2:2  3  4  5  6  7  8  9  10 11 12 13 14 15 16 17 18 19 20 21
Row 3:3  4  5  6  7  8  9  10 11 12 13 14 15 16 17 18 19 20 21 22
Row 4:4  5  6  7  8  9  10 11 12 13 14 15 16 17 18 19 20 21 22 23
Row 5:5  6  7  8  9  10 11 12 13 14 15 16 17 18 19 20 21 22 23 24
Row 6:6  7  8  9  10 11 12 13 14 15 16 17 18 19 20 21 22 23 24 25
Row 7:7  8  9  10 11 12 13 14 15 16 17 18 19 20 21 22 23 24 25 26
Row 8:8  9  10 11 12 13 14 15 16 17 18 19 20 21 22 23 24 25 26 27
Row 9:9  10 11 12 13 14 15 16 17 18 19 20 21 22 23 24 25 26 27 28
```

Analysis

This program declares a 2-D array called a2DArray. It also declares some variables that are used as loop counters. It enters a set of two nested for loops. The outer for loop, on lines 9–15, performs one iteration for each row in the array. The inner for loop iterates once for each column. Therefore, every time the program executes the outer loop, it executes the inner loop 20 times. The variable i tracks the current row. The variable j tracks the current column. As the program iterates through the pair of loops for each row and column, it stores the value of i+j in each location in the array.

The program then enters another pair of nested for loops, beginning on line 17. It uses these for loops to iterate through each row and column in the 2-D array. For every element in the 2-D array, the program prints the value in each column to the screen. It also uses an if statement to add some blank space as padding between the values it prints. If the value is less than 10, the number being printed (0 through 9) is one digit long. Therefore, the program prints two spaces to the screen. If the number is not less than 10, the program tests to see if it is less than 100. Since the numbers 10–99 are all two digits long, the program prints only one space to the screen. This set of chained if statements ensures that the columns of output line up when the program prints them on the display.

This program demonstrates how elements are accessed in a 2-D array. Each element is specified by the array name, followed by its row and column number.

11.4   Initializing Multidimensional Arrays

Like single-dimensional arrays, multidimensional arrays can be initialized when they are declared. Example 11.2 demonstrates how this is done.

EXAMPLE 11.2   Initializing Multidimensional Arrays

```
int a2DIntArray[3][4] = {{1,2,3,4},
                         {4,5,6,7},
                         {7,8,9,10}};
int a3DArray[2][2][2] = {{{1,2},{3,4}},
                         {{4,3},{2,1}}};
```

This example shows how C programs initialize 2-D and 3-D arrays. Each array element can be individually initialized. The initializations for each row are set off in braces. The indentation shown in Example 11.2 is not required by the C language or compiler. However, it helps us visualize a 2-D array as a table if we line up the rows and columns.

To understand the initialization for the 3-D array, we can visualize it as a table with depth to it. It is as if we have placed a 2-D array on a desk in front of us and put another one on top of it. The array has height, width, and depth. The initialization must reflect that.

Higher-order arrays, such as 4-D or 5-D arrays, extend this same initialization pattern into as many dimensions as defined by the array.

11.5   Using Multidimensional Arrays In Programs

Let's get some experience with multidimensional arrays by using one in a program.

Hands On 11.2

Objective

Write a program that:
Creates a constant called DISPLAY_AREA_SIZE and sets it to 20.
Declares and initializes a 2-D array of characters.
Declares a character variable called tempChar and initializes it to a space.
Declares an integer variable called top and initializes it to 0.
While the user has not typed 'Q' or 'q',
    If the user enters a 'U' or 'u',
        Decrements the variable top by DISPLAY_AREA_SIZE.
    If the user enters a 'D' or 'd',
        Increments the variable top by DISPLAY_AREA_SIZE.
    If top is now outside the bounds of the array,
        Adjusts top to be inside the array boundaries.
    Clears the screen.
Displays each row of the array starting with line indicated by top and ending with top+DISPLAY_AREA_SIZE.
Prompts the user for input.
Gets input from the user.

Experiment

Because this program is lengthy, it is provided for you on the Examples CD that accompanies with this book. The Chapt11 directory in the Examples directory contains a file called EditV1.C. Load the program into your text editor or IDE. Compile, link, and run it.

```
 1    //------------------------------------------------------------
 2    /*
 3    File Name:    EditV1.c
 4
 5    Remarks:      This is the first version of what will become
 6                  a text editor.
 7    */
 8
 9
10    //------------------------------------------------------------
11    // Include Files
12    //------------------------------------------------------------
13
14    #include <stdio.h>
15
16    // End Include Files------------------------------------------
17
18
19
20    //------------------------------------------------------------
21    // Constants
22    //------------------------------------------------------------
23
24    const int MAX_BUFFER_ROWS         = 100;
25    const int MAX_BUFFER_COLS         = 60;
26    const int DISPLAY_AREA_SIZE       = 20;
27    const int SCREEN_SIZE             = 25;
28
29    // End Constants----------------------------------------------
30
31
32
33
34    int main()
35    {
36          char textBuffer[MAX_BUFFER_ROWS][MAX_BUFFER_COLS];
37          int i,j;
38          char tempChar;
39          int top;
40
41          // Fill the buffer with characters.
42          // For each row...
43          for (i=0,tempChar=' ';i<MAX_BUFFER_ROWS;i++)
44          {
45                // For each column...
46                for (j=0;j<MAX_BUFFER_COLS-1;j++)
47                {
48                      // Store a character in the buffer.
49                      textBuffer[i][j]=tempChar++;
50
51                      // If tempChar was incremented past z...
52                      if (tempChar>'z')
53                      {
54                            // Reset tempChar to space.
55                            tempChar=' ';
56                      }
57                }
58                textBuffer[i][MAX_BUFFER_COLS-1]='\0';
```

```
59              }

60
61              // While the user doesn't want to quit...
62              top=0;
63              for (tempChar=' ';
64                  (tempChar!='q') && (tempChar!='Q');
65              scanf("%c",&tempChar))
66              {
67                      // Scroll the screen up or down based on user input.
68                      switch (tempChar)
69                      {
70                          case 'U':
71                          case 'u':
72                              top -= DISPLAY_AREA_SIZE-1;
73                          break;

74
75                          case 'D':
76                          case 'd':
77                              top += DISPLAY_AREA_SIZE-1;
78                          break;
79                      }

80
81                      /* If the index of the first line of text to be
82                      displayed is now outside the boundaries of the
83                      array, adjust it so that it is inside. */
84                      if (top<0)
85                      {
86                              top=0;
87                      }
88                      else if (top >= MAX_BUFFER_ROWS)
89                      {
90                              top=MAX_BUFFER_ROWS-DISPLAY_AREA_SIZE;
91                      }

92
93                      // Clear the screen.
94                      for (i=0;i<SCREEN_SIZE;i++)        // For each row...
95                      {
96                              // Print an endline.
97                              printf("\n");
98                      }

99
100                     // For each row of text...
101                     for (i=top,j=0;
102                         (i < top+DISPLAY_AREA_SIZE) &&
103                             (i < MAX_BUFFER_ROWS);
104                         i++,j++)
105                     {
106                             printf("%s\n",textBuffer[i]);
107                     }

108
109                     // Display a status line.
110                     if (top==0)
111                     {
112                             printf("\nBeginning of buffer\n");
113                     }
114                     else if (top+DISPLAY_AREA_SIZE>=MAX_BUFFER_ROWS)
115                     {
```

```
116                    printf("\nEnd of buffer\n");
117            }
118            else
119            {
120                    printf("\n\n");
121            }
122
123            // Prompt the user for a command.
124            printf("COMMAND:");
125        }
126
127
128        return (0);
129 }
130
131 //-----------------end EditV1.C-----------------------
```

Results

When the program starts, it will display the screen shown in Figure 11.3. If the user presses 'd' or 'D' on the keyboard until the program gets to the end of the array, the screen will resemble Figure 11.4.

FIGURE 11.3 Output from EditV1.C

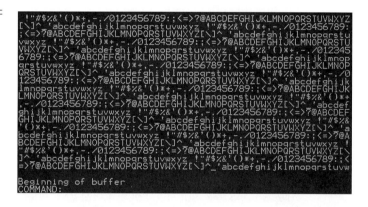

FIGURE 11.4 Scrolling the Array

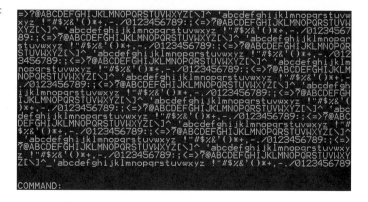

Analysis

The first thing you'll probably notice about this program is that it is more heavily commented than the programs presented so far. Now that we're beginning to write real programs, we need to document them more like real programs. The name of this file is EditV1.c. The "Edit" part of the name is short for text editor. "V1" stands for version 1.

You'll see a comment banner at the beginning of EditV1.c. The banner lists the file name. It also provides a section for comments about what the file contains. Every C source file you create should have a banner like this. Many companies also insist you include a modification history in the file banner.

After the file banner, there are comments that indicate where the include files should go. We'll discuss the details of include files in Chapter 16. The only include file we use in this program is the same one we have always used, stdio.h.

Next is a section for constants. As discussed in Chapter 10, many programmers prefer to declare constants near where they are used. Others declare them all together in one place. Throughout the remainder of this book, you'll see both styles used so their respective merits can be demonstrated.

In this program we use a 2-D array of characters. I've arbitrarily set the number of rows in the array to 100. The number of columns is set to 60. Most computer screens display 80 characters across in text mode. Some display more. If you want to, you can adjust the number of columns to whatever will fit on one line of your display.

The constant SCREEN_SIZE indicates the number of rows on the screen in text mode. The program uses this constant to clear the screen each time the user scrolls the display. Many computer screens display 24 rows. I set the screen size to one more than the actual number of rows on the screen to ensure that it is entirely blanked. If your computer displays more lines of text on your screen, adjust the constant SCREEN_SIZE to be one more than that number.

In the main() function the program declares a 2-D array of characters called textBuffer. When a program sets aside a large chunk of memory to store data, we say that it has allocated a **buffer**. Although there are other ways of creating buffers, it is not unusual to implement a buffer using an array. In this case, the buffer textBuffer holds the text that will be scrolled in the program.

The main() function uses two for loops to store characters into the array. The inner loop, which begins on line 46, iterates through every column. Each time through the inner loop, the program stores the value from the variable tempChar into textBuffer[i][j]. It then increments tempChar. It also checks the value in the tempChar to ensure it doesn't go beyond lowercase 'z'. If it does, it is reset to a space (ASCII character 32).

The inner for loop executes once for each column in a row. After the loop finishes, the program uses an assignment statement to store a null character in the last position in the current row. Remember that if there are 60 characters in the row, they are numbered 0 through 59. In order to access the last position in the row, we use MAX_BUFFER_COLS-1, not MAX_BUFFER_COLS. This also explains why the condition on the inner for loop is j<MAX_BUFFER_COLS-1. If MAX_BUFFER_COLS is set to 60, then the loop quits when j equals 59. Characters are stored in locations 0 through 58. When j becomes 59, the loop quits and the assignment statement that follows it (line 58) will assign a null character into location 59.

I emphasize this behavior of arrays because it is often a source of confusion with programmers. In fact, it's very common for even experienced programmers to make mistakes on the **boundary conditions** of their loops. The boundary conditions are the initial and final values of the variables that control a loop.

After the text buffer has text in it, we want this program to display the text and allow the user to scroll it up and down. To accomplish this, we use another pair of for loops. This is similar to examples we saw in Chapter 10. A switch statement is used to adjust the first line of the array that will be printed on the screen. If the user enters 'u' or 'U', the program decrements the variable top by one less than the display area size. If the user inputs 'd' or 'D', the program increments top by one less than the display area size.

If the top line has been incremented or decremented to a value outside of the array boundaries, the program adjusts it so that it is inside the array (lines 84–91). It then clears the screen by printing newlines. If a program prints enough newlines, whatever is currently on the screen will eventually scroll off.

There are better ways to clear a display. Each type of display has at least one, and they are not the same from display type to display type. The method we use here is the only one that works on any text mode display.

Once the screen is clear, `main()` is ready to display each row of text. Notice that throughout this program we've always used two subscripts with the array `textBuffer`. To access a single element in the array, we've used `textBuffer[i][j]`. However, in the `for` loop that prints each row (lines 101–107), we use only one subscript. Why?

Remember that a 2-D array is an array of arrays. In other words, one row in `textBuffer` is an array. The row `textBuffer[0]` is an array of characters. So is `textBuffer[1]`, and so on. The C compiler treats character arrays terminated by the null character as strings. Therefore, each row in `textBuffer` is a string. By leaving off one subscript, we access an entire string of characters rather than an individual character element. C programmers often do this with character arrays.

After it displays a portion of the text buffer on the screen, `main()` displays a status line. This is a common technique. Graphical user interfaces (GUIs) will typically have a status bar on the bottom of an application's window. It serves the same purpose that the status line does here. It allows us to give messages to the user based on the current state of the program.

In this case, `main()` utilizes a set of chained `if-else` statements (lines 110–121) that test to see whether the user has scrolled to the beginning or the end of the text buffer. If the program encounters the beginning of the buffer, it prints the message "Beginning of buffer" to the status line on the screen. If it reaches the end of the buffer, it prints the message "End of buffer" to the status line. If neither of those conditions is true, the program leaves status line blank.

At the end of the loop, the program prompts the user for input (line 124). It retrieves the input in the increment/decrement section of the `for` loop (line 65).

TECHNICAL NOTE 11.3
Leaving one of the subscripts off of a 2-D array gives you access to an entire "row" of data. This is useful with 2-D character arrays. By leaving off the subscript for the second dimension, each "row" can be treated as a single string.

TIP 11.1
Most programs today use some kind of status bar. When you develop the user interface for your program, you should seriously consider using a status bar.

Try This

Set the named constant `MAX_BUFFER_COLS` to 100. Recompile, link, and run the program. What happens to the output?

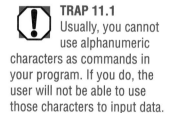

TRAP 11.1
Usually, you cannot use alphanumeric characters as commands in your program. If you do, the user will not be able to use those characters to input data.

TIP 11.2
To enable users to enter keyboard commands, programs typically take one of two approaches. Either they alternate between command mode and input mode, or they use command characters that users never enter as data.

With this example, we are beginning to build a text editor. However, we can't keep using characters such as `'u'` and `'d'` to send scrolling commands to our program. If we did, users wouldn't be able to type `'u'` or `'d'` into their documents.

Traditionally, there are two ways to solve this problem. The first is to have the program run in two different modes, command mode and edit mode. When it is in command mode, it interprets all input from the keyboard as commands. One of the commands puts the program in edit mode. In this mode, the program stores all keyboard input as text in the text buffer. Usually, the user gets back to command mode by pressing the Escape key. The text editor vi, which is often included with the Unix operating system, works in this way.

The other traditional way to send user commands to the program is to assign commands to keys that users would never use for their documents. For example, instead of using `'u'` and `'d'` for scrolling up and down, we could use Ctrl+u and Ctrl+d. Ctrl+u is often abbreviated ^u or ^U. Ctrl+d is abbreviated ^d or ^D.

Both of these characters are in the ASCII set. However, there is no character representation for them. We can't put the statement `if (tempChar != '^u')` in our programs. What we can do is define a named constant to represent these characters. Example 11.3 illustrates how constants can be declared to represent Ctrl+u and Ctrl+d. The values for Ctrl+u and Ctrl+d come from the ASCII table in Appendix B. In Example 11.3 we create named constants of type `char` to represent the ASCII values for Ctrl+u and Ctrl+d. To do this, we need a type cast to change the integer values into characters.

EXAMPLE 11.3 Declaring Character Constants

```
const char CTRL_U = (char)21;
const char CTRL_D = (char)4;
```

My students often wonder why we don't use the Page Up and Page Down keys on the keyboard to scroll up and down one screenful at a time. The answer is that these keys, as well as the arrow keys and the function keys, are not part of the ASCII set. The C Standard Library input and output functions allow us to use only characters in the ASCII set. If we want to get input from keys that are not represented in the ASCII set, we must use other methods that are often not portable.

For instance, MS Windows, Macintosh OS, and Unix XWindows-based interfaces all provide methods to access keyboard keys that are not in the ASCII set. Unfortunately, the access methods are different for each. To write completely portable programs, we must stick to the ASCII set. However, most professional programmers find this restriction too limiting. They will typically use the method provided by the operating system or user interface library for accessing all keys (or most) on the keyboard. If the program needs to be ported, they will rewrite the portions that get input. Although it's more work, it produces a more professional interface.

11.6 Troubleshooting Guide

After reading this section, you should be able to:

- Recognize problems that can occur with complex array initializations.
- Find and fix problems with declaring large arrays.

11.6.1 Complex Array Initializations

The initialization of a multidimensional array can rapidly get very complex. For instance, Example 11.4 declares and initializes a 3-D array. Can you tell which parts of the array are initialized and which parts aren't?

EXAMPLE 11.4   A Complex Array Initialization

```
1              int a3DArray[2][4][5] =
2              {
3                      {{1,2,},
4                      {1,2,,3},
5                      {,1,2,3,4},
6                      {1,2,3,4,5}},
7                      {{5,},
8                      {5,4},
9                      {5,4,,,},
10                     {5,4,3,2,1}}
11             };
```

This three dimensional array is 2x4x5. That is, it contains two 2-D arrays. Each of the 2-D arrays are four rows by five columns. The initialization is laid out to aid this discussion. You may or may not want to align your initializations this way.

Line 3 of Example 11.4 initializes a3DArray[0][0][0] to 1 and initializes a3DArray[0][0][1] to 2. The comma after the 2 explicitly commands the compiler to leave a3DArray[0][0][2] uninitialized. Most compilers will follow this command, so it will probably contain a random value. There are no initializations given for a3DArray[0][0][3] and a3DArray[0][0][4]. Many compilers will initialize them to zero.

Following this same pattern, line 4 initializes a3DArray[0][1][0] to 1, a3DArray[0][1][1] to 2, leaves a3DArray[0][1][2] uninitialized, sets a3DArray[0][1][3] to 3, and may or may not initialize a3DArray[0][1][4] to 0.

Line 5 leaves a3DArray[0][2][0] uninitialized, sets a3DArray[0][2][1] to 1, stores a 2 in a3DArray[0][2][2], sets a3DArray[0][2][3] to 3, and puts a 4 in a3DArray[0][2][4].

Line 6 stores the values 1,2,3,4,5 in locations a3DArray[0][3][0], a3DArray[0][3][1], a3DArray[0][3][2], a3DArray[0][3][3], and a3DArray[0][3][4] respectively.

The statements on lines 7–11 initialize the other half of the array. As you can see, this initialization is not easy to read. In fact, even people who have been programming for C for many years may have to make a chart to figure this initialization out.

The best advice I can give you is to avoid initializations like this one. If you absolutely *must* do something like this, comment it heavily so that anyone attempting to read your initialization can understand it easily.

11.6.2 Declaring Large Arrays

Some compilers have trouble allocating and accessing large arrays. Just exactly how "large" is defined depends on the compiler.

Arrays larger than 64 kilobytes (64K) have traditionally been a problem for MS DOS-based compilers. When a PC is running MS DOS as its operating system, it uses a **segmented memory architecture**. This means that memory is accessible in 64K chunks. The result is that it is difficult for DOS-based PCs to allocate arrays larger than 64K. Typically, compiler manufacturers provide memory models of different sizes. We don't have to know the details of DOS memory models to use them. If you are declaring arrays that are larger than 64K, you need to use the Large or Huge memory model (whichever your compiler provides).

The Macintosh operating system, Windows 95/98, Windows NT, Windows 2000, and the various varieties of Unix all use a **flat memory architecture**. This means that you should have no problems declaring large arrays.

TECHNICAL NOTE 11.4
All programs have a stack, which is an area of memory programs use for allocating variables.

However, if your compiler gives you an error when declaring a large array, you may need to make your **stack** larger. The stack is an area of memory that programs use for allocating variables. Each program has its own stack. If your program crashes unexpectedly when it encounters the declaration of an array, your program's stack is more than likely too small. Your compiler documentation will tell you how to adjust the size of your program's stack.

SUMMARY

Arrays can be declared with more than one dimension. A 2-D array can be thought of as a table with rows and columns. In memory, it is actually an array of arrays.

Multidimensional arrays are initialized by indicating values for each element. The values for each row are in braces, and the sets of row values are separated from each other with commas.

Multidimensional arrays elements are accessed by specifying an index number for each dimension. A 2-D array would require the row and column number of an element to access that element.

TECHNICAL NOTES

11.1 Programmers use 3-D and even 4-D arrays in computer graphics, engineering, and scientific computing.

11.2 The maximum number of dimensions you can declare on an array is set by the manufacturer of your compiler. Most compilers will allow you to declare up to seven dimensions.

11.3 Leaving one of the subscripts off of a 2-D array gives you access to an entire "row" of data. This is useful with 2-D

character arrays. By leaving off the subscript for the second dimension, each "row" can be treated as a single string.

11.4 All programs have a stack, which is an area of memory programs use for allocating variables.

TIPS

11.1 Most programs today use some kind of status bar. When you develop the user interface for your program, you should seriously consider using a status bar.

11.2 To enable users to enter keyboard commands, programs typically take one of two approaches. Either

they alternate between command mode and input mode, or they use command characters that users never enter as data.

TRAP

11.1 Usually, you cannot use alphanumeric characters as commands in your program. If you do, the user will not be able to use those characters to input data.

REVIEW QUESTIONS

1. What is a multidimensional array?

2. Why don't programmers normally use 4-D or 5-D arrays?

3. How are array elements initialized by default in a multi-dimensional array?

4. What is another name for an array of characters?

5. How can an entire row in an array of characters be printed to the screen at once?

6. In Hands On 11.2, the first pair of nested `for` loops stores characters in each row of the 2-D array. Why is a null character appended to the end of each row?

7. What does it mean to say that a 2-D array is an array of arrays?

8. Why didn't the program in Hands On 11.2 use the PageUp and PageDown keys?

9. How can text editors tell whether the user's input is a command or text to store in the text buffer? What are the two traditional ways of solving this problem?

10. Where do you think named constants should appear, together at the beginning of a program or near where they are used? Why?

EXERCISES

1. Fill in the blank.

   A two-dimensional array can be thought of as an _____ of _____.

2. Fill in the blank.

   All of the elements in an array must be of the same _____.

3. Fill in the blank.

   The array declaration
   ```
   int anArray[10][10];
   ```
   allocates space in memory for _____ integers.

4. Fill in the blank.

   The array declaration
   ```
   int anArray[10][10] = {{1,2,3,4},
                          {5,6,7,8}};
   ```
   allocates space in memory for _____ integers.

5. Find the two errors in the following array initialization.
   ```
   int a3DArray[2][4][5] = {{{1,2,},{1,2,,3},{,1,2,3,4},{1,2,3,4,5}}
                            {{5,},{5,4},{5,4,,,},{5,4,3,2,1}}};
   ```

6. Fill in the blank.

   The number in square brackets that is used to access an array element is called the _____.

7. Use the array declaration below and fill in the blanks in the following statement.
   ```
   int anIntArray[10][20];
   ```
   The element in the fourth column of the tenth row of the array `anIntArray` is accessed using the subscript index numbers `anIntArray[ _ ][ _ ]`.

8. Explain what boundary conditions are and why they are a source of programming errors.

9. Write a program that creates a 12x12 array of integers. Use a pair of nested `for` loops to generate a multiplication table for the numbers 0–11 and store the results in the array locations. If the array is called `timesTable`, then the result of the multiplication 2x3 should be stored in `timesTable[2][3]`, the result of the multiplication of 2x4 should be stored in `timesTable[2][4]`, and so on. After all of the values have been calculated and stored in the array, use another pair of nested `for` loops to print the times table.

10. Write a program that calculates the grade point averages (GPAs) of a group of students. The program should declare a 3x5 array of floating-point values. It will need to prompt the user for the grades of three students. Each student's grades will be stored in a row of the array. After your program has retrieved five grades for every student, calculate and print the GPA for each student. Assume that 4.0 is the highest grade a student can earn and 0.0 is the lowest. The method for calculating a student's GPA is to add up all of the grades in a row and divide by the number of grades.

11. Add error checking to the program in Exercise 10. When the user types in a grade, use a loop to make sure that he/she cannot enter a grade lower than 0.0 or higher than 4.0.

12. Modify the program in Hands On 11.2 so that it uses the command Ctrl+U to scroll toward the beginning of the text buffer and Ctrl+D to scroll toward the end of the text buffer. Use named constants in your program.

13. Modify your program from Exercise 12 so that it prints the contents of the variable `top` onto the status line. Ensure that it prints this information each time the screen is scrolled.

14. Modify your program from Exercise 13. Replace the `switch` statement with an equivalent set of chained `if-else` statements.

15. Modify your program from Exercise 14. Make it scroll toward the beginning of the buffer one line at a time when the user types Ctrl+B. Make it scroll toward the end of the buffer one line at a time when the user enters Ctrl+E.

16. Modify your program from Exercise 15. Make it exit the program when the user types Ctrl+X.

17. Modify your program from Exercise 16. When the user types Ctrl+S, the status line should be toggled on or off. By default the status line should be displayed. When the user enters Ctrl+S, your program sets a variable that indicates that the status line should not be displayed. If the user enters Ctrl+S again, the variable is set to indicate that the status line should be displayed.

18. Modify your program from Exercise 17 so that it uses `while` loops rather than `for` loops. Explain which you think is more appropriate for this program, the `while` loop or the `for` loop, and why.

19. Write a program that stores integer values in a 3-D array. The 3-D array should be 50 rows by 20 columns and 5 elements deep. The value that is stored in each array element should be the sum of the row number plus the column number plus the depth number. After the values are stored in the array, print them to the screen.

20. Demonstrate how a 3-D array is initialized by giving at least 2 examples other than those shown in this chapter.

21. Write a program that stores integer values in a 4-D array. The 4-D array should be 50 by 20 by 10 by 5. The value that is stored in each array element should be the sum of the four index numbers of each element. After the values are stored in the array, print them to the screen.

22. Write a program that uses a 2-D character array to store 100 strings. Each string should be 40 characters in length. Set each string in the 2-D array to any group of printable characters you would like to use. After your program stores characters in the strings, it should print them to the screen. Next, swap the characters in the first string with the characters in the last string. Swap the characters in the second string with the characters in the second-to-the-last string, and so on. Once the swapping is complete, your program should print all of the strings. Your program *must* move the character data. It cannot achieve the desired output by printing the array in reverse order.

23. The use of the C Standard Library `rand()` function was demonstrated in the Exercises for Chapter 10. Write a program that uses the `rand()` function to fill a 1000x10 array of integers with values. If the value generated by the `rand()` function is greater than 1000, divide it by 10 until it is less than or equal to 1000. Once the array is filled with integers whose values are between 0 and 1000 inclusive, print the table row by row. Calculate the average value for each row. Print the row's average value after the last value for that row. For each row, print the 10 integers and their average. Reminder: you must put the statement

```
#include <stdlib.h>
```

at the beginning of your program so that you can use the `rand()` function.

24. Engineers often are interested in the frequency with which events occur. Modify the program you wrote for Exercise 23. Add a 1-D array of 1000 integers. Initialize every element in the 1-D array to 0. After your program does everything required in Exercise 23, it should use a pair of nested loops to iterate through the 2-D array. Each time it encounters an integer, it should use that integer as an index into the 1-D array and increment the value in the 1-D array location. For example, every time the program finds the number 500 in the 2-D array, it should increment the value in location number 500 of the 1-D array by 1. When these nested loops finish, they will have counted the frequency with which all of the numbers 0 through 1000 appear in the 2-D array. After your program has found the frequency data, it should print that data.

25. The potential difference in electrical current across a conducting material, such as a wire, can be calculated using Ohm's law for a steady electrical current. The formula is

$$V = IR$$

where V is the potential difference across the conductor, I is the current, and R is the resistence. Write a program that:
　　Declares a 2-D array of `double` values. The array should have 10 rows and 10 columns.
　　Prompts the user for starting and ending values of I.
　　Gets the starting and ending values of I from the user.
　　Prompts the user for the starting and ending values of R.
　　Gets the starting and ending values of R from the user.
　　Calculates the I increment as:
　　　　(Ending I Value – Starting I Value)/10
　　Calculates the R increment as:
　　　　(Ending R Value – Starting R Value)/10

For each row in the array,
    For each column in the array,
        Calculates V for the current values of I and R. Store V in the array.
        Increments I and R.
    Prints the contents of the array as a table with column and row headings.

GLOSSARY

Buffer   A block of contiguous memory used to store data.

Flat Memory Architecture   All available memory is directly addressable without resorting to segments and offsets, which are used in a segmented memory architecture.

Boundary Conditions   The starting and ending values of a loop's control variable.

Segmented Memory Architecture   Memory in the computer is Allocating arrays and buffers larger than the fixed-size blocks can be problematic.

Stack   An area of memory programs use for allocating variables.

12

User I/O, Strings, and String Functions

OBJECTIVES

After reading this chapter, you should be able to:

- Use C Standard Library functions to perform input and output (I/O).
- Use C Standard Library functions to process characters and strings.

OUTLINE

PREVIEW

Humans communicate with words. Computers are useful tools that aid us in processing words into forms that are meaningful to other people. Words are usually processed by programs in the form of characters and strings. Therefore, it is important for C programmers to develop competency in writing programs that handle characters and strings. This chapter presents some of the C Standard Library functions that are designed to make string and character handling easier.

12.1   Input and Output of Characters and Strings

A frequent task of computer programs is interacting with program users. That interaction often takes the form of characters and strings. Throughout this book, the code examples and programs have used the `printf()` and `scanf()` functions for user interaction. In an effort not to present too much information at one time, only the basic details of these two functions have been covered. In reality, there is much more to the `printf()` and `scanf()` functions.

In addition, the C Standard Library offers several other functions performing user input and output. Each of them has its own particular uses.

It's important to note that most computers use **buffered input** for their keyboards. A **keyboard buffer** is a small amount of memory that the operating system sets aside to store the user's keystrokes. All of the most popular operating systems use a keyboard buffer. Data in a buffer is not available to the program until something flushes the buffer. **Line buffers,** such as the keyboard buffer, are flushed each time the user presses the Enter key on the keyboard. As a result, the C Standard Library input functions do not see any input until the Enter key is pressed. This is true even when you want to get input one character at a time. Other types of buffers flush only when they are full. The C Standard Library functions provide ways to manually flush them. Figure 12.1 illustrates how data buffers work.

For some programs, buffered input is a problem. Section 12.3.3 in the Troubleshooting Guide near the end of this chapter gives some tips on how this problem can be resolved.

FIGURE 12.1 **Data Buffers**

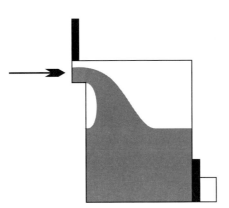

Data flows into the stream buffer.

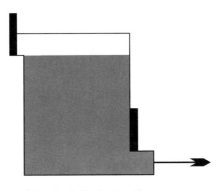

When the buffer flushes, the
data flows out byte by byte.

12.1.1   The `printf()` Function

The `printf()` function is probably the most essential output function in the C Standard Library. However, in today's world of graphical user interfaces, the C Standard Library `printf()` function is not widely used.

These two statements may seem contradictory at first. However, experience shows otherwise. GUI-based operating systems provide functions for outputting strings to the user. Some of these are based on the `printf()` function. Even if they are not, it is extremely common to use variations of the `printf()` function in a GUI-based environment.

For instance, when programming for Microsoft Windows, one of the most commonly used string output functions is `TextOut()`. The `TextOut()` function requires that all formatting be done on the string prior to invoking the `TextOut()` function. As we will see later in this chapter, the `sprintf()` function can be used for exactly this purpose. If you write programs for Windows, X Windows, or the Macintosh, you will use `sprintf()` frequently. As the name implies, `sprintf()` is a variation of the `printf()` function. A solid understanding of `printf()` is an invaluable aid in C programming for nearly all operating systems.

The `printf()` function accepts a variable number of parameters. There must be at least one. As the examples in this book have demonstrated, the first parameter must be a string. That string can contain **formatting specifiers**. For instance, to print the contents of a string variable, `printf()` uses the `"%s"` format specifier. To print a decimal integer, it uses `"%d"`.

If the first parameter to `printf()` contains formatting specifiers, it is called a **format string**. A definition of a `printf()` formatting specifier is shown in Definition 12.1.

TECHNICAL NOTE 12.1
Formatting specifiers are also called conversion specifiers because they specify how the `printf()` function converts data into a displayable form.

DEFINITION 12.1   Definition of `printf()` Formatting Specifiers

```
%[flag(s)][width][.precision][modifier]type
```

In this definition, *flag(s)*, *width*, *precision*, *modifier*, and *type* each represent one component of the formatting specifier. The square brackets around *flag(s)*, *width*, *precision*, and *modifier*, indicate that they are each optional. They may or may not appear in the formatting specifier.

Table 12.1 shows a list of the values that are used for *type*.

TABLE 12.1 Type Specifiers for the `printf()` Function

Type Specifier	Outputs	Example
c	A character.	`"%c"`
d	A signed decimal integer.	`"%d"`
e	A floating-point number using e-notation.	`"%e"`
E	A floating-point number using E-notation.	`"%E"`
f	A floating-point number using decimal notation.	`"%f"`
g	A floating-point number using %e or %f, whichever is shorter.	`"%g"`
G	A floating-point number using %E or %f, whichever is shorter.	`"%G"`
i	A signed decimal integer, exactly the same as %d.	`"%i"`
o	An unsigned octal (base 8) integer.	`"%o"`
p	A pointer.	`"%p"`
s	A string of characters.	`"%s"`
u	An unsigned decimal integer.	`"%u"`
x	An unsigned hexadecimal (base 16) integer. Uses lowercase for the digits a–f.	`"%x"`
X	An unsigned hexadecimal integer. Uses uppercase for the digits A–F.	`"%X"`
%	A percent sign.	`"%%"`

Programs print integer values using the `"%d"`, `"%i"`, `"%o"`, `"%u"`, `"%x"` and `"%X"` formatting specifiers. The `"%d"` and `"%i"` specifiers are interchangeable. They are both used to output decimal integers that can be positive or negative. The `"%u"` specifier is used for unsigned integers. The `printf()` function uses `"%o"` specifier to print octal numbers. Octal numbers are in base 8.

When `printf()` encounters a `"%x"` or `"%X"` in a format string, it prints the corresponding parameter as a hexadecimal number, which is base 16. Programmers use hexadecimal numbers extensively. For more information on hexadecimal numbers, please see Appendix D. The only difference between `"%x"` and `"%X"` is that `"%x"` prints lowercase letters for the digits a–f, while `"%X"` prints uppercase.

The `"%e"`, `"%E"`, `"%f"`, `"g"` and `"%G"` specifiers are used for floating-point numbers. Floating-point numbers can be printed with decimal notation or scientific notation. Table 12.2 shows numbers printed in both formats.

TABLE 12.2 Floating-Point Numbers in Decimal and Scientific Formats

Decimal Format	Scientific Notation
12345600000000.0	1.23456×10^{13}
602200000000000000000000	6.022×10^{23}
0.0000979	9.79×10^{-5}
–0.69300181	$-6.9300181 \times 10^{-1}$

Scientists and engineers commonly need to print numbers that are extremely large or extremely small. For example, Avogadro's number, which is used in chemistry and physics, specifies the number of atoms in exactly 12 grams of carbon-12. The value Avogadro's number in scientific notation is 6.022×10^{23}. That is 6.022 multiplied by 100,000,000,000,000,000,000,000. Because numbers containing that many zeros are not very convenient to write, scientific notation is used. It saves us from having to write out all of the digits of a very large number.

In C programming, the letters e or E are used to represent the x10 in scientific notation. If a program outputs Avogadro's number with `printf()` and the `"%e"` specifier, it prints as 6.022e23. If the `"%E"` specifier is used, the result is 6.022E23. Table 12.3 repeats the numbers from Table 12.2 that were in scientific notation. It shows them as they might appear when printed with the `printf()` function using the `"%e"` and `"%E"` formatting specifiers.

TABLE 12.3 Floating-Point Numbers Printed with the `"%e"` and `"%E"` Specifiers

%e	%E
1.234560e+013	1.234560E+013
6.022000e+023	6.022000E+023
9.790000e-005	9.790000E-005
–6.930018e-001	–6.930018E-001

Note: The output shown here may differ slightly from the output of these same numbers on your computer. The actual output depends on the compiler you use.

In addition to the specifiers, `printf()` recognizes a set of modifiers that enable programs to more accurately tell `printf()` the type of the data type be printed. Table 12.4 shows the valid modifiers. In Definition 12.1, these correspond to *modifiers*.

TABLE 12.4 Formatting Modifiers

Modifier	Description	Example
h	Used with integer formatting specifiers to indicate a short integer or unsigned short integer.	`"%hi"`, `"%hd"`, `"%hu"`
l	Used with integer formatting specifiers to indicate a long integer or unsigned long integer.	`"%li"`, `"%ld"`, `"%lu"`
L	Used with floating-point formatting specifiers to indicate a long `double` value.	`"%Lf"`, `"%Le"`, `"%LE"`, `"%Lg"`, `"%LG"`

Note: Not all compilers support these modifiers.

The *width* and *precision* portions of Definition 12.1 provide more particular control over the format of the output. *width* specifies the minimum number of characters to print for the column or field. A wider field will be used if the number or string won't fit.

The *precision* portion of Definition 12.1 specifies the precision for floating-point numbers. For `"%e"`, `"%E"`, and `"%f"`, this specifies the number of digits to the right of the decimal point. With `"%g"` and `"%G"`, it specifies the number of significant digits. A dot with no digits following it specifies a zero to the right of the decimal point. `"%s"` specifies the maximum number of characters to be printed. For integer formatting specifiers, this sets the minimum number of digits to appear. Leading zeros are added if needed.

The values for *flags* are shown in Table 12.5.

Your particular compiler may support additional values for each of the formatting specifier components given in Definition 12.1. However, you should carefully consider whether to use those that are not in the ANSI C standard. They may provide convenience, but you may sacrifice portability when you use them.

Although the value is seldom used, the `printf()` function does return a number. The value that it returns is the number of characters it prints.

TRAP 12.1
Most compilers provide additional specifiers that can be used for the *flag(s)*, *width*, *precision*, *modifier*, and *type* portions of Definition 12.1. Using them may be convenient, but they can make your code less portable.

**TABLE 12.5   Possible Values
for the *flags* Modifier**

Flag Value	Description
–	Left justify the item to be printed.
+	Signed values greater than zero are displayed with a plus sign. Signed values less than zero are displayed with a minus sign.
space	Signed values greater than zero are displayed with a leading space. Signed values less than zero are displayed with a minus sign.
#	Use an alternative format for the formatting specifier. When used with %o, a leading 0 is printed. With %x or %X, a leading 0x or 0X is printed. For floating-point formatting specifiers, a decimal point is printed even if no digits follow. %g and %G prevent trailing zeros from being deleted.
0	Pad numbers with leading zeros to fill the field or column width. This flag is ignored if the - flag also is used or if precision is specified for integer formatting specifiers.

12.1.2   The `scanf()` Function

Like the `printf()` function, the `scanf()` function has a wide range of data formatting options. As with `printf()`, the `scanf()` function takes a variable number of parameters. It must have at least two. The first is a format string containing formatting specifiers. The `scanf()` function reads in characters and formats them based on the formatting specifiers. Definition 12.2 gives the definition of `scanf()` formatting specifiers.

DEFINTION 12.2   Definition of `scanf()` Formatting Specifiers

```
%[*][width][modifier]type
```

Only the % and *type* portions are required. The *, *width*, and *modifier* portions are optional. Table 12.6 gives the set of types that can be used in `scanf()` formatting specifiers.

In addition to the type specifiers shown in Table 12.6, your compiler may also support additional non-ANSI type specifiers.

The rest of the parameters to `scanf()` are variables in which the formatted input will be stored. If the variables are atomic data types, they must each be preceded by an ampersand (&). If they are character arrays, they do not need the ampersand. If your program is using `scanf()` to read in a character string, it should pass the array name without an ampersand. Example 12.1 shows some calls to the `scanf()` function with various formatting specifiers.

EXAMPLE 12.1   Calling `scanf()`

```
int anInteger, anotherInteger;
float aFloatingPointValue;
char aCharacterArray[80];

scanf("%d",&anInteger);
scanf("%d %i",&anInteger,&anotherInteger);
scanf("%f",&aFloatingPointValue);
scanf("%s",aCharacterArray);
```

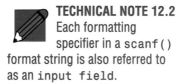

TECHNICAL NOTE 12.2
Each formatting specifier in a `scanf()` format string is also referred to as an `input field`.

Each type in a formatting specifier can be coupled with a type modifier, which corresponds to the *modifier* portion of Definition 12.2. The `scanf()` function uses the same set of type modifiers as the `printf()` function. These appear in Table 12.4.

The *width* portion of Definition 12.2 specifies a positive decimal integer which controls the maximum number of characters to be read. It can be thought of as the width of the input field. The `scanf()` function will not read more than *width* characters for the particular formatting specifier. If `scanf()` encounters a whitespace character (newline, tab, or space), it will read fewer than *width* characters. It will also read fewer than *width* characters if it reads a character that cannot be formatted according to the formatting specifier.

TABLE 12.6 Type Specifiers for the `scanf()` **Function**

Type Specifier	Outputs	Example
c	A character.	`"%c"`
d	A signed decimal integer.	`"%d"`
e	A floating-point number using e-notation.	`"%e"`
E	A floating-point number using E-notation.	`"%E"`
f	A floating-point number using decimal notation.	`"%f"`
g	A floating-point number using %e or %f, whichever is shorter.	`"%g"`
G	A floating-point number using %E or %f, whichever is shorter.	`"%G"`
i	A signed decimal integer, exactly the same as %d.	`"%i"`
o	An unsigned octal (base 8) integer.	`"%o"`
p	A pointer.	`"%p"`
s	A string of characters.	`"%s"`
u	An unsigned decimal integer.	`"%u"`
x	An unsigned hexadecimal (base 16) integer. Uses lowercase for the digits a–f.	`"%x"`
X	An unsigned hexadecimal integer. Uses uppercase for the digits A–F.	`"%X"`

An asterisk (*) after the percent sign in a formatting specifier causes the input for the next formatting specifier in the format string to be read, but it will not let a value be stored in the variable.

On some compilers programs may be able to read in strings that include white space. This is done by substituting square brackets for the *s* in the `"%s"` specifier. The corresponding input is read until `scanf()` encounters characters that are not in the square brackets. If the first character is a caret (^), the effect is reversed. The `scanf()` function reads input until it encounters the one of the characters inside the square brackets.

Example 12.2 demonstrates a `scanf()` formatting specifier that reads strings containing the characters `'A'` through `'Z'` or `'a'` through `'z'`, the characters `'0'` through `'9'`, and the space character. If it encounters a character that is not one of these, it will stop reading input.

EXAMPLE 12.2 Selecting Characters for `scanf()` to Read

```
"%[A-Z, a-z,' ',0-9]"
```

TIP 12.1
Many compilers enable your program to use `"%[]"` to specify what characters `scanf()` will read. This is not part of the ANSI standard, but it is widely supported.

This style of formatting specifier is not part of the ANSI standard, and your compiler may not allow it. However, it is widely supported. For example, both Microsoft Visual C++ and the Gnu C/C++ compiler support it. You can ensure that your compiler supports this feature by writing a short test program that utilizes it.

The `scanf()` function returns the number of input fields that it reads into the program.

12.1.3 The `getchar()` and `putchar()` Functions

In addition to `printf()` and `scanf()`, the C Standard Library provides the `getchar()` and `putchar()` functions for reading input and performing output. The `getchar()` function reads one character at a time. It takes no parameters, and its return value is the character it reads. The `putchar()` function outputs a single character. It takes the character to output as its only parameter. It returns the character it outputs. Example 12.3 contains a short program demonstrating the use of `getchar()` and `putchar()`.

EXAMPLE 12.3 **Using `getchar()` and `putchar()`**

```
1   #include <stdio.h>
2
3   int main()
4   {
5         char inputString[80];
6         int i,done;
7
8         printf("Please enter an input string.\n");
9         for (i=0,done=0;(i<80) && (!done);i++)
10        {
11              inputString[i] = getchar();
12              if ((inputString[i] == '\n') || (i==79))
13              {
14                    done = 1;
15                    inputString[i]='\0';
16              }
17        }
18
19        for (i=0;(i<80) && (inputString[i]!='\0');i++)
20        {
21              putchar(inputString[i]);
22        }
23
24        return (0);
25  }
```

TRAP 12.2
On systems using buffered keyboard input, `getchar()` will not receive any characters from the operating system until the user presses the Enter key on the keyboard.

This program reads input one character at a time until it gets 79 characters or encounters a newline. When either one of these conditions occurs, it sets the variable `done` to 1 so that the first `for` loop will end. It also puts a null character at the end of the string. The second `for` loop prints the string using the `putchar()` function.

On computers using buffered keyboard input (most do), the `getchar()` function will not receive any input until the user presses the Enter key. After the Enter key is pressed, repeated calls to `getchar()` can pull the user's keystrokes from the keyboard buffer. The newline will also be in the buffer.

12.1.4 The `gets()` and `puts()` Functions

Programs can use the `gets()` and `puts()` functions to retrieve string input from the user. They are more straightforward to use than `scanf()` and `printf()`. However, they are more specialized toward getting and printing strings.

The `gets()` function takes a string as its only parameter. When the user presses Enter, `gets()` will store the user's input into its parameter. This string will include any spaces or tabs that the user types. However, the newline character will not be in the string. Instead, `gets()` replaces the newline with a null character.

The `puts()` function prints a string. Its only parameter is the string to be printed. After it prints the string, it prints a newline.

Example 12.4 demonstrates the use of `gets()` and `puts()`.

EXAMPLE 12.4 **Using `gets()` and `puts()`**

```
1   #include <stdio.h>
2
3   int main()
4   {
5         char inputStrings[5][80];
6         int i;
7
8         printf("Please enter 5 strings. ");
9         printf("End each one by pressing Enter\n");
```

```
10          for (i=0;i<5;i++)
11          {
12                  gets(inputStrings[i]);
13          }
14
15          putchar('\n');
16
17          for (i=0;i<5;i++)
18          {
19                  puts(inputStrings[i]);
20          }
21
22          return (0);
23    }
```

TRAP 12.3
The gets() function
may overwrite memory
or cause your program to crash
if the user enters more
characters than the string in its
parameter list will hold.

TECHNICAL NOTE 12.3
To avoid the potential
problems gets() has
when the user enters too many
characters, programs can use
getchar() and allocate space
for strings on a character-by-
character basis. This technique is
demonstrated in Chapter 18.

The short program in this example uses gets() to read a group of strings. The strings are stored in a 2-D array of characters. It uses the puts() function to print the strings.

Each row of the 2-D array contains enough space for 80 characters. If the user types in five strings that are 80 characters or less, this program will function perfectly. However, there is a problem when the user enters a string that is longer than 80 characters.

If the user types in more than 80 characters, there will not be enough space in the row to store them all. This will cause a memory overwrite. Data may be lost, or the program may crash. Exactly what happens can't be predicted in advance.

To avoid this problem, most programs that use gets() create a string that is much larger than any input the user might reasonably type in. However, this strategy will not guarantee that your program will function properly.

The most common solution to this problem is simply not to use gets(). Many programs use getchar() instead. This enables them to count the number of characters the user types in and stop reading when there are too many.

12.2   String Handling Functions

The C Standard Library provides a variety of functions for dealing with strings. Their prototypes can be found in the Standard Library header file string.h.

12.2.1   The strlen() Function

The strlen() function counts the number of characters in a string (not including the null character) and returns that count. Its single parameter is the string whose length will be returned. Finding the length of a string is such a common task that you will probably use this function in most of the programs you write. Example 12.5 demonstrates how strlen() is used.

EXAMPLE 12.5   Using strlen()

```
1    #include <stdio.h>
2    #include <string.h>
3
4    int main()
5    {
6          char inputString[80];
7
8          printf("Please enter a string, and then press Enter: ");
9          gets(inputString);
10         printf("The string you entered was %d characters long",
11                 strlen(inputString));
12
13         return (0);
14   }
```

In Example 12.5, the program prompts the user for a string, which is retrieved with a call to `gets()`. The `strlen()` function is then called in conjunction with a call to `printf()`. `strlen()` finds the length of the string, and `printf()` prints that value. Notice that the statement on line 6 allocates enough space for 80 characters. However, in all likelihood, `strlen()` will not return the value 80 when this program is run. The `strlen()` function does not return the number of characters that are allocated to a string. It returns the number of locations in the string that are actually being used to store characters.

12.2.2 The `strcpy()` Function

To copy characters from one string into another, the C Standard Library contains the `strcpy()` function. This function takes two parameters. They are the destination and source strings for the copy (in that order). `strcpy()` copies all of the characters in the source string to the destination string. This includes the null character. Example 12.6 illustrates its use.

EXAMPLE 12.6 Using `strcpy()`

```
1    #include <stdio.h>
2    #include <string.h>
3
4    int main()
5    {
6          char aString[80];
7          char anotherString[80];
8
9          strcpy(aString,"This is a string of characters\n");
10         printf("%s",aString);
11
12         strcpy(anotherString,aString);
13         printf("%s",anotherString);
14
15         return (0);
16   }
```

As shown in this example, the `strcpy()` function can copy characters from a literal string (line 9) or a string variable (line 12).

Note that it is up to you as the programmer to ensure that there is enough space in the destination string for all of the characters in the source string. For instance, if we changed line 6 of Example 12.6 to

```
char aString[10];
```

then the call to `strcpy()` on line 9 would attempt to copy too many characters into the variable `aString`. More than likely, the program would crash.

TRAP 12.4
When calling `strcpy()`, it is your job to make sure that the destination string is large enough to hold the characters from the source string. Trying to copy too many characters will very likely crash your program.

12.2.3 The `strcat()` Function

The `strcat()` function concatenates one string onto the end of another. As with `strcpy()`, it requires two parameters. The first is the destination string, which will be changed by the concatenation. The second is the source string. Example 12.7 shows how `strcat()` can be used. Figure 12.2 gives the output from the program.

EXAMPLE 12.7 Using `strcat()`

```
1    #include <stdio.h>
2    #include <string.h>
3
4    int main()
5    {
6          char aString[80];
7          char anotherString[80];
```

```
8
9          strcpy(aString,"The first string.");
10         printf("%s\n",aString);
11
12         strcpy(anotherString,"The second string.");
13         printf("%s\n",anotherString);
14
15         strcat(aString,anotherString);
16         printf("The variable aString is now %s\n",
17                 aString);
18         printf("The variable anotherString is still %s\n",
19                 anotherString);
20
21         return (0);
22   }
```

FIGURE 12.2   The Output of Example 12.7

The first string.
The second string.
The variable aString is now The first string.The second string.
The variable anotherString is still The second string.

It is your job to ensure that there is enough space in the destination string to hold all of the characters from the source and destination strings. The strcat() function will not do that for you. If your program tries to concatenate too many characters onto the destination string, it may crash.

TECHNICAL NOTE 12.4
Most implementations of the strcmp() function compare strings by starting at the beginning of both strings and subtracting the ASCII value of the first character in the second string from the first character in the first string. If the value is zero, strcmp() moves to the next character and repeats the subtraction. It continues in this manner until it either reaches the end of one of the strings or the subtraction yields a non-zero value.

12.1.4   The strcmp() Function

Strings can be compared to one another by invoking the strcmp() function. This function compares the characters in the first parameter to those in the second. If the first string is less than the second based on the ASCII values of their characters, the strcmp() function returns a value less than zero. If they are the same, strcmp() returns zero. If the first string is greater than the second string based on ASCII values, then strcmp() returns a value greater than zero.

The strcmp() function is case sensitive. To strcmp(), the string "ABC" is different than the string "ABc". If one of the two strings in the parameter list is shorter than the other, it is viewed by strcmp() as being less than the other string. So the string "ABC" is less than the string "ABCD".

12.2.5   The strncpy(), strncat(), and strncmp() Functions

The Standard Library supports variations on the strcpy(), strcat(), and strcmp() functions. In particular, it provides the functions strncpy(), strncat(), and strncmp(). These three functions perform their operations on portions of strings. The *n* in the middle of the name of each function stands for an additional parameter n, which specifies the number of characters on which to perform the operation.

For instance, strncpy() takes three parameters. The first two are the destination and source strings. The last is an integer specifying the number of characters to copy from the source string into the destination string. If the null character is not within the first n characters, it is not copied and strncpy() will not add it.

Likewise, the strcat() function takes three parameters, a destination string, a source string, and an integer n. It concatenates the first n characters from the source string onto the end of the destination string. If the null character is not within the first n characters, it is not copied and strncat() will not add it.

The strncmp() function has one more parameter than strcmp(). It compares the first n characters of the two strings in its parameter list. Its return values are the same as strcmp().

12.2.6 The `sprintf()` Function

One of the primary variations on the `printf()` function is `sprintf()`. The `sprintf()` function prints formatted output into a string rather than on the screen. It is widely used when programming for GUI-based operating systems such as the Macintosh OS and Microsoft Windows.

The `sprintf()` requires one more string parameter than `printf()` at the beginning of the parameter list. When the function finishes, the first string in the list will contain the output of the function. The second parameter is a format string whose specifications are identical to the format string used by `printf()`. Any other parameters are variables as indicated by the format string. Example 12.8 contains a simple demonstration of how programs use the `sprintf()` function. Figure 12.3 gives the output of the program.

EXAMPLE 12.8   Using the `sprintf()` Function

```
1   #include <stdio.h>
2
3   int main()
4   {
5           int anInteger = 150;
6           float aFloatingPointNumber = 56.789;
7           char destinationString[256];
8
9           sprintf(destinationString,
10                  "This is an integer %d. This is a float %f.\n%s",
11                  anInteger,
12                  aFloatingPointNumber,
13                  "This is a string.");
14
15          printf("%s",destinationString);
16
17          return (0);
18  }
```

FIGURE 12.3   The Output of Example 12.8

> This is an integer 150. This is a float 56.789001.
> This is a string.

This short program demonstrates how the `sprintf()` function prints formatted information into a string. That information can come from variables, literal numeric values, or literal strings. Unlike this rather contrived example, formatted strings created with `sprintf()` are rarely printed with `printf()`. Instead, they are used with other string output functions.

Example 12.9 contains a code fragment showing how the `sprintf()` function can be used to prepare output for the MS Windows `MessageBox()` function. The error information and an output string are printed into the string variable `outputString`. This is then used as the text for a pop-up message box warning the user that something rather drastic has occurred.

EXAMPLE 12.9   Using `sprintf()` in a Microsoft Windows Program

```
sprintf(outputString,
        "Error %d has occurred.\nProgram aborting...",
        errorNumber);
MessageBox(NULL, outputString, "Fatal Error",MB_OK);
```

Other graphical user interfaces, such as the Macintosh operating system and XWindows-based libraries for Unix, provide functions similar to `MessageBox()`. The `sprintf()` function is commonly used with all of them.

12.2.7 Other C String Functions

The ANSI C Standard Library specifies many string handling functions that are not presented here. Table 12.7 summarizes some of the more popular functions. In addition, many compilers offer handy functions that are not specified in the ANSI C Standard. Table 12.8 lists a few of the most widely implemented string functions.

TABLE 12.7 Other ANSI C String Functions

Function Name	Description
memcmp()	Similar to strcmp(). Compares bytes instead of characters.
memcpy()	Similar to strcpy(). Compares bytes instead of characters.
memmove()	Moves data from possibly overlapping memory regions.
memset()	Sets an entire group of bytes (or string) to the specified value.
strchr()	Finds the first occurrencze of a character in a string.
strstr()	Finds the first occurrence of a substring inside a string.
strtok()	Finds the next occurrence of the specified token in a string.

TABLE 12.8 Common Non-ANSI C String Functions

Function Name	Description
strcmpi() or stricmp()	Compares strings without case sensitivity.
strdup	Copies a string by allocating memory for the destination string and copying characters from the source string into the newly-allocated memory.
strrev	Reverses the order of the characters in the specified string.

12.3 Troubleshooting Guide

After reading this section, you should be able to:

- Be aware of possible pitfalls associated with I/O functions.
- Remove extraneous characters from the keyboard buffer.
- Use unbuffered keyboard input.
- Understand and avoid the problems associated with unterminated strings.

12.3.1 Using scanf(), gets(), and getchar() Together in a Program

All of the ANSI input and output (I/O) functions can be used together in a program without any problem if the developer understands how they all work. However, it has been my experience as a teacher that students new to C usually have an easier time if they do not use scanf() in the same program with gets() and getchar().

One reason for this difficulty is that scanf() often leaves characters in the keyboard buffer that students do not anticipate being present. Remember that, by default, scanf() stops reading characters whenever it encounters white space (the space character, the tab character, or the newline character). To use scanf() in the same program as getchar() and gets(), you must anticipate the possible presence of leftover characters in the keyboard buffer.

This is not hard to do once you have some experience with these functions. In general, a common rule of thumb is to remove all extra characters from the keyboard buffer before calling any input function. Section 12.3.2 of this chapter explains how this can be done.

Also, some early implementations of the C Standard Library had quirks in them that caused additional problems with using scanf() in the same program as getchar() and gets(). I have not seen this problem in some years. However, if you are using an old compiler and having unexplained problems with the input functions, you may need to update it.

The best thing you can do to resolve problems with using `scanf()` in the same program as `getchar()` and `gets()` is to read thoroughly the reference page for the `scanf()` function in your compiler's documentation.

12.3.2 Clearing the Keyboard Buffer

Most computers today use buffered keyboard input. When your program calls any of the Standard Library input functions, it receives characters from the keyboard buffer. Your program generally does not have a means of determining how long these characters have been in the buffer. It is possible that they are left over from a previous input operation.

In many cases, programs are written with the assumption that there is no existing input in the keyboard buffer when it calls an input function. However, that may not actually be the case. If your program is written with this assumption, you must clear the keyboard buffer before you get input. There are many ways of doing this.

The first and easiest to implement is to make sure that your program never leaves characters in the keyboard buffer when it gets input. This requires your program to read input until it finds the newline character. Usually, programs use the `gets()` function to accomplish this. If every input operation reads all of the characters currently in the keyboard buffer, there will not be any extra characters in the buffer when the next input function is called.

At first glance, it may seem that the main drawback to this approach is that all of your input is retrieved as strings. If your program is retrieving numeric input, your program must validate that the string contains a number in the proper format. It must also convert the data to a number.

In reality, this is not a drawback. Checking input data to ensure that it is in the proper format is something that programs must do anyway. It is called data validation. The most common technique for data validation is to read input as a string, validate that it is in the proper format, and convert it to the type your program needs. This technique not only improves the robustness of your program, but it also ensures that there are no extra characters in the keyboard buffer.

Some compilers provide an additional means of clearing the keyboard buffer. They contain a non-ANSI function that enables your program to check the keyboard buffer for keystrokes. Usually the function is named something similar to `_kbhit()`, `keybdhit()`, `keyhit()`, or `keypressed()`. If your compiler includes such a function in its library, your program can call it before each input operation. If there are keystrokes in the keyboard buffer, your program can use `getchar()` to remove them. Example 12.10 shows a code fragment from a Windows 98 console application that uses the `_kbhit()` function to clear the keyboard buffer. The `_kbhit()` function is available with Microsoft Visual C/C++.

EXAMPLE 12.10 Clearing the Keyboard Buffer

```
1   while ( _kbhit() )
2   {
3           getchar();
4   }
```

The `while` loop in Example 12.10 calls the Microsoft Visual C/C++ library function `_kbhit()` to look into the keyboard buffer. If there is a keystroke in the buffer, `_kbhit()` returns a non-zero value. This evaluates to true, which causes the body of the loop to be executed. Inside the loop, the code fragment calls the `getchar()` function to remove the character from the keyboard buffer.

Check your compiler documentation to see if your compiler supports this method of clearing the keyboard buffer. If you are not using Visual C/C++ it is likely that the name of the function your program needs to use is different. You will have to search for it in your compiler's documentation.

12.3.3 Unbuffered Keyboard Input

Buffered keyboard input is not appropriate for every program. There are methods of retrieving unbuffered input from the keyboard. However, these methods are not specified in the ANSI standard. They vary from compiler to compiler and from operating system to operating system. You will have to look in your compiler's documentation to see which you can use.

The libraries that come with many compilers offer unbuffered input functions for C programs. Usually, these are named `getch()` and `getche()`.

The `getch()` function retrieves a character directly from the keyboard. Your program does not have to wait for the user to press Enter to retrieve the character. As soon as the user presses a keystroke, the `getch()` function will return the input. The `getch()` function does not echo the character to the screen. When the user presses a character he/she will not see it on the display, but it will be available immediately to the program.

The `getche()` function works almost exactly like the `getch()` function. The only difference is that the `getche()` function echos the input character to the screen.

C libraries for Unix systems may not offer the `getch()` and `getche()` functions. Instead, they often enable programs to turn off buffered input using a function called `ioctl()`, which is short for input/output control. Once a program turns off input buffering with `ioctl()`, `getchar()` retrieves characters directly from the keyboard without waiting for the user to press Enter.

SUMMARY

In C, data I/O and string handling are tasks that are handled primarily by functions in the Standard Library. The input functions that are most often utilized to interact with the user are `scanf()`, `getchar()`, and `gets()`. The `printf()`, `putchar()`, and `puts()` functions are commonly used output functions.

Strings are implemented as arrays of characters terminated with a null character. The C Standard Library provides several functions for processing strings. Among those used most often in programs are `strlen()`, `strcpy()`, `strcat()`, `strcmp()`, `strncpy()`, `strncmp()`, `strncat()`, `strset()`, and `sprintf()`. These functions are used for such tasks as initializing, copying, comparing, and concatenating strings, as well as finding the lengths of

strings. The C Standard Library also provides other string handling functions.

Typically, it is useful to clear the keyboard buffer before or after each input operation. The easiest way to handle this task is to retrieve all the input the keyboard buffer contains each time data is read. This is typically done using functions such as `getchar()` and `gets()`. There are other techniques for clearing the keyboard buffer that involve functions that are widely implemented but not part of the ANSI C Standard.

Most computers today use buffered keyboard input. As a result, no input is given to the Standard Library input functions until the user presses Enter. Most compilers provide methods of performing unbuffered keyboard input. However, these are not part of the ANSI C Standard.

TECHNICAL NOTES

12.1 Formatting specifiers are also called conversion specifiers because they specify how the `printf()` function converts data into a displayable form.

12.2 Each formatting specifier in a scanf() format string is also referred to as an input field.

12.3 To avoid the potential problems `gets()` has when the user enters too many characters, programs can use `getchar()` and allocate space for strings on a character-by-character basis. This technique is demonstrated in Chapter 18.

12.4 Most implementations of the `strcmp()` function compare strings by starting at the beginning of both strings and subtracting the ASCII value of the first character in the second string from the first character in the first string. If the value is zero, `strcmp()` moves to the next character and repeats the subtraction. It continues in this manner until it either reaches the end of one of the strings or the subtraction yields a non-zero value.

TIP

12.1 Many compilers enable your program to use `"%[]"` to specify what characters `scanf()` will read. This is not part of the ANSI standard, but it is widely supported

TRAPS

12.1 Most compilers provide additional specifiers that can be used for the *flag(s)*, *width*, *precision*, *modifier*, and *type* portions of Definition 12.1. Using them may be convenient, but they can make your code less portable.

12.2 On systems using buffered keyboard input, `getchar()` will not receive any characters from the operating system until the user presses Enter on the keyboard.

12.3 The `gets()` function may overwrite memory or cause your program to crash if the user enters more characters than the string in its parameter list will hold.

12.4 When calling `strcpy()`, it is your job to make sure that the destination string is large enough to hold the characters from the source string. Trying to copy too many characters will very likely crash your program.

REVIEW QUESTIONS

1. How do C programs retrieve input from the keyboard and send output to the screen?
2. What are the differences between calling the `gets()` function and calling the `scanf()` function with the `"%s"` formatting specifier?
3. What are the differences between calling the `puts()` function and calling the `printf()` function with the `"%s"` formatting specifier?
4. How can strings containing white space be read into a program?

5. What does the `strlen()` function do?
6. What do the `strcpy()` and `strncpy()` functions do?
7. What do the `strcat()` and `strncat()` functions do?
8. What do the `strcmp()` and `strncmp()` functions do?
9. What does the `strset()` function do?
10. Why does the C Standard Library contain the `sprintf()` function when it also has the `printf()` function?

EXERCISES

1. Fill in the blanks.
   A string is an array of _____. Therefore, an array of strings is an array of _____ arrays.
2. Explain what a keyboard buffer is and why you think operating systems might use them. Also describe the difference between buffered and unbuffered keyboard input.
3. Write a program that uses *buffered* input to do the following:
   Read a string of no more than 80 characters. The string should be read character-by-character.
   Output the string to the screen.
4. If your system supports it, write a program that uses *unbuffered* input to do the following:
   Read a string of no more than 80 characters. The string should be read character-by-character.
   Output the string to the screen.
5. Write a program that reads a string containing white space from the keyboard. Print the string to the screen.
6. Write a program that does the following:
   Fills a 2-D array of characters with random strings.
   Prints the unsorted strings.
   Invokes the `strcpy()` and `strcmp()` functions to sort each row in the 2-D array.
   Prints the sorted strings.
7. Write a program that does the following:
   Prompts the user for a number between 1 and 80.
   Reads the number and stores it in a variable called `charCount`.
   Prompts the user to input a string.
   Reads `charCount` characters from the keyboard, including blanks and tabs.
   Prints the input string.

8. Write a program that does the following:
   Fills a 2-D array of characters with five strings input by the user.
   Prints the unsorted strings.
   Invokes the `strcpy()` and `strcmp()` functions to sort each row in the 2-D array without case sensitivity. If your compiler provides a `stricmp()` or `strcmpi()` function, do not use it. Hint: The C Standard Library contains a function called `toupper()` that converts characters to uppercase.
   Prints the sorted strings.
9. Write a program that does the following:
   Gets a string from the user.
   Gets a character from the user.
   Prints the string "Found" if the character is in the string.
   Prints the string "Not Found" if the character is not in the string.
10. Write a program that uses the `strncpy()` function to copy the first eight characters of the string "This is a null terminated string." into a string variable. It should then use the `printf()` function to print the contents of the string variable. Explain what happened and why.
11. Write a program that uses the `strncat()` function to concatenate the first eight characters of the string "This is a null terminated string." into a string variable containing the string "A short string". It should then use the `printf()` function to print the contents of the string variable. Explain what happened and why.
12. Write a program that retrieves a string from the user, reverses the order of the characters, and prints the reversed

string. If your compiler provides a function to do this, do not use it in your program.

13. In your compiler's documentation, look up the `vsprintf()` function. Explain what it does and how you think it might be useful in programs.

14. Write a program that retrieves two strings from the user. It should use the `strstr()` function to search for the second string in the first string. If it is found, print the string "Found". If not, print "Not Found".

15. Look up the `scanf()` formatting specifiers in your compiler's documentation. Make a list of the specifiers your compiler supports that are not in this chapter. Explain what each does.

16. Look up the `printf()` formatting specifiers in your compiler's documentation. Make a list of the specifiers your compiler supports that are not in this chapter. Explain what each does.

17. Write `printf()` formatting specifiers that:
    Prints a long double in a column that is 10 characters wide. The output should have no more than three digits to the left of the decimal point.
    Prints signed integers with a + sign if they are positive and a − sign if they are negative. They should print in a column 12 characters wide.
    Prints hexadecimal numbers in a 10 character column.

18. Write a `scanf()` formatting specifier that:
    Reads a string which may only contain uppercase characters.
    Reads a hexadecimal integer.
    Reads a string that is no more than 10 characters long.

19. Write a program that retrieves six floating-point numbers from the user and prints them in scientific notation using the letter E as a replacement for the x10.

20. Write a program that gets two strings from the user, prints them into a character array using the `sprintf()` function, and prints the resulting string.

21. Write a program that uses `getchar()` to retrieve a string from the user. The string must not be more than 30 characters long. It may contain only uppercase and lowercase letters. Your program should validate that each character is a letter as it reads in the character. If the character is invalid, print an error message and exit the program. If the entire string contains valid characters, print the string on the screen.

22. Write a program that uses `getchar()` to retrieve a string from the user. The string can only contain the digits 0–9. The program should validate each character in the string as it reads them. If it retrieves an invalid character, it should beep the computer's speaker using the statement

    ```
    printf("%c",(char)7);
    ```

    When it has validated all of the characters in the input, it should convert the string to an integer.

23. In your compiler's documentation, look up the `sscanf()` function. Explain what it does and how you think it might be useful in programs.

24. Search your compiler's documentation for string or character functions not mentioned in this chapter. If there are any, list them in a table. List the names of the functions in the first column of the table. In the second column, write a brief description of each function in the list.

25. Read your compiler's documentation on the `strtok()` function. Write a program that demonstrates the use of the `strtok()` function. It should tokenize the string "C makes it easy to shoot yourself in the foot; C++ makes it harder, but when you do, it blows away your whole leg. —Bjarne Stroustrup (the inventor of C++)" using the space character as the delimiter.

GLOSSARY

Buffered Input   Input data that is stored in memory until the input process is finished.

Formatting Specifiers   A special set of character codes that describe the format of data for the `printf()` and `scanf()` functions.

Format String   A string which contains formatting specifiers.

Input Field   Another name for a formatting specifier.

Keyboard Buffer   An area of memory in which user keystrokes are stored until the user presses the Enter key.

Line Buffer   An input or output buffer that holds one line of data.

13

Structured Design with Functions

OBJECTIVES

After reading this chapter, you should be able to:

- Explain the basics of structured design.
- Explain functions and their purposes.
- Explain the essential principles of designing functions.
- Write functions.
- Pass information into functions.
- Get information from functions.
- Use function prototypes.

OUTLINE

PREVIEW

Professional programs are seldom as short as the example programs in this book. Many commercial application programs are hundreds of thousands of lines of source code. Some are millions of lines in length. It is normal for programs to be written by large teams. In fact, their size makes it nearly impossible for one person to write them in a timely manner.

It would not be reasonable for a program that is hundreds of thousands of lines of source code to fit into main(). *A program must be broken into manageable pieces. That is one of the primary reasons for functions.*

It is not enough, however, to build programs from manageable pieces. The pieces must have a definite design to them, or they won't be worth creating.

This chapter introduces functions and describes the part they play in well-designed C programs. It also presents some of the fundamentals of software design.

13.1   Structured Design

Function-oriented languages like C have been in use for decades. Experience shows that building programs from functions is beneficial, especially when structured design techniques are used.

So what is structured design, and why do we use it? To answer this, we'll first examine the reasons for using structured design, then we'll look at what it is.

13.1.1   Why Structured Design?

The most important reasons for structured software design are derived from the software life cycle.

The Software Life Cycle   One of the most valuable tools to come into use in the 1970s was the concept of a **software life cycle** for dealing with the differing tasks of the software development process. By isolating tasks and specifying areas of focus, it became possible to do a more efficient and accurate job of producing software within budget and on time.[1]

Software is useful for a limited length of time. The lifespan of some software is short. Most software for the CP/M operating system came and went rather quickly. Other pieces of software continued for a long time. The vi editor for Unix is nearly as old as I am.

During the life cycle of a program, there are several distinct phases. Analysis and design is usually the first phase, followed by development and, finally, maintenance. During the maintenance phase, all bug fixes and enhancements are done. Figure 13.1 shows the software life cycle.

FIGURE 13.1   The Software Life Cycle

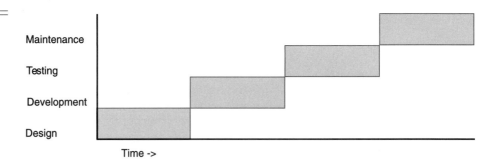

There are many views of just what phases the software life cycle should contain. The information here is not meant to reflect any one software design methodology. Instead, it is a generic summary of the main phases of the software life cycle. The concepts presented here will help provide an understanding of the basics. That is enough to begin to design and develop robust and reusable software.

The Design Phase   The design phase occurs first in the software life cycle. When software is well-designed, it generally contains far fewer errors than if it is just thrown together.[2]

During the design phase, the designers gather a list of requirements from the people that will use or sell the software. They may examine competing products. They often do surveys of potential users. If they are writing the software to take the place of a paper-based system, they will look at the printed forms. This preparation helps them find out what information the current system gathers and processes.

The general goals of the design phase are to communicate accurately and completely with the users and to provide them with all the information necessary for them to

---

[1]For references from this time period, see Philip W. Metzger, *Managing a Programming Project* (Englewood Cliffs, NJ: Prentice Hall, Inc., 1981) P. Bruce and S. M. Pederson, *The Software Development Project: Planning and Management* (John Wiley & Sons, 1981).

[2]The importance of good software design was recognized as far back as the 1960s. See C. Bohn and G. Jacopini, "Flow Diagrams, Turing Machines and Languages with Only Two Formation Rules," Communications of the ACM, Vol. 9, No. 5 (May 1966) pp. 366–71. See also Edsgar Djikstra, "Go To Statement Considered Harmful," Communications of the ACM, Vol 11 No. 3 (March 1968), pp. 147–48.

determine what they need from the software. The designer must then create a software model that accurately reflects the users' specifications. This model is usually a combination of diagrams that show the architecture of the software and a text description of how the software works. The model must be easy to modify and maintain.

Specific goals of the software design phase are as follows:

- Determine what is and is not part of the system.
- Determine which parts of the system can be automated and/or computerized.
- Create a model of the existing system that includes both the data and the processes that manipulate the data.
- Design a specification document that reflects the ways in which the users of the system do business.
- Write the specification to enhance information hiding, code reusability, and independence from the operating environment.
- Eliminate as many design errors as possible before coding begins.
- Enhance the specification to reflect modular design.

The Development Phase   The development phase is the period of time when programmers actually write the code. The general goal for the programming phase is to create a software system that will be efficient, robust, and modifiable, as well as meet all of the specifications.

Specific goals are as follows:

- Write the program according to the design specification and the model.
- Write the program in a way that makes the software robust and modular.
- Eliminate errors and document any programmer assumptions.

The Testing Phase   Once the software has been developed, it must be tested. The general goal of the testing phase is to be certain that the application is robust, runs correctly, and meets the specifications.

The Maintenance Phase   After the initial release of the software, it enters the maintenance phase. During this time, programming errors are fixed and new features are added to the software. Programming errors are called **bugs**. New features added to software are called **enhancements**.

The general goal for this phase of the software life cycle is to quickly get the user up and running on the program. This includes getting the program installed and giving the user enough information or training so that he/she can learn the software quickly.

The software must then be maintained as needed. Maintenance requires adding new features when the users request them and fixing errors. The code must be re-tested as it is maintained. The engineers who are doing the maintenance must also modify the documentation to reflect changes in the code.

Finding Problems Early   Of the four phases shown in Figure 13.1, which do you think costs the most?

Most of my students usually answer that development is the most expensive, but that's not correct. It's maintenance. 75 to 85 percent of the cost of software is often spent on fixing bugs, adding new features, and other maintenance tasks. In my experience, the average is closer to 85 percent than to 75 percent. This means that anything we can do to bring down the cost of maintenance will save money.

Many large software companies have found that extra time and money spent in design can lead to huge savings during maintenance. Almost without exception, developers use the extra time in the early phases of the project to do structured design and development.

In software development projects, it's always true that the earlier you find a problem, the less expensive it is to fix. Bugs found in a piece of software after it is released (the maintenance phase) are a very expensive problem. Some companies actually have had to distribute free versions of their software with fixes for serious bugs that were found by users. This is very costly, and it hurts a company's reputation.

If software errors are found during testing, the developers can typically fix them for less than one tenth of what it would cost to fix them during maintenance.

If bugs are found during development, the cost of fixing them is usually less than one tenth of what would be spent to fix them during testing.

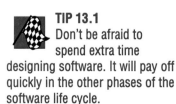
TIP 13.1
Don't be afraid to spend extra time designing software. It will pay off quickly in the other phases of the software life cycle.

TRAP 13.1
Rushing into development without adequate design can drive up the cost of software.

TIP 13.2
Increasing the reusability of your code makes you more productive in less time.

TIP 13.3
Always try to make your programs easy for other programmers to read and understand.

TIP 13.4
Well-designed programs tend to be more readable. Programs that are readable are easier for maintenance programmers to understand and modify in a reliable way.

If problems are discovered during design, the price of fixing them is normally less than a tenth of the cost of fixing them during development.

The result is that if it costs $10 to fix a bug during the design phase, it will cost $100 to fix during development. This same bug will cost at least $1,000 to repair during testing and $10,000 to fix during maintenance. Clearly, good design saves the most money.

Extending And Modifying Programs   I was in computing for several years before I realized one basic fact: computer programs aren't written to be read by computers, they're written so humans can read them.[3] In fact, a leading software design expert states:

> A program is a communication between programmers; it is a technical exposition describing information and how it is processed.[4]

Surprised? It's true. There's not a single computer on the market today that can read a C program directly. All of them need a compiler or interpreter to translate C to binary.

If programs are meant to be read by humans, then we should make them as readable as possible. Programs that are easy for maintenance programmers to read are less expensive to maintain and enhance than programs that are hard to read. Structured design techniques assist us in creating readable programs.

Structured design also will help us build software modules that are easily integrated into a large variety of programs.[5] And that's what I like—getting the most mileage out of my efforts. I tell my students that, in programming, laziness is a virtue. The more use they can get out of a piece of code they have written, the more successfully lazy they have been. When a hardworking programmer is given a task, he goes directly to his computer and starts coding. When a successfully lazy (and smart) programmer is given a task, she tries to find as much code from reusable libraries that will fit the task as she can. Successfully lazy programmers get more done in less time.

Another reason for using these techniques is that your success at a company is influenced by the quality of your code. Other people will at some point take over the maintenance of the program. If so, you'll have a much better reputation in the company if it's well organized and easily maintainable.

Portability   When a company produces a program which turns out to be popular, they often rewrite it so that it can run on new operating systems or hardware. The process of making it run on different hardware or under a different operating system is called **porting** the program.

Writing portable software can save the company you work for significant amounts of money. This is not an exaggeration. I have had job experiences where the software engineering team I was on saved our employer literally millions of dollars by designing and developing our software with portability in mind.

Structuring a program correctly in the design phase can make writing highly portable programs a much simpler task.

Reliability   Structured design naturally results in programs that are broken into small, reusable pieces. Each piece can be tested on its own. The benefit of this approach is that individual pieces of the program can be tested much sooner than the whole program. In fact, there can be (and should be) a lot of overlap between the development and testing phases of the software life cycle.

Because program pieces can be tested as development proceeds, testers can spend much more time testing them. The result is more reliable programs built from reusable, well-tested pieces.

---

[3]For a similar discussion, see Edward Yourdon and Carl Argila, *Case Studies in Object Oriented Analysis and Design* (Upper Saddle River, NJ: Prentice Hall, Inc., 1996), pp. 5–6.

[4]Michael Marcotty, *Software Implementation* (Hertfordshire, UK: Prentice Hall International (UK), Ltd., 1991), p. xv.

[5]See Michael Marcotty, *Software Implementation* (Hertfordshire, UK: Prentice Hall International (UK), Ltd., 1991), pp. 70–74.

13.1.2 Using Structured Design

At this point, I'll climb down off of my soapbox and stop preaching the benefits of structured design. Instead, let's take a look at how it's done.

Hitting The Bull's Eye

The three principal factors in a programming project are the following:

- Quality
- Cost
- Time

The main task when managing a programming project is optimizing these three factors. In practical experience, companies are too often extremely short-sighted and will sacrifice quality to optimize cost and time. Companies that take this approach do themselves no favors. Sacrificing quality to cost and time in the short term often leads to higher costs and wasted time later.

Quality can be increased without adding significantly to cost and time by using what is known as a "bull's eye" approach to software development, which is shown in Figure 13.2.

FIGURE 13.2 Bull's Eye Software Development

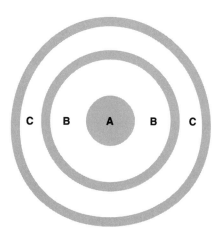

A—Early version of the program with only the essential features of the program completed.

B—Project nearing the halfway mark. Many features are in place. Fixes and enhancements of the early features are complete.

C—Project finished. The errors are corrected and the software is documented.

Figure 13.2 shows us that projects can be developed in stages. We start by implementing the core feature set. Once it's done, the testers can begin testing it. We can demonstrate it to the user and get feedback for **design reviews**. A design review is a meeting where a team gets together and reviews the robustness, effectiveness, and usability of their software design. Because design problems may be found during development, it is important for a team to have regular design reviews.

As the project approaches the halfway point, many of the program's features should be up and running. We may even allow users to install the software and begin using it so they can provide feedback.

Based on the feedback from the previous two stages, we can target the software more accurately to the users' needs. We clean up any final bugs, write the documentation, and release the software.

Decisions about which features should be implemented in stage A depend on the situation. Some common priorities are the following:

- The most "important" features are finished first.
- The most quickly implemented features are finished first.
- The most easily implemented features are finished first.

Ways of implementing the priorities above might include the following:

- Simulation of the user interface(s).
- Rapid prototyping of the potential product.
- Simulation of the software system using off-the-shelf components.
- Coding the critical modules first.
- Top-down development.

The bull's eye approach helps identify errors early. The earlier an error is found, the less costly it is is to fix it.

Top-Down Design   There are many excellent books on structured design and development.[6] In this book, we won't try to cover the specific, formal structured design methods they teach. Instead, we'll look at a generic approach that will help you move later into whatever design methodology you think is best. This simple and direct method of software design is **top-down design**.

The essence of this technique is to start with the most general statement of what a program does. From there, you break the general task into more specific tasks. These tasks are broken down into subtasks until the lowest level is reached. When is the lowest level reached? There is no hard and fast rule that answers this question. However, a good guideline to start you off is this: you're done when your design results in programs made up of functions that are shorter than one or two printed pages in length.

Let's look at an example. Let's say that we're building a computer game that we'll call Space Attackers. Space Attackers will be a game in which there are several rows of evil, mean, nasty, and incredibly bad-mannered attackers from outer space slowly moving back and forth across the screen together. When they reach the left or right edges of the screen, every row will move down some, and they'll start marching back the other way. Periodically, the attackers will fire their guns downward at the defender.

The defender will be drawn as a tank at the bottom of the screen. It will be able to move back and forth and shoot at the attackers. If any of the attackers' bullets hit the defender, or if any of the attackers reach the bottom of the screen, the defender dies. An attacker dies when it is hit by the defender's bullet.

Between the attackers and the defender are a few barriers that the defender can use for shelter. Figure 13.3 illustrates what Space Attackers might look like.

By describing the game, we've stated its **functional specification**. A functional specification lists everything that a program does. You must generate this before you start writing the program, or you won't know when it's finished.

Once we write a functional specification, we can start the design. First we draw a diagram that gives the most general statement of what the program does, as shown in Figure 13.4.

The first-level design diagram can be very simple. However, its value becomes clearer when we start to break this task down. Figure 13.5 shows the first level or so of subtasks.

As you can see, the diagram is beginning to be helpful to a C programmer. The major tasks necessary for running the Space Attacker game are now shown. All of them except Init Game are done repeatedly until the game ends.

---

[6]Some of my favorites are Michael Marcotty, *Software Implementation* (Hertfordshire, UK: Prentice Hall International (UK), Ltd., 1991), Alka Jarvis and Vern Crandall *Inrodes to Software Quality* (Upper Saddle River, NJ: Prentice Hall, Inc., 1997), and Rodney C. Wilson, *Software Rx* (Upper Saddle River, NJ: Prentice Hall, Inc., 1997).

FIGURE 13.3 Space Attackers

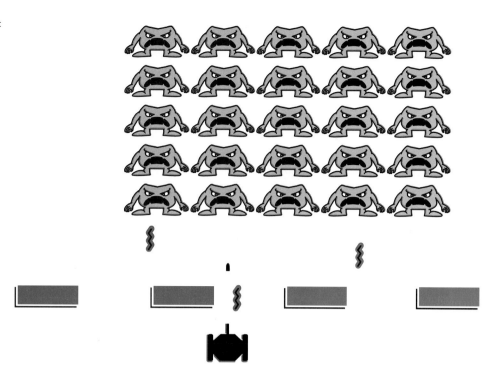

FIGURE 13.4 The First-Level Design Diagram for Space Attackers

Space Attackers

FIGURE 13.5 Space Attackers Diagram with Subtasks

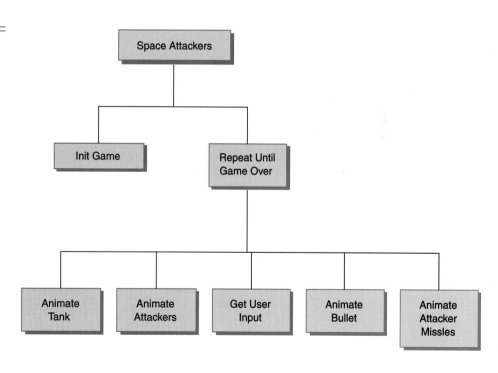

Let's focus on the task of animating the evil horde of Space Attackers. If we were to draw the next level of subtasks for that task, it would look like Figure 13.6.

This is top-down design in action. We started with a very general diagram of what the program does. Each successive diagram is getting more and more specific. If we were doing a diagram for a game we really wanted to implement, we would need to break down each of the second-level tasks just as we did with Animate Attackers.

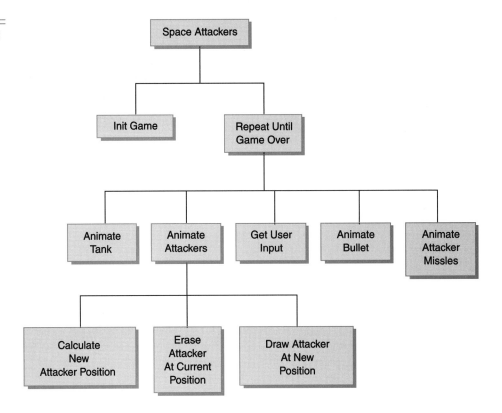

FIGURE 13.6 **Space Attackers with More Subtasks**

Modularizing Programs   As Figures 13.4–13.6 show, top-down design means breaking a program down into progressively more specific tasks. Breaking programs into small, reusable pieces is called **modularization**. Any computer program can be broken down into clearly defined modules.

13.2   Creating a Function

C functions give us a way to create C programs that are composed of modules. These modules often correspond directly to the boxes in a top-down design diagram. If we were writing the Space Attackers program, we would create functions for each of the boxes in Figures 13.5 and 13.6.

You already know how to write functions in C. We have been using a function in every program we've written. It's called `main()`.

Creating any C function is done in essentially the same way as creating `main()`. Every function that you write must have a unique name, a return type, a parameter list, a code block, and a prototype. Each of these is discussed in the remaining sections of this chapter.

Hands On 13.1 illustrates how to create a function by showing a program that calls a function to clear the screen.

Hands On 13.1

Objective

Write a program that:
       Calls a function to clear the screen.
       Declares a 2-D array of integers.
       Fills the integer array.
       Displays the contents of the integer array.

Experiment

Because this program is somewhat long, it is provided for you on the Examples CD included with this book. On the CD is a directory called Examples. In the Examples directory is a directory called Chapt13. In Chapt13 you will find a file named Ho13_1.c Copy the file to your hard drive. Compile, link, and run it.

```c
1    //------------------------------------------------------------
2    // Include Files
3    //------------------------------------------------------------
4
5    #include <stdio.h>
6
7    // End Include Files------------------------------------------
8
9
10   //------------------------------------------------------------
11   // Prototypes
12   //------------------------------------------------------------
13
14   void ClearScreen(void);
15
16   // End Prototypes---------------------------------------------
17
18
19   int main()
20   {
21       // Local constants.
22       const int MAX_ARRAY_ROWS = 10;
23       const int MAX_ARRAY_COLS = 10;
24       int a2DArray[MAX_ARRAY_ROWS][MAX_ARRAY_COLS];
25       int i,j;
26       int tempInt;
27       char inputChar;
28
29       ClearScreen();
30       for (i=0;i<MAX_ARRAY_ROWS;i++)
31       {
32           for (j=0;j<MAX_ARRAY_COLS;j++)
33           {
34               a2DArray[i][j]=i*j+j;
35           }
36       }
37
38       printf("The current contents of the array are:\n");
39
40       for (i=0;i<MAX_ARRAY_ROWS;i++)
41       {
42           for (j=0;j<MAX_ARRAY_COLS;j++)
43           {
44               printf("%d",a2DArray[i][j]);
45
46               if (a2DArray[i][j] < 10)
47               {
48                   printf(" ");
49               }
50               else if (a2DArray[i][j] < 100)
51               {
52                   printf(" ");
```

```
53                      }
54              }
55              printf("\n");
56      }

58      for (i=0;i<MAX_ARRAY_ROWS;i++)
59      {
60              for (j=0;j<MAX_ARRAY_COLS;j++)
61              {
62                      if (i<j)
63                      {
64                              tempInt=a2DArray[i][j];
65                              a2DArray[i][j]=a2DArray[j][i];
66                              a2DArray[j][i]=tempInt;
67                      }
68              }
69      }

71      printf("\nPress any character, then press Enter to ");
72      printf("continue.");
73      scanf("%c",&inputChar);
74      ClearScreen();

76      printf("The current contents of the array are:\n");

78      for (i=0;i<MAX_ARRAY_ROWS;i++)
79      {
80              for (j=0;j<MAX_ARRAY_COLS;j++)
81              {
82                      printf("%d",a2DArray[i][j]);

84                      if (a2DArray[i][j] < 10)
85                      {
86                              printf("  ");
87                      }
88                      else if (a2DArray[i][j] < 100)
89                      {
90                              printf(" ");
91                      }
92              }
93      printf("\n");
94      }
95      return (0);
96  }



100  void ClearScreen(void)
101  {
102      int i;

104      // Local constant
105      const int MAX_SCREEN_ROWS = 25;

107      for (i=0;i<MAX_SCREEN_ROWS;i++)
108      {
109              printf("\n");
110      }
111  }
```

Results

When we run the program, it will first display the output shown in Figure 13.7.

After the user presses any character key and then presses Enter, the screen shown in Figure 13.8 will appear.

FIGURE 13.7 **The Program's Initial Output**

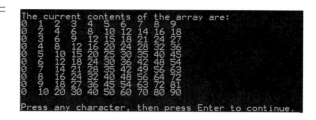

FIGURE 13.8 **The Program's Final Output**

Analysis

This program loads a 2-D array with integer values and prints them to the screen. It then swaps them to a different location in the array and prints them again.

Notice that this program declares all constants near where they are used. If there was a global constant, its declaration would occur near the top of the program so that it would be visible to all functions.

Before it does anything else, the program calls the function `ClearScreen()`. As the name indicates, the function clears the screen. The function is called again after the contents of the array are printed for the first time.

The `ClearScreen()` demonstrates how a function is defined. Figure 13.9 shows the generic form of a function definition.

```
return_typeFunctionName[parameter]_type parameterName], parameter2_type parameterName2....parameter[\] type parameterNameN]
{
  C++ statements
}
```

FIGURE 13.9 **The Generic Form of a Function Definition**

The first thing a function must have is a return type. The return type can be any valid C data type, such as `int` or `char`. Functions send data back to the program that called them. A function's return type tells the program the type of the data that the function sends back. In this case, the `ClearScreen()` function does not send back any data. We call it to clear the screen. It doesn't need a return type, so we use the type `void`. The `void` type tells the program that `ClearScreen()` does not send information back to the function which called it.

All functions in a C program must have a unique function name. The name is followed by a parameter list in parentheses. The parameter list can have any number of parameters, each with their own data type (`int`, `char`, `double`, and so on). Programs use parameter lists to send information to functions they call.

The program in this Hands On example doesn't send any information to the `ClearScreen()` function. Because `ClearScreen()` doesn't use any parameters, we put the type `void` in the parentheses. Whenever you write a function that doesn't need any information passed to it through the parameter list, you should put the type `void` in the function's parameter list.

Figure 13.9 shows that every function has a block of code associated with it. A function's code block is also called its body. The body of the function is contained in the braces. The program executes the body when it calls the function. A function is called when its name appears in another function. For example, the name `ClearScreen()` appears twice in `main()` in the program in Hands On 13.1. Each time the name `ClearScreen()` appears, program execution jumps to the `ClearScreen()` function and its code block is executed.

If a function declares a variable within its code block, the variable is only visible within that function. The `main()` and `ClearScreen()` functions both have a variable called `i` declared inside them. These are two different variables with the same name, but they are not accessible outside of the function in which they are declared. Because they are in two different code blocks, they are two different variables. It does not matter that they have the same name.

The `main()` function also declares a variable named `j`. This variable is accessible only in `main()`. Example 13.1 has a version of the `ClearScreen()` function that tries to increment the variable `j`. If you tried to use the variable `j` in the `ClearScreen()` function, as the example shows, your compiler would tell you that the variable `j` is an undeclared identifier.

EXAMPLE 13.1 An Undeclared Identifier

```
1   void ClearScreen(void)
2   {
3        int i;
4        for (i=0;i<MAX_SCREEN_ROWS;i++)
5        {
6             /* This is not allowed. j has not been declared
7             in this function. */
8             j++;
9             printf("\n");
10       }
11  }
```

When a variable is declared in a function, it is accessible and usable from the point at which it is declared to the end of that code block.

Although the `ClearScreen()` function in Hands On 13.1 is about the simplest type of function we can create, it demonstrates all the essentials of functions. First, it has a name that is unique in the program. There can be no other function in the program named `ClearScreen()`. Second the `ClearScreen()` function has a return type, which is `void`. In addition, it has a parameter list, which is empty. It also has a code block and a prototype. The next few sections describe each of these parts of a function.

13.2.1 Naming Functions

Every function must have a name. There are a few simple rules for naming functions. First, function names must start with a letter or an underscore character (_). The rest of the function name can contain numbers, letters, or the underscore character. The letters in a function name can be uppercase or lowercase.

The ANSI C standard states that function names can be up to 1024 characters long. However, not all compilers support function names of that length. It's generally not convenient to make your function names longer than 30 or 40 characters anyway. They become too tedious to type.

When naming a function, uppercase letters are recognized by the compiler as being different than lowercase letters. For example, the function `thisfunc()` is seen by the compiler as being different than the functions `ThisFunc()` and `thisFunc()`.

No spaces are allowed in function names. Table 13.1 shows some valid and invalid function names.

TABLE 13.1 Valid and Invalid Function Names

Valid Function Names	Invalid Function Names
CalculateInterestRate	Calculate Interest Rate
merge_text	merge-text
CleanupAndExit	Cleanup&Exit
Find100Ways	100Ways

A function name should always describe the action that the function performs. Function names like DoStuff() or CalcValues() are often useless to the maintenance programmer because they're too vague.

Similarly, a function name should be understandable to most ordinary human beings. For instance, I once worked on a project on which a programmer named a function GP1toGP2CCDtaXfr4Rl(). Do you have any idea what that function does? Neither do most people from this planet.

On the other hand, what would you think a function named CalcInterestRate() does? That's right. It calculates the interest rate. Not only is this name understandable to most people, but it also gives the context in which it is used. You can expect that a function called CalcInterestRate() is appropriate for some sort of financial application.

Good function names describe what the function does. They do it in a way that is understandable to most maintenance programmers. They all contain a verb. Most contain a direct object in the name as well. The verb states what the function does. The direct object states what the verb's action is performed on.

If the function name does not contain an object, the meaning of the verb must be obvious. For instance, the function name Print() is acceptable because programmers understand that printing something sends output to the screen or printer. It would be better, however, to specify where the output is going—to the screen or the printer. The function name Calculate() is too vague to be useful. Calculate what? It is not clear what is being calculated, even if you know the type of program for which the function is being written.

For the most part, words in good function names should be completely written out. They should not contain cryptic abbreviations. A function name like GP1toGP2CCDtaXfr4Rl() doesn't do anyone any good. If a function name contains any abbreviations, they should be abbreviations that most people use and understand.

Bad function names are vague, undescriptive, or contain too many abbreviations. They do not give any information about the context in which they are used. They do not contain verbs. Table 13.2 shows some good and bad function names.

TABLE 13.2 Good And Bad Function Names

Good Function Names	Bad Function Names
CalcInterestRate	DoStuff
TransferData	GP1toGP2CCDtaXfr4Rl
DisplayPicture	Picture
CloseWindow	FiniWin

13.2.2 What Happens When a Function Is Called?

When a function is called, we also say that it is invoked. Program execution jumps from the spot in the program where the function is invoked to the beginning of the function. At the end of the function, program execution returns to the point where the function was called.

For example, in Hands On 13.1, the first action of the main() function was to call the function ClearScreen(). Whenever this happens, program execution jumps to the ClearScreen() function. The program executes all of the statements in the function's code block. At the end of the ClearScreen() function, program execution returns to the point where ClearScreen() was invoked.

13.2.3 Passing Information to a Function

We often need to pass information to functions. This is done through the parameter list. The parameter list may contain as many parameters as you like within the limits of your computer's memory.

Example 13.2 demonstrates how parameters can be passed to a function through the parameter list. It shows the `ClearScreen()` function with one parameter. The parameter contains the number of lines on the screen. Notice that the parameter has a name and a type, just like a variable. A parameter is only visible in the code block of the function to which it belongs.

EXAMPLE 13.2   A Verion of `ClearScreen()` with a Parameter

```
1    void ClearScreen(int maxScreenRows)
2    {
3         int i
4         for (i=0;i<maxScreenRows;i++)
5         {
6              printf("\n");
7         }
8    }
```

When this version of the `ClearScreen()` function is called, an integer value must be passed to it or the program will not compile. Example 13.3 demonstrates different ways the `ClearScreen()` function from Example 13.2 can be called.

EXAMPLE 13.3   Calling the `ClearScreen()` Function from Example 13.2

```
1    int main()
2    {
3         int rows=100;
4
5         ClearScreen(25);
6         ClearScreen(rows);
7         return (0);
8    }
```

In Example 13.4 the program calls the `ClearScreen()` function twice. The first time, it passes the function a literal integer value, 25. The second time, it passes an integer variable called `rows` through the parameter list. The value in rows is 100. It makes no difference to the operation of the `ClearScreen()` function whether we pass it a literal integer value or an integer variable. `ClearScreen()` works correctly with either because it is getting an integer.

Example 13.4 demonstrates some problems that can occur if we use the `ClearScreen()` function improperly. In this example, the program calls `ClearScreen()` three times. The first time, the program tries to pass `ClearScreen()` a character. Even though this is an odd thing to do, it can work because a character can evaluate to a number. Most C compilers will output an error when they see this. However, if we adjust the compiler settings, we can force it to change this error to a warning. This is never a good idea.

EXAMPLE 13.4   Calling `ClearScreen()` with Wrong Parameters

```
1    int main()
2    {
3         float badValue=25.25;
4
5         ClearScreen('C');
6         ClearScreen(badValue);
7         ClearScreen("If a function expects an int, never give it a string.");
8         return (0);
9    }
```

If a function expects a parameter of a certain type, we should pass it a value of that type. We can get around this to a certain extent by using type casting. Be very careful with type casting parameters. It is far better to always pass an integer to a function that expects an integer than it is to type cast the parameter to an `int`.

Example 13.4 also demonstrates an attempt to call `ClearScreen()` with a floating point number in its parameter list. This also can work. However, we may have to adjust the compiler settings. By default, most compilers will report this as an error. If it does work, the fractional part of the floating-point number will most likely be truncated.

In the last attempt to call `ClearScreen()` in Example 13.4, the program tries to pass it a string. This is extremely bad programming practice. It should be reported as an error by your compiler.

If a function expects more than one parameter, the parameters are separated by commas. Each parameter must have its own type declared, even if it is the same type as the parameter before it. For example, it a function has two integer parameters in its parameter list, the type `int` must appear before each parameter name. Each parameter declaration must have a comma separating it from the next parameter declaration.

Example 13.5 demonstrates a program that calls a function expecting two parameters. The example illustrates that the parameters can be of different types. It also demonstrates that arrays can be passed as parameters. Notice that the size of the array is not specified in the parameter list on line 16. C allows this so we can use the same function on different-sized arrays. Remember that an array of characters is a string. In C, strings are terminated by the null character. So we know how long the array of characters is by the position of the null character.

EXAMPLE 13.5   A Function That Takes Two Parameters

```
1    #include <stdio.h>
2
3    void RepeatString(int repetitionCount,char outputString[]);
4
5    int main()
6    {
7         int count=100;
8         char aString[]="This is another string";
9
10        RepeatString(10,"This is a string");
11        RepeatString(count,aString);
12        return (0);
13    }
14
15
16    void RepeatString(int repetitionCount,char outputString[])
17    {
18         int i;
19
20         for (i=0;i<repetitionCount;i++)
21         {
22              printf("%s\n",outputString);
23         }
24    }
```

This short program declares a function called `RepeatString()`, which prints a string to the screen repeatedly. Both the string and the repetition count are passed into the function as parameters. The `RepeatString()` function is called on lines 10 and 11 of the `main()` function. Notice that it does not make any difference whether `main()` passes literal values, as it does on line 10, or values stored in variables, as shown on line 11. As long as the number and types of the parameters are correct, the program will compile. If the programmer using the `RepeatString()` function fails to pass two parameters from `main()` to `RepeatString()`, the program will not compile. The program will not also compile if the parameters are not the correct type.

I have stated repeatedly that `main()` is a function. It may occur to you that `main()` should have parameters. That is true. It is possible to pass values to `main()`. These parameters are values that the user types in on the command line when he or she runs the program. Command line parameters are presented in Chapter 20.

In previous chapters, I have left the parameter list of `main()` empty. If you want to, you can put the word `void` into the parentheses for `main()`. You can also just leave them blank.

13.2.4 Returning a Value from a Function

Information is passed into a function through the parameter list. It is passed out of a function using the return value. To send a value out of a function, you must use the C keyword `return`. The type of the data must match the return type of the function. Figure 13.10 shows a function from Hands On 13.2, which appears after the figure. This function, called `Max()`, returns the value in the variable `maxValue`. Notice that the type in front of the function name and the type of `maxValue` are the same. If this is not the case, your compiler will at least generate a warning. It will probably generate an error.

Note that it is possible to use a type cast when the return value does not match the return type of a function. Theoretically, this should be fairly straightforward. In practice, however, I have found that some compilers have quirks that make this an inconsistent operation. They each seem to handle the process a bit differently. Therefore, I recommend against using this technique until you are sure what your compiler will do with the value.

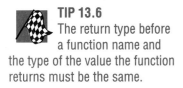

TIP 13.6
The return type before a function name and the type of the value the function returns must be the same.

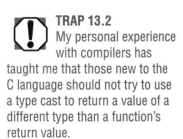

TRAP 13.2
My personal experience with compilers has taught me that those new to the C language should not try to use a type cast to return a value of a different type than a function's return value.

FIGURE 13.10   A Function That Returns a Value

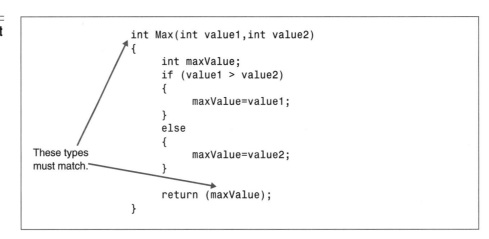

```
int Max(int value1,int value2)
{
        int maxValue;
        if (value1 > value2)
        {
                maxValue=value1;
        }
        else
        {
                maxValue=value2;
        }
        return (maxValue);
}
```

These types must match.

Hands On 13.2 illustrates how functions can return values to programs.

Hands On 13.2

Objective

Write a program that uses a function to find the maximum of two values entered by the user.

Experiment

Type the following program into your IDE or text editor. Compile, link, and run it.

```
1    #include <stdio.h>
2
3    int Max(int value1,int value2);
4
5    int main()
6    {
7            int inputValue1,inputValue2,maxValue;
```

```
 8
 9            printf("Please enter a number and press Enter:");
10            scanf("%d",&inputValue1);
11
12            printf("Please enter another number and press Enter:");
13            scanf("%d",&inputValue2);
14
15            maxValue=Max(inputValue1,inputValue2);
16
17            printf("\n");
18            printf("The maximum of the two values you typed ");
19            printf("in was: %d\n",maxValue);
20
21            return (0);
22    }
23
24
25    int Max(int value1,int value2)
26    {
27            int maxValue;
28
29            if (value1 > value2)
30            {
31                    maxValue=value1;
32            }
33            else
34            {
35                    maxValue=value2;
36            }
37
38            return (maxValue);
39    }
```

Results

Please enter a number and press Enter: **10**
Please enter another number and press Enter: **20**
The maximum of the two values you typed in was: 20

Analysis

This program calls a function named `Max()`. The `Max()` function finds the maximum of two integers that are passed into it as parameters. It returns the maximum to the `main()` function.

When the program executes, it asks the user for two integer values. After the user types them in, the program invokes the `Max()` function. `Max()` uses a simple `if-else` statement to determine which of the two is the maximum value. It returns the largest value using the statement

```
return (maxValue);
```

TIP 13.7
It is helpful to put a function's return value in parentheses.

The data that the `Max()` function returns does not have to be put in parentheses as I do throughout this book. When I was first programming in C, I encountered a few compilers that wouldn't evaluate return values properly unless they were in parentheses. I got in the habit of putting return values in parentheses and have never stopped. I continue this habit because I think it makes the code clearer. It eliminates the possibility of misunderstanding. The compiler can't misunderstand, and neither can the maintenance programmer.

In the program in Hands On 13.2, `main()` calls `Max()`. As far as `main()` is concerned, the `Max()` function evaluates to a value. It can be treated just like any other value. Function calls can be used just the way any Rvalue would be used. Functions that return values cannot be used as Lvalues. Recall that an Rvalue is anything on the right side of an assignment operator (=). An Lvalue is anything that can be put on the left of the = sign.

Try This

Try modifying the `Max()` function so that it finds the maximum of three values passed in as parameters.

All functions are capable of returning a value. We saw earlier in this chapter that functions which do not return a value should have a return type of `void`.

Because `main()` is a function, it also can return a value. In all of the programs we wrote so far, we returned the value zero from `main()`. This is because many operating systems expect programs to return a value. Typically, they want a zero if the program terminates normally. Most operating systems expect programs to return a non-zero value if there was an error.

13.2.5 Function Prototypes

Every function that we write in our C programs, with the exception of `main()`, should have a prototype. A **prototype** is a declaration of a function's name, return type, and parameter list. It enables the C compiler to do type checking on the return type and parameter list whenever the function is called.

A function prototype looks exactly like the first line of the function. The only difference is that the prototype is terminated by a semicolon (;). Example 13.6 repeats the program that was given in Example 13.5. The prototype for the `RepeatString()` function appears on line 3 before `main()`.

TECHNICAL NOTE 13.2
We use function prototypes in our programs to make our functions callable by all functions in the program. Using prototypes also enables the compiler to check the types of the return value and parameters at every point in the program where functions are called.

TIP 13.8
Create a prototype for every function that you write except `main()`. The prototypes should go at the beginning of your program files.

TRAP 13.3
Do not create a prototype for the `main()` function. Do not try to call the `main()` function. That is done for you.

EXAMPLE 13.6 A Program That Calls a Function

```c
1   #include <stdio.h>
2
3   void RepeatString(int repetitionCount,char outputString[]);
4
5   int main()
6   {
7       int count=100;
8       char aString[]="This is another string";
9
10      RepeatString(10,"This is a string");
11      RepeatString(count,aString);
12      return (0);
13  }
14
15
16  void RepeatString(int repetitionCount,char outputString[])
17  {
18      int i;
19
20      for (i=0;i<repetitionCount;i++)
21      {
22          printf("%s\n",outputString);
23      }
24  }
```

218   Chapter 13

By putting function prototypes at the beginning of program files, you enable the prototype to be visible from the point it is declared to the end of the file. The result is that any function in the program file can call any other function, and type checking will be done for all calls.

The `main()` function never needs a prototype. It is called by the operating system. Don't ever try to call `main()` yourself. That is a very quick way to crash your program.

The easiest way to create a function prototype is to use your text editor's copy function. Simply copy the first line of every function to the top of the program file. Terminate each prototype with a semicolon, as shown in Example 13.6.

13.3 Structured Design with Functions

Functions give us the ability to create programs that are structured using the top-down design techniques presented earlier in this chapter. For example, let's look again at the Space Attackers game.

Figure 13.11 repeats Figure 13.6, which shows a partial design of the Space Attackers game. From this design, it is easy to create functions. In fact, each box in the diagram corresponds to one function. The box labeled "Space Attackers" is implemented in the `main()` function. There would also be a function, probably called `InitGame()`, that would implement the tasks represented by the box labeled Init Game. The same would be true for all the other boxes on the diagram.

FIGURE 13.11 A Partial Design for Space Attackers

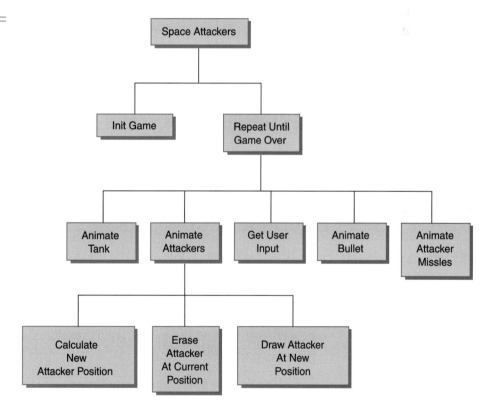

If we were writing this game together, we could easily use the diagram to divide up the work of the project. Top-down design makes it much simpler for members of programming teams to work together.

Most design methodologies have you create some type of design diagrams. They are not always the top-down charts presented here. However, their purpose is to define specific programming tasks. Generally, design methodologies next have you create a text definition for each box in your diagram. From that text definition, you write your functions. In this book, we will use pseudocode as our text definition of the functions we will write.

Although top-down design helps us structure our programs, the individual functions we write must be structured as well. To properly structure our functions, they should all follow some basic guidelines. Specifically, they should be modular and they should hide their implementation whenever possible.

13.3.1 Modular Functions

A modular function has a name that describes what it does. It may seem odd to repeat such a small detail. However, if you can't give your function a short name that tells what the function does, it probably does too much. You may need to break it down into a group of smaller functions.

To be modular, all functions should have one entry point and one exit point. It is possible to put multiple `return` statements in a function. Avoid the temptation to do that. Multiple exit points in a function make it harder to maintain. It unnecessarily increases the possible paths through the function. Example 13.7 demonstrates a function that has multiple exits.

EXAMPLE 13.7   A Function with Multiple Exits

```
1   int AFunction(int aParameter)
2   {
3         if (aParameter > 0)
4               return -1;
5         return 1;
6   }
```

Multiple exits don't do much damage to a short function like this. However, real functions that you write in commercial applications tend to be much longer than this. Multiple exits from a long function can very easily confuse a maintenance programmer or a tester.

Multiple exit points create many execution paths through a function. The execution paths grow exponentially as the number of exit points increases. The result is that multiple exit points from a function can create so many execution paths through the code that it is literally impossible to test every path.

Functions should always have clearly defined interfaces. All information that goes into a function should be passed in through the parameter list. All information that is passed out of a function should be passed out through the return value.

All functions in a program should be no more than two printed pages of code in length. This is a general rule of thumb, not a law written in stone. There will always be some functions in your program that are several pages long. However, if the majority of your functions in your program are longer than about two printed pages, you should think about redesigning your program.

TECHNICAL NOTE 13.5
It is possible to pass information out of a function through the parameter list. There are very valid and logical reasons for doing so. See section 18.4 in Chapter 18 for more information. On the whole, the majority of the functions in your program should return information through the return value whenever possible.

13.3.2   A Black Box

All functions should hide their implementation. Example 13.8 illustrates this idea. It shows a program that we saw earlier in this chapter. The program calls a function named `ClearScreen()`.

EXAMPLE 13.8   A Function That Hides Its Implementation

```
1   int main()
2   {
3         ClearScreen(25);
4         int rows=100;
5         ClearScreen(rows);
6         return (0);
7   }
```

Let's say that you are writing a program that calls the `ClearScreen()` function. Let's also suppose that you and I are working on the same project and that I wrote the `ClearScreen()` function for you.

Do you care about the internal workings of the `ClearScreen()` function? Probably not. You shouldn't have to. As long as it does its job of clearing the screen to your satisfaction, that's all that concerns you.

As much as possible, this is the way that all functions should be written. Each function should perform a task. Other programmers using functions that we've written should not have to know the algorithm of the function to use it. As long as the functions produces the correct results, they're happy.

When a function is written in this manner, we say that it is a **black box**. The name black box indicates that the function does its task without us knowing how.

You use many black boxes every day. Do you know all of the internal workings of your telephone? How about your microwave oven? If you're like me, you may know the inner workings of a computer in great detail but have no idea how to fix a car. To me, a car is a big rolling black box. Others see computers that way.

The black box approach helps us to simplify our world. That includes the programs that we write. We learn just enough about them to make them do what we want.

13.4   Troubleshooting Guide

After reading this section, you should be able to:

- Recognize and fix errors that are commonly made when creating functions.
- Use debugging programs.

13.4.1   Mistakes Programmers Commonly Make When Creating Functions

There are some mistakes that everyone makes when they first start writing C functions. Among the most common are misplaced semicolons, misplaced or forgotten braces, unreachable code, missing return values, and unenforced programmer assumptions.

Misplaced Semicolons   One common error that programmers encounter when creating functions is to accidentally put a semicolon (;) on the end of the first line of the function. If you do this, the compiler will think that you are declaring a prototype. It may tell you that it's found an unexpected opening brace ({) in your program. If you see such an error at the beginning of a function, check to make sure that there is not a semicolon after the function's parameter list.

Missing or Misplaced Braces   It is easy to forget the closing brace (}) on a function. If your compiler tells you that it has found an unexpected end of file in your program, it may be that a closing brace is missing. If it tells you that a semicolon should appear before the opening brace of a function, you may have left the opening or closing brace off of the previous function in the file.

Unreachable Code   If you get an error that some code at the end of your function is unreachable, you've probably ignored my advice about not using multiple `return` statements. Rewrite your function so that you can take the extra `return` statements out. This should solve the problem.

Missing `return` Statement   All functions must return a value if they do not have the `void` return type. Forgetting the `return` statement at the end of a function is a common mistake. You will know you have done this when your compiler tells you that your function must return a value.

Unenforced Programmer Assumptions   A common source of errors in functions occurs when programmers assume something to be true but don't enforce that assumption. Example 13.9 shows a code fragment of a function with a programmer assumption. Can you spot it?

EXAMPLE 13.9   A Function with a Programmer Assumption

```
1   void SomeFunction(int upperLimit,int anArray[])
2   {
3        int i;
```

```
4
5          for (i=0;i<upperLimit;i++)
6          {
7                  anArray[i] = i;
8          }
9    }
```

The function `SomeFunction()` in Example 13.9 is written with the assumption that the parameter `upperLimit` is greater than or equal to zero. You can tell this because `upperLimit` is used to control access to an array. Arrays are never indexed with numbers that are less than zero. The programmer who wrote `SomeFunction()` assumed that it would never be called with the `upperLimit` parameter set to a negative value. While this may be a valid way to use this function, it is unreasonable to assume that every programmer will recognize this restriction.

There is nothing in the function that enforces the assumption that `upperLimit` is greater than or equal to zero. However, the C Standard Library provides the `assert()` function for enforcing such assumptions. The `assert()` function takes a logical condition for its only parameter. If the condition evaluates to true, `assert()` does nothing. If it evaluates to false, it will stop the program and print an error message. In effect, the `assert()` function asserts that the condition is true. Example 13.10 contains a rewritten version of `SomeFunction()` with an assertion.

EXAMPLE 13.10   An Enforced Programmer Assumption

```
void SomeFunction(int upperLimit,int anArray[])
{
     int i;
     assert(upperLimit >= 0);
     for (i=0;i<upperLimit;i++)
     {
             anArray[i] = i;
     }
}
```

When you call `assert()` in your functions, it is a very in-your-face way of catching programmer errors. This is very desirable. As much as possible, we want to communicate to other programmers using our functions that they have given our functions incorrect values. We do not want them to be able to miss the error. If the program aborts due to an assertion, the problem will be noticed. That's always a good thing.

The majority of the functions you write will be written with programmer assumptions. As a result, you should always take time to determine exactly what your assumptions are and enforce them with assertions.

There are certain types of errors that should be handled with assertions, and others that should not. Assertions are strictly for handling errors that programmers might make. They are not for handling runtime errors or user errors.

For instance, if your program runs out of memory while it is executing, it should enable the user to save any unsaved data and shut down gracefully. This cannot be done with assertions. It generally requires `if-else` statements or something similar. Runtime errors such as this should not be handled with assertions.

An example of a user error might be typing in an incorrect or invalid name when prompted for a file name. If that is handled with an assertion, the program will crash every time the user makes a typing mistake. That will not make your program very popular.

When you use the `assert()` function, you must include the C Standard Library header file assert.h. Most compilers will let you compile both debug and release versions of your program. The debug version contains debugging information that slows the program down but helps you find errors. The release version does not contain the debugging information, so it is faster. If your compiler supports this feature, it will automatically remove assertions in the release version of the program. So although the call to the `assert()` function will remain in your C source code, the compiler will simply ignore it in the release version of the program. It will work only in the debug version.

This is as it should be. Programming errors that are normally caught by assertions should be found and fixed before the program is released.

13.4.2 Using Debugging Programs

The use of functions enables programs to be larger and more complex than the simple programs presented so far in this book. Anyone writing a large, complex program soon realizes that a debugging program is something every programmer should have. Most commercial compilers today come with debugging programs. If your compiler does not have a debugging program, it is wise to invest in one as soon as possible. Debugging programs will save you large amounts of time and effort.

Programmers often refer to debugging programs as "debuggers." Most debuggers allow you to set breakpoints, single-step through programs, set variable watches, alter the values of variables, and evaluate expressions.

Setting Breakpoints   Setting a breakpoint with a debugger causes the program you're working on to execute until it reaches the breakpoint. When it does, the debugger stops program execution and displays the source code of the program. You can then examine the state of the program.

Advanced debuggers will allow you to set conditional breakpoints. When the breakpoint is encountered, a condition is checked. If the condition is true, the debugger halts program execution. If not, it just continues. For instance, you can set a breakpoint condition to stop the program on the tenth time the debugger encounters the breakpoint.

When you test your program and find that it crashes, the first thing you'll need to do is find the location in the code where the crash occurs. An easy way to do this is to set a breakpoint at a likely spot in the code and run the program. If the program crashes before the debugger encounters the breakpoint, you should move the breakpoint closer to the beginning of the program. You might try setting several breakpoints throughout the program and executing from breakpoint to breakpoint until the crash occurs. This strategy narrows your search to the statement causing the crash.

Once you find where the program crashes, set a breakpoint just before the problem statement and run the program again. When the program encounters the breakpoint, you can examine its state just before it crashes and look for clues as to why it fails.

Single-Stepping Through Programs   Setting breakpoints enables us to skip over large sections of our programs that we know are working. It is often very beneficial, however, to step through our programs one line at a time. Debugging programs enable us to do exactly that.

We use the ability to step into each program statement when the statement is a function call and we want to see the function execute. This ability enables us to single-step through the current function and all functions that it calls.

As we step through the program, we can watch the changes in the variables. We can also view the program logic, which is not always what we expect it to be.

Setting Variable Watches   To be valuable, debuggers must enable us to examine the state of program variables. This ability is crucial to understanding the current state of a program. Most program crashes are due to variables taking on wrong or unexpected values. The incorrect or unexpected values put the program into an invalid state. The result is that the program doesn't function correctly.

To find the cause of the problem, we must be able to see how the values of variables change as the program executes. We do this by setting a watch. When we set a watch, we are telling the debugger that we want to watch the contents of a variable. The program will usually display the variable and its current contents somewhere on the screen. As we step through the program, we can watch the variable's value change.

Altering Variable Values   Advanced debuggers enable us to set the value of variables as a program executes. We can use this ability to force the program down a particular logic path. That is, we can use it to make loops start or stop, or to make a program execute an `if` or `else` statement. This capability is highly desirable when testing programs.

Evaluating Expressions   Programs use conditions to control loops and program branches. Debuggers give us the ability to evaluate conditions. This enables us to see why a particular condition may be evaluating to unexpected values. It also enables us to evaluate complex conditions a piece at a time.

Other Debugger Features   Most debuggers can either step over or into a function. Stepping over a function means executing it without showing the code being executed. When you step into a function, the debugger displays each line of the function it executes. You step over a function when you know it works and you just want the results it produces. You step into a function when you want to debug it.

Many debuggers automatically display the return value of a function. This feature is especially helpful when you do not have the source code for a function that you are using in your program. If you linked your program to a commercial library, you may have the object code for a function but not the source code

SUMMARY

Structured program design requires that we break programs down into sections or modules. Each module should perform a single task or a group of highly related tasks. In C, these program modules are called functions.

There are many reasons that a program must use functions for structure. Most of these reasons are derived from the software life cycle. The software life cycle is the useful lifespan of a program. Research and experience have shown that maintenance is by far the most expensive phase of the software life cycle. Structured design helps reduce the cost and effort of maintenance.

Top-down design is a method of structured design that developers have used for many years. Top-down design is done by breaking a program down into subtasks. These sub-

tasks are in turn broken down into smaller subtasks until the subtasks are small enough. Finding the point at which they are small enough is mainly a matter of experience.

We use functions to create C program modules. Every function must have a name. It also must have a return type, a parameter list, and a function body. Information is input into a function through the parameter list. It is output from a function through the return type. You should create a prototype for every function that you write except main().

In general, functions should follow the black box rule. That is, a programmer should not have to know the internal workings of a function to use it. If the interface is completely specified, any programmer should be able to invoke and use a function that you write.

TECHNICAL NOTES

13.1   Remember that every program has a stack. The stack is an area of the computer's memory that the program uses for a function's variables and parameters. Parameters are passed to functions by copying them onto the program's stack. The number of parameters and variables a function may have depends on the amount of memory available for the stack.

13.2   We use function prototypes in our programs to make our functions callable by all functions in the program. Using prototypes also enables the compiler to check the types of the return value and parameters at every point in the program where functions are called.

13.3   The main() function does not need a prototype because its prototype is defined by the C language specification.

13.4   When you compile your code, your compiler attaches a block of executable code to your program called the startup code. Among other things, these statements allocate the program's stack and call the main() function. We generally say that main() is called by the operating system. However that's not strictly true. The operating system calls the startup code and the startup code calls main().

13.5   It is possible to pass information out of a function through the parameter list. There are very valid and logical reasons for doing so. See section 18.4 in Chapter 18 for more information. On the whole, the majority of the functions in your program should return information through the return value whenever possible.

TIPS

13.1   Don't be afraid to spend extra time designing software. It will pay off quickly in the other phases of the software life cycle.

13.2   Increasing the reusability of your code makes you more productive in less time.

13.3   Always try to make your programs easy for other programmers to read and understand.

13.4   Well-designed programs tend to be more readable. Programs that are readable are easier for maintenance programmers to understand and modify in a reliable way.

13.5   Always pass data of the correct type to a function. If it expects an integer type, pass an integer. If it expects a character, pass it a character, etc.

13.6 The return type before a function name and the type of the value the function returns must be the same.

13.7 It is helpful to put a function's return value in parentheses.

13.8 Create a prototype for every function that you write except `main()`. The prototypes should go at the beginning of your program files.

TRAPS

13.1 Rushing into development without adequate design can drive up the cost of software.

13.2 My personal experience with compilers has taught me that those new to the C language should not try to use a type

cast to return a value of a different type than a function's return value.

13.3 Do not create a prototype for the `main()` function. Do not try to call the `main()` function. That is done for you.

REVIEW QUESTIONS

1. What is structured design?
2. What is the software life cycle?
3. What are the phases of the software life cycle?
4. Which phase of the software life cycle is most expensive?
5. What is top-down design?
6. What is a function?
7. How can functions be used in structured design?
8. How is information passed to a function?
9. How do you get information out of a function?
10. What is a function prototype? How is it created? What does it do?

EXERCISES

1. Fill in the blanks.

   Top-down design breaks programs down into chunks of code called _____. We implement these in C using _____.

2. Identify which statements are true.
   a. Functions should be implemented as a white box.
   b. If a function is a black box, programmers do not have to know its internal workings to use it.
   c. We implement functions as black boxes to make them easier to use.
   d. Functions implemented as black boxes cannot be maintained.

3. Fill in the blanks.

   All functions should be written using _____ _____. They should _____ their implementation.

4. Define the term *software life cycle*. Name the primary phases of the software life cycle, and explain their major goals.

5. Explain the process of bull's eye software development. Describe its possible advantages.

6. Explain why using top-down design to break a program down into smaller tasks might be helpful.

7. Fill in the blanks.

   All functions must have a unique _____. They must also have a _____ _____ that specifies the _____ that they send back to the calling function. If a function does not _____ a value, its _____ _____ should be `void`. In addition, every function must have a _____. Programs use this to pass information into a function. If the function does not need information passed to it, it should have the type `void` in its _____ _____. Functions also must have a code block, which is also called the _____ of the function.

8. Function prototypes turn on type checking of a function's _____ _____ and _____ at every point where the function is called.

9. Explain why software designers generally discourage multiple exit points from functions.

10. Explain the rules for naming functions.

11. Write a program that uses a function to square a number. Call the function `Squared()`. Your program should invoke `Squared()` to calculate the squares of 2, 10, and –5. The square of a number is that number times itself.

12. Write a program that uses a function called `Power()`. The `Power()` function should match the following prototype exactly.

    ```
    int Power(int aNumber,int thePower);
    ```

    The `Power()` function should raise the number in the `aNumber` parameter to the power in the `thePower` parameter. Your program should demonstrate the `Power()` function by calculating the answers to the following: 2^5, 10^3, and -3^7.

The `Power()` function needs to handle only positive powers. The user should not be able to pass in a negative value for `thePower`. Enforce this programmer assumption.

13. Write a program that uses a function called `PrintPrimes()`. The `PrintPrimes()` function should calculate all of the prime numbers between 1 and the number that is passed in, and print them to the screen. It should match the following prototype exactly.

       int PrintPrimes(int upperLimit);

    If `PrintPrimes()` is successful at finding some prime numbers, it should print them out and return the total number of prime numbers that it found. Hint: The most straightforward way to find prime numbers is to iterate through every number between 1 and `upperLimit` inclusive. Divide each number by all of the numbers below it. This implies a loop in a loop.

14. Write a program that uses a function which calculates the area of a rectangle. The area is found by multiplying the length of the rectangle by its width. The function should match the following prototype exactly:

       int RectangleArea(int length, int width);

    It should calculate the area using the parameters `length` and `width` and return the answer. Demonstrate that your function works by having your program calculate the areas of the following rectangles:

Rectangle	Width	Length
1	10	12
2	81	3
3	9	9
4	50	21
5	11	183

15. Write a program that uses a function which calculates the area of a circle. The area of a circle is found using the formula πr^2, where p is the value 3.14159 and r is the radius of the circle. Your function should match the following prototype:

       double CircleArea(double radius);

    Demonstrate that it works by having your program find and print the area of circles with the following radii: 10, 5.5, 0.453, and 20.

16. Modify the program in Example 13.6. Your program should get a string from the user. It should also ask the user how many times to repeat the string. It should then call the `RepeatString()` function to print the string the specified number of times.

17. Write a program that uses a function to calculate the perimeter of a rectangle. The perimeter is found by adding two times the length to two times the width (2L + 2W). The function should match the following prototype:

       RectanglePerimeter (int length, int width);

    It should calculate the perimeter using the parameters `length` and `width` and return the answer. Demonstrate that your function works by having your program calculate the perimeter of the following rectangles:

Rectangle	Width	Length
1	10	12
2	81	3
3	9	9
4	50	21
5	11	183

18. Write a program that uses a function to calculate the circumference of a circle. The circumference of a circle is found using the formula $2\pi r$, where π is the value 3.14159 and r is the radius of the circle. Your function should match the following prototype:

       double CircleCircumference(double radius);

    Demonstrate that it works by having your program find and print the circumference of circles with the radius 10, 5.5, 0.453, and 20.

19. Write a program that calls a function to print a string in reverse order. The function should take any size character array in its parameter list. The program should demonstrate that the function works by invoking it at least three times with three different strings. If your compiler provides a function that reverses strings, do not use it.

20. Write a program that calls a function named `StringLength()`. The `StringLength()` function should have the following prototype:

```
int StringLength(char inputString[]);
```

This function should count the number of printable characters (excluding the null character) in the parameter `input-String`. It should return the total as the return value. Have your program demonstrate that the function works correctly by calling it at least three times with three different strings as input.

21. The equation for a line is

$$y = mx + b$$

where m is the slope of the line, x is the x coordinate of a point on the line, and b is the y intercept. Write a function that calculates and returns the y coordinate for any given x coordinate on a line. The function should match the following prototype:

```
double FindYValue(double slope,
                  double xValue,
                  double yIntercept);
```

Write a program that demonstrates that your function works.

22. The power that a heater consumes can be calculated using the formula

$$p = vi$$

where p represents the power, v stands for the voltage, and i is the current. Write a function that calculates and returns p when given specific values for v and i. The function should match the following prototype:

```
double HeaterPower(double voltage, double current);
```

Write a program that demonstrates that your function works.

23. The force on an object can be calculated by the equation

$$F = ma$$

where F is the force, m represents the mass of the object, and a is the object's acceleration. Write a function that performs this calculation. It should have two parameters, the mass and the acceleration. Have it return the value it calculates. Write a program that demonstrates that your function works.

24. The Greek mathematician Euclid developed an algorithm for finding the greatest common divisor of two integers, integer1 and integer2. The algorithm is as follows:
    a. If the remainder of integer1/integer2 is zero, then integer2 is the greatest common divisor.
    b. If the remainder is not zero, then assign the value in integer2 to integer1. Assign the remainder to integer2.
    c. Repeat the process from step a.
    Write a function that implements this algorithm. It should take two integer parameters and return the greatest common divisor.

25. Three-dimensional computer graphics programs often use matrix multiplication to move (translate), rotate, and scale 3-D figures. Specifically, they multiply every vertex in the figure by a 4×4 transformation matrix. The general form of the multiplication is

$$[X_P\, Y_P\, Z_P\, 1] \begin{bmatrix} M_{00} & M_{01} & M_{02} & M_{03} \\ M_{10} & M_{11} & M_{12} & M_{13} \\ M_{20} & M_{21} & M_{22} & M_{23} \\ M_{30} & M_{31} & M_{32} & M_{33} \end{bmatrix} = [X_R\, Y_R\, Z_R\, 1]$$

In this equation, x_p, y_p, and x_p represent the x, y, and z coordinates of the point to be transformed. The values of the 4×4 transformation matrix are represented by M_{00}, M_{01}, and so forth, with the subscripts giving the row and column numbers of each value on the matrix. The values x_R, y_R, and x_R represent the x, y, and z coordinates of the resulting point. The equations for the matrix multiplication are

$$x_p = (x_p * M_{00}) + (y_p * M_{10}) + (z_p * M_{20}) + (M_{30})$$
$$y_p = (x_p * M_{01}) + (y_p * M_{11}) + (z_p * M_{21}) + (M_{31})$$
$$z_p = (x_p * M_{02}) + (y_p * M_{12}) + (z_p * M_{22}) + (M_{32})$$

Write a program that transforms a point using the equations above. Your function will have three parameters, and match the following function signature exactly:

```
void TransformPoint(double thePoint[3],
                    double transformationMatrix[4][4],
                    double resultPoint[3]);
```

Make the function use the values in the arrays `thePoint` and `transformationMatrix` to calculate the resulting point. Store the *x*, *y*, and *z* values of the resulting point in `resultPoint`. Write a program that calls the `TransformPoint()` function three times. Make it use the point (10, 20, 30) and the following transformation matrices to demonstrate the use of your function. Your program must call `TransformPoint()` once for each matrix.

$$\begin{bmatrix} 1 & 0 & 0 & 0 \\ 0 & 1 & 0 & 0 \\ 0 & 0 & 1 & 0 \\ 0 & 0 & 0 & 1 \end{bmatrix} \quad \begin{bmatrix} 1 & 0 & 0 & 0 \\ 0 & 1 & 0 & 0 \\ 0 & 0 & 1 & 0 \\ 5 & 9 & 3 & 1 \end{bmatrix} \quad \begin{bmatrix} 2 & 0 & 0 & 0 \\ 0 & 3 & 0 & 0 \\ 0 & 0 & 4 & 0 \\ 0 & 0 & 0 & 1 \end{bmatrix}$$

GLOSSARY

Black Box   A modular unit of program code, such as a function, that will perform a task without our knowing about how it is implemented.

Bugs   Programming errors in the software.

Design Review   A meeting where a team gets together and reviews the robustness, effectiveness, and usability of their software design.

Enhancements   Features that are added to the software after its initial release.

Functional Specification   A list of everything a program does.

Modularization   Breaking programs into reusable blocks of code with clearly-defined interfaces.

Porting   Rewriting software so that it will run on another operating system and/or different kind of computer.

Prototype   A declaration of a function's name, return type, and parameter list.

Software Life Cycle   The useful lifespan of software.

Top-Down Design   The process of designing software by starting with a general statement of what the software does. This is broken into more specific sub-tasks. These, in turn, may also be divided into increasingly specific sub-tasks until the program is understood well enough to be written.

14

Programmer-Defined Data Types

OBJECTIVES

After reading this chapter, you should be able to:

- Use structures to create programmer-defined types.
- Use unions to make data types.
- Define types and specify groups of related constants with enumerated types.
- Use the `typedef` keyword to create an alias for a type.

OUTLINE

PREVIEW

Using functions and the design techniques presented in Chapter 13, developers can create structured programs. Top-down design structures a program based on the way that the program processes data.

In addition to structuring the processes that a program performs, C enables developers to structure the data itself. This chapter presents the C language elements that you can use to structure data in your programs.

14.1   Modeling Data

We saw in Chapter 13 that functions give us a way to encapsulate and structure the code needed to perform a particular task. Programmer-defined data types do the same thing for data.

The ability to create our own data types enables us to structure the data to reflect the programming situation. When we do this, we say that we are creating a **data model**. Modeling data makes data processing easier and more intuitive. The data models we create model things that exist in the real world. They also model things that don't exist, as well as ideas.

14.1.1   Modeling the Real World

An architectural design program might enable us to create a wall of a house. In software, we would want that wall to behave exactly as a real wall does, or as close to it as possible. The wall in software is not a real wall. It exists only as data in the computer.

Creating a software model of the real world enables us to manipulate the data as if we were manipulating a real object. In the preceding example, I might use several walls to build a model of a house in the computer. I could look at the house, repaint it, possibly even navigate my way through it. All of this can be done without actually building the house.

14.1.2 Modeling Ideas

Another example of a data model is a dragon. I spent part of my career as a programmer writing computer games. I actually have had occasion to create a dragon data type in software. Dragons don't exist, but you and I as software developers are not limited by that. We can easily model dragons in software.

It's also common in the business world to model things that exist only as ideas. One example is a bank account. A bank account is not a physical object. You can't paint it, you can't touch it, and you can't take it home and put it in your closet. It doesn't exist except as an idea.

The idea of a bank account is modeled often in software. In fact, a significant percentage of all of the software ever written was created primarily for dealing with bank accounts.

14.1.3 Encapsulation

Why do we model data? Simply put, data models enable us to group related data together and provide functions that perform specific operations on it. The functions define the list of operations that can be performed on the data. As long as we access the data type through the functions that go with it, the data will stay in a valid state (if there are no errors in the functions). This is called **data encapsulation** or **data hiding**.

There are many programs filled with global variables. A global variable is a variable that is accessible from any function in the program. When some part of the program puts bad data into the global variable, it is difficult to track down the offending code. For this reason, we should avoid global variables.

Even if we don't use global variables, encapsulation helps us write better software. With programmer-defined types, we have the opportunity to provide a consistent and safe way to access the data in the types we define. We can set limits on the values that the data can receive. We can validate the data in any way needed as it is set. All of this control helps us ensure that the variable contains valid data at all times.

In our earlier example of a dragon data type for a game, all of the information that the software needs about the dragon should be put together into a `dragon` data type. We can also provide a set of functions that perform operations on a dragon, such as making it breathe fire or fly. Programs use these functions to change the data in a variable of type `dragon`. No other part of the software should directly access the data in the `dragon` data type. This ensures that the dragon object is properly initialized, and that it behaves in the way dragons should.

Encapsulating data into types we define also simplifies our programs. For instance, suppose you were writing a program to help design airplanes, and you decided to create a data type called `wing`. The `wing` data type would contain all of the information that the software needs to describe and simulate a plane's wing. Once you define a `wing` data type, you can declare variables of type `wing` in your program. You can pass those variables to functions in much the same way you pass integers or strings. Rather than pass each data item needed to simulate a wing individually, you can pass them as a group. This makes the interfaces to your functions much simpler and easier to understand.

14.2 Structures

One of the most powerful tools that C gives us for creating our own data types is the structure. C structures can contain data. Each data item is called a **member**. Collectively, all of the data items together are called the structure's **member data**.

14.2.1 Defining Structures

Figure 14.1 gives the general form of a structure. Programmers define structures using the `struct` keyword. The `struct` keyword is followed by the name of the type, which is indicated in the figure by *type_name*. A pair of opening and closing braces follow. These

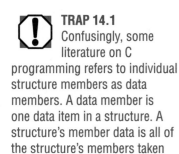

TRAP 14.1
Confusingly, some literature on C programming refers to individual structure members as data members. A data member is one data item in a structure. A structure's member data is all of the structure's members taken together.

FIGURE 14.1 The General
Form of a Structure

```
struct type_name
{
     member_type1 memberName1;
     member_type1 memberName1;
     .
     .
     .
     member_typeN memberNameN;
};
```

mark the beginning and ending of the structure's definition. Inside the braces, programs declare data members in just the same way they declare variables. Just as with variables, each structure member needs a type and a name.

Example 14.1 illustrates the way we define structures. This example defines a new data type for complex numbers. Complex numbers are numbers with real and imaginary parts. The imaginary portion of a complex number is marked with the letter i and the real part with the letter j. Complex numbers are used in engineering tasks such as integrated circuit design.

The `complex_number` data type contains two members of type `double`, called i and j. These contain the imaginary and real parts of the complex number.

EXAMPLE 14.1   The complex_number Data Type

```
struct complex_number
{
     double i,j;
};
```

It is not necessary for the member data of a structure to be all of the same type. Each member can be a different type. You can even define structures that contain arrays.

14.2.2   Declaring and Using Structure Variables

Defining a structure with the `struct` keyword does not allocate any memory for data. It does nothing more than define a type. To allocate memory for the structure, we must declare a variable of the structure's type.

Declaring a structure variable is similar to declaring variables of atomic data types. Your program must state the type and the name of the variable. Because the type is a structure, you must also use the word `struct`. Example 14.2 demonstrates how to declare a structure variable of type `complex_number`, which was defined in Example 14.1.

EXAMPLE 14.2   Declaring a Structure Variable

```
struct complex_number aComplexNumber;
```

The declaration of a structure allocates enough memory to hold all of the structure's members. In this example, the program will allocates enough space for two values of type `double`.

After a structure variable is declared, your program can use it to store values in structure members. It does this by stating the variable name, followed by a period and a member name. Example 14.3 illustrates how to store a values in a variable of type `complex_number`.

EXAMPLE 14.3   Storing Values in a Structure Variable

```
aComplexNumber.i=13.99;
aComplexNumber.j=-26.001;
```

Hands On 14.1 defines and declares a new data type using a structure. It also demonstrates how programs access structure members.

TECHNICAL NOTE 14.1
Once a structure is defined, the type is visible and available for use from the point it is defined until the end of the file.

TIP 14.1
Structures must be both defined and declared before they can be used in a program.

TECHNICAL NOTE 14.2
Although a structure's type name may be visible through an entire file, a structure variables follow the same rules as other variables. They are visible only in the functions in which they are declared.

Hands On 14.1

Objective

Define a data type for complex numbers.
Declare two variables of type `complex_number`.
Prompt the user for two complex numbers.
Add the complex numbers the user enters.
Print the results.

Experiment

Copy this program from the Examples CD included with this book onto your hard drive. The file name is Ho14_1.c. You will find it in the Chapt14 directory, which is in the Examples directory. Compile, link, and run this program.

```
1   #include <stdio.h>
2
3   struct complex_number
4   {
5        double i,j;
6   };
7
8
9   int main()
10  {
11       struct complex_number aComplexNumber;
12       struct complex_number anotherComplexNumber;
13       struct complex_number result;
14
15       printf("\nPlease enter a complex number. Type the\n");
16       printf("imaginary part of the number, then press Enter.");
17       printf("\nNext, type the real part of the ");
18       printf("number.\n");
19       printf("Imaginary part: ");
20       scanf("%lf",&aComplexNumber.i);
21       printf("Real part: ");
22       scanf("%lf",&aComplexNumber.j);
23
24       printf("\nPlease enter another complex number. \n");
25       printf("Imaginary part: ");
26       scanf("%lf",&anotherComplexNumber.i);
27       printf("Real part: ");
28       scanf("%lf",&anotherComplexNumber.j);
29
30       result.i = aComplexNumber.i + anotherComplexNumber.i;
31       result.j = aComplexNumber.j + anotherComplexNumber.j;
32
33       printf("\n");
34       printf("  (%lfi + %lfj)\n",
35               aComplexNumber.i,
36               aComplexNumber.j);
37       printf("+ (%lfi + %lfj)\n",
38               anotherComplexNumber.i,
39               anotherComplexNumber.j);
40       printf("---------------------------\n");
41       printf("  (%lfi + %lfj)\n",
42               result.i,
43               result.j);
```

```
44        printf("\n");
45
46        return (0);
47   }
```

Results

Please enter a complex number. Type the
imaginary part of the number, then press Enter.
Next, type the real part of the number.
Imaginary part: **12.3**
Real part: **23.4**

Please enter another complex number.
Imaginary part: **34.5**
Real part: **45.6**

$$\begin{array}{r} (12.300000i + 23.400000j) \\ + \ (34.500000i + 45.600000j) \\ \hline (46.800000i + 69.000000j) \end{array}$$

Analysis

This program uses a structure to define the type `complex_number`. In the `main()`
function, it declares three variables of type `complex_number`: `aComplexNumber`,
`anotherComplexNumber`, and `result`. Each of these has two members of type
`double`. Therefore, when these variables are declared, the program allocates
enough space to hold six `double` values.

As this program shows, you can use the members of a structure anywhere
you would use a variable of that type. The `double` values in the three structure
variables were used with `printf()`, `scanf()`, and the addition operator. The fact
that these were structure members did not make a difference. They can be used
as LValues or RValues, just like variables of atomic data types.

14.2.3   Structure Parameters and Return Values

Like any other type of variable, structures can be passed to functions as parameters. They
also can be used as a function's return values. Hands On 14.2 modifies the program from
Hands On 14.1. In addition to defining the type `complex_number`, it provides some functions to perform operations on `complex_number` variables. These functions take parameters of type `complex_number` and return `complex_number` values.

Hands On 14.2

Objective

Define a data type for complex numbers.
Declare two variables of type `complex_number`.
Prompt the user for two complex numbers.
Add the complex numbers the user enters.
Print the results.

Experiment

Copy this program from the Examples CD that accompanies this book onto your
hard drive. The file name is Ho14_2.c. You will find it in the Chapt14 directory,
which is in the Examples directory. Compile, link, and run this program.

```c
1   #include <stdio.h>
2
3   struct complex_number
4   {
5           double i,j;
6   };
7
8
9   struct complex_number GetComplexNumber(void);
10  void PrintComplexNumber(
11                  struct complex_number numberToPrint);
12  struct complex_number AddComplexNumbers(
13                          struct complex_number firstNumber,
14                          struct complex_number secondNumber);
15
16
17  int main()
18  {
19          struct complex_number aComplexNumber;
20          struct complex_number anotherComplexNumber;
21          struct complex_number result;
22
23          printf("\nPlease enter a complex number. Type the\n");
24          printf("imaginary part of the number, then press Enter.");
25          printf("\nNext, type the real part of the ");
26          printf("number.\n");
27          aComplexNumber = GetComplexNumber();
28
29          printf("\nPlease enter another complex number. \n");
30          anotherComplexNumber = GetComplexNumber();
31
32          result = AddComplexNumbers(aComplexNumber,
33                                      anotherComplexNumber);
34
35      printf("\n");
36      printf("  ");
37      PrintComplexNumber(aComplexNumber);
38      printf("\n");
39      printf("+ ");
40      PrintComplexNumber(anotherComplexNumber);
41      printf("\n");
42      printf("-------------------------\n");
43      printf("  ");
44      PrintComplexNumber(result);
45      printf("\n");
46
47      return (0);
48  }
49
50
51  struct complex_number GetComplexNumber(void)
52  {
53          struct complex_number theNumber;
54
55      printf("Imaginary part: ");
56      scanf("%lf",&theNumber.i);
57      printf("Real part: ");
58      scanf("%lf",&theNumber.j);
```

```
59
60        return (theNumber);
61    }
62
63    void PrintComplexNumber(
64            struct complex_number numberToPrint)
65    {
66        printf("(%lfi + %lfj)",
67            numberToPrint.i,
68            numberToPrint.j);
69    }
70
71
72    struct complex_number AddComplexNumbers(
73                        struct complex_number firstNumber,
74                        struct complex_number secondNumber)
75    {
76        struct complex_number result;
77
78        result.i = firstNumber.i + secondNumber.i;
79        result.j = firstNumber.j + secondNumber.j;
80
81        return (result);
82    }
```

Results

Please enter a complex number. Type the imaginary part of the number, then press Enter. Next, type the real part of the number.
Imaginary part: **23.4**
Real part: **34.5**

Please enter another complex number.
Imaginary part: **45.6**
Real part: **56.7**

$$
\begin{array}{r}
(23.400000i + 34.500000j) \\
+\ (45.600000i + 56.700000j) \\
\hline
(69.000000i + 91.200000j)
\end{array}
$$

Analysis

This version of the complex number program provides functions that perform operations on variables of type complex_number.

The GetComplexNumber() function enables a user to enter a complex number from the keyboard. It declares a complex_number variable called theNumber. This variable is only available inside the function GetComplexNumber(). The function prompts the user for the imaginary and real parts of the number. These are stored in the members of the variable theNumber. When the function ends, it uses the return statement to send the contents of the variable theNumber back to main().

PrintComplexNumber() prints a complex number to the screen in the proper format for complex numbers. The number to be printed is passed into this function as a parameter.

AddComplexNumbers() adds two complex numbers. It takes these numbers as parameters. This function adds the imaginary parts of the two numbers together and stores the answer in the appropriate structure member of the variable result. It does the same for the real parts of the two parameters. It's important to remember that variables are accessible only in the function in which they are declared. The variable `result` in the `AddComplexNumbers()` is not the same variable that is declared in `main()`. It does not matter that they have the same name.

After the `AddComplexNumbers()` function calculates the result of adding the two parameters, it returns the answer with the statement on line 81.

 Try This

Add a function to this program that subtracts two complex numbers. Complex number subtraction is performed by subtracting the imaginary part of the second number from the imaginary part of the first number and subtracting the real part of the second number from the real part of the first number.

Hands On 14.2 demonstrates the approach that C programmers commonly use when they create new data types. As shown in the Hands On program, it is advisable to provide a set of functions that perform operations on variables of that type. In doing so, you provide structure for both the source code and the data. The data types you create help structure the data, and the functions you provide to go with the data types help structure the program.

This effort is worthwhile. It helps structure your program into a highly maintainable format. Other programmers can understand the code more easily. Both you and they can get much more mileage out of your efforts when you use this technique.

There is another important thing to note about the programs in Hands On 14.1 and 14.2. They use only atomic data types. However, we are not limited to these data types. We can use arrays in structures. Example 14.4 illustrates this technique.

EXAMPLE 14.4   Using Arrays in a Structure

```
1   struct customer
2   {
3          char name[60];
4          char address1[60];
5          char address2[60];
6          char city[60];
7          char state[3];
8          unsigned zip;
9   };
```

Example 14.4 defines a structure type called `customer`. The `customer` type contains character arrays that provide storage for a customer's name, address, city, and state. It also contains an unsigned integer that is used to store a zip code.

Accessing a character in an array that is also a structure member is not much different than accessing a character in a normal array variable. The program must state the name of the structure variable, followed by a period and the name of the array member. The array subscript is also required. Example 14.5 demonstrates this. It initializes the first character in each of its arrays to null characters. It also sets the zip code to zero. This indicates that there is no customer information stored in the structure variable.

EXAMPLE 14.5   Accessing an Element in an Array Structure Member

```
1   struct customer aCustomer;
2   aCustomer.name[0] = '\0';
3   aCustomer.address1[0] = '\0';
4   aCustomer.address2[0] = '\0';
5   aCustomer.city[0] = '\0';
6   aCustomer.state[0] = '\0';
7   aCustomer.zip = 0;
```

14.2.4   Arrays of Structures

Like other data types, structures can be used as array elements. Example 14.6 shows the declaration of an array of the `customer` structures defined in Example 14.4.

EXAMPLE 14.6   An Array of Structures

```
struct customer allCustomers[100];
```

The array `allCustomers` contains 100 `customer` structures. Their indexes are numbered 0–99. Each one of them has six members, five of which are arrays. To access an individual structure, you must specify its index number, as shown in Example 14.7.

EXAMPLE 14.7   Accessing an Array of Structures

```
allCustomers[5].name[0] = '\0';
allCustomers[98].zip = 98765;
allCustomers[33].state[2] = '\0';
```

The first statement in this example accesses array element number 5 in the array `allCustomers`. This element is a structure. The statement sets the first character of the `name` member of the structure equal to the null character.

The second statement accesses array element number 98. It sets the zip member of that structure to 98765.

The last statement in the example accesses array element whose index number 33. It stores the null character in the third element of the `state` member.

14.2.5   Nested Structures

Structures can contain members of virtually any data type, including data types we define. Simply put, structures can have members that are structures. In fact, you can build types that are as complex as you'd like. For example, you can create an array of structures that each contain an array of structures that each contain an array of characters.

Structures which contain members that are structures are called **nested structures**. Example 14.8 illustrates the use of nested structures.

EXAMPLE 14.8   Nested Structures

```
1    struct name
2    {
3            char first[30];
4            char middleInitial;
5            char last[30];
6    };
7
8    struct address
9    {
10           char street1[40];
11           char street2[40];
12           char city[40];
13           state[3];
14           unsigned zip;
15   };
16
17   struct customer
18   {
19           struct name customerName;
20           struct address customerAddress;
21   };
```

This example shows a type called `customer` on lines 17–21. It has two members. The first, `customerName`, is of type `name`. The `name` type is a structure containing three members.

The second member of the `customer` structure is called `customerAddress`. It is of the type `address`, which contains five members.

Nested structures are declared and accessed using the rules already presented. Example 14.9 shows the declaration of a customer variable called `thisCustomer`. The statement on line 3 accesses the first character of the first name. To do so, it begins by declaring the variable name, `thisCustomer`. Because `thisCustomer` is a structure, any of its members must be accessed using the period, followed by the member name. The member `customerName` is a structure of type `name`. To access a member of the `name` structure, the example again uses the period followed by the member name, `first`. The member `first` is an array. Storing a value in an individual array element requires the use of the array subscript.

EXAMPLE 14.9   Accessing a Member of a Nested Structure

```
1    struct customer thisCustomer;
2
3    thisCustomer.customerName.first[0] = '\0';
4    thisCustomer.customerName.middleInitial = 'Z';
5    thisCustomer.customerAddress.state[0]='N';
6    thisCustomer.customerAddress.state[1]='Y';
7    thisCustomer.customerAddress.state[2]='\0';
8    thisCustomer.customerAddress.zip = 98765;
```

Nesting structures is a powerful way to create complex types. Be aware, however, that nested structures can result in types that require large amounts of memory. These days, memory is becoming less of an issue. However, in some situations, memory is at a premium. If this is the case, using nested structures may not be a good idea.

14.3   Unions

A union is a C language element that enables programmers to define variable types. Unions encapsulate multiple data types into the same memory space. You define a union in a way similar to the way a structure is defined.

Like a structure, a union stores data in its members. However, unlike structures, the members in unions all share the same memory space. The C compiler allocates memory for the largest member in the union. You can access that memory using any of the union members. However, no matter which member you use, you are accessing the same memory location.

Like structures, unions define a type. The definitions of unions are handled in almost exactly the same way as the definitions of structures. The only real difference is that they begin with the keyword `union` instead of `struct`. The definition of a simple union type is given in Example 14.10.

EXAMPLE 14.10   Defining a Union

```
union character
{
        char asChar;
        int asInt;
};
```

In this example, the type `character` is defined. It contains a member of type `char` and a member of type `int`. When a variable of type `character` is declared, the program allocates enough space for the largest member of the union. In this case, the largest member is probably the `int`.

Once union variables are declared, programs can use any of their members. However, the members all access the same memory space. Example 14.11 uses the type `character` from Example 14.10 to declare and access a union variable. Recall that the amount of memory allocated for the types `char` and `int` are different on different types of computers. For this example, we'll assume that a `char` is 8 bits and an `int` is 32 bits.

EXAMPLE 14.11   Declaring and Using a Union Variable

```
1    union character aCharacter;
2
3    aCharacter.asChar = 'Q';        /* Stores a 'Q' in the first 8 bits of the
```

TRAP 14.3
Variables whose types are built from nested structures can consume large amounts of memory. You must weigh the benefits of using nested structures against the need, if any, to conserve memory.

TECHNICAL NOTE 14.3
The C compiler allocates enough memory for only the largest member of a union. All union members share that memory.

```
  4                            variable. */
  5  printf("%c",aCharacter.asChar);
  6  aCharacter.asInt = 7;          // Uses all 32 bits. Stores Ctrl+G.
  7  printf("%c",aCharacter.asChar);
```

TRAP 14.4
Because union
members all access the
same memory, using them can
be confusing to maintenance
programmers. In general, it's
wise to use them sparingly and
document their use with lots of
comments.

Although these statements may look unusual, they are perfectly valid in C. Line 1 declares a union variable called aCharacter. The character 'Q' is stored in aCharacter on line 3. The program allocates 32 bits for the variable aCharacter because its largest member is of type int. The member asChar is of type char, so the statement on line 3 stores the 'Q' in the first 8 bits of the memory allocated for the variable aCharacter.

Once a value is stored into the variable aCharacter, we can access it using either the member asChar or the member asInt. On line 5, the memory for the variable is accessed through the asChar member. It is treated just like any other variable of type char.

Line 7 accesses the memory for aCharacter through the member asInt. This overwrites the 'Q' because both members of the union use the same memory space. The statement stores the number 7 into the variable. This can then be accessed either as a char or as an int. In fact, on line 8, the asChar member is used to retrieve the value and print it as a char. This statement will beep the speaker of most computers.

14.4   Enumerated Types

It's not unusual to need to define lists of related constants. C provides a method of creating groups of constants and associating them with a type. Because this method enumerates values for a type, it is called an **enumerated type**. The values associated with the enumerated type are called **enumerants**, or **enumerated values**.

Declare enumerated types with the C keyword enum. The enumerated values are actually integers in disguise. Technically speaking, enumerated values are mapped onto the set of integers.

Hands On 14.3 illustrates one way to use an enumerated type.

Hands On 14.3

Objective

Write a program that uses an enumerated type to enumerate colors.

Experiment

Type the following program into your IDE or text editor. Compile, link, and run it.

```
 1   #include <stdio.h>
 2
 3   enum colors
 4   {
 5           BLACK,
 6           RED,
 7           GREEN,
 8           BLUE,
 9           YELLOW,
10           CYAN,
11           MAGENTA,
12           DARK_RED,
13           DARK_GREEN,
14           DARK_BLUE,
15           BROWN,
16           DARK_CYAN,
17           PURPLE,
```

```
18          WHITE
19   };
20
21
22   int main()
23   {
24          enum colors rainbow;
25
26          for (rainbow=BLACK; rainbow<=WHITE; rainbow++)
27          {
28                  printf("%d\n",rainbow);
29          }
30
31          rainbow = 45;
32
33          return(0);
34   }
```

Results

```
0
1
2
3
4
5
6
7
8
9
10
11
12
13
```

Analysis

This program enumerates a group of related constants. The constants are colors. Using the enum keyword, it creates a list of constants and associates them with the type color. The program declares a variable of type color, assigns color values to it, and uses it in a for loop.

The for loop iterates through the list of color values. Because color values are actually integers, programs can use any operator on color variables that they can use on integer variables. In this case, the program uses the ++ operator to increment rainbow each time the for loop iterates. It also uses the <= operator to perform a comparison.

The Results section shows the values rainbow takes on each time through the loop. The first constant in the list is assigned the value of zero. Every subsequent constant is one greater than the constant before it.

The statement

```
rainbow = 45;
```

TIP 14.2
You may need to modify your compiler settings so that it will generate an error when your program treats enumerated types as integers. This is usually a good change to make.

on line 31 shows that any integer can be assigned to a variable of an enumerated type. This is true even if the integer value is not one of the enumerated values. However, your compiler may give you a warning about this. It may tell you that the program is trying to assign an integer value to an enumerated type. Most of the compilers that flag this with a warning will allow you to upgrade that warning to an error.

Enumerated types are used primarily for documenting programs. They can help you make your programs much clearer to read. If I wrote the loop in Hands On 14.3 like this

```
for (int i=0; i<=13; i++)
{
        printf("%d\n",i);
}
```

the intent of the loop would not be at all clear. Using the type name `color` and the enumerated color values clarifies that the `for` loop iterates through a list of colors.

Enumerated types are also a convenient way of defining lists of constants. Many programs define their error codes as enumerated types. Example 14.12 demonstrates this technique.

EXAMPLE 14.12   Defining Error Codes with enum

```
1   enum error_code
2   {
3           NO_ERROR,
4           NOT_ENOUGH_MEMORY,
5           INVALID_NUMERIC_VALUE,
6           INPUT_STRING_TOO_LONG,
7           EMPTY_INPUT_STRING,
8           VALUE_OUT_OF_RANGE,
9           INVALID_INPUT_DATA,
10          FILE_READ_ERROR,
11          FILE_WRITE_ERROR,
12          CANT_FIND_FILE,
13          INVALID_DIRECTORY_NAME,
14          INVALID_FILE_NAME,
15          NO_FILE_READ_PERMISSION,
16          NO_FILE_WRITE_PERMISSION
17  };
```

In professional programs, these lists of error codes can get *very* long. I personally have seen programs with literally thousands of enumerated error codes. It would be a real chore to maintain a list of error codes if they all were declared as constant integers.

Declaring error codes as enumerated values makes the compiler assign them values. You can switch them around, add new ones, or delete values from the list without having to renumber anything yourself.

You can also assign specific integer values to enumerants. Example 14.13 demonstrates this.

EXAMPLE 14.13   Assigning an Integer Value to Enumerants

```
1   enum error_code
2   {
3           NO_ERROR,
4           NOT_ENOUGH_MEMORY,
5           INVALID_NUMERIC_VALUE,
6           INPUT_STRING_TOO_LONG,
7           EMPTY_INPUT_STRING = 10,
8           VALUE_OUT_OF_RANGE,
9           INVALID_INPUT_DATA,
10          FILE_READ_ERROR,
11          FILE_WRITE_ERROR,
12          CANT_FIND_FILE,
13          INVALID_DIRECTORY_NAME = 100,
14          INVALID_FILE_NAME,
15          NO_FILE_READ_PERMISSION,
16          NO_FILE_WRITE_PERMISSION
17  };
```

As in Example 14.12, the constant NO_ERROR is assigned the value zero. The next three constants are assigned the values 1, 2, and 3, respectively. The constant EMPTY_INPUT_STRING is assigned the value 10 with the assignment statement. The following values increase by one. VALUE_OUT_OF_RANGE is assigned 11, INVALID_INPUT_DATA is assigned 12, and so on. INVALID_DIRECTORY_NAME is assigned the value 100. From there the values increase by one.

14.5 typedef

Type definitions are a way to rename a type. In C programming literature, this is also said to be a way of creating an "alias" for a type name. You can rename any type to another name regardless of whether it is a built-in type or a type that you create. Example 14.14 shows a few type definitions.

EXAMPLE 14.14 Some Type Definitions

```
typedef int integer;
typedef float real;
typedef struct a_structure_type another_structure_type;
```

The type definitions in this example each rename an existing type to new name. The first renames int to integer. The second renames float to real. After these type definitions, you can use both type names in your program. You can declare variables of type real or float. Both are valid type names after the compiler processes the typedef.

You can rename atomic types, structures, unions, or enumerated types. The statement

```
typedef struct a_structure_type another_structure_type;
```

renames the structure a_structure_type to another_structure_type. Again, both type names are valid after the type definition. You can declare variables of type a_structure_type or another_structure_type.

When you use type definitions with structures, unions, and enumerated types, you can give names to anonymous types. An anonymous type is a type that doesn't have a name. However, the type definition gives it a name.

Example 14.15 illustrates a structure that creates an anonymous type. What makes it anonymous is the fact that there is no type name after the keyword struct. Everything from the keyword struct to the closing brace (}) defines the type. The typedef statement renames that type from nothing to my_struct.

EXAMPLE 14.15 Renaming an Anonymous Type

```
typedef struct
{
        int intData;
        double doubleData;
} my_struct;
```

This style of programming is common in C. It enables us to use the word struct less frequently in our programs. After the compiler has processed the type definition in Example 14.15, the program can declare variable of type my_struct, as shown in Example 14.16.

EXAMPLE 14.16 Using a Renamed Structure Type

```
my_struct thisVariable;
```

There is no need to use the keyword struct before the type name my_struct. This helps us create types that look more like the atomic data types.

Renaming anonymous unions is like renaming anonymous structures. The only difference is that you use the word union instead of struct in the definition.

As Example 14.17 shows, the same technique can be used on an enumerated type.

EXAMPLE 14.17 Renaming an Anonymous Enumerated Type

```
1    typedef enum
2    {
3            BLACK,
4            RED,
5            GREEN,
6            BLUE,
7            YELLOW,
8            CYAN,
9            MAGENTA,
10           DARK_RED,
11           DARK_GREEN,
12           DARK_BLUE,
13           BROWN,
14           DARK_CYAN,
15           PURPLE,
16           WHITE
17   } color;
```

This statement creates an anonymous enumerated type and defines a group of constants to go with it. The effect of the typedef is to rename the anonymous type from no name to the name colors. Once that has been done, the program can declare variables of type color without needing to repeat the keyword enum, as Example 14.18 demonstrates.

EXAMPLE 14.18 Declaring Variables of Type color

```
1    color allColors;
2
3    for (allColors = BLACK;allColors<=WHITE;allColors++)
4    {
5            printf("The color is %d\n",allColors);
6    }
```

After the anonymous type has been renamed with the typedef statement, we can just use the type name to declare variables. Most programmers prefer this technique.

14.6   Troubleshooting Guide

After reading this section, you should be able to:

- Recognize and avoid problems stemming from creating duplicate enumerated values.
- Use type definitions to avoid portability problems.

14.6.1   Duplicate Enumerated Values

It's possible to create two or more enumerated values in an enumerated type that have exactly the same value. Example 14.19 shows how this problem occurs.

EXAMPLE 14.19 Duplicate Enumerated Values

```
1    enum my_values
2    {
3            VALUE1 = 1,
4            VALUE2 = -1,
5            VALUE3,  // =0
6            VALUE4   // =1
7    };
```

The enumerated value VALUE1 in this example is assigned the value 1. VALUE2 receives the value −1. The other enumerated values in the enumerated type are not explicitly assigned a value by a programmer. The C compiler will give VALUE3 a value of one more than the value of VALUE2. Therefore, VALUE3 is assigned 0, as the comment indicates. The C compiler increases the value of VALUE3 by one and assigns it to VALUE4, which is 1. This gives VALUE4 the same values as VALUE1. Example 14.20 contains a fragment of a C program. The program fragment tests the value of a variable to see if it is equal to VALUE4. Because VALUE1 and VALUE4 are equal, the test will evaluate to true. Usually, this is an error.

EXAMPLE 14.20　A Logical Error

```
1   my_values aValue = VALUE1;
2
3   if (aValue == VALUE4)
4   {
5           // Do some processing
6   }
```

The way to avoid this problem is to make sure that you never define the same value twice in an enumerated type. With *very* rare exceptions, each enumerated value should be unique.

14.6.2　Using typedef for Portability

When we're creating programs, it's easy to assume that the purpose of the software we're writing will always be the same. In practice, that's seldom true. Developers' assumptions often come back to haunt maintenance programmers.

In Example 14.21, we see the definition of a very useful structure type for a graphics program. For the simple task it accomplishes, it's globally well-designed. However, if you look at the example closely, you'll see that the structure contains a potentially serious error. Can you tell what it is?

EXAMPLE 14.21　A Seemingly Well-Designed Structure

```
1   typedef struct
2   {
3           int red;
4           int green;
5           int blue;
6   } rgb_color;
```

Any programmer defining a type such as this makes one basic assumption that is probably not true. The assumption is that the program will never be ported to a another type computer or another operating system.

The rgb_color type is intended for use in a graphics-oriented program. It defines a type that stores red, green, and blue color levels. The color values are defined as integers. On an operating system with a 16 bit integer, there are 65536. However, half of those are negative. Most hardware can't deal with negative color values. So a programmer who defines a type like this is probably assuming that the values will never be negative. That means there are really 32,768 possible color values each for red, green, and blue. This may be exactly what the programmer wants, given the computer and operating system for which he or she is developing the program.

Now let's suppose the company that produces this program decides to port it to many other computers and operating systems. On some of these systems, the number of possible colors is only 256 each for red, green, and blue. On some of the target systems there are over 4 million possible colors. On some, there are billions.

Do you see the porting problem here? On some systems, every occurrence of the word int must be changed to short. On others, it needs to be unsigned, long, or unsigned long. This does not initially seem like a large task. However, when programmers use structures such as this, they tend to define temporary variables to help them process the data in the structures. In the case of the type in Example 14.21, the temporary variables sprinkled throughout the program would be of type int. If the program were ported to another system, those same variables might need to be changed to short, long, unsigned long, or whatever else is appropriate.

TRAP 14.5
The Year 2000 bug is a perfect example of an incorrect programmer assumption. The original developers of many programs written in the 1960's, 1970's, and 1980's incorrectly assumed that their programs would not be in use in the year 2000. To save memory, they wrote their programs so that they represented dates using only the last two digits of the year. Because of this, their programs would not properly handle the transition to the new century. Although the spectacular Hollywood explosions and shut-downs predicted in the popular media did not occur, companies lost millions of dollars worth of data over this problem. Wise programmers build their software in such a way that their assumptions can easily be changed later.

One or more maintenance programmers must search through the entire program looking for integer variables that must be changed to another type. With each occurrence they find, they'll be cursing the name of the original developer of this data type (not really, but they won't be happy).

Example 14.22 illustrates an easy way to avoid this entire problem. It uses a `typedef` statement to create a type called `color_value`. When the program is ported, the developer doing the port has to change only the `int` in the `typedef` statement to `short` (or `long`, or `unsigned`, or whatever else is appropriate) and then recompile. The job will be done. If you design software this way, maintenance programmers will sing your praises for generations to come (another exaggeration, but they'll be a lot happier).

TIP 14.3
One way to increase the portability of your program is to use a `typedef` to easily create aliases for types that would change when the program is rewritten for the new computer or operating system.

EXAMPLE 14.22   A More Portable `rgb_color` Class

```
1   typedef int color_value;
2   typedef struct
3   {
4        color_value red;
5        color_value green;
6        color_value blue;
7   } rgb_color;
```

SUMMARY

In addition to the built-in types, C provides structures, unions, enumerated types, and type definitions. You can use all of these to create types for your programs.

Structures enable developers to define complex data types. Data for structures is stored in the structure's members. Structure members may be of any type.

Unions are similar to structures. However, unlike structures, all of the data members of unions share the same memory space. When a program declares a union variable it allocates only enough space for the largest data member. All of the union's data members share that same memory space.

Enumerated types give us a way to create a type and associate constants with it. The compilers map the enumerated values onto the set of integers.

Type definitions give you a way to rename types. This helps document your program. It can also increase your program's portability.

TECHNICAL NOTES

14.1   Once a structure is defined, the type is visible and available for use from the point it is defined until the end of the file.

14.2   Although a structure's type name may be visible through an entire file, a structure variables follow the same rules as other variables. They are visible only in the functions in which they are declared.

14.3   The C compiler allocates enough memory for only the largest member of a union. All union members share that memory.

TIPS

14.1   Structures must be both defined and declared before they can be used in a program.

14.2   You may need to modify your compiler settings so that it will generate an error when your program treats enumerated types as integers. This is usually a good change to make.

14.3   One way to increase the portability of your program is to use a `typedef` to easily create aliases for types that would change when the program is rewritten for the new computer or operating system.

TRAPS

14.1   Confusingly, some literature on C programming refers to individual structure members as data members. A data member is one data item in a structure. A structure's member data is all of the structure's members taken together.

14.2 When you first start using arrays and structures together, it can be confusing. However, it is easier if you remember a few simple rules:

- If the variable is an array of structures, every structure in the array must be accessed with an array subscript. The array subscript must be attached to the variable name.

- If a structure contains a member that is an array, each element in the array must be accessed with an array subscript. The array subscript must be attached to the member name.

- If the variable is an array of structures that have members that are arrays, both the variable name and the member name must have subscripts.

14.3 Variables whose types are built from nested structures can consume large amounts of memory. You must weigh the benefits of using nested structures against the need, if any, to conserve memory.

14.4 Because union members all access the same memory, using them can be confusing to maintenance programmers. In general, it's wise to use them sparingly and document their use with lots of comments.

14.5 The Year 2000 bug is a perfect example of an incorrect programmer assumption. The original developers of many programs written in the 1960s, 1970s, and 1980s incorrectly assumed that their programs would not be in use in the year 2000. To save memory, they wrote their programs so that they represented dates using only the last two digits of the year. Because of this, their programs would not properly handle the transition to the new century. Although the spectacular Hollywood explosions and shut-downs predicted in the popular media did not occur, companies lost millions of dollars worth of data over this problem. Wise programmers build their software in such a way that their assumptions can easily be changed later.

REVIEW QUESTIONS

1. What is the difference between a structure and a union?
2. How are structure members accessed?
3. What is an enumerated type?
4. What are some of the advantages of using enumerated types? What are some of the disadvantages?
5. Why would having duplicate enumerated values be a potential problem in a program?
6. What does a type definition do?
7. What is an anonymous type? How are they used in conjunction with `typedef` statements?
8. How can type definitions be used to increase the portability of a program?
9. How can programmer assumptions cause problems later in a program's life cycle?
10. What are some of the techniques you've learned in this book to decrease potential maintenance problems in your software?

EXERCISES

1. Fill in the blanks.

   Programmer-defined types such as _____, _____, _____ _____, and _____ _____ enable developers to create types that model their data.

2. Explain how programmer-defined types can be used to model ideas, things in the real world, and things that don't exist.

3. Fill in the blanks.

   Enumerated values are really _____. Variables of enumerated types can be assigned any valid _____ value. However, if you assign such a variable an _____ value instead of one of the type's enumerated values, your compiler may give you a warning.

4. Describe the differences between structures and unions.

5. Fill in the blank.

   The `typedef` statement creates an _____ for a type name.

6. Explain how programmer-defined types can be used to enhance a program's portability.

7. Write a program that uses the `typedef` and `enum` statements to define a type called `day_of_week`. Your enumerated type should also define the following constants: SUNDAY, MONDAY, TUESDAY, WEDNESDAY, THURSDAY, FRIDAY, and SATURDAY. Prompt the user for an integer in the range of 1–7. If the user enters a 1, your program should print the string `"Sunday"`. If the user enters a 2, your program should print the string `"Monday"`, and so on.

8. Arrays are homogenous (all of the same type) collections of data. Structures and unions enable programmers to create nonhomogenous (not all of the same type) collections of data. Explain why both are needed in the C programming language.

9. Examine the following structure. Notice that it contains a member called selfReference.

```
struct this_type
{
        char aString[10];
        int stringLength;

        struct this_type selfReference;
};
```

Write a program that defines this structure and uses it. Compile the program and explain your results. Explain why you think this should or should not be allowed by the C programming language. Hint: How much memory should the program allocate for this structure when your program declares a variable of type this_type?

10. Write a program that uses a union called type_change. The union should have two data members. The first should be an integer, and the second should be a floating-point number. In your program, declare a type_change variable and store the value 123.456 into it as a floating-point number. Retrieve the value from the variable as an integer and print it. Explain the results.

11. Write a program that uses a union called int_to_char. The union should have an integer and a character data member. Declare a variable of type int_to_char. Store the values 7, 10, and 65 into the variable as integers. Retrieve them as characters and print each character.

12. Create an enumerated type called logical. The logical type should have the constants FALSE and TRUE associated with it. The value of TRUE should be one. The constant FALSE should equal zero. Write a program that demonstrates your enumerated type. Do not use #define statements in this program.

13. Suppose you are writing a multiplayer network game. Create an enumerated type called network_message. Imagine that the game uses this enumerated type to send event messages over the network. Associate ten constants that you make up with the network_message type. These should indicate player events such as PLAYER_MOVED_LEFT, PLAYER_MOVED_RIGHT, and so on. In addition, include a constant at the beginning called NETWORK_MESSAGE_FIRST and another at the end of the list called NETWORK_MESSAGE_LAST which indicates the lowest and highest message values. Write a program that prompts the user for an integer between the highest and lowest message value. If the user inputs a value outside that range, your program should output an error message. If the user inputs a valid value, print a message indicating that a network message was received. Also print its value and a text description of it.

14. Design a portable type called point_3d. The point_3d type should have data members that contain X, Y, and Z values of a point in 3-D space. On some systems, the X, Y, and Z components of the point will need to be integers. On others, they will need to be floating point numbers or doubles. Design your type appropriately. Initially, they should be integers. Write a program to demonstrate your point_3d type.

15. Use the point_3d type you designed for Exercise 14. Change the type so that it stores the X, Y, and Z values as floating point numbers instead of integers. Recompile your program and demonstrate that it works. You should need to change only one statement in your program.

16. Design a portable type called rgb_color. The rgb_color type should contain three members, called red, green, and blue. On some computers, these members will be of type int. On others, they will be short or long. Design your type appropriately. Initially, they should be integers. Write a program to demonstrate that your rgb_color type.

17. Use the rgb_color type you designed for Exercise 16. Change the type so that it stores the red, green, and blue values as long integers instead of integers. Recompile your program and demonstrate that it works. You should need to change only one statement in your program.

18. Write a program that uses the nested structures defined in Example 14.8. Your program should declare an array of 5 structures of type customer. It must then prompt the user to enter the customer information for each customer structure in the array. Finally, it should print the information in the array of structures.

19. Using the typedef and struct statements create a type called date_type. The date_type type should contain integer fields for the day, month, and year. Write a program that prompts the user for ten dates and stores them in an array of date_type structures. After the user has entered the dates, the program should print them.

20. Use the program you wrote for Exercise 19. Add a structure called time_type that contains fields to store the hour, minute, and seconds values. Also create a type called date_time_stamp which contains a date and a time. Instead of an array of ten date_type structures, your program should use an array of ten date_time_stamp structures. Your program should prompt the user for ten dates and times. It should ensure that the dates and times are valid. After it has retrieved ten dates and times from the user and stored them in the array of date_time_stamp structures, your program should print them.

21. Use the program you wrote for Exercise 20. Your program should print the array of date_time_stamp structures in unsorted order after it has retrieved ten date and time values from the user. It will then use the pseudocode algorithm

presented below to sort the structures in the array of `date_time_stamp` structures. This algorithm is called the Bubble Sort. After the structures are sorted, it must print the structures in sorted order. Note: The algorithm below assumes that the array of `date_time_stamp` structures is called `allTimeStamps`.

```
// For each array element...
for (i=0;i<10;i++)
{
        // For each element less than the current element
        for (j=0;j<i;j++)
        {
                if (the date and time in allTimeStamps[i] <
                    the date and time in allTimeStamps[j])
                {
                    /* Swap the values in
                    allTimeStamps[i] and
                    allTimeStamps[j]. */
                }
        }
}
```

22. Write a reservation program for MegaProp Airlines. This airline has one plane which seats 10 people. The reservation program should declare an array of ten structures of type `seating_reservation`. The `seating_reservation` structure should contain a structure of type `name`. The `name` structure should contain members for an individual passenger's first and last names. The `seating_reservation` structure should also contain a structure called `seat_identifier`. The `seat_identifier` structure should have members to hold the seat's row numbers and seat letters. Row numbers range from 1 to 3. The first row contains two seats, A and B. These are both window seats. Rows two and three contain four seats each, A, B, C, and D. A and B are on the left side of the aisle as you face the back of the plane. C and D are on the right. A and D are the window seats. Your program should display the following menu:

```
Select an option:
A) Show All Empty Seats
B) Show All Empty Aisle Seats
C) Show All Empty Window Seats
D) Assign a Customer to a Seat
E) Delete a Seat Assignment
F) Show All Seat Assignments
```

When the user enters a selection of A–F, your program should perform the requested function. Make sure that users cannot enter invalid row and seat identifiers.

23. Electrical engineers use complex numbers in integrated circuit design. Complex numbers are numbers that have a real part and an imaginary part. The imaginary part is a number that is multiplied by the square root of −1. The imaginary part of a complex number is represented by a number and the letter i. For instance, 5i is an imaginary part of a complex number. The real part is represented by a number and the letter j. 10j would be an example of a real part of a complex number. So the resulting complex number would be $5i + 10j$.

Two complex numbers are added by adding their respective imaginary parts together and then adding their respective real parts together. For example, adding the complex number $5i + 10j$ to $20i + 30j$ is done as follows:

$$
\begin{array}{r}
5i + 10j \\
+\ 20i + 30j \\
\hline
25i + 40j
\end{array}
$$

Define a structure called `complex_number` that implements the complex number data type. Write a function that takes two `complex_number` parameters, adds them together, and returns the result. Write a program that demonstrates that your function works.

24. Complex numbers can be subtracted from one another by subtracting the real part of the first number from the real part of the second and subtracting the imaginary part fo the first number from the imaginary part of the second.

For example, subtracting the complex number $5i + 10j$ from $20i + 30j$ is done as follows:

$$
\begin{array}{r}
20i + 30j \\
-\ 5i + 10j \\
\hline
15i + 20j
\end{array}
$$

Use the `complex_number` type you created in Exercise 23. Write a function that takes two complex numbers as parameters, subtracts them, and returns the result. Write a program that demonstrates that your function works.

25. Create a table like the one below. Have it list every C language statement presented in this chapter that is used to create programmer-defined data types. For every statement, it should contain a description of what the statement does, and when to use it.

C Language Statement	What It Does	When To Use It

GLOSSARY

Data Encapsulation   Creating a type that combines related data into a unit. Variables of the new data type should be accessed through a set of functions that are provided with the type. Through this means, programs do not access data items in the type directly. The associated functions provide safe access to the type.

Data Hiding   See **Data Encapsulation**.

Data Model   Data that is structured to fit the current programming situation.

Enumerant   Another name for an enumerated value.

Enumerated Type   A type definition that defines not only a type but also a group of constants associated with the type.

Enumerated Value   A constant defined in an `enum` statement.

Member   One data item in a structure or union.

Member Data   All of the data items in a structure or union taken together.

Nested Structure   A structure which has one or more members that are also structures.

15

Designing Data Types

OBJECTIVES

After reading this chapter, you should be able to:

- Determine the essential attributes of a type.
- Determine the essential operations on a type.

OUTLINE

PREVIEW

This chapter deals with the skills that required for designing and developing robust, useful C types. Be sure to attempt as many of the Exercises at the end of the chapter as you can. They will walk you through the process of designing types.

15.1   Type Attributes

Recall that programmer-defined types are used to model things in the real world, things that don't exist, and ideas.

In C terminology, structure and union types are composed of member data. The member data describes whatever the type models. They are its **attributes**. You and I have attributes (height, weight, hair color, and so on) that describe us. All data types have attributes as well. Once we determine that a type is required in the software we are writing, we must ask ourselves what attributes are important for the type to have.

15.1.1   Finding Essential Attributes

The essential attributes that a type requires depend entirely on the context of the type. For instance, a customer record type in a database program for a software store would probably include attributes such as name and address. It would probably not include shoe size. However, shoe size might be an important attribute in a customer record type of a database for a shoe store. Both databases need a customer record type. However, the importance of certain attributes is different in each context.

Software usually responds to **events**. An event is some stimulus that generates a reaction from the program. Think about living things, like the person sitting next to you. If you poke that person, you will usually provoke a reaction. The act of poking your neighbor (not a suggested activity) is an event. What your neighbor does when the event occurs is the reaction.

Events come from a variety of sources. The person using the software triggers most of the events to which a program responds. For instance, when a user selects an item from a menu, that action is an event. The software must respond to that event. Pressing keys on the keyboard, moving the mouse, and clicking mouse buttons all cause events that the software may need to handle. Events also can be caused by the passage of time (a timed backup, for instance).

The events a type responds to can help you determine what attributes the type requires. As an example, if you are writing a simulation of a hockey game, you will undoubtedly need a puck type in the software. The primary event to which a puck type must

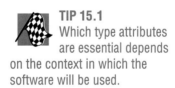
TIP 15.1
Which type attributes are essential depends on the context in which the software will be used.

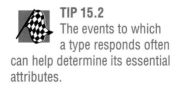
TIP 15.2
The events to which a type responds often can help determine its essential attributes.

respond is coming into contact with something else in the game (hockey sticks, goal nets, walls, and so on). The puck must react by changing position, speed, or direction. Therefore, the puck must keep track of its current position, speed, and direction. These are its essential attributes.

TIP 15.3
Design reviews in which you describe your types to another software engineer are a great tool for designing types.

Another helpful way to isolate the important attributes of types is to describe them. Several software design methodologies require a written description of each type in the program. You may or may not want your programming to be that formal. However, it can still be helpful to sit down with another software engineer on the project and describe your software types to him or her. As you do, the other software engineer can write down a list of the important attributes. See how well your lists agree. Conducting design reviews such as this can help every member of your team design a better set of types.

15.1.2 Choosing Attribute Types

After you've identified what attributes (member data) a programmer-defined type needs, you must choose the type of each attribute. This choice also frequently depends on the context.

TIP 15.4
The appropriate type for each member of a structure depends on the software's context and goals.

For example, if you are writing a 3-D aircraft simulation, you will need to keep track of the plane's current position as it flies through the 3-D simulated world. You can use floating-point numbers for these attributes, or you can use integers. Using floating-point numbers normally results in greater accuracy. This can be very important for a simulator that is used to train commercial airline pilots. However, for a game that people play on their personal computers, accuracy is often not as important as smooth animation. To get the performance you need on a personal computer, you may choose to sacrifice accuracy for speed. Tracking the user's position using integers is typically faster on microcomputers because they may not have the capability to process floating-point numbers that high-end hardware has.

As you select the type of each attribute, you must strive to be as flexible as possible. All too often, designers of databases forget that people have a wide variety of names. I have a friend whose last name is Vander Hooven. He often complains to me about computer systems for businesses and government agencies that choke on his name. They were designed for people with a single last name, and they can't handle it when users enter two words for a last name. Often, he gets mail addressed to Vanderhooven, which makes him angry, or Van Derhooven, which he usually just throws away.

TIP 15.5
It's helpful to be as flexible as possible when you are picking the types for member data.

Unfortunately, systems designers often don't account for non-English punctuation in names. There are punctuation marks that are used in Spanish, French, and German names that are not used in English names. The same is true of names from many other languages. When we select or create types for structure attributes, they must account for all possibilities.

In actual practice, it's next to impossible to account for all future possibilities when you select type attributes. Therefore, you must design your types in such a way that you can change the type of attributes without impacting other types in the system.

15.2 Operations on Programmer-Defined Types

For the important types that we create as structures, we need to provide a set of functions that perform operations on variables of that type. This approach gives both us and others working with us a set of standard ways to operate on that type.

Example 15.1 repeats the program from Hands On 14.2. In addition to defining the `complex_number` type, it provides two functions, `PrintComplexNumber()` and `AddComplexNumbers()`. Once these functions are written, the processes of printing complex numbers to the screen and adding them together are standardized. Neither we nor other programmers using our `complex_number` type ever have to write code for those tasks again.

EXAMPLE 15.1   A Type with a Set of Type Operations

```
1   #include <stdio.h>
2
3   struct complex_number
```

```
 4   {
 5        double i,j;
 6   };
 7
 8
 9   struct complex_number GetComplexNumber(void);
10   void PrintComplexNumber(
11                struct complex_number numberToPrint);
12   struct complex_number AddComplexNumbers(
13                        struct complex_number firstNumber,
14                        struct complex_number secondNumber);
15
16
17   int main()
18   {
19        struct complex_number aComplexNumber;
20        struct complex_number anotherComplexNumber;
21        struct complex_number result;
22
23        printf("\nPlease enter a complex number. Type the\n");
24        printf("imaginary part of the number, then press Enter.");
25        printf("\nNext, type the real part of the ");
26        printf("number.\n");
27        aComplexNumber = GetComplexNumber();
28
29        printf("\nPlease enter another complex number. \n");
30        anotherComplexNumber = GetComplexNumber();
31
32        result = AddComplexNumbers(aComplexNumber,
33                                   anotherComplexNumber);
34
35        printf("\n");
36        printf("  ");
37        PrintComplexNumber(aComplexNumber);
38        printf("\n");
39        printf("+ ");
40        PrintComplexNumber(anotherComplexNumber);
41        printf("\n");
42        printf("-------------------------\n");
43        printf("  ");
44        PrintComplexNumber(result);
45        printf("\n");
46
47        return (0);
48   }
49
50
51   struct complex_number GetComplexNumber(void)
52   {
53        struct complex_number theNumber;
54
55        printf("Imaginary part: ");
56        scanf("%lf",&theNumber.i);
57        printf("Real part: ");
58        scanf("%lf",&theNumber.j);
59
60        return (theNumber);
61   }
```

```
62
63    void PrintComplexNumber(
64             struct complex_number numberToPrint)
65    {
66         printf("(%lfi + %lfj)",
67             numberToPrint.i,
68             numberToPrint.j);
69    }
70
71
72    struct complex_number AddComplexNumbers(
73                    struct complex_number firstNumber,
74                    struct complex_number secondNumber)
75    {
76         struct complex_number result;
77
78         result.i = firstNumber.i + secondNumber.i;
79         result.j = firstNumber.j + secondNumber.j;
80
81         return (result);
82    }
```

In a commercial application, there would be many more functions provided with a type that implements complex numbers. Exactly what those functions should be depends on a number of factors. In a program that makes only light use of complex numbers, developers may be able to get away with writing a very small group of functions. High-end programs that perform complicated calculations and make heavy use of complex numbers would need a very large and complete set of functions to operate on them.

In programming literature, the functions provided with a programmer-defined type are often referred to as its **type interface**. They can also be called its **application program interface** (API).

Our task in designing the interface for a type is to create an interface that is minimal but complete.

TECHNICAL NOTE 15.1
The set of functions provided to perform operations on a programmer-defined type can be called its application program interface (API), its type interface, or just its interface.

TIP 15.6
Type interfaces should be both minimal and complete.

15.2.1 Designing a Minimal Interface

It's easy to create too many functions in a type's interface. We want our types to be convenient and powerful to use. As a result, we tend to add more functions than are really needed.

On most projects, other programmers will use our types. They may find our types difficult to understand if the types' interfaces are overburdened with extra functions. They tend to get lost in a maze of detail.

In addition, it's not up to us as programmers to predict all possible future uses of our types. That doesn't mean we should disregard all future needs. However, with some planning and forethought, we can create types that others can easily extend and enhance. If our types employ a well-designed and minimal set of functions for their interfaces, enhancing them later is generally straightforward.

TIP 15.7
A type's interface of functions should not contain extra or duplicate functions.

Suppose, for example, that we create a type that has a function called Copy(). Some users may prefer the name of the function to be Duplicate(). Others might it to be Clone(). We can accommodate them all by creating Duplicate() and Clone() functions that call the Copy() function. However, we are not creating a minimal interface. Some programmers will inevitably wonder what the difference between Duplicate(), Clone(), and Copy() is. Using three function names in an interface to do exactly the same thing will generate more confusion than is worthwhile.

15.2.2 Designing a Complete Interface

Type interfaces should also be complete. They must allow programmers to do anything with the type that they might reasonably expect to do. The definition of reasonable is very subjective. However, there are a few guidelines that you can follow that will help.

TIP 15.8
When designing and developing types, look for repetitive tasks that you perform on types which require large chunks of code. Consider making these tasks interface functions.

TIP 15.9
When designing and developing types, add interface functions that reduce the likelihood of programmer errors.

As you design and develop your software, look for tasks that you perform on types repetitively. Are these tasks simple functions calls? Or do you repeatedly need to write many lines of code to complete the task? If it's the latter, you might think about including a function in the type's interface that performs the task.

Also, we should ask ourselves if there are errors programmers repeatedly make whenever they use our types. If so, we may need to examine what they are trying to get our types to do. If they are using our types in unexpected ways, we may need to add interface functions to accommodate them.

15.3   Identifying Essential Types in a Program

Before we start designing types in the software we write, we must identify the types we will use to construct our programs. Many books which expound a large variety of software design methods are currently available. Each has its own unique way of identifying the types that are essential to a software system. However, most of them share some common ideas.

The first is an idea we've already mentioned: types usually react to one or more events.

When you design types, it can be helpful to pretend that you are the type. Make it justify its existence. Say,

"I am a *type_name*. My purpose is to *type_action*. The events that I react to are *event_list*."

where *type_name* is the name of the type you are testing, *type_action* is the type's primary purpose or action, and *event_list* is the group of events to which it reacts.

If you have trouble stating the primary purpose of a type or find that it does not react to any events, you probably don't need the type in the software.

The top-down design techniques in Chapter 13 identify the tasks that a program must perform. Knowing the tasks a program must accomplish helps us determine the events which cause a response from the software. It is often helpful to use a spreadsheet program to make a list of all of the tasks that the program has to handle. From this, generate the group of events that would cause each task to begin.

For instance, a text editor must save a document to a file. That is one of its tasks. It performs that task when particular events occur. One of the events is the selection of Save from the File menu by the user. Another might be the user clicking a mouse button on a Save icon in a toolbar. Another might be a timed backup.

Once you identify the tasks and events, select the appropriate type to handle the event. Here again, a spreadsheet can be useful. Start with a list of tasks in a column. In the next column, list the events that cause the task to be performed. In another column, list the types that handle the event. Table 15.1 shows a partial list for a text editor.

TABLE 15.1   A Partial List of Types for a Text Editor

Task	Trigger Event	Type
Save a file.	Selecting Save from the File menu.	`menu, menu_item, text_buffer`
Load a file.	Selecting Load from the File menu.	`menu, menu_item, text_buffer`
Move cursor left.	Pressing the left arrow key.	`screen_cursor, insertion_point_cursor`

TIP 15.10
If a type is used to accomplish only one task in a program, then it should be left out if it does not simplify or modularize the software or make it more portable.

The table shows that two or more tasks can require the same types. This indicates that these are important types in the program. If a type is needed to accomplish only one task, it's always good to ask if the type is really necessary. If the type simplifies or modularizes the software, it is worth creating. Also, if it makes the software more portable, it may be worth creating. If it doesn't do any of these things, it's better to leave the type out.

You may also find it helpful to imagine your system without the type you are designing. Would it make a difference in the software if the type was eliminated? The larger the impact, the more likely that the type should be in the software.

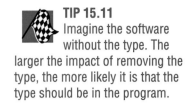

TIP 15.11
Imagine the software without the type. The larger the impact of removing the type, the more likely it is that the type should be in the program.

As you are designing, you periodically encounter type operations and attributes that naturally cluster together. These usually indicate the need for a new type. Example 15.2 shows a `customer_info` structure which could be used in software for a video rental store.

EXAMPLE 15.2   A customer_info Structure

```
1    struct
2    {
3           char firstName[40];
4           char middleInitial;
5           char lastName[40];
6           char address1[40];
7           char address2[40];
8           char city[40];
9           char state[3];
10          unsigned zip;
11          char moviesRented[100];
12          int movieListLength;
13   } customer_info;
```

Notice that certain attributes form natural groups. There are three attributes associated with the customer's name. There are five attributes associated with the customer's address. Two attributes are used for keeping a list of movies that the customer has rented. A program using this type would undoubtedly contain functions for setting and retrieving the value of each of these attributes.

This type should be broken down into more types. The name attributes, the address attributes, and the list attributes should each be clustered together into their own types. Example 15.3 demonstrates how the `customer_info` type might be revised.

EXAMPLE 15.3   A Revised customer_info Structure

```
1    typedef struct
2    {
3           char firstName[40];
4           char middleInitial;
5           char lastName[40];
6    } customer_name;
7
8    typedef struct
9    {
10          char address1[40];
11          char address2[40];
12          char city[40];
13          char state[3];
14          unsigned zip;
15   } customer_address;
16
17   typedef struct
18   {
19          char moviesRented[100];
20          int movieListLength;
21   } rental_list;
22
23   typedef struct
24   {
25          customer_name name;
26          customer_address address;
27          rental_list movieList;
28   } customer_info;
```

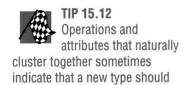

TIP 15.12
Operations and attributes that naturally cluster together sometimes indicate that a new type should be created.

Breaking a large structure into smaller structures in this way can make it much easier to modify and enhance a program later. For example, we may need to add a member for the apartment number in an address. If we're using the `customer_info` structure from Example 15.2, it's likely that adding the extra field would force us to change many functions in a program. Isolating the address into a separate structure will generally mean that changes to the address will impact a smaller number of functions.

Breaking large structures into a collection of smaller structures whose attributes naturally cluster together may make the program easier to maintain.

15.4   Troubleshooting Guide

After reading this section, you should be able to:

- Recognize and fix problems with type attributes.
- Recognize and fix problems with type interfaces.

15.4.1   Troubles with Attributes

When determining type attributes, it's easy to create problems as we try to solve them. Let's take a look at some of the most common types of errors novice C programmers make as they choose type attributes.

TECHNICAL NOTE 15.2
When we decrease the amount of memory a program uses, we say that we are reducing its memory footprint.

Too Few Attributes   Let's face it, no matter how much memory is installed on a computer, it's never enough. As developers, we're constantly looking for ways to reduce the amount of memory our programs use. One of the easiest ways to do this is to reduce the amount of data that each type stores. While this is generally a good goal, it can lead to problems.

One way to tell that you've packaged too little information in a type is if you are constantly calculating values that you will use with a type.

TIP 15.13
If you (or other programmers) are repeatedly calculating values for use with a type, your type may not have enough attributes.

Let's say I create a type called `parts_list` that does not store the length of the list. Let's also suppose I don't provide a function that calculates the length of the list. If you are using my `parts_list` type, you will need to repeatedly write loops that scan the list and count the number of items in it. This need indicates a problem with the design. If memory is so limited that I don't think it best to store the length of the list in the type, then I should provide a function which performs that calculation. If the memory requirements for my application are not that stringent, I should store the length in my `parts_list` type.

TIP 15.14
If other programmers are all adding the same attributes to types that we create, then we've left an important attribute out.

When other programmers on our current project can't seem to use our types without adding more attributes to them, we probably need to take a look at our design. It may be that there are many different uses for the types we've designed. It's possible that it is most efficient for other programmers to extend our design in ways that suit them. However, we should ask ourselves if there is common information that most of the other programmers are adding. If so, we have a strong indication that we've left an important attribute out.

Too Many Attributes   Imagine I'm writing the Space Attackers game from Chapter 13. I determine that I need a type to represent attackers in software. Example 15.4 shows one possible version of that type.

EXAMPLE 15.4   An attacker Class

```
1   typedef struct
2   {
3          int upLeftX,upLeftY,lowRigthX,lowRightY;
4          int height, width;
5          bitmap attackerImage;
6          int speed, acceleration;
7          movement_direction currentDirection;
8   } attacker;
```

This `attacker` type contains four integers which define a rectangle for the attacker's image. Positions on computer screens are commonly defined by pixel locations. A pixel is a tiny dot in the screen that lights up with a color specified by software. Each pixel

TECHNICAL NOTE 15.3
A pixel is an abbreviation for **pi**cture **el**ement. A pixel is one tiny dot on your computer screen. Your program can turn it on and set its color.

location has an *x* and *y* coordinate associated with it. These coordinates represent the column and row number of each pixel. The `attacker` type keeps track of the pixel location of the upper left and lower right corners of the attacker's image.

The `attacker` type also contains the height and width, in pixels, of the attacker's image. This is redundant information. My `attacker` type takes up more memory than it should. If the `attacker` type contains the two corner positions, I can calculate the height and width when it is needed. If it contains the height and width, I can leave out one of the corner positions. With one corner and the height and width, I can calculate the position of the other corner.

You justifiably might ask if having both the corner positions and the height and width would save some time. After all, it would decrease the number of calculations my program needs to perform. To a certain extent, that is correct. However, there is overhead associated with passing information to functions. In this case, the extra overhead incurred when I pass `attacker` variables to functions could decrease performance enough to offset any increase I might get in not calculating the information.

This example may seem to conflict with the previous section, which warns against having too few attributes. Competing considerations such as these are common. As you design types, you are constantly pulled in two directions. You want the type to contain all of the information it should. However, you don't want to put so much information into it that it degrades performance. Much of programming ends up being a balancing act between how much memory and how much microprocessor time a program uses.

Irrelevant Attributes   All of the attributes in a type should be related to each other and to the type itself. They should describe whatever is being modeled by the type. That may seem to be a somewhat obvious statement. However, you'll find types you encounter on the job may not follow this guideline.

One common method programmers use to get rid of global variables is to package them all together into a structure and to pass the structure to functions in the program. The resulting structure contains attributes that are not related to the structure itself or to each other. Packaging the global variables into a structure enables programmers to turn global variables into local variables. They can then pass the structure to all functions that would reference a global variable. Unfortunately, this technique doesn't solve the problem of global variables.

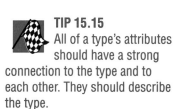

TIP 15.15
All of a type's attributes should have a strong connection to the type and to each other. They should describe the type.

Global variables create too strong of a connection between program modules.[1] It's hard to use or enhance any one piece of the program without affecting the rest. Often, programmers who enhance a program find that they must throw away and rewrite large parts of it because it depends on global variables. Simply combining unrelated global variables into a single type doesn't remove the connection between the program modules.

TIP 15.16
Make attribute names self-documenting.

Poor Attribute Names   Type attributes are variables. Like all variables, they should be well-named. Avoid cryptic abbreviations. In general, programmers looking at your code will not find one-letter variable names helpful. The exceptions to this are when you are writing an extremely trivial application or when you are writing a computer graphics applications that uses *x*, *y*, and *z* coordinates.

For the most part, variables with names like `q`, `r`, or `dx` don't communicate enough information to maintenance programmers to be useful. Choose names that document themselves. Instead of `dx`, try `deltaX` to indicate a change in *x* position. Rather than a variable named `r`, use one named `radius` to store the radius of a circle.

15.4.2   Trouble with Operations

The operations on a type can suffer from the same difficulties as the attributes. The same general rules apply. We mentioned earlier in this chapter that we should try to create types with interfaces which contain enough functions, but not too many. All of the functions which perform operations on a type should relate directly to the type itself. They should also relate to each other. The name of each function should be a short but specific description of what the function does.

---

[1]They create too much cohesion between program modules. See Maureen Sprankle, *Problem Solving and Programming Concepts,* (Upper Saddle River, NJ: Prentice Hall, Inc., 1992), pp. 66–67.

SUMMARY

When designing software, we must identify the tasks the software must perform. We use this information to generate a list of events to which the software will respond. From that, we can identify and design the software types. This process includes identifying the types that are needed, the data they contain, and the operations that can be performed on the data.

Well-designed types contain a minimal but complete set of attributes. They support a minimal but complete set of

interface functions. The interface is appropriate for the type. It provides the set of operations that programmers would reasonably expect from the type.

Types that are easy to use are well-named. So are their member data and interface functions.

TECHNICAL NOTES

15.1 The set of functions provided to perform operations on a programmer-defined type can be called its application program interface (API), or just its interface.

15.2 When we decrease the amount of memory a program uses, we say that we are reducing its memory footprint.

15.3 A pixel is an abbreviation for **pi**cture **el**ement. A pixel is one tiny dot on your computer screen. Your program can set its color.

TIPS

15.1 Which type attributes are essential depends on the context in which the software will be used.

15.2 The events to which a type responds often can help determine its essential attributes.

15.3 Design reviews in which you describe your types to another software engineer are a great tool for designing types.

15.4 The appropriate type for each member of a structure depends on the software's context and goals.

15.5 It's helpful to be as flexible as possible when you are picking the types for member data.

15.6 Type interfaces should be both minimal and complete.

15.7 A type's interface of functions should not contain extra or duplicate functions.

15.8 When designing and developing types, look for repetitive tasks that you perform on types which require large chunks of code. Consider making these tasks interface functions.

15.9 When designing and developing types, add interface functions that reduce the likelihood of programmer errors.

15.10 If a type is used to accomplish only one task in a program, then it should be left out if it does not simplify or modularize the software, or make it more portable.

15.11 Imagine the software without the type. The larger the impact of removing the type, the more likely it is that the type should be in the program.

15.12 Operations and attributes that naturally cluster together sometimes indicate that a new type should be created.

15.13 If you (or other programmers) are repeatedly calculating values for use with a type, your type may not have enough attributes.

15.14 If other programmers are all adding the same attributes to types that we create, then we've left an important attribute out.

15.15 All of a type's attributes should have a strong connection to the type and to each other. They should describe the type.

15.16 Make attribute names self-documenting.

REVIEW QUESTIONS

1. How do you identify the essential types in a software system?
2. How can you identify types that may not be needed in the software?
3. How do you select the most important attributes for a type?
4. What guidelines are important to consider when selecting types for member data?
5. In what ways can you determine whether or not your type's set of interface functions is minimal?
6. In what ways can you determine whether or not your type's set of interface functions is complete?
7. How can you tell when you have too many or too few attributes in a type?
8. What guidelines should you follow to ensure your types attributes and operations are relevant?
9. How do you pick good names for your types, member data, and interface functions?
10. What should be your most important goals when designing software types?

1. Fill in the blanks.

   An _____ is a data item that describes the types characteristics. An _____ is a stimulus to which a type reacts.

2. Describe the method presented in this chapter for determining what types are needed to implement a program.

3. Fill in the blanks.

   The set of functions provided with a programmer-defined type is called the type's _____ _____ _____.

4. List the advantages and disadvantages of providing a set of interface functions with a programmer-defined type.

5. Explain what it means to define a minimal but complete set of interface functions with a programmer-defined type.

6. Tell whether you think making an interface of functions complete or minimal is more important. Explain why.

7. Describe a method of increasing the portability of programmer-defined types.

8. Explain what a design review is and how it might help you design types for a program.

9. Describe conditions that might indicate your program needs an additional type defined in it.

10. Explain how to tell if your type has too many or too few attributes.

11. Give five examples of good attribute names and five examples of bad attribute names. Explain why they are good or bad.

12. Use a structure and a `typedef` to create a `customer` data type for a software store. Explain why the attributes you chose are essential and relevant to the context in which the program will be used.

13. Modify the `customer` data type that you created for Exercise 12 so that it will be useful for a video tape rental store. Explain why you made the modifications you did. Tell why the attributes you chose are more relevant for the context in which the program will be used.

14. The top-down design diagram in Figure 15.1 shows a partial design of a simple text editor. Continue this design by filling in greater detail.

FIGURE 15.1 A Partial Design of the Text Editor

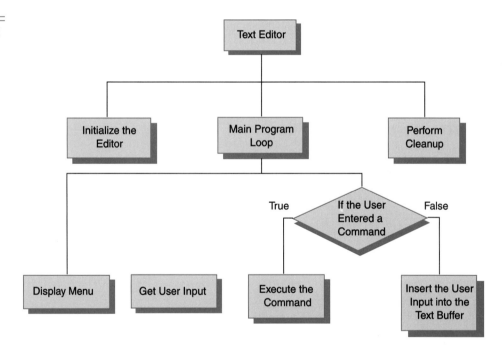

15. Table 15.2 on page 263 contains a list of all of the tasks the text editor should perform. Use this information to create a list of all events to which the text editor should respond.

16. Make a list of all of the types that you think are necessary for the text editor.

17. Use the list of events from Exercise 15 and the list of types from Exercise 16. Make a list of each event and the type that will respond to it.

18. Use the list of types you created for Exercise 16. Write down a brief justification for the existence of each type in your system.

19. Use the list of types that you created for Exercise 16. Define structures for each type. Select the structure members for each type. Choose the type of each attribute. Explain why you chose the attribute types that you did.

20. Use the structures you created for Exercise 19. Create a set of interface functions for each type. Explain why you think each type needs the functions you included.

21. Select a type from the structures you created for Exercise 19. Explain why you think that type's interface of functions is both minimal and complete.

TABLE 15.2 The Text Editor's Task List

Task	Comment
Load a file.	Load an ASCII text file from the disk into the text buffer.
Save a file.	Save ASCII text from the buffer onto the disk.
Display a menu.	Display a list of commands that the editor recognizes.
Display the text.	Display the current contents of the text buffer.
Get user input.	Get input from the keyboard.
Interpret keyboard input.	Distinguish between user commands and text for the buffer.
Insert text.	If the user inputs text for the buffer, insert it into the text buffer.
Delete text.	Delete text from the buffer when the user presses the backspace key.

22. Select a type from the structures you created for Exercise 19. Explain how you chose the attribute names. Make a list of alternate names for each of the type's attributes. Explain how these names are better or worse.

23. Use the list of interface functions you created for Exercise 20. Explain how you chose the interface's function names. Make a list of alternate names for each of the type's member functions. Explain whether these names are better or worse.

24. Design a type called `customer_name` for a software store, and define a structure for it. Also define the list of interface functions the `customer_name` type would require.

25. Use the `customer_name` type you created for Exercise 24. Explain how the type you defined, and its functions, would handle names such as John Paul Van Valkenberg and Gina Marie Ellen Martinez-Smith.

GLOSSARY

Application Program Interface (API)   See **Type Interface**.

Attribute   A piece of data which describes the item being modeled by a type.

Event   A stimulus to which the software reacts.

Type Interface   A set of functions that perform a group of standard operations on a programmer-defined type.

16

Preprocessor Directives

OBJECTIVES

After reading this chapter, you should be able to:

- Use preprocessor directives to define constants.
- Use preprocessor directives to define macros.
- Use preprocessor directives to perform conditional compilation.
- Use preprocessor directives to control compilation options.

OUTLINE

PREVIEW

In this chapter, we'll discuss the C preprocessor. The preprocessor is an extremely powerful tool useful for writing professional-caliber C programs. Surprisingly, it is often overlooked in discussions of C programming.

In this chapter, we'll first look at the purposes and uses of the C preprocessor. We'll then discuss the commands, or directives, that the preprocessor understands.

16.1   What Is the Preprocessor?

In Chapter 2 I said that we develop C programs by compiling source code into object code. We then link the object code into executable code. This process was illustrated in Figure 2.1, which is repeated here in Figure 16.1 for convenience.

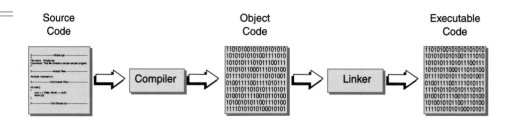

Figure 16.1 does not quite show a complete picture of the process of creating a computer program. There is one more step. Before your compiler ever sees the source file, it is automatically processed by the C preprocessor, as shown in Figure 16.2.

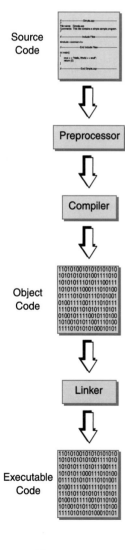

The preprocessor executes **preprocessor directives** in your source code. Table 16.1 shows the most commonly used directives. We'll cover each of these directives in this chapter.

Directive	Meaning
`#define`	Defines named constants and macros.
`#ifdef-#else-#endif`	Provides conditional compilation capabilities.
`#ifndef-#else-#endif`	Provides conditional compilation capabilities.
`#if defined()`	Same as `#ifdef`.
`#if !defined()`	Same as `#ifndef`.
`#include`	Includes a header file.
`#pragma`	Compiler-dependent directives.

TABLE 16.1   Common Preprocessor Directives

16.2   #define

C programs use the preprocessor `#define` statement to create named constants and **macros**.

16.2.1   Creating Named Constants with #define

We saw in Chapter 10 that we can create named constants with the `const` keyword. The preprocessor `#define` directive can be used for the same purpose. The `#define` directive is not a C command. It is a preprocessor directive. Example 16.1 shows a named constant created with the `#define` directive.

EXAMPLE 16.1   Creating a Named Constant with #define

```
#define MAX_STUDENTS_PER_CLASS 100
```

TECHNICAL NOTE 16.1
Some preprocessors create an intermediate file with a .i extension. The compiler then compiles the .i file.

This example creates a named constant called `MAX_STUDENTS_PER_CLASS`. When we compile the program, the compiler automatically invokes the C preprocessor. Everywhere the preprocessor finds the constant `MAX_STUDENTS_PER_CLASS`, it will substitute the value 100. The output of the preprocessor goes directly into the compiler. The preprocessor does not change your source files in any way.

Creating a named constant with `#define` is not the same as creating it with the `const` keyword. The `const` keyword is a C statement. It is processed by the C compiler. Constants created with the `const` keyword are visible in the code block in which they are created.

Named constants created with the `#define` directive are different. If a named constant is created with `#define`, it is visible from the point at which it is defined to the end of the file. Whether or not the `#define` directive appears in a code block does not matter. Example 16.2 demonstrates both ways of creating constants.

EXAMPLE 16.2   Using #define

```
1   #include <stdio.h>
2
3   #define A_CONSTANT      20
4
5   void PrintConstants(void);   // Prototype
6
7   int main()
8   {
9           #define ANOTHER_CONSTANT = 2.3;
10          const int AN_INTEGER_CONSTANT = 11;
11
12          PrintConstants();
13          return (0);
14  }
15
16  void PrintConstants(void)
```

```
17  {
18          printf("%d\n",A_CONSTANT);            // This is okay.
19          printf("%f\n",ANOTHER_CONSTANT);      // This also works.
20          printf("%d\n",AN_INTEGER_CONSTANT);   // This will not work.
21  }
```

This program creates two constants with the preprocessor's #define statement and one with the const keyword. The constants A_CONSTANT and ANOTHER_CONSTANT are visible from the point at which they are defined until the end of the file. The preprocessor does not see that ANOTHER_CONSTANT is defined inside a code block. AN_INTEGER_CON-STANT, however, is different.

Because AN_INTEGER_CONSTANT is created with the const keyword, it is processed by the compiler. Unlike the preprocessor, the compiler is programmed to understand the rules of the C language. It sees that AN_INTEGER_CONSTANT is created in the code block of the main() function. Therefore, AN_INTEGER_CONSTANT is not visible in the PrintConstants() function. The compiler will indicate that there is an error in this program on line 20.

Before the compiler ever reads the source code, the preprocessor goes through the program and substitutes the value 20 everywhere it finds the constant A_CONSTANT. It substitutes the value 2.3 everywhere it finds ANOTHER_CONSTANT. It does not do this for AN_INTEGER_CONSTANT. Example 16.3 demonstrates this.

EXAMPLE 16.3 The Output of the Preprocessor

```
1   void PrintConstants(void);    // Prototype
2
3   int main()
4   {
5          const int AN_INTEGER_CONSTANT = 11;
6
7          PrintConstants();
8          return (0);
9   }
10
11  void PrintConstants(void)
12  {
13          printf("%d\n",20);                    // This is okay.
14          printf("%f\n",2.3);                   // This also works.
15          printf("%d\n",AN_INTEGER_CONSTANT);   // This will not work.
16  }
```

Example 16.3 demonstrates that constants created with the #define directive are never seen by the compiler. Before the compiler sees the source file, the preprocessor removes all of the named constants and substitutes their values. This is not done for constants created with the const keyword.

It's important to remember that the preprocessor does not change the contents of your C source file. It takes what you see in Example 16.2 and turns it into what you see in Example 16.3. It then feeds that result directly into your compiler without your ever seeing it and without changing your .C file.

As you can see from these examples, the use of const gives you much stricter control over the visibility of constants than #define does. This is one of the reasons that C programmers today generally prefer to create constants with const rather than #define.

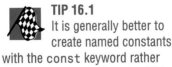

TIP 16.1
It is generally better to create named constants with the const keyword rather than the #define directive. This gives you much more control over the visibility of the constant in your program.

16.2.2 Macros

The #define directive can be used to create named constants. It can also be used to create macros. A macro looks like a function, and usually acts like one. However, because a macro is created with the #define statement, it is not a function. Instead, the preprocessor inserts the code for the macro into the program everywhere it finds the name of the macro.

Hands On 16.1 demonstrates how to create a macro.

Hands On 16.1

Objective

Write a program that uses a macro to square a number. It must:
    Use the macro to square the literal value 25.
    Print the result.
    Store the value 35 in a variable.
    Use the macro to square the value in the variable.
    Print the result.

Experiment

Type the following program into your IDE or text editor. Compile, link, and run it.

```
1    #include <stdio.h>
2
3    #define Squared(aNumber) aNumber*aNumber
4
5    int main()
6    {
7            int anIntegerVariable = 35;
8
9            printf("Did you know that 25 squared is ");
10           printf("%d?\n",Squared(25));
11
12           printf("Did you know that 35 squared is ");
13           printf("%d?\n",Squared(anIntegerVariable));
14
15           return (0);
16   }
```

Results

Did you know that 25 squared is 625?
Did you know that 35 squared is 1225?

Analysis

This program creates a macro that squares the number passed to it. The macro looks like a function. However, it is not. Program execution does not jump to the macro code as it does with a function. Instead, the macro code is substituted into the program by the preprocessor. Whenever the preprocessor finds the Squared() macro, it substitutes the macro's source code into the program code. That is, when the preprocessor finds the call

        Squared(25)

it inserts

        25*25

instead. Wherever it sees

        Squared(anIntegerVaraible)

it substitutes

        anIntegerVaraible*anIntegerVaraible

in its place. Of course, the substitution is not performed in your .C file. The preprocessor reads the .C file, performs the substitutions, and feeds the result directly to your compiler.

TIP 16.2
Macros are generally faster than functions, but they increase a program's size. You must decide which is more important, speed or size.

Using macros has definite advantages. Whenever program execution jumps to a function, it incurs some overhead. Macros do not have that overhead. However, because the macro's code is substituted throughout the program, it increases the size of the program. Using macros heavily can greatly increase your program's memory footprint, so you must strike a balance between size and speed.

Macros have another advantage: they don't do type checking on their parameters. For instance, Example 16.4 shows a macro named `Max()`. This macro finds the maximum of two values. The values can be integers, unsigned, floats, or any other numeric data type.

EXAMPLE 16.4   The Macro `Max()`

```
#define Max(value1,value2)  (value1>value2) ? value1:value2
```

Defining this macro for use with numeric data types can save us much effort. Example 16.5 shows the equivalent functions that you would need in order to accomplish the same task that the `Max()` macro does.

EXAMPLE 16.5   `Max()` Functions

```
1   short MaxShort(short value1,short value2)
2   {
3           return ((value1>value2) ? value1:value2);
4   }
5
6   int MaxInt(int value1,int value2)
7   {
8           return ((value1>value2) ? value1:value2);
9   }
10
11  long MaxLong(long value1,long value2)
12  {
13          return ((value1>value2) ? value1:value2);
14  }
15
16  unsigned short MaxUnsignedShort(unsigned short value1,unsigned short value2)
17  {
18          return ((value1>value2) ? value1:value2);
19  }
20
21  unsigned MaxUnsigned(unsigned value1,unsigned value2)
22  {
23          return ((value1>value2) ? value1:value2);
24  }
25
26  unsigned long MaxUnsignedLong(unsigned long value1,unsigned long value2)
27  {
28          return ((value1>value2) ? value1:value2);
29  }
30
31  float MaxFloat(float value1,float value2)
32  {
33          return ((value1>value2) ? value1:value2);
34  }
35
36  double MaxDouble(double value1,double value2)
37  {
38          return ((value1>value2) ? value1:value2);
39  }
40
41  long double MaxLongDouble(long double value1,long double value2)
```

```
42  {
43        return ((value1>value2) ? value1:value2);
44  }
```

As you can see, this a quite a bit of code.

Not doing type checking on parameters is also a disadvantage of macros. To see why, look at Example 16.6. This program fragment declares an array of characters and passes it to the Squared() macro from Hands On 16.1. It also declares an integer array and passes the integer array and the character array to the Max() macro. The preprocessor has no problem with this because it doesn't do any type checking on the parameters of a macro. No matter how ridiculous it is to attempt to square an array, the preprocessor will not stop us from doing so.

EXAMPLE 16.6   One Weakness of Macros

```
1   #define Squared(x) x*x
2   int anIntArray[10];
3
4   char aCharArray[100];
5   char aChar;
6   aChar=Squared(aCharArray);
7   aChar=Max(anIntArray,aCharArray);
```

TECHNICAL NOTE 16.2
Compilers that treat array names as unsigned integers are rare. You'll usually find this behavior only in compilers written for highly specialized hardware. This technique is not fully compatible with ANSI C, but it makes compilers so much easier to write that some companies will do it just to be able to ship a compiler with their hardware. When you call them up to complain about the incompatibilities, they usually try to convince you that you need to upgrade to the new version of the compiler (for a fee).

There is an outside possibility that the compiler will not catch this error at all. Although it is rare, there actually are some compilers that treat all array names as unsigned integers which contain the starting memory address of the array. Therefore, they allow you to do bizarre math like this on array names.

Therefore, the lack of type checking can be both a strength and a weakness for macros.

Example 16.7 illustrates another common problem with macros. In this program, we repeat the Squared() macro from Hands On 16.1.

EXAMPLE 16.7   A Precedence Problem

```
1   #include <stdio.h>
2
3   #define Squared(aNumber) aNumber*aNumber
4
5   int main()
6   {
7        int anIntegerVariable = 35;
8        printf("%d\n", Squared(anIntegerVariable+3));
9
10       return (0);
11  }
```

As the title of the example indicates, there is a precedence problem in the example. When the preprocessor performs its substitution on the Squared() macro, it changes

```
Squared(anIntegerVariable+3)
```

to

```
anIntegerVariable+3*anIntegerVariable+3
```

which will not give us the answer we expect. The rules of precedence say that the multiplication is performed before both of the additions on the line. Therefore, the program will first multiply 3*anIntegerVariable. It will then add anIntegerVariable. Finally, it will add 3. This does not give us the answer we are looking for.

The solution to precedence problems in macros is to put parentheses around your parameter names nearly everywhere they occur. Example 16.8 demonstrates this technique with the Squared() macro.

EXAMPLE 16.8 **Fixing the Precedence Problem in the Squared() Macro**

```
#define Squared(aNumber) (aNumber)*(aNumber)
```

If we use this version of the macro in Example 16.7, the preprocessor will change

```
Squared(anIntegerVariable+3)
```

to

```
(anIntegerVariable+3)*(anIntegerVariable+3)
```

which will give the correct answer.

Macros can span more than one line of text if you use the continuation character, which is the backslash (\). Example 16.9 shows a macro version of the ClearScreen() function from earlier chapters. This macro spans more than one line. In fact, it even defines an entire code block, just like a function. The preprocessor allows macros to do this.

EXAMPLE 16.9 **A Macro That Spans More Than One Line**

```
1    #define ClearScreen(totalScreenLines)              \
2        {                                              \
3            for (int i=0;i<totalScreenLines;i++)       \
4            {                                          \
5                printf("\n");                          \
6            }                                          \
7        }
```

TRAP 16.1
If used frequently in a program, macros that span more than one line can rapidly increase the size of your program.

Remember that the preprocessor substitutes all of the macro code wherever the macro name appears. Using large, multiline macros can rapidly increase the memory footprint of your program.

16.3 *#ifdef - #else - #endif*

C preprocessor directives enable us to define blocks of code that are conditionally compiled. This means that the code may or may not be included in the program, depending on conditions at compile time. The #ifdef directive tells the preprocessor to conditionally include a block of code for compilation if a particular named constant is defined. All of the code that is being conditionally compiled must occur between the #ifdef and #endif statements. Hands On 16.2 demonstrates a block of code that is compiled conditionally.

Hands On 16.2

Objective

Write a program that conditionally compiles a block of code.

Experiment

Type the following program into your IDE or text editor. Make sure that you define the constant COMPILE_THIS_CODE in the program. Then compile, link, and run the program. After you view the results, delete the definition of the named constant COMPILE_THIS_CODE. Compile, link, and run the program again.

```
1    #include <stdio.h>
2
3    #define COMPILE_THIS_CODE
4
5    int main()
6    {
7            #ifdef COMPILE_THIS_CODE
```

```
 8        printf("This code is conditionally ");
 9        printf("compiled and executed.\n");
10        #endif
11
12        printf("This code is always compiled ");
13        printf("and executed.\n");
14
15        return (0);
16   }
```

Results

First run

This code is conditionally compiled and executed.
This code is always compiled and executed.

Second run, after recompilation

This code is always compiled and executed.

Analysis

For the first run, the named constant COMPILE_THIS_CODE was defined, as shown in the code in the Experiment section. Because the preprocessor detected that the constant COMPILE_THIS_CODE was defined in the program, it included the block of code between the #ifdef and the #endif for compilation. Those lines of the program were compiled and executed.

It does not matter that the constant COMPILE_THIS_CODE is not defined to a value. If we define a constant and put nothing after it, the C preprocessor still sees it as being defined. Wherever it encounters the constant COMPILE_THIS_CODE, it substitutes nothing. An exception to this is in #ifdef statements. It does not perform the substitution in this case. Instead, it tests to see if the constant is defined.

Before the second run of the program, I commented out the line

```
#define COMPILE_THIS_CODE
```

by changing it to

```
// #define COMPILE_THIS_CODE
```

so that the constant was no longer defined. When the preprocessor checked this source file, it did not find the constant COMPILE_THIS_CODE. The condition of the #ifdef evaluated to false. Therefore, the preprocessor did not pass the code between the #ifdef and the #endif to the compiler. As far as the compiler could detect, that code did not exist. The output for the second run in the Results section demonstrates that these lines of code did not become part of the final executable program.

TECHNICAL NOTE 16.3
Substitution of defined constants is not performed in the #ifdef, #ifndef, #if defined(), and #if !defined() statements. Instead, the preprocessor performs a test to see whether the specified constant is defined.

As with C language if statements, preprocessor #ifdef directives can have else clauses. An else clause for an #ifdef directive uses the #else directive. Example 16.10 demonstrates an #ifdef directive with an #else clause.

EXAMPLE 16.10   An #ifdef with an #else Clause

```
1   #ifdef COMPILE_THIS_CODE
2   printf("This code is conditionally ");
3   printf("compiled and executed in the #ifdef.\n");
4   #else
5   printf("This code is conditionally ");
6   printf("compiled and executed in the #else.\n");
7   #endif
```

If the constant COMPILE_THIS_CODE is defined in the program before this #ifdef statement, the preprocessor sends the statements in the #ifdef block to the compiler. If COMPILE_THIS_CODE is not defined, the preprocessor sends the statements in the #else block to the compiler.

16.4 #ifndef - #else - #endif

In addition to the #ifdef directive, the preprocessor uses an #ifndef directive. This name is an abbreviation for "if not defined." It works in exactly the opposite way that #ifdef does. If the constant that is being testing for is *not* defined, then preprocessor sends the code block of the #ifndef directive to the compiler. If it *is* defined, none of that code is compiled. Hands On 16.3 demonstrates the use of #ifndef, along with #else and #endif.

Hands On 16.3

Objective

Write a program that demonstrates the use of #ifndef - #else - #endif.

Experiment

Type the following program into your IDE or text editor. Make sure that you do *not* define the constant DONT_COMPILE_THIS_CODE in the program. Compile, link, and run the program. After you view the results, add the definition of the named constant DONT_COMPILE_THIS_CODE. Compile, link, and run the program again.

```
1    #include <stdio.h>
2
3    #define DONT_COMPILE_THIS_CODE
4
5    int main()
6    {
7         #ifdef DONT_COMPILE_THIS_CODE
8         printf("This code is conditionally ");
9         printf("compiled and executed in the #ifndef.\n");
10        #else
11        printf("This code is conditionally ");
12        printf("compiled and executed in the #else.\n");
13        #endif
14
15        return (0);
16   }
```

Results

First run

This code is conditionally compiled and executed in the #else.

Second run

This code is conditionally compiled and executed in the #ifndef.

Analysis

For the first run of this program, I did not define the named constant DONT_COMPILE_THIS_CODE. Because preprocessor did not find the constant

`DONT_COMPILE_THIS_CODE` in the program, it included the block of code between the `#else` and the `#endif` for compilation. Those lines of the program were compiled and executed.

Before the second run of the program, I added the line

```
#define DONT_COMPILE_THIS_CODE
```

to the program before the `#ifndef`. When the preprocessor checked the source file, it found the constant `DONT_COMPILE_THIS_CODE`. The condition of the `#ifndef` evaluated to true. Therefore, the preprocessor passed the code between the `#ifdef` and the `#else` to the compiler. The output for the second run in the Results section demonstrates that these lines of code became part of the final executable program.

16.5 `#if defined()` and `#if !defined()`

Early versions of C limited the length of identifiers, keywords, and preprocessor directives to eight characters. That's why directives such as `#ifdef` and `#ifndef` are so terse. Over time, C compilers became able to handle longer names. Programmers wanted preprocessor directives that were easier to read and more self-documenting. Therefore, the ANSI C committee added the preprocessor directives `#if defined()` and `#if !defined()`. They do exactly the same thing as `#ifdef` and `#ifndef`. The code fragments in Example 16.11 demonstrate their use.

EXAMPLE 16.11   Using `#if defined()` and `#if !defined()`

```
 1   #if defined(COMPILE_THIS_CODE)
 2   printf("This code is conditionally ");
 3   printf("compiled and executed in the #if defined().\n");
 4   #else
 5   printf("This code is conditionally ");
 6   printf("compiled and executed in the #else.\n");
 7   #endif
 8
 9   #if !defined(DONT_COMPILE_THIS_CODE)
10   printf("This code is conditionally ");
11   printf("compiled and executed in the #if !defined().\n");
12   #else
13   printf("This code is conditionally ");
14   printf("compiled and executed in the #else.\n");
15   #endif
```

16.6 `#elif`

The C preprocessor also provides an `#elif` directive, which is short for "else if." You can use it with `#ifdef`, `#ifndef`, `#if defined()`, and `#if !defined()`. With it, you can create a series of chained if conditions. Example 16.12 demonstrates one possible use of a series of code blocks that are conditionally compiled.

EXAMPLE 16.12   Using `#elif`

```
 1   #ifdef OS_MSDOS
 2   #define ClearScreen() system("cls")
 3   #elif defined(OS_UNIX)
 4   #define ClearScreen() system("clear")
 5   #elif defined(OS_BRACKENBUSH)
 6   #define ClearScreen() system("clrscr")
```

```
 7   #else
 8   #define ClearScreen()                                        \
 9           {                                                    \
10                   for (int i=0;i<25;i++)                       \
11                           printf("\n");                        \
12           }
13   #endif
```

This example demonstrates a way to write macros that are portable across any operating system. In this case, the `#elif` directive enables us to create a definition of the `ClearScreen()` macro for multiple operating systems.

The `#ifdef` in this code fragment tests whether the constant `OS_MSDOS` is defined. If it is, the fragment defines the `ClearScreen()` macro as a call to the C `system()` function. This function is part of the C Standard Library. It executes a command that the current operating system recognizes. The format of these commands are completely dependent on the operating system. In the case of MS DOS, the command to clear the screen is `"cls"`.

If the constant `OS_MSDOS` is not defined, the code fragment uses the `#elif` and `defined()` directives to test whether `OS_UNIX` is currently defined. If it is, it defines the `ClearScreen()` macro as a call to the C `system()` function. In this case, it passes the string `"clear"` to the operating system because that is the command to clear the screen under Unix.

If the constant `OS_UNIX` is not defined, the fragment tests whether the constant `OS_BRACKENBUSH` is defined. I often use a made-up computer and operating system called the Brackenbush 5000 in my classroom examples. The command to clear the screen on this imaginary system is `"clrscr"`. If this code fragment detects that the constant `OS_BRACKENBUSH` is defined, it then defines the `ClearScreen()` macro as a call to the C `system()` function with the string `"clrscr"` to clear the screen.

If the none of the constants this code fragment tests for are currently defined, the fragment creates a `ClearScreen()` macro that clears the screen by printing 25 newline characters. This is a reasonable default action for this macro.

16.7 `#include`

We have been using the `#include` directive in every C program so far. This directive instructs the preprocessor to read a file into the current file. The file it reads in is called an include file. This instruction enables us to create definitions that we can use in many C files. The preprocessor reads in all of the definitions in the include file as if we typed the definitions into the C file at the point where the `#include` directive occurs.

As you know, C files have the extension .c on the end. The files that we include are called **header files**. Header files have traditionally used a .h extension. However, that is only a convention. C compilers do not force you to use this extension on your files.

The C Standard Library comes with a set of header files. They contain definitions that are widely used. For instance, the file stdio.h contains the prototypes for the `printf()` and `scanf()` functions. Input from the keyboard and output to the screen is not actually part of the C language itself. It is added on through functions whose prototypes are defined in the C Standard Library. This is the reason that we needed to include stdio.h in all of our programs.

For information on the content of header files and C source files, see Chapter 17.

Whenever you include header files from the C Standard Library, you need to put the name of the header file in angle brackets (< and >). Because we have primarily been using the C Standard Library file stdio.h, we have been using these brackets. They tell the preprocessor to search in its standard include directory for the header file.

When we create our own header files, we should not put them in the compiler's standard include directory. We don't want to get our header files mixed up with those that come with the compiler. Often, we keep the header files that we create in the current directory for the project we are working on. To get the compiler to check the current directory for the header file, we simply put the header file name in quotes, like this

```
#include "MyFile.h"
```

TIP 16.3
It is a convention for C source files to have a .c extension and for header files to have a .h extension. It is a good idea for you to use this style of naming files as well.

TECHNICAL NOTE 16.4
The path to the standard `include` directory is compiler-dependent. Most compilers will let you set it manually.

Using quotation marks rather than angle brackets tells the preprocessor to look in the current directory for the specified header file. If it does not find the file, it may look in the Standard Library include directory. However, this behavior is compiler-dependent.

16.8   #pragma

No matter what type of product a company manufactures, they always want to distinguish themselves from the competition. One way to do this is to add features that the competition doesn't have. Companies that produce C compilers are no different.

Using the #pragma directive, the C preprocessor enables our programs to access compiler-specific features in a compiler-independent way. Any #pragma directives that the compiler doesn't recognize, it ignores.

In a #pragma directive, the compiler-specific command appears immediately after the #pragma. See Example 16.13.

EXAMPLE 16.13   Using the #pragma Directive

```
#pragma auto_inline
```

The directive in Example 16.13 is specific to Microsoft's Visual C++. Other compilers may or may not support the auto_inline directive. If they don't, they just ignore the entire #pragma statement.

Because all #pragma options are specified by the manufacturer of your compiler, you must look in the compiler's documentation to learn which options it supports.

16.9   Troubleshooting Guide

After reading this section, you should be able to:

* Use preprocessor directives to keep header files from being included more than once.
* Use preprocessor directives to help you debug your programs.

16.9.1   Header Files That Include Header Files

It is often the case in C programming that you define a type for use with another type. For example, many games use sprites. A sprite is an animated object that moves on the screen. A sprite has a bitmap image and a current position. The sprite type in Example 16.14 follows this pattern.

EXAMPLE 16.14   A sprite Object

```
1   typedef struct
2   {
3           bitmap bitmapImage;
4           point upperLeft;
5   } sprite;
```

In a professional program, this definition of the sprite type would go into a file called Sprite.h. Notice that it makes use of a bitmap type and a point type. These are programmer-defined types that would be created in the files Bitmap.h and Point.h. That means Sprite.h would need to include those two files.

It is possible that another file might need to include Sprite.h. The programmer using the sprite type, for very good reasons, might also include Bitmap.h and Point.h in her header file. The result is that Bitmap.h and Point.h would be included twice. Figure 16.3 illustrates this problem.

The compiler will definitely not like this situation. It will see the definitions of the bitmap and point types twice in the file MyFile.h.

The way we resolve this problem is to use preprocessor directives to keep track of when a header file has already been included. Example 16.15 illustrates this technique.

FIGURE 16.3   A Problem with
Header Files

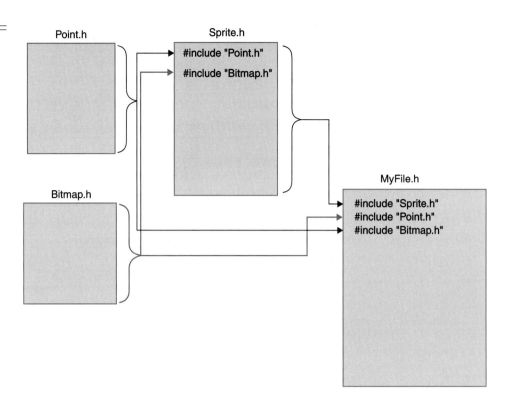

EXAMPLE 16.15   **Preventing Multiple Definitions**

```
1    // This is the file Bitmap.h
2    #if !defined(BITMAP_H)
3    #define BITMAP_H
4
5    typedef struct
6    {
7         // Definition details go here.
8    } bitmap;
9
10   #endif
```

The line 2 of the header file Bitmap.h contains the preprocessor directive

```
#if !defined(BITMAP_H)
```

This tells the preprocessor to send the code block of the `#if !defined` directive to
the compiler if the named constant `BITMAP_H` is not defined. The very first item in the
`#if !defined` directive's code block is the statement on line 3 that reads

```
#define BITMAP_H
```

Once the header file Bitmap.h has been included once, the constant `BITMAP_H` is defined. If Bitmap.h is included again, the preprocessor will begin to process each statement
in the file again. The first statement is, of course, the

```
#if !defined(BITMAP_H)
```

directive. This time, the constant `BITMAP_H` is defined. Therefore, nothing between the
`#if !defined()` directive and the `#endif` is sent to the compiler. The preprocessor prevents all of the definitions in Bitmap.h from appearing more than once in a file.[1]

---

[1] When I was learning C programming in college, I worked this technique out for myself. I actually thought I was
the first to invent it and spent about three weeks congratulating myself on what a clever programmer I was. Then
I found the technique explained in a C programming book that had been written years prior to that time. That experience taught me that it's sometimes better to be well-read than clever.

16.9.2 Using Preprocessor Directives for Debugging

Debugger programs aren't always available for the environment in which we're working. Even if they are, there are ways to ease our debugging burdens using the C preprocessor.

Marking Code for Debug   One common debugging strategy is to define code as being for debugging purposes only. Suppose you create a function that writes the current status of a program out to a log file. This enables you to, among other things, print the log file and review it together with co-workers who might be able to help you fix problems. In the version of the program that you release to the public, you don't want the program to save its status in a log file. That will slow it down considerably. In this scenario, you can use the preprocessor to conditionally compile code only in the debug version. Example 16.16 demonstrates this technique.

EXAMPLE 16.16   Defining Code for Debug

```
#if defined(DEBUG)
SaveProgramStatusToLogFile();
#endif
```

As you can see, the preprocessor will pass the call to the function `SaveProgramStatusToLogFile()` to the compiler only if the constant DEBUG is defined. As long as you are working on your program, it can contain the definition of the constant DEBUG. As soon as you are ready for release, delete or comment out the defintion of DEBUG and recompile. The preprocessor will not pass the call to `SaveProgramStatusToLogFile()` to the compiler.

Simulating Breakpoints   If a debugger isn't available for the hardware or operating system you're using, you can still put breakpoints in your program using the preprocessor. Example 16.17 shows a macro called `Breakpoint()`. This macro will cause a program to display a message and pause until the user presses the Enter key on the keyboard. The message can be any string which contains program status information. A macro such as this enables your program to print the contents of variables or other program status information. The program will wait until you have finished reviewing the status message. When you press Enter, the program continues.

EXAMPLE 16.17   Simulating Breakpoints

```
 1  #if defined(DEBUG)
 2  #define Breakpoint(msgstr)                              \
 3          {                                               \
 4              aChar;                                      \
 5              printf("%s\n",msgstr);                      \
 6              printf("Press any key to continue...");     \
 7              scanf("%c",&aChar);                         \
 8          }
 9  #else
10  #define Breakpoint(msgstr)
11  #endif
```

Notice also that this example uses the technique described in the previous section. That is, if the constant DEBUG is defined, the preprocessor defines the `Breakpoint()` macro with the code block shown in the example. If it isn't, the preprocessor defines the `Breakpoint()` macro as nothing. Everywhere the call to the `Breakpoint()` macro occurs in the source code, the preprocessor substitutes nothing. The compiler never sees the macro or any references to it in the source code.

SUMMARY

Every time you compile a program, it is automatically processed by the C preprocessor before it is compiled. We can put the C preprocessor directives in our programs to control the preprocessor's behavior.

The preprocessor is used to define named constants, define macros, and perform conditional compilation. Named constants and macros can be created using the #define directive. The preprocessor can perform conditional compilation with the `#ifdef, #ifndef, #else, #elif, #if de-fined()`, and `#if !defined()` directives.

C programmers put the type and constant definitions that are used in more than one file into header files. This enables them to include the header file in another file which needs the definitions. Use the `#include` directive to include a file.

The `#pragma` directive enables us to access compiler-specific features in a portable way. If a compiler doesn't support a particular `#pragma` option it ignores the option.

TECHNICAL NOTES

16.1   Some preprocessors create an intermediate file with a .i extension. The compiler then compiles the .i file.

16.2   Compilers that treat array names as unsigned integers are rare. You'll usually find this behavior only in compilers written for highly specialized hardware. This technique is not fully compatible with ANSI C, but it makes compilers so much easier to write that some companies will do it just to be able to ship a compiler with their hardware. When you call them up to complain about the incompatibilities, they usually try to convince you that you need to upgrade to the new version of the compiler (for a fee).

16.3   Substitution of defined constants is not performed in the `#ifdef, #ifndef, #if defined()`, and `#if !defined()` statements. Instead, the preprocessor performs a test to see whether the specified constant is defined.

16.4   The path to the standard `include` directory is compiler-dependent. Most compilers will let you set it manually.

TIPS

16.1   It is generally better to create named constants with the `const` keyword rather than the `#define` directive. This gives you much more control over the visibility of the constant in your program.

16.2   Macros are generally faster than functions, but they increase a program's size. You must decide which is more important, speed or size.

16.3   It is a convention for C source files to have a .C extension and for header files to have a .H extension. It is a good idea for you to use this style of naming files as well.

TRAP

16.1   If used frequently in a program, macros that span more than one line can rapidly increase the size of your program.

REVIEW QUESTIONS

1. What is the C preprocessor? What is it used for?
2. How do you define a named constant with the `#define` directive? Where in a file is a defined constant visible?
3. How do you define a macro with the `#define` directive?
4. What are some of the advantages of macros when compared to functions? What are some of the disadvantages?
5. What preprocessor directives are used to perform conditional compilation?
6. What are three reasons you might want to do conditional compilation?
7. What does the `#include` directive do?
8. Why do we use header files?
9. What is one potential problem with include files? How do you solve this problem?
10. How can you use preprocessor directives to aid you in debugging your programs?

EXERCISES

1. Explain the differences between defining a constant with the `#define` directive and declaring a constant using the `const` keyword.
2. Describe the advantages and disadvantages of using macros rather than functions in programs.
3. Tell why you think programmers might use conditional compilation to mark code for debugging even if they have a debugger program.
4. Describe how conditional compilation can be used to make source code more portable.

5. Fill in the blanks.

The _____ preprocessor directive tests to see if a named constant is defined. The _____ _____ directive does the same thing, but it is a bit more readable.

6. Fill in the blanks.

The _____ preprocessor directive tests to see if a named constant is not defined. The _____ _____ directive does the same thing, but it is a bit more readable.

7. Fill in the blanks.

The _____ preprocessor directive is used with the _____, _____, _____ _____, or _____ _____ directives to create a series of chained if-else directives for conditional compilation.

8. Fill in the blanks.

The _____ preprocessor directive must appear at the end of a conditional compilation directive created with _____, _____, _____ _____, or _____ _____.

9. Define a macro called Cube() that cubes any number that you pass to it. In other words, if you pass it 5, it should evaluate to 5*5*5. Write a program which demonstrates that your macro works.

10. Change the program that you wrote for Exercise 9. Declare an integer variable called anInteger. Initialize anInteger to 5. Your program should call the Cube() macro you wrote in Exercise 1 and pass it anInteger+2. If it does not give the correct answer, fix it so that it does.

11. Explain how you can write highly portable macros using conditional compilation.

12. Tell why you think C programmers use header files. Explain how their programs would be different if they did not.

13. Explain why a header file must not be included more than once. Write a program which demonstrates how to use conditional compilation to prevent including a header file more than once.

14. Define a macro called Max3() that finds the maximum of three values. Write a program that demonstrates the macro.

15. Write a macro called Max4() that finds the maximum of four values. Hint: This is easier if you use the Max3() macro from Exercise 14.

16. Write a program that uses a for loop to count from 0 to 999. Inside the loop, call a function called Print-Counter() that prints the current value of the loop counter variable to the screen. Make the call to the function conditionally compiled. If the constant PRINT_COUNTER is defined, then the call to the Print-Counter() function should be compiled. If it is not defined, the compiler should not compile the call to PrintCounter().

17. Look in your compiler's documentation and find three #pragma options that are specific to your compiler. Briefly explain each.

18. Write programs that demonstrate the use of the three #pragma directives you explained in Exercise 17.

19. Write a program which demonstrates the use of the Breakpoint() macro in the Troubleshooting Guide in this chapter.

20. Write a program that uses conditional compilation to define a named constant called ARRAY_LENGTH. If the constant SMALL_ARRAY is defined, the value of ARRAY_LENGTH should be 20. If the constant BIG_ARRAY is defined, the value of ARRAY_LENGTH should be 1000. If neither of these constants are defined, the value of ARRAY_LENGTH should be 100. Your program should declare an array of characters of length ARRAY_LENGTH. It should use a for loop to fill the array with characters and then print the characters to the screen.

21. Look in your compiler's online documentation or a book about the C Standard Library for information about a function called abort(). Use the abort() function to define a macro called DebugAbort(). The DebugAbort() macro should print an error message to the screen and then abort the program. The macro should be included in the compiled program only if the constant DEBUGGING is defined. Write a program which demonstrates that your macro works.

22. Early personal computers did not perform floating-point calculations as efficiently as integer calculations. Therefore, graphics programs, which require intensive processing, used integers rather than floating-point numbers. As specialized floating point hardware became more available, programs had to be written so that they could easily be changed to use floating point math. Use conditional compilation to define a portable data type called point_3d. Create the point_3d type with the struct and typedef statements. The structure should contain three members, xCoordinate, yCoordinate, and zCoordinate. If the constant INTEGER_PROCESSING is defined in the program, make the data type of the xCoordinate, yCoordinate, and zCoordinate members int. If the constant FLOATING_POINT_PROCESSING is defined, make their data types double.

23. Use conditional compilation to write a macro called DebugPrintString(). The DebugPrintString() macro should print a string to the screen if the constant DEBUGGING is defined. If it is not defined, all calls to DebugPrintf() should automatically be removed from the code by the preprocessor. Write a program to demonstrate that your macro works.

24. Use conditional compilation to write a macro called DebugPause(). If the constant DEBUGGING is defined in the program, the DebugPause() macro should pause program execution until the user presses the Enter key. If it is not defined, all calls to DebugPause() should be removed automatically from the code by the preprocessor. Write a program to demonstrate that your macro works.

25. An advanced use of preprocessor directives and conditional compilation is to use multiple macros to build program sections. Write a macro called DebugRepeat-

TaskStart(). This macro should take one parameter that specifies the number of times to repeat a task. If the constant DEBUGGING is defined in the program, this macro should insert the code for the first part of a for loop into the program. Also write a macro called DebugRepeatTaskEnd(). The DebugRepeat-TaskEnd() macro also performs its code substitution if the constant DEBUGGING is defined. It takes no parameters and inserts the code to end a for loop. The use of these two macros looks like the following:

```
DebugRepeatTaskStart(100);
printf("This is a string.\n");
DebugRepeatTaskEnd();
```

This should cause a for loop to be inserted around the statement

```
printf("This is a string.\n");
```

that repeats 100 times. Write a program to demonstrate that your macros work.

GLOSSARY

Header File   A file which contains definitions that are used in more than one .C file. A header file uses the .H extension.

Macro   A block of code resembles a function, but is created as part of a #define statement.

Preprocessor Directive   A command that is understood and processed by the C preprocessor.

17

Organizing Programs

OBJECTIVES

After reading this chapter, you should be able to:

- Organize programs composed of multiple files.

- Explain what goes into a header file.

- Explain what goes into a .C file.

OUTLINE

PREVIEW

Most commercial programs are composed of a large number of files. Designing and developing an application requires programmers to know how to organize the source code. This skill is basic to building working systems in a team environment. This chapter introduces some common organizational conventions used by C programmers.

17.1   Organizing Files

In most development environments, programs must be divided into many files. When you are working as part of a development team, working in the same file or files as other developers is generally too difficult to be worthwhile. You often end up overwriting each other's work. As a result, development teams ordinarily divide a program into parts and assign each team member to write a type or a group of types. They agree on the interface to each type. The team members each implement their parts of the program. When they are finished, all of the pieces must fit together. Therefore, they must all agree on and use the same method of organizing their files.

The most common method of ensuring consistency is to put the definition of shared types into header files, which use the .h extension on their file names. The functions for the types go into a .c file. Using this style, types tend to stand on their own better, and more than likely they can be used in other programs.

17.1.1   Header Files

Header files are the most common tool for sharing information between .c files. Used properly, they can be a tremendous aid in writing portable, reusable types.

What To Put in a Header File   What goes into a header file?

Remember that one of the goals structured programming is encapsulation. No type should have to "know" how any other type is implemented. If you and I are working on a project together, I should be able to change the implementation of any of my types without making you change the implementation of any of your types. As long as the interfaces to my types stay the same, changes in the implementation of my type shouldn't affect your work at all.

Using this philosophy, a header file should contain only the things that two or more .c files need to share. Any time we put something into a header files, we should ask ourselves if it is needed in more than one .c file. If not, it should not go into a header file.

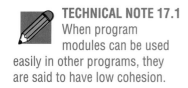

TECHNICAL NOTE 17.1
When program modules can be used easily in other programs, they are said to have low cohesion.

TIP 17.1
Header files should contain only information that is shared between two or more .c files.

Table 17.1 contains a list of everything that normally goes into a header file. In general, programmers follow the order of arrangement shown in the table. That is, include files come before global constants. Global constants come before types, and so on. Keep in mind that this table does not reflect rules set in stone. It presents common practice. If you've got a good reason to use a different style that the one shown here, by all means discuss it with your team members.

TABLE 17.1 The Contents of a Header File

Item	Explained In
Include Files	Chapter 16
Global Constants	Chapter 10, Chapter 16
Type definitions	Chapter 14, Chapter 15
Enumerated Types	Chapter 14, Chapter 15
Structures and Unions	Chapter 15, Chapter 15
Macros	Chapter 16
Prototypes	Chapter 13

Header files often include other header files. All `#include` directives generally go together at the beginning of a file. A header file includes another a header file when the definitions in the first header file use the definitions in another. Therefore, the include files generally come first so that their definitions are available to everything else in the header file.

It is typically best to declare constants close to where they are used. However, if constants are used widely throughout a program, programmers often declare them together in a header file. It's not unusual for the value of a constant to be dependent on the value of a constant in another header file. Therefore, the section for the global constants comes after the `#include` directives. It's also not unusual for type definitions, enumerations, class definitions, and other header file items to use the global constants. As a result, programmers often put global constants just after the include directives.

Type definitions, enumerated types, structures, and unions are all ways of creating your own types. Your types form the building blocks of a program and its functions. So programmers generally insert these items next.

As we saw in Chapter 13, macros do not check the types of their parameters. They can occur virtually anywhere in the header file. The typical style is to put them after the type definitions, enumerated types, structures, and unions. However, because they do not depend on any type definitions, some programmers put them together with the global constants. Usually the other members of your team will not mind if you choose to use this style of implementation.

Because the function prototypes commonly depend on the definitions of the constants and types, they usually come last in a header file.

What Not to Put in a Header File   Header files never contain functions. If you were to put a function into a header file, it would undoubtedly be included in more than one .c file. When you compiled your program, the linker would detect two (or more) identical versions of your functions. It would not know which one to link to, and your link would fail. For this same reason, you should never include a file with a .c extension.

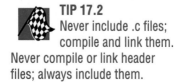

TRAP 17.1
Putting functions in header files will generally result in the linker finding multiple versions of the functions. It will not know which to use, and the link will fail.

TIP 17.2
Never include .c files; compile and link them. Never compile or link header files; always include them.

17.1.2 C Source Files

Header files contain the definitions a program needs. C source files (.c files) contain its implementation. A .c file can contain anything that a header file contains. It also contains functions. Table 17.2 displays the contents of a .c file in the order in which the items typically occur. Notice that the only difference between header files and .c files is that .c files also contain functions.

How do you know when a type definition, for instance, goes into a .h file and when it goes into a .c file? I'll answer that question with a question. Is the type definition shared? If the information is not a function and must be shared between two or more .c files, it goes into a header file. If not, it goes into a .c file.

Item	Explained In
Include Files	Chapter 16
Global Constants	Chapter 10, Chapter 16
Type Definitions	Chapter 14, Chapter 15
Enumerated Types	Chapter 14, Chapter 15
Structures and Unions	Chapter 15, Chapter 15
Macros	Chapter 16
Prototypes	Chapter 13
Functions	Chapter 13

Typically, programmers organize their header and .c files around their types. That is, for each type that is shared, they create a header file to hold the type definition. They also make a .c file that contains the functions associated with the type.

Let's suppose that we're working on a text editor together. The text editor uses a text buffer. Each line of the text buffer contains a string. We decide that you will implement a string type called `text_string`, and I will use that to implement a `text_buffer` type. You will need to create a file called Tstring.h. You should also make a file called Tstring.c.

The file Tstring.h will hold the definition of the `text_string` type. It will also contain any other types, constants, prototypes, and so on that may be needed to use the `text_string` type.

Tstring.c will have the functions associated with the `text_string` type. There may also be other types, constants, functions, and so forth, that you must use to implement the `text_string` type. Because these are not shared, there should be no mention of them in the Tstring.h header file. Therefore, other team members will not need to know anything about them when they try to use your `text_string` type.

If I am writing the files to implement the `text_buffer` type, I will include your header file TString.h in my file, Tbuffer.h. This file has the type definition of the `text_buffer` type. I will also need to write a file called Tbuffer.c.

In addition, we will also need to create a file for the `main()` function of our program. It will declare and manipulate a `text_buffer` type, get user input, and interpret user commands. There may be functions in addition to `main()` in this file that are not called by functions in any other file.

Figure 17.1 shows the organization of the text editor.

FIGURE 17.1 **One Possible Organization of a Text Editor Program**

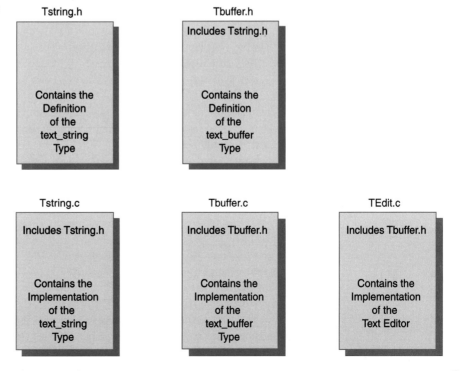

Tstring.h

Contains the Definition of the text_string Type

Tbuffer.h

Includes Tstring.h

Contains the Definition of the text_buffer Type

Tstring.c

Includes Tstring.h

Contains the Implementation of the text_string Type

Tbuffer.c

Includes Tbuffer.h

Contains the Implementation of the text_buffer Type

TEdit.c

Includes Tbuffer.h

Contains the Implementation of the Text Editor

This style of organization affords several advantages. It helps hide the implementation of each type by sharing only the type definition in the header file. The implementation is hidden in a .c file. This lessens the dependence between type implementations and increases encapsulation. It helps other programmers figure out how the program works and enables them to quickly find type definitions and implementations.

17.2   Troubleshooting Guide

After reading this section, you should be able to:

- Find and fix circular inclusions.
- Understand the advantages and disadvantages of using one central include file.

17.2.1   Circular Inclusions

When you follow the file organization style described in this chapter, you will find that it has one characteristic that can be either an advantage or a disadvantage, depending on your point of view.

Suppose we have three header files, A.h, B.h, and C.h. Figure 17.2 shows fragments of these three files. Notice that the file B.h includes A.h. C.h includes B.h. A.h includes C.h.

FIGURE 17.2   Circular Inclusion

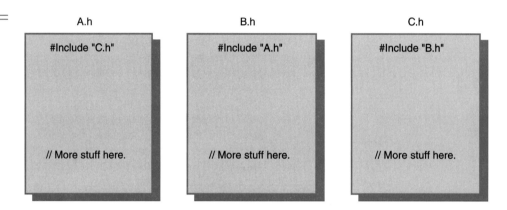

C compilers don't allow this. By separating every type definition into its own header file, it becomes harder to prevent circular inclustions. You've got to expect that programmers using your types may run into this problem.

This difficulty is not necessarily bad. In my personal experience, circular inclusions always indicate a design flaw. Every time I've run into this, I've found that my types were too interdependent. Sometimes I just had to redesign their interfaces. Other times, I needed to create additional types in the program. Sometimes I had to combine two or more types into one. In each instance, I was able to come up with a better design that did not suffer the circular inclusion problem.

For this reason, I think of circular inclusions as a benefit, not a disadvantage. They tell me when I have a design problem. However, many other programmers see circular inclusions as a serious disadvantage.

17.2.2   One Big Inclusion

Some programmers include all of their header files in one file. Figure 17.3 demonstrates this technique. It uses the header files from Figure 17.1 and adds an additional header file called Tedit.h. This file includes all other header files created for the program. All .c files include the header file Tedit.h. They do not include any other header file.

You can extend this technique to solve the problem of circular includes. Example 17.1 shows the contents of the three header files from Figure 17.2. It also adds a fourth header file, D.h.

FIGURE 17.3   An All-Inclusive Include File

Tstring.h

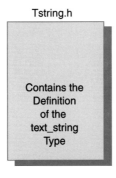

Contains the
Definition
of the
text_string
Type

Tbuffer.h

Includes Tstring.h

Contains the
Class Definition
of the
text_buffer
Type

TEdit.h

Includes Tstring.h
Includes Tbuffer.h

Tstring.cpp

Includes TEdit.h

Contains the
Implementation
of the
text_string
Type

Tbuffer.cpp

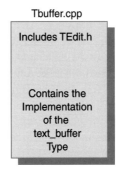

Includes TEdit.h

Contains the
Implementation
of the
text_buffer
Type

TEdit.c

Includes Tbuffer.h

Contains the
Implementation
of the
Text Editor

EXAMPLE 17.1   Solving the Circular Inclusion Problem

```
1   // Beginning of A.h
2   #define A_H
3   #if !defined(D_H)
4   #include D.h
5   #endif
6
7   // More stuff here.
8
9   // End of A.h
```

```
1   // Beginning of B.h
2   #define B_H
3   #if !defined(D_H)
4   #include D.h
5   #endif
6
7   // More stuff here.
8
9   // End of B.h
```

```
1   // Beginning of C.h
2   #define C_H
3   #if !defined(D_H)
4   #include D.h
5   #endif
6
7   // More stuff here.
8
9   // End of C.h
```

```
 1  // Beginning of D.h
 2  #define D_H
 3  #if !defined(A_H)
 4  #include A.h
 5  #endif
 6  #if !defined(B_H)
 7  #include B.h
 8  #endif
 9  #if !defined(C_H)
10  #include C.h
11  #endif
12  // End of D.h
```

Let's suppose that the preprocessor is currently working on the file A.h. The file A.h defines the constant A_H. Because the constant D_H is not defined, it includes the file D.h. The first thing that D.h does is define the constant D_H. Next, it tests to see whether A_H is defined. Because A_H is defined at this point, D.h does not include A.h. It does include B.h and C.h. The files B.h and C.h will not include D.h because D_H is currently defined.

The processing of B.h and C.h follow the same pattern. Using this technique, you can include one header file in every other header file and every .c file in a program. It will automatically include every other header file. There can never be a circular inclusion in your program.

The disadvantage of this, however, is that your program grows by leaps and bounds. This technique causes *everything* (macros, types, constants, and so on) to be defined in *every* .c file. Your compiler might optimize away things that are not used, or it might not.

Using an all-inclusive include file also increases the time it takes to compile your program. For a large professional program, compilation can literally take hours. An all-inclusive header file can literally double or triple an already long compile time. Although such a header file may simplify your coding effort, you pay a price for it.

SUMMARY

C programmers normally put type definitions into a header file. The functions associated with it go into a .c file. Together, the header file and the .c file form the definition and implementation of a type.

Header files should contain information that needs to be shared between two or more .c files. Anything that is required by only one .c file should go into only that .c file.

Following this style of implementation can lead to circular inclusions, which usually indicate a design problem. You can eliminate the circular inclusion problem by using one all-inclusive include file. However, it may make your program larger, and it will compile more slowly.

TECHNICAL NOTE

17.1   When program modules can be used easily in other programs, they are said to have low cohesion.

TIPS

17.1   Header files should contain only information that is shared between two or more .c files.

17.2   Never include .c files; compile and link them. Never compile or link a header files; always include them.

TRAP

17.1   Putting functions in header files will generally result in the linker finding multiple versions of the functions. It will not know which to use, and the link will fail.

REVIEW QUESTIONS

1. What does a .h file contain?
2. What does a .c file contain?
3. How do you decide whether something should go in a .H file or a .c file?
4. What is circular inclusion?
5. How might circular inclusion be a benefit?
6. How does the possibility of circular inclusion place a burden on the programmer?
7. How does an all-inclusive include file ease the burden on the programmer?
8. What penalty is paid for using an all-inclusive include file?
9. Why should header files never include .c files?
10. Why should .c files never include other .c files?

EXERCISES

1. Explain why C programs generally are not kept in one file. Tell how breaking up a program into smaller files helps the programmers on a project.
2. In your own words, describe what goes into a header (.h) file and why.
3. In your own words, describe what goes into a C source file (.c) and why.
4. Explain the advantages of using header files in C programs. Explain any disadvantages. Tell how you might overcome these disadvantages.
5. Explain how the sample organization of the text editor in this chapter helps program development.
6. Look back at the diagrams for the Space Attackers game in Chapter 13. Name at least three types you would create for this game. Describe how you would organize the files for these three types, and explain your reasons for organizing the files the way you did.
7. This chapter, and some of the previous chapters, presented the concept of organizing programs around their types. For each programmer-defined type, developers create a header file and a C source file. Describe any advantages of organizing a program around its types. Tell what disadvantages you think this might create.
8. Some programmers organize their files around the tasks a program performs rather than around the types it uses. Tell what you think of this technique. Explain the reasons for your viewpoint.
9. Suppose you are designing a customer database program for a software store. Name at least three types you would create for this program. Describe how you would organize the files for these three types. Explain your reasons for organizing the files the way you did.

Exercises 10–25 use the files in the Chapt17 directory on the Examples CD included with this book. These files form the basis of a text editor. You will find the Chapt17 directory in the Examples directory on the CD. Copy the files from the CD to your hard drive. If you are using Visual C, which is also on the CD, use the following instructions to compile the program.

For Windows 95/98, Windows NT, or Windows 2000:

- Start Visual C++.
- From the main menu, select File. Chose **New** from the **File** menu.
- When the dialog box appears, choose **Win32 Console Application**. Type in a name for the project. Click **OK**. Click **Finish**. Click **OK**.
- From the main menu, select Project, then choose **Add to Project**. Click **Files**.
- In the dialog box that appears, navigate to the directory containing the source files you copied from the CD. Select Tedit.c, T.buffer.c, and Tstring.c. Click **OK**.

10. Open the file Tstring.h. Notice that it defines the type `text_string` on line 51. It is defined as an array of characters. Any `text_string` variable declared like this

    ```
    text_string aVariableName;
    ```

    will be an array of characters. Tell whether you think it is better to implement the type this way or declare an array of characters every time you need a text string in the program. Explain why you think the implementation you've chosen is better.

11. The file Tstring.h contains prototypes for six functions. These are used to perform various tasks on the `text_string` type. Tell why you think these functions do or do not form a good set of interface functions for the `text_string` type.

12. Open the file Tstring.c. Part of the function `TextStringSetString()` is not yet written. The part that's missing should be inserted at line 88. Replace the comment

    ```
    // Insert a for loop here.
    ```

    with a `for` loop that copies the characters one by one from `charArray` into `theString`. Do not use the Standard Library `strcpy()` function.

13. Replace the `for` loop you wrote for Exercise 13 with a call to the `strcpy()` function. Be sure to include the Standard Library file string.h at the beginning of Tstring.c.

14. The file Tstring.h contains a function called `TextStringSetCharacter()`. The `for` loop in this function (lines 166–173) finds the length of a `text_string`. Replace this loop with a call to the C Standard Library `strlen()` function, which does the same thing. Be sure to include the Standard Library file string.h at the beginning of Tstring.c.

15. The function `TextStringGetCharacter()` in Tstring.c is not finished. Use the comments as a guide for writing the code that is missing. This function returns an integer. If there is an error, it returns –1 instead of the ASCII value of a character. Explain why this is or is not a good way to implement error handling in this function.

16. The function `TextStringGetCharacter()` in Tstring.c is not properly documented. Finish the documentation at the beginning of the function. Also, write and document the function `TextStringAppendCharacter()`.

17. The file Tbuffer.c contains a macro called `SelectValue3()`. As the comment on line 22 indicates, there is something wrong with the macro. Explain what it is. Either fix the macro, or rewrite it as a function. Explain why you chose the implementation you did. Tell why you think the macro is in Tbuffer.c rather than Tbuffer.h.

18. Finish and document the function `TextBufferSetRow()` in the file Tbuffer.c.

19. Document the functions `TextBufferGetRow()` and `TextBufferSetCharacter()` in the file Tbuffer.c.

20. Finish and document the function `TextBufferGetCharacter()` in the file Tbuffer.c.

21. Modify the file Tedit.c so that the program displays a status line on the line before the prompt for the user's command. When the user scrolls the buffer to the beginning, the program should print `"Beginning of buffer."` on the status line. When the user scrolls to the end, the program should print `"End of buffer."` on the status line.

22. Add a default case to the `switch` statement in the `main()` function in the file Tedit.c. If the user types invalid input, then beep the computer's speaker by printing ASCII character 7.

23. The named constants `CONTROL_D` and `CONTROL_U` are created using `#define` statements rather than the `const` keyword. This is because some compilers will not let you use constants created with the `const` keyword in the cases of `switch` statements. Change the constants `CONTROL_D` and `CONTROL_U` so that they are created with `const` rather than `#define`. Recompile the program and run it. Explain what happened. Tell which of these two you think is a better implementation. Tell why. Explain why the names of these two constants are or are not well chosen.

24. In the file Tedit.c, `ClearScreen()` is implemented as a macro. Tell whether or not you think this would be better implemented as a function.

25. The file Tedit.c is not properly documented. Finish the documentation in this file.

18

Pointers

OBJECTIVES

After reading this chapter, you should be able to:

- Explain the purposes and uses of pointers.

- Declare pointers and use them to point at data.

- Dereference pointers with pointer or array notation.

- Use pointers with functions.

- Declare and use character pointers for strings.

OUTLINE

PREVIEW

C is a flexible and efficient programming language. Much of its flexibility comes from its use of pointers. However, because the use of pointers is such a powerful and flexible tool, it is also a constant source of programmer errors.

This chapter presents essential techniques for using pointers. It also contains warnings about ways to help prevent pointer errors. Nearly any technique that reduces the likelihood of pointer errors is worth using. Pointer problems are notoriously difficult to find and can be excruciatingly difficult to fix. Nevertheless, pointers are such powerful tools that developers writing professional C programs can rarely get by without them.

18.1 What Is a Pointer?

A pointer is a variable that does not contain data. It contains the address of data. Every location in a computer's memory has an address. Normally, we give names to memory locations by declaring variables. That way, we don't have to know or deal with absolute addresses in memory. Pointers enable us to use and manipulate memory addresses in a hardware-independent way. We can use addresses to locate data without knowing the address itself.

Computer hardware relies heavily on the use of addresses. Because pointers enable us to utilize addresses in our programs, we have the ability to communicate with the computer in a manner that is close to the way it "thinks." It is often said that "pointers take programmers closer to the hardware." This characteristic of pointers makes our programs both more efficient and more powerful.

18.2 Using Pointers

Like all variables, pointers must be declared. They can be initialized when they are declared. To access the data to which a pointer points, our programs need to dereference pointers.

18.2.1 Declaring Pointers

To declare a pointer variable, programs declare the type of the pointer, indicate that it is a pointer rather than data, and declare the variable name. Figure 18.1 illustrates how this is done.

FIGURE 18.1 The Declaration of a Pointer to Integers

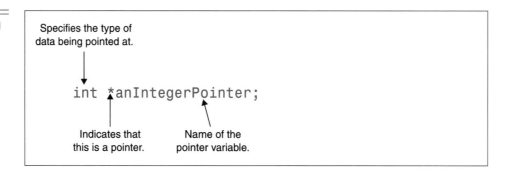

As Figure 18.1 shows, the type name at the beginning of the pointer declaration specifies the type of data that will be pointed at by the pointer variable. The asterisk (*) shows that this variable contains a pointer to data and not the data itself.

Pointers can point to any type of data. Example 18.1 demonstrates the declaration of pointer variables. Each variable in the example points at a different type of data.

EXAMPLE 18.1 Declaring Pointer Variables

```
1   int *anIntegerPointer;
2   char *aCharacterPointer;
3   unsigned long *anotherPointer;
4   double *aPointerToDouble;
5   customer *customerPointer;
6   void *aPointerToAnything;
```

The first declaration in Example 18.1 declares a pointer to integers. The variable `aCharacterPointer` on line 2 declares a pointer to characters. This variable can be used to point one character or a group of characters. In fact, any pointer can point to a group of data items, just like an array.

TECHNICAL NOTE 18.1
Pointers can point at single data items. They can also point at groups of data items, just as if they were arrays.

The third and fourth declarations in Example 18.1 declare pointers to the types un-signed long and double, respectively. The variable customerPointer does not point at an atomic data type. The customer type, which is shown on line 5, is a structure type that was created in the examples in Chapter 14. Pointers can point to any type of data. It doesn't matter whether the data is an atomic data type or a programmer-defined type.

The last declaration in Example 18.1 shows a pointer to void. When our programs use the keyword void as a return type on a function, it indicates that no data is returned. When programs use void in a function's parameter list, it states that there are no parameters. This logically leads many people learning C to assume that a pointer to void is a pointer to nothing. Although that is a logical assumption, it is not correct.

Variables of type void * are generic pointers which can point to any type of data. Software designers generally recommend against using them. It is usually better to state the type of the data being pointed at. However, there are times when we do not know in advance what data type a pointer will be used with. In these situations, the use of a void pointer may be unavoidable. Be aware, though, that using void pointers is not as straightforward as using other types of pointers. The potential problems are discussed in Section 18.7.3 later in this chapter.

18.2.2 Initializing Pointers

Pointers are initialized in much the same manner as other variables. Whenever you declare a pointer, it is wise to initialize it immediately. Never let a pointer contain an unknown value. Because pointers are so powerful, accidentally using an uninitialized pointer can be a disastrous error. The program may actually work for quite a while and then suddenly not work. Or it can work sometimes but not others. This type of error is *very* difficult to track down. Modern debugging tools can help, but it's a whole lot easier to just get into the habit of initializing every pointer.

Pointer variables are typically initialized to the value NULL, as shown in Example 18.2. NULL is a constant that is declared in the C Standard Library files stdio.h and stdlib.h. To use the value NULL, at least one of these two files must be included in your program.

EXAMPLE 18.2   Initializing Pointer Variables

```
1   int *anIntegerPointer = NULL;
2   char *aCharacterPointer = NULL;
3   unsigned long *anotherPointer = NULL;
4   double *aPointerToDouble = NULL;
5   customer_record *customerPointer = NULL;
6   void *aPointerToAnything = NULL;
```

18.2.3 Pointing to Data

The primary purpose of a pointer variable is to point at data. It does this by storing the memory address where the data is located. C provides the ampersand operator (&) for the task of finding the address of data.

Example 18.3 demonstrates the use of the ampersand operator for obtaining the address of data.

EXAMPLE 18.3   Obtaining the Address of Data

```
1    int anInteger;
2    int *anIntegerPointer = &anInteger;
3    char aCharacter = 'C';
4    char *aCharacterPointer = &aCharacter;
5    unsigned long anUnsignedLongValue = 10000;
6    unsigned long *anotherPointer = &anUnsignedLongValue;
7    double aDouble = 0;
8    double *aPointerToDouble = &aDouble;
9    customer aCustomer;
10   customer *customerPointer;
11   customerPointer = &aCustomer;
```

TIP 18.2
When programmers
read statements
such as

`anIntegerPointer = &anInteger;`

they read them as,
"anIntegerPointer equals
the address of anInteger."

Line 1 of this example declares an integer variable. Line 2 declares a pointer to an integer and uses the ampersand operator to find the address of `anInteger`. The variable `anInteger` is not initialized. It contains a random value. The variable `anInteger-Pointer` contains the memory address of `anInteger`.

Similarly, the declarations on lines 3 and 4 of the example create two variables. Line 3 declares a character variable called `aCharacter`. Line 4 declares the variable `aChar-acterPointer` and initializes it with the address of `aCharacter`. As a result, `aCharac-terPointer` points to `aCharacter`. This is illustrated in Figure 18.2.

FIGURE 18.2 A Character Variable and a Character Pointer

This figure shows that the character variable contains the character `'C'`. The character pointer variable contains the address in memory where the character variable is located. Rather than show the actual address in binary or hexadecimal, I've followed the convention of most C and C++ literature and depicted the pointer with an arrow. However, let me emphasize that nothing magical, mysterious, or even symbolic is stored in pointer variables. They contain a memory address in binary.

Note that initializing the pointer does not initialize the data. Initializing the data does not initialize the pointer. These are two separate operations. The character variable can be set to any character. That does not change the contents of the pointer variable. The pointer variable can be set to point at any other character anywhere else in memory. That does not change the contents of the character variable.

Suppose you wrote a program that contained the following statements:

```
char aCharacter = 'Q';
char anotherChar = 'D';
char *aCharacterPointer;
aCharacterPointer = &aCharacter;
```

These statements create three variables. The first, `aCharacter`, contains the character `'Q'`. The variable `anotherChar` contains the character `'D'`. The statement

```
aCharacterPointer = &aCharacter;
```

stores the address of `aCharacter` in `aCharacterPointer`. Figure 18.3 illustrates this.

FIGURE 18.3 Two Variables and a Pointer

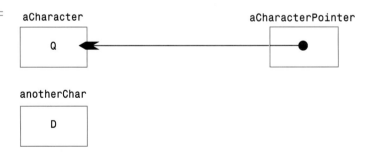

If the program contained the statement

```
aCharacterPointer = &anotherChar
```

the address contained in `aCharacterPointer` would change, as shown in Figure 18.4.

Reassigning the address in `aCharacterPointer` does not change the contents of `aCharacter` and `anotherChar`. Likewise, if the program contained the statements

```
aCharacter = 'X';
anotherChar = 'Z';
```

FIGURE 18.4 Reassigning the Pointer

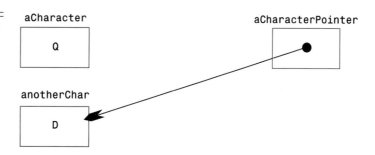

the address in the pointer variable would not change. These are important points to remember. As programmers, we must be able to distinguish between statements that change pointers and statements that change data.

If we look back at Example 18.3, we see that the other statements declare variables of a variety of types and declare pointers to those variables. Notice especially that finding the address of a variable that is of a programmer-defined type is no different than finding the address of a variable of an atomic data type. Line 9 shows the declaration of a variable of type `customer`. As line 11 demonstrates, finding the address of this programmer-defined structure variable requires the use of the ampersand operator just as if `customer` were an atomic data type.

18.2.4 Dereferencing Pointers

The purpose of pointing a pointer at data is to store, access, and process the data. When a program access the memory location indicated by a pointer variable, we say that it **dereferences** the pointer.

Programs use the asterisk operator (*) to dereference pointers. The code fragment in Example 18.4 declares an integer variable and an integer pointer.

EXAMPLE 18.4   Dereferencing a Pointer

```
1   int anInteger = 5;
2   int *anIntegerPointer = &anInteger;
3   printf("%d\n",*anIntegerPointer);
```

The third statement in this example prints the data in the memory location pointed at by `anIntegerPointer`. The value that is printed is 5 because `anIntegerPointer` points at `anInteger`, which contains 5. The statement

```
    *anIntegerPointer
```

accesses the contents of the memory location pointed to by `anIntegerPointer`. Confusingly, many C programmers read the statement

```
    *anIntegerPointer
```

as, "the contents of `anIntegerPointer`." Although this is common, it is not accurate. The contents of `anIntegerPointer` is an address. The statement

```
    *anIntegerPointer
```

does not give a program access to the address in `anIntegerPointer`. It provides access to the contents of the memory location pointed at by the address in `anIntegerPointer`. The way this statement should be read is "the contents of the memory location pointed to by `anIntegerPointer`."

To emphasize this idea further, Example 18.5 expands on the code fragment from Example 18.4.

EXAMPLE 18.5   Changing Pointer Data and Addresses

```
1   int anInteger = 5;
2   int *anIntegerPointer = &anInteger;
3   printf("%d\n",*anIntegerPointer);
```

```
4   *anIntegerPointer = 20;
5   printf("%d\n",*anIntegerPointer);
6   printf("%d\n",anInteger);
7   anIntegerPointer = 20;   // This is probably wrong!
```

If this code fragment were executed in a program, the value 5 would be printed to the screen, as in Example 18.4. However, the statement on line 4 changes the contents of the memory location that is pointed at by `anIntegerPointer`. Because `anIntegerPointer` points to `anInteger`, it also changes the contents of `anInteger` to 20. This is demonstrated by lines 5 and 6 of the example. They both print the value 20 to the screen.

When line 7 is executed, there is no dereference operator (the * symbol). Therefore, the statement stores the value 20 in the variable `anIntegerPointer`. This causes `anIntegerPointer` to point at the absolute memory address 20 in system RAM. That is almost always an error. If you're using MS DOS, you've just pointed the pointer to a section of memory called the Interrupt Vector Table. If you then assign a value into `*anIntegerPointer`, you'll discover that your computer will stop working rather quickly. If you're using another operating system, this may or may not work.

Figure 18.5 shows the difference between executing the statements in lines 4 and 7 of Example 18.5.

FIGURE 18.5 Assigning a Value to a Dereferenced and Undereferenced Pointer

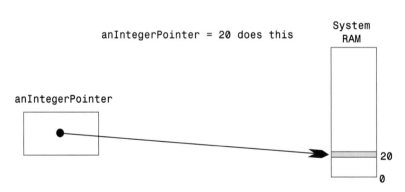

Usually, you don't want to point a pointer at an absolute address in memory. Most of the time, assigning a numeric value to a pointer (instead of the contents of the location it points at) is a mistake.

18.2.5 Pointing to Structures and Unions

When programs declare a structure or union variable, they access the individual members of the structure or union with the dot notation. To do so, they refer to the variable name, followed by the dot and the member name. This is shown in Example 18.6, which uses the `customer` structure defined in Chapter 14.

EXAMPLE 18.6 Accessing a Structure Variable's Member

```
customer aCustomer;
aCustomer.zip = 87654;
```

To get access to a structure or union member with a pointer, programs must dereference the pointer. As with variables of atomic data types, this is done with the asterisk operator (*). When a program dereferences a pointer to a structure (or union), it evaluates to a structure (or union). Programs must then use the dot notation to access individual members. The notation for this is demonstrated in Example 18.7.

EXAMPLE 18.7   Accessing a Structure Member with a Pointer

```
customer aCustomer;
customer *customerPointer;
customerPointer = &aCustomer;
*customerPointer.zip = 98765;
```

Using the asterisk and dot notations together can get somewhat tedious. So C provides the arrow operator (–>) as a shorthand notation. Example 18.8 illustrates its use.

EXAMPLE 18.8   Accessing a Structure Member with a Pointer

```
customer aCustomer;
customer *customerPointer;
customerPointer = &aCustomer;
customerPointer->zip = 98765;
```

Most programmers use the arrow notation. In professional programs, it is very rare to see the notation shown in Example 18.7.

18.3   Pointers and Arrays

Any pointer can point at a single piece of data or at a collection of data. If it points at a collection of data, the data must all be of the same type. This is another way of saying that a pointer can be used as an array.

In C, array names are pointers in disguise. Every array name contains the address of the data to which it points. Specifically, an array name contains the address of the first byte of the first element in the array. When you leave the subscript operator (the square brackets) off of an array, the array name evaluates to a pointer.

There are two primary differences between an array and a pointer that points at a block of data:

- The array points at a fixed location in memory. The pointer can point to any memory location.
- The amount of memory allocated for the array is fixed, or static. It is determined when you write the program and it does not change as the program runs. Pointers can point to memory blocks of different sizes.

18.3.1   Pointing to Arrays

Unlike atomic data types, programs do not need to use the ampersand operator to point a pointer at an array. Because an array name evaluates to the address of the first byte in the array, only the assignment operator is required. Once a pointer contains the starting address of the array, a program can access the individual array elements using the **base address** in the pointer and an **offset**. Example 18.9 illustrates these techniques.

EXAMPLE 18.9   Accessing an Array Using a Pointer

```
1   int anInteger;
2   int *aPointer;
3   int anArray[10] = {0,1,2,3,4,5,6,7,8,9};
4
5   aPointer = anArray;
6   anInteger = *aPointer;        // Gets the first integer.
7   anInteger = *(aPointer + 1);  // Gets the second integer.
```

Lines 1–3 of this example declare an integer variable, an integer pointer, and an array of integers. The array is initialized to contain the numbers 0–9. On line 5, the address of the first byte in the array is stored in aPointer. The ampersand operator is not needed in front of anArray because it is an array name. An array name with no subscripts evaluates to the starting address of the array.

Another way to obtain the first byte in an array is to use both the subscript and ampersand operators. For instance, we could change line 5 to read

```
aPointer = &anArray[0];
```

This change would not change the meaning of the statement. They say exactly the same thing. In fact, this notation was preferred in early C programs. Early versions of C did not support the notation on line 5 of Example 18.9. However, the notation used on line 5 is the preferred style today. As a result, some modern compilers will not recognize the statement

```
aPointer = &anArray[0];
```

To get the first integer in the array using the pointer, the code fragment in Example 18.9 uses the asterisk operator (line 6). Getting access to other elements in the array is not quite as straightforward. Programs must calculate the address of each successive element and then dereference the address. Line 7 of Example 18.9 demonstrates this.

Addresses in C are numbers. The C language enables us to add integer values to addresses. To calculate the address of the second element in the array, we must add an offset to the base address of the array. The base address is the address of the first byte in the array. The offset is the element number being accessed. Line 7 adds the number 1 (the offset) to the base address contained in aPointer. It then uses the asterisk to dereference the address it calculated. Figure 18.6 illustrates base addresses and offsets.

FIGURE 18.6 Adding Offsets to Base Addresses

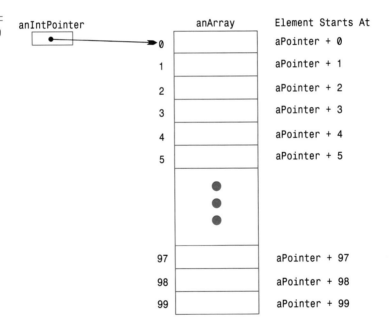

Notice that the statement

```
*(aPointer + 1)
```

uses parentheses to force precedence. The precedence of the dereference operator (the asterisk) is higher than the precedence of the addition operator. If the statement were

```
*aPointer + 1
```

precedence would force the pointer to be dereferenced first. The value 1 would then be added to whatever was at that location in memory. To gain access to the second element in the array, the program must perform the addition first and then dereference the address.

It is important to note that the statement

```
*(aPointer + 1)
```

does not add one *byte* to the address. It adds one times the size of the element. Line 2 of Example 18.9 states that aPointer points at integers. Because of this, the C compiler knows that adding one (or any other value) to aPointer means that we want to add one times the size of an integer to the base address it contains. If aPointer pointed at another data type, such as a float or a structure, it would add one times the size of that data type. The same is true when using the ++ or -- operators. They increment or decrement pointers by one times the size of the data being pointed at.

Because pointer notation can be cumbersome, many programmers find it easier and more efficient to increment or decrement pointers. Example 18.10 demonstrates this technique.

EXAMPLE 18.10   Incrementing a Pointer

```
1   int i, *aPointer;
2   int anArray[10] = {0,1,2,3,4,5,6,7,8,9};
3
4   aPointer = anArray;
5   for (i=0;i<10;i++)
6   {
7           printf("%d\n",*aPointer++);
8   }
```

Like Example 18.9, this example declares an integer, an integer pointer, and an array of integers. It points the integer pointer at the array. The code fragment then enters a for loop, which it uses to walk through the array. The first time through the loop, it dereferences the pointer to retrieve the integer value stored at the location specified by the address in aPointer. Because aPointer contains the address of the first element in the array, the integer value 0 is printed by the call to printf(). The postincrement operator increments the pointer after the 0 is printed.

On the second pass through the loop, aPointer contains the address of the second integer in the array. Instead of adding an offset to the base address on each pass through the loop, the code fragment increments the pointer. Figure 18.7 illustrates the operation of this for loop.

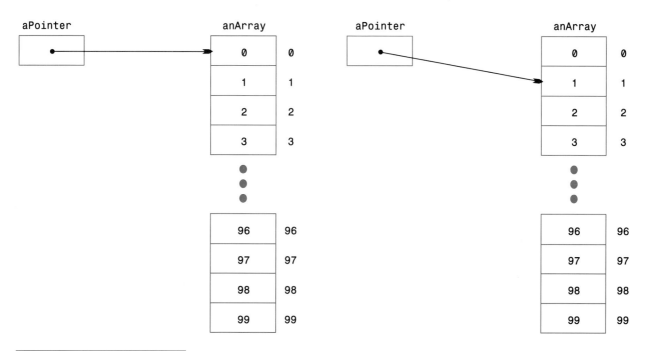

FIGURE 18.7   Incrementing a Pointer

When the loop finishes, the pointer points to an address that is beyond the end of the array. If we want the pointer to point to the beginning of the array again, we must insert the statement

```
aPointer = anArray;
```

after the end of the `for` loop.

18.3.2 Pointer and Array Notation

Because there is a fundamental equivalence between pointers and arrays, it is possible to use array notation with pointers and pointer notation with arrays. These techniques are demonstrated in Hands On 18.1.

Hands On 18.1

Objective

Write a program that:
> Declares an array of 100 integers.
> Declares a pointer to integers.
> Sets the pointer to the starting address of the array.
> Using the pointer and array notation, loops through the array and initializes
>> each item in it.
> Using the array and pointer notation, loops through the array and prints the
>> values in each item.

Experiment

Type the following program into your IDE or text editor. Compile, link, and run it.

```
1   #include <stdio.h>
2
3   int main()
4   {
5       int anArray[100];
6       int *anIntPointer = NULL;
7       int i;
8
9       anIntPointer = anArray;
10
11      // Array notation with the pointer name.
12      for (i=0;i<100;i++)
13      {
14          anIntPointer[i] = i;
15      }
16
17      // Pointer notation with the array name.
18      for (i=0;i<100;i++)
19      {
20          printf("%d\n",*(anArray+i));
21      }
22
23      return (0);
24  }
```

Results

The output of this program has been shortened to save space.

0
1

```
2
3
4
5
6
7
8
9
10
.
.
.
95
96
97
98
99
```

Analysis

This sample program begins by declaring an array of integers and a pointer to integers. It then points `anIntPointer` at the array.

Using a `for` loop, it loads integer values into the array. However, it does not use the array name. Rather, it uses the pointer name to store data. In addition, the loop treats the pointer name exactly as if it is an array name. That's because it *is* an array name for as long as it points at the array.

The second loop in this program (lines 18–21) accesses each element in the array through the array name. However, it does not use array notation, it uses pointer notation. This is not something programmers generally do. For the most part, developers find array notation easier to deal with than pointer notation. For this reason, many programmers use it rather than pointer notation when they can.

TECHNICAL NOTE 18.7
When compilers see array notation in programs, they convert it to pointer notation internally. The final binary executable contains pointers and offsets. Essentially, the compiler invisibly converts all array notation to pointer notation in the executable code.

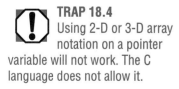

TRAP 18.4
Using 2-D or 3-D array notation on a pointer variable will not work. The C language does not allow it.

Hands On 18.1 demonstrates the fundamental equivalence of pointers and arrays. Because C arrays are really pointers, compilers generally translate all array notation in our programs to pointer notation. You and I don't see that. The compiler does it internally without changing our source code, so it doesn't matter to the compiler which notation we use. For this reason, programmers often prefer to use array notation with pointers whenever they can.

An important limitation on this concept is that it does not extend into higher-dimensional arrays. We cannot point a pointer to a 2-D or 3-D array and use 2-D or 3-D array notation on the pointer. This technique works only with arrays of a single dimension.

This is not as serious a limitation as it might seem at first. Chapter 19 will show how programs can use pointers to pointers to simulate a 2-D array.

Chapter 10 stated that although some programming languages prevent programmers from accessing memory outside arrays, C does not. Our programs are perfectly able to access memory outside an array. The equivalence of pointers and arrays tells us why.

Part of the flexibility of the C language is its ability to use pointers to point at blocks of memory. For C to be effective in that task, it must treat pointers and arrays the same. Pointers store only the address of data. To be as efficient as possible, they cannot store the size of the data block at which they point. It is therefore not possible for the C compiler to enforce array boundaries. To do so would create a fundamental difference between pointers and arrays, which would severely limit the uses of pointers or degrade their performance. Therefore, the designers of C just decided to let you and I handle that ourselves.

The equivalence of pointers and arrays has many advantages. Hands On 18.2 demonstrates one of them.

Hands On 18.2

Objective

Write a program that:
> Declares a 2-D array of characters.
> Declares an array of pointers to characters.
> Fills the 2-D array with strings.
> Points each pointer in the array of pointers to characters to the beginning of each row in the 2-D array.
> Uses the array of pointers to print each string in the 2-D array.
> Uses the array of pointers to sort the strings.
> Uses the array of pointers to print the sorted strings.

Experiment

The following program can be found in the Examples directory on the Examples CD included with this book. It is in the Chapt18 directory in a file called Ho18_2.c. Load it into your IDE or text editor. Compile, link, and run it.

```
1   #include <stdio.h>
2   #include <string.h>
3
4   #define ARRAY_SIZE 30
5   #define CHARS_PER_STRING 40
6
7   int main()
8   {
9       static char a2DCharArray[ARRAY_SIZE][CHARS_PER_STRING];
10      char *charPointerArray[ARRAY_SIZE];
11      int i,j;
12      char tempChar;
13      char *tempPointer = NULL;
14
15      for (i=0,tempChar = 'A';i<ARRAY_SIZE;i++)
16      {
17          for (j=0;j<CHARS_PER_STRING-1;j++)
18          {
19              if (tempChar > 'z')
20              {
21                  tempChar = 'A';
22              }
23
24              a2DCharArray[i][j] = tempChar++;
25          }
26          a2DCharArray[i][CHARS_PER_STRING-1] = '\0';
27      }
28
29      for (i=0;i<ARRAY_SIZE;i++)
30      {
31          charPointerArray[i] = a2DCharArray[i];
32      }
33
34      printf("\nThe unsorted array...\n");
35      for (i=0;i<ARRAY_SIZE;i++)
36      {
37          printf("%s\n",charPointerArray[i]);
```

```
38              }
39
40       for (i=1;i<ARRAY_SIZE;i++)
41       {
42               for (j=0;j<i;j++)
43               {
44                       if (strcmp(charPointerArray[i],
45                               charPointerArray[j]) < 0)
46                       {
47                               tempPointer = charPointerArray[i];
48                               charPointerArray[i] = charPointerArray[j];
49                               charPointerArray[j] = tempPointer;
50                       }
51               }
52       }
53
54   printf("\nThe sorted array...\n");
55       for (i=0;i<ARRAY_SIZE;i++)
56       {
57               printf("%s\n",charPointerArray[i]);
58       }
59
60       return (0);
61   }
```

 Results

```
The unsorted array...
ABCDEFGHIJKLMNOPQRSTUVWXYZ[\]^_`abcdefg
hijklmnopqrstuvwxyzABCDEFGHIJKLMNOPQRST
UVWXYZ[\]^_`abcdefghijklmnopqrstuvwxyzA
BCDEFGHIJKLMNOPQRSTUVWXYZ[\]^_`abcdefgh
ijklmnopqrstuvwxyzABCDEFGHIJKLMNOPQRSTU
VWXYZ[\]^_`abcdefghijklmnopqrstuvwxyzAB
CDEFGHIJKLMNOPQRSTUVWXYZ[\]^_`abcdefghi
jklmnopqrstuvwxyzABCDEFGHIJKLMNOPQRSTUV
WXYZ[\]^_`abcdefghijklmnopqrstuvwxyzABC
DEFGHIJKLMNOPQRSTUVWXYZ[\]^_`abcdefghij
klmnopqrstuvwxyzABCDEFGHIJKLMNOPQRSTUVW
XYZ[\]^_`abcdefghijklmnopqrstuvwxyzABCD
EFGHIJKLMNOPQRSTUVWXYZ[\]^_`abcdefghijk
lmnopqrstuvwxyzABCDEFGHIJKLMNOPQRSTUVWX
YZ[\]^_`abcdefghijklmnopqrstuvwxyzABCDE
FGHIJKLMNOPQRSTUVWXYZ[\]^_`abcdefghijkl
mnopqrstuvwxyzABCDEFGHIJKLMNOPQRSTUVWXY
Z[\]^_`abcdefghijklmnopqrstuvwxyzABCDEF
GHIJKLMNOPQRSTUVWXYZ[\]^_`abcdefghijklm
nopqrstuvwxyzABCDEFGHIJKLMNOPQRSTUVWXYZ
[\]^_`abcdefghijklmnopqrstuvwxyzABCDEFG
HIJKLMNOPQRSTUVWXYZ[\]^_`abcdefghijklmn
opqrstuvwxyzABCDEFGHIJKLMNOPQRSTUVWXYZ[
\]^_`abcdefghijklmnopqrstuvwxyzABCDEFGH
IJKLMNOPQRSTUVWXYZ[\]^_`abcdefghijklmno
pqrstuvwxyzABCDEFGHIJKLMNOPQRSTUVWXYZ[\
]^_`abcdefghijklmnopqrstuvwxyzABCDEFGHI
JKLMNOPQRSTUVWXYZ[\]^_`abcdefghijklmnop
qrstuvwxyzABCDEFGHIJKLMNOPQRSTUVWXYZ[\]
^_`abcdefghijklmnopqrstuvwxyzABCDEFGHIJ
```

```
The sorted array...
ABCDEFGHIJKLMNOPQRSTUVWXYZ[\]^_`abcdefg
BCDEFGHIJKLMNOPQRSTUVWXYZ[\]^_`abcdefgh
CDEFGHIJKLMNOPQRSTUVWXYZ[\]^_`abcdefghi
DEFGHIJKLMNOPQRSTUVWXYZ[\]^_`abcdefghij
EFGHIJKLMNOPQRSTUVWXYZ[\]^_`abcdefghijk
FGHIJKLMNOPQRSTUVWXYZ[\]^_`abcdetfghijkl
GHIJKLMNOPQRSTUVWXYZ[\]^_`abcdefghijklm
HIJKLMNOPQRSTUVWXYZ[\]^_`abcdefghijklmn
IJKLMNOPQRSTUVWXYZ[\]^_`abcdefghijklmno
JKLMNOPQRSTUVWXYZ[\]^_`abcdefghijklmnop
UVWXYZ[\]^_`abcdefghijklmnopqrstuvwxyzA
VWXYZ[\]^_`abcdefghijklmnopqrstuvwxyzAB
WXYZ[\]^_`abcdefghijklmnopqrstuvwxyzABC
XYZ[\]^_`abcdefghijklmnopqrstuvwxyzABCD
YZ[\]^_`abcdefghijklmnopqrstuvwxyzABCDE
Z[\]^_`abcdefghijklmnopqrstuvwxyzABCDEF
[\]^_`abcdefghijklmnopqrstuvwxyzABCDEFG
\]^_`abcdefghijklmnopqrstuvwxyzABCDEFGH
]^_`abcdefghijklmnopqrstuvwxyzABCDEFGHI
^_`abcdefghijklmnopqrstuvwxyzABCDEFGHIJ
hijklmnopqrstuvwxyzABCDEFGHIJKLMNOPQRST
ijklmnopqrstuvwxyzABCDEFGHIJKLMNOPQRSTU
jklmnopqrstuvwxyzABCDEFGHIJKLMNOPQRSTUV
klmnopqrstuvwxyzABCDEFGHIJKLMNOPQRSTUVW
lmnopqrstuvwxyzABCDEFGHIJKLMNOPQRSTUVWX
mnopqrstuvwxyzABCDEFGHIJKLMNOPQRSTUVWXY
nopqrstuvwxyzABCDEFGHIJKLMNOPQRSTUVWXYZ
opqrstuvwxyzABCDEFGHIJKLMNOPQRSTUVWXYZ[
pqrstuvwxyzABCDEFGHIJKLMNOPQRSTUVWXYZ[\
qrstuvwxyzABCDEFGHIJKLMNOPQRSTUVWXYZ[\]
```

Analysis

The underlying concept behind this program is the same technique that database programs use. Like database programs, this sample program sorts an index of data without moving the data itself.

An index in software is very much like the index of this book. If you look at it, you'll see that this book's index contains an alphabetical list of topics, and page numbers where those topics can be found. You can think of those page numbers as pointers to pages in the book. In programs, an index works the same way. It contains a sorted list of key words related to some important information. It also contains pointers to where the information can be found.

This Hands On program uses an array of pointers to characters to create an index. It sorts the index by sorting the pointers. Programs that use this technique are much more efficient because they do not have to move large blocks of data. They just shuffle pointers.

The program begins by declaring some constants, two arrays, and some temporary working variables that it needs. One of the arrays is a 2-D array of characters. Each row in this array is a string. The other array is a 1-D array of pointers to characters. Recall that, in C, a pointer to characters is another form of a string.

The program enters a pair of nested `for` loops which fill the array a2DCharArray with characters. Because strings in C must be terminated by a null character, the program also puts a null character on the end of each row.

Next, the program uses another `for` loop to point each of the pointers in charPointerArray to the beginning of a row in a2DCharArray. Notice that the statement

```
charPointerArray[i] = a2DCharArray[i];
```

omits one dimension of the array a2DCharArray. When you leave the second set of square brackets off of a two dimensional array, it evaluates to a pointer. The pointer contains the address of the first item in the row. So the statement above gets the address of the first character in each row and stores that address in the array of pointers. The statement

```
charPointerArray[i] = &a2DCharArray[i][0];
```

is another way to do the same thing.

The Hands On program prints each string using charPointerArray. This proves that the strings are not in sorted order. It then enters pair of nested for loops on lines 40–52 which sort the strings using the Bubble Sort we used in previous chapters. The program makes use of the Standard C Library string function strcmp() to compare two strings. If the first string is less than the second string, strcmp() returns a number that is less than zero. If they are equal, it returns zero. If the string in the first parameter is greater than the string in the second parameter, strcmp() returns a number greater than zero. Recall that the order which the strcmp() function uses is based on the ASCII chart. Any string beginning with uppercase letters will come before any string beginning with lowercase letters. Uppercase letters occur before lowercase letters in the ASCII chart.

If strcmp() detects that the string indicated by charPointerArray[i] is less than the string pointed at by charPointerArray[j], the body of the if statement swaps them by swapping the pointers. The strings themselves are never moved. This is exactly the same concept that is used in index files in database programs. It's generally much more efficient and more flexible to sort an index than to sort data.

The program finishes up by printing the sorted array of pointers.

18.4 Pointers and Functions

Pointers are often used as parameters to functions and as return values from functions.

18.4.1 Pointers as Parameters

Chapter 13 demonstrated that changes our programs make to parameter values in functions do not affect anything outside the functions. This is because the values in a function's parameters are copies of the values that were passed to the function.

This rule implies that we can move information into a function through its parameter list, but we can't get information back out through the parameter list. Pointers provide a way to get around that limitation.

If a program passes a pointer in a function's parameter list, it is passing the address of data rather than the data itself. If the data is changed by the function, it will remain changed after the function has ended. Example 18.11 illustrates this idea.

EXAMPLE 18.11   **Changing Data in a Function**

```
1   #include <stdio.h>
2
3   void AFunction(int intParameter,int *intPointerParameter);
4
5   int main()
6   {
7         int anInteger = 10;
8         int anotherInteger = 20;
9
10        printf("anInteger = %d\n",anInteger);
11        printf("anotherInteger = %d\n",anotherInteger);
12
```

```
13          AFunction(anInteger,&anotherInteger);
14
15          printf("anInteger = %d\n",anInteger);
16          printf("anotherInteger = %d\n",anotherInteger);
17
18          return (0);
19     }
20
21
22     void AFunction(int intParameter,int *intPointerParameter)
23     {
24          intParameter = 50;
25          *intPointerParameter = 60;
26
27          printf("intParameter = %d\n",intParameter);
28          printf("intPointerParameter = %d\n",*intPointerParameter);
29     }
```

Example 18.11 contains a small program which declares a function. Figure 18.8 shows the program's output. On lines 7 and 8, the program declares two integers and initializes them. It prints their values. On line 13, the program calls the function AFunction(). It passes the value in anInteger as the first parameter to AFunction(). The second parameter is the address of anotherInteger.

When the program jumps to AFunction(), the value in anInteger is copied into intParameter. The address of anotherInteger is copied into intPointerParameter. The statement on line 24 changes the value in intParameter. However, that does not change the value in anInteger because intParameter is a copy of anInteger. Changing the copy does not change the original.

The statement on line 25 changes the contents of the memory location pointed to by intPointerParameter. Because intPointerParameter points to the memory location used by anotherInteger, this statement will change the contents of anotherInteger. Figure 18.9 illustrates this concept.

The statements on lines 27–28 of Example 18.11 print the data contained in intParameter and pointed to by intPointerParameter. When the function AFunction() ends, program execution jumps back to line 13. Lines 15–16 print the contents of anInteger and anotherInteger. As you can see from Figures 18.8 and 18.9, the value of anotherInteger was changed by AFunction().

A more concrete demonstration of pointer parameters is shown in Example 18.12. The program creates a function called StringLength(), which works in exactly the same manner as the Standard Library function strlen(). Although the StringLength() function takes a pointer parameter, it uses array notation.

EXAMPLE 18.12   A Function with a Pointer Parameter

```
1   #include <stdio.h>
2
3   int StringLength(char *aString);
4
5   int main()
```

FIGURE 18.9 The Effect of a
Pointer Parameter

Before AFunction() Is Called

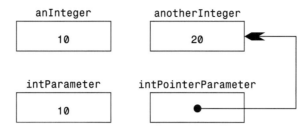

At the Beginning of AFunction()

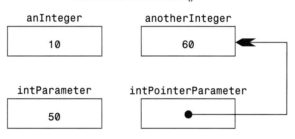

At the End of AFunction()

After AFunction() Returns

```
 6   {
 7          char tempString[] = "A short string.";
 8
 9          printf("The length of the string is %d\n",
10                  StringLength(tempString));
11
12          return (0);
13   }
14
15
16   int StringLength(char *aString)
17   {
18          int i;
19          for (i=0;aString[i]!='\0';i++)
20                  /* Empty loop body */  ;
21          return (i);
22   }
```

The StringLength() function in Example 18.12 does not change the data in the aString parameter. It is often the case that programmers pass pointers to data because passing the data itself would require too much overhead. For this reason, the StringLength() function takes a pointer to characters as its parameter.

Pass by Value, Pass by Address   Passing data to a function is called **pass by value**. When a program passes a parameter by value, it copies the value being passed into the parameter. Changing the copy does not change the original. Pass by value parameters transmit data *into* a function only. This is the parameter passing method introduced in Chapter 13.

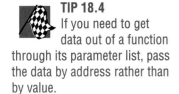

When a program passes a pointer to data in a function's parameter list, it is referred to as **pass by address**. Passing by address means that the address of the data is copied into a pointer parameter. Changing the data being pointed at within a function means the changes will persist after the function ends. The original data is being changed, not a copy. Pass by value parameters can move data both into *and* out of a function through the parameter list.

So when should we use pass by value and pass by address?

As often as possible, parameters should be passed by value. Passing by value prevents functions from accidentally changing data when they should not. However, pass by value is very inefficient when programs pass large pieces of data. Nested structures, in particular, can grow to be quite large. Passing large amounts of data by value forces the program to spend a lot of time creating multiple copies of the data.

Passing by address is more efficient when dealing with large blocks of data. Only the address is copied into the parameter. The program does not make a new copy of the data as it does when using pass by value. However, passing the address of data to a function means that the function can change the data. This leaves programs open to unintended side effects.

There are times when we *want* functions to change the values we pass as parameters. In fact, the C language would be hobbled if it *didn't* provide pass by address. This is one of the techniques that enable us to get more than one value out of a function when it returns. Recall that a function can return only one value at a time. If we want a function to pass back more than one value when it ends, we must pass those values through the parameter list using pass by address or pass by reference.

The most common reasons for passing parameters by address are the following:

- We need to get information out of a function through the parameter list.
- A function needs to return more than one value.
- Our program needs to change data inside a function and have that data remain changed after the function ends.
- The data is too large to pass by value efficiently.

For all other cases, the general preference among experienced C developers is to use pass by value.

Using `const` with Pointer Parameters   The program in Example 18.12 demonstrated an instance in which it is sensible to use pass by value even though the function does not change the data. If the `StringLength()` function were to change the data, it would be a serious program flaw.

In cases such as this, it is advisable to mark pointer parameters as unable to change the data to which they point. We can do this by adding the `const` keyword to the parameter declaration. Example 18.13 repeats the program in Example 18.12. However, in this version, the parameter list contains the word `const`. This prevents the function from changing the data.

EXAMPLE 18.13   A `const` Parameter

```
1    #include <stdio.h>
2
3    int StringLength(const char *aString);
4
5    int main()
6    {
7         char tempString[] = "A short string.";
8
9         printf("The length of the string is %d\n",
10                StringLength(tempString));
11
12        return (0);
13   }
14
15
```

```
16   int StringLength(const char *aString)
17   {
18           int i;
19           for (i=0;aString[i]!='\0';i++)
20                   /* Empty loop body */  ;
21           return (i);
22   }
```

Adding the `const` keyword before the type name of a pointer parameter prevents the function from changing the data. It is also possible to use `const` to prevent the function from changing the pointer. To do so, add the word `const` between the asterisk and the parameter name. Table 18.1 lists the ways that the `const` keyword can be used to prevent changes to pointers and data.

TABLE 18.1 Constant Pointer Parameters

Parameter Declaration	Description
`char *aString`	Neither the data nor the pointer are constant.
`const char *aString`	The data cannot be changed by the function. The pointer can be changed.
`char * const aString`	The data can be changed by the function. The pointer cannot.
`const char * const aString`	Neither the data nor the pointer can be changed by the function.

Table 18.1 uses the parameter for the `StringLength()` function shown in Examples 18.12 and 18.13. It illustrates that we can prevent functions from changing pointers, changing data, or both. However, programmers often ask, is this really necessary?

The answer is no and yes. Strictly speaking, there is no harm in the `StringLength()` function in Example 18.12. The fact that there is no `const` in the parameter list doesn't hurt the function. As long as the maintenance programmers remembers that the `StringLength()` function is not supposed to change data, everything will be fine. However, you should ask yourself, how likely is it that a programmer hired two or three years after you left the company will know exactly which functions you wrote should not change the data pointed to by their pointer parameters?

If you think that all maintenance programmers will always figure out which data is not supposed to be changed by a function, then you probably will not use the `const` keyword in your parameter lists. However, if you think that maintenance programmers just might make a mistake, then you'll probably consider the use of the `const` keyword essential.

TIP 18.6
Use the const keyword as often as possible with pointer parameters.

My recommendation is to use the `const` keyword as often as you can in parameter lists. If a maintenance programmer comes behind you and tries to modify data or pointers you've marked as `const`, he or she will most probably stop and do some serious thinking. Either the word `const` needs to be removed from the parameter list or the maintenance programmer is doing something wrong. Usually, it's the latter, not the former.

18.4.2 Pointers as Return Values

Just as with any other type, programs can use pointers as function return values. This enables functions to return arrays. It also helps us when we want to return large structures from a function. As with passing parameters, it is more efficient to return a pointer to a structure than the structure itself.

When returning pointers from a function, it is vital that we never try to return a pointer to a local variable. Example 18.14 demonstrates this mistake.

EXAMPLE 18.14 Returning a Pointer to a Local Variable

```
1   char *StringCombine(char *string1, char *string2)
2   {
3           char temp[256];
```

```
 4          char *tempPointer;
 5
 6          strcpy(temp, string1);
 7          strcat(temp, string2);
 8          tempPointer = temp;
 9          return (tempPointer);
10      }
```

The StringCombine() function in this example concatenates two strings in a local variable called temp. It returns the address of temp. Recall that the memory for local variables in functions comes from the program's stack. When the return statement at the end of StringCombine() is executed, the program sends the address in tempPointer back to the function which called StringCombine(). That address is the beginning of the array temp. It points to a location on the program's stack. When StringCombine() ends, the memory for temp will be given back to the stack. More than likely, the program will immediately use that area of the stack for something else. Even if it doesn't, the pointer will be pointing to an area of memory that is no longer is use. Either way, it is a recipe for disaster.

Usually, returning a pointer to a local variable causes programs to crash. Unfortunately, it can also work just fine for long periods of time. It all depends on how the compiler allocates stack space and how the program uses it. Errors like this can be extremely difficult to find. It is vital that you avoid this mistake.

Hands On 18.3 demonstrates the use of pointers as parameters and return values.

TRAP 18.5
Returning a pointer to a local variable in a function can cause numerous problems.

Hands On 18.3

Objective

Write a program that:
Defines a new type called text_string.
Provides the following functions for the text_string type:
    SetFromTextString()—Sets a text_string from another text string.
    SetFromCharArray()—Sets a text_string from a character array.
    ConcatenateCharArray()—Concatenates a character array to a text_string.
    AppendTextString()—Appends a text_string to a text_string.
    AppendCharArray()—Appends a character array to a text_string.
    AppendChar()—Appends a character to a text_string.
    Printf()—Performs the same task as printf(), but on a text_string.
    Scanf()—Performs the same task as scanf(), but on a text_string.
    Length()—Calculates and returns the length of a text_string.
The program should test each of these functions.

Experiment

The following program is provided on the Examples CD included with this book. In the Examples directory is a directory called Chapt18. The Chapt18 directory contains the files TString.h, TString.c, and StrTest.c. Load these three files into your text editor or IDE. Compile and link them. Run the resulting program.
This is the file StrTest.c.

```
 1  #include "TString.h"
 2
 3  int main()
 4  {
 5          text_string string1;
 6          text_string string2;
 7          text_string string3;
```

```
8          TextStringSetFromCharArray(&string2,"This is ");
9          TextStringSetFromCharArray(&string3,"a string.");
10         TextStringConcatenateTextString(&string1,
11                                         &string2,
12                                         &string3);
13
14         TextStringAppendChar(&string1,'\n');
15         TextStringPrintf(&string1);
16
17         TextStringSetFromCharArray(&string2,"This is ");
18         TextStringConcatenateCharArray(&string1,&string2,"another string.");
19
20         TextStringAppendChar(&string1,'\n');
21         TextStringPrintf(&string1);
22
23         TextStringSetFromCharArray(&string2,"Is this");
24         TextStringSetFromTextString(
25                 &string1,
26                 TextStringAppendCharArray(&string2," also a string?"));
27
28         TextStringAppendChar(&string1,'\n');
29         TextStringPrintf(&string1);
30
31         TextStringSetFromCharArray(&string1,"Here is ");
32         TextStringSetFromCharArray(&string2,"another string.");
33         TextStringAppendTextString(&string1,&string2);
34
35         TextStringAppendChar(&string1,'\n');
36         TextStringPrintf(&string1);
37
38         printf("The length of the string is ");
39         printf("%d\n",TextStringLength(&string1));
40
41         printf("Please type in a string and press Enter\n");
42         TextStringScanf(&string1);
43
44         printf("The string you typed in was:");
45         TextStringPrintf(&string1);
46         printf("\n");
47
48         return (0);
49  }
```

This is the file TString.h.

```
1   #if !defined(TSTRING_H)
2   #define TSTRING_H
3
4   #include <stdio.h>
5
6   #define MAX_TEXT_STRING_LENGTH 60
7
8   typedef struct
9   {
10          char charString[MAX_TEXT_STRING_LENGTH];
11          int length;
12  } text_string;
13
14
```

```
15   void TextStringSetFromTextString(text_string *destination,
16                                    const text_string *source);
17
18   void TextStringSetFromCharArray(text_string *destination,
19                                   const char * const source);
20
21   void TextStringConcatenateTextString(text_string *destination,
22                                        const text_string *string1,
23                                        const text_string *string2);
24
25   void TextStringConcatenateCharArray(text_string *destination,
26                                       const text_string *string1,
27                                       const char * const charArray);
28
29   text_string *TextStringAppendTextString(text_string *string1,
30                                           const text_string *string2);
31
32   text_string *TextStringAppendCharArray(text_string *string1,
33                                          const char * const charArray);
34
35   text_string *TextStringAppendChar(text_string *string1,
36                                     const char aCharacter);
37
38   int TextStringPrintf(const text_string *source);
39   int TextStringScanf(text_string *destination);
40
41   int TextStringLength(const text_string *theString);
42
43
44   #endif
```

This is the file TString.c.

```
1    #include "TString.h"
2
3    void TextStringSetFromTextString(
4              text_string *destination,
5              const text_string *source)
6    {
7         int i;
8
9         for (i=0;
10             (i<MAX_TEXT_STRING_LENGTH-1) &&
11                  (source->charString[i]!='\0');
12             i++)
13         {
14             destination->charString[i]=source->charString[i];
15         }
16         destination->charString[i]='\0';
17         destination->length=i;
18   }
19
20
21   void TextStringSetFromCharArray(
22              text_string *destination,
23              const char * const source)
24   {
25         int i;
26
```

```
27          for (i=0;
28               (i<MAX_TEXT_STRING_LENGTH-1) &&
29                    (source[i]!='\0');
30               i++)
31          {
32               destination->charString[i]=source[i];
33          }
34          destination->charString[i]='\0';
35          destination->length=i;
36     }
37
38
39     void TextStringConcatenateTextString(text_string *destination,
40                                          const text_string *string1,
41                                          const text_string *string2)
42     {
43          int i,j;
44
45          // Copy the characters from string1.
46          TextStringSetFromTextString(destination,string1);
47
48          // Copy the characters from string2.
49          for (i=string1->length,j=0;
50               (i<MAX_TEXT_STRING_LENGTH-1) &&
51                    (string2->charString[j]!='\0');
52               i++,j++)
53          {
54               destination->charString[i]=string2->charString[j];
55          }
56          destination->charString[i]='\0';
57          destination->length=i;
58     }
59
60     void TextStringConcatenateCharArray(text_string *destination,
61                                         const text_string *string1,
62                                         const char * const charArray)
63     {
64          int i,j;
65
66          // Copy the characters from string1.
67          TextStringSetFromTextString(destination,string1);
68
69          // Copy the characters from string2.
70          for (i=string1->length,j=0;
71               (i<MAX_TEXT_STRING_LENGTH-1) &&
72                    (charArray[j]!='\0');
73               i++,j++)
74          {
75               destination->charString[i]=charArray[j];
76          }
77          destination->charString[i]='\0';
78          destination->length=i;
79     }
80
81
82     text_string *TextStringAppendTextString(
83                         text_string *string1,
84                         const text_string *string2)
```

```
85    {
86         int i,j;
87
88         // Copy the characters from string2.
89         for (i=string1->length,j=0;
90              (i<MAX_TEXT_STRING_LENGTH-1) &&
91                   (string2->charString[j]!='\0');
92              i++,j++)
93         {
94              string1->charString[i]=string2->charString[j];
95         }
96         string1->charString[i]='\0';
97         string1->length=i;
98
99         return (string1);
100   }
101
102
103   text_string *TextStringAppendCharArray(
104                        text_string *string1,
105                        const char * const charArray)
106   {
107        int i,j;
108
109        // Copy the characters from string2.
110        for (i=string1->length,j=0;
111             (i<MAX_TEXT_STRING_LENGTH-1) &&
112                  (charArray[j]!='\0');
113             i++,j++)
114        {
115             string1->charString[i]=charArray[j];
116        }
117        string1->charString[i]='\0';
118        string1->length=i;
119
120        return (string1);
121   }
122
123
124   text_string *TextStringAppendChar(text_string *string1,
125                               const char aCharacter)
126   {
127        if (string1->length<MAX_TEXT_STRING_LENGTH-2)
128        {
129             string1->charString[string1->length] = aCharacter;
130             string1->length++;
131             string1->charString[string1->length] = '\0';
132        }
133        return (string1);
134   }
135
136
137   int TextStringPrintf(const text_string *source)
138   {
139        return (printf("%s",source->charString));
140   }
141
142
```

```
143   int TextStringScanf(text_string *destination)
144   {
145          return(scanf("%s",destination->charString));
146   }
147
148   int TextStringLength(const text_string *theString)
149   {
150          return (theString->length);
151   }
```

Results

This is a string.
This is another string.
Is this also a string?
Here is another string.
The length of the string is 24
Please type in a string and press Enter
astring
The string you typed in was:astring

Analysis

As a demonstration of the design and development techniques presented in previous chapters, this Hands On program defines a type called `text_string`. It also provides a set of functions that programs can use to perform operations on `text_string` variables. Following the guidelines given in Chapter 17, the `text_string` type is defined in TString.h. The implementation of the `text_string` functions appear in TString.c.

The file StrTest.c contains the program which uses the `text_string` type and functions. It begins by including TString.h. The `main()` function declares three `text_string` variables. On line 9, it calls the function `TextStringSetFromCharArray()` to store characters into a `text_string` variable.

The `TextStringSetFromCharArray()` function is on lines 21–36 of TString.c. Its prototype appears on lines 18–19 of TString.h. The function takes two parameters. The first is a pointer to a `text_string` structure. The second is a pointer to characters. It copies characters from the parameter `source` to the character array in the `text_string` parameter `destination`. In addition, it appends a null character onto the end of the string and saves the string's length in the structure.

Once the `TextStringSetFromCharArray()` function ends, the program returns to line 9 of StrTest.c. The `main()` function again calls `TextStringSetFromCharArray()` to store "a string." into the `text_string` variable `string3`. On lines 10–12, it calls `TextStringConcatenateTextString()`, which can be found on lines 39–58 of TString.c.

The `TextStringConcatenateTextString()` takes three parameters. The second and third are the two strings which will be concatenated. The first is the `text_string` into which the results will be stored. This function calls `TextStringSetFromTextString()` to copy characters from `string1` into `destination`. The code for `TextStringSetFromTextString()` is shown on lines 3–18 of TString.c. It is nearly identical to `TextStringSetFromCharArray()`. The primary difference is that `TextStringSetFromTextString()` copies characters from a `text_string` variable rather than a character array.

`TextStringConcatenateTextString()` enters a loop on line 49. The loop sets the variable `i` to contain the length of `string1`. This is also the index number of the location into which the next character in `destination` will be copied. The loop starts at that point in `destination` and copies characters from `string2`. When all of the characters have been copied, it appends a null character and saves the length of the string.

Returning from `TextStringConcatenateTextString()` takes program execution back to lines 10–12 of StrTest.c. The `main()` function invokes `TextStringAppendChar()` on line 14. This causes program execution to jump to line 124 of TString.c. The `TextStringAppendChar()` appends a single character onto the end of a `text_string` variable. It uses an `if` statement (line 127) to ensure that there is room in the `text_string` for one more character. If there is room, it inserts the character, increments the string's length, and appends the null character. When it ends, it returns a pointer to the `text_string`.

On line 15 of StrTest.c, `main()` calls the `TextStringPrintf()` function. This function performs essentially the same task as `printf()`, except that it prints `text_string` variables.

Lines 23–29 of StrTest.c show more calls to the functions `TextStringSetFromCharArray()` and `TextStringSetFromTextString()`. The `main()` function also invokes `TextStringAppendCharArray()` on line 26. This function appends a character array to a `text_string` variable. When it does, it changes the contents of the `text_string`. Because `TextStringAppendCharArray()` returns a pointer to its first parameter, its return value can be used as a parameter for any other function which takes a pointer to a `text_string`. This is exactly how `TextStringAppendCharArray()` is used on line 26 of StrTest.c. The code for `TextStringAppendCharArray()` is on lines 103–121 of TString.c.

The `TextStringAppendCharArray()` function uses a `for` loop to copy characters onto the end of its `string1` parameter. The loop sets `i` to the length of `string1`. This makes copying begin at the end of `string1`, overwriting the null character at the end. The other loop variable, `j`, is set to the value 0. This is used as the index number of the character to be copied. The loop runs while `i` is less than `MAX_TEXT_STRING_LENGTH-1` and the character in location `j` of `charArray` is not equal to the null character. On each iteration of the loop, both `i` and `j` are incremented. When the loop finishes, the function appends a null character and saves the length of the string.

On line 33 of StrTest.c, `main()` calls the `TextStringAppendTextString()` function. Its code is nearly identical to `TextStringAppendCharArray()`. The only difference is that `TextStringAppendTextString()` copies characters from a `text_string` rather than a character array.

Line 42 of StrTest.c invokes the function `TextStringScanf()`. This function uses `scanf()` to read a `text_string` from the keyboard.

All of the `text_string` functions have at least one pointer parameter. Many of them return a pointer. In instances where the function should not change what is being pointed at, the pointer is marked by the keyword `const`.

 Try This

Insert the keyword `const` into the parameter lists of the `text_string` functions that do not use it. How does this change the operation of the functions?

18.5 Pointers and Strings

The fundamental equivalence of pointers and arrays means that you can choose which notation you want to use based on your needs. You can select the notation that's fastest or the one that easiest to read.

Example 18.15 shows a function called `StringCopy()`, which is based on the Standard Library `strcpy()` function. The `StringCopy()` function uses array notation. It is easy and straightforward for most programmers to read.

EXAMPLE 18.15 The `StringCopy()` Function

```
1  char *StringCopy(char destinationString[],char sourceString[])
2  {
3        int i;
```

```
 4
 5          for (i=0; sourceString[i]!='\0'; i++)
 6          {
 7                  destinationString[i]=sourceString[i];
 8          }
 9          destinationString[i]='\0';
10
11          return (destinationString);
12   }
```

The for loop in Example 18.15 copies characters from the source array to the destination array. The condition on the for loop prevents the function from copying the null character to the destination string. As soon as the loop finds the null character in the source string, the condition evaluates to false. When this happens, the body of the loop and the increment are not executed. To ensure that the destination string has a null character on the end, the StringCopy() function explicitly puts one there before it returns.

Example 18.16 contains a version of the StringCopy() function that takes pointers for its parameters instead of arrays. It makes no difference how the function works. Pointers can be treated as arrays.

EXAMPLE 18.16 StringCopy() with Pointer Parameters

```
 1    char *StringCopy(char *destinationString,char *sourceString)
 2    {
 3          int i;
 4
 5          for (i=0; sourceString[i]!='\0'; i++)
 6          {
 7                  destinationString[i]=sourceString[i];
 8          }
 9          destinationString[i]='\0';
10
11          return (destinationString);
12    }
```

The StringCopy() function can also use equivalent pointer notation. Example 18.17 contains a version of StringCopy() with pointer notation.

EXAMPLE 18.17 StringCopy() with Pointer Notation

```
 1    char *StringCopy(char *destinationString,char *sourceString)
 2    {
 3          int i;
 4
 5          for (i=0; *(sourceString+i)!='\0'; i++)
 6          {
 7                  *(destinationString+i) = *(sourceString+i);
 8          }
 9          *(destinationString+i)='\0';
10
11          return (destinationString);
12    }
```

We can use pointer notation inside the StringCopy() function whether we declare the parameters as pointers or arrays. The C compiler will not generate an error either way. If we do use pointer parameters for the StringCopy() function, we can eliminate the integer variable i by incrementing the pointers. Example 18.18 demonstrates this technique.

EXAMPLE 18.18 Eliminating i from StringCopy()

```
 1   char *StringCopy(char *destinationString,char *sourceString)
 2   {
 3          char *temp = destinationString;
```

```
 4
 5        for (;*sourceString != '\0'; sourceString++,destinationString++)
 6        {
 7                *destinationString = *sourceString;
 8        }
 9        *destinationString='\0';
10
11        destinationString = temp
12
13        return (destinationString);
14   }
```

Although this version of the function looks quite different, it does exactly the same thing as previous versions. When a program calls this function, it passes StringCopy() two pointers to characters. It can also pass arrays. It makes no difference.

Let's suppose that a program calls the StringCopy() function with the statement

```
StringCopy(string1,string2);
```

where string1 and string2 are pointers to characters. The strings pointed to by string1 and string2 are passed by address. *The pointers themselves are passed by value.* This is an important detail to remember. The variables string1 and string2 are pointers. The addresses in those two pointers are *copied* into the parameters destinationString and sourceString when the StringCopy() function begins. The parameters destinationString and sourceString contain copies of the addresses in string1 and string2. You can change the copies of the addresses if you want to, but that doesn't change the addresses that string1 and string2 contain.

The for loop in Example 18.18 does not need anything in its initialization section. The two pointer parameters are already set to point at the beginning of the strings when the function is called. Therefore, the first thing the loop does is perform its test. Each time the test on the for loop evaluates to true, it executes the body of the loop. Inside the loop's body, the statement

```
*destinationString = *sourceString;
```

copies a character from the memory location pointed to by the pointer sourceString. It stores the character in the memory location pointed to by destinationString.

After the function executes the loop's body, it performs the increments. The for loop increments the addresses in the parameters destinationString and sourceString. Let me emphasize that this does not change the addresses in the calling program (string1 and string2 in our example). The parameters destinationString and sourceString are copies of the original pointers that were passed into StringCopy().

Although incrementing the parameters destinationString and sourceString does not change string1 and string2, it does change the addresses that destinationString and sourceString contain. On line 13, the StringCopy() function returns that destinationString contains. When the for loop finishes, destinationString contains the address of the end of the string, not the beginning. As a result, the StringCopy() function declares a temporary variable on line 3 to save the address of the beginning of the destination string. On line 11, StringCopy() assigns that address back into destinationString. It then returns the address.

Example 18.19 also shows a version of the StringCopy() function. This time, the test in the for loop has been made more efficient. This version still tests for the null character. However, it performs the test by evaluating the character itself. Because the null character evaluates to zero, the test will evaluate to false when it encounters the null character.

EXAMPLE 18.19   Eliminating the Comparison from StringCopy()

```
 1   char *StringCopy(char *destinationString,char *sourceString)
 2   {
 3        char *temp = destinationString;
 4
 5        for (;*sourceString; sourceString++,destinationString++)
```

```
 6          {
 7                  *destinationString = *sourceString;
 8          }
 9          *destinationString='\0';
10
11          destinationString = temp
12
13          return (destinationString);
14   }
```

We can make this function even more efficient by using an assignment. An assignment statement evaluates to a value. The value of the assignment statement is the value which is assigned. We can use this fact to make our loop even more concise, as shown in Example 18.20.

EXAMPLE 18.20   A Terse Version of `StringCopy()`

```
 1   char *StringCopy(char *destinationString,char *sourceString)
 2   {
 3          char *temp = destinationString;
 4
 5          for (;*destinationString = *sourceString;
 6                  sourceString++,destinationString++)
 7          {
 8          }
 9
10          destinationString = temp
11
12          return (destinationString);
13   }
```

The body of the `for` loop is now empty. All of the work is done in the control portion. The assignment statement

```
    *destinationString = *sourceString
```

assigns the value in the memory location that `sourceString` points at to the memory location pointed to by `destinationString`. The value of that assignment is the character that was assigned. If the character is the null character, the assignment evaluates to zero, or false. If it is any other value, it evaluates to true.

Because the assignment statement is now in the test portion of the `for` loop, the null character is copied to the destination string. We no longer need the extra assignment of the null character just before the `return` statement.

It is actually possible to make this function even more efficient and concise. Example 18.21 shows how.

EXAMPLE 18.21   A Bare Bones `StringCopy()` Function

```
 1   char *StringCopy(char *destinationString,char *sourceString)
 2   {
 3          char *temp = destinationString;
 4
 5          while (*destinationString++ = *sourceString++)
 6          {
 7          }
 8
 9          return (temp);
10   }
```

In this version the `for` loop becomes a `while` loop. The increments are done in the test. The C compiler will not see anything wrong with that. Because the loop uses postincrements, the dereferences and the assignment are performed first. Each time the function executes this loop, it performs the test. To evaluate the test, it must perform the assignment. To do the assignment, the function must dereference the pointers, so it gets the character in the memory location pointed to by `sourceString`. It assigns the character into the memory location pointed to by `destinationString`. The value of the assignment is the value of the character. As long as the null character is not assigned, the loop continues. After the function performs the assignment and the test, it increments the pointers to the next location in memory.

There are trade-offs to using pointer notation this way. Programmers may find it hard to read. Many more programmers are familiar and comfortable with array notation than with this style of pointer notation. The version of `StringCopy()` in Example 18.21 is extremely efficient. However, some programmers may not understand how it works. Therefore, you've got to decide what's more important, code readability or efficiency.

To stress this point even further, I'll provide one more example before we move on to another topic. Because the body of the `while` loop in Example 18.21 was empty, we can omit it completely. However, we must terminate the `while` loop with a semicolon. Example 18.22 contains a final version of the `StringCopy()` function.

EXAMPLE 18.22   The Final `StringCopy()` Function

```
1   char *StringCopy(char *destinationString,char *sourceString)
2   {
3         char *temp = destinationString;
4
5         while (*destinationString++ = *sourceString++);
6
7         return (temp);
8   }
```

As brief as this function is, it still does everything the original did. As you can see, it uses far less code than the original.

If you do choose to use these pointer techniques, it's a good idea to include plenty of comments explaining what you did. Adding comments goes a long way toward helping new programmers on the project understand the code they're reading.

18.6   Using Pointers in the Text Editor

The availability of pointers puts us one step closer to creating a text editor like those that have actually been used by professional programmers. As with all good software, a design of the text editor must be done first.

18.6.1   Statement of Purpose

Following the design techniques presented in Chapter 13, we'll start the design of the text editor by creating a statement of purpose. It's important to be able to state the purpose of every program we write. We must know why the software will be useful before we bother to write it.

Our statement of purpose will simply be to write a text editor to demonstrate how complete programs (not just small examples) are written.

18.6.2   The Functional Specification

The next step in designing a program is a functional specification. As you may recall, a functional specification is a list of everything a program does. Table 18.2 gives a functional specification for this version of the text editor.

18.6.3   Program Design Charts

Using the functional specification, we can create some top-down design charts for the text editor. Figure 18.10 shows the design chart.

TABLE 18.2 A Functional Specification for the Text Editor

Task	Description
Create a buffer for text.	Allocate memory for a fixed-size text buffer.
Fill the buffer.	Generate and store strings of varying length in the text buffer.
Clear the screen.	Remove any text that may be displayed on the screen.
Display the buffer.	Print one page of text to the screen. A page is defined as enough rows of text to fill the text area.
Display a menu.	Display the menu of valid commands.
Get user input.	Retrieve a command character from the user. The program will take action based on the user's command.
Scroll up one line.	Scroll the text one line toward the beginning of the buffer.
Scroll up one page.	Scroll the text one page toward the beginning of the buffer.
Scroll down one line.	Scroll the text one line toward the end of the buffer.
Scroll down one page.	Scroll the text one page toward the end of the buffer.
Edit a row.	Enable the user to edit one row of text.
Quit.	Exit the program.

FIGURE 18.10 A Top-Down Design of the Text Editor

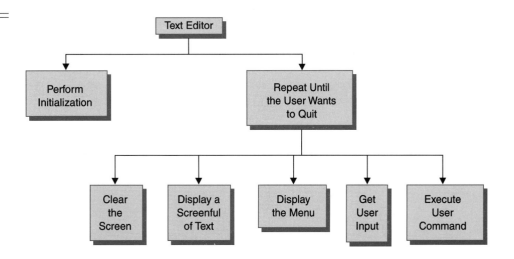

The design chart shows that the program performs its necessary initialization and then enters a loop. Until the user wants to quit, the program clears the screen and displays one page of text. The editor uses a portion of the screen as its text area. A page of text is considered to be the number of lines of text that fit into the text area.

In addition to displaying the page of text, the editor prints a menu of commands that it recognizes. It asks the user to enter a command and retrieve the user's input. The program uses a series of logical conditions to determine which command was entered. It then executes the appropriate response. Figure 18.11 gives more detailed view of the Execute User Command task from Figure 18.10.

18.6.4 Designing the Types

The types which will be used in the text editor need to be designed next. The editor will create and manipulate a buffer of text. We could use just a 2-D array of characters for the buffer. However, doing so would present us with some problems.

The declaration of the 2-D array tells us how many rows of text the array can *potentially* contain. However, it does not tell us how many of the rows actually contain text. For this version of the text editor, that is not particularly important because the program fills all rows of the buffer. It might seem that a 2-D array is exactly what we need.

There is, however, one other piece of information that the editor needs associated with the text buffer. To scroll the text buffer, the editor will need to know the line number

FIGURE 18.11 **Executing the User's Command**

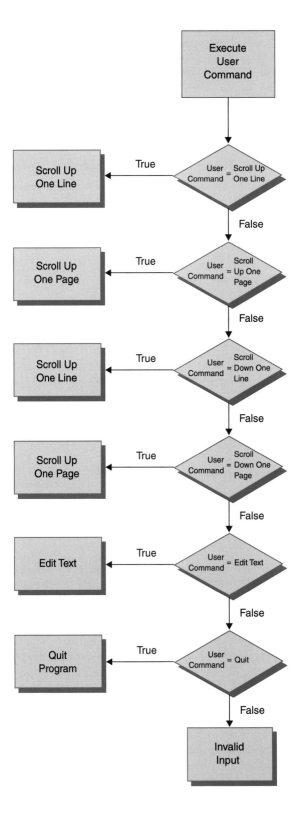

of the first line of the buffer that is displayed on the screen. We could declare that as an integer variable in main() and pass it to all functions which require it. However, if we are passing an array and an associated integer to several functions, it indicates that these pieces of information need to be packaged together into a single type. This was discussed in Chapter 15.

For these reasons, the text editor defines a type called text_buffer. The text_buffer type will contain a 2-D array of characters and an integer. Using the list of tasks in Table 18.2 as a guide, we can create a list of functions to go with the text_buffer type. Table 18.3 gives this list.

Function	Description
TextBufferInitialize()	Initializes a variable of type text_buffer to a known state.
TextBufferSetRow()	Copies a string into a specified row in a text buffer.
TextBufferGetRow()	Copies a row of characters from a text buffer into a string.
TextBufferScrollUp()	Scrolls upward a specified number of lines.
TextBufferScrollDown()	Scrolls downward a specified number of lines.
TextBufferGetTopLine()	Retrieves the first line of the buffer to be displayed in the text area on the screen.

TABLE 18.3 Functions for the text_buffer Type

Table 18.2 tells us that a text buffer will need to be initialized, scrolled up, and scrolled down. For simplicity, this will be done on a row-by-row basis. Therefore, the text_buffer type requires functions to get and set the contents of a row. To display the buffer's contents, the program will need to retrieve the index number of the first row to be displayed. The functions in Table 18.3 fulfill all of these requirements.

According to the design specifications created so far, this is the only type needed to create the text editor program. Therefore, the program will be divided into three files. The first, TEdit.c, will contain the highest-level functions in the program. The other two, TBuffer.h and TBuffer.c, will contain the definition and implementation of the text_buffer type.

18.6.5 Moving To Pseudocode

Before writing program code, our next task should be to write the pseudocode for each function. Example 18.23 contains one possible version of the pseudocode for TEdit.c. Example 18.24 shows the type definition of the text_buffer type. Example 18.25 contains the pseudocode for TBuffer.c.

EXAMPLE 18.23 The Pseudocode for TEdit.c

```
1  //---------------------------------------------------------
2  /*
3  File Name:    TEdit.c
4  Comments:     This file contains the functions which
5                implement the text editor.
6  */
7  //---------------------------------------------------------
8
9
10 void InitializeTextBuffer(text_buffer *tBuffer);
11 void ClearScreen(void);
12 void DisplayText(const text_buffer * const tBuffer);
13 void PrintMenu(void);
14 char GetUserCommand(void);
15
16
17 int main()
18 {
19       // Initialize the text buffer.
20
21       // While the user does not want to quit...
22             // Clear the screen.
23             // Display a page of text.
24             // Display the menu.
25             // Get the user's command.
26             // If the user wants to scroll up one line...
27                   // Scroll the buffer up one line.
```

```
28                    // If the user wants to scroll up one screenful...
29                            // Scroll the buffer up one screenful.
30                    // If the user wants to scroll down one line...
31                            // Scroll the buffer down one line.
32                    // If the user wants to scroll down one screenful...
33                            // Scroll the buffer down one screenful.
34                    // If the user wants to edit text...
35                            // Prompt the user for the line to edit.
36                            // Get the user's input.
37                            // Prompt the user for a line of text.
38                            // Get the user's input.
39                            // Store the new text in the specified row.
40                    // If the user wants to quit...
41                                // Set the loop control variable to exit.
42                    // Else the command is not recognized...
43                            // Print an error message.
44    }
45
46
47    //-----------------------------------------------------------
48    /*
49    Function Name:      InitializeTextBuffer
50    Parameters:
51         In:           None.
52         Out:          tBuffer - A pointer to the buffer which
53                               will be filled by this function.
54         In/Out:       None.
55    Return Values:     None.
56    Comments:          This function fills the specified text buffer
57                       with rows of text of varying length.
58    */
59
60    void InitializeTextBuffer(text_buffer *tBuffer)
61    {
62         // Set the text buffer to a known state.
63
64         // For each row in the buffer...
65              /* Generate a random number between 5 and the
66              maximum length of a row. This will be the length
67              of the string to store in the current row. */
68              /* Generate a string of text of the calculated
69              length. */
70              // Store the string in the current row.
71    }
72
73    // End InitializeTextBuffer
74    //-----------------------------------------------------------
75
76
77    //-----------------------------------------------------------
78    /*
79    Function Name:      ClearScreen
80    Parameters:
81         In:           None.
82         Out:          None.
83         In/Out:       None.
84    Return Values:     None.
85    Comments:          This function clears the screen by printing newlines.
```

```
86    */
87
88    void ClearScreen(void)
89    {
90         // For each line on the screen...
91              // Print a newline.
92    }
93
94    // End ClearScreen
95    //------------------------------------------------------------
96
97
98    //------------------------------------------------------------
99    /*
100   Function Name:    DisplayText
101   Parameters:
102        In:          tBuffer - A pointer to the text buffer
103                          that will be displayed on the screen.
104        Out:         None.
105        In/Out:      None.
106   Return Values:   None.
107   Comments:        This function starts with the current top
108                    row in the text buffer and prints
109                    successive rows of text from the buffer
110                    to the screen. It stops when it reaches
111                    the maximum number of rows to be displayed.
112   */
113
114   void DisplayText(const text_buffer * const tBuffer)
115   {
116        // For each row to be displayed...
117             // Get a row of text.
118             // Print it to the screen.
119   }
120
121   // End DisplayText
122   //------------------------------------------------------------
123
124
125   //------------------------------------------------------------
126   /*
127   Function Name:    PrintMenu
128   Parameters:
129        In:          None.
130        Out:         None.
131        In/Out:      None.
132   Return Values:   None.
133   Comments:        The PrintMenu function prints the menu of
134                    text editor commands to the screen.
135   */
136
137
138   void PrintMenu(void)
139   {
140        // Print the commands recognized by the text editor.
141   }
142
143   // End GetUserCommand
```

```
144     //------------------------------------------------------------
145
146
147     //------------------------------------------------------------
148     /*
149     Function Name:      GetUserCommand
150     Parameters:
151             In:             None.
152             Out:            None.
153             In/Out:         None.
154     Return Values:      This function returns a single-character
155                         user command.
156     Comments:           The GetUserCommand function retrieves a
157                         character command from the keyboard. The
158                         user must type the character, followed by
159                         the Enter key. If the Enter key is not
160                         pressed, this function waits until it is.
161
162                         After the command is retrieved, there is
163                         still a newline character left in the
164                         keyboard buffer. This function will pull
165                         it out and throw it away.
166     */
167
168     char GetUserCommand(void)
169     {
170             // Get the user's command from the keyboard.
171             // Throw away the newline.
172             // Return the command.
173     }
174
175     // End GetUserCommand
176     //------------------------------------------------------------
177
178
179     // End TEdit.c
180     //------------------------------------------------------------
```

EXAMPLE 18.24   The Definition of the `text_buffer` Type

```
1   typedef struct
2   {
3       char allRows[TBUFFER_LENGTH][TBUFFER_ROW_LENGTH];
4       int topLine;
5   } text_buffer;
```

EXAMPLE 18.25   The Pseudocode for TBuffer.c

```
1    //------------------------------------------------------------
2    /*
3    File Name:   TBuffer.c
4    Comments:    This file contains the functions which
5                 implement all of the valid operations on the
6                 text_buffer type.
7    */
8    //------------------------------------------------------------
9
10
11   //------------------------------------------------------------
```

```
12    /*
13    Function Name:      TextBufferInitialize
14    Parameters:
15          In:           None
16          Out:          None.
17          In/Out:       tBuffer - Contains the address of the
18                             text buffer to initialize
19    Return Values:      None.
20    Comments:           This function sets the text buffer into a
21                        known state. It does this by initializing
22                        the top line to zero and setting the first
23                        character in each row to the null
24                        character.
25    */
26
27    void TextBufferInitialize(text_buffer *tBuffer)
28    {
29          // Initialize the first row to zero.
30
31          // For each row of the buffer...
32                /* Set the first character in each row to the
33                null character. */
34    }
35
36    // TextBufferInitialize
37    //------------------------------------------------------------
38
39
40    //------------------------------------------------------------
41    /*
42    Function Name:      TextBufferSetRow
43    Parameters:
44          In:           rowNumber - Specifies the index number of
45                             the row to set.
46                        textString - Contains a string of
47                             characters that will be copied into
48                             the specified row.
49          Out:          None.
50          In/Out:       tBuffer - Contains the address of the
51                             text buffer that the text string
52                             will be copied into.
53    Return Values:      None.
54    Comments:           Use this function to copy a string of
55                        characters into a row in the text buffer.
56    */
57
58    void TextBufferSetRow(int rowNumber,
59                          const char * const textString,
60                          text_buffer *tBuffer)
61    {
62          // If the row is in range...
63                /* Copy the characters from the text string to the
64                specified row. */
65    }
66
67    // End TextBufferSetRow
68    //------------------------------------------------------------
69
```

```
70
71   //------------------------------------------------------------
72   /*
73   Function Name:      TextBufferGetRow
74   Parameters:
75       In:             rowNumber - Specifies the index number of
76                           the row to get.
77                       tBuffer - Contains the address of the
78                           text buffer that the text string
79                           will be copied from.
80       Out:            textString - Contains a string of
81                           characters that the specified row will
82                           be copied into.
83       In/Out:         None.
84   Return Values:      None.
85   Comments:           Applications use this function to copy
86                       the specified row from the text buffer
87                       into a string of characters.
88   */
89
90   void TextBufferGetRow(int rowNumber,
91                         char *textString,
92                         const text_buffer * const tBuffer)
93   {
94       // If the row is in range...
95               /* Copy the characters from the specified row into
96               the text string.
97   }
98   // End TextBufferGetRow
99   //------------------------------------------------------------
100
101
102  //------------------------------------------------------------
103  /*
104  Function Name:      TextBufferScrollUp
105  Parameters:
106      In:             linesToScroll - Contains the number of
107                          lines to scroll up.
108      Out:            None.
109      In/Out:         None.
110  Return Values:      None.
111  Comments:           This function scrolls the buffer up by
112                      the number of lines specified in the
113                      linestoScroll parameter. Scrolling the
114                      buffer up means moving the displayable
115                      area toward the beginning of the buffer.
116                      This is done by setting the top row of
117                      the buffer.
118
119                      If scrolling the buffer results in the
120                      top row of the buffer taking on a value
121                      that is less than zero, the top row is
122                      set to zero.
123  */
124
125  void TextBufferSetRow(int linesToScroll,
126                        text_buffer *tBuffer)
127  {
```

332 Chapter 18

```
128          // Move the top row up.
129
130          // If the top row is less than zero...
131                // Set the top row to zero.
132    }
133
134    // End TextBufferScrollUp
135    //--------------------------------------------------------------
136
137
138    //--------------------------------------------------------------
139    /*
140    Function Name:      TextBufferScrollDown
141    Parameters:
142        In:            linesToScroll - Contains the number of
143                             lines to scroll down.
144        Out:           None.
145        In/Out:        None.
146    Return Values:     None.
147    Comments:          This function scrolls the buffer down by
148                       the number of lines specified in the
149                       linestoScroll parameter. Scrolling the
150                       buffer down means moving the displayable
151                       area toward the end of the buffer.
152                       This is done by setting the top row of
153                       the buffer.
154
155                       If scrolling the buffer results in the
156                       top row of the buffer taking on a value
157                       that is greater than the last line of
158                       the buffer minus the number of rows in
159                       the on-screen text area, the top row is set
160                       to the last line of the buffer minus the
161                       number of rows in the on-screen text area,
162    */
163    void TextBufferScrollDown(int linesToScroll,
164                              int displayAreaHeight,
165                              text_buffer *tBuffer)
166    {
167         // Move the top row down.
168
169         /* If the top row is greater than the last line of
170         the buffer minus the number of rows in the on-screen text
171         area... */
172                /* Set the top row to the last line of the buffer
173                minus the number of rows in the on-screen text area. */
174    }
175
176    // End TextBufferScrollDown
177    //--------------------------------------------------------------
178
179
180    //--------------------------------------------------------------
181    /*
182    Function Name:      TextBufferGetTopLine
183    Parameters:
184        In:            tBuffer - Contains a pointer to the text
185                             buffer.
```

```
186          Out:        None.
187          In/Out:     None.
188   Return Values:     This function returns the curren top row
189                      number.
190   Comments:          See Return Values.
191   */
192
193   int TextBufferGetTopLine(const text_buffer * const tBuffer)
194   {
195          // Return the top row number.
196   }
197
198   // End TextBufferGetTopLine
199   //---------------------------------------------------------
200
201
202   // End TBuffer.c
203   //---------------------------------------------------------
```

The pseudocode shown in these examples is only one possible version. To aid students in coding their programs, I find it easier to present pseudocode which resembles C. This method also enables the pseudocode to be written into C source files as comments. When the C code is written, the result will be a program that is very well documented.

Many designers do not like this approach. They prefer that pseudocode be written in a style that more closely resembles a human language such as English. The primary (and compelling) advantage of this is that designers do not have to commit to a particular programming language until after the program is designed. They can decide which language best fits the task that the pseudocode describes.

If the company you work for does not have pseudocoding standards, you must decide which style of pseudocode works best for your situation.

18.6.6   Writing the Program

Hands On 18.4 presents the text editor as we have designed it. Because it is somewhat long, the code is not shown here in the book. Instead, you will find it on the Examples CD included with this book.

Hands On 18.4

Objective

Write a text editor that:
    Fills a buffer with text.
    Enables the user to edit the text one line at a time.
    Enables the user to scroll the text up or down.
    Enables the user to exit the program.

Experiment

The files for this Hands On program are found on the Examples CD included with this book. They are the files TEdit.c, TBuffer.h, and TBuffer.c. You'll find them in the Ho18_4 directory. The Ho18_4 directory is in the Chapt18 directory, which is in the Examples directory.

Results

Figure 18.12 shows the initial screen displayed by the text editor program.

FIGURE 18.12   The Initial
Output of the Text Editor

```
Display  Buffer
Line     Line
Number   Number
   0        0      ABCDEFGHIJKLMNOPQRSTUVWXYZ[\]^_`abcdefg
   1        1      hijklmnopqrstuvwxyzABCDEFGHIJKLMNOPQRST
   2        2      UVWXYZ[\]^_`abcdefghijklmnopqrstuvwxyzA
   3        3      BCDEFGHIJKLMNOPQRSTUVWXYZ[\]^_`abcdefgh
   4        4      ijklmnopqrstuvwxyzABCDEFGHIJKLMNOPQRSTU
   5        5      VWXYZ[\]^_`abcdefghijklmnopqrstuvwxyzAB
   6        6      CDEFGHIJKLMNOPQRSTUVWXYZ[\]^_`abcdefghi
   7        7      jklmnopqrstuvwxyzABCDEFGHIJKLMNOPQRSTUU
   8        8      WXYZ[\]^_`abcdefghijklmnopqrstuvwxyzABC
   9        9      DEFGHIJKLMNOPQRSTUVWXYZ[\]^_`abcdefghij
  10       10      klmnopqrstuvwxyzABCDEFGHIJKLMNOPQRSTUUW
  11       11      XYZ[\]^_`abcdefghijklmnopqrstuvwxyzABCD
  12       12      EFGHIJKLMNOPQRSTUVWXYZ[\]^_`abcdefghijk
  13       13      lmnopqrstuvwxyzABCDEFGHIJKLMNOPQRSTUUWX
  14       14      YZ[\]^_`abcdefghijklmnopqrstuvwxyzABCDE
Press one of the following keys to issue a command, then press the Enter key.
U Scroll up one line.  D Scroll down one line.  B Scroll up one page.  F Scroll
down one page.  E Edit text.  Q Quit.
COMMAND>>>
```

Analysis

The main() function for this Hands On program resides in the file TEdit.c. As with most C source files, TEdit.c contains a section for include files. It also has a specific section for constants used throughout the program. In addition, it defines an enumerated type called boolean on lines 45–49.

The boolean type did not appear in the design. This is a design flaw. It is often easy to accidentally omit the design of small types such as this one. However, designs should be detailed enough to account for them. If we overlook details such as this, there will be some confusion on the part of developers working from our designs. If small details such as the boolean type do not appear in the design, it is likely that developers on the project will create their own. One of the developers may create a boolean type exactly as it appears on lines 45–49. Another may create a type called bool. Some programmers prefer the name logical for this type. Others prefer BOOL or BOOLEAN. It is easy in this situation for many programmer-defined types which do exactly the same task to be created. Only one is needed throughout the entire program. It should be defined and included in the design.

Lines 59-63 of TEdit.c contain the prototypes of the functions which are defined in TEdit.c and called only by main(). For this reason, their prototypes do not appear in a header file.

The main() function begins on line 71. It declares three variables, one of which is the text buffer. Because of stack size the limitations of some compilers, it was necessary to declare textBuffer as static. The details of the keyword static are presented in Chapter 21. On line 81, main() invokes the InitializeTextBuffer() function. The address of textBuffer is passed as the only parameter.

The code for the InitializeTextBuffer() is on lines 176–234. It calls TextBufferInitialize() to set the text buffer into a known state. It then uses the C Standard Library rand() function to fill each row of the buffer with strings of random length. You may wonder why this code isn't moved into TextBufferInitialize(). The reason goes back to the software life cycle. To decrease the cost of maintenance and to increase the reusability of the text_buffer type, the TextBufferInitialize() function was written in a generic way. Initializations specific to this program are performed in InitializeTextBuffer(). This style of implementation slightly increases the amount of code in the program, but helps make the text_buffer type completely independent of all functions in TEdit.c.

After the InitializeTextBuffer() finishes, the main() function enters a for loop on line 84. This is the primary loop of the program. It clears the screen and displays one page of text by calling DisplayText().

The DisplayText() function calls the TextBufferGetTopLine() function to retrieve the row number of the first row of buffer text to be displayed in the screen. It enters a for loop on line 294. Within the loop, the printf() statements print the line number of the text area, the buffer line number, and the row of text.

TRAP 18.6
Forgetting to include small details in a design can cause confusion among programmers on a development project.

The design for the text editor did not contain any information about the format of the program's output. This is also a design flaw. On a project with many developers, everyone has to know in advance what information the program will print on the screen. They must also know the exact arrangement of the information on the screen. It is not unusual for designs to specify program output right down to the pixel level.

When the `DisplayText()` function ends, the program jumps back to line 90 of TEdit.c. The `main()` function invokes `PrintMenu()` to print the program's main menu on the screen. On line 96, it calls `GetUserCommand()` to retrieve a character command from the user.

A look at `GetUserCommand()`, which appears on lines 369–406 of TEdit.c, shows that the function does more than just read a character. In addition, this function removes the remaining newline character out of the keyboard buffer. However, this assumes there *is* a keyboard buffer. For the most part, that is a safe assumption. However, that assumption is not documented in the Comments section of the function's banner. It should be. Programmer assumptions such as this are very easy to overlook. We must be careful to document them.

When `GetUserCommand()` ends, the program returns to line 96 of TEdit.c. After a user command has been retrieved from the keyboard, the `main()` function uses a `switch` statement, beginning on line 98, to determine which command was entered by the user. If the user entered the command to scroll up one line, the program calls `TextBufferScrollUp()` on line 103.

The code for the `TextBufferScrollUp()` function is on lines 134–172 of TBuffer.c. Its prototype is on lines 46–47 of TBuffer.h. The function takes two parameters. The first is the number of lines to scroll. The second is a pointer to the `text_buffer` variable to be scrolled. When `TextBufferScrollUp()` is called, it decrements the `topLine` member of the `text_buffer` structure by the value in `linesToScroll`. If `topLine` becomes less than zero, it is set to zero. This prevents the function from scrolling beyond the beginning boundary of the array. When `TextBufferScrollUp()` finishes, the program returns to line 103 of TEdit.c.

If the user enters the command to scroll down one line, the `main()` function invokes `TextBufferScrollDown()` on line 117. The prototype for this function is on lines 48–50 of TBuffer.h. The code for it appears on lines 176–221 of Tbuffer.c. This function takes three parameters. The first is the number of lines to scroll. The second is the size of the on-screen text area. The third is a pointer to the buffer to be scrolled.

`TextBufferScrollDown()` operates in a manner that is very similar to `TextBufferScrollUp()`. However, it has some additional constraints it must handle. It must leave at least one page of text on the screen. It cannot let the user scroll the screen until the screen is blank. If this happens, the user could easily become confused and frustrated. Therefore, the function cannot allow the top line of the buffer to be scrolled by more than the total length of the buffer minus the height of the on-screen text display area. If this happens, it adjusts the top line of the buffer. When it ends, program execution goes back to line 117 of TEdit.c.

The `TextBufferScrollUp()` and `TextBufferScrollDown()` functions are also called on lines 110 and 124, respectively, of TEdit.c. These calls are made in response to the scroll page up and scroll page down commands.

If the user enters the command to edit text, the `switch` statement in `main()` selects the `case` statement which begins on line 130. Notice that there are opening and closing braces between the `case` and `break` statements. The braces define a new block of code. Local variables may be defined in any code block, as the variables `lineNumber` and `tempString` are.

Within the code block of the `case` statement, the program prompts the user for the buffer line number of the row to edit. It then prompts the user and calls the `scanf()` function get the text which will be stored in the row. When this text is retrieved, the program uses `TextBufferSetRow()` to store it in the text buffer.

If the user types in the quit command, the `switch` statement jumps to the case beginning on line 156 of TEdit.c. This case sets the variable done to TRUE. When it does, the `for` loop beginning on line 84 exits.

In situations where the user enters a command not recognized by the program, it jumps to the `default` statement, which begins on line 162. The `default` prints an error message and waits for the user to press Enter.

The program in Hands On 18.4 illustrates the attention to detail that software designers need in order to properly design software. Although it seemed as if the design for the program was good, it contained important omissions. Paying attention to detail is part of becoming a professional programmer.

18.7 Troubleshooting Guide

After reading this section, you should be able to:

- Recognize and fix uninitialized pointers.
- Read complex pointer declarations.
- Understand the complications which result from using void pointers.

18.7.1 Uninitialized Pointers

Forgetting to initialize pointers is a common source of pointer problems in C. In Example 18.26, the program fragment declares a pointer to an integer. It also assigns a value into the location pointed to by `anIntegerPointer`. We can't tell where that location is just by looking at these statements.

EXAMPLE 18.26   An Assignment to an Uninitialized Pointer

```
1   int *anIntegerPointer;
2   *anIntegerPointer = 5;
```

If you accidentally forget to initialize a pointer (and we all do eventually), you may be lucky enough to have a compiler that will catch this error. If it doesn't, your compiler may automatically initialize all uninitialized data to zero. If that is the case, then you'll get an error when you run the program. The text for the run time error will probably be "Null pointer assignment." or something similar. Alternatively, the operating system may generate an error. Typically it will display a message telling you that your program caused a "General Protection Fault" or an "Unrecoverable Error."

If your compiler doesn't automatically initialize uninitialized data to zero, your program can work just fine for a while. The pointer will contain a random value. The value might by chance be a valid memory address. If it is, the program will work. The random value may also point to an area of memory that already stores data. In that case, you'll get a memory overwrite. Literally anything can happen to your program when it encounters a memory overwrite. The result is completely unpredictable.

The easiest way to eliminate many pointer errors is to always initialize every pointer to NULL when you declare it.

18.7.2 Complex Pointer Declarations

Pointers enable programmers to accomplish very complex tasks in very efficient ways. However, this sometimes necessitates pointer declarations which are not very straightforward. For example, Example 18.27 shows some declarations that some programmers will not find easy to read.

EXAMPLE 18.27   Complex Pointer Declarations

```
1   int **anArray[];
2   int *AFunction();
3   int **AFunction();
```

The key to being able to read statements like these is to follow precedence. You start with the identifier name and end with the type name. In between, you use the precedence chart to determine what is being declared.

To read the first statement in Example 18.27, start with the name `anArray`. If you check a precedence chart, you'll see that the array subscript operator ([]) has higher precedence than the pointer declaration (*). Therefore `anArray` is an array, as the name of the variable suggests. Each element in `anArray` is a pointer to a pointer to an integer.

Reading the declaration on line 2 of Example 18.27 requires the same technique. The identifier is `AFunction`. Because the parentheses have higher precedence than the asterisk, `AFunction` is a function. `AFunction()` returns a pointer to an integer. What we are looking at here is a function prototype. The same is true of the third declaration in Example 18.27. It is a function that returns a pointer to a pointer to an integer.

One technique for simplifying pointer declarations is to use `typedef` statements to break them into smaller pieces. For instance, Example 18.28 shown an alternative way to create the declaration on line 1 of Example 18.27.

EXAMPLE 18.28   Simplifying Pointer Declarations

```
1   typedef int ** pointer_to_int_pointer;
2   pointer_to_int_pointer anArray[];
```

The `typedef` statement on line 1 of this example creates an alias, or new name, for pointers to pointers to integers. The statement on line 2 uses the alias to declare the array. There can be no real doubt about what is being declared here. It is an array of pointers to integer pointers (which is another way of saying pointer to pointer to `int`).

18.7.3   Complications with `void` Pointers

Programs can use `void` pointers as generic pointers to any type of data. However, they are not as straightforward to use as other types of pointers. Example 18.29 demonstrates `void` pointers.

EXAMPLE 18.29   Using void Pointers

```
1   #include <stdio.h>
2
3   int main()
4   {
5        int intData[5] = {5,6,7,8,9};
6        int *intPointer;
7        float floatData[5] = {0.1,0.2,0.3,0.4,0.5};
8        float *floatPointer;
9        void *genericPointer;
10       int i;
11
12       // These two loops are ok.
13
14       intPointer = intData;
15       for (i=0;i<5;i++)
16       {
17            printf("%d\n",*intPointer++);
18       }
19
20       floatPointer = floatData;
21       for (i=0;i<5;i++)
22       {
23            printf("%f\n",*floatPointer++);
24       }
25
26       // These two loops won't work.
27       genericPointer = intData;
28       for (i=0;i<5;i++)
29       {
```

```
30                      printf("%d\n",*genericPointer++);
31              }
32
33              genericPointer = floatData;
34              for (i=0;i<5;i++)
35              {
36                      printf("%f\n",*genericPointer++);
37              }
38
39              return (0);
40      }
```

The short program in this example declares two arrays, one of type `int` and the other of type `float`. The first two loops in the program demonstrate that typed pointers can be used to step through arrays of data. When the program dereferences the pointers `intPointer` and `floatPointer`, it knows how many bytes of data to retrieve from memory because the types of the pointers are stated.

Let's suppose that both an `int` and a `float` are four bytes. Line 6 tells the compiler that `intPointer` points at integer data. When the dereference statement on line 17 is compiled, the compiler generates code to retrieve four bytes of integer data. Likewise, when it compiles the dereference statement on line 23, the compiler generates code to retrieve four bytes of floating-point data.

In addition, the compiler must know the type of the data in order to perform increments and decrements on pointers. The increment statements on lines 17 and 23 work because the compiler knows how many bytes are in an `int` and a `float`.

The same is not true for the two loops on lines 27–37. According to the rules of C, it is perfectly acceptable to point a `void` pointer to typed data. This is shown on lines 27 and 33. The C compiler will have no problem with these two statements.

However, because the compiler does not know the types of the data being pointed at, the statements on lines 30 and 36 will not work. The compiler will not be able to generate code to dereference or increment `genericPointer`.

The easiest way to solve this is to type cast the `void` pointer whenever the program performs a dereference, increment, or decrement on it. Example 18.30 illustrates this technique with the program from Example 18.29.

EXAMPLE 18.30 Type Casting `void` Pointers

```
1   #include <stdio.h>
2
3   int main()
4   {
5           int intData[5] = {5,6,7,8,9};
6           int *intPointer;
7           float floatData[5] = {0.1,0.2,0.3,0.4,0.5};
8           float *floatPointer;
9           void *genericPointer;
10          int i;
11
12          // These two loops are ok.
13
14          intPointer = intData;
15          for (i=0;i<5;i++)
16          {
17                  printf("%d\n",*intPointer++);
18          }
19
20          floatPointer = floatData;
21          for (i=0;i<5;i++)
22          {
```

```
23                  printf("%f\n",*floatPointer++);
24          }
25
26          // These two loops also work.
27          genericPointer = intData;
28          for (i=0;i<5;i++)
29          {
30                  printf("%d\n",*((int *)genericPointer)++);
31          }
32
33          genericPointer = floatData;
34          for (i=0;i<5;i++)
35          {
36                  printf("%f\n",*((float *)genericPointer)++);
37          }
38
39          return (0);
40  }
```

This version of the program will work correctly. The type cast of the void pointer tells the compiler the size of the data. When the void pointer is dereferenced or incremented, the compiler will generate the appropriate code.

It is not always possible to type cast the void pointer. There are other, more advanced, solutions to this problem. However, they require a knowledge of C language features that are beyond the scope of this book.

SUMMARY

A pointer is a variable which contains the address of data rather than the data itself. The address of a data item can be stored in a pointer using the & and = operators. When a program accesses the data being pointed at, it uses the dereference operator (*).

Programs can use pointers to contain the addresses of atomic data types or programmer-defined types. When accessing structure or union members, programs can use the –> operator.

Pointers can also point at arrays. Because arrays and pointers are essentially the same thing, pointer notation can be used with array names. Programs can use array notation with pointers. However, only the notation for 1-D arrays can be used.

Programs can pass pointers as parameters to functions. When they do, it is termed pass by address. Passing the data itself is called pass by value. If a pointer to data must be passed to a function but the function should not change the data, the keyword const can be used to enforce the constancy of the data.

Pointers can also be used as return values from functions. A function should never return a pointer to a variable that is local to itself.

To prevent possible problems, programs should always initialize pointers to NULL upon declaration. Complex pointer declarations should be avoided if possible. If not, they can be simplified with typedef statements. Although pointers of type void * can be used as generic pointers, the complications that result from their use limit their value.

TECHNICAL NOTES

18.1   Pointers can point at single data items. They can also point at groups of data items, just as if they were arrays.

18.2   Pointers can point a atomic data types. They can also point at programmer-defined types.

18.3   Pointers can also be used to point at functions. However, that is an advanced topic that is beyond the scope of this book.

18.4   The technique of assigning absolute hardware addresses was commonly used by graphics and game programmers under MS DOS. In order to squeeze maximum perfor-

mance out of the hardware, programmers accessed the memory on the display adaptor, called video RAM or VRAM, directly. They would do this by declaring a pointer and setting it to point at the beginning of VRAM. This method is still used by programmers writing software for embedded systems.

18.5   Some operating systems present programs with a virtual address space which they then map to physical addresses. This enables the operating system to convince programs that they have much more memory than is physically installed. The extra memory is supplied by swapping portions of programs and data out to the disk. Windows, Unix, and the Macintosh OS all use this technique. The result of this process is that assigning an absolute address on an OS such as Unix may not cause the program to crash. However, it is probably not correct because it doesn't enable you to set a pointer to an actual hardware address.

18.6   In addition to adding offsets to base addresses contained in pointers, programs can also subtract offsets from base addresses. They can also use the increment and decrement operators on pointers. No other arithmetic operators can be used with pointers.

18.7   When compilers see array notation in programs, they convert it to pointer notation internally. The final binary executable contains pointers and offsets. Essentially, the compiler invisibly converts all array notation to pointer notation in the executable code.

18.8   It is not strictly the case that functions return only a single value. It is possible to return two values from a C function. However, this is not widely used in industry because so many programmers are unfamiliar with the technique. Even if you know how to do it, the maintenance programmer probably won't. It's usually best just to avoid returning multiple values.

18.9   Declaring an array of pointers to pointers is one way of declaring a 3-D array.

TIPS

18.1   Always initialize all pointers. It goes a long way toward preventing pointer problems in programs.

18.2   When programmers read statements such as

        anIntegerPointer = &anInteger;

they read them as, "anIntegerPointer equals the address of anInteger."

18.3   The ampersand operator can be used to find the address of any type of variable. It doesn't matter whether the variable is an atomic data type or a programmer-defined type.

18.4   If you need to get data out of a function through its parameter list, pass the data by address rather than by value.

18.5   With some specific exceptions, it is generally better to pass parameters by value.

18.6   Use the `const` keyword as often as possible with pointer parameters.

TRAPS

18.1   Dereferencing a pointer does not give access to the address it contains. It gives access to the data to which it points.

18.2   It is usually a mistake to assign an absolute numeric value to a pointer variable.

18.3   When dereferencing an address calculated by adding an offset to a base address, leaving off parentheses will give an incorrect result. Programs must use parentheses to force the address to be calculated first, and then the address can be dereferenced.

18.4   Using 2-D or 3-D array notation on a pointer variable will not work. The C language does not allow it.

18.5   Returning a pointer to a local variable in a function can cause numerous problems.

18.6   Forgetting to include small details in a design can cause confusion among programmers on a development project.

18.7   The layout of a program's output should not be omitted from its design. Major misunderstandings between programmers can occur if the screen output and printed reports are not designed before the program is written.

REVIEW QUESTIONS

1. What is a pointer?
2. Why should pointers be initialized to NULL when they are declared?
3. How do programs dereference pointers to atomic data?
4. How do programs dereference pointers to programmer-defined types?
5. In what ways are pointers and arrays similar? In what ways are they different?
6. What is the difference between pass by value and pass by address?
7. When would programmers use pass by value rather than pass by address?
8. When would programmers use pass by address rather than pass by value?
9. When is it appropriate to use the `const` keyword in pointer parameter declarations?
10. What happens when a function returns a pointer to a variable that is declared inside itself? Why does this happen?

EXERCISES

1. Fill in the blanks.

   A pointer contains the _____ of _____ rather than the _____ itself.

2. Name three uses of pointers.

3. Demonstrate how the addresses of data are stored in pointers. Show both atomic data types and programmer-defined types.

4. Demonstrate how pointers are dereferenced. Show both atomic data types and programmer-defined types.

5. Explain the difference between the following two statements.

   ```
   *intPointer = 20;
   intPointer = 20;
   ```

   Explain any possible problems with the second statement.

6. This chapter contains several warnings of potential problems you might encounter with pointers. Make a list of them. Tell whether you think pointers are a good feature in the C language. Explain why.

7. When assigning a pointer to point at the beginning of an array, the & operator is not needed on the array name. Explain why.

8. Explain the differences between pointers and arrays. Describe the similarities.

9. The `text_string` type created for Hands On 18.3 does not use any of the C Standard Library functions. Rewrite the `text_string` type so that it uses as many Standard Library string functions as possible. Be sure to include the header file string.h in TString.c.

10. Write a program that attempts to use 2-D array notation on a pointer which points to a 2-D array. Explain what happened and why.

11. Explain the use of a base address and an offset in accessing a group of data items with an array. Tell why this technique makes it impossible for the C language to check array boundaries.

12. Write a program which contains a function called `Swap()`. The `Swap()` function must take two integer pointers as parameters. It should swap the values in the memory locations pointed to by the parameters.

13. Write a function called `StringReverse()`. Have the `StringReverse()` function take two parameters, a source string and a destination string. Make it copy the characters from the source string into the destination string in reverse order. For example, the first character in the source string should be the last character in the destination string, and so forth. Use arrays and array notation. Write a program that demonstrates that your `StringReverse()` function works.

14. Rewrite the `StringReverse()` function you wrote for Exercise 13 so that it uses pointers and pointer notation. Make the function as efficient as possible.

15. Write a function called `PrintMessages()`. The `PrintMessages()` funtion should print a group of strings that are passed into it. Have the `PrintMessages()` function take two parameters. The first should be an array of strings. None of the strings should be longer than 80 characters. The second parameter should be an integer that tells how many strings are in the array of strings. Write a program that demonstrates that your `PrintMessages()` function works. Make it call `PrintMessages()` at least three times. Each time that the program calls `PrintMessages()`, it should pass in a different array of strings. Each array should contain a different number of strings.

16. Write a program that defines and uses the following types.

    ```
    typedef enum
    {
            SPADES,
            CLUBS,
            HEARTS,
            DIAMONDS
    } card_suit;

    typedef enum
    {
            ACE,
            TWO,
            THREE,
            FOUR,
            FIVE,
            SIX,
    ```

```
        SEVEN,
        EIGHT,
        NINE,
        TEN,
        JACK,
        QUEEN,
        KING
} face_value.

typedef struct
{
        card_suit suit;
        face_value value;
};
```

Your program should declare an array of cards. Initialize the array so that it contains cards in random order. You can use the C Standard Library `rand()` function if you want. Also declare an array of pointers. Set each pointer to point at a structure in the array of cards. Print the array of cards using the array of pointers. Sort the cards by suit by sorting the array of pointers. Use the suit order defined by the `card_suit` enumerated type. Within each suit, sort the cards into the order defined by the `face_value` enumeration. Print the sorted cards.

17. A data structure is a method of organizing data in software. Data structures and C `struct` statements are not the same thing. A common data structure used in programs is a stack. One way to implement a stack is to use a C `struct` statement. For a stack of integers, the `struct` can contain an array of `int` values. It also needs an integer member called `top`. There are three basic operations on a stack: initialize, push, and pop. When a program creates a stack, it should initialize it into a known state. In this state, the value of `top` is set to zero. A stack is a last in, first out data structure (LIFO). The last item that the program puts onto the stack is the first one it takes off. Therefore, the act of putting a value onto the stack is called pushing it. Removing a value from the stack is called popping it. Write a program that implements a stack of 100 integers. The initialize, push, and pop operations should match the following function prototypes.

```
/* This function must set the stack into a known state.*/
void StackInitialize(stack *theStack);

/* The Push() function puts the value in theItem into the array in
theStack. It goes into the array location specified by the top member.
After the item has been pushed onto the stack, the Push() function must
increment top. If the stack is full, the Push() function returns zero.
If there was room on the stack to push the item on, Push() returns one.
*/
int Push(stack *theStack,int theItem);

/* The Pop() function decrements the top member and puts the value it
finds at that location in the array into the parameter theItem. If the
stack is empty (top is zero), the memory location pointed to by theItem
should be set to zero and the Pop() function should return zero. If the
item was successfully popped from the stack, it should be stored in the
memory location pointed to by theItem, and Pop() should return one. */
int Pop(stack *theStack,int *theItem);
```

Write a program that implements the stack type, all of its functions, and demonstrates that the stack works properly.

The following exercises use the text editor program in Hands On 18.4.

18. Examine the output of the text editor program. Notice that the output is not very attractive. For instance, the menu could be neater and more organized. Rewrite the program to make the output look better. Explain what you did and why.

19. There is a program error in the text editor. Run the program and type E. Press the Enter key. Now type 0, followed by Enter. When prompted, type the string "alineoftext" without the quote marks. Now enter any command, followed by Enter. Notice that, although the program redraws the screen. It does not execute the command. Find why and fix it.

20. Explain why you can't have spaces in the text you type into the text editor as it's currently written. Modify the program so you can.

21. The `GetUserInput()` function is written with the assumption that the user has typed in one character followed by a newline. However, the user may not do that. Modify the `GetUserInput()` function such that when the user types in more than one character, it throws away all characters but the first.

22. If your computer supports unbuffered input, modify the `GetUserInput()` function to use unbuffered input. Change the user prompts as well.

23. The code in the `InitializeTextBuffer()` function which is supposed to generate a random line length doesn't work. All lines are the maximum length. Add a loop which iterates while the random number is greater than the maximum line length. Each time through the loop, it should divide the random number by 10.

24. The `DisplayText()` function is written with the assumption that the top line of the text buffer is never greater than the length of the buffer minus `TEXT_AREA_HEIGHT`. Explain whether you think this is a safe assumption. Modify the function so that it does not contain this assumption.

25. Modify the text editor so that is uses the `text_string` type from Hands On 18.3 rather than arrays of characters and character pointers.

GLOSSARY

Base Address   The address of the first byte in the array.

Dereference   The act of accessing the contents of the memory location pointed to by a pointer.

Offset   The element number being accessed.

Pass by Address   Passing the address of data to a function.

Pass by Value   Passing data to a function.

19

Dynamic Memory Allocation

OBJECTIVES

After reading this chapter, you should be able to:

- Allocate and deallocate memory as a program runs.
- Dynamically allocate memory for atomic data.
- Dynamically allocate arrays.
- Dynamically allocate memory for objects.

OUTLINE

PREVIEW

Pointers are powerful tools in C. However, their real strength becomes available to us as programmers when we combine pointers with dynamic memory allocation. When a program does dynamic allocation, it allocates memory as it runs. So far, we've only examined static allocation. Using static allocation, the amount of memory is determined at compile time rather than at run time.

This chapter examines how programs perform dynamic memory allocation. It presents techniques for growing and shrinking the data areas in memory according to how much memory the user needs. At the end of the chapter, you'll find a version of the text editor that can grow a text buffer to the limits of memory.

19.1   Allocation and the Heap

A computer's memory is a limited resource. No matter what kind of computer your program is running on, there is a physical limit to the amount of memory the program can use. Often, programs must share the available memory with other programs running on the system. The free memory that is not being used by any program is called the **heap**.

As programs run, they may need an increasing or decreasing amount of memory. To get more memory, they allocate it from the heap. When they are finished using it, they deallocate it so that it returns to the heap.

19.2   Allocation and Deallocation

In C, programs dynamically allocate and deallocate memory using the C Standard Library memory management functions. When a program allocates a block of memory, it must store the address of the memory block in a pointer variable.

19.2.1   Memory Management Functions

Dynamic allocation from the heap is handled through the C Standard Library functions `malloc()`, `calloc()`, `realloc()`, and `free()`. All C source files which use these functions should include the C Standard Library header file stdlib.h.

Programs use the `malloc()` function to allocate a block of contiguous memory. It does not initialize the memory it allocates. Therefore, we must assume that the block of memory contains random values.

The `calloc()` function allocates multiple contiguous blocks of memory and initializes them to zero. Because it performs this initialization, it is slower than `malloc()`. However, the initialization makes it a safer function to use.

The `realloc()` function reallocates memory previously allocated with `malloc()` or `calloc()`. It can make dynamically allocated blocks of memory grow or shrink. If the memory block is supposed to grow, `realloc()` does not initialize the new portion of memory it allocates. The data remains in the previously allocated section. For example, if a program doubles the size of a memory block from 2048 bytes to 4096 bytes, the data in the first 2048 bytes remains. The newly-allocated 2048 bytes are not initialized.

In addition, if the block of memory grows, `realloc()` may need to allocate the new, larger block in a different location on the heap. If it does, it will move the data from the old block into the new block of memory.

The `realloc()` function takes two parameters. The first is a pointer to the memory block to be reallocated. The second is the size of the new block in bytes. If it is successful, `realloc()` returns a pointer to the resized memory block. If it cannot perform the reallocation, it returns NULL.

Applications use the `free()` function to deallocate memory allocated with `malloc()`, `calloc()`, or `realloc()`. Once the block of memory has been freed, the pointer to that memory is no longer valid. Attempts to store data to a freed block of memory is a sure way to crash a program. To use the pointer again, programs must set it to point at a valid block of memory.

19.2.2   Allocating and Deallocating Atomic Data

To allocate any atomic data type, a program must first declare a pointer to contain the address of the data. It uses a C Standard Library function such as `malloc()` to allocate the memory. When it finishes with the dynamically allocated block of memory, it must call `free()` to return the block to the heap.

Hands On 19.1 illustrates how programs dynamically allocate atomic data types.

Hands On 19.1

Objective

Write a program that:

Uses an integer pointer to dynamically allocate an integer.

Initializes the integer to 50.

Prints the address of the dynamically allocated integer and value it contains.

Uses a pointer to dynamically allocate a `double`.

Initializes the `double` to 123.45.

Prints the address of the dynamically allocated `double` and value it contains.

Experiment

Type the following program into your IDE or text editor. Compile, link, and run it.

```
1   #include <stdio.h>
2   #include <stdlib.h>
3
4   int main()
5   {
6           int *intPointer=NULL;
7           double *doublePointer=NULL;
8
9           intPointer = malloc(sizeof(int));
10          *intPointer = 50;
11          printf("The memory location %p contains %d\n",
12                  intPointer, *intPointer);
13
14          doublePointer = calloc(1,sizeof(int));
15          *doublePointer = 123.45;
16          printf("The memory location %p contains %lf\n",
17                  doublePointer, *doublePointer);
18
19          free(intPointer);
20          free(doublePointer);
21
22          return (0);
23  }
```

Results

The memory location 02412930 contains 50
The memory location 02414700 contains 123.450000

Analysis

This short program declares two pointers to atomic data types. On line 9, it allocates memory for an `int` using the C Standard Library function `malloc()`. The address of the first byte of the block of memory allocated from the heap by `malloc()` is assigned into the pointer variable `intPointer`. On line 10, the program assigns the value 50 into the allocated memory. Notice that when a program uses a pointer to store data into dynamically allocated memory, it uses the pointer dereference operator.

On lines 11 and 12, the program prints the address stored in the integer pointer. It also prints the value contained in that address.

The program repeats the same process on lines 14–17 using a pointer to a `double` value.

Just before it ends, the program uses the function `free()` to deallocate the memory that it allocated. Your program must deallocate allocate all memory that it dynamically allocates.

This program uses two different memory allocation functions. On line 9, it allocated a single integer by calling the `malloc()` function. The only parameter to `malloc()` is the number of bytes of memory to allocate. The `malloc()` function returns the address of the memory block it allocates. The program obtains this by using the `sizeof()` operator. If `malloc()` fails to allocate memory, it returns NULL.

The `calloc()` function, which is invoked on line 14, takes two parameters. The first is the number of memory blocks to allocate. The second is the size of an individual block. Like `malloc()`, it returns the address of the allocated memory if the memory was successfully allocated. If not, it returns NULL.

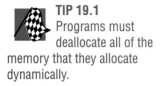

TIP 19.1
Programs must deallocate all of the memory that they allocate dynamically.

TIP 19.2
Every time you allocate memory, check to ensure that the allocation was successful.

19.2.3 Checking the Allocation

Computers have a limited amount of memory installed. It seems that no matter how much memory is available, programs want more. Therefore, it is likely that at some point your program will try to allocate more memory than the operating system can give it. If you don't check for allocation failures, your program will crash.

If the operating system can't give your program the memory it's trying to allocate, the memory allocation functions will return the value NULL. Whenever it allocates memory, a program should use an `if` statement to test for a NULL value.

Example 19.1 contains a version of the program from Hands On 19.1. This version checks the allocations it performs.

EXAMPLE 19.1 Checking Dynamic Memory Allocation

```
1   #include <stdio.h>
2   #include <stdlib.h>
3
4
5   int main()
6   {
7           int *intPointer=NULL;
8           double *doublePointer=NULL;
9
10          intPointer = malloc(sizeof(int));
11          if (intPointer != NULL)
12          {
13                  *intPointer = 50;
14                  printf("The memory location %p contains %d\n",
15                          intPointer, *intPointer);
16                  free(intPointer);
17          }
18          doublePointer = calloc(1,sizeof(int));
19          if (doublePointer != NULL)
20          {
21                  *doublePointer = 123.45;
22                  printf("The memory location %p contains %lf\n",
23                          doublePointer, *doublePointer);
24                  free(doublePointer);
25          }
26
27          return (0);
28  }
```

If the allocation fails, this version of the program will not try to use the pointers. Doing so when there is an allocation failure would cause the program to crash.

Developers should not use assertions to check for memory allocation failures. Allocation failures are seldom a programmer error. They are one possible runtime error over which programmers have little or no control. As a developer, the only thing that you can do is write your software so that it will recover gracefully from a memory allocation failure.

19.2.4 Allocating and Deallocating Structures

Programmer-defined types such as structures and unions are allocated and deallocated in exactly the same manner as atomic data types. Because dynamic allocation requires the use of pointers, we must use the -> operator to access individual members of a dynamically-allocated structure. Example 19.2 demonstrates the allocation of a structure. Figure 19.1 shows the output from this program.

EXAMPLE 19.2 **Dynamic Allocation of a Structure**

```
1   #include <stdio.h>
2   #include <stdlib.h>
3
4
5   #define FIRST_NAME_LENGTH           25
6   #define LAST_NAME_LENGTH            25
7
8   #define STREET_ADDRESS_LENGTH               25
9   #define CITY_NAME_LENGTH                    25
10  #define STATE_OR_PROVINCE_NAME_LENGTH       3
11  #define COUNTRY_NAME_LENGTH                 25
12
13  typedef struct
14  {
15        char first[FIRST_NAME_LENGTH];
16        char mi;
17        char last[LAST_NAME_LENGTH];
18  } customer_name;
19
20  typedef struct
21  {
22        char street1[STREET_ADDRESS_LENGTH];
23        char street2[STREET_ADDRESS_LENGTH];
24        char city[CITY_NAME_LENGTH];
25        char stateProvince[STATE_OR_PROVINCE_NAME_LENGTH];
26        unsigned zipMailCode;
27        char country[COUNTRY_NAME_LENGTH];
28  } customer_address;
29
30
31  typedef struct
32  {
33        unsigned customerID;
34        customer_name name;
35        customer_address address;
36  } customer;
37
38
39
40  int main()
41  {
42        customer *theCustomer=NULL;
43
```

```
44        theCustomer = malloc(sizeof(customer));
45
46        theCustomer->customerID = 14153;
47        strcpy(theCustomer->name.first,"Bob");
48        theCustomer->name.mi = 'B';
49        strcpy(theCustomer->name.last,"Bumper");
50
51        strcpy(theCustomer->address.street1,"1234 SW Elberta Blvd.");
52        theCustomer->address.street2[0] = '\0';
53        strcpy(theCustomer->address.city,"Hilldale");
54        strcpy(theCustomer->address.stateProvince,"NM");
55        theCustomer->address.zipMailCode = 87654;
56        strcpy(theCustomer->address.country,"USA");
57
58        printf("Customer ID:    %u\n",theCustomer->customerID);
59        printf("Name:           %s %c. %s\n",
60              theCustomer->name.first,
61              theCustomer->name.mi,
62              theCustomer->name.last);
63        printf("Address:        %s\n                          %s\n",
64              theCustomer->address.street1,
65              theCustomer->address.street2);
66        printf("                %s  %s\n                          %u\n",
67              theCustomer->address.city,
68              theCustomer->address.stateProvince,
69              theCustomer->address.zipMailCode);
70        printf("                %s\n",
71              theCustomer->address.country);
72        free(theCustomer);
73        return (0);
74    }
```

FIGURE 19.1 **Program Output**

```
Customer ID:    14153
Name:           Bob B. Bumper
Address:        1234 SW Elberta Blvd.

                Hilldale   NM
                87654
                USA
```

This program defines some constants it needs and then defines three types using structures. These structures are called customer_name, customer_address, and customer. The customer_name structure contains data members for an individual's first and last names, as well as a middle initial. The customer_address structure has data members for two lines of the customer's street address (the second is usually used for apartment numbers) and data members for the customer's city, state or province, zip or mail code, and country.

The customer type is a nested structure because it contains members that are also structures. In addition, it contains a member that is not a structure.

The program's main() function declares a variable that is a pointer to a customer structure. On line 44, it uses this variable to contain the address of a block of memory it allocates with the malloc() function. Once the memory has been allocated, the program can store information into the individual structure members. For example, line 46 demonstrates how the program stores an unsigned integer into the customerID member.

To save a string into the customer's first name, the program uses the -> notation on line 47 to access the name member of the customer structure. However, because name is

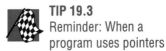

TIP 19.3

Reminder: When a program uses pointers to structures, it must access the structure members with the -> notation. If it does not use pointers, it must access structure members with the . notation.

also a structure, the program must specify which field in the customer_name structure it needs to access. Therefore, it uses the . notation to gain access to the first field.

Understanding when to use -> and when to use . can be tricky at first. Any questions about this can be resolved by looking at the types of the structure variables. The variable theCustomer is a pointer. Whenever a program accesses a structure member using a pointer to a structure, it must put the -> after the pointer name. The name and address members of the customer structure are not pointers to structures. They are structures. The -> notation cannot be used with structures, only with pointers to structures. Whenever structures variables appear, programs must use the . notation to access their memebers.

Line 47 illustrates how to access the first member in the name member of the-Customer. Because first is an array of characters (a string), the easiest way to store a string into it is to call the C Standard Library function strcpy(). The strcpy() function copies the characters from its second parameter into its first parameter.

Lines 48 and 49 demonstrate how the mi and last members of the name member of theCustomer are accessed. The mi member is a single character. The program can use the assignment operator to store information into it. The last member is another character array, so the program uses strcpy().

The program uses the same techniques on lines 51–56 to save information into the members of the address member of theCustomer. All of the information in theCus-tomer is printed on lines 58–71.

19.2.4   Allocating and Deallocating Arrays

Programs can set a pointer at a group of data elements. Once a program does, it can treat the group of data as an array. C enables us to dynamically allocate arrays. After they are allocated, dynamically allocated arrays are not much different than statically allocated arrays in many ways.

The main advantage of dynamically allocated arrays is that they can change size. An array that we allocate statically, such as this one

```
char anArray[100];
```

may never change size. However, dynamically allocated arrays can shrink or grow as the program runs. The amount of memory they use can be different each time the program runs.

Allocating an array is similar to allocating one item. When programs allocate arrays, they usually use the calloc() function rather than malloc(). However, either can be used. Hands On 19.2 illustrates the process of allocating a single-dimensional array.

Hands On 19.2

Objective

Write a program that allocates an array of characters. The program should fill the array with characters, then print them to the screen. It should then allocate a larger array of characters, fill the array, and print its contents.

Experiment

Type the following program into your IDE or text editor. Compile, link, and run it.

```
1   1#include <stdio.h>
2   #include <stdlib.h>
3
4
5   #define ARRAY1_SIZE    20
6   #define ARRAY2_SIZE    60
7
8   int main()
```

```
 9   {
10           char *charArray=NULL;
11           char tempChar;
12           int i;
13
14           charArray = calloc(ARRAY1_SIZE,sizeof(char));
15
16           for (i=0,tempChar='A';i<ARRAY1_SIZE-1;i++)
17           {
18                   charArray[i]=tempChar++;
19           }
20           charArray[ARRAY1_SIZE-1] = '\0';
21
22           printf("%s\n",charArray);
23
24           free(charArray);
25
26           charArray = calloc(ARRAY2_SIZE,sizeof(char));
27
28           for (i=0;i<ARRAY2_SIZE-1;i++)
29           {
30                   charArray[i]=tempChar++;
31                   if (tempChar>'z')
32                   {
33                           tempChar = 'A';
34                   }
35           }
36           charArray[ARRAY2_SIZE-1] = '\0';
37
38           printf("%s\n",charArray);
39
40           free(charArray);
41
42           return (0);
43   }
```

Results

ABCDEFGHIJKLMNOPQRS
TUVWXYZ[\]^_`abcdefghijklmnopqrstuvwxyzABCDEFGHIJKLMNOPQRST

Analysis

The program in this Hands On example declares a character pointer and some constants that it needs. It uses the `calloc()` function to allocate memory for an array of characters. Once the memory is allocated, the program can treat it just like any other single-dimensional array. It can use pointer notation or array notation, whichever you decide is best.

After the program allocates memory for the first array, it enters a `for` loop to fill the array with characters. It then appends a null character at the end of the array and prints the string.

On line 24, the program frees the array so that its memory goes back to the heap. It allocates a larger block of memory on line 26 and repeats the process of filling the new array with characters, appending a null character and printing the string.

Just before the `main()` function returns, it frees the second block of memory it allocated for the array.

Try This

Replace line 14 of this program with the statement

```
charArray = malloc(ARRAY1_SIZE * sizeof(char));
```

How does this change the program?

19.2.5 Allocating and Deallocating Multidimensional Arrays

In addition to dynamically allocating single-dimensional arrays, your program also can allocate arrays that have two or more dimensions. However, this is not as straightforward as allocating a single-dimensional array.

Recall that an array name is a pointer to the first element in the array. However, unlike single-dimensional arrays, you cannot use array notation with dynamically allocated multidimensional arrays. Example 19.3 demonstrates one technique for dynamically allocating multidimensional arrays.

EXAMPLE 19.3   Dynamically Allocating 2-D arrays

```
 1   #include <stdio.h>
 2   #include <stdlib.h>
 3
 4
 5   #define TOTAL_ROWS       10
 6   #define TOTAL_COLS       20
 7
 8
 9   int main()
10   {
11          int *p=NULL;
12          int i,j;
13
14          p = malloc(TOTAL_ROWS*TOTAL_COLS*sizeof(int));
15
16          for (i=0;i<TOTAL_ROWS;i++)
17          {
18                  for (j=0;j<TOTAL_COLS;j++)
19                  {
20                          *(p+(i*TOTAL_COLS)+j) = i*j;
21                  }
22          }
23
24          for (i=0;i<TOTAL_ROWS;i++)
25          {
26                  for (j=0;j<TOTAL_COLS;j++)
27                  {
28                          printf("%d\n", *(p+(i*TOTAL_COLS)+j));
29                  }
30          }
31
32          free(p);
33   };
```

One of the most common methods of dynamically allocating a 2-D array in C is to allocate a 1-D array and treat it like a 2-D array. That's how Example 19.3 works. It's fast and efficient. However, if your program uses this method, it cannot use array notation. You must use pointer notation. Examples of this appear on lines 20 and 28.

The statement on line 20 stores a value in the array. To get the address of the array location, it must calculate the current position using the row and column numbers. Lines

16–22 show a pair of nested `for` loops. The loop control variables, i and j, are used as the current row and column numbers. The statement

$$*(p+(i*TOTAL\_COLS)+j)$$

is a bit hard to read for some programmers, but using precedence helps us understand it. The parentheses force precedence so that the statement multiplies the variable i by TOTAL_COLS. When added to the starting address of the array, this calculates the address of the current row. The value in j is the current column number within the current row.

If i and j are 0, then the statement evaluates to

$$*(p+0+0)$$

which is the starting address of the array. If i is 0 and j is 1, then the statement evaluates to

$$*(p+0+1)$$

This is the address of the second element in the array. Incrementing j enables the program to move down the column. To get to the next row, the program must multiply the current row number by the number of items in a row. That is accomplished by the statement

$$(i*TOTAL\_COLS)$$

This value is then added to the current column number and the base address of the array.

While this method does not dynamically allocate a true 2-D array, it accomplishes essentially the same thing. It is a fast and efficient way of indexing into the array. Unfortunately, there are a fair number of programmers that could misinterpret the pointer notation this method uses.

Another way to accomplish the same thing, and to be able to use array notation, is to allocate a pointer to a group of pointers. Each of the pointers in the group points to the first element of one row in the 2-D array. Hands On 19.3 demonstrates this technique.

Hands On 19.3

Objective

Write a program that:
Dynamically allocates an array of pointers to characters.
Dynamically allocates strings for each row.
Fills the strings with characters.
Prints the characters.

Experiment

Use the file Ho19_3.c for this Hands On program. You will find it in the Chapt19 directory on the Examples CD inlcuded with this book. The Chapt19 directory is located in the Examples directory. Compile, link, and run the program.

```
1   #include <stdio.h>
2   #include <stdlib.h>
3
4   #define TOTAL_ROWS      10
5   #define TOTAL_COLS      20
6
7
8   typedef enum
9   {
10          FALSE,
11          TRUE
12  } boolean;
```

```
13
14
15  int main()
16  {
17        int i,j;
18        char **allRows=NULL;
19        char *oneRow=NULL;
20        char tempChar;
21        boolean memoryError=FALSE;
22
23        allRows = calloc(TOTAL_ROWS,sizeof(char *));
24        if (allRows == NULL)
25        {
26             memoryError=TRUE;
27        }
28        else
29        {
30            for (i=0,tempChar='A';
31                 (i<TOTAL_ROWS) && (!memoryError);
32                 i++)
33            {
34                 allRows[i] = calloc(TOTAL_COLS,sizeof(char));
35                 if (allRows[i] == NULL)
36                 {
37                      memoryError=TRUE;
38                      for (j=0;j<i;j++)
39                      {
40                           free(allRows[j]);
41                      }
42                      free(allRows);
43                 }
44                 else
45                 {
46                      oneRow = allRows[i];
47                      for (j=0;(j<TOTAL_COLS) && (!memoryError);j++)
48                      {
49                           oneRow[j] = tempChar++;
50                           if (tempChar>'z')
51                           {
52                                tempChar = 'A';
53                           }
54                      }
55                 }
56            }
57
58            for (i=0;(i<TOTAL_ROWS) && (!memoryError);i++)
59            {
60                 printf("Row %d:%s\n",i,allRows[i]);
61            }
62        }
63
64        if (memoryError)
65        {
66             printf("Could not allocate memory. Program aborting...\n");
67        }
68        else
69        {
70            for (i=0;i<TOTAL_ROWS;i++)
```

```
71                  {
72                          free(allRows[i]);
73                  }
74                  free(allRows);
75          }
76
77          return (0);
78  }
```

Results

```
Row 0:ABCDEFGHIJKLMNOPQRST
Row 1:UVWXYZ[\]^_`abcdefgh
Row 2:ijklmnopqrstuvwxyzAB
Row 3:CDEFGHIJKLMNOPQRSTUV
Row 4:WXYZ[\]^_`abcdefghij
Row 5:klmnopqrstuvwxyzABCD
Row 6:EFGHIJKLMNOPQRSTUVWX
Row 7:YZ[\]^_`abcdefghijkl
Row 8:mnopqrstuvwxyzABCDEF
Row 9:GHIJKLMNOPQRSTUVWXYZ
```

Analysis

By declaring a pointer to a pointer to characters (line 18), this program creates a variable that it can use much like a 2-D array. It allocates an array of pointers to characters on line 23. Each of the character pointers in the array will point at one row of integers.

The program checks the memory allocation on line 24. If it fails, the value of allRows will be NULL. In that case, the program sets the variable memoryError to TRUE.

If the allocation is successful, the program uses a for loop to allocate each row of characters (line 34). The allocation of each row must also be checked. If the allocation of a row fails, the program frees all rows that have been allocated. It then frees the array of pointers. However, if the program was able to allocate all of the rows, it sets a pointer to the beginning of the current row. This pointer can be treated just like any other string.

To review: the program simulates a dynamically allocated 2-D array by allocating an array of pointers. Each pointer is used to keep track of the beginning of a row of characters. It then allocates space for each row of characters.

Recall that a 2-D array is an array of arrays. The array of pointers to arrays that this program creates is very similar. Using this technique, programs can dynamically allocate as many rows as needed. The array of pointers can grow or shrink as required. Although this program creates rows that are all the same length, the individual rows can all be different lengths if you like. This method also enables programmers to use array notation to access each row (see line 46) as well as each character in each row (see line 49).

Because a pointer to a character is a string in C, the program can pass each individual pointer to any function that expects a string. An example of this appears on lines 58–61. A for loop is used to iterate through the array of pointers. It passes each individual pointer to the printf() function. The "%s" in printf()'s format string tells it to expect a string variable as the input.

The program ends by printing an error message if there was a memory allocation error. If no error occurred, it uses the free() function to release the memory allocated to each row. It then frees the array of pointers.

It is important that memory is released in this order. If the program freed the memory for allRows first, all of the pointers to the rows would be lost. The program would have no way of releasing the memory allocated to the individual rows.

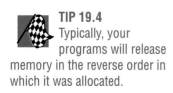

TIP 19.4
Typically, your programs will release memory in the reverse order in which it was allocated.

In general, your programs will follow this pattern of allocating and releasing memory. The last memory allocated will often be the first to be freed.

Try This

Try rewriting this program so that each line of text is a different length. What changes did you have to make?

As we have seen, C supplies us with at least two methods of dynamically allocating memory that we can treat as a multidimensional array. There are other methods, but most of them are more complex than those shown here.

Allocating a 1-D array and treating it like a 2-D array using pointer notation is faster. However, there are a fair number of programmers who will struggle with reading the resulting code. Allocating an array of pointers to arrays means that array notation can be used throughout the program. However, it is slightly slower. In the end, you must decide which technique is most appropriate for your program.

19.3   Dynamic Allocation in the Text Editor

Prior versions of the text editor all statically allocated memory to hold the characters. The editor created a `text_buffer` object. The `text_buffer` object in turn created an array of strings.

With dynamic memory allocation, we can modify the `text_string` functions and the `text_buffer` functions so that they do not allocate space for characters until the memory is actually needed. The text editor then requires only the memory it actually uses. Hands On 19.4 demonstrates how dynamic allocation can be used in the text editor.

Hands On 19.4

Objective

Write a version of the text editor that uses dynamic allocation. Each `text_string` in the `text_buffer` should allocate memory only when the program stores characters in the string. The `text_buffer` should not allocate memory for empty strings.

Experiment

Use the following program from the Examples CD. The program is in the TEdit directory, which is in the Chapt19 directory. The Chapt19 directory can be found in the Examples directory. Compile, link, and run the program. This program consists of five files: TEdit.c, TString.h, TString.c, TBuffer.h, and TBuffer.c. Because the full program is quite long, the code will not be shown here. Please refer to the files on the disk.

Results

Figure 19.2 shows the output of this program after two lines of text have been typed into the buffer.

Analysis

Hands On examples in previous chapters demonstrated that we can change the implementation of types significantly without making numerous changes to the rest of the program. These new versions of the `text_string` and `text_buffer`

FIGURE 19.2   **Output of the Text Editor Program**

```
Display  Buffer
Line     Line
Number   Number
1        1            The first line of text.
2        2
3   .    3
4        4
5        5
6        6
7        7
8        8
9        9
10       10
11       11
12       12
13       13
14       14       Another line of text.
15       15
Press one of the following keys to issue a command, then press the Enter key.
U Scroll up one line.   D Scroll down one line.   B Scroll up one page.
F Scroll down one page.   E Edit text.   Q Quit.
COMMAND>>>
```

types use dynamic allocation. Yet, their function interfaces remain very similar to the previous versions. The primary difference is that new functions have been added.

This version of the text editor is not limited to a fixed-size buffer. The buffer can grow to the limits of memory. Each row of the buffer can be a different length. The program also includes additional error checking.

A look at the `text_buffer` and `text_string` types shows that both types now use pointers to enable dynamic memory allocation. The `allRows` member of the `text_buffer` structure is a pointer to `text_string` structures. As it executes, the text editor will use the functions in TBuffer.c to allocate as many `text_string` structures as it needs. Each `text_string` holds one row of text. Whenever the program needs more rows for text, it allocates a larger array of `text_string` structures.

Even when `text_string` structures are allocated, memory for the actual characters is not. No memory for characters is allocated until the program actually tries to store characters in a `text_string`. Line 36 of TString.h shows that the `charArray` member of the `text_string` structure is a pointer to characters. The structure also contains a member called `charsAllocated`. This keeps track of the actual number of character spaces the functions in TString.h allocate, including the memory used by the null character. It is possible that the number of characters in a `text_string` is less than the number of memory spaces allocated. The end of the `text_string` is marked by a null character.

The `main()` function is located in the file TEdit.c. TEdit.c begins with a file banner, which is followed by the list of include files. The program then declares the constants it needs. Some constants are created with the `const` keyword. Others use the `#define` preprocessor directive. If your compiler supports the use of constants created with `const` as size specifiers for arrays and as constants in `case` statements, then you can change these so that they are all created with `const` rather than `#define`.

The program defines the `boolean` enumerated type on lines 50–54 of TEdit.c. Some compilers already provide this type even though it is not part of the ANSI C Standard. If yours does, it will indicate an error or warning on lines 50–54 when you compile the program. To get rid of the error or warning, comment out the statements on lines 50–54.

The definition of the `boolean` type is followed by the declaration of several function prototypes. These functions are used only by `main()`. Therefore, their prototypes do not go into a header file.

The `main()` function begins on line 76 of TEdit.c. After declaring some variables it needs, it invokes `TextBufferInitialize()` to set the text buffer into a known state.

The code for `TextBufferInitialize()` appears on lines 50–76 of TBuffer.c. This function is written with the assumption that the parameter tBuffer will never contain the value `NULL`. Therefore, `TextBufferInitialize()` calls the `assert()` function to ensure that is true. In fact, almost all of the functions in

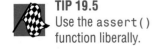

TIP 19.5
Use the `assert()` function liberally.

TBuffer.c and TString.c use assertions to document programmer assumptions. To create robust programs, most experienced developers recommend using this technique.

Remember that you should not use assertions to check for runtime errors. If, for instance, the user tries to load a file into the text editor that doesn't exist, your program should not use an assertion to handle the error. Imagine trying to use a text editor that aborted every time you typed in an incorrect file name.

`TextBufferInitialize()` sets the `text_buffer` into a known state by setting all three of its members to 0 or `NULL`. If this function is not called before a `text_buffer` is used, it is likely that the program will crash.

After `TextBufferInitialize()` ends, program execution returns to the `main()` function. `main()` enters a `for` loop (line 87 of TEdit.c) that continues until the user quits, or until there is a fatal program error. First, the loop calls the `ClearScreen()` function to clear the screen. It uses the `DisplayText()` function to display the current contents of the `text_buffer`. At this point, the buffer is empty. However, the user needs to see that the buffer is empty so that he or she will know that the program is ready to accept input.

The primary difference between this version of `DisplayText()` and the version presented in Chapter 18 is that this version must call the `TextStringInit-String()` and `TextStringFree()` functions. In order for the memory allocation code in TString.c to work properly, a `text_string` must be in a known state before it is used. If a program tries to use functions in TString.c before it calls `TextStringInitString()`, it is likely to crash.

In addition, all programs that declare `text_string` variables must free the memory for those variable when they are no longer in use. If a program does not do this, memory leaks will probably occur. Memory leaks are discussed in the Troubleshooting Guide near the end of this chapter. TString.c provides the `TextStringFree()` for freeing memory used by a `text_string`.

After `DisplayText()` finishes, program execution returns to `main()` on line 93 of TEdit.c. Next, it calls `GetUserCommand()`, which is shown on lines 327–364 of TEdit.c. This function uses the C Standard Library function `getchar()` to get characters from the user. The version in Chapter 18 used `scanf()`. You may wonder why this function was changed.

Later in this program, the text editor uses `gets()` rather than `scanf()` to get strings of text from the user. Recall that `scanf()` uses spaces as well as newlines to delimit input strings. If the user types in a string that contained spaces, as most do, `scanf()` would see that as multiple strings. Using `scanf()` might cause the program to think the user was trying to store more than one string on one line of the buffer. Using `gets()` is a simple way around that.

What does this have to do with the `GetUserCommand()` function? In short, experience has taught me that the `gets()` and `scanf()` functions generally should not be used in the same program. Using `scanf()` in the `GetUserCommand()` function will probably cause characters to be left in the keyboard buffer when the program does not expect them. The only way to ensure that this does not happen is to empty the keyboard buffer every after every user command. It is simpler to use `getchar()` and `gets()` together in a program than it is to use `scanf()` and `gets()`. `getchar()` and `gets()` are made to be used together in programs. There are compilers whose implementations of the `scanf()` and `gets()` functions can be used together perfectly well with no problems. However, my experience is that this is not true with all compilers. I've been plagued by this problem more than once, so I avoid using them in the same program.

Because most computers used buffered keyboard input, `getchar()` will not return a character until the user presses the Enter key. The `getchar()` function retrieves only one character, so the newline character will be left in the keyboard buffer. `GetUserCommand()` calls `getchar()` again on line 375 to pull the newline out of the buffer.

When the `GetUserCommand()` function ends, the program returns to line 99 of TEdit.c. On line 101, it uses a `switch` statement to determine what command the user typed. If the user entered the command to scroll up one line or one screenful of text, the program calls TextBufferScrollUp(). Its source code is on lines 205–247 of TBuffer.c. It decrements the topLine member of the text_buffer and checks to see whether topLine contains a value that is less than 0. If so, it sets topLine to 0.

If the switch statement beginning on line 101 of TEdit.c determines that the user entered the command to scroll down one line or one screenful of text, main() calls TextBufferScrollDown(). Lines 252–316 of TBuffer.c contain the code for TextBufferScrollDown(). The TextBufferScrollDown() function increments the top line of the buffer. It then checks to see whether the top row is greater than the last line of the buffer minus the number of rows in the displayable area. If so, it sets the top row to the last line of the buffer minus the number of rows in the displayable area. If the current buffer size is less than the number of lines in one screenful of text, it is possible for this function to set the top line to a number less than 0. TextBufferScrollDown() checks for this condition and adjusts the top line if needed.

If the switch statement beginning on line 101 of TEdit.c determines that the user entered the command to edit a line of text, the program calls the Edit-Buffer() function. Lines 369–480 of TEdit.c contain the code for EditBuffer().

The EditBuffer() function declares some variables it requires and then calls the TextStringInitString() to initialize the variable tempString to a known state. It also invokes TextStringSetFromCharArray() to store 40 blank spaces into tempString. This is one method of increasing the speed of the program. On line 457 of TEdit.c the program calls TextStringScanString() to enable the user to type in a line of text. As we will see shortly, the TextStringScanString() function allocates additional characters one at a time when tempString becomes full. By initializing tempString to 40 spaces, it performs one memory allocation for the first 39 characters that the user types. When the 40th character is typed in, the TextStringScanString() function allocates each additional character one at a time.

TECHNICAL NOTE 19.2
When using dynamic memory allocation, there often is a trade-off between allocating extra memory to increase the program's speed and possibly wasting memory. You must decide for yourself which is more important to the program you are writing.

TECHNICAL NOTE 19.3
In addition to the atoi() function, the C Standard Library function also provides other routines to convert strings to numbers. For example, atol() converts an ASCII string to a long, and atof() converts a string to a float. For more detail, see your compiler's documentation.

The intent here is to save some time during the execution of the Edit-Buffer() function. However, if the user types in less than 40 characters, some memory might be wasted. This is a common trade-off when writing programs. Often, allocating more memory speeds up the program at the expense of possibly wasting memory. You must decide which is more important to the program you are writing.

After EditBuffer() sets tempString to 40 blank spaces, it uses an if statement to ensure that the memory for tempString was allocated. If there was no error, the function gets the top line of the text_buffer. It enters a do-while loop on line 415. Inside the loop, the function prompts the user for the buffer line number of the line to edit. It uses the gets() function to retrieve the line number as a string.

On line 424 of Tedit.c, the EditBuffer() function calls the C Standard Library function atoi() to convert the ASCII character string retrieved by gets() into an integer. If atoi() fails, it returns 0. This is one reason why this version of the text editor tells the user that buffer line numbering begins with 1 rather than 0. Otherwise, the program would have trouble telling whether the user wanted to edit line 0 or she/he mistyped the line number. By telling the user that the line numbers begin with 1, there can only be one condition under which atoi() will return zero. That condition occurs when the user mistypes the line number.

Another reason that the user is told in the DisplayText() function that line numbering begins with 1 rather than 0 is that it is more intuitive for the user. However, the actual line numbers used by the software must begin with 0 rather than 1. As a result, the line number must be decremented by 1 after it is retrieved. The decrement is shown on line 459.

On line 427 of TEdit.c, the program tests the input to see whether the user simply pressed Enter rather than type in a line number. If so, it sets the variable done to TRUE so that the loop will end and program execution will return to main().

If not, it tests whether the user entered valid input. If the input is valid, it sets the variable `gotValidInput` to `TRUE`. This terminates the loop. If the user did not enter valid input, the `else` statement on lines 439–445 prints an error message. The `do-while` loop exits when the user either presses Enter or types in valid input.

If the user typed in a valid line number, the `EditBuffer()` function prompts the user for a line of text. It calls `TextStringScanString()` to retrieve the user's input.

The code for `TextStringScanString()` is on lines 448–505 of TString.c. After it declares the variables it uses, `TextStringScanString()` calls `TextStringGetLength()` to get the length of the `text_string` where the user's input will be stored. On line 474 of TString.c, it enters the `for` loop it uses to retrieve the user's input. The loop runs while the user has not typed an end-of-file character nor pressed Enter. Recall that the end-of-file character can be different on each operating system. However, it is represented by the Standard Library constant `EOF`.

Each time the loop performs its test, it calls `getchar()`. Notice that the statement

```
(inputChar = getchar()) != EOF
```

has a pair of parentheses around

```
(inputChar = getchar())
```

These parentheses are necessary. Precedence rules dictate that the `!=` operator has higher precedence than `=`. If the parentheses are omitted, the statement will be

```
inputChar = getchar() != EOF
```

Because the `!=` operator has higher precedence, this statement will first compare the return value from `getchar()` to the Standard Library constant `EOF`. If they are not equal, the comparison will evaluate to 1. The 1 will be stored in `inputChar`. That is not what we want this loop to do. The parentheses around

```
(inputChar = getchar())
```

force the assignment to be done first. The value that is assigned is then compared to `EOF`.

If the character the user types is not equal to `EOF` or `'\n'`, the body of the `for` loop executes. In the loop, `TextStringScanString()` tests whether the number of characters the user typed is less than the length of the destination string. If it is, `TextStringScanString()` calls `TextStringSetCharacter()` to store the character the user entered into the destination string. If the number of characters the user types is greater than or equal to the length of the destination string, `TextStringScanString()` invokes `TextStringAppendCharacter()` to add the character onto the end of the string. Because this changes the length of the destination string, the variable `destinationStringLength` is updated by calling `TextStringGetLength()`.

The code for `TextStringAppendCharacter()` appears on lines 312–408 of TString.c. This is a more complex function than most of the other functions in this program. The primary reason is that it does dynamic allocation under a variety of circumstances.

On line 344 of TString.c, `TextStringAppendCharacter()` uses an `if` statement to determine whether character locations have already been allocated for the destination string. If memory has been allocated, `TextStringAppend-Character()` calls the C Standard Library function `strlen()` to get the length of the string. It uses another `if` statement (lines 351–356) to determine whether the string's length is less than the number of characters allocated. If it is, then there is still room in the string to add the new character. Therefore, `TextStringAppendCharacter()` adds it and appends a null character. If not, there is no room in the string. More memory must be allocated before the character can be appended.

If there is no room in the destination string because it is empty, `TextStringAppendCharacter()` allocates enough space for the new character and the null character. It stores them both in the string (lines 362–367), if the allocation was successful. If the memory allocation fails, the function sets an error status variable to `TSE_CANT_ALLOCATE_STRING`.

If the destination string is not empty and has no room for the new character, `TextStringAppendCharacter()` allocates space for the new character. If the allocation is successful, the characters in the destination string are copied into the newly allocated memory (line 383). The new character and the null character are appended to the string. The character array for the old string is freed on line 390. The address of newly allocated array of characters is saved in the `charArray` of the `text_string` structure on line 393. Line 396 increments the number of characters allocated to the destination string. If the memory allocation could not be performed, an error status variable is set on line 400.

When `TextStringAppendCharacter()` returns, the program jumps back to `TextStringScanString()`. On line 499 of TString.c, `TextStringScanString()` ensures that there is a null character on the end of the destination string. It then returns the number of characters it read from the keyboard.

After `TextStringScanString()` exits, the program returns to the `Edit-Buffer()` function in TEdit.c. Line 459 of TEdit.c decrements the row number. Next, `EditBuffer()` calls `TextBufferSetRow()`. This function, which is on lines 81–144 of TBuffer.c, also performs dynamic allocation.

If the destination row number is valid, the `TextBufferSetRow()` function uses `TextStringSetFromTextString()` to copy the string into the selected row and to handle any errors that might occur while this happens. If the buffer is not currently large enough to contain the selected row, `TextBufferSetRow()` calls `Allo-cateRows()` to allocate enough `test_string` structures so that the buffer will contain the selected row. If the memory is allocated, `TextBufferSetRow()` invokes `TextStringSetFromTextString()` to copy the characters into the destination row.

After the end of the `TextBufferSetRow()` function, the program returns to `EditBuffer()` in TEdit.c. If the temporary `text_string` variable contains characters (it won't if the user presses Enter when asked to input a line of text), its memory is released back to the heap on line 473 of TEdit.c.

When the `EditBuffer()` function terminates, the program jumps back to the `switch` statement in `main()`. The `for` loop, which begins on line 87 of TEdit.c, iterates and gets another command from the user. If the user types in the command to quit, the `switch` statement on line 101 jumps to the `case` statement on line 138. This `case` statement sets the variable `done` to `TRUE`. If, instead, the user types in a command that the program doesn't recognize, the default `case` on line 144 of TEdit.c will execute. This prints an error message and enables the user to continue.

The `for` loop on lines 87–151 of TEdit.c will repeat until the user enters the quit command, or until there is an error. If an error does occur, the `if` statement on lines 154–158 will print an error message.

Whether there was an error or not, the program frees the memory for the `text_buffer` (line 160) before it exits `main()`.

19.4   Troubleshooting Guide

After reading this section, you should be able to

- Perform "safe" pointer comparisons.
- Prevent memory leaks.

19.4.1   Pointer Comparisons

A pointer is an integer memory address. C enables programs to manipulate the addresses in pointers directly. For instance, a program can add integers to pointers. It can also subtract integers from pointers. Sometimes, it is tempting to try to compare the addresses in pointers. For instance, it is possible in some circumstances to test for the end of a string using pointers. Example 19.4 demonstrates this technique.

EXAMPLE 19.4 **Comparing Pointers**

```
1    char *aString = new char [80];
2    char *pointer1, *pointer2;
3    char outputCharacter;
4
5    strcpy(aString,"This is a string.");
6    pointer1 = &aString[0];
7    pointer2 = &aString[17];
8    while (pointer1 < pointer2)
9    {
10        outputCharacter = *pointer1;
11        printf("%c",outputCharacter);
12        pointer1++;
13   }
```

The program fragment in this example declares two pointers, `pointer1` and `pointer2`. It sets `pointer1` to the beginning of a string. The program fragment uses the C Standard Library function `strcpy()` to copy characters into the string it allocates dynamically. It points `pointer2` at the end of the string. The example uses a `while` loop to iterate through the string and print each character to the screen. Syntactically, there is no reason why this program fragment should not work. However, that won't prevent it from crashing in some circumstances. The potential problem is in the way memory is organized on some computers.

Recall that programs allocate memory dynamically from the heap. The operating system may allocate heap memory with addresses that increase or decrease. The C languages definition does not specify whether successive blocks of memory have addresses that get larger or smaller. In programming terms, we say that the heap can grow up (toward larger addresses) or down (toward smaller addresses).

Look again at the program fragment in Example 19.4. If this program runs on a computer which allocates memory in increasing order, it will run just fine. It will increment `pointer1` until it gets to the same address as `pointer2`. However, what do you think will happen if it runs on a computer that allocates memory in decreasing order?

The answer is that the program fragment won't work. It increments the pointer through memory, expecting to eventually encounter `pointer2`. If memory is allocated in decreasing order, the address in `pointer2` will be smaller than the address in `pointer1`. Each time the `while` loop increments the address in `pointer1`, `pointer1` points at a location that is increasingly distant from `pointer2`. The `while` loop will continue until the user manually terminates the program or reboots the computer, or until the program crashes.

Because you can't tell by looking at program code whether pointer comparisons are safe or not, you must assume they are not. The only absolutely safe pointer comparisons are shown in Table 19.1. Table 19.2 contains pointer comparisons that are usually safe.

TABLE 19.1 **Safe Pointer Comparisons**

Comparison	Example
Pointer equal to NULL.	`thisPointer == NULL`
Pointer not equal to NULL.	`thisPointer != NULL`

TABLE 19.2 **Mostly Safe Pointer Comparisons**

Comparison	Example
Pointer equal to pointer.	`thisPointer == thatPointer`
Pointer not equal to pointer	`thisPointer != thatPointer`

You can, under most circumstances, compare two pointers to see whether they are equal. Most computers these days present a program with **normalized memory addresses**. When memory addresses are normalized, there is only one way to represent an address. A normalized memory addressing architecture is also referred to as a flat memory architecture.

On the other hand, some computers use **segmented memory addressing**. Computers that run MS DOS use segmented memory addressing. They represent memory addresses with segment/offset pairs. The segment and offset are combined to form a single memory address. One drawback to segmented memory architectures is that there are many different segment/offset pairs that refer to any given memory address. Under MS DOS a pointer comparison like

```
if (thisPointer == thatPointer)
```

may not work because the variables `thisPointer` and `thatPointer` can use two different sets of numbers to refer to the same location in memory.

Computers that use segmented memory addressing are increasingly rare. Popular commercial operating systems such as Windows 95/98, Windows NT, Windows 2000, MacOS, BeOS, Linux, NextStep, and Unix all use normalized, or flat, memory addressing. All of the pointer comparisons listed in Tables 19.1 and 19.2 are safe under these operating systems.

19.4.2   Memory Leaks

TECHNICAL NOTE 19.4
Leaking memory also can be called memory orphaning.

In programs that perform many dynamic memory allocations, an easy mistake to make is to set a pointer to a new address before deallocating the memory to which it points. Figure 19.3 shows a pointer that points to a dynamically allocated block of memory. Without deleting the dynamically allocated block, the program stores another address in the pointer. Because the address of the memory block is lost, the program can't use or deallocate the block. It becomes unusable until the program terminates. This is called a **memory leak**.

The only way to absolutely prevent memory leaks is to be sure to deallocate every block of memory you allocate. That's very easy to say, but not so easy to do. This is especially true in large, complex programs. Memory leaks are one of the most common errors in C programming.

If you look in any software development magazine that is oriented toward C programmers, you'll see many advertisements for products which detect memory leaks. It is generally a good idea to read product reviews for these types of software tools. Finding one that fits your needs and investing in it may save you many hours of difficult debugging.

19.4.3   Portable Memory Allocation

Although it hasn't been directly mentioned, the code in this chapter has demonstrated one technique for portable dynamic memory allocation, using the `sizeof()` operator rather than specifying a specific number of bytes to allocate.

For instance, the program in Hands On 19.1, which is repeated in Example 19.5, showed how to allocate integers using `malloc()` and `calloc()`.

EXAMPLE 19.5   Dynamic Allocation and the `sizeof()` Operator

```
1   #include <stdio.h>
2   #include <stdlib.h>
3
4
5   int main()
6   {
7         int *intPointer;
8         double *doublePointer;
9
10        intPointer = malloc(sizeof(int));
11        *intPointer = 50;
12        printf("The memory location %p contains %d\n",
```

FIGURE 19.3 **A Memory Leak**

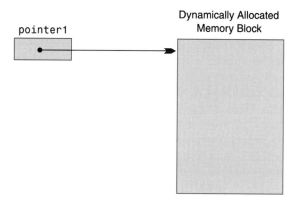

pointer1

Dynamically Allocated
Memory Block

Program Sets pointer1
to Point at New Memory Block

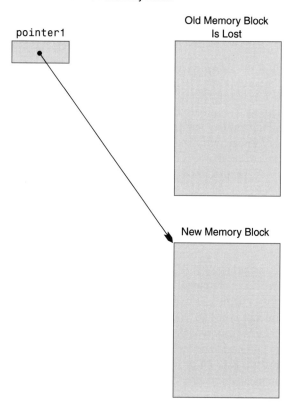

pointer1

Old Memory Block
Is Lost

New Memory Block

```
13                      intPointer, *intPointer);
14
15          doublePointer = calloc(1,sizeof(int));
16          *doublePointer = 123.45;
17          printf("The memory location %p contains %lf\n",
18                  doublePointer, *doublePointer);
19
20          free(intPointer);
21          free(doublePointer);
22
23          return (0);
24  }
```

Notice that the calls to `malloc()` and `calloc()` on lines 10 an 15 use `sizeof(int)` to specify the number of bytes to allocate. It is possible to put in a number instead. For example, line 10 could be changed to

```
intPointer = malloc(4);
```

TIP 19.7

To keep code portable, it is wise to use the `sizeof()` operator to help your program specify the number of bytes to dynamically allocate.

TIP 19.8

To enable your code to be compiled by a larger number of compilers without generating warnings, type cast the return values of `malloc()`, `calloc()`, and `realloc()`.

Programs which do this will run properly only on computers and operating systems that use a 4-byte integer. If the program is ever ported to a computer or operating system which uses a larger or smaller integer, it won't work. For this reason, hard-coding the number of bytes to be allocated should generally be avoided.

Another technique for increasing portability is to type cast the return type of `malloc()`, `calloc()` and `realloc()`. All three functions return a pointer to the type `void`. When a function returns `void`, it does not return a value. However, when it returns `void *`, it returns a generic pointer that can be used to point to any type of data.

Many compilers will give a warning if `void` pointers are assigned to a typed pointer such as `int *`. You can make your program more portable between compilers by type casting the return value of `malloc()`, `calloc()`, and `realloc()` to match the type of the variable in which the address is being stored.

For example, to increase portability, line 10 of Example 19.5 should read

```
intPointer = (int *)malloc(sizeof(int));
```

Line 15 of Example 19.5 should read

```
doublePointer = (double *)calloc(1,sizeof(int));
```

19.4.4 Memory Fragmentation

As a program runs, it can allocate and deallocate memory. As a program deallocates memory, it is possible for the heap to contain spaces between the allocated blocks. This is called **memory fragmentation.**

As memory becomes increasingly fragmented, it becomes harder for the program to allocate large blocks of memory from the heap. It may have plenty of space on the heap to satisfy the allocation request. However, if the available memory is scattered in small spaces in between allocated blocks, it can't be allocated.

One method of fixing this problem is called **garbage collection**. When garbage collection is performed, the allocated blocks of memory are shifted together so that there is no space between them. The result is one contiguous block of free memory that can be used to satisfy allocation requests.

Garbage collection is best handled by the operating system. Increasingly, manufacturers of operating systems are building in garbage collection. However, not all of the operating systems you will use have it. If your operating system doesn't support garbage collection and you find your program needs it, you can purchase commercial C libraries that perform memory allocation and have garbage collection built in. Unless you are a high-powered programmer, garbage collection is not usually something you want to build into your program yourself. It is time-consuming to create and very complex. Garbage collection also can incur very high overhead in a program. Using it can significantly slow a program down.

A simpler technique is to allocate all of the memory your program might need at once. If your program needs more memory as it runs, it can allocate another large block when required. This will probably result in wasting a lot of memory. However, it is a very simple and brute-force way of reducing fragmentation.

Many programmers faced with memory fragmentation problems will allocate memory in fixed-size blocks. For example, we could modify the text editor created in this chapter so that it allocates automatically 80 characters for every `text_string`. If the user adds more than 80 characters to a `text_string`, the program could allocate an additional 80 characters.

Although this will waste some memory, allocating fixed-size blocks means that all of the free holes in memory are the same size. Any of them can be used to satisfy an allocation request.

SUMMARY

Programs can allocate and free memory as they run. This is called dynamic memory allocation. Dynamically allocated memory comes from a program's heap. The heap is a section of memory a program can use for dynamic allocation.

Programs allocate memory using the C Standard Library functions `malloc()`, `calloc()`, and `realloc()`. They deallocate memory with the `free()` function. If there is not enough memory to satisfy an allocation request, `malloc()`, `calloc()`, and `realloc()` return NULL. Functions must declare pointer variables to store the address of the memory blocks they allocate.

You can allocate memory for atomic data types, programmer-defined types, and arrays.

Every dynamic allocation should be checked to ensure it was successful.

When using pointers, programmers should be aware that there are pointer comparisons that are safe and those that are unsafe. Comparing a pointer to NULL is always safe.

If a pointer contains the address of a memory block, the memory block must be freed before a new address can be assigned to the pointer. If the block is not freed, a memory leak will result.

To make allocations portable, programs should use the `sizeof()` operator with a type name rather than specifying an exact number of bytes to allocate. They also should type cast the return values of `malloc()`, `calloc()`, and `realloc()`.

If programs allocate and deallocate many blocks of memory, it is possible for free space on the heap to become fragmented.

TECHNICAL NOTES

19.1 There can be more than one heap available to a program. Every program has a local heap assigned to it. Programs may also have access to a global heap shared by all of the applications that are executing at that moment.

19.2 When using dynamic memory allocation, there often is a trade-off between allocating extra memory to increase the program's speed and possibly wasting memory. You must decide for yourself which is more important to the program you are writing.

19.3 In addition to the `atoi()` function, the C Standard Library function also provides other routines to convert strings to numbers. For example, `atol()` converts an ASCII string to a long, and `atof()` converts a string to a `float`. For more detail, see your compiler's documentation.

19.4 Leaking memory also can be called memory orphaning.

TIPS

19.1 Programs must deallocate all of the memory that they allocate dynamically.

19.2 Every time you allocate memory, check to make sure that the allocation was successful.

19.3 Reminder: When a program uses pointers to structures, it must access the structure members with the `->` notation. If it does not use pointers, it must access structure members with the `.` notation.

19.4 Typically, your programs will release memory in the reverse order in which it was allocated.

19.5 Use the `assert()` function liberally.

19.6 Use assertions to handle programmer errors. Use `if` or `switch` statements to handle user input and other runtime errors.

19.7 To keep code portable, it is wise to use the `sizeof()` operator to help your program specify the number of bytes to dynamically allocate.

19.8 To enable your code to be compiled by a larger number of compilers without generating warnings, type cast the return values of `malloc()`, `calloc()`, and `realloc()`.

TRAP

19.1 After a block of memory is free, the pointer to that block is no longer valid. Do not try to store data in freed memory blocks.

REVIEW QUESTIONS

1. What is dynamic memory allocation? What is static memory allocation?
2. How do you use the functions `malloc()`, `calloc()`, `realloc()`, and `free()`?
3. How do you dynamically allocate atomic data types?
4. How do you dynamically allocate a single-dimensional array?
5. How do you dynamically allocate a multidimensional array?
6. How do you dynamically allocate programmer-defined types?
7. What are memory leaks? How do they cause problems for programs which use dynamic memory allocation?
8. What is memory fragmentation? How do you prevent it?

9. What are some techniques for increasing the portability of C source code that performs dynamic memory allocations?

10. How do you check a memory allocation to see whether it was successful? Why is it important to check every memory allocation?

EXERCISES

1. Write a program that dynamically allocates an array of 1,000 integers. It should fill the array with random integers, sort them, and print them out.

2. Write a program that allocates a 2-D array of integers. It should first allocate an array of pointers to integers. Next, the program must allocate a row of integers for each pointer in the array of pointers to integers. It should fill each row of the array with random integers. The program should sort the integers in each individual row into ascending order. It should then print out the contents of the entire array.

3. Enhance the program in Hands On 19.3. Modify it so that it dynamically allocates an array of 200 pointers of type char *. Have it allocate a string for each pointer in the pointer array. Fill the strings with characters. Print the array of strings. Sort the strings in ascending order and print the sorted strings. Your program should not move the characters in the strings. It must sort the strings by sorting the pointers.

4. Modify the program in Hands On 19.4. Increase the portability of the program by type casting the return values from calloc() and realloc().

5. Examine the code for the TextStringScanString() function in Hands on 19.4. Notice that it uses gets() rather than scanf(). Explain why you do or do not think the name of this function should be TextStringGetString() rather than TextStringScanString().

6. Create a design for the text editor based on the source code provide for Hands On 19.4. The design must include:
   A statement of purpose for the program that is no more than one paragraph in length.
   A functional specification.
   A hierarchical chart showing the program's design.
   A pseudocode version of the program.

7. The text editor in Hands On 18.6 (in Chapter 18) did not have an EditBuffer() function. However, the version of the editor in Hands On 19.4 does. Explain why you do or do not think this function is necessary.

8. Explain what improvements you think could be made to the output and error messages of the text editor in Hands On 19.4. Tell why you think the output and error messages are or are not user friendly.

9. Examine the code for the text editor in Hands On 19.4. On lines 30–35 of the file TEdit.c, constants are defined that are used to represent the character commands which the editor recognizes. Explain why this is or is not helpful in writing the program.

10. Compile, link, and run the text editor program from Hands On 19.4. When you are prompted for a command, type **E** to edit text. When prompted for the line number of the row to edit, type

   The first line of text.

   Explain the resulting output of the program. This problem is caused by the call to gets() on line 423 of TEdit.c. Explain specifically why the program acted as it did. Rewrite the EditBuffer() function to fix this problem. Explain what your solution was and why you chose that particular answer to the problem.

11. Examine the GetUserCommand() function in Hands On 19.4. Explain what would happen if the user typed in a string of characters rather than one single character. Fix this function so that, after it retrieves the first character in the keyboard buffer, it keeps pulling characters out of the keyboard buffer until it finds the '\n'. It should throw away all of the extra characters it finds, as well as the '\n'.

12. Rewrite the TextStringAppendCharacter() function in Hands On 19.4 so that it uses realloc() rather than calloc() on line 377 of TString.c. Explain what other changes you needed to make to the program as a result of the modifying line 377.

13. In the discussion of memory fragmentation in section 19.4.4, one of the techniques suggested for reducing fragmentation is to allocate fixed-size blocks. Modify the program in Hands On 19.4 so that all of the functions in TString.c that allocate memory allocate it in 80-character blocks. For example, when the TextStringAppendCharacter() function detects that a string is full, make it allocate space for an additional 80 characters rather than space for just two. Explain why you think these modifications are or are not necessary for this program.

14. Modify the text editor from Hands On 19.4. Add a command to the program's main menu that enables the user to sort the text in the buffer. When the user selects the Sort command, the program should sort the strings in the buffer in ascending order.

15. Using the program in Hands On 19.4, write a function that converts a group of numeric characters in a `text_string` to an integer. Given the string "1234", your function should return the integer value 1,234. The function should match the following prototype *exactly*:

```
int TextStringToInteger(const text_string * const sourceString);
```

Do not use any C Standard Library function in the `TextStringToInteger()` function. Modify the `EditBuffer()` function so that it uses a `text_string` and the `TextStringToInteger()` function rather than a character array and the `atoi()` function to retrieve a line number from the user.

16. Examine the source code for Hands On 19.4. Notice that lines 146–148 of TEdit.c display an error message to the user and get input. Explain what might happen to the text editor if the user typed in some characters and then pressed Enter. Modify the program so that it does not have that problem.

17. Using the code from Hands On 19.4, create a type called `text_buffer_list`. This type should contain a dynamically allocated array of `text_buffer` structures. It also should contain an integer member called `currentBuffer`, which will contain the index number of the currently selected buffer in the list of buffers. Also write the following functions:

```
text_bufferList_error TextBufferListSetCurrentBufferNumber(
                         text_buffer_list *tBufferList,
                         int bufferNumber);
```

Sets the `currentBuffer` member of the `text_buffer_list`.

```
int TextBufferListGetCurrentBufferNumber(
         const text_buffer_list * const tBufferList);
```

Retrieves the index number of the current buffer in the list.

```
text_buffer *TextBufferListGetCurrentBuffer(int bufferNumber);
```

Retrieves a pointer to the current `text_buffer` in the list.

18. Using the `text_buffer_list` you wrote for Exercise 17, rewrite the text editor in Hands On 19.4 so that it enables the user to create and edit up to 10 buffers. Add a command to the menu to enable the user to select the current buffer. When a new buffer is selected, display the contents of that buffer and enable the user to edit it. Allocate only as many buffers as are needed.

19. Use the `text_string` type from Hands On 19.4 in a new program. Add the following functions to TString.c and their prototypes to TString.h. Write a program which demonstrates that they work. Explain the purpose of any additional error values you needed to add to the `text_string_error` enumerated type.

```
text_string_error TextStringAppendTextString(
                         text_string *destinationString,
                         const text_string * const sourceString);
```

Appends `sourceString` onto the end of `destinationString`. The result is stored in `destinationString`.

```
text_string_error TextStringAppendCharArray(
                         text_string *destinationString,
                         const char * const sourceArray);
```

Appends the characters from `sourceArray` onto the end of `destinationString`. The result is stored in `destinationString`.

```
long TextStringToLong(const text_string * const theString);
```

Converts the characters in `theString` to a long. If any of the characters are not the digits 0–9, a plus sign, or a minus sign, the function should return 0.

20. Use the `text_string` type from Hands On 19.4 in a new program. Add the following functions to TString.c and their prototypes to TString.h. Write a program which demonstrates that they work. Explain the purpose of any additional error values you needed to add to the `text_string_error` enumerated type.

```
text_string_error TextStringInsertTextString(
                         text_string *destinationString,
                         const text_string * const sourceString,
                         int startPosition);
```

Inserts `sourceString` into `destinationString` starting at the location indicated by `startPosition`.

```
text_string_error TextStringInsertCharArray(
                         text_string *destinationString,
```

```
                  const char * const sourceArray,
                  int startPosition);
```

Inserts `sourceArray` into `destinationString` starting at the location indicated by `startPosition`.

21. Data structures are ways of organizing data in software. One common type of data structure is a linked list. A linked list can grow to the limits of memory. Write a program that uses a linked list of `customer` structures. Use the following definition for the `customer` type.

```
typdef struct
{
        char customerName[80];
        char addressLine1[80];
        char addressLine2[80];
        char addressLine3[80];
        char cityName[80];
        char stateProvince[80];
        char postalCode[10];
} customer;
```

Each item in a linked list is called a node. Linked list nodes contain data and pointers. The pointers hold the address of the previous and next node in the list. This links ever node to the one before it and the one after it. Use the following definition for the linked list:

```
typedef struct _linked_list_node
{
        customer theCustomer;
        struct _linked_list_node *next, *previous;
} linked_list_node;
```

Your program should declare a variable called `theList`, that is a pointer to the list. This variable will hold the address of the first item on the list. If the list is empty, `theList` will contain NULL. Have your program get customer information from the user for each customer. Each time the user inputs the customer information, dynamically allocate a node for the list. When you allocate a node, be sure that you initialize the `next` and `previous` pointers to NULL. Store the customer information in the node. Write a function that inserts the node into the list. If the list is empty, point `the-List` at the node. If the list is not empty, the program should follow the `next` links from node to node until it reaches the end of the list. It encounters the end of the list when the `next` pointer of the current node is NULL.It should then insert the node at the end of the list. After it has built a list of at least five nodes, your program must print the customer data in the list.

22. Modify the program you created for Exercise 21 so that it builds a circular linked list. A circular linked list is a linked list in which the `next` pointer of the list node in the list pointer to the first node in the list. The `previous` pointer of the first node points to the last node.

23. Modify your program from Exercise 22. Add an integer `customerID` member to the customer structure. When your program adds a node to the linked list, it should generate a unique customer identification number and store it in the node's `customerID` member. Add the following menu to your program.

    A) Add a customer to the list.
    D) Delete a customer from the list.

If the user selects A, add a customer to the circular linked list as before. However, if the user selects D, print a list of customer names and customer ID numbers. Prompt the user for an ID. Remove the selected node from the list. When you delete a node from a linked list, copy the address in the current node's `next` pointer into the `next` pointer of the node preceding it in the list. Copy the address in the current node's `previous` pointer into the `previous` pointer of the node after it in the list.

24. Use the program you wrote for Exercise 23. Add an option to the menu that enables the user to search for a particular node in the list by its ID number and edit the customer information in the node.

25. Look at the program you wrote for Exercises 21–24. Evaluate your design. Compare your design to the guidelines presented in the previous chapters. If you put the `customer` and `linked_list_node` types into their own .h and .c files, explain why. If you did not, explain why. Describe how your design makes it easy or hard to develop the program. For each of these types, make a list of the functions in its interface of functions. Explain why you think each function is needed. Tell why the interface is or is not minimal and complete.

GLOSSARY

Garbage Collection   The collection of free memory blocks scattered throughout the heap into one contiguous block of memory.

Heap   A pool of free memory that a program can use for dynamic allocation.

Memory Fragmentation   The accumulation of small free spots between allocated blocks in the heap where memory has been freed.

Memory Leak   The loss by the program of the address of a dynamically allocated block of memory, or the failure of a program to free a memory block that it allocated.

Normalized Memory Addresses   Addressing memory such a way that there is only one unique address number for each location in memory.

Segmented Memory Addresses   A memory addressing scheme that uses segment/offset pairs to address each location in memory. Many different segment/offset pairs can be used to access any particular memory address.

20

Encapsulating Data

OBJECTIVES

After reading this chapter, you should be able to:

- Understand and explain the concept of data encapsulation.
- Understand and explain the concept of scope.
- Use scope and persistence to control encapsulation.
- Understand and explain the concept of persistence.
- Use `const` to increase data encapsulation.
- Use storage classes to control scope and persistence.

OUTLINE

PREVIEW

To develop robust software, programmers must use the techniques provided by the C language for encapsulating data and controlling access to it. Chapter 14 introduced the idea of using encapsulation to hide data from program code that doesn't need to access it. Good encapsulation helps us ensure our data maintains its integrity. It also helps keep our programs in valid operational states.

This chapter introduces some common methods of data encapsulation in C. In particular, it presents techniques for overseeing access to data by controlling its scope and persistence.

20.1   Scope and Persistence

As stated in previous chapters, the **scope** of a variable is the portion of the program code where the variable can be accessed. For example, local variables can be accessed only in the function where they are declared. Therefore, the scope of a local variable is the function in which it is declared.

The **persistence** of a variable is the time of its existence. Local variables exist for only as long as the function in which they are declared is running. Their scope and persistence are both limited to the function. A variable's scope and persistence don't have to be the same. They are controlled through storage classes.

20.2   Storage Classes

The C language provides us with multiple storage classes. A variable's storage class sets its scope and persistence. There are five different storage classes: `auto`, `static`, `register`, `extern`, and `volatile`.

20.2.1   `auto`

The `auto` storage class specifies automatic variables. Automatic variables are the easiest storage class to deal with because we can completely ignore it. Automatic variables are local variables in a function. Every local variable we've created so far in this book has been an `auto` variable. We've already demonstrated the scope of automatic variables. They can be seen only in the function which declares them. We've also seen their persistence. They exist only for as long as the function which declares them is running.

Because local variables have the storage class `auto` by default, we don't need to put the keyword `auto` anywhere in our programs. However, you can insert it if you want. Example 20.1 shows how.

EXAMPLE 20.1   **An `auto` Variable**

```
1   void MyFunction(void)
2   {
3          auto int aVariable = 10;
4
5          // More C statements here.
6   }
```

TECHNICAL NOTE 20.1
The initialization of an auto variable is done each time the function that declares it is called.

Automatic variables cease to exist when the function that declares them finishes executing. They are recreated every time the function is called again. Example 20.1 shows an `auto` variable with an initial value. Each time this function begins to execute, it creates the automatic variable `aVariable`. It also initializes the variable to 10 every time `MyFunction()` is called.

20.2.2   `static`

The `static` storage class is the most complex. Using the `static` keyword has a different effect on different C program elements. You can use the `static` storage class on local variables, module global variables, and functions.

`static` Variables   Local variables with the storage class static have the same scope as automatic variables. They can be seen only in the function in which they are declared. However, they do not have the same persistence.

An automatic variable ceases to exist when the function that declares it finishes executing. Variables with the storage class `static` don't. They still exist, but no other function can access them. Example 20.2 demonstrates a `static` local variable in a function.

EXAMPLE 20.2   **A `static` Variable**

```
1   typedef enum {FALSE, TRUE} boolean;
2   void MyFunction(void)
3   {
```

```
   4        static bool beenCalled = false;
   5
   6        if (!beenCalled)
   7        {
   8            beenCalled = true;
   9        }
  10   }
```

TECHNICAL NOTE 20.2
The initialization of a static variable in a function is done the first time the function is called.

The function in this example declares a static variable named `beenCalled`. This variable can be seen only in the function `MyFunction()`. No other function can access it. `MyFunction()` sets `beenCalled` to FALSE. However, this initialization is done only once. No matter how many times the program calls `MyFunction()`, the initialization is never done again.

Just before it ends, `MyFunction()` sets `beenCalled` to TRUE. When `MyFunction()` finishes executing, `beenCalled` will not lose its value. The next time the program calls `MyFunction()`, the variable `beenCalled` will still contain the value TRUE.

In addition to `static` local variables, you can also use the `static` keyword to declare **module global variables**. The scope of a module global variable is limited to the .C file in which it is declared. It can't be seen outside of that one .C file.

Module global variables are a double-edged sword. They can be used to increase data encapsulation. However, like global variables, they also can seriously undermine a program's encapsulation depending on how you use them.

Let's suppose, for example, that we're creating a windowing system for a program that's running on an operating system which doesn't come with a graphical user interface. Figure 20.1 shows how part of that program might look.

The file Win.h in the figure contains the prototypes of functions which create, destroy, and manipulate windows on the screen. The file Win.c contains the implementations of those functions. It also declares a `static` variable at the beginning of the file. This variable is not declared inside a function. It is visible to every function in the file Win.c. However, because it is `static`, it is not visible to any function outside that file, so it is a module global variable. It is not global to the entire program.

TECHNICAL NOTE 20.3
The initialization of a `static` module global variable is performed when the program loads.

Note that the initialization on `static` module global variables is performed when the operating system loads the program. It is not done again until the program is restarted.

The variable in this example is a dynamically allocated array of windows. Whenever a program calls `CreateWindow()`, a `window` is created and added to the array. The `window` functions perform various tasks on individual windows in the array. The program selects the `window` to perform operations on by passing in the `window_id` (short for window identifier) it received from `CreateWindow()`. A `window_id` is really a zero-based index number into the array of `window` structures. When the program is done with a `window`, it calls `DeleteWindow()` to remove it from the array.

This technique is essentially a way of doing object-oriented programming, similar to what is done in C++, Java, and C#. The C programming language doesn't have the object-oriented extensions provided in C++, Java, or C#. However, you can achieve much of the same level of encapsulation by using module global variables.

With this method, the definition of the `window` type is not seen outside of the file Win.c. The designer of the `window` type can prevent programmers from accessing the members of the `window` structure. All operations on the `window` type must be performed by functions whose prototypes are contained in Win.h. The program selects a window to perform an operation by passing its window identifier. Other modules in the program have access only to the window identifiers, not to the windows themselves. The windows are kept in the dynamically allocated list of windows structures pointed to by the module global variable `windowList`.

Using module global variables can have a down side as well. They suffer from the same problems as global variables, but on a smaller scale. Because all of the functions in the file Win.c can see the variable `windowList`, any of them can change it. If the data in one of the `window` structures gets into an invalid state, it is harder to track down the function responsible. However, if they are carefully handled, the encapsulation that module global variables provide can make it worth using them.

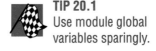

TIP 20.1
Use module global variables sparingly.

```
//--------------------------------------------
// Win.h
//--------------------------------------------

typedef int window_id;

void window_id CreateWindow(int height,int width);
void MoveWindow(window_id theWindow);
void ResizeWindow(window_id theWindow,
                  int newHeight,
                  int newWidth));
void DrawWindow(window_id theWindow);
void DeleteWindow(window_id theWindow);
```

```
//----------------------------------------------------
// Win.c
//----------------------------------------------------

#include "win.h"

typedef struct
{
  // Structure members go here.
} window;

static window *windowList = NULL;

window_id CreateWindow(int height,int width)
{
  // Function body goes here
}

void MoveWindow(window_id theWindow)
{
  // Function body goes here
}

void ResizeWindow(window_id theWindow,
                  int newHeight,
                  int newWidth))
{
  // Function body goes here
}

void DrawWindow(window_id theWindow)
{
  // Function body goes here
}

void DeleteWindow(window_id theWindow)
{
  // Function body goes here
}
```

FIGURE 20.1   **A Module Global
Variable**

static Functions   Like static module global variables, static functions cannot be seen outside of the file in which they are defined. Functions with the static storage class are used as support functions to hide implementation.

As an example, Figure 20.2 shows the same pair of files that appeared in Figure 20.1. The file Win.c now contains a function called RecalcWindowSize(). Because it has the storage class static, the scope of this function is limited to the file in which it is defined. It can be called only by other functions in Win.c, such as ResizeWindow(). Functions in other files cannot access RecalcWindowSize(). Any function in Win.c needing access to RecalcWindowSize() can call it.

The RecalcWindowSize() function is completely dependent on the current implementation. If we change how windows are implemented, it's likely that this function will change or disappear entirely. For this reason the static keyword is used to prevent other files from accessing this function.

20.2.3 register

The storage class register declares variables with the same scope and persistence as automatic variables. Unlike other storage classes, the keyword register is a hint to the

```
//--------------------------------------------------
// Win.h
//--------------------------------------------------

typedef int window_id;

void window_id CreateWindow(int height,int width);
void MoveWindow(window_id theWindow);
void ResizeWindow(window_id theWindow,
                  int newHeight,
                  int newWidth));
void DrawWindow(window_id theWindow);
void DeleteWindow(window_id theWindow);
```

```
//--------------------------------------------------
// Win.c
//--------------------------------------------------

#include "win.h"

typedef struct
{
    // Structure members go here.
} window;

static window *windowList = NULL;


static void RecalcWindowSize(
                    window *theWindow);


window_id CreateWindow(int height,int width)
{
   // Function body goes here
}

void MoveWindow(window_id theWindow)
{
   // Function body goes here
}

void ResizeWindow(window_id theWindow,
                  int newHeight,
                  int newWidth))
{
   // Function body goes here
}

void DrawWindow(window_id theWindow)
{
   // Function body goes here
}

void DeleteWindow(window_id theWindow)
{
   // Function body goes here
}


static void RecalcWindowSize(
                    window *theWindow)
{
   // Function body goes here
}
```

FIGURE 20.2 A static Function

TECHNICAL NOTE 20.4
Reminder: CPU stands for central processing unit. It is the part of the microprocessor that executes instructions.

compiler, rather than a command. It tells the compiler that a variable will be heavily used. The compiler may ignore the `register` storage class entirely. If it does not, the compiler will try, as much as possible, to keep `register` variables in the microprocessor's on-chip registers. Doing so will increase the speed at which the CPU can access the variables. The CPU has very fast access to its registers. Anytime the CPU must access a device (such as RAM) that is not on board the microprocessor chip, the CPU must wait. By declaring frequently used variables as having the storage class `register`, you might increase the speed of your program.

Example 20.3 demonstrates the declaration of a `register` variable.

EXAMPLE 20.3 Declaring a `register` Variable in a Function

```
1    void AFunction(void)
2    {
3         register int i;
```

```
4
5          for (i=0;i<10000;i++)
6          {
7                  // Do some processing here.
8          }
9    }
```

Be aware, however, that microprocessors have only a limited number of on-chip registers. If your function declares many `register` variables, the compiler likely will ignore the suggestion on at least some of them.

How do you know if you've declared too many `register` variables? Basically, you don't. If you have a background in Assembly Language programming, you can look at the executable code your compiler generates for your program. This will tell you how the program uses the CPU's registers. When looking at C source code there is no way to tell which `register` variables are being kept in the CPU's registers and which are being kept in RAM.

TRAP 20.1
Declaring *all* of your local variables to be `register` variables gives very much the same results as if you declared *none* of them as `register` variables.

20.2.4 `extern`

C programs use the `extern` keyword to declare global variables. It tells the compiler that memory is allocated elsewhere for a variable being referred to in the current file. Figure 20.3 shows two files. The file This.c declares a global variable. A function in the file That.c accesses the global variable.

FIGURE 20.3 Using extern to Declare a Global Variable

This.c

```
int aGlobalVariable;



//C functions go here.
```

That.c

```
extern int aGlobalVariable;



//C functions go here.
```

To make the global variable visible to the functions in That.c, the program must declare the variable as `extern` in That.c. Doing so tells the compiler that you are allowing access to the global variable and prevents the compiler from allocating memory for it in That.c. Memory for the global variable is allocated in This.c. When you link the program, the linker will check to ensure that memory is allocated for the global variable somewhere in the program's code.

Notice in the figure that there are multiple declarations of `aGlobalVariable`, one with the keyword `extern` and one without it. Let's suppose that there are 1,000 files that make up the program our team of developers is working on. This is not at all unusual in a professional program. Let's also suppose that all 1,000 of them must access the global variable. That means that there will be 1,000 declarations of `aGlobalVariable`. 999 of them will contain the keyword `extern` and one won't. In addition, *all* of the files depend on the presence of This.c in the program. None of the files can be used in another program unless we also use This.c. It is actually very likely that we won't be able to use *any* of these 1,000 files in another program. This equates to a lot of wasted effort.

Now let's suppose that, for some reason, we find that `aGlobalVariable` should be a `long` rather than an `int`. We must now go back and change all 1,000 declarations of `aGlobalVariable`. Maintenance difficulties such as this are typical when you use global variables. The Troubleshooting Guide at the end of this chapter contains some techniques that will help lessen this problem.

TRAP 20.2
Using global variables generally complicates your program code.

20.2.5 `volatile`

If you develop operating systems or device drivers, you may find occasion to use the storage class `volatile`. Declaring a variable as `volatile` means that something other than the software can change the variable's value.

When you write operating systems and device drivers, your compiler may allow you to map variables in your program to specific locations in memory. Developers use this ability to declare a variable name for I/O ports, hardware registers, and other hardware devices that may reside in the microprocessor's memory space. They can treat the port (or other hardware device) as if it is a variable in memory. Not only is the software able to read values from and write values to the variable, but the hardware can too. For this reason, you can never depend on the variable having any particular value. The hardware may change its value at any time.

Unless you are developing a program that interacts with computer hardware directly, you will probably not find a use for the `volatile` keyword.

20.3 const

In addition to using storage classes to control scope and persistence, we can increase encapsulation by using the `const` keyword to restrict changes to program data.

As previous chapters demonstrated, `const` can be used to declare constants. We also can apply it to function parameters ensure that they are not changed inside the function. In addition, functions can return `const` values.

Returning `const` values from functions increases encapsulation when it is used with programmer-defined types such as structures. One example of why we may want return `const` values can be shown from the `text_string` type used in previous chapters. The file TString.h, which appeared in Chapter 19, is repeated in Example 20.4 for convenience.

EXAMPLE 20.4   TString.h

```
1    //----------------------------------------------------------
2    /*
3    File name:   Tstring.h
4    Comments:    This file contains the definitions needed to
5                 use the text_string type.
6    */
7    //----------------------------------------------------------
8
9    #ifndef TSTRING_H
10   #define TSTRING_H
11
12
13
14   //----------------------------------------------------------
15   // Enumerated types
16
17   typedef enum
18   {
19        TSE_NO_ERROR = 0,
20        TSE_CANT_ALLOCATE_STRING
21   } text_string_error;
22
23   // End enumerated types
24   //----------------------------------------------------------
25
26
27
28
29   //----------------------------------------------------------
30   // Type definitions
31
32   typedef struct
33   {
34        char *charArray;
```

```
35        int charsAllocated;
36  } text_string;
37  // End type definitions
38  //-----------------------------------------------------------
39
40
41
42
43  //-----------------------------------------------------------
44  // Prototypes
45
46  /* The TextStringInitString function must be called on a
47  text_string variable before it is used.*/
48  void TextStringInitString(text_string *theString);
49
50  text_string_error TextStringSetFromCharArray(
51                          text_string *destinationString,
52                          const char * const charArray);
53
54  text_string_error TextStringSetFromTextString(
55                          text_string *destinationString,
56                          const text_string * const sourceString);
57
58  void TextStringSetCharacter(text_string *theString,
59                          char theCharacter,
60                          int characterIndex);
61
62  char TextStringGetCharacter(const text_string * const theString,
63                          int characterIndex);
64
65  text_string_error TextStringAppendCharacter(
66                          text_string *theString,
67                          char theCharacter);
68
69  int TextStringPrintString(const text_string * const theString);
70  int TextStringScanString(text_string *theString);
71
72  int TextStringGetLength(const text_string * const theString);
73
74  void TextStringFree(text_string *theString);
75
76  // End prototypes
77  //-----------------------------------------------------------
78
79
80
81  #endif
82
83  // End Tstring.h
84  //-----------------------------------------------------------
```

Now suppose we need to use the text_string type with the sprintf() function. However, we can't pass a text_string as a parameter to sprintf(). Example 20.5 demonstrates one way around the problem.

EXAMPLE 20.5 Using a text_string Variable with sprintf()

```
1  /* This example assumes that the variable errorMessage is of type text_string.
2  It also assumes that errorNumber is an integer and outputMessage is an
3  array of characters. */
4  sprintf(outputMessage,"Error %i: %s\n",errorNumber,errorMessage.charArray);
```

The technique used in Example 20.5 is not very desirable. It accesses a structure member directly. Encapsulation encourages us to avoid that. For better encapsulation, software designers create a type and a set of interface functions which go with the type. For safety's sake, all access to the structure's members is performed through the interface functions.

It would be nice to be able to get the address contained in `errorMessage.charArray` without accessing it directly. Therefore, the designer of the type must provide an interface function. It might look something like this

```
char *TextStringToCharPointer(const text_string const *theString);
```

This function returns the starting address of its parameter's character array. This is a nice solution. It retrieves the address we need without requiring us to access the structure member directly. However, it creates a problem of its own. Having the address in the pointer means that programs can change the data being pointed at without using the `text_string` interface functions. For instance, Example 20.6 contains code which passes the pointer it obtains to the `gets()` function.

EXAMPLE 20.6 Creating an Alias to a Structure Member

```
1   char *aString;
2
3   aString = TextStringToCharPointer(&aTextString);
4   gets(aString);
```

This example saves the return value of `TextStringToCharPointer()` in a character pointer variable. In programming terms, we say that it creates an **alias** for the structure member. The call to `gets()` uses the alias to change the contents of the `text_string` variable aTextString. However, it does so without calling any `text_string` interface functions. As the old saying goes, this can be a recipe for disaster.

Using the `const` keyword provides us a way out of this dilemma. If we use `const` on the return type of the `TextStringToCharPointer()` function, it cannot be changed. The prototype for `TextStringToCharPointer()` would look like this

```
const char *TextStringToCharPointer(const text_string const *theString);
```

Example 20.7 demonstrates how this function must be used.

EXAMPLE 20.7 Returning a const Value

```
1  /* This example assumes that the variable errorMessage is of type text_string.
2  It also assumes that errorNumber is an integer and outputMessage is an
3  array of characters. */
4  const char *aConstPointer;
5
6  aConstPointer = TextStringToCharPointer(&errorMessage);
7  sprintf(outputMessage,"Error %i: %s\n",errorNumber,errorMessage.charArray);
```

Now that `TextStringToCharPointer()` returns a `const` pointer, the return value must be stored in a `const` variable. As a result, the alias cannot be used to change the contents of the character array in the `text_string` variable.

20.4 Troubleshooting Guide

After reading this section, you should be able to:

- Correctly define global variables in a header file.
- Use `static` functions for better interface design.

20.4.1 Defining Global Variables

Let's look back at Figure 20.3. It clearly shows that we end up with multiple declarations of every global variable in a program. That's because we need to declare a global variable in every file that accesses it. We could use one declaration if we put it in a header file. Figure 20.4 demonstrates this technique.

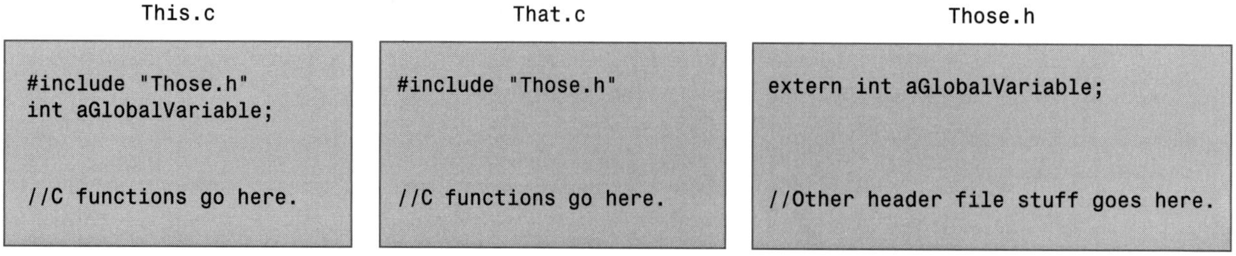

This.c
```
#include "Those.h"
int aGlobalVariable;


//C functions go here.
```

That.c
```
#include "Those.h"


//C functions go here.
```

Those.h
```
extern int aGlobalVariable;


//Other header file stuff goes here.
```

FIGURE 20.4   A Global Variable in a Header File

There's a problem here, however. We can't include the header file in This.c. If we did, it would result in two declarations of aGlobalVariable in the same file. This will at least cause warning and probably will cause an error during compilation.

We can move the declaration of aGlobalVariable into the header file *and* include the header file in all of the C files (such as This.c) if we use a conditional compilation trick. Example 20.8 illustrates how this is done.

EXAMPLE 20.8   One Definition for a Global Variable

```
1   // MyProg.c
2   #include <stdio.h>
3
4   #define EXTERN
5   #include "global.h"
6
7   int main()
8   {
9       theGlobalVariable = 5;
10
11      printf("theGlobalVariable = %d\n",theGlobalVariable);
12
13      AFunction();
14
15      return (0);
16  }
```

```
1   // Global.h
2   #ifndef GLOBAL_H
3   #define GLOBAL_H
4
5   #if !defined(EXTERN)
6   #define EXTERN extern
7   #endif
8
9   EXTERN int theGlobalVariable;
10
11  void AFunction(void);
12
13  #endif
```

```
1   // AFile.c
2   #include "global.h"
3
4
5   void AFunction(void)
```

```
6   {
7           printf("theGlobalVariable = %d\n",theGlobalVariable);
8   }
```

The program in Example 20.8 is made up of three files. MyProg.c, Global.h, and AFile.c. Its output appears in Figure 20.5. The main() function is in MyProg.c. Line 4 of MyProg.c defines the constant EXTERN. By putting nothing else on line 4, the program defines EXTERN as a blank.

FIGURE 20.5   Printing the Global Variable

```
theGlobalVariable = 5
theGlobalVariable = 5
```

Line 5 includes the header file Global.h. This causes the compiler to read Global.h into MyProg.c. As it does, it preprocesses and compiles the statements in Global.h. Line 4 of Global.h tests to see if EXTERN is not defined. When the preprocessor reads Global.h into MyProg.c, it will detect the definition of EXTERN from line 4 of MyProg.c. Because it is defined, the conditional compilation statements on lines 4–6 are skipped.

The variable definition on line 8 of Global.c begins with the constant EXTERN. At this point, it is defined as a blank. Therefore, the preprocessor substitutes a blank in the place of EXTERN, effectively removing it. The results are the declaration of the global variable theGlobalVariable and the allocation of memory for that variable. The compiler and the preprocessor then process and compile the rest of MyProg.c and Global.h.

Next, AFile.c is processed and compiled. Notice that there is no definition of the constant EXTERN in AFile.c. Like MyProg.c, AFile.c includes Global.h.

When it reads Global.h into AFile.c, it will again process the statement on line 4. This time the constant EXTERN is not defined, so the statement on line 5 of Global.h is processed. It defines the constant EXTERN as the C keyword extern. So when the preprocessor processes line 8 of Global.c, it will substitute the keyword extern for the constant EXTERN. This declares the global variable theGlobalVariable as an external variable, meaning that memory for it is not allocated in AFile.c. This is just what we want.

Using this technique, all of the files in the program use the declaration of theGlobalVariable in Global.h. However, memory for theGlobalVariable is allocated only in the file which contains the definition of the constant EXTERN. This file is MyProg.c, which contains the main() function.

After the program is compiled, the variable theGlobalVariable is visible to all functions in MyProg.c and AFile.c. They both demonstrate this by printing its value.

This example should illustrate that using global variables is a lot of work. They cause numerous maintenance headaches that you can only get around with tricky code. Even then, they are still hard to debug when something goes wrong.

TIP 20.2
When using the constant EXTERN to define global variables, the #define EXTERN statement should appear only in the file containing the main() function.

20.4.2   Encapsulation and Interface Design

As this chapter has shown, using static function and static module global variables can aid you significantly in encapsulating the types you create. However, this method has both positives and negatives.

In general, your types will have a .h and a .c file associated with them. The use of static module global variables enables your program to keep a list of **instances** of each type. Each time your program allocates memory for a type, it creates an instance of that type.

For example, a program may use the text_string type from Chapter 19. Each time it declares a text_string variable, it allocates memory. So the variable is an instance of the text_string type. Likewise, a program may allocate an array of text_string structures. Each text_string in the array is an instance of the text_string type.

What's nice about using module global variables to keep a private list of instances is that it forces all programmers using that type to call a Create() function, as in Figure 20.1. The program had to call CreateWindow() to create an instance of a window. Like all such Create() functions, CreateWindow() returns an identifier. To perform any operations on an instance of a window (such as moving or resizing it), the program must call one of the functions in Win.c and pass it the window identifier. The program cannot directly access the window instance. It cannot even access the `window` type.

In addition, this method enables your program to automatically initialize the type. Recall that in Chapter 19, the `text_string` type required the function `TextStringInitString()`. Using a private instance list in a static module global variable eliminates the need for the `TextStringInitString()`. If TString.c kept a private list of all text_string structures used in the program, it would provide a function called `TextStringCreate()`. The `TextStringCreate()` would automatically initialize every `text_string` structure it allocated. There would be no need for other programmers using the `text_string` type to call `TextStringInitString()`.

This chapter also demonstrated that `static` functions enable the creation of functions which are private to a file. Functions cannot call `static` functions in other files.

Therefore, using both `static` variables and `static` functions provides a high level of encapsulation of a type. This can be very good. However, we must weigh the benefits of this style of programming against the costs.

Whenever we use any type of global variable in a program, even module global variables, we make the program harder to debug and maintain. This has been well demonstrated by many software designers over the years.

Also, keeping a private instance list of every type we create means extra overhead in list management. It forces us to use pointers and dynamic allocation. Both of these are a constant source of errors in C programs. They also slow programs down.

In addition, these methods force programmers to call functions to operate on structures and unions. Calling functions is slower than operating on them by accessing their members directly. However, it's generally safer and more portable.

We've got to ask ourselves what the primary goals of our project are. If we're more interested in writing the fastest software possible and we don't care about portability, then the encapsulation techniques presented in this chapter are of little use to us. However, if portability, encapsulation, and reusability are priorities for the project, then it's wise to apply the methods demonstrated in this chapter.

SUMMARY

One method of increasing the robustness and reusability of software is data encapsulation. Encapsulating data controls access to it. This enables software modules to control how data changes.

We encapsulate data by controlling its scope and persistence. Scope is the visibility of data in a program. Persistence can be thought of as the "lifetime" of the data.

Programmers can use storage classes to control the scope and persistence of data. Most variables in a C program are automatic variables declared locally in a function. Local variables have `auto` storage class by default. Automatic variables are created at the point they are declared in a function. They go out of scope when the function terminates.

We can control the restrict changes to data with the keyword `const`. C allows `const` variables, `const` parameters, and `const` return values.

The storage class `static` changes both scope and persistence. We can apply it to variables declared in functions, to variables declared outside of functions, and to functions.

The `register` storage class has the same scope and persistence as the `auto` storage class. Variables declared with the storage class `register` are kept in the CPU's on-chip registers as much as possible. The use of the `register` storage class may speed up programs.

The `external` storage class is used for global variables.

The `volatile` storage class tells the compiler that something other than the software can change the value in a variable. This is provided primarily for programming directly to the hardware.

TECHNICAL NOTES

20.1 The initialization of an auto variable is done each time the function that declares it is called.

20.2 The initialization of a static variable in a function is done the first time the function is called.

20.3 The initialization of a `static` module global variable is performed when the program loads.

20.4 Reminder: CPU stands for *central processing unit*. It is the part of the microprocessor that executes instructions.

TIPS

20.1   Use module global variables sparingly.

20.2   When using the constant EXTERN to define global variables, the #define EXTERN statement should appear only in the file containing the main() function.

TRAPS

20.1   Declaring *all* of your local variables to be register variables gives very much the same results as if you declared *none* of them as register variables.

20.2   Using global variables generally complicates your program code.

REVIEW QUESTIONS

1. What is scope?
2. What is persistence?
3. What is data encapsulation?
4. What techniques can be used to encapsulate the implementation of a type?
5. How can the keyword const be used to control changes to data?
6. What are automatic variables? What scope and persistence do they have?

7. What scope and persistence do of the following?
   a. static local variables
   b. static module global variables
   c. static functions
8. What scope and persistence do the storage classes register, extern, and volatile have?
9. How can storage classes be used to help design robust and modular interfaces?
10. What are the problems associated with global variables?

EXERCISES

1. Explain the pros and cons of module global variables.
2. Write a paragraph each on the benefits of software modularity, reusability, data encapsulation, and implementation encapsulation.
3. Explain the scope and persistence of each of the following:
   a. An auto variable declared in a function.
   b. A volatile variable declared in a function.
   c. An extern variable declared outside a function.
   d. A static variable declared in a function.
   e. A static variable declared outside a function.
   f. A static function.
4. For simple types created with structures and unions, some software designers do not write a set of interface functions. Instead, they write preprocessor macros that look like functions to access individual structure members. Describe the reasons that this approach might be beneficial. Explain problems that might occur with this implementation.
5. Describe the similarities and differences of auto and volatile variables.
6. Use a structure to create a type that you think might be useful in business, graphics, scientific, or engineering software. Do not use any of the types presented to this point in this book. Explain how you would design the type and its interfaces for maximum encapsulation and modularity.
7. If a parameter is passed by value to a function, some software designers do not think it is necessary to make it a const parameter. Others disagree. Explain whether you think the word const is really necessary in this situation. Give specific reasons.
8. Many software libraries declare a global variable which reports the current error status. Describe the advantages and disadvantages of this approach. Give at least one other method of accomplishing the task of reporting a library's error status.
9. Imagine that you have been asked to write a drawing program for a personal computer. Among other things, the drawing program will enable the user to create circles, draw them, change their color, change their size, and move them. Use a structure to create a circle type and any other types or constants needed to use it. Explain why you chose the structure members you did. Tell whether you would use a static module global variable as a list for storing all instances of the circle type. Also explain why you would or would not use this technique.
10. Using the circle type you designed in Exercise 9, write the prototypes for the circle interface functions.

11. Suppose that you have been asked by your boss to be part of a team writing a wildlife simulation program. Your job will be to simulate rabbits in software. You will need to create the type `rabbit` and write a set of functions for performing operations on `rabbit` variables. Your type must keep track of the rabbit's age. It must also store a percentage, from 0% to 100%, that represents the rabbit's health. At 0%, the rabbit is dead. At 100%, the rabbit is in perfect health. In addition, the type must store a percentage representing the rabbit's hunger level. At 0%, the rabbit is completely full. At 100%, the rabbit has starved to death. Also store a percentage representing the rabbit's thirst level. The rabbit will require regular sleep. Information should be kept that indicates how tired the rabbit is. Use a structure called `internal_rabbit` to design the type. Make the structure visible only in the file Rabbit.c. Use a `typedef` in Rabbit.h to define the `rabbit` type as integer identifiers. Specify the prototypes for the set of `rabbit` interface functions. Explain why you chose the functions you did.

12. Modify the rabbit type you created for Exercise 11. Add a structure member which tracks the rabbits' colors. Assume that the rabbits can be either brown, black, grey, or white. When the rabbits reproduce, some of the offspring will have their father's color and some their mother's color. The litters may vary in size. Add functions to the `rabbit` API to manage these new attributes. Also add a function called `RabbitReproduce()`. Explain why you added the functions you did. Give the reasons for selecting the parameters you chose for the `RabbitReproduce()` function.

13. Write API functions for the following `list` type:

```
typedef void * list_item_pointer;
typedef struct
{
        list_item_pointer *theList;
        int listLength;
} list;
```

This type uses a dynamically allocated array of pointers to list items. The pointers to list items are really `void` pointers, so they can point at any type. Programs must allocate the list items and then call an API function that you will write to add the item to the list. They must pass a pointer to a `list` item to the function. The list must be able to grow to the limits of memory. Write a function to enable programs to remove items from the list. When a program removes an item from the list, it must return a pointer to the item and store the value NULL where the item was in the list. Design the API functions required for the `list` type. Write a program that demonstrates that all of your API functions work.

14. Use the `list` type you created for Exercise 13. Explain the advantages and disadvantages of using the `list` type in your programs to keep instance lists.

The following exercises use source code from the Examples CD included with this book. A directory called Chapt20 is in the Examples directory. The Chapt20 directory contains a directory called TEdit. In the TEdit directory are the files TEdit.c, TBuffer.h, TBuffer.c, TString.h, and TString.c.

15. Examine the text editor files provided for this chapter. Some of the prototypes in TString.h contain `const` parameters. Others do not. Make a table with 3 columns. In the first column, list the name of the function. Put the each parameter name in the second column. In the third column, write a brief explanation of whether or not the parameter is `const` and why. The table will resemble Table 20.1.

TABLE 20.1   A Sample Parameter Table

Function Name	Parameter Name	Description
FirstFunction	FirstParameter	Description text.
	Second Parameter	Description text.
SecondFunction	FirstParameter	Description text.
	Second Parameter	Description text.
	ThirdParameter	Description text.

16. The file TEdit.c provided for this chapter contains the functions `ClearScreen()` and `DisplayMenu()`. Should these functions be `static`? Why or why not?

17. Examine the text editor files provided for this chapter. Give the name of any local variables that you think should use the storage class `register`. Explain your reasons.

18. Using the text editor files provided for this chapter, rewrite the files TString.h and TString.c. Change the name of the `text_string` structure to `internal_text_string` and move it to TString.c. In TString.h, use a `typedef` to create a type named `text_string` that is an integer. Create a `static` module global variable in TString.c that holds a list of all instances of the `internal_text_string` type. Delete the function `TextStringInitString()`, and add a function

called `TextStringCreate()`. Make the `TextStringCreate()` function dynamically allocate an instance of the internal_text_string structure, initialize it, and store it in the list of instances. Have it return a unique identifier for each `internal_text_string` it creates. These identifiers will be of type `text_string`. Rewrite all other `text_string` API functions to perform operations on `internal_text_string` structures in the list of instances. Instead of taking `text_string` structures or pointers to `text_string` structures as parameters, the functions will use the unique identifiers returned from `TextStringCreate()`. Write a program that demonstrates that your new versions of TString.h and TString.c work properly.

19. Use the text editor files provided for this chapter. Rewrite the files TBuffer.h and TBuffer.c to use the versions of TString.c and TString.h you wrote for Exercise 18.

20. Modify the versions of TBuffer.h and TBuffer.c you wrote for Exercise 19. Change the name of the `text_buffer` structure to `internal_text_buffer` and move it to TBuffer.c. In TBuffer.h, use a `typedef` to create a type named `text_buffer` that is an integer. Create a `static` module global variable in TBuffer.c that holds a list of all instances of the `internal_text_buffer` type. Delete the function `TextBufferInitialize()` and add a function called `TextBufferCreate()`. Make the `TextBufferCreate()` function dynamically allocate an instance of the internal_text_buffer structure, initialize it, and store it in the list of instances. Have it return a unique identifier for each `internal_text_buffer` it creates. These identifiers will be of type `text_buffer`. Rewrite all other `text_buffer` API functions to perform operations on `internal_text_buffer` structures in the list of instances. Instead of taking `text_buffer` structures or pointers to `text_buffer` structures as parameters, the functions will use the unique identifiers returned from `TextBufferCreate()`. Integrate these new versions of TBuffer.h, TBuffer.c, TString.h, and TString.c into the text editor. Demonstrate that your new version of the text editor works.

In the following exercises, you will create a data structure called a linked list. A linked list groups data together in an organized way. Linked lists can grow to the limits of memory. Each item in a linked list is called a node. Unlike an array, the items, or nodes, in a list, do not have to be in contiguous memory. Each node in the list contains data (or a pointer to the data) and links (pointers) to the next and previous items in the list. When a list node is created, the pointers to the next and previous nodes must be initialized to NULL. For the first node in the list, the pointer to the previous node is NULL. For the last item in the list, the pointer to the next node is NULL. Programs using the linked list must keep a variable that points to the first node in the list. The first node is usually referred to as its head. The last node is called its tail.

21. Use the following types to create a linked list.

```
typedef void *data_item_pointer;
typedef struct _linked_list_node
{
        data_item_pointer theData;
        struct_linked_list_node *previous, *next;
} linked_list_node;
```

Design the prototypes for the API functions for a linked list from the following table. You will not be using instance lists to implement the linked list.

22. Review the API function prototypes you created for Exercise 21. If you did not use the `const` keyword in your parameter lists, go back and put it in wherever you think it is needed. Tell which function parameters should be `const` and which should not. Explain why.

Function Name	Description
LinkedListCreateNode( )	Allocates a `linked_list_node` and initializes its members to NULL. Returns a pointer to the node, if it could be allocated. Otherwise, it returns NULL.
LinkedListAddNode( )	Adds a node to the end of the list. If the list is empty, the node becomes the head of the list.
LinkedListGetNode( )	Retrieves a node from the list when given a zero-based index number. For example, if passed the integer 5, this function returns a pointer to the sixth node in the list. If the node is not found, this function returns NULL.
LinkedListRemoveNode( )	Removes a node from the list when given a zero-based index number. If the node is not found, this function returns NULL. Otherwise, it returns a pointer to the node.
LinkedListAddNodeData( )	Adds a data item to a node when given a pointer to a node and the address of the data item. Returns a nonzero value ifthe data item was successfully added to the node. Otherwise, it returns zero.
LinkedListGetNodeData( )	Returns the data item from a node when given a pointer to a node. If the node has no data item, this function returns NULL.
LinkedListRemoveNodeData( )	Removes a data item from a node when given a pointer to a node. Returns the address of the data item. If the node contains no data item, this function returns NULL.

23. Write the API functions for the linked list that you designed in Exercises 21 and 22. Write a program to demonstrate that they work. Use the following structure for your data items.

```
typedef struct
{
        char customerName[80];
        char streetAddress[3][80];
        char cityName[80];
        char stateProvince[80];
        char zipPostalCode[11];
} customer;
```

Do not use magic numbers in your program. When you pass a pointer to a customer structure to your linked list functions, such as LinkedListAddNodeData, you must type cast the pointer to the type data_item_pointer.

24. Write a program that uses the linked list you created for Exercises 21–23. Use the following customer type instead of the one provide in Exercise 23.

```
typedef struct
{
        int customerID;
        char customerName[80];
        char streetAddress[3][80];
        char cityName[80];
        char stateProvince[80];
        char zipPostalCode[11];
} customer;
```

Notice that this version of the customer type contains an integer identifier for each customer. Modify your LinkedListAddNode() function so that each time it inserts a node into the list, it checks to ensure that the customer ID number is unique. If there is a duplicate, it should not add the node to the list, and it should return zero. If the node was inserted, make LinkedListAddNode() return a nonzero value.

25. Exercises 15–20 have you write a version of the text editor that uses instance lists. Compare types such as those to the linked list you created for Exercises 21–24. Specifically, explain any differences in encapsulation and whether you think the efforts to create types with instance lists is or is not worthwhile.

GLOSSARY

Alias   An additional name for a variable, type, structure member, or union member.

Instance   The memory allocation, either static or dynamic, of a type.

Module Global Variables   Variables that can be seen by all functions in a .C file.

Persistence   The length of time a variable exists.

Scope   The portion of the program in which a variable is visible.

21

File Input and Output

OBJECTIVES

After reading this chapter, you should be able to:

- Name and use the standard C files.
- Read and write formatted data.
- Read data from files.
- Write data to files.
- Use command-line arguments.
- Print text to a printer

OUTLINE

PREVIEW

Most of the topics presented so far in this book have dealt with C language tools that help us process data. However, processing data is only one third of what a computer does. It must also read data in from various sources and send data out to various destinations. Data input and output are the topics of this chapter.

21.1   The Standard Files

There are no statements in the C language to do data input and output (data I/O). This is sometimes surprising to programmers with experience in languages such as Basic or Pascal. The C Standard Library adds data I/O through the use of files. Files are a data type defined by the C Standard Library. There are a set of functions in the Standard Library that perform operations on files. Every compiler manufacturer implements a version of the file type and the file functions for its compiler's target hardware and operating system. The underlying details of this implementation are normally different for every type of computer and operating system. However, the interface of file functions is the same on all computers and all operating systems. Using C files helps us write portable C code.

All of the standard data sources are implemented as files. We normally think of files as something we store on disks and tapes. However, C also implements devices as files. To a C program, the keyboard and the screen are files, as is the printer.

The C Standard Library defines three standard files. They are `stdin`, `stdout`, and `stderr`. These are abbreviations for standard input, standard output, and standard error, respectively. Many compilers also define the file `stdprn`, which is short for standard printer. The file `stdin` is connected to the keyboard, and `stdout` is connected to the display. If it is supported, `stdprn` sends output to the default printer.

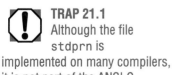

TRAP 21.1
Although the file `stdprn` is implemented on many compilers, it is not part of the ANSI C definition. If you need your code to be extremely portable, you must not depend on the presence of the file `stdprn`.

The file `stderr` is, by default, connected to the display. Programs use it to send error messages to the user. The C standard defines this special file for error messages because it is possible to redirect the output of the file `stdout`. This ability can be used to redirect `stdout` to send its output into another program. Because the output no longer flows to the screen, users will not see any error messages if they are sent to `stdout`. If your program sends error messages to `stderr` instead, users will see them even if `stdout` is redirected.

In C literature, files are also referred to as **streams**. As a result, you'll often see the standard files called the standard streams instead.

File I/O can be buffered or unbuffered. As we've previously noted, unbuffered input makes data immediately available to the program. Likewise, unbuffered output goes directly to its destination device.

On the other hand, data from buffered input goes into a data buffer. Data buffers are flushed automatically when full. The C Standard Library also provides a function which programs can use to manually flush a file buffer.

TECHNICAL NOTE 21.1
Because files are sometimes called streams in C literature, the standard files are also referred to as the standard streams.

21.2 File Input and Output

Computer programs store data in files. To process data, our programs must be able to read from and write to data files.

There are two basic types of files, text and binary files. Our programs use the C file functions to read from and write to either type of file. The file functions require the use of the `FILE` type defined by the C Standard Library.

21.2.1 The `FILE` Type

Every implementation of the C Standard Library defines a structure called `FILE`. The Standard Library is written so that we don't need to know the implementation details of the `FILE` type.

To process data in a file, programs must create a file variable and open the file. They read data from the file using the file input functions. They can also write to the file using the file output functions. When they finish, they close the file.

Example 21.1 demonstrates how programs declare a `FILE` variable.

EXAMPLE 21.1 Declaring a `FILE` Variable

```
1    #include <stdio.h>
2
3    int main()
4    {
5            FILE *filePointer = NULL;
```

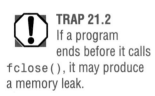

TRAP 21.2
If a program ends before it calls `fclose()`, it may produce a memory leak.

The `FILE` type is declared in the header file stdio.h. Note that programs must declare the variable as a pointer to a `FILE`, not as just a `FILE`. Programs allocate the memory for the `FILE` structure by calling the Standard Library function `fopen()`. The memory for a structure of type `FILE` is released by calling the Standard Library `fclose()` function. It is important that programs call the `fclose()` function before they end. If a program terminates before calling `fclose()`, there may be a memory leak. Most modern operating systems clean up memory leaks produced in this way. However, you cannot depend on it.

Whenever a program opens a file, it must specify the type of file to open. It may select either a text file or a binary file. Either type of file can be opened for input, output, or both.

No matter which mode they use, programs call the `fopen()` function to open a file. The first parameter to `fopen()` is a string containing the name of the file. If the file is on a disk or tape, the program must follow the operating system's conventions for specifying the path. One example of this is the difference in path names between Windows and Unix. On a computer running Windows, path names are specified using the `'\'` character. Unix uses the `'/'` character.

If the file being opened is a device, such as a printer, the program must follow the operating system's conventions for naming the device. For instance, DOS programs can open the device `"LPT1"`. Many Unix programs use the string `"/dev/lp0"`.

The second parameter to the `fopen()` function is a string containing one or more file mode specifiers. The list of available file mode specifier strings appears in Table 21.1.

TABLE 21.1 `fopen()` **Mode Specifiers**

Specifier String	Description
`"r"`	Opens a text file for reading. If the file does not already exist, it is not created.
`"w"`	Opens a text file for writing. If the file already exists, it is truncated to contain zero bytes of data. If it does not exist, it is created.
`"a"`	Opens a text file for writing. New data is appended to the end of the file. If the file does not exist, it is created.
`"r+"`	Opens a text file for both reading and writing. Reading is assumed to occur first, so the current location pointer is set to the beginning of the file. If the file does not exist already, it is not created.
`"w+"`	Opens a text file for both reading and writing. Writing is assumed to occur first. If the file already exists, it is truncated to contain zero bytes of data. If it does not exist, it is created.
`"a+"`	Opens a text file for both reading and writing. Writing is assumed to occur first. The current location pointer points to the end of the file. The entire file can be read, but existing data cannot be overwritten. If the file does not exist, it is created.
`"rb"`	Same as `"r"`, but uses binary mode.
`"wb"`	Same as `"w"`, but uses binary mode.
`"ab"`	Same as `"a"`, but uses binary mode.
`"wb+"`	Same as `"w+"`, but uses binary mode.
`"ab+"`	Same as `"a+"`, but uses binary mode.

TIP 21.1
You don't have to worry about accidentally moving a file's current location pointer before the beginning of a file or after its end. The Standard Library file functions prevent your program from doing that.

When `fopen()` opens a file, it allocates a structure of type `FILE`. The structure contains a member called the **current location pointer**. The current location pointer contains the location in the file where the next read or write will take place. We can think of a file as an array of bytes. If the current location pointer contains the number zero, it is pointing to the first byte in the file. A valid current location pointer can never contain a number less than zero.

You and I don't have to worry about manipulating a file's current location pointer directly. The C Standard Library provides functions to do that for us.

21.2.2 Text Files

A text file contains characters from the ASCII character set. Using the modes specified in Table 21.1, programs can open text files for reading, writing, or both.

Reading from Text Files   The default file type when a program opens files for input or output is a text file. Generally, a program processes a text file by starting at the beginning and reading until it reaches the end of the file. It can determine when that occurs by invoking the `feof()` function. It reads data from a file using one of the functions in Table 21.2.

TABLE 21.2 **Input Functions for Text Files**

Function	Description
`fgetc()`	Retrieves a character from a file.
`fgets()`	Retrieves a string from a file.
`fscanf()`	Same as `scanf()`, but used on files.

Hands On 21.1 demonstrates the use of the file functions for opening a text file, reading characters, and closing a file.

Hands On 21.1

Objective

Write a program that opens a text file, reads its contents one character at a time, and prints out each character it reads.

Experiment

Copy the file DI.TXT from the Examples CD onto your hard disk. Put it in the same folder or directory as the executable program you create from the C source code below. The file DI.txt can be found in the Chapt21 directory, which is in the Examples directory on the CD.

Type the following program into your IDE or text editor. Compile, link, and run it.

```
1   #include <stdio.h>
2
3   int main()
4   {
5        FILE *filePointer;
6        int tempChar;
7
8        filePointer = fopen("DI.txt","r");
9
10       while (!feof(filePointer))
11       {
12            tempChar = fgetc(filePointer);
13            if (!feof(filePointer))
14            {
15                 putchar(tempChar);
16            }
17       }
18       fclose(filePointer);
19       return (0);
20  }
```

Results

THE DECLARATION OF INDEPENDENCE

When in the Course of human events, it becomes necessary for one people to dissolve the political bands which have connected them with another, and to assume, among the Powers of the earth, the separate and equal station to which the Laws of Nature and of Nature's God entitle them, a decent respect to the opinions of mankind requires that they should declare the causes which impel them to the separation.

We hold these truths to be self-evident, that all men are created equal, that they are endowed by their Creator with certain unalienable Rights, that among these are Life, Liberty, and the pursuit of Happiness. That to secure these rights, Governments are instituted among Men, deriving their just powers from the consent of the governed, That whenever any Form of Government becomes destructive of these ends, it is the Right of the People to alter or to abolish it, and to institute new Government, laying its foundation on such principles and organizing its powers in such form, as to them shall seem most likely to effect their Safety and Happiness. Prudence, indeed, will dictate that Governments long established should not be changed for light and transient causes; and accordingly all experience hath shown, that mankind are more disposed to suffer, while evils are sufferable, than to right themselves by abolishing the forms to which they are accustomed. But when a long train of abuses and usurpations, pursuing invariably the same Object evinces a design to reduce them under absolute Despotism, it is their right, it is their duty, to throw off such Government, and to provide new Guards for their future security. Such has been the patient sufferance of these Colonies; and such is now the necessity which constrains them to alter their former Systems of Government.

Analysis

As the Results section demonstrates, this program reads a text file called DI.txt. As line 1 of the program demonstrates, the file stdio.h must be included for the program to access the definition of the FILE type and the Standard Library file functions.

The program's main() function declares a pointer to a FILE structure on line 5. It also declares a variable it uses to store the characters it reads from the text file.

On line 8, the program invokes the fopen() function to open the file DI.txt. The first parameter to fopen() is a string containing the name of the text file to open. The source code is written with the assumption that DI.txt is in the same directory as the executable program. If it is not, the program will do nothing.

If the file could not be opened, fopen() will return NULL. When it enters the while loop on line 10, the program passes the value in filePointer to feof(). If filePointer is NULL, many implementations of the feof() function will return 1, indicating that the end of the file is reached. However, some will not. They may assume that your program checked to make sure the value of the parameter is not NULL before calling feof(). Because of this uncertainty, every program you write should check all file pointers to ensure that their files are open before the pointers are used. If, like this Hands On example, your program doesn't perform that check, it may crash on certain types of computers.

If the file DI.txt was successfully opened, the return value of feof() will be 0, indicating that the end of the file has not been reached. The logical NOT operator (!) evaluates to 1 when feof() returns 0. Therefore, the while loop will execute. Inside the loop, the program uses the Standard Library function fgetc() to read a single character from the file. The return type of fgetc() is int, rather than char. If fgetc() reads beyond the end of the file, it will return the value EOF. This value is not in the ASCII set, so the type char cannot be returned. It must be int. For this reason, the variable tempChar is also declared int.

On line 13, the program uses an if statement to test for the end of the file again. You may wonder if we can omit the if statement, as shown in Example 21.2.

EXAMPLE 21.2 The Hands On Program with No `if` Statement

```
1    #include <stdio.h>
2
3    int main()
4    {
5         FILE *filePointer;
6         int tempChar;
```

TRAP 21.3
Before calling any file functions, always check that the file pointer variable does not equal NULL.

```
 7
 8          filePointer = fopen("DI.txt","r");
 9
10          while (!feof(filePointer))
11          {
12                  tempChar = fgetc(filePointer);
13                  putchar(tempChar);
14          }
15          fclose(filePointer);
16          return (0);
17     }
```

If we were to use the version of the program shown in Example 21.2, the program would not operate correctly. To understand why, we must step through the program when it reads the last character from the file.

When the program reads the last character from the text file, it has not yet reached the end of the file. Even though there is no more data, the feof() function does not detect that yet. Therefore, the condition on the while loop will evaluate to true. When the fgetc() function is called on line 12 of Example 21.2, it detects that there is no more data in the file. It sets a member of the FILE structure pointed to by filePointer to TRUE. This data indicates that the end of the file has been reached. On line 13 of Example 21.2, there is no if statement to test for the end of the file. The call to the putchar() function attempts to write the character in tempChar out to the screen. However, tempChar contains the EOF character, which should never be printed. Therefore, it is necessary to check to ensure data was read before processing or outputting it.

After the Hand On program reads all printable characters from the file DI.txt, the feof() function returns 1 to indicate that the end of file has been reached. This terminates the while loop, and the program exits.

 Try This

Delete the file DI.txt from the directory containing the executable program for this Hands On example, or rename it. Verify that the program does not read the file. Are there any errors when you run it?

With minor modifications, the program in Hands On 21.1 could use the fgets() or fscanf() functions rather than fgetc(). Example 21.3 contains a version of the Hands On program that reads strings from the text file with fgets().

EXAMPLE 21.3   Reading a Text File with fgets()

```
 1    #include <stdio.h>
 2
 3    #define MAX_INPUT_STRING_LENGTH 100
 4
 5
 6    int main()
 7    {
 8          FILE *filePointer;
 9          char tempString[MAX_INPUT_STRING_LENGTH];
10
11          filePointer = fopen("DI.txt","r");
12
13          while (!feof(filePointer))
14          {
15                  if (fgets(tempString,
16                          MAX_INPUT_STRING_LENGTH,
```

```
17                          filePointer) != NULL)
18              {
19                      puts(tempString);
20              }
21      }
22      fclose(filePointer);
23      return (0);
24  }
```

FIGURE 21.1 Partial Output of Example 21.3

THE DECLARATION OF INDEPENDENCE

When in the Course of human events, it becomes necessary
for one people to dissolve the political bands which have
connected them with another, and to assume, among the Powers
of the earth, the separate and equal station to which the
Laws of Nature and of Nature's God entitle them, a decent
respect to the opinions of mankind requires that they should
declare the causes which impel them to the separation.

We hold these truths to be self-evident, that all men are

TECHNICAL NOTE 21.2
Every line of text in a text file ends with a newline character rather than a null character.

In memory, strings end with a null character. However, in text files every line of text ends with a newline character. The fgets() function reads a line of text, up to and including the newline character.

The first parameter to fgets() is the character array in which the text will be stored. The second parameter is the maximum number of characters to be stored in the array. The name of the second parameter is n. The fgets() function reads n-1 characters and appends a '\0' to the string. The third parameter to fgets() is a pointer to the text file from which it will read.

Figure 21.1 shows that the output of Example 21.3 has a blank line between each line of text. This is caused by using fgets() and puts() together. The fgets() function reads an entire line of text from a text file, including the '\n' character. It appends a '\0' after the '\n'. The puts() function prints a string followed by a '\n'. Using these two functions together results in two newlines being printed, which causes the blank lines in the output.

In this program, the if condition inside the while loop is different than that given in Hands On 21.1. The fgets() function returns NULL if it was not able to read a string from the file. The program calls fgets() and checks for the NULL value on lines 15–17. If the result of fgets() is not NULL, the string was read from the text file. The program invokes puts() to print the string.

Example 21.4 shows a version that uses fscanf().

EXAMPLE 21.4 Reading a Text File with fscanf()

```
1   #include <stdio.h>
2
3   #define MAX_INPUT_STRING_LENGTH 100
4
5   int main()
6   {
7       FILE *filePointer;
8       char tempString[MAX_INPUT_STRING_LENGTH];
```

```
9        int returnStatus;
10
11       filePointer = fopen("DI.txt","r");
12
13       while (!feof(filePointer))
14       {
15               returnStatus = fscanf(filePointer,"%s",tempString);
16               if ((returnStatus != EOF) && (returnStatus>0))
17               {
18                       printf("%s\n",tempString);
19               }
20       }
21       fclose(filePointer);
22       return (0);
23   }
```

FIGURE 21.2   Partial Output of Example 21.4

```
THE
DECLARATION
OF
INDEPENDENCE
When
in
the
Course
of
human
events,
it
becomes
necessary
for
one
people
to
dissolve
the
political
bands
which
have
connected
```

TECHNICAL NOTE 21.3
The fscanf() function can be used to read from any input file, including the file stdin. So the calls

scanf("%s",aString);

and

fscanf(stdin,"%s",aString);

do exactly the same thing.

As its first parameter, fscanf() takes a pointer to the text file to be read. The rest of the parameters are exactly the same as scanf(). In fact, the only difference between scanf() and fscanf() is that scanf() can read only from the file stdin. The fscanf() function can read from any input file.

Figure 21.2 demonstrates that the output of this version of the program is considerably different than the output of previous versions. Like scanf(), the fscanf() stops reading when it encounters white space. This includes the space character and the '\n'. While reading this file, fscanf() sees each word in the file as a separate string. As each string is read, the program prints it on a line by itself.

The fscanf() function returns either the constant EOF or the number of fields it reads. If it reads successfully, the return value will be greater than zero. If not, it will be zero. If the end of the file is encountered, it returns EOF. For this reason, the program in Example 21.4 uses an if statement, beginning on line 16, to ensure that the read was successful and the end of the file has not been reached. If the program is able to read a string, it prints the string by calling the printf() function on line 18.

Writing to Text Files   To write text to a file, programs must open the file for writing using one of the fopen() mode specifiers in Table 21.1. Once files are open for writing, programs use the file output functions shown in Table 21.3.

Hands On 21.2 provides a simple demonstration of how programs write text to files with the fputc() and fputs() functions.

TABLE 21.3 Output Functions for Text Files	Function	Description
	fputc()	Writes a character to a file.
	fputs()	Writes a string to a file.
	fprintf()	Same as printf(), but used on files.

Hands On 21.2

Objective

Write a program that:
Opens a text file.
Prompts for and retrieves text from the user.
Writes the text to the text file.

Experiment

Type the following program into your IDE or text editor. Compile, link, and run it.

```
1    #include <stdio.h>
2
3    #define INPUT_LINE_LENGTH 40
4
5    int main()
6    {
7          FILE *outputFile=NULL;
8          char quitChar;
9          char inputText[INPUT_LINE_LENGTH];
10
11         outputFile = fopen("outfile.txt","w");
12
13         if (outputFile)
14         {
15               for (quitChar='N';(quitChar != 'y') && (quitChar != 'Y');)
16               {
17                     printf("Enter a string of no more than 40 characters\n");
18                     printf(">>> ");
19                     gets(inputText);
20                     fputs(inputText,outputFile);
21                     fputc('\n',outputFile);
22
23                     printf("\nQuit? Y/N: ");;
24                     quitChar=getchar();
25
26                     while (getchar()!='\n');
27
28                     putchar('\n');
29                     putchar('\n');
30               }
31
32               fclose(outputFile);
33         }
34
35         return (0);
36   }
```

Results

This program displays the following on the screen:

Enter a string of no more than 40 characters
>>> a string of characters

Quit? Y/N: **n**

Enter a string of no more than 40 characters
>>> another string of characters

Quit? Y/N: **y**

The output file contains the following:
a string of characters
another string of characters

Analysis

This program reads character input from the keyboard and writes it to a text file. It begins by declaring a file pointer and opening a text file for writing. The name of the file is outfile.txt.

If fopen() is able to open the output file, the program enters a for loop. Inside the loop, it prompts the user to enter a string of no more than 40 characters. It reads the characters in from the keyboard by calling the gets() function. To send the characters out to the file, it invokes the puts() function. It also used the putchar() function to send a newline to the file after each string.

After the line of text is sent to the file, the program prints a prompt on the screen asking whether to continue (line 23). Because the user must type in a character and then press the Enter key, the program uses a while loop to throw away the newline character. If the user types in a string, this loop also ensures that only the first character in the buffer is used as a command. The putchar() function is called twice to print two blank lines on the screen.

When the user types 'Y' or 'y', the for loop terminates. The program calls the fclose() function to close the file.

With minimal changes, the program in Hands On 21.2 could be rewritten to use the fprintf() function rather than fputc() and fputs(). Example 21.5 contains the source code listing for a version of the program utilizing fprintf().

EXAMPLE 21.5 Writing to a Text File with fprintf()

```
1    #include <stdio.h>
2
3    #define INPUT_LINE_LENGTH 40
4
5    int main()
6    {
7         FILE *outputFile=NULL;
8         char quitChar;
9         char inputText[INPUT_LINE_LENGTH];
10
11        outputFile = fopen("outfile.txt","w");
12
13        if (outputFile)
14        {
15             for (quitChar='N';(quitChar != 'y') && (quitChar != 'Y');)
```

```
16              {
17                      printf("Enter a string of no more than 40 characters\n");
18                      printf(">>> ");
19                      gets(inputText);
20                      fprintf(outputFile,"%s\n",inputText);
21
22                      printf("\nQuit? Y/N: ");;
23                      quitChar=getchar();
24
25                      while (getchar()!='\n');
26
27                      putchar('\n');
28                      putchar('\n');
29              }
30
31              fclose(outputFile);
32      }
33
34      return (0);
35 }
```

TIP 21.2
The only difference between `printf()` and `fprintf()` is that `printf()` prints its output to the file `stdout`, while `fprintf()` can print to any file. Because of this, the calls

`printf("%s",aString);`

and

`fprintf(stdout,"%s",aString);`

are identical.

The only change to the version of the program in Example 21.5 is replacing the calls to `fputs()` and `fputc()` with a single call to `fprintf()`.

21.2.3   Binary Files

Binary files are not limited to holding only ASCII characters. They contain any valid binary number. Most programs that are more complex than a text editor save their data in binary files.

Programs use many of the same techniques to process binary files as they do text files. However, when opening binary files, programs must specify binary mode. To do this, they must pass one of the strings from Table 21.1 that contains the letter b as the second parameter to `fopen()`. When a program opens an existing binary file for reading, it can use the string `"rb"`.

Reading from Binary Files   Programs can read data from binary files one byte at a time. They can also read entire blocks of data at once. Table 21.4 contains the Standard Library file functions which can be used to read file data in binary mode.

TABLE 21.4   Input Functions for Binary Mode

Function	Description
fgetc()	Reads a byte of data from a file.
fread()	Reads a block of data from a binary file.

In binary mode, the `fgetc()` function reads a byte rather than a character. Hands On 21.3 demonstrates the use of the `fgetc()` function in binary mode.

Hands On 21.3

Objective

Write a program that:
>   Prompts the user for a file name.
>   Retrieves the file name from the user.
>   Reads any file, whether in text or binary format, as a binary file.
>   Labels each row of output with the addresses of the row of bytes in hexadecimal format. The address of a byte is the distance of its offset number from the beginning of the file.
>   Outputs the contents of the file in hexadecimal format in rows of eight bytes.

Experiment

The program for this Hands On is located in the file Ho21_3.c on the Examples CD. A directory called Chapt21 is in the Examples directory. Ho21_3.c is in the Chapt21 directory. Load this program into your text editor or IDE. Compile, link, and run it.

Results

The first screenful of output will resemble Figure 21.3.

FIGURE 21.3　**Output from Hands On 21.3**

```
0x0-0x7:      23    69    6E    63    6C    75    64    65
0x8-0xF:      20    3C    73    74    64    69    6F    2E
0x10-0x17:    68    3E    D     A     D     A     23    64
0x18-0x1F:    65    66    69    6E    65    20    46    49
0x20-0x27:    4C    45    5F    4E    41    4D    45    5F
0x28-0x2F:    4C    45    4E    47    54    48    9     32
0x30-0x37:    35    36    D     A     D     A     63    6F
0x38-0x3F:    6E    73    74    20    69    6E    74    20
0x40-0x47:    52    4F    57    5F    4C    45    4E    47
0x48-0x4F:    54    48    20    3D    20    38    3B    D
0x50-0x57:    A     63    6F    6E    73    74    20    69
0x58-0x5F:    6E    74    20    52    4F    57    53    5F
0x60-0x67:    50    45    52    5F    53    43    52    45
0x68-0x6F:    45    4E    20    3D    20    32    35    3B
0x70-0x77:    D     A     63    6F    6E    73    74    20
0x78-0x7F:    69    6E    74    20    50    41    47    45
0x80-0x87:    5F    4C    45    4E    47    54    48    20
0x88-0x8F:    3D    20    32    30    3B    D     A     63
0x90-0x97:    6F    6E    73    74    20    63    68    61
0x98-0x9F:    72    20    54    41    42    5F    43    48
Press the Enter key to continue...
```

Analysis

The output of this Hands On program will consist of a series of bytes in hexadecimal format. The first column of output contains the addresses of the bytes in the row. For example, the first row is labled 0x0-0x7. The eight bytes that follow are bytes 0 through 7 in the file.

The program source code contains sections for its include files, constants, types, and prototypes. When you run this program, it will prompt you for a file name (lines 77–82). On line 85, the program attempts to open the file as a binary file in read-only mode. If the file can't be opened, the program executes the `else` statement on lines 150–155.

If the file can be opened, the program calls the `ClearScreen()` function on line 96. It enters a `for` loop, which begins on line 99. The loop executes until it has printed a page of output or it has reached the end of the file. It will also terminate if there is some sort of file error.

On lines 104–106, the program prints the addresses of the current row of bytes. Each row consists of eight bytes. The addresses are printed in hexadecimal format.

After the address range of the current row is displayed, the program enters a `for` loop which prints each byte. It uses the Standard Library `fgetc()` function to read a byte from the file. If the byte was read, it is printed on the screen (line 120) in hexadecimal format.

If program could not read the byte, it sets the variable `done` to TRUE (line 125), which ends all three loops. If the byte could not be read but the program has not reached the end of the file, an error has occurred. The program sets a variable containing the error status. If the byte could not be read and there was no error, the program prints a message to the user indicating that the end of the file was reached.

A screenful of output is called a page. Each time the program prints a page, it also prints a prompt to the user (line 143). This prompt tells the user that the program is waiting. When the user presses the Enter key, the program continues.

Try This

This Hands On program can open either binary or text files. Either way, the contents of the files are printed as hexadecimal numbers. Try using this program to open the file Ho21_3.c. Then use it to open the executable version of the program. What differences do you see?

In addition to reading binary files one byte at a time, programs can read data from binary files in blocks. Programs can retrieve the contents of an entire structure or array from a file in one read operation. To perform block reads, programs use the `fread()` function.

The `fread()` function takes four parameters. The first is the memory address where the data will be stored when it is read from the file. The second is the size of each data item. If, for instance, the program is reading a group of integers from a file, this parameter should be set to `sizeof(int)`.

The third parameter to `fread()` is the number of items to read. If the program is reading a group of ten integers, the value of the third parameter will be 10.

The last parameter to the `fread()` function is a pointer to the file from which the data will be read. Example 21.6 contains a portion of a program showing how `fread()` can be used to read a group of integers.

EXAMPLE 21.6   Reading Integers with `fread()`

```
1   int main()
2   {
3           int integerArray[100];
4           FILE *fp=NULL;
5
6           fp = fopen("INTS.DAT","rb");
7           if (fp)
8           {
9             fread((void *)integerArray,
10                  sizeof(int),
11                  100,
12                  fp);
13          }
14   }
```

Line 3 of the code fragment in Example 21.6 declares an array of 100 integers. Line 4 declares a pointer to a file. The statement on line 6 opens a file called INTS.DAT. The file is opened in read-only, binary mode.

If the file is successfully opened, the example calls the `fread()` function. It passes the starting address of the integer array as the first parameter. The address should be type cast because the data type of first parameter to `fread()` is `void *`. If the program does not type cast the first parameter, some compilers will report a warning. While most experienced programmers will not be flustered by this warning, new programmers maintaining your code may think something is wrong. Adding the type cast takes very little effort, and it decreases the number of warnings produced at compile time.

The same basic technique can be used to read the contents of a structure from a binary file. Programs can read the structures one at a time. They can also fill entire arrays of structures with one read. These abilities are widely used in database programs. Hands On 21.4 contains the source code for a simple program that reads a structure from a binary file. The structure contains customer information.

TIP 21.3
When your program passes a pointer as the first parameter to `fread()`, it is a good idea to type cast the pointer to `void *`. This decreases the number of warnings the compiler produces.

Hands On 21.4

Objective

Write a program that reads a structure from a file. It should print the information it retrieves from the file onto the screen.

Experiment

Load the following program into your IDE or text editor. Compile, link, and run it. When you run the program, be sure the file data.bin is in the same directory as the executable program. You will find data.bin on the Examples CD included with this book. A directory called Chapt21 is in the Examples directory. The file data.bin is in the Chapt21 directory. To save you some typing, the source code for this example is also in the Chapt21 directory. It is in a file named Ho21_4.c.

```
1   #include <stdio.h>
2
3   #define MAX_STRING_LENGTH 256
4   #define STATE_NAME_LENGTH 3
5
6
7   typedef enum
8   {
9       NO_ERROR = 0,
10      CANT_OPEN_FILE,
11      FILE_IO_ERROR
12  } error_status;
13
14  typedef struct
15  {
16      char name[MAX_STRING_LENGTH];
17      char streetAddress1[MAX_STRING_LENGTH];
18      char streetAddress2[MAX_STRING_LENGTH];
19      char city[MAX_STRING_LENGTH];
20      char state[STATE_NAME_LENGTH];
21      unsigned zip;
22  } customer;
23
24
25  int main()
26  {
27      int errorStatus = 0;
28      customer aCustomer;
29      FILE *fp = NULL;
30
31
32      fp = fopen("data.bin", "rb");
33
34      if (!fp)
35      {
36          printf("Could not open file\n");
37          errorStatus = CANT_OPEN_FILE;
38      }
39
40      if (errorStatus == NO_ERROR)
41      {
```

```
42              aCustomer.name[0] = '\0';
43              aCustomer.streetAddress1[0] = '\0';
44              aCustomer.streetAddress2[0] = '\0';
45              aCustomer.city[0] = '\0';
46              aCustomer.state[0] = '\0';
47              aCustomer.zip = 0;
48
49              if (fread((void *)(&aCustomer),sizeof(customer),1,fp) != 1)
50              {
51                  errorStatus = FILE_IO_ERROR;
52              }
53              else
54              {
55                  printf("%s\n",aCustomer.name);
56                  printf("%s\n",aCustomer.streetAddress1);
57                  printf("%s\n",aCustomer.streetAddress2);
58                  printf("%s\n",aCustomer.city);
59                  printf("%s\n",aCustomer.state);
60                  printf("%u\n",aCustomer.zip);
61                  printf("Press Enter to continue...");
62                  getchar();
63              }
64          }
65      if (fp)
66      {
67          fclose(fp);
68      }
69      return (errorStatus);
70  }
```

Results

Bill Williams
1234 5th St
Apt. #24
Big City
NM
87654
Press Enter to continue...

Analysis

This small program reads a binary file called data.bin. If the file is not in the same directory as the executable program, the program will not be able to read the file.

The first portion of the program defines an enumerated type containing error status identifiers. It also defines a `customer` structure, similar to those used in previous chapters.

The `main()` function declares the variables it needs and attempts to open the file data.bin for reading in binary mode. If it cannot open the file, it sets an error condition. If it succeeds, it initializes the variable `aCustomer` to indicate that it is empty. While this isn't strictly necessary, it's a good precaution.

Next, the program attempts to read a customer structure from the file using the Standard Library `fread()` function. The address of the structure variable is type cast to a `void` pointer to prevent compilers from issuing warnings about mismatched parameter types.

If the read is successful, `fread()` will return the number of items (not bytes) it read. This program reads only one item, so if the number returned by `fread()` is not 1, something is wrong. In that case, the program sets an error condition. If the read was successful, the program prints the information in the structure variable.

The program in Hands On 21.4 contains no pointers. Structures and arrays that contain no pointers can easily be written to a disk or tape. It is also straightforward to read them from a disk or tape. Reading or writing structures and arrays that contain pointers, however, is not as easy.

When a structure or array contains one or more pointers, the pointers hold the address in memory of some data. If a program writes the structure or array to a disk, it will write only the structure or array. Therefore, the information pointed to by the pointers in the structure or array will not be written. That must be saved to disk or tape in an additional write operation.

As a result, programs which write structures or arrays containing pointers into files must perform one write operation for the structure or array and an additional write operation for each pointer in the structure or array.

TRAP 21.4
When using `fread()` to read structures or arrays containing pointers, a program must allocate memory for each pointer to point at. It must also perform a read operation for each pointer. If this algorithm is not followed, the data will not be read properly.

When reading in structures or arrays containing pointers, programs must read the structure or array. They also must perform a read operation for each pointer in the structure or array. This usually requires allocating a block of memory for each pointer in the structure or array. This must be done prior to the read operation for the pointer. The block of memory is then used to store the data associated with the pointer.

For instance, Example 21.7 shows a version of the `customer` structure which contains pointers. This enables data for a members of the `customer` type, such as the name, to be dynamically allocated. Dynamically allocating the name is desirable because some people have long names. Others have short names. Dynamic allocation efficiently accommodates them both.

EXAMPLE 21.7   A `customer` Structure with Pointers

```
1   typedef struct
2   {
3           char *name;
4           char *streetAddress1;
5           char *streetAddress2;
6           char *city;
7           char *state;
8           unsigned zip;
9   } customer;
```

If a program uses the `customer` structure in Example 21.7, it must read the structure. The memory pointed at by each pointer member of the `customer` structure must be allocated by the program. It is not automatically allocated by the read operation. Once it has been allocated, the program must perform separate read operations for each pointer member in the structure.

Writing to Binary Files   Programs write information to binary files in much the same way that they read it. However, the flow of information is reversed. Programs can write data to binary files one byte at a time. Additionally, they can write entire blocks of data at once. Table 21.5 contains the Standard Library file functions which can be used to write file data in binary mode.

As with the `fgetc()` function, `fputc()` operates on a byte rather than a character. The `fwrite()` function is the counterpart to `fread()`. It writes blocks of data to files. Hands On 21.5 illustrates its use.

TABLE 21.5   Output Functions for Binary Mode

Function	Description
`fputc()`	Writes a byte of data from a file.
`fwrite()`	Writes a block of data from a binary file.

Hands On 21.5

Objective

Write a program that writes the information in a customer structure to a file.

Experiment

Load the following program into your IDE or text editor. Compile, link, and run it. To save you some typing, the source code for this example is in the Chapt21 directory, which you will find in the Examples directory on the Examples CD. The code for this Hands on program is in a file named Ho21_5.c.

```c
1   #include <stdio.h>
2
3   #define MAX_STRING_LENGTH 256
4   #define STATE_NAME_LENGTH 3
5
6
7   typedef enum
8   {
9         NO_ERROR = 0,
10        CANT_OPEN_FILE,
11        FILE_IO_ERROR
12  } error_status;
13
14  typedef struct
15  {
16        char name[MAX_STRING_LENGTH];
17        char streetAddress1[MAX_STRING_LENGTH];
18        char streetAddress2[MAX_STRING_LENGTH];
19        char city[MAX_STRING_LENGTH];
20        char state[STATE_NAME_LENGTH];
21        unsigned zip;
22  } customer;
23
24
25  int main()
26  {
27        error_status errorStatus = NO_ERROR;
28
29
30        customer aCustomer = {"Bill Williams",
31                              "1234 5th St",
32                              "Apt. #24",
33                              "Big City",
34                              "NM",
35                              87654};
36        FILE *fp = NULL;
37
38        fp=fopen("data.bin","wb");
39        if (!fp)
40        {
41              printf("Could not open file\n");
42              errorStatus = CANT_OPEN_FILE;
43        }
44        else
```

```
45              {
46                      if (fwrite((void *)(&aCustomer),sizeof(customer),1,fp) != 1)
47                      {
48                              errorStatus = FILE_IO_ERROR;
49                      }
50                      else
51                      {
52                              fclose(fp);
53                      }
54              }
55
56      if (errorStatus == NO_ERROR)
57      {
58              fp = fopen("data.bin", "rb");
59
60              if (!fp)
61              {
62                      printf("Could not open file\n");
63                      errorStatus = CANT_OPEN_FILE;
64              }
65      }
66
67      if (errorStatus == NO_ERROR)
68      {
69              aCustomer.name[0] = '\0';
70              aCustomer.streetAddress1[0] = '\0';
71              aCustomer.streetAddress2[0] = '\0';
72              aCustomer.city[0] = '\0';
73              aCustomer.state[0] = '\0';
74              aCustomer.zip = 0;
75
76              if (fread((void *)(&aCustomer),sizeof(customer),1,fp) != 1)
77              {
78                      errorStatus = FILE_IO_ERROR;
79              }
80              else
81              {
82                      printf("%s\n",aCustomer.name);
83                      printf("%s\n",aCustomer.streetAddress1);
84                      printf("%s\n",aCustomer.streetAddress2);
85                      printf("%s\n",aCustomer.city);
86                      printf("%s\n",aCustomer.state);
87                      printf("%u\n",aCustomer.zip);
88                      printf("Press Enter to continue...");
89                      getchar();
90              }
91      }
92
93      if (fp)
94      {
95              fclose(fp);
96      }
97
98      return (errorStatus);
99 }
```

Results

Bill Williams
1234 5th St
Apt. #24
Big City
NM
87654
Press Enter to continue...

Analysis

This program is an expanded version of the program from Hands On 21.4. It declares a variable of type `customer`, which it initializes. Next, it opens a binary file for output. It calls `fwrite()` to write the contents of the structure to the output file. If it is successful, it clears the contents of the `customer` variable. It then uses `fread()` to read the data back into aCustomer.

Random Access Programs seldom access data in files in sequential order. In other words, they usually do not start at the beginning and process the data from the first byte to the last. More typically, they allow **random access** to the data in the file. When a program uses random access, it can access any byte of data in any order.

In C, random access is provided through the use of the `fseek()` and `ftell()` functions. Programs use these functions to control a file's current location pointer so that they do not have to do it directly. Recall that the current location pointer is the byte offset from the beginning of the file where the next read or write will take place.

If a program needs to find where the current location pointer is in a file, it calls the `ftell()` function. To move the current location pointer, programs invoke `fseek()`.

The `ftell()` function takes one parameter, a pointer to a file. It returns the byte offset contained in the file's current location pointer. The offset specifies the distance, in bytes, from the beginning of the file, where the next read or write will take place.

The `fseek()` function requires three parameters. The first is a pointer to file. The second parameter is the number of bytes to move. Programs use the `fseek()` function's third parameter to specify the initial position from which the seek will be performed. Table 21.6 contains the constants that can be passed to `fseek()` for its third parameter.

TABLE 21.6 Initial Position Specifiers for the `fseek()` Function

Constant	Description
SEEK_SET	Seek from the beginning of the file.
SEEK_CUR	Seek from the current position of the current location pointer.
SEEK_END	Seek from the end of the file.

If SEEK_SET is used as the third parameter to `fseek()`, the number in the second parameter specifies a byte offset from the beginning of the file. So, for example, the call

```
fseek(fp,5,SEEK_SET);
```

moves the current location pointer to sixth byte of the file (the first byte is byte 0). If the end of the file is encountered before the specified number of bytes, the current location pointer will point to the end of the file. A program cannot move the current location pointer beyond the end of the file. Also, a program cannot move the current location pointer to a point before the beginning of a file. So the call

```
fseek(fp,-10,SEEK_SET);
```

will always fail. It attempts to move the current location pointer to a byte offset that is before the beginning of the file. If this call is executed in a program, the current location pointer will be set to the beginning of the file.

If, on the other hand, a program invoked the `fseek()` function like this

```
fseek(fp,-10,SEEK_CUR);
```

the call can work. This invocation of `fseek()` moves the current location pointer from its current position 10 bytes toward the beginning of the file. If the beginning of the file is encountered before the current location pointer is moved the specified number of bytes, the current location pointer points to the beginning of the file.

If the third parameter to `fseek()` is SEEK_END, the second parameter must be negative. In this case, it specifies the number of bytes to move toward the beginning of the file from the end.

The return value of `fseek()` is the number of bytes it actually moves.

21.2.4 Other File Functions

In addition to the functions already presented, the C Standard Library provides other file functions. Among the most often used are `ungetc()`, `rewind()`, `fflush()`, and `ferror()`.

The `ungetc()` Function   Recall that C files are also viewed as streams of information. Sometimes programs may want to read a character or byte from an input stream, see what it is, and put it back onto the stream to be read by another part of the program. For this situation, the C Standard Library provides the `ungetc()` function.

In text mode the `ungetc()` function will put characters back onto a stream. In binary mode it puts bytes onto the input stream. The ANSI standard states that all implementations of `ungetc()` must be able to push one character or byte back onto the stream before the next read occurs. Some implementations enable your program to push back more than one character or byte. With these versions, your program can read several characters and then push them all back onto the stream. When the program begins reading again, the characters or bytes will be read in the reverse order in which they were pushed onto the stream.

If you want your code to be portable between compilers, you must not depend on the ability to push more than one character back onto a stream at a time.

The `ungetc()` function takes two parameters, the character to push back onto the stream and the stream onto which the character will be pushed.

The `rewind()` Function   Some programs process files by reading them sequentially, beginning with the first byte in the file and reading byte-by-byte until the end of the file. When the end of the file is reached, programs may need to start again at the beginning of the file. To make this easy, the C Standard Library provides the `rewind()` function. It is so named because, in the days when computers used tape drives instead of disk drives, a call to this function actually rewound the tape.

In more recent implementations, the `rewind()` function positions a file's current location pointer to the start of the file. This function takes one parameter, a pointer to the file.

In addition to moving the current location pointer to the beginning of the file, the `rewind()` function clears any file errors that might currently be flagged on the stream.

Many of the example programs presented so far in this book have needed to clear the keyboard buffer. For the most part, the `getchar()` function was used to pull the remaining keystrokes out of the keyboard buffer.

However, this assumes that there is at least one keystroke waiting in the keyboard buffer. In reality, there may not be. If there is not, the program will hang until the user presses the Enter key. The `rewind()` function provides us with a way around that limitation. Every implementation with which I am familiar enables programs to call `rewind()` and pass it the stream `stdin`. This will clear the keyboard buffer. This simple call provides us with a straightforward and portable way to clear the keyboard buffer.

The `fflush()` Function   At times, before a program can continue processing, it may need to ensure that everything it's written to a stream has reached the stream's destination.

TIP 21.4
Although some implementations of the C Standard Library enable your program to call `ungetc()` more than once between read operations from a stream, you must not depend on this if you want your code to be portable.

TIP 21.5
To clear the keyboard buffer, call the `rewind()` function and pass it the stream `stdin`. This technique works with every implementation of `rewind()` with which I'm familiar.

For the most part, stream buffers are managed by the operating system. They are flushed when they are full, when the stream is closed, or when the program exits normally. However, there are also times when programs need to manually flush a stream's buffers. Programs use the C Standard Library function `fflush()` to accomplish this task.

The `fflush()` function takes a pointer to a file as its only parameter. It returns zero if the buffer was successfully flushed. It also returns zero when the stream has no buffer or when it has been opened for reading only. If there is an error, `fflush()` returns EOF.

If the stream is opened for output, `fflush()` writes the contents of the stream's buffer to the stream's destination. Usually, this means that the data in the stream's buffer is written to a disk or tape. If the stream is opened for input rather than output, calling `fflush()` will clear the contents of the stream's buffer. The call

```
fflush(NULL);
```

flushes the buffers of all open output streams.

The `ferror()` Function   Programs that process information in files must ensure that the file operations were successful. One way to do this is by calling `ferror()`.

The `ferror()` function takes one parameter, which is a pointer to a file. If no error has occurred on that stream, it returns zero. If there was an error, it returns a nonzero value. The meaning of the value depends on the compiler you are using. You will need to look in your compiler's reference documentation to find out exactly what the error number indicates. You also can convert the error numbers to error messages using the `strerror()` and `perror()` functions. These are presented in the Troubleshooting Guide near the end of this chapter in Section 21.6.1.

21.3   Printing Text

At its most basic level, a C program sees printers as text mode output files. In actual practice, printing output can be a real problem for a programmer. All printers accept ASCII text. However, each type of printer also has its own unique set of **control codes**. These control codes are used to enable and disable the unique features the printer offers.

When MS DOS was the most popular operating system, it was nearly impossible to accommodate every type of printer available. There were certain groups of command codes that most printers recognized. Generally, programmers limited themselves to using only these control codes.

With the advent of more sophisticated operating systems, programs can communicate with printers in standardized ways. This enables nearly any program to use nearly any printer.

The downside of this increased compatibility is that the source code for printing must be specific to a particular operating system. If you want truly portable code, you can only send text output to a printer.

Because C programs see printers essentially as text output files, you can write text to a printer using the C Standard Library file functions. Some compilers provide a stream called `stdprn`, which stands for standard printer. It is connected to the default printer.

If your compiler does not provide such a stream, your program can create one itself. Example 21.8 shows a code fragment that opens a stream called `stdprn`.

EXAMPLE 21.8   Opening a Printer for Output

```
1   FILE *stdprn;
2
3   #ifdef (MSDOS_WINDOWS_VERSION)
4   stdprn = fopen("PRN","w");
5   #elif defined(UNIX_VERSION)
6   stdprn = fopen("/dev/lpt0","w");
7   #endif
```

The code fragment in Example 21.8 uses preprocessor directives to conditionally compile statements for different operating systems.

If the constant MSDOS_WINDOWS_VERSION is defined, the statement on line 4 is compiled. This statement opens a file called stdprn. Under MS DOS and MS Windows, the name for the default printer is PRN.

If, instead of MSDOS_WINDOWS_VERSION, the constant UNIX_VERSION is defined, the statement on line 6 is compiled. With many versions of UNIX, the first available printer is named "/dev/lpt0".

Once the printer has been opened as a file, programs can use text-mode Standard Library functions to write text to the file. The functions fprintf(), fputc(), and fputs() all will work.

21.4 Adding File I/O to the Text Editor

Now it's time to pull together many of the ideas that we've discussed throughout this chapter and write a version of the text editor that loads and saves files.

Hands On 21.6

Objective

Write a text editor that enables a user to load, edit, and save a text file. It also should enable the use to scroll the text on the screen upward and downward.

Experiment

Load the following program into your IDE or text editor. Compile, link, and run it. This program is composed of six files, Tedit.c, Tstring.h, Tstring.c, Tbuffer.h, Tbuffer.c, and MiscType.h. On the Examples CD, there is a directory called Examples. A directory called Chapt21 is in the Examples directory. In Chapt21 is the HO21_6 directory. The files for this program are in the HO21_6 directory. To save space, the code is not shown here. Please refer to the files on the disk.

Results

When the program starts, the screen will resemble Figure 21.4.

FIGURE 21.4 The Initial Output of the Editor

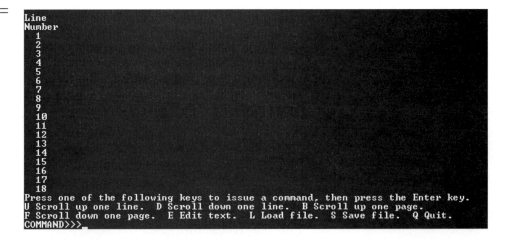

Press L, and then press Enter. When prompted, type the file name TEdit.c. Your screen will resemble Figure 21.5.

FIGURE 21.5   Loading a File

```
Line
Number
    1    //-------------------------------------------------------------
    2    /*
    3    File Name:        TEdit.c
    4    Comments:         This file contains the functions which
    5                             implement the text editor.
    6    */
    7    //-------------------------------------------------------------
    8
    9
   10
   11
   12    //-------------------------------------------------------------
   13    // Include files
   14
   15    #include <stdio.h>
   16    #include <stdlib.h>
   17    #include "MiscType.h"
   18    #include "TBuffer.h"
Press one of the following keys to issue a command, then press the Enter key.
U Scroll up one line.  D Scroll down one line.  B Scroll up one page.
F Scroll down one page.  E Edit text.  L Load file.  S Save file.  Q Quit.
COMMAND>>>_
```

Analysis

Congratulations! You have just created a working text editor that loads and saves files. As you run this program, test out each of the commands. Notice that the layout of the files follows the design ideas we covered in previous chapters. Following those design guidelines helps us produce a text editor that is easy for maintenance programmers to understand and enhance.

This text editor functions very much like some of the first text editors that programmers commonly used. However, it is more limited in its functionality than most of them were. It makes some of the same design compromises that were common back then, and it makes them for the same reasons. For instance, this text editor only uses command characters that are in the ASCII set of characters. This helps ensure portability across multiple hardware and operating system platforms.

The program begins in the file Tedit.c by including the header files it requires. It defines some constants and an enumerated type containing error identification numbers. It also declares the prototypes for some general purpose functions which are called only by functions in TEdit.c.

As with most functions, `main()` starts off by declaring some variables. One of them is the actual text buffer. It initializes the buffer with a call to `TextBufferInitialize()`. The program enters a loop on line 96 which continues until the user enters the Quit command. Inside the loop, it clears the screen and displays a screenful of text.

A quick look that the `DisplayText()` function on lines 236–304 shows that it has been modified from versions in previous chapters. It no longer displays both the display and buffer line numbers. This version prints only the display line numbers. As with previous versions, the program completely redraws the screen each time the user enters a command. Users generally don't care for that. However, it gives us an easy and portable way to implement the text editor.

After the program prints a screenful of text, `main()` calls `PrintMenu()` to display the menu. Next, it invokes `GetUserCommand()` to retrieve input from the user. The `GetUserCommand()` function appears on lines 349–386 of TEdit.c. The primary difference between this version of `GetUserCommand()` and previous versions is that it uses the `rewind()` function from the C Standard Library to clear the keyboard input buffer.

Like many programs, the text editor uses a `switch` statement to interpret the input. It begins on line 110 of TEdit.c. The user can enter commands to scroll up a page, scroll up one line, scroll down a page, or scroll down a line. The software also recognizes commands to edit a line of text, save the contents of the buffer to a file, and load the buffer from a file. All other input causes the default case of the `switch` statement to be executed. The default case prints a message telling the user that the input was incorrect.

The cases for the Scroll Up and Scroll Down commands simply call the appropriate `text_buffer` functions. The Edit, Save, and Load commands invoke other functions in TEdit.c. They then use `text_buffer` functions to edit, save, or load the file.

If the user selects the Edit command, `main()` invokes the `EditBuffer()` function, which is on lines 391–506 of TEdit.c. The `EditBuffer()` function initializes a `text_string` variable and stores a string of 40 space characters in it. This causes the program to allocate space for 40 characters at once rather than performing an allocation for each character stored into the `text_string`. As was discussed in Chapter 20, this improves program speed but may waste memory.

Next, the `EditBuffer()` function retrieves the top line number of the buffer. It enters a `do-while` loop (line 438) and displays a prompt asking for the number of the line to edit (lines 441–442). The program gets the line number from the user as a string and converts it to a number. That way, if the user types in anything other than a number, the program can do error checking on the input. The text editor program uses the Standard Library function `atoi()` to convert the string of ASCII characters to an integer. If the user enters data that is not an integer, the `atoi()` function returns zero.

If the user enters a valid line number, the program displays a prompt asking the user to enter new text for that line. Although there were actually text editors which functioned this way, users found them annoying. Even if they only wanted to change one character on the line, they had to re-enter the entire line of text. Users don't appreciate that.

Modern text editors enable users to move the cursor to a particular line on the screen and edit that line. Remember that the arrow keys are not in the ASCII set. For portability, we are using only ASCII characters. Many text editors in the past have used characters in the ASCII set for cursor movement. We could do the same. However, cursor movement is often dependent on the hardware, operating system, and compiler you are using. Is there a portable way to do hardware-dependent operations like clearing the screen and moving the cursor?

Well, no and yes. There is no standard, portable way built into C to do these operations. However, we can use preprocessor directives to conditionally compile macros that perform these tasks.

After `EditBuffer()` gets a line of input from the user, it calls `TextBufferSetRow()` on line 485 to store the string into a row of the buffer. The `TextBufferSetRow()` function is on lines 83–152 of TBuffer.c. Notice that an `if` statement has been added on lines 143–146. If there is no error in the process of storing the string into the buffer, this `if` statement sets a member of the `text_buffer` structure called `isDirty` to `TRUE`. The `isDirty` member was added to the `text_buffer` definition in TBuffer.h for this version of the text editor. If the contents of the buffer have been changed since it was last saved, programmers say that the buffer is "dirty." Once it has been saved to a file, it is "clean" again.

When a `text_buffer` is initialized with `TextBufferInitialize()`, the value of the `isDirty` member is set to `FALSE`. The `text_buffer` functions set this member to `TRUE` whenever they change the contents of the buffer. Changing the contents of the buffer is exactly the purpose of the `TextBufferSetRow()` function. If it is successful, it marks the buffer as dirty.

When the `TextBufferSetRow()` function ends, program execution returns to `EditBuffer()`. On lines 496–500 of TEdit.c, an `if` statement tests whether the variable `tempString` was used by the function. If the user typed any characters in, it was. However, if the user just pressed Enter when prompted for a new string, then `tempString` will be empty. When it is not empty, it must be cleaned up properly before the function ends. This is done by calling the `TextStringFree()` function and passing it a pointer to `tempString`. After `EditBuffer()` finishes, program execution returns to `main()`.

If the `switch` statement in `main()` determines that the user entered the Save command, program execution jumps to line 147 of TEdit.c. This `case` statement invokes the `SaveBuffer()` function. If the call to `SaveBuffer()` is not successful, the `if` statement on lines 148–155 of TEdit.c prints an error message.

The code for the `SaveBuffer()` function appears on lines 511–566 of TEdit.c. It declares some variables it needs, including a `text_string` variable called `fileName`. Next, the function uses `TextStringInitString()` to initialize `fileName`. It prompts the user for the name of the file and uses the `TextStringScanString()` function to read it in.

You might ask why the program does not just use `scanf()` or `gets()` to read the line of text into the program. It could, but there would be trade-offs. These two C Standard Library functions require programs to allocate, in advance, enough memory to hold the strings they retrieve from the user. When we are writing programs, you and I have no way to determine how many characters the user will type. The typical strategy for coping with this is to allocate more memory than the user will possibly fill. However, when the user only types a few characters, that technique is extremely wasteful of memory. The `text_string` type, which first appeared in Chapter 19, can grow to the limits of memory one character at a time. This is where that effort really pays off. By using a `text_string` to store input and calling `TextStringScanString()`, the program can read in as many characters as the user types, up to the limits of memory. The program doesn't have to waste memory by allocating more than the user will possibly fill up.

TIP 21.6

When faced with the constant dilemma of whether to optimize memory usage or program speed, ask yourself how much waiting the program is doing. If the program is getting input from the user, most of its time is spent waiting. Therefore, slowing the program down to save memory is probably a good choice. If the program can complete its task before the user presses the next keystroke, the user won't notice the extra time the program spends on the task.

The drawback to this technique is that the program will be performing an allocation for each character the user types into the editor. This requires a lot of overhead and slows the program down. However, in this case, that doesn't matter. When the program is reading input from the user, the slowest part of the whole process is the user. Computers are so much faster than humans that adding extra overhead to the input process may not matter. The user will not see any difference in the speed of the program. Even with the extra overhead, the computer is still faster than the person using it.

If the user enters a valid file name, the program calls `TextBufferSaveFile()`. This function is on lines 533–614 of TBuffer.c. It uses an `if` statement to determine whether the buffer is dirty. If the buffer is clean, the function just returns. If it is dirty, `TextBufferSaveFile()` attempts to open the file specified by the parameter `fileName`.

The function may not be able to open the file. There are a variety of reasons for this. For example, the user may have specified a file name that is not valid for the operating system. The user might not have write privileges on the disk, such as when they attempt to save a file onto a CD ROM. If, for whatever reason, the file cannot be opened for writing, the `TextBufferSaveFile()` function sets an error status variable and returns.

If the file can be opened, the `TextBufferSaveFile()` function enters a `for` loop on line 568. The loop iterates through every line of the buffer. If the line is not empty, the `TextBufferSaveFile()` calls `fprintf()` to write it to the file. If the line does not contain any characters, `TextBufferSaveFile()` prints a newline to the file.

On line 589, `TextBufferSaveFile()` calls the Standard Library `ferror()` function to test for a file write error. If one is found, it sets an error status variable. Otherwise, the loop continues to iterate.

When the loop finishes without error, the statement on line 599 marks the text buffer as being clean. The call to `fclose()` on line 602 closes the file. The function exits by returning the value in the error status variable. When it does, program execution returns to `SaveBuffer()` in TEdit.c. If the buffer was written without error, `SaveBuffer()` calls `TextStringFree()` on line 560 of TEdit.C to prevent a memory leak.

When the user enters the Load command at the main menu of the text editor, the `switch` statement in `main()` jumps to the `case` statement on line 159 of TEdit.c. The `case` statement invokes the `LoadBuffer()` function. If this function is not successful at loading a file into the buffer, the `if` statement on lines 160–167 set an error status variable.

The code for the `LoadBuffer()` function is on lines 571–627 of TEdit.c. Like `SaveBuffer()`, `LoadBuffer()` initializes a `text_string` variable and uses the variable to store a file name it gets from the user. It calls `TextBufferLoadFile()` to load the file into the buffer.

The `TextBufferLoadFile()` function can be found on lines 429–528 of TBuffer.c. The function attempts to open the specified text file. If it is not successful, it sets an error status variable. If the file can be opened, `TextBuffer-LoadFile()` enters a `for` loop to read in the contents of the file. Inside the `for` loop, the function uses a `while` loop to read each line of the file one character at a time. This enables the program to read the line of text into a `text_string` variable. Because it does, the line of text can be any length up to the limits of memory.

After the `while` loop reads a line of text from the file, TextBufferLoadFile() calls `TextBufferSetRow()` to save the text into a row of the buffer. The first condition in the `if` statement on lines 491–498 tests whether there has been an error. If there was, we don't want the program to try and store the contents of the string into a buffer row. The first condition also checks to determine whether the end of file has been reached. If so, the variable `tempString` does not contain valid input, so the program should not save its contents into the buffer. The last condition in this `if` statement calls the `TextBufferSetRow()` function and tests its return value. If it returns any type of error, the statement on line 497 sets an error status variable.

Each time the `for` loop iterates, it invokes `TextStringSetCharacter()` on line 504 of TBuffer.c to blank out the line of text. It does this by saving a null character in location 0 in the temporary string. A look at `TextStringSetCharacter()` on lines 221–270 of TString.c shows that the function has been modified to enable this type of assignment.

In particular, the call to the `assert()` function on lines 261–263 of TString.c has been added. This assertion uses a conditional operator. Recall that any condition can be used in an assertion. The conditional operator evaluates to a value. If that value is zero, it is false. Otherwise, it is true. The conditional operator in the parameter list of this call to `assert()` tests whether the character index and the length of the string are both zero. If so, it evaluates to the statement on line 262. This statement is also a condition. It tests to ensure that there is at least one character allocated. If the character index and the length are not zero, the conditional operator evaluates to the result of the condition on line 263. This condition ensures that the character index is less than the length of the string.

Once the `TextStringSetCharacter()` function has set the temporary string to the null character, program execution returns to the `for` loop in `TextBuffer-LoadFile()`, which is in TBuffer.c. This loop repeats until the program reaches the end of the input file. When it terminates, `TextBufferLoadFile()` frees the temporary text string (line 508 of TBuffer.c) and closes the input file (line 510). If the file was successfully loaded, the statement on line 521 marks the buffer as dirty. `TextBufferLoadFile()` ends and program execution returns to `LoadBuffer()` in TEdit.c.

If any error was encountered in loading the file, the `if` statement on lines 602–607 of TEdit.c sets an error status variable. `LoadBuffer()` frees its local `text_string` variable and returns the error status. The program jumps back to `main()`. If `LoadBuffer()` returned an error, the `if` statement on lines 160–167 of TEdit.c prints an error message to the user. However, this is not considered a fatal error in the program, so it continues.

The program executes until the user enters the Quit command. When this occurs, `main()` frees the text buffer (line 195) and exits.

21.5   Parsing Command-Line Arguments

Through the use of pointers, C supports a rich set of very powerful programming techniques. For example, pointers enable programmers to pass a variable number of parameters to a function. A common use of this capability is to pass parameters to the `main()`

function in a program. Many programs, especially programs which load files, use this feature to enable the user to specify which file to load when the program starts.

Whenever we run a C program, the operating system calls `main()`. We can pass arguments (parameters) from the operating system to `main()`. The `main()` function takes two parameters, `argc` and `argv`. Example 21.9 shows a `main()` function with arguments.

EXAMPLE 21.9 A `main()` Function with Arguments

```
1   int main(int argc,char *argv[])
2   {
3       // Program statements go here.
4   }
```

The parameter name `argc` is short for "argument count." It contains the number of items on the command line, including the program name itself. The parameter name `argv` stands for argument vector. It programming terminology, an array is sometimes referred to as a vector. The parameter `argc` contains the number of items in the array `argv`. The `argv` parameter is an array of pointers to characters. Because each pointer to characters is a string, `argv` is an array of strings. Each string is one item that was typed on the command line.

Let's suppose that I type the program name `MyProg` at my operating system's prompt and then press Enter. When the program starts, the operating system will pass the string `"MyProg"` in `argv[0]`. The parameter `argc` will contain a 1. The operating system will set `argv[1]` to NULL.

Example 21.10 demonstrates another command line. At the operating system prompt, the user has entered the program name

```
c:\mydir\myprog
```

The user also typed three file names. Whatever the program `myprog` does, the user wants it done to these three files.

EXAMPLE 21.10 Entering Arguments at the Command Prompt

```
d:\>c:\mydir\myprog this.txt that.txt those.txt
```

When `myprog` starts, `argc` contains the value 4. The string in `argv[0]` is `c:\mydir\myprog`, and `argv[1]` contains the string `"this.txt"`. The string `"that.txt"` is stored in `argv[2]`, and `"those.txt"` is stored in `argv[3]`. A NULL is in `argv[4]`.

You can treat `argv` like any other array of strings. You can parse it, pass it to other functions, and so on. If you don't want your program to support command-line arguments, just leave the parameter list of `main()` empty.

21.6   Troubleshooting Guide

After reading this section, you should be able to

- Obtain more specific error informaiton.
- Use file I/O as a debugging tool.

21.6.1   Getting File I/O Error Information

As discussed in Section 21.2.4, the C Standard Library provides the `ferror()` function to tell our programs when file errors occur. The `ferror()` function returns an error number. It does not tell us what the error means. For that, the C Standard Library contains the `strerror()` and `perror()` functions.

The `strerror()` Function   C programs call the `strerror()` function to convert an error number obtained from `ferror()` into a string. The error numbers and error strings are completely dependant on the operating system under which the program is running. Example 21.11 shows how `strerror()` can be used.

EXAMPLE 21.11 Using `strerror()`

```
1   /* This code fragment assumes that errorNumber is an integer, and fp is a
2   valid pointer to an open file. */
3   errorNumber = ferror(fp);
4   if (errorNumber!=0)
5   {
6          printf("%s",strerror(errorNumber));
7   }
```

The `perror()` Function When programs call the `perror()` function, it prints an error message supplied by the program to the `stderr` stream. It also prints a message which corresponds to the current error. The current error is stored in a global variable called `errno`, which is defined in the Standard Library header file errno.h. The number in `errno` is used as an index into a list of error strings. The list is also defined in errno.h.

The `perror()` function first prints the string it receives through its parameter. Next, it prints the error message it obtains using the value in `errno`.

21.6.2   Using Error Log Files to Debug Programs

Many programmers find **log files** to be a handy debugging aid. Programs write status and error information into log files as they execute. Log files supplement the use of debugging programs. They also can be used in situations where debugging programs are not available or not desirable.

For instance, many game programmers use log files to debug their games. Typically, games take over the entire screen. If you use a debugging program on a computer with one screen while developing games, the debugging program will pop up its window to show status information while the game is executing. This can interfere with the color palette or obscure a critical part of the screen image. Writing program status information to a log file provides a way to get debugging information without disrupting the images on the screen.

21.6.3   A Simple Debugging System

Hands On 21.7 demonstrates one simple approach to a debugging system that uses log files.

Hands On 21.7

 Objective

Write a debugging system that logs errors to files. Write a program to that:
Opens a log file.
Executes a loop 100 times.
On each loop iteration, writes the loop counter to the log file.
Closes the log file.

 Experiment

Type the following program into your IDE or text editor. Compile, link, and run it. This program consists of two files, main.c and debugger.h.

This is the file main.c.

```
1   #include <stdio.h>
2
3   #define DEBUGGING
4   #define EXTERN
5   #include "Debugger.h"
6
7   int main()
8   {
9          char logMessage[80];
```

```
10          int i;
11
12
13          OpenLogFile("log.txt");
14
15          WriteToLogFile("Entering for loop\n");
16
17          for (i=0;i<100;i++)
18          {
19                  sprintf(logMessage,"i=%d\n",i);
20                  WriteToLogFile(logMessage);
21          }
22
23          WriteToLogFile("Exiting for loop\n");
24
25          CloseLogFile();
26
27          return (0);
28  }
```

This is the file debugger.h

```
1   #ifndef DEBUGGER_H
2   #define DEBUGGER_H
3
4   #ifdef DEBUGGING
5   #include <stdio.h>
6   #include <stdlib.h>
7
8   #if !defined(EXTERN)
9   #define EXTERN extern
10  #else
11  #define EXTERN
12  #endif
13
14  EXTERN FILE *logFile;
15
16
17  #define OpenLogFile(logFileName)                    \
18          {                                           \
19              logFile = fopen(logFileName,"w");       \
20              if (!logFile)                           \
21              {                                       \
22                  abort();                            \
23              }                                       \
24          }
25
26  #define WriteToLogFile(data)     fprintf(logFile,"%s",data);
27
28  #define CloseLogFile()   fclose(logFile)
29
30  #else
31
32  #define OpenLogFile(logFileName)
33  #define WriteToLogFile(data)
34  #define CloseLogFile()
35
36  #endif   // end #ifdef DEBUGGING
37
38  #endif   // end #ifndef DEBUGGER_H
```

Results

Note: The output of this program has been shortened to save space. All of the values between 10 and 90 have been omitted.

Entering for loop
i=0
i=1
i=2
i=3
i=4
i=5
i=6
i=7
i=8
i=9
i=10
.

.

.
i=90
i=91
i=92
i=93
i=94
i=95
i=96
i=97
i=98
i=99
Exiting for loop

Analysis

You'll undoubtedly notice some odd-looking `#define` statements at the beginning of this program. I'll explain the purpose of these shortly.

This program demonstrates the log file system by using three macros. The first, `OpenLogFile()`, does just what the name suggests. The log file must be open before program status information can be written to it. You can use this debugging system in a program made up of many C files. The only requirement is that they all include the file Debugger.h. The `OpenLogFile()` macro needs to be called once at the beginning of the program. After that, the log file debugging system is available to all functions and all files in your program.

Programs use the second debugging macro, `WriteToLogFile()`, for writing information to the error log file. Notice that the program uses the `WriteToLog-File()` macro to write strings. If the program has other types output to store in the log file, it must convert the output to a string. In this Hands On program, the conversion is done with a call to `sprintf()`.

When the program finishes with the error logging system, it uses the `CloseLogFile()` macro to close the log file.

You'll find the implementation of the log file debugging system in the file Debugging.h. It begins with the standard method of using `#ifndef` (or `#if   !defined()`) to keep this header file from defining its contents more than once in any single C source file. It also contains a statement that reads

```
#ifdef DEBUGGING
```

This statement forms one of the key aspects of the log file debugging system. If the constant `DEBUGGING` is defined, this file defines all of the debugging macros. If it is not defined, the `#else` clause is processed by the preprocessor. It defines all of the debugging macros as nothing but blank lines. Because these macros are defined as being nothing but blank lines, the preprocessor removes the macros from the source code when it does a pass over a .c file. When the constant DEBUGGING is not defined, the preprocessor substitutes blank lines where the debugging macros appear in the source code. This effectively turns off the debugging system. When you want to use it again, simply define DEBUGGING in your .c file before the #include "Debugging.h" statement.

That's exactly what the sample program does. Line 3 of main.c contains a statement defining the constant DEBUGGING. The statement

```
#include "Debugging.h"
```

is on line 5. Because DEBUGGING is defined before the include statement on line 5, the #ifdef statement on line 4 of Debugging.h will compile all of the statements between the #ifdef (line 5) and the #else (line 30), which enables the debugging system.

If the constant DEBUGGING is defined, the debugging system includes some files from the Standard Library that it needs. It then contains a set of statements that read

```
#if !defined(EXTERN)
#define EXTERN extern
#else
#define EXTERN
#endif
```

These statements use the technique demonstrated in Chapter 20 for handling global variables. The statement that follows these declares a global FILE pointer variable for the debugging system. This is one of the few situations where a global variable might be useful in a program. That is primarily because it is removed automatically from the final version of the program. Under most circumstances, global variables cause far, far more problems than they solve.

This set of statements tells the preprocessor that, if the constant EXTERN is not defined, the preprocessor should define EXTERN as the C keyword extern. When you use a global variable, only one file in your program can actually declare the variable. The other files use the extern keyword to tell the compiler that they are referencing a global variable declared in another file. The set of statements on lines 8–12 of Debugging.h automatically use the extern keyword to indicate that the global variable is declared in another .c file.

One of the .c files in the program must have the constant EXTERN declared in it. You'll see that declaration at the beginning of the file main.c. If EXTERN is declared, the statement on line 11 of debugger.h redefines EXTERN as blank. This effectively declares the global variable in the .c file.

If all of this seems somewhat complicated, that's only because it is. This is one of the many reasons that global variables should not find their way into released versions of a program.

The OpenLogFile() macro uses the global stream variable to open the log file. If it can't open the log file, the program calls the Standard Library abort() function to halt program execution.

The macro WriteToLogFile() uses the fprintf() function to print strings into the log file. Finally, the CloseLogFile() macro calls the fclose() function for the global log file variable.

SUMMARY

C programs use files, also called streams, to write data to and read data from devices. These devices include the keyboard, the screen, disks, and tapes. The C Standard Library provides the streams are stdin, stdout, and stderr.

Streams can be buffered or unbuffered. Unbuffered streams make data available immediately to the device or program. Buffered streams do not make the data available until the buffer is flushed.

Streams can be used for input, output, or both. For long-term storage, data is stored in files. These typically reside on disks, but they can exist on any valid data storage device. Files contain either text or binary data.

All files must be opened before programs can read from them or write to them. They should be closed before the program terminates. Programs can retrieve data from files using the `fscanf()`, `fgetc()`, `fgets()`, and `fread()` functions. They write data to files using the `fprintf()`, `fputc()`, `fputs()`, and `fwrite()` functions.

C files use current location pointers to keep track of where the next read or write will occur. Your program can control the position of the current location pointer with the `fseek()` function. It can find out where the current location pointer is in a file with the `ftell()` function. These two functions enable programs to access data in random order rather than sequentially.

Other file functions provided by the C Standard Library include `ungetc()`, which puts a character back onto a stream. In addition, it provides the `rewind()` function to set a file's current location pointer back to the beginning of the file. It contains `fflush()`, which flushes a stream's buffer. It also provides the `ferror()` function to test for errors during file errors.

C programs see printers as files. Therefore, data can be printed to files using the C Standard Library file function.

When a program starts, the operating system passes information to the program through the `main()` function's `argc` and `argv` parameters. Often, these parameters include the names of files to load.

C programs translate the error numbers obtained from `ferror()` into text error messages using the `strerror()` and `perror()` functions.

TECHNICAL NOTES

21.1 Because files are sometimes called streams in C literature, the standard files are also referred to as the standard streams.

21.2 Every line of text in a text file ends with a newline character rather than a null character.

21.3 The `fscanf()` function can be used to read from any input file, including the file `stdin`. So the calls

        scanf("%s",aString);

and

        fscanf(stdin,"%s",aString);

do exactly the same thing.

21.4 In programming literature, collections of items, such as arrays, are sometimes referred to as vectors.

TIPS

21.1 You don't have to worry about accidentally moving a file's current location pointer before the beginning of a file or after its end. The Standard Library file functions prevent your program from doing that.

21.2 The only difference between `printf()` and `fprintf()` is that `printf()` prints its output to the file `stdout`, while `fprintf()` can print to any file. Because of this, the calls

        printf("%s",aString);

and

        fprintf(stdout,"%s",aString);

are identical.

21.3 When your program passes a pointer as the first parameter to `fread()`, it is a good idea to type cast the pointer to `void *`. This decreases the number of warnings the compiler produces.

21.4 Although some implementations of the C Standard Library enable your program to call `ungetc()` more than once between read operations from a stream, you must not depend on this if you want your code to be portable.

21.5 To clear the keyboard buffer, call the `rewind()` function and pass it the stream `stdin`. This technique works with every implementation of `rewind()` with which I'm familiar.

21.6 When faced with the constant dilemma of whether to optimize memory usage or program speed, ask yourself how much waiting the program is doing. If the program is getting input from the user, most of its time is spent waiting. Therefore, slowing the program down to save memory is probably a good choice. If the program can complete its task before the user presses the next keystroke, the user won't notice the extra time the program spends on the task.

TRAPS

21.1 Although the file `stdprn` is implemented on many compilers, it is not part of the ANSI C definition. If you need your code to be extremely portable, you must not depend on the presence of the file `stdprn`.

21.2 If a program ends before it calls `fclose()`, it may produce a memory leak.

21.3 Before calling any file functions, always check that the file pointer variable does not equal `NULL`.

21.4 When using `fread()` to read structures or arrays containing pointers, a program must allocate memory for each pointer to point at. It must also perform a read operation for each pointer. If this algorithm is not followed, the data will not be read properly.

REVIEW QUESTIONS

1. What is the purpose of the files `stdin`, `stdout`, and `stderr`?
2. Why does the C Standard Library provide both the `stdout` and `stderr` stream?
3. What is buffered I/O? What is unbuffered I/O? What is line-buffered input? How can a program manually flush a stream buffer?
4. How does a program open a stream to read from a text file? How does a program open a stream to read from a binary file?
5. How does a program open a stream to write to a text file? How does a program open a stream to write to a binary file?
6. How does a program empty the keyboard buffer with just one function call?
7. How do programs control the current location pointer?
8. How do you use the `fread()` function to read data from a binary file?
9. How does a program retrieve command-line parameters?
10. How can programs detect errors? How do programs convert file error numbers to meaningful messages.

EXERCISES

1. Name the standard C streams and explain what each does.
2. If all information on computers is ultimately stored as binary numbers, explain why there are binary and text files in C.
3. Explain the difference between sequential and random file access.
4. Explain why parsing command-line arguments might be important to programs that load data files.
5. Make a table with two columns. Have the left column contain a list of all of the file functions presented in this chapter. Have the right column contain a brief description of each function.
6. Write a program that gets input from the keyboard, writes it to a text file, and prints it on the screen. If the output file already exists, the program should overwrite any text that it contains.
7. Write a program that gets input from the keyboard writes it to a text file, and prints it on the screen. If the file exists, do not overwrite the existing data. Append the new text to the end of the file.
8. Write a program which prints to the screen all of the strings it receives in the `argv` parameter of `main()`.
9. Fill in the blanks.

   Like `printf()` and `scanf()`, the _____ and _____ functions write and read data. However, unlike `printf()` and `scanf()`, these two functions enable the program to specify the file to write or read.
10. Fill in the blanks.

    Programs use the _____ and _____ functions to enable random access to file data.
11. Indicate which of the following statements are true.
    a. A file's current location pointer keeps track of where the file is located.
    b. Programs can move the current location pointer toward the beginning or end of the file.
    c. A file's current location pointer enables random data access.
    d. Most C Standard Library file functions have no effect on the current location pointer.
    e. The movement of a current location pointer can be relative to the beginning of the file, to the end of the file, or to the pointer's current position.

12. Write a function called `CopyFile()`. The `CopyFile()` function should take two parameters, `sourceFileName` and `destinationFileName`. Have it open both files in binary mode, and copy all data in `sourceFileName` into `destinationFileName`. It must match the following prototype exactly.

        int CopyFile(char *sourceFileName,char *destinationFileName);

    The `CopyFile()` function should return zero if it is successful. If it cannot open the source file, it should return –1. I f it cannot open or write to the destination file, it should return –2. Write a program to demonstrate that the `CopyFile()` function works.

13. Write a program which compares two text files. It should take the names of the two files as command-line parameters. Have the program print the first line of the first file, followed by the first line of the second file. Make it repeat the process for the second line of each file, and so on.

14. Write a program that takes the name of a text file on its command line. The program should prompt the user for a character position in the file. Assume that the first character position is zero, the second is one, and so on. When the program receives a character position, have it begin printing characters from that position until it encounters a newline, a space, or the end of the file.

15. Write a program that takes the name of a text file and a string as command-line parameters. The program must search the text file for all occurrences of the string and print each line which contains the string. The program must validate the parameters the user types on the command line.

16. Increase encapsulation in the text editor in Hands On 21.6 by adding the keyword `const` to wherever is appropriate. Explain where you added the word `const` and why.

17. The text editor in Hands On 21.6 may append empty lines at the end of files it saves. One possible way to eliminate this problem would be to add a member to the `text_buffer` structure which keeps track of the last line number in the buffer that contains text. Another approach would be to allocate only the number of lines that are actually used. Fix this problem using one of these two solutions. Explain which solution you chose and why.

18. Use the `strerror()` or `perror()` function to enhance the text editor in Hands On 21.6. Modify it so that `main()` prints more specific error messages to the user. You may have to add new error codes or change how error codes are handled.

19. Use the debugging system from Hands On 21.7 to enhance the text editor from Hands On 21.6. Modify the editor so that errors of any kind are logged to a file called Editor.log.

20. Modify the text editor from Hands On 21.6 so that it recognizes the string `"-c"` on its command line. When the editor receives the `"-c"` option, it logs all of user's commands to a file called Edcmd.log.

21. Modify the text editor program from Hands On 21.6 so that it reads a file name from the command line. It should load the specified file into the text buffer.

22. The text editor in Hands On 21.6 allows the user to exit the program even if the buffer is dirty. Modify the editor programs so that, if the buffer is dirty, it asks the user whether the buffer should be saved before exiting.

23. The text editor in Hands On 21.6 loads a file even if the current buffer is dirty. Modify the program to prompt the user and ask whether the current contents of the buffer should be saved before loading a new file.

24. The text editor in Hands On 21.6 contains what many would consider a flaw in the user interface. If the buffer is clean and the user selects Save from the main menu, the program does not save the buffer and it does not tell the user. Rewrite the program to inform the user that the buffer does not need to be saved if it is clean. Explain the approach you used to solve this problem. Tell why you think your solution reflects good user interface design.

25. Write a program than enables the user to type a text file name on its command line. Have the program load the file into a buffer. It must then count the occurrences of each word in the file. Have it print each word, followed by the total number of times that word appears in the file.

GLOSSARY

Control Codes   Printer control codes control features that are specific to the particular type of printer.

Current Location Pointer   A pointer in a file which indicates where the next read or write will take place.

Log File   A file a program can use to store status or error messages.

Random Access   The ability to read or write any piece of data at any time without searching sequentially through the file.

Stream   Another name for a file.

22

Fiddling with Bits

OBJECTIVES

After reading this chapter, you should be able to:

- Use bitwise operators to manipulate bits and bytes of data directly.
- Define structures with fields of specific bit widths.

OUTLINE

PREVIEW

Because the C language was created by programmers for high-powered programming tasks, its designers gave it the ability to manipulate data directly on a bit-by-bit level. This chapter presents the operators and techniques for performing bitwise operations.

22.1   Bytes and Bits

Chapter 1 presented the idea that all data and instructions in computers are ultimately stored as binary numbers. If you feel you need a review of binary numbers, please see Appendix D.

Each digit, or bit, in a binary number is either a one or a zero. The digits are grouped into bytes, which each contain eight bits. Bytes are grouped into words. The number of bytes in a word differs with each type of computer and each operating system. A word on a computer is the same size as its integer.

C provides a set of operators which enable us to directly set the binary digits of data. These bitwise operators are one of the features that make C so well-suited to programming hardware directly. Developers who write operating systems, hardware drivers, test equipment software, networking software, and graphics software use the bitwise operators extensively.

22.1.1   Signed and Unsigned Integers

To use the bitwise operators, programmers must understand how computers represent signed and unsigned integers. Typically, bit patterns that programs operate on are stored in unsigned integers. However, some operators also require an understanding of how computers represent signed integers.

The designers of each type of computer determine how signed numbers (numbers that can be positive or negative) are represented. This cannot be defined by the C language. Most computers use one bit to represent the positive or negative sign. It is usually the left-most bit, which is also called the most significant bit (MSB). Figure 22.1 illustrates this.

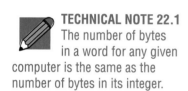

TECHNICAL NOTE 22.1
The number of bytes in a word for any given computer is the same as the number of bytes in its integer.

TECHNICAL NOTE 22.2
The highest-order bit, which is usually shown as the left-most bit in diagrams, is called the most significant bit (MSB). The lowest-order bit, which is usually depicted as the right-most bit, is called the least significant bit (LSB).

FIGURE 22.1   A Number with a Sign Bit

```
1001111010010101
```

The number in Figure 22.1 uses the left-most bit as the sign bit. If that bit is zero, the number is positive. If the bit is one, the number is negative. The number in the figure is a 16-bit signed integer. If all of the bits were used to represent numbers, a 16-bit integer could represent 65,536 different numbers. Using one bit as the sign bit divides that number of integers into half for the range of positive numbers and half for negative numbers. A 16-bit signed integer can represent 2^{15} positive numbers and 2^{15} negative numbers. The range of a 16-bit signed integer is –32768 to +32767.

Unsigned numbers do not have a sign bit. Therefore, in a 16-bit integer, all 16 bits are devoted to representing positive integers. As a result, the range of an unsigned 16-bit integer is 0 to +65535.

If we use one bit of a signed number as the sign bit, there will be two representations of zero, one with the bit pattern (assuming a 16-bit integer) 0000000000000000 and one with the bit pattern 1000000000000000. This gives +0 and -0. This style of number representation is called the **one's complement** method.

Because it is wasteful to use two bit patterns to represent one value, computers generally use a **two's complement number representation**. The two's complement also uses the left-most bit as the sign bit. However, to find the bit pattern of a negative number, we must start with the positive number, invert the bits, and add one.

Let's suppose we want to find the two's complement bit pattern for negative three. First, we start with the bit pattern for +3, which is 00000011 if we use an 8 bit signed integer. To get –3, we invert the bit pattern, giving 11111100. Next, we add 1, resulting in 11111101. This is the binary bit pattern for –3.

Under the two's complement method, there is only one representation for zero. Using an 8-bit signed integer, the binary pattern for zero is 00000000. If we then invert the bits, we get 11111111. Finally, when we add one, the result is 100000000. However, because this result is 9 bits long, the left-most bit is thrown away. This leaves 00000000, which is what we started with.

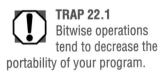

TECHNICAL NOTE 22.3
Computers generally use the two's complement method to represent binary numbers.

22.1.2   Hexadecimal Numbers

C programmers generally do bit manipulation using hexadecimal (base 16) numbers. If you feel you need a review of hexadecimal numbers, please see Appendix D.

Hexadecimal numbers are easily converted to binary numbers. The reverse is also true. To convert hexadecimal to binary, simply convert each hexadecimal digit to its 4-bit binary equivalent, and then group all of the bits together.

For instance, if we convert the individual hexadecimal digits of the number AF38 to binary, the result is 1010 1111 0011 1000. To obtain the final answer, we just group the bits together to get 1010111100111000.

To convert the binary bit pattern 1110010101111111 to hexadecimal, separate the bits into groups of four. This gives 1110 0101 0111 1111. Next, convert each group of bits to its equivalent hexadecimal digit. In this example, the result is C57F.

For a more complete discussion of these conversion techniques, please see Appendix D.

In C programs, literal hexadecimal numbers in program code must be preceded by the prefix 0x. So, for instance, the hexadecimal number C57F in a program would be written as 0xC57F.

22.2   Bitwise Operators

The bitwise operators provided by the C language enable us to shift groups of bits to the right or left. We also can use them to turn bits on or off (change them to one or zero). However, this ability comes at a price.

All bitwise operations do not work exactly the same way on every type of computer. How they work is determined by hardware-dependant factors. In fact, even though the examples in this chapter are written as generically as possible, they may not work on your computer. It's a good idea to test them to be sure.

The fact that bitwise operations tend to be hardware-specific is usually not a problem. Most of the people who use bitwise operators are writing software that interacts directly with a specific type of computer. Therefore, portability is often not a concern. This issue is addressed more fully in the Troubleshooting Guide at the end of this chapter.

TRAP 22.1
Bitwise operations tend to decrease the portability of your program.

22.2.1 Shifting Bits

The >> right shift operator shifts all the bits in a value to the right by a specified number of places. It is a binary operator, meaning that it requires two operands. The value being shifted goes on the left of the operator. The number of bit positions to shift is placed on the right of the operator, as shown in Example 22.1

EXAMPLE 22.1 Using the Right Shift Operator

```
aValue >> 8
```

The right shift operator does not change the value of its operands. It evaluates to the shifted bit pattern. In Example 22.1, the number in aValue would not be changed.

Hands On 22.1 illustrates the use of the right shift operator.

Hands On 22.1

Objective

Write a program that:

Initializes an unsigned integer to a hexadecimal value.

Uses a loop to shift the bits in the unsigned integer by an increasing number of bit positions. The loop should stop when the answer is one.

Prints the value being shifted, the loop counter, and the result of the right shift operator each time through the loop.

Experiment

Type the following program into your IDE or text editor. Compile, link, and run it.

```
1   #include <stdio.h>
2
3   int main()
4   {
5        unsigned aValue = 0xC57F;
6        unsigned theAnswer;
7        int i;
8
9        for (i=0;i<16;i++)
10       {
11            theAnswer = aValue >> i;
12            printf("aValue = %x   ",aValue);
13            printf("i=%i   ",i);
14            printf("theAnswer = %x\n",theAnswer);
15       }
16
17       return (0);
18  }
```

Results

aValue = c57f i=0 theAnswer = c57f
aValue = c57f i=1 theAnswer = 62bf
aValue = c57f i=2 theAnswer = 315f
aValue = c57f i=3 theAnswer = 18af
aValue = c57f i=4 theAnswer = c57
aValue = c57f i=5 theAnswer = 62b
aValue = c57f i=6 theAnswer = 315
aValue = c57f i=7 theAnswer = 18a

aValue = c57f i=8 theAnswer = c5
aValue = c57f i=9 theAnswer = 62
aValue = c57f i=10 theAnswer = 31
aValue = c57f i=11 theAnswer = 18
aValue = c57f i=12 theAnswer = c
aValue = c57f i=13 theAnswer = 6
aValue = c57f i=14 theAnswer = 3
aValue = c57f i=15 theAnswer = 1

Analysis

This program declares some variables and enters a for loop. The loop iterates 16 times. Inside the loop, the right shift operator is used to show the value to which C57F evaluates when it is shifted by the number of bits specified in the variable i. The first time through the loop, the value of i is zero. The statement on line 11 shifts the value in aValue zero bits to the right. So, of course, the result is the same as the starting value.

The next time the loop iterates, i is equal to 1. When the statement on line 11 is executed, it shifts aValue to the right by one bit. The result is the hexadecimal number 62bf. The loop repeats this until it has iterated 16 times.

TECHNICAL NOTE 22.4 Reminder: An Rvalue is a value on the right side of an assignment operator.

The Results section of this Hands On example demonstrates that the right shift operator does not change the value of its operands. Instead, it evaluates to the shifted value. That value can then be treated the same as any other Rvalue.

If you print the values in theAnswer as decimal numbers (base 10), rather than hexadecimal, you'll undoubtedly notice that each answer is the same as if you performed an integer division on the one before it. Shifting a value one bit to the right is the same as dividing it by 2.

Try This

Modify this Hands On program so that it prings theAnswer in decimal and octal in addition to hexadecimal.

The C language also provides the << left shift operator. It is used in exactly the same way as the right shift operator. Example 22.2 shows a version of the program from Hands On 22.1. The only difference is that this program performs a left shift rather than a right shift on line 11.

EXAMPLE 22.2   Using the Left Shift Operator

```
1    #include <stdio.h>
2    int main()
3    {
4          unsigned aValue = 0xC57F;
5          unsigned theAnswer;
6          int i;
7
8          for (i=0;i<16;i++)
9          {
10               theAnswer = aValue << i;
11               printf("aValue = %x   ",aValue);
12               printf("i=%i   ",i);
13               printf("theAnswer = %x\n",theAnswer);
14         }
15
16         return (0);
17   }
```

TECHNICAL NOTE 22.5 Shifting a value to the right by one bit divides it by two. Shifting it left one bit multiplies it by two.

When the left or right shift is performed, the empty positions in the value are normally filled with zeros. However, there are some older systems that do not follow this convention when performing a right shift. They use a technique called *sign extension*. Sign extension is discussed in the Troubleshooting Guide at the end of this chapter.

Since shifting a value one position to the left increases it by a power of two, performing a left shift is the same as multiplying by two.

22.2.2 Bitwise AND

Chapter 7 introduced the && logical AND operator. The C language also defines a & bitwise AND operator. The bitwise AND operator performs an AND operation on each bit in its operands. Figure 22.2 illustrates how it works.

FIGURE 22.2 A Bitwise AND Operation

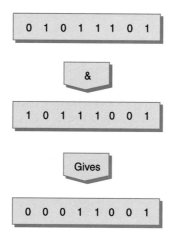

As Figure 22.2 shows, the bitwise AND operator requires two operands. It compares the left-most bit in the first operand to the left-most bit in the second. It does the same for each bit in turn. The result of the bitwise AND operation is determined by the truth table given in Table 22.1.

TABLE 22.1 Truth Table for Bitwise AND

Bit from First Operand	Bit from Second Operand	Result
0	0	0
0	1	0
1	0	0
1	1	1

Truth tables were introduced in Chapter 7. Table 22.1 shows that when the bitwise AND operator compares two bits, it evaluates to one only if both bits are one. In all other cases, the result is zero.

Bitwise AND operations enable programs to evaluate individual bits in a variable. In Example 22.3, the code fragment performs a bitwise AND on a variable. It uses a **bit-mask**, also just called a mask, to select the bit to be tested. Figure 22.3 illustrates how this code fragment works.

EXAMPLE 22.3 Masking Bits

```
1    unsigned aValue = 0x51D3;
2    unsigned oneBit = aValue & 0x02;
3    printf("%u\n",oneBit);
```

Line 2 of Example 22.3 performs a bitwise AND on the value in the variable aValue. It uses the bitmask value 0x02. Figure 22.3 shows that all bits in the bitmask are zero except one. When a bitwise AND is performed using this mask, the zeros force the re-

FIGURE 22.3   Using a Bitmask

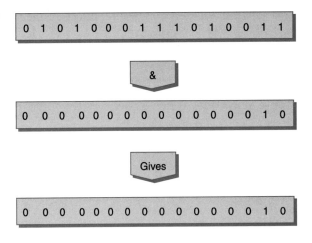

sult to be zeros for those bit positions. In any position in the bitmask containing a one, the result will be determined by the corresponding bit in the value being tested.

The one in the bitmask in the second position from the right in Figure 22.3 selects the bit in aValue to be tested. If the second bit from the right in aValue is zero, the result of the bitwise AND operation is zero. If the second bit from the right in aValue is one, the result of the bitwise AND will contain a one in the corresponding bit position.

The bitwise AND can also be used to set bits in a value to zero. In Example 22.4, the code fragment performs a bitwise AND operation. In this case, the bitmask contains all ones, except for the right-most bit. That is the bit being set to zero, or "turned off."

EXAMPLE 22.4   Setting a Bit to Zero

```
1   unsigned aValue = 0x51D3;
2   unsigned result = aValue & 0xFFFE;
3   printf("%u\n",result);
```

Anywhere a one appears in the bitmask in Example 22.4, the bits in the variable result will be determined by the corresponding bit values in aValue. This is illustrated in Figure 22.4. The zero in the right-most position of the bitmask forces the right-most bit in result to be zero. In this way, any single bit or any group of bits in a value can be set to zero.

FIGURE 22.4   Setting a Bit to Zero with a Bitmask

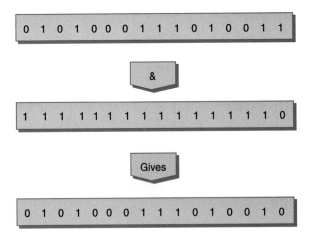

22.2.3   Bitwise OR

Like the bitwise AND operator, the bitwise OR operator evaluates corresponding pairs of bits in its two operands. The bitwise OR operator is a vertical line, |. On many keyboards, this is typed using the same key as the \ symbol. The bitwise OR operator uses the truth table shown in Table 22.2 to perform the evaluation.

TABLE 22.2 Truth Table for Bitwise OR	Bit from First Operand	Bit from Second Operand	Result
	0	0	0
	0	1	1
	1	0	1
	1	1	1

The only time a bitwise OR operation evaluates to zero is when the corresponding bits in both of its operands are zero. Figure 22.5 illustrates the use of the bitwise OR operation.

FIGURE 22.5   A Bitwise OR Operation

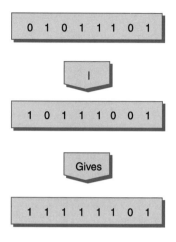

When combined with a bitmask, programs often use the bitwise OR operator to set individual bits in a value to one. Example 22.5 demonstrates this technique.

EXAMPLE 22.5   Setting a Bit to One with Bitwise OR

```
1    unsigned aValue = 0x7F11;
2    unsigned result = aValue ¦ 0x02;
3    printf("%u\n",result);
```

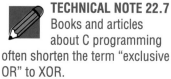

TIP 22.3
Use a bitmask and the bitwise OR operator to set bits, or groups of bits, to one.

Figure 22.6 shows that the bitwise OR operation forces the second bit from the right in the variable `result` from Example 22.5 to be a one.

FIGURE 22.6   Using a Bitmask with Bitwise OR

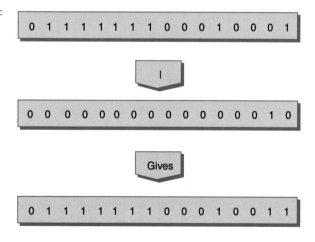

TECHNICAL NOTE 22.7
Books and articles about C programming often shorten the term "exclusive OR" to XOR.

22.2.4   Exclusive OR

The C language uses the ^ symbol, which is called a caret, for the bitwise exclusive OR operator. This is often abbreviated as XOR in C programming literature.

The bitwise XOR operator follows the truth table shown in Table 22.3.

	Bit from First Operand	Bit from Second Operand	Result
TABLE 22.3 Truth Table for Bitwise XOR	0	0	0
	0	1	1
	1	0	1
	1	1	0

Unlike bitwise OR, XOR evaluates to zero if both of its operands are one or both of them are zero. As a result, bitwise XOR is often a handy way to toggle bits from zero to one and one to zero. The program in Hands On 22.2 demonstrates how this is done.

Hands On 22.2

Objective

Write a program that:

Defines the type `toggle_switch` and the associated constants `TOGGLE_SWITCH_OFF`, `TOGGLE_SWITCH_ON`, `TOGGLE_SWITCH_MASK`.

Declares a `toggle_switch` variable and sets the toggle switch to `TOGGLE_SWITCH_ON`.

Repeats a loop 10 times. If the toggle switch is on, have the loop print the string `"The switch is on.\n"`. Otherwise, have it print the string `"The switch is off.\n"`. Each time the loop iterates, the program should toggle the value in the toggle switch.

Experiment

Type the following program into your IDE or text editor. Compile, link, and run it.

```
1   #include <stdio.h>
2
3   typedef enum
4   {
5           TOGGLE_SWITCH_OFF = 0x0,
6           TOGGLE_SWITCH_ON,
7           TOGGLE_SWITCH_MASK = 0x1
8   } toggle_switch;
9
10
11  int main()
12  {
13          toggle_switch lightSwitch = TOGGLE_SWITCH_ON;
14          int i;
15
16          for (i=0;i<10;i++)
17          {
18                  if (lightSwitch)
19                  {
20                          printf("The switch is on.\n");
21                  }
22                  else
23                  {
24                          printf("The switch is off.\n");
25                  }
26
```

```
27              lightSwitch = lightSwitch ^  TOGGLE_SWITCH_MASK;
28          }
29
30          return (0);
31      }
```

Results

The switch is on.
The switch is off.
The switch is on.
The switch is off.
The switch is on.
The switch is off.
The switch is on.
The switch is off.
The switch is on.
The switch is off.

Analysis

A toggle switch is a switch that can be turned on or off, like a light switch. This program defines the software equivalent of a toggle switch.

After including the file stdio.h, this program defines the enumerated type toggle_switch. It enumerates the constants TOGGLE_SWITCH_OFF, TOGGLE_SWITCH_ON, and TOGGLE_SWITCH_MASK. Notice that the constants TOGGLE_SWITCH_ON and TOGGLE_SWITCH_MASK have the same value. Chapter 14 indicated that it is generally a good idea to avoid having duplicate values in an enumerated type. This Hands On program demonstrates a possible reason to break that rule.

The constants TOGGLE_SWITCH_OFF and TOGGLE_SWITCH_ON are states to which toggle switches can be set. Variables of type toggle_switch can be on or off. The constant TOGGLE_SWITCH_MASK is not a state value. It is a mask used to toggle the current state of the toggle switch. Because TOGGLE_SWITCH_MASK is not a state value, some software designers have no problem with the fact that it has the same value as TOGGLE_SWITCH_ON.

Other designers would disagree. They say that, since state information is defined in the enumeration, the constant TOGGLE_SWITCH_MASK should be defined separately, as shown in Example 22.6.

EXAMPLE 22.6   Defining the Mask Separately

```
1   typedef enum
2   {
3           TOGGLE_SWITCH_OFF = 0x0,
4           TOGGLE_SWITCH_ON
5   } toggle_switch;
6   #define TOGGLE_SWITCH_MASK 0x1
```

This style of definition eliminates the duplicate values in the enumerated type. Also, only state values are defined in the enumeration. The mask is still associated with the enumerated type, but it is defined separately.

Personally, I prefer the style of definition shown in Example 22.6. However, the other style was shown in the Hands On program because you'll see it on the job.

On line 27 of this Hands On program, the statement

```
lightSwitch = lightSwitch ^  TOGGLE_SWITCH_MASK;
```

uses an XOR operation to toggle the current value of the toggle_switch variable. If the value of lightSwitch is 1, XOR'ing it with TOGGLE_SWITCH_MASK will make it 0. If it is 0, XOR'ing it with TOGGLE_SWITCH_MASK will make it 1.

TIP 22.4
Use bitmasks and the exclusive OR operator to toggle bits or groups of bits.

22.2.5 Bit Negation

The ~ bit negation operator inverts each bit in a value. All of the ones become zeros and the zeros become ones. This is not the same thing as taking the negative value. Hands On 22.3 illustrates the difference.

Hands On 22.3

Objective

Write a program that:
    Prompts the user for a value.
    Outputs negation of the input value.
    Outputs the negative of the input value.

Experiment

Type the following program into your IDE or text editor. Compile, link, and run it.

```
1   #include <stdio.h>
2
3   int main()
4   {
5           int inputValue;
6
7           printf("Please enter a number. :");
8           scanf("%i",&inputValue);
9
10          printf("The value %i in hexadecimal is %x.\n",
11                  inputValue,inputValue);
12          printf("The bitwise negation of %i is %x.\n",
13                  inputValue,~inputValue);
14          printf("The negative of %i in hexadecimal is %x.",
15                  inputValue,-inputValue);
16
17          return (0);
18  }
```

Results

First run.

Please enter a number. :**25**
The value 25 in hexadecimal is 19.
The bitwise negation of 25 is fffffe6.
The negative of 25 in hexadecimal is fffffe7.

Second run.

Please enter a number. :**0**
The value 0 in hexadecimal is 0.
The bitwise negation of 0 is ffffffff.
The negative of 0 in hexadecimal is 0.

Third run.

Please enter a number. :**–1**
The value -1 in hexadecimal is ffffffff.
The bitwise negation of -1 is 0.
The negative of -1 in hexadecimal is 1.

Analysis

This program was run three times. The computer on which the program was run uses a 32-bit integer.

During the first run, the number 25 was entered at the input prompt. The program output both the negation and the negative of 25 in hexadecimal. The negation operator gives the one's complement of a number. The negative operator gives its negative value using the two's complement method.

On the second run of the program, the input value was zero. The negation operator inverts all of the bits to ones. If we were to print this value as a decimal integer, it would be −1. On the other hand, because computers represent negative numbers using the two's complement method, the negative of zero is zero.

The third run demonstrates the use of the program on a negative input value. In this case, the input number is −1. The negation of −1 is zero. However, the negative of −1 is 1.

> **TRAP 22.2**
> Bitwise negation is not the same thing as finding the negative of a number with the unary minus operator.

22.2.6 Bitwise Assignment Operators

Most of the bitwise operators also have a corresponding bitwise assignment operator. Table 22.4 contains the bitwise assignment operators provided by C.

TABLE 22.4 The Bitwise Assignment Operators

Operator	Description	Example
>>=	Performs a right shift. Assigns the result to the operand on the left.	`aValue >>= 5;`
<<=	Performs a left shift. Assigns the result to the operand on the left.	`aValue <<= 5;`
&=	Performs a bitwise AND. Assigns the result to the operand on the left.	`aValue &= 0x01;`
|=	Performs a bitwise OR. Assigns the result to the operand on the left.	`aValue |= 0x01;`
^=	Performs a bitwise XOR. Assigns the result to the operand on the left.	`aValue ^= 0x01;`

Each of these operators performs its operation and then assigns the results into the operand on the left.

22.3 Bitfield Structures

In C, programmers can define structures whose members have specific widths. As we define these types, we can tell the compiler how many bits to allocate for each structure member. Structures defined in this way are called **bitfield structures**. All bitfield structure members are unsigned integers. C does not allow them to be any other type. Example 22.7 demonstrates how bitfield structure members are defined.

EXAMPLE 22.7 Defining Bitfield Structure Members

```
1  typedef struct
2  {
3    unsigned aDataMember:3;
4    unsigned anotherDataMember:1;
5    unsigned lastDataMember:7;
6  } some_bits;
```

The structure in Example 22.7 contains a member called `aDataMember`. This member is 3 bits wide. It also contains `anotherDataMember` and `lastDataMember`. The widths of these members are 1 and 7 bits, respectively. The total width of the type `some_bits` is 10 bits.

Members of bitfield structures are accessed in exactly the same way as any other structure. For instance, the statements

```
some_bits theseBits;
theseBits.lastDataMember = 100;
```

assign the value 100 into the member `lastDataMember` in the structure variable `theseBits`.

At first glance, it may appear that bitfield structures are a great way to save memory. For example previous chapters defined the type `boolean` as an enumerated type. Using that definition, every variable of type `boolean` is actually a integer. It seems that memory could be saved by defining the `boolean` type as a bitfield structure, as shown in Example 22.8.

EXAMPLE 22.8   An Alternate Definition of the `boolean` Type

```
1  typedef struct
2  {
3          unsigned boolValue:1;
4  } boolean;
```

The `boolean` type needs only one bit to store all of the information it requires. In theory, this looks like a great way to accomplish that. Unfortunately, that is not generally the case. On most types of computers, the minimum data size is either an integer or a byte. Therefore, on almost every type of computer, the structure in Example 22.8 would be the minimum data size (either an integer or a byte). The fact that the structure defines a type that is one bit wide does not matter. If the minimum data size for a particular type of computer is a 32-bit integer, variables of the `boolean` type defined in Example 22.8 would be 32 bits. Only one bit would be used. The rest would be unused by the program.

You can pad the bitfields in a structure with unnamed "holes" of a specified width. An unnamed field width of zero forces the next bitfield to align with the next integer boundary in memory. Example 22.9 demonstrates unnamed bitfields.

EXAMPLE 22.9   Unnamed Bitfields

```
1  typedef struct
2  {
3          unsigned aDataMember      :3;
4          unsigned                  :2;
5          unsigned anotherDataMember:1;
6          unsigned                  :0;
7          unsigned lastDataMember   :7;
8  } some_bits;
```

The structure member `aDataMember` in Example 22.9 is 3 bits wide. It is followed by a "gap" of 2 unused bits. The member `anotherDataMember` is 1 bit wide. It is followed by `lastDataMember`, which is aligned on the next available integer boundary in memory. The alignment is caused by the statement on line 6.

Bitfield structures enable programmers to pack data very tightly in memory. Suppose, for example, we're part of a team that is writing a game. We want to encode the attributes of the game's main character, who is a type of creature called a "trog," into a single, tightly-packed unit. The attributes being used for the trog are shown in Table 22.5.

The information in Table 22.5 leads very easily to the structure definition in Example 22.10.

TABLE 22.5   **Trog Attributes**

Attribute	Bit Width	Values
Age	6	0-64
Fur Color	4	0: White
		1: Red
		2: Blue
		3: Green
		4: Magenta
		5: Yellow
		6: Cyan
		7: Grey
		8: Dark Red
		9: Dark Blue
		10: Dark Green
		11: Purple
		12: Brown
		13: Orange
		14: Navy Blue
		15: Black
Total Eyes	2	Can be 0, 1, 2, or 3.
Rows of Teeth	1	0: One row
		1: Two rows

EXAMPLE 22.10   **The Definition of the `trog` Type**

```
1   typedef struct
2   {
3           unsigned age       :6;
4           unsigned furColor  :4;
5           unsigned totalEyes :2;
6           unsigned rowsOfTeeth:1;
7           unsigned           :3;     // Unused bits.
8   } trog;
```

The unused bits at the end of the `trog` structure force the width of the structure to 16 bits. Most computers handle data types more efficiently if their width is a power of two (0, 2, 4, 8, 16, 32, 64, and so on). The structure definition in this example encodes all of the information the game needs about a trog into a single, 16-bit quantity. The individual pieces of information are as easily retrievable as information in structure.

Other uses of bitfield structure include hardware-intensive programming and artificial intelligence. Developers writing software to control hardware directly often encode hardware attributes into bitfield structures. Programmers who are writing programs that learn sometimes use genetic algorithms. Data operated on by these algorithms is often encoded into bitfield structures.

22.4   Troubleshooting Guide

After reading this section, you should be able to:

- Understand and explain zero-filling and sign extension.
- Understand the portability problems which can occur when using bit manipulation techniques.

22.4.1   Zero-Filling and Sign Extension

When programs perform a left or right shift, they usually fill the empty positions in the value with zeros. This is called **zero-filling**. However, some older hardware, and some embedded systems, do not follow this convention when performing a right shift. They use a technique called **sign extension**. Computers that use sign extension copy the value of the sign bit into empty bit positions when they do a right shift.

If, as an example, the instructions

```
int aValue = -15599;
aValue >>= 5;
```

are executed on a computer that does sign extension and uses a 16-bit integer, the sign bit will be copied 5 times to the right. Figure 22.7 illustrates this example.

FIGURE 22.7   **Sign Extension**

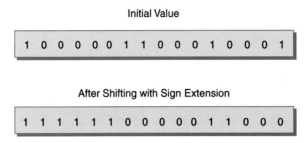

Initial Value

| 1 | 0 | 0 | 0 | 0 | 0 | 1 | 1 | 0 | 0 | 0 | 1 | 0 | 0 | 0 | 1 |

After Shifting with Sign Extension

| 1 | 1 | 1 | 1 | 1 | 1 | 0 | 0 | 0 | 0 | 0 | 1 | 1 | 0 | 0 | 0 |

TIP 22.5
If you are working on hardware that is more than 10 years old, or you are writing software for an embedded system, it is wise to find out whether the hardware does zero-filling or sign extension before you use the right shift operator.

Figure 22.7 demonstrates that shifting bits to the right on hardware that does sign extension can cause unexpected results for those unused to it. For instance, if you are using a right shift operation as a quick way to divide a number by a power of two, sign extension will complicate the process. If you are aware that your hardware uses sign extension and you write your program accordingly, it is usually not a problem.

22.4.2 Portability Concerns with Bitwise Operators and Bitfield Structures

Incorporating bitwise operations and bitfield structures into programs can sometimes make it complicated to port code. There are several reasons why this is so.

Often, when we write code that uses bitwise operations, it is because we are programming directly to the hardware or operating system. One common use of this style of programming is in computer graphics. When writing software to edit or process images, programmers use bitwise operators extensively. The images they process may be stored in a format that is dependant on the hardware or operating system. The BMP image file format was designed for Microsoft Windows. The PICT format for image files was designed for the Apple Macintosh.

Because modern software is flexible, most programs and operating systems can read files in their "non-native" format. MS Windows and Apple Macintosh computers can both read images in the BMP and PICT formats. As a result, some portability concerns are eliminated.

Even so, bitwise operations are performed differently on different image file formats. The algorithms to lighten or darken an image may be the same for all image file formats. However, the actual bitwise operations your program needs to perform may have to be implemented slightly differently.

A common way to deal with such problems is to write multiple functions to perform a particular task. Each function performs the task for a different image file format. They are often called from a single, generic function. If I were writing a function called `Light-enImage()`, which made an image brighter, I might write functions named `Light-enBMPImage()` and `LightenPICTImage()`. One of the parameters might be an enumerated type which could be set to the constant `IMAGE_FORMAT_BMP` or `IMAGE_FORMAT_PICT`. If the parameter value was `IMAGE_FORMAT_BMP`, `LightenImage()` would lighten the image by calling `LightenBMPImage()`. If the parameter was set to `IMAGE_FORMAT_PICT`, `LightenImage()` would call `LightenPICTImage()`.

A common use of bitfield structures is for communicating directly with hardware ports. This communication is completely hardware-dependant. To help improve portability, programs can use conditional compilation to define bitfield structures for each operating system or hardware type.

If you are writing a program for multiple types of hardware, and one of them supports sign extension rather than zero-filling, it is wise to use conditional compilation for portability. The code oriented toward dealing with sign extension will not work on systems that do zero-filling.

If your program contains bitwise operations dependant on the hardware or operating system, and the code for the operations is not long, you might consider putting the code into a preprocessor macro. A different version of the macro can be compiled for each operating system or hardware type.

SUMMARY

Bitwise operators enable C programmers to manipulate data on a bit-by-bit basis.

The bitwise AND operator compares corresponding bits from its two operands. The corresponding bit position in the result contains a one if both of the operand bits are one. Otherwise, the resulting bit is zero.

The bitwise OR operator also compares corresponding bits from its two operands. The corresponding bit position in the result contains a one if either of the operand bits are one. Otherwise, the resulting bit is zero.

When performing the bitwise exclusive OR operation, a bit position in the result contains a one if either one (but not both) of the operand bits is one the other is zero. Otherwise, the resulting bit is zero.

Bitwise negation inverts all of the one bits in a data item to zeros and all of the zeros to ones.

As a shorthand, C provides the bitwise assignment operators >>=, <<=, &=, |=, and ^=. Each of these performs its operation in the and stores the result in left-hand operand.

Bitfield structures provide programs with a way of defining types with specific bit formats. All bitfield structure members are unsigned integers. No other data type is allowed by the rules of the C language.

Using bitwise operators and bitfield structures may decrease a program's portability. Macros, conditional compilation, and writing multiple versions of functions can help increase portability.

TECHNICAL NOTES

22.1 The number of bytes in a word for any given computer is the same as the number of bytes in its integer.

22.2 The highest-order bit, which is usually shown as the left-most bit in diagrams, is called the most significant bit (MSB). The lowest-order bit, which is usually depicted as the right-most bit, is called the least significant bit (LSB).

22.3 Computers generally use the two's complement method to represent binary numbers.

22.4 Reminder: An Rvalue is a value on the right side of an assignment operator.

22.5 Shifting a value to the right by one bit divides it by two. Shifting it left one bit multiplies it by two.

22.6 Programmers often refer to the act of setting bits to zero as "turning the bits off."

22.7 Books and articles about C programming often shorten the term "exclusive OR" to XOR.

TIPS

22.1 Any single bit or any group of bits in a value can be tested using a bitwise AND with a bitmask.

22.2 Bitmaps can be used with the bitwise AND operator to set a bit, or a group of bits, to zero.

22.3 Use a bitmask and the bitwise OR operator to set bits, or groups of bits, to one.

22.4 Use bitmasks and the exclusive OR operator to toggle bits or groups of bits.

22.5 If you are working on hardware that is more than 10 years old, or you are writing software for an embedded system, it is wise to find out whether the hardware does zero-filling or sign extension before you use the right shift operator.

TRAPS

22.1 Bitwise operations tend to decrease the portability of your program.

22.2 Bitwise negation is not the same thing as finding the negative of a number with the unary minus operator.

REVIEW QUESTIONS

1. How are signed numbers represented using the one's complement method? What are the disadvantages of this method?

2. How are signed numbers represented using the two's complement method? What are the advantages of this method when compared with the one's complement method?

3. Why do C programmers generally use hexadecimal numbers when performing bitwise operations?

4. What are zero-filling and sign extension? Why are they important considerations when shifting bits?

5. How is the bitwise AND operation performed? Give an example other than those presented in this chapter. How can bitwise AND be used to set bits in a value to zero?

6. How is the bitwise OR operation performed? Give an example other than those presented in this chapter. How can bitwise OR be used to set bits in a value to one?

7. How is the bitwise XOR operation performed? Give an example other than those presented in this chapter. How can bitwise XOR be used to toggle bits in a value?

8. What are bitfield structures? How are they defined?

9. Why are bitfield structures used in programs?

10. What portability concerns are associated with the use of bitwise operators and bitfield structures?

EXERCISES

1. Fill in the blanks.
   a. The bitwise AND operator is often used to set bits in a value to _____. Programmers also refer to this as turning the bits _____.
   b. The bitwise OR operator is often used to set bit in a value to _____. Programmers also refer to this as turning the bits _____.
   c. The bitwise AND, OR, and XOR operators are often used with a _____ to set or toggle bits in a value.
   d. The bitwise negation operator sets all of the ones in a value to _____, and all of the zeros to _____.

2. State whether each of the following are true or false. If the statement is false, explain why.
   a. All computers use zero-filling when shifting bits.
   b. Bitwise operators enable programs to manipulate data on a bit-by-bit level.
   c. Bitfield structure members must be unsigned integers.

3. State whether each of the following is true or false. If the statement is false, explain why.
   a. Bitfield structures which are defined as smaller than one byte definitely save memory.
   b. Programs using the bitwise operators or bitfield structures are never portable.
   c. Shifting bits to the right is a fast way of dividing by a power of two.

4. Write a program that demonstrates whether your computer uses zero-filling or sign extension.

5. Write a program that prompts the user for a signed integer. Have it use a bitwise OR and a bitmask to determine if the number is positive or negative. If it is positive, have it output the string `"positive"`. Otherwise, it should output the string `"negative"`.

6. Write a function that converts a string containing hexadecimal digits to a hexadecimal number. That is, if the function is passed the string `"A1F0"`, it will return the hexadecimal value A1F0. Write a program which demonstrates that your function works.

7. Write a function that converts a string containing binary digits to a hexadecimal number. That is, if the function is passed the string `"10100001"`, it will return the hexadecimal value A1. Write a program which demonstrates that your function works.

8. Write a program that gets a string from the user. The string must contain hexadecimal digits. If any of the digits are invalid, it should output an error message and terminate. If the string contains valid hexadecimal digits, it should print the binary bit pattern of the equivalent binary number. Print a space between the bits for each hexadecimal digit. Therefore, when the user enters the string `"A2"`, the program should print the string `"1010 0010"`.

9. Write a program that gets a string from the user. The string must contain binary digits. If any of the digits are invalid, it should output an error message and terminate. If the string contains valid binary digits, it should print the hexadecimal digits of the equivalent hexadecimal number. Therefore, when the user enters the string `"10100010"`, the program should print the string `"A2"`.

10. Right shifting an unsigned integer is the same as dividing it by a power of two. Write a function that takes a number and a power. Have it use the right shift operator to divide the number by the specified power of two. In other words, the function should calculate the result of

$$\frac{number}{2^{power}}$$

Write a program that demonstrates that your function works.

11. Write a function that takes an unsigned integer as its parameter. Have it returns the number of one bits in the parameter. Write a program which demonstrates that your function works.

12. Write function that takes an unsigned integer and a bit position. The function should return 1 if there is a one in

that bit position. Otherwise, it should return 0. Write a program which demonstrates that your function works.

13. Write a function that takes an unsigned integer and the number of bit positions to shift right. The bits lost off of the right end should reappear on the left end of the unsigned integer. That is, the bit shifted off the right end of the value should be placed in the left-most position. Write a program which demonstrates that your function works.

14. Write a function that takes an unsigned integer as its parameter. Have it reverse the order of the bits in its parameter and return that value. Write a program which demonstrates that your function works.

15. Write two functions. The first, called `LowByte()`, takes an unsigned integer in hexadecimal format. It should return the contents of the rightmost eight bits. The second, called `HighByte()`, should return the contents of the second group of eight bits from the right. Write a program which demonstrates that your functions work.

16. Write two Macros. The first, called `LowByte()`, type casts its parameter to an unsigned integer and treats it as a hexadecimal number. It should evaluate to the contents of the rightmost eight bits. The second, called `HighByte()`, should evaluate to the contents of the second group of eight bits from the right. Write a program which demonstrates that your macros work.

17. Give the definition of a 64-bit structure called `hardware_configuration` which contains the following:

A member that indicates what kind of removable media drives are installed. A value of 0x0 indicates no drives, 0x01 specifies the presence of one or more floppy disk drives, 0x2 indicates one or more CD ROM drives, 0x4 indicates the presence of one or more DVD drives, and 0x8 specifies the presence of one or more Zip drive.

A bitfield of 1 unused byte.

A member specifying the amount of system RAM installed. This can be a number from 0 to 1 gigabyte.

A member specifying the presence of a game port. A value of 0 indicates no game port. A value of 1 specifies that a game port is present.

A member specifying the presence of a network interface card. A value of 0 indicates no network card. A value of 1 specifies that a network card is present.

A member specifying the number of serial ports installed. This member can contain a value in the range of 0–15.

A member specifying the number of parallel ports installed. This member can contain a value in the range of 0–3.

A bitfield of 1 unused byte.

The following exercises demonstrate simplified versions of techniques used by graphics programs to combine images using the bitwise operators.

18. Convert the following 8x8 and 32x32 binary bit patterns into two groups of hexadecimal numbers:

```
00000000
00001000
00011100
```

```
00111110
00011100
00011100
00011100
00000000
```

```
00000110000000110000000000000000
00000110000000110000000000000000
00000110000000110000000111100000000
00000110000000110000000111100000000
00000110000000110000000111100000000
00000110000000110000000111100000000
00000110000000110000000111100000000
00000110000000110000000111100000000
00000110000000110000000000000000
00000110000000110000000111100000000
00000110000000110000000111100000000
00000110000000110000000111100000000
00000110000000110000000111100000000
00000110000000110000000111100000000
00001111111110000000111100000000
00001111111110000000111100000000
00001111111110000000111100000000
00001111111110000000111100000000
00000110000000110000000111100000000
00000110000000110000000111100000000
00000110000000110000000111100000000
00000110000000110000000111100000000
00000110000000110000000111100000000
00000110000000110000000111100000000
00000110000000110000000111100000000
00000110000000110000000111100000000
00000110000000110000000111100000000
00000110000000110000000111100000000
00000110000000110000000111100000000
00000110000000110000000111100000000
00000110000000110000000111100000000
00000110000000110000000111100000000
00000110000000110000000111100000000
```

Write a program that uses the patterns to print two images. For each bit position, print an asterisk (*) if the bit position contains a one. Print a space if the bit position contains a zero. The first image should be 8 rows by 8 columns. The second image should be 32 rows by 32 columns. Combine the two images using a bitwise XOR operation. When combining the two images, XOR the hexadecimal number representing the first row of the 8x8 bit pattern with the hexadecimal number representing the first row of the 32x32 bit pattern. XOR the hexadecimal number representing the second row of the negated 8x8 bit pattern with the hexadecimal number representing the second row of the 32x32 bit pattern, and so on. Print the resulting image using the same technique you used to print the bit patterns.

19. Convert the following 8x8 and 32x32 binary bit patterns into two groups of hexadecimal numbers:

```
00000000
00001000
```

```
00011100
00111110
00011100
00011100
00011100
00000000
```

```
00001100000001100000000000000000
00001100000001100000000000000000
00001100000001100000011100000000
00001100000001100000011100000000
00001100000001100000011100000000
00001100000001100000011100000000
00001100000001100000011100000000
00001100000001100000011100000000
00001100000001100000000000000000
00001100000001100000011100000000
00001100000001100000011100000000
00001100000001100000011100000000
00001100000001100000011100000000
00001100000001100000011100000000
00001111111111100000011100000000
00001111111111100000011100000000
00001111111111100000011100000000
00001111111111100000011100000000
00001100000001100000011100000000
00001100000001100000011100000000
00001100000001100000011100000000
00001100000001100000011100000000
00001100000001100000011100000000
00001100000001100000011100000000
00001100000001100000011100000000
00001100000001100000011100000000
00001100000001100000011100000000
00001100000001100000011100000000
00001100000001100000011100000000
00001100000001100000011100000000
00001100000001100000011100000000
00001100000001100000011100000000
```

Write a program that uses the patterns to print two images. For each bit position, print an asterisk (*) if the bit position contains a one. Print a space for each bit position that contains a zero. Have the program use the bitwise negation operator to invert the images. Print the inverted images using the same technique you used to print the images.

20. Use the program you wrote for Exercise 17. In addition to having it print the images and inverted images, use the bitwise AND operation to combine the negated 8x8 image with the initial 32x32 image. When combining the two images, bitwise AND the hexadecimal number representing the first row of the negated 8x8 bit pattern with the hexadecimal number representing the first row of the 32x32 bit pattern. Bitwise AND the hexadecimal number representing the second row of the negated 8x8 bit pattern with the hexadecimal number representing the second row of the 32x32 bit pattern, and so on. Print the resulting image using the same technique you used to print the bit patterns.

21. Use the program you wrote for Exercise 18. After combining the negated 8x8 image with the 32x32 image, have it combine the 8x8 image with the 32x32 image using a bitwise OR operation. Print the resulting image by printing an asterisk (*) if the bit position contains a one. Print a space if the bit position contains a zero.

22. Review the result of the programs you created for Exercises 21–24. Explain what the result is when you combine two images using the following steps:
    a. Negate the small image.
    b. Combine the negated small image with the large image using a bitwise AND operation.
    c. Combine the small image with the large image using a bitwise OR operation.

    FYI: If your computer uses a GUI-based operating system, this is the method it utilizes to draw the mouse cursor on the screen.

GLOSSARY

Bitfield Structures   A structure which contains members whose width in bits is specified in the type definition.

Bitmask   A pattern of bits which programs use in conjunction with bitwise AND and OR operations to select bits in a value to be tested or set.

One's Complement Number Representation   A method of representing signed numbers which uses one bit as the sign bit.

Sign Extension   Filling empty positions with the value of the sign bit when right shifts are performed.

Two's Complement Number Representation   A method of representing signed numbers that uses one bit as the sign bit, but negative numbers are found by inverting the bits in a positive number and adding one.

Zero-Filling   Filling empty bit positions with zeros when left or right shifts are performed.

23

Designing the Text Editor

OBJECTIVES

After reading this chapter, you should be able to:

- List the objectives for writing a program.
- Make a program specification.
- Design the functionality of a program.
- Design the types and functions in a program.
- Use the bull's-eye approach to make a project plan.
- Pseudocode a program.

OUTLINE

PREVIEW

This chapter is the beginning of where the "rubber meets the road" so to speak. Throughout the course of this book, I've attempted to present a balanced approach between C language proficiency, software design skills, and practical programming skills. In this chapter, we attempt to pull everything together to design a working text editor.

23.1   The Purpose of the Program

We write software for definite reasons. If we can't state those reasons in one paragraph or less of written text, we probably should not write the software. This applies to any software project you will ever do.

Here is our statement of purpose:

> The program we will write for this chapter is a text editor. It is first and foremost a teaching tool. It will demonstrate how to design and develop a robust program in C.

This statement tells us exactly what we are creating and why. Because this program is primarily a teaching tool, we will have a certain set of priorities while developing it. These are:

1. *The software must teach as many of the techniques presented in this book as possible.* Because of this need, the design of the software will probably not be as consistent with itself as a real, professional program. That is, you'll see that I sometimes design and implement the same task two different ways just to demonstrate both methods.
2. *The source code must be easy to understand.* As you look through the code presented in the remaining chapters, you may see ways that the program could be made more efficient. Sometimes I've deliberately sacrificed efficiency for clarity. There are things you'll be able to do to make the program use less memory and run faster. However, they will make the program less readable to those new to C.

3. *The software must work reasonably well.* The error checking and error handling are not done as well in this text editor as they would be in professional software. This program must be easy to understand. Error checking and error handling statements tend to make a program's logic less clear. Therefore, I've omitted some of it. There is enough error checking and error handling to demonstrate the techniques, but not enough for this to be a professional program. Also, I've deliberately left some errors in the program for you to find and debug in the Exercises at the end of the remaining chapters.

4. *The program should be as close to a real text editor as can reasonably be expected.* Let's face it: No one can implement a top-notch, professional programmer's text editor with all the bells and whistles in a one semester class. However, the goal of writing this program is to create a situation that is as close to real job experience as possible within the limits of your time.

5. *The software must be extensible and portable.* C is available on a variety of hardware platforms using a variety of operating systems. This book must be usable with all of them. So must the software. However, there are constraints on the size of this book and the time limitations in producing it. Therefore, only the MS DOS version of the text editor will be demonstrated in the remaining chapters. However, the text editor will be built in such a way that it will be straightforward enough for you to create a version for any operating system on any computer.

23.2 The Program Specification

Knowing the purpose of a program enables developers to create a program specification. A program specification is a list of everything the program does. This is often harder to determine than it sounds. We typically write our programs for users other than ourselves. In fact, most programs are used by people who are not programmers. Because the vast majority of users are not familiar with software development, they often have difficulty stating what they want the software to do. Few users can specify all of the features of a program in the terms that programmers use.

I've learned by experience that one helpful way to design the program in a way that the users will understand is to design the user interface first. Most of the tasks the software performs are done in response to a user command. When the user types something on the keyboard, uses the mouse, or selects a menu item, the software must respond. Therefore, designing the user interface first shows the user most of what the program does. Seeing the user interface helps the user get a clear understanding of the program's features. When the user understands and approves of the features, software designers can create a program specification.

Modern computer programs use graphical user interfaces which include menus, dialog boxes, and mouse input. However, implementing that kind of interface requires more time than most students have available. Therefore, the final version of the text editor will use the style of interface used in previous chapters. This type of interface was widely used in the software industry for years.

Like earlier versions of the text editor, this version will be a line-oriented editor. When users edit text, they will specify which line to edit and type in their changes for just that one line. Early text editors were often implemented in this line-oriented style. Most editors today are screen-oriented. Users can move the program's cursor anywhere on the screen and edit the text at that point.

One of the goals of this project is to write a very portable text editor. Implementing a full-screen editor requires writing the program for a specific operating system and type of computer. Because this does not fit with the stated goals of the program, we will be implementing a line-oriented editor.

Figure 23.1 shows the text-based menu that the editor will display to the user. As in previous chapters, the user will communicate with the software using keyboard commands. Table 23.1 specifies the keyboard commands.

TECHNICAL NOTE 23.1
Designing a program's user interface may not tell us everything the program does. The software may also respond to events not generated by the user. For instance, a program may perform specific tasks at a certain day and time. In this case, it is responding to the system clock, not the user. This capability might not be reflected in the user interface.

TECHNICAL NOTE 23.2
Screen-oriented editors are also called full-screen editors because they allow the use of the full screen.

TECHNICAL NOTE 23.3
It is possible to implement a full-screen text editor that is also quite portable. However, it is very difficult. The information required to write such a program is beyond the scope of this book.

FIGURE 23.1   The Menu
System for the Text Editor

Press one of the following keys to issue a command, then press the Enter key.
U, D, B, F, A, Z, E, L, S, Q, Or Press H for Help

TABLE 23.1   Text Editor Keyboard Commands

Keyboard Command	Action
U or u	Scroll the text up one line.
D or d	Scroll the text down one line.
B or b	Scroll the text up one page.
F or f	Scroll the text down one page.
A or a	Scroll the text to the beginning of the buffer.
Z or z	Scroll the text to the end of the buffer.
E or e	Edit a line of text.
L or l	Load a file into the buffer.
S or s	Save the buffer into a file.
H or h	Get help.
Q or q	Quit the program.

By looking at menu and command characters in the user interface, we can tell that the user must be able to use the program to do the following:

1. Enter text into the current text file.
2. Load a text file.
3. Save a text file.
4. Exit the program.
5. Scroll the text up one screenful at a time. The user should not be able to scroll beyond the beginning of the buffer.
6. Scroll the text down one screenful at a time. The user should not be able to scroll beyond the end of the buffer.
7. Scroll the text up one line at a time. The user should not be able to scroll beyond the beginning of the buffer.
8. Scroll the text down one line at a time. The user should not be able to scroll beyond the end of the buffer.
9. Scroll to the end of the text buffer.
10. Scroll to the beginning of the text buffer.
11. Obtain help about the menu commands.

This is the specification for the text editor. In the world of professional programming, there are actually many types of program specifications. Common names for them are *functional specification, internal specification,* and *external specification.* The types of specifications you use depend on the software design methodology your company uses. The specification presented here is a generic approach to program specifications.

23.3   Top-Down Design

The program specification in the previous section describes most of the functionality of the text editor. The top-down design shows it graphically.

We start the top-down design with the most generic statement of what the program does. Figure 23.2 shows the first level of the top-down design.

FIGURE 23.2   The First Level of the Top Down Design

Text Editor

Next, we break the program down into some of its specific tasks. The text editor, like most programs, will need to perform some initializations when it starts up. While the user doesn't want to quit, the editor will get user input, execute the user's commands, and enter the user's text into the text buffer. When the user wants to quit, the program will perform any necessary clean-up and exit. See Figure 23.3.

FIGURE 23.3   Designing the Sub-Tasks of the Editor

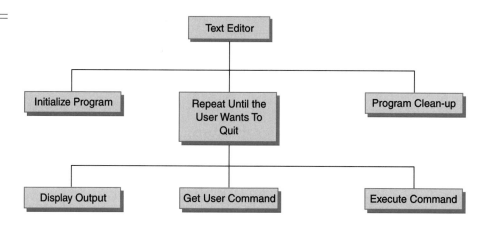

FIGURE 23.3   Designing the Sub-Tasks of the Editor

TIP 23.1
If you get into the habit of designing a message loop into your programs, programming for GUIs will be easier.

The box in Figure 23.3 labeled "Repeat until the user wants to quit" is called the program's **message loop**. The main message loop of a program displays the program's output and reacts to the user's input. Most programs today are structured in this way. This is especially true of programs using GUIs.

The diagram in Figure 23.3 does not specify the commands to which the program will react. Therefore, we need another diagram that shows more of the details of executing user commands.

Figure 23.4 shows the commands to which the text editor will respond. These commands were taken from the specification we saw earlier. The each box on this diagram represents a function. Each function is a response to a particular command.

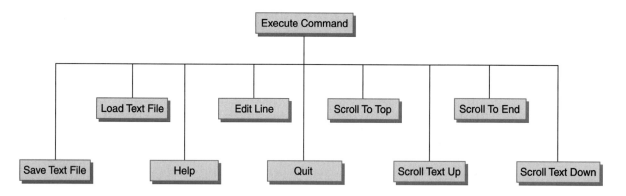

FIGURE 23.4   The Details of Execute Command

Notice that the Scroll Text Up and Scroll Text Down functions don't specify how much to scroll. That information is part of the command. As with earlier versions of the editor, this version will contain a function which will scroll text up by any number of lines. The program will use that function to scroll the text up a line at a time. It will call the same function to scroll the text up a screenful at a time. The Scroll Text Down function will work in a similar manner.

23.4   Designing the Program's Types

Our next step is to design the types that will form the building blocks of the program. Of course, the program will need a text string for each row of text. It will store the text strings in a text buffer. However, unlike previous versions of the text editor, the program will completely encapsulate implementation of text strings. It will use an instance list to store all text strings in a list that is visible only to text string functions. Instance lists were first presented in Chapter 20.

Because the program will use an instance list, it will need to define a type for instance lists and a set of instance list functions.

So now we have three of the types the editor need:

1. The text string.
2. The text buffer.
3. The instance list.

Once the program's primary types are specified, our next job is to define the data they contain and design their functionality.

23.4.1 Text Strings

We've been using various definitions of text string types throughout this book. At this point, we need to decide on a design for this version of the text editor.

Because I want to demonstrate dynamic allocation and instance lists, I'll decide rather arbitrarily that the text string type will use these two techniques.

Some versions of the text string type allocated a default number of character locations in memory for every text string. Pre-allocating memory in this manner generally makes the program run faster. However, it can waste large amounts of memory. This version of the text string type will use a style of dynamic allocation called **lazy allocation**. A text string will not allocate memory for characters until the program tries to store them in memory. As a result, the program wastes as little memory as possible.

Because text strings will be implemented with an instance list, only the text string functions will have access to the text string type. The rest of the program will operate on text strings by passing identifiers to the text string functions.

Using instance lists essentially creates an internal view of text strings and an external view. The internal view is the actual instances on which the text string functions would operate. The external view is the instance identifiers.

Suppose you and I were part of a development team, and I was the programmer implementing text strings. I would provide you with a file called TString.h to include in your .c source files. I would also provide the development team with a file called TString.obj, which would be linked to the final program. I would create TString.obj from TString.c. I would be the only one who sees or works on the contents of TString.c.

This is good for the rest of the team because no one besides me needs to know how text strings are implemented. In TString.h, the team members would have access to a type named `text_string`. Variables of the type `text_string` would actually be unique identifiers of text string instances. Variables of `text_string` forms the external view of a text string.

In the file TString.c, I would define a type called `internal_text_string` (another good name for the type might be `text_string_instance`). The `internal_text_string` type is the actual implementation of text strings. This is the internal view of text strings.

Although this may seem somewhat complicated, it is a good approach for a programming team. It completely hides the implementation of a text string. The other members of the team must know only two things about the use of text strings:

1. Variables of type `text_string` are identifiers, not instances. Therefore, memory for instances is allocated only when the program calls the `TextStringCreate()` function. Instances are only deallocated when a program calls `TextStringFree()`.
2. All operations on an instance of a text string must be performed by text string functions. These are listed in TString.h.

The effect of using instance lists to encapsulate the text string type means that I can completely change the internal implementation of a text string without impacting the other programmers on my team. As long as I do not change the interface of the text string functions, I can make any necessary changes without requiring anyone else on the team to change their portions of the software. If you and I are on a team together, then this is very good for you. You would not want to have to change your code every time I change mine.

The internal and external views of a text string will need to be defined. The external view will be available in TString.h. The internal view will be visible only in TString.c. Example 23.1 gives the definition of the `text_string` type that appears in TString.h. Example 23.2 shows the definition of the type `internal_text_string`, which occurs in TString.c.

EXAMPLE 23.1   The External Definition of the Text String Type

```
typedef instance_identifier text_string;
```

EXAMPLE 23.2   The Internal Definition of the Text String Type

```
1   typedef struct
2   {
3         char *charArray;
4         int charsAllocated;
5   } internal_text_string;
```

The `charArray` member of the `internal_text_string` type is a pointer to the memory containing the string's characters. The memory will be dynamically allocated so that a text string can be any length. The `charsAllocated` member of the structure will be used to keep track of the number of characters (including the null character) that have been allocated to a text string. It is possible that the text string may contain fewer characters than have been allocated. For instance, if the user stores the string "This is a rather long string of characters" into a text string, the program will allocate 46 character locations for the string. The string will contain 45 printable characters plus the null character. If the program later sets location 0 in the text string to `'\0'`, then the length of the string will be zero. However, it will still have 46 character spaces allocated in memory. Therefore, the length of the string and the number of spaces allocated for it may not be the same.

As mentioned previously, using an instance list for text strings requires the presence of a function called `TextStringCreate()` in the text string interface. Applications may need to test a `text_string` variable to be sure it contains a valid instance identifier. So the text string type should provide a function called `TextStringIsValid()`.

In addition, programmers using the text string type will need to set the characters it contains. They probably will want to be able to copy the characters from another text string or from an array of characters. They may also want to get and set individual characters in the string. They'll probably need to append characters to an existing string.

Programs will need to read text strings from the keyboard and print them to the screen. They will need to read text strings in from files and write them out to files. They must be able to get the length of a text string. Also, we will probably want to use the text string type with C Standard Library functions. To do that, we must convert text strings to C character arrays. When we are finished using an instance of a text string, we will need a way to free the memory it uses.

Table 23.2 shows the list of text string functions that we will be implementing for the text editor.

It is possible that not all of these functions will be used by the text editor. The question is, should we write the functions that are not used? The answer is, it depends.

If there are only a few extra short functions, we may want to go ahead and write them to provide a complete interface for text strings. This is especially true if text editor is likely to be enhanced later. However, if our project is behind schedule, it is not wise to spend time writing functions that are not used by the current version of the software.

We also must consider whether our code will be used in other programs. If text strings will be incorporated into programs other than the text editor, it is wise to spend time writing the extra functions.

23.4.2   The Text Buffer

The text editor must contain at least one text buffer. The program will use a text buffer to display and edit text.

Function	Description
TextStringCreate()	Allocates and initializes an instance of a text string.
TextStringIsValid()	Returns TRUE if the instance ID is valid, or FALSE if not.
TextStringSetFromCharArray()	Copy the characters in an array into a text string.
TextStringSetFromTextString()	Copy the character in a text string into another text string.
TextStringSetCharacter()	Copy a character into a specified position in a text string.
TextStringGetCharacter()	Get the specified character from a text string.
TextStringAppendCharacter()	Append a character to the end of a text string.
TextStringPrintString()	Print a text string to stdout.
TextStringScanString()	Read a text string from stdin.
TextStringFGetString()	Read a text string from a file.
TextStringFPutString()	Write a text string to a file.
TextStringGetLength()	Find the length of a text string.
TextStringCopyAsCharArray()	Allocate a character array, and copy the characters from a text string into it.
TextStringFree()	Free the memory used by the instance of the text string.

TABLE 23.2 **The Text String Functions**

The text buffer should be able to grow to the limits of memory. It will need a member that is a pointer to text strings so it can dynamically allocate an array of text strings. It also needs a member to keep track of the number of text strings allocated in the array. The text buffer type will store the row number of the first line of text that the buffer is currently displaying.

In addition to containing the array of text strings, the length of the array, and the first line displayed, the text editor must know whether the text strings in the buffer have been modified by the user. In programmer jargon, it has to keep track of whether the buffer is dirty. If it's been modified since it was saved, it's dirty and needs to be saved again. If the buffer is dirty, the program should ask whether the user wants to save before it exits.

The text buffer is one of the more complex types in this program. It will need a uniform method of handling errors. One option is to make all of the text buffer member functions return error codes. Another is to have the text buffer type contain an error status variable. Whenever the program needs to check the error status, it can call a member function to get the value of the error status data member.

So the next logical question is, which method do you use and why?

Having member functions return error codes is good to do when there are many instances of an object in the program. For example, the text editor uses a lot of text strings. If we were to make the text string structure contain an error status member, there would be an error status value for each text string in the text buffer. We would end up using a large amount of memory. Having member functions return error codes saves that memory.

However, having member functions return error codes also causes complications of its own. You may find that the place where you need to test for and handle an error is in a function other than where it occurred.

Suppose the function DoSomething() is currently executing. DoSomething() was called by ThatFunction(). DoSomething() calls a function named Evaluate(). Also suppose that any errors occurring in Evaluate() need to be handled in ThatFunction(), not in DoSomething(). If an error occurs while Evaluate() is running, its error code will have to be passed by Evaluate() to DoSomething(). The function DoSomething() will have to pass it to ThatFunction().

This situation can make it difficult to also pass back other kinds of errors that occur in DoSomething(). If a type contains an error status data member, ThatFunction() can call a function which reports the error status of the type. This leaves DoSomething() to return error codes that deal with its own errors.

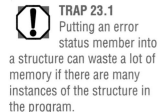

TRAP 23.1
Putting an error status member into a structure can waste a lot of memory if there are many instances of the structure in the program.

TIP 23.2
If there are few instances of a structure in a program, it may be a good idea for the structure to have an error status member.

If there are many instances of a type in a program, it probably shouldn't contain an error status data member. If there are only a few, then having an error status data member can be a real advantage.

These are not hard and fast rules, just guidelines. Some companies write all functions so that they return error codes. Any other information that must come out of the functions must be passed back using pointers in the parameter lists.

We now have enough information to design the `text_buffer` type. This is given in Example 23.3.

EXAMPLE 23.3 The `text_buffer` Type

```
1   typedef struct
2   {
3           text_string *allRows;
4           int totalRows;
5           int topLine;
6           boolean isDirty;
7           text_buffer_error errorStatus;
8   } text_buffer;
```

The text buffer type must provide functions to initialize a buffer, set a row of text, and get a row of text. It also needs functions to scroll the buffer up and down. It will have functions for loading and saving files. The `text_buffer` type should provide a function that returns the row number of the first line of text to be displayed on the screen. The program must be able to query a buffer's length. It should provide a function that reports whether the text buffer is dirty. It also will have one function to report the error status and another to clear it. Lastly, it must provide a function for freeing the memory a buffer occupies.

Table 23.3 gives a list of the functions for the `text_buffer` type.

TABLE 23.3 The `text_buffer` Functions

Function	Description
TextBufferInitialize()	Set the `text_buffer` to a known state.
TextBufferSetRow()	Store text in a row of the buffer.
TextBufferGetRow()	Get text from a row in the buffer.
TextBufferScrollUp()	Scroll the buffer up by a specified number of lines.
TextBufferScrollDown()	Scroll the buffer down by a specified number of lines.
TextBufferScrollToBeginning()	Scroll the text to the beginning of the buffer.
TextBufferScrollToEnd()	Scroll the text to the end of the buffer.
TextBufferGetTopLine()	Get the row number of the first line of text to be displayed on the screen.
TextBufferSaveToFile()	Save the contents of the buffer to a file.
TextBufferLoadFromFile()	Load the contents of a file to the buffer.
TextBufferGetBufferLength()	Get the total number of rows in a buffer.
TextBufferGetError()	Report the buffer's current error status.
TextBufferClearError()	Reset the buffer's error status to `TBE_NO_ERROR`.
TextBufferFree()	Free the memory used by a text buffer.

23.4.3 Instance Lists

Text strings will be based on instance lists. Therefore, the text editor requires a type called `instance_list`. The instance list must be able to store data items of any type. The list will have to grow to the limits of memory. In addition to holding the list itself, it will need to store the list length and the list's error status.

As previously mentioned, implementing a type such as text strings using creates an internal and an external view of the type. Recall that the `text_string` type defined in TString.h actually holds a unique identifier of an instance of an `internal_text_string`. Identifiers used by instance lists must all be of the same type. Therefore, InstList.h must contain a type definition for instance list identifiers. The type definition for instance list identifiers is shown in Example 23.4.

EXAMPLE 23.4   Other Types Used with Instance Lists

```
typedef int instance_list_size;
typedef instance_list_size instance_identifier;
```

Two types are created in this example. The first is used to specify the length of an instance list. It also is used to declare loop counter variables that process instance lists. The name `instance_list_size` is used instead of `int`. This enables a maintenance programmer to easily change all variables that deal with the list length to `long`, `unsigned`, or `unsigned long` if the need arises.

The second type defined in Example 23.4 is the instance list identifier. When using instance lists for a type, as is done with text strings, programmers rename the type `instance_identifier` as needed using a `typedef` statement. This was demonstrated in Example 23.1. The alias `text_string` was created for the `instance_identifier` type.

Any types using instance lists must define the instance identifiers in this way. If a programmer is on team writing a game involving dragons and he wanted to use instance lists to implement the `dragon` type, he would define the type `dragon` as an alias for `instance_identifier`, as shown in Example 23.5. The actual information about a dragon would be kept in a type called `internal_dragon` (or possibly `dragon_instance`).

EXAMPLE 23.5   Creating Another Alias for the `instance_identifier` Type

```
typedef instance_identifier dragon;
```

The instance list will be a dynamically allocated array of pointers to data. Because the pointers must point to any type of data, we will have to use `void` pointers. To make it easier for programmers using instance lists, InstList.h will define a type called `instance_list_item`. Its definition is shown in Example 23.6.

EXAMPLE 23.6   The `instance_list_item` Type

```
typedef void * instance_list_item;
```

The definition of the `instance_list` type is given in Example 23.7.

EXAMPLE 23.7   The `instance_list` Type

```
1   typedef struct
2   {
3           instance_list_item *itemArray;
4           instance_list_size listLength;
5           instance_list_error errorStatus;
6   } instance_list;
```

All instance lists must be declared and initialized in the same way. For the convenience of programmers using the `instance_list` type, it is a good idea to provide a macro that performs the declaration and initialization. Example 23.8 contains the definition of this macro.

EXAMPLE 23.8   The `DeclareInstanceList()` Macro

```
1   #define DeclareInstanceList(listName)                    \
2               static instance_list listName = {            \
3                               NULL,                        \
4                               0,                           \
5                               ILE_NO_ERROR}
```

This macro must be used at file scope level. In other words, it can be used only outside a function. `DeclareInstanceList()` creates a module global variable accessible to all functions in the current .c file. It should never be used in a .h file.

To declare an instance list for text strings, we will put the statement

```
DeclareInstanceList(stringList);
```

near the beginning of the file TString.c.

A set of functions is also associated with the `instance_list` type. Programs must be able to add items to the list. They will need to get items without removing them. Also, programs must be able to remove items from the list completely. They will need functions to get the length of the list, query its error status, and clear the error status. The instance list functions are given in Table 23.4.

TABLE 23.4   The Instance List Functions

Function	Description
`InstanceListAddItem()`	Add an item to an instance list.
`InstanceListGetItem()`	Retrieve an item from the list.
`InstanceListGetLength()`	Get the number of item spaces allocated for the list.
`InstanceListRemoveItem()`	Delete an item from the instance list.
`InstanceListGetLastError()`	Retrieve the current error condition.
`InstanceListClearError()`	Reset the error status to `ILE_NO_ERROR`.

23.5   Filling Out Function Parameter Lists

Designing the types and functions gives us the basic building blocks of a program. However, it lacks some important information. Specifically, we need to know exactly what parameters will be passed into each function. We also must specify every function's return value. Simply put, we must specify the prototype for every function in the program.

To figure out what information each function needs and what it will return, software designers examine carefully what the function does.

TECHNICAL NOTE 23.4 Literal values specified in the program's source are said to be **hard-coded** into the program.

For example, the `TextBufferInitialize()` function sets a text buffer's structure members to a group of predetermined values. These values never change. They are literal values specified directly in the program's source code. This function needs no information in its parameter list other than the address of the text buffer. It does not need to return a value.

To continue the example, `TextBufferSetRow()` also requires a pointer to a text buffer. To set a specific row in the buffer to a text string, the function requires the row number and the string. Because we've already decided that the text buffer type will contain an error status member, `TextBufferSetRow()` does not need to return an error status value. There is no other information it might need to return, so its return type will be `void`.

Examples 23.9, 23.10, and 23.11 show the prototypes for the text string, text buffer, and instance list functions.

EXAMPLE 23.9   Prototypes for the Text String Functions

```
1   text_string TextStringCreate(text_string_error *errorStatus);
2
3   text_string_error TextStringSetFromCharArray(
4                       text_string destinationString,
5                       const char * const charArray);
6
7   text_string_error TextStringSetFromTextString(
8                       text_string destinationString,
```

```
 9                                          text_string sourceString);
10
11   text_string_error TextStringSetCharacter(text_string theString,
12                                             char theCharacter,
13                                             int characterIndex);
14
15   char TextStringGetCharacter(text_string sourceString,
16                               int characterIndex);
17
18   text_string_error TextStringAppendCharacter(
19                               text_string destinationString,
20                               char theCharacter);
21
22   int TextStringPrintString(text_string sourceString);
23
24   int TextStringScanString(text_string destinationString);
25
26   text_string_error TextStringFGetString(
27                               text_string theString,FILE *inputFile);
28
29   text_string_error TextStringFPutString(
30                               text_string theString,FILE *outputFile);
31
32   int TextStringGetLength(text_string sourceString);
33
34   text_string_error TextStringCopyAsCharArray(
35                               text_string sourceString,
36                               char **destinationArray);
37
38   void TextStringFree(text_string theString);
```

EXAMPLE 23.10   Prototypes for the Text Buffer Functions

```
 1   void TextBufferInitialize(text_buffer *tBuffer);
 2
 3   void TextBufferSetRow(text_buffer *tBuffer,
 4                         int rowNumber,
 5                         text_string textString);
 6
 7   void TextBufferGetRow(const text_buffer * const tBuffer,
 8                         int rowNumber,
 9                         text_string *textString);
10
11   void TextBufferScrollUp(text_buffer *tBuffer,
12                           int linesToScroll);
13
14   void TextBufferScrollDown(text_buffer *tBuffer,
15                             int linesToScroll,
16                             int displayAreaHeight);
17   void TextBufferScrollToBeginning(text_buffer *textBuffer);
18
19   void TextBufferScrollToEnd(text_buffer *textBuffer);
20
21   int TextBufferGetTopLine(const text_buffer * const tBuffer);
22
23   void TextBufferSaveToFile(text_buffer *textBuffer,
24                             text_string fileName);
25
26   void TextBufferLoadFromFile(text_buffer *textBuffer,
```

```
27                          text_string fileName);
28
29    int TextBufferGetBufferLength(
30                const text_buffer * const tBuffer);
31
32    text_buffer_error TextBufferGetError(text_buffer *tBuffer);
33
34    void TextBufferClearError(text_buffer *tBuffer);
```

EXAMPLE 23.11   **Prototypes for the Instance List Functions**

```
 1    instance_identifier InstanceListAddItem(
 2                              instance_list *theList,
 3                              instance_list_item theItem);
 4
 5    instance_list_item InstanceListGetItem(
 6                              instance_list *theList,
 7                              instance_identifier itemID);
 8
 9    instance_list_size InstanceListGetLength(
10                              instance_list *theList);
11
12    instance_list_item InstanceListRemoveItem(
13                              instance_list *theList,
14                              instance_identifier itemID);
15
16    instance_list_error InstanceListGetLastError(
17                              instance_list *theList);
18
19    void InstanceListClearError(instance_list *theList);
```

23.6   Pseudocoding the Text Editor

TECHNICAL NOTE 23.5
Most software design methodologies will have you produce more design diagrams than we have using the generic methods shown in this chapter. They'll also require you to some sort of textual explanation (such as pseudocode) of the processes in your program.

Before you begin writing the C source code for a program, it's good to pseudocode it. The process of pseudocoding a program forces developers to think about the design of each type and function before they actually write it.

One technique for pseudocoding is to create a function as if you were really going to write it. Instead of writing C statements in the body of the function, write comments. Example 23.12 shows pseudocode for the text editor's main() function.

EXAMPLE 23.12   **Pseudocode for the main() Function**

```
 1    int main()
 2    {
 3            // Initialize the text buffer.
 4            // Enter the message loop.
 5
 6            // If there was an error...
 7                    // Print an error message.
 8
 9            // Free the text buffer.
10
11            // Return the error status.
12    }
```

The main() function is quite short, but it is all that is needed. Following the design diagrams shown previously in this chapter, most of the work of the program is done by the function's main() calls to execute its message loop. Example 23.13 shows the MessageLoop() function.

EXAMPLE 23.13   Pseudocode for the MessageLoop() Function

```
 1   //--------------------------------------------------------
 2   /*
 3   Function Name:              MessageLoop
 4   Parameters:
 5       In:                     None.
 6       Out:                    None.
 7       In/Out:                 None.
 8   Return Values:              This function returns PE_NO_ERROR if no error
 9                               occurred. Otherwise, it returns the error
10                               codes it receives from the functions it
11                               calls.
12   Comments:                   The MessageLoop() function is the main message
13                               loop of the program. It displays the program's
14                               output and reacts to the user's input.
15   */
16
17   static program_error MessageLoop(text_buffer *textBuffer)
18   {
19       // While the user does not want to quit...
20           // Clear the screen.
21           // Display a page of text.
22           // Display the menu.
23           // Get the user's command.
24           // Respond to the user's command.
25               // If the user wants to scroll up one line...
26                   // Scroll the buffer up one line.
27               // If the user wants to scroll up one screenful...
28                   // Scroll the buffer up one screenful.
29                   // Leave an overlap of one line.
30               // If the user wants to scroll down one line...
31                   // Scroll the buffer down one line.
32               // If the user wants to scroll down one screenful...
33                   // Scroll the buffer down one screenful.
34               // If the user wants to edit text...
35                   // Edit the text.
36               /* If the user wants to scroll to the
37               beginning of the buffer... */
38                   // Scroll to the beginning.
39               /* If the user wants to scroll to the end of the
40               buffer... */
41                   // Scroll to the end.
42               // If the user wants to load a file...
43                   // Load the file.
44               // If the user wants to save a file...
45                   // Save the file.
46               // If the user needs help...
47                   // Help the user.
48               // If the user wants to quit...
49                   // Set the loop control variable to exit.
50               // Else the command is not recognized...
51                   // Print an error message.
52
53       // Return the error status.
54   }
55
56   // End MessageLoop
57   //--------------------------------------------------------
```

Each function in the program can be pseudocoded in the method shown in these examples. Doing so enables developers to work out the logic of the program completely before it is coded in C.

Designing software is an iterative process. Often, many of the implementation details are not clear on the first design pass. Writing a pseudocode version of each function before we implement it helps focus us on the details we may have missed.

For instance, specifying the prototypes for the text editor's functions and writing pseudocode make it clear that there are details omitted from the text editor's design. The `MessageLoop()` function in Example 23.13 uses a loop control variable. When the user wants to quit, this variable is set to a value that makes the loop condition evaluate to false. The simplest way to do this is to use a `boolean` variable. This implies we need to define the type `boolean` in the program. However, the `boolean` type does not appear in the current design. This is a mistake. It should be included.

In addition, functions for text strings, text buffers, and instance lists should have enumerated types for error values. The program itself should also have an enumerated type which enumerates all possible program error conditions.

Software designers must carefully think about the possible error conditions which can occur as each function executes. The designer of a function determines what type of error a particular problem is. It can be either a runtime error or a programmer error.

Recall that a runtime error is caused by conditions at the time the program executes. Runtime errors include such problems as running out of memory, as well as incorrect input typed by the user. Runtime errors are handled with program logic such as `if` statements.

Programmer errors, on the other hand, are errors caused by programmers calling functions with improper values, at incorrect times, or in the wrong order. Functions typically respond to programmer errors with `assert()` statements. These crash the program and force the developers to fix the error before shipping the software.

After developers find design problems by pseudocoding, they update the designs. By the time they write the actual program code, most of the details are ironed out.

If you use the pseudocoding style shown in Examples 23.12 and 23.13, you are actually documenting your program before you write it. The pseudocode can be saved in .c files as comments. You then fill in the appropriate C statements after each comment.

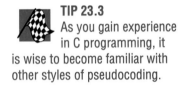

TIP 23.3

As you gain experience in C programming, it is wise to become familiar with other styles of pseudocoding.

Although many C programmers use this style of pseudocoding, software design methodologies seldom do. For very good reasons, the creators of software design methodologies prefer styles of pseudocode that don't look so much like C. Using the style of pseudocode shown in Examples 23.12 and 23.13 helps programmers figure out exactly what C statements are needed. Therefore, it is well suited to the purposes of this book.

23.7   A Project Plan for the Text Editor

A solid design gives developers a good idea of what code they'll be writing for a program and how much effort it will require. In a real job situation, a developer would next produce a project schedule.

To create a realistic schedule, programmers have to determine what needs to be implemented first. They can then estimate how long it will take to write and debug the code. Many use the bulls-eye approach presented in Chapter 13.

For the text editor, a programer may decide to write a simple `main()` function and implement instance lists. Her `main()` function would call and test each of the instance list functions. Next, she could implement text strings and modify `main()` to test text strings. Once text strings were working properly, she could implement text buffers and, finally, the text editor itself.

This approach gives her much of the core functionality of the text editor early in the project. Each successive version of the text editor adds more of the types needed for the final program. Before she moves on to the next version, she can thoroughly test the types and functions she's already implemented. If an error occurs while writing the text string functions, the chances are good that the problem is in the text string functions, not in the instance list functions. When text strings are written and tested, implementation problems will probably be in the text buffer functions, not in text strings or instance lists.

A project plan for a program shows the completion date of the core system. It also contains the dates on which each module of code will be written, tested, and integrated into the program. This is an important point. When you write a schedule, you must allow time for integrating the new code into the software. It's very rare that a component will go into a program without any hitches.

Table 23.5 illustrates a possible project schedule for the text editor.

TABLE 23.5   A Schedule for Implementing the Text Editor

Component(s)	Start Date	Code Completion Date	Testing and Debugging Completion Date	Integration Completion Date
Instance list, simple version of `main()`	Sept 1	Sept 20	Oct 5	Oct 20
Text strings	Oct 21	Nov 5	Nov 20	Dec 5
Text buffers	Dec 6	Dec 20	Jan 10	Jan 25
Complete text editor	Jan 26	Feb 15	Feb 25	Mar 10

TRAP 23.2
Developers tend to be optimistic people. It is normal for developers to underestimate the amount of time required for a task. This can lead to schedule slips and unplanned delays.

TIP 23.4
Experienced software developers often estimate their schedules and then double their original estimates. This practice helps them create realistic schedules for their projects.

TIP 23.5
If you are leading a team of programmers, doubling the team members' schedule estimates will help you produce a realistic schedule.

Tasks that are started and ended on the dates in a schedule are called **milestones**. Any schedule you make must allow for holidays, sick time, personal time, and so forth. Many software engineers estimate their milestones and then double their estimates.

If you are managing a team of developers, you will divide up the code modules among the members of your team. Typically, you'll ask them to estimate their milestone schedules. When experienced managers receive the team's estimates, they often double them. This is true even if the members of the team have already doubled their original estimates.

When creating schedules, it is important to allow enough time for testing the software. Testing can take days, weeks, or months. Software testing is an art in itself. Many testers are people who have worked in development. Software testing provides an alternative career path for those with development skills.

The approach shown in the schedule in Table 23.5 is not the only one you can use. You may decide that it's most important to get the user interface up and running first so you can plug each additional software module into a working environment. With this approach, you'd first write and debug the functions in TEdit.c. They would not actually do anything other than display the user interface. Next, you'd create the text buffer using character arrays. After that, the text string and instance list functions would be written. The schedule you use depends on the priorities of your project.

23.8   Troubleshooting Guide

After reading this section, you should be able to:

- Avoid potential problems in stating the purpose of a program.
- Avoid selecting types that do not belong in the program.
- Do iterative design to find details you've previously omitted.

23.8.1   What's the Purpose?

You'll find as you go through your career that users sometimes cannot clearly state the purpose of the software they want produced. Typically, this is because they have not studied the need that the software is intended to fit. They hired you to do that for them. Your job is to study the situation and suggest one or more solutions.

The problem comes when they don't tell you that this is why you're being hired. They make a general statement like, "We need to computerize our business." Naturally, they hire you because you're the local computer expert. They tell you, "We need a computer system." After a brief pause, they usually add, "But we need one that doesn't cost too much."

The company's need here is real. Management genuinely needs to computerize parts of the business. However, they can't specify which parts unless they have carefully studied how the business operates.

You know you're in this situation when the people hiring you can't clearly state what the software is for in one paragraph or less. If they use broad, general terms to describe what the program does, they don't know what they really want.

Another problem occurs when management tells you, "We want you to computerize what Jane does." Your logical response is "What does Jane do?" If the reply is something like, "She coordinates customer relations information" then you're in trouble. There are many situations in which a person's job can't be done by a computer. Management recognizes that Jane performs valuable functions. She may have been doing her job for many years. Someone suggests that it would be good to capture her knowledge in software before Jane retires. This may or may not work.

You may find that you can get a computer to do some of what Jane does by putting a web page on the company's Internet server. You can write a program that interfaces with the web page and collects information from customers. The program can then route the information where it needs to go.

However, the essence of doing many jobs well lies in the judgement and experience of the person doing them. A computer will never learn every customer's face and ask them about their spouse's operation, child's baseball league, and so on. These things may be the most important factors in getting Jane's job done.

Although this may sound like it has nothing to do with software design, in fact it does. To be successful, you must be able to see clearly what the software should do and what it should not do. You must be willing and able to propose both software and nonsoftware solutions. In the example presented here, the solution might be to create a customer database and have Jane input her extensive knowledge of the customers. It also might require suggesting to management that Jane pick and train the person who's going to replace her when she retires. The situation requires both a software and a non-software solution.

Whenever the statement of purpose for the software is vague or involves names of specific people, be careful. Tell management that you must study the problem for awhile before you can begin to design the system. Suggest a schedule which will allow you to identify the company's software needs and report back. When you present your report, suggest alternatives. Describe what each alternative will cost and what the company will get for its money.

To be a software designer, you must work at developing all of these skills. The primary task of a software designer is communication. You must be able to communicate with management, users, and technology workers.

When you present your proposal and management selects one of the alternatives you've given them, you should have a short, clear statement of purpose for your program. Only then can you move forward with the project.

23.8.2 Watch Out for Improper Types

When designing program components, be wary of types that have only verbs in their names. For example, avoid types with names such as `calculate`, `print`, or `manage`. A type's name is ideally a noun. It should not be `print`, but rather `report_printer`. Or better yet, `report_generator` so that the generated report can be stored or printed. There should not be a type in your program called `manage_windows`. It should be a `window_manager`.

If you can't state the name of a type as a noun, it probably shouldn't be a type. It should be a function. Programmer-defined types represent something. They act as models of *things*. It is the job of a type's API functions to perform actions, not the type itself.

Types with verbs for names will almost always make your system more complex and less structured. They indicate a need to redesign the software.

23.8.3 Play It Again, Sam

Designing software is an iterative process. Developers will always have to go back and redesign parts of the system when they implement it. Therefore, they need to plan for change. Design software so that it can be easily modified and extended because it probably will be before version 1.0 is released.

Also, try do as much design as you can the first time around. Attempt to anticipate everything you'll need to implement in the software. For example, some items were omitted from the initial design of the text editor. These were discovered during pseudocoding. Each time we design software, there will be things we leave out. As we discover them, we need to update the design and go through the entire process again.

Many programmers consider writing pseudocode a waste of time. However, writing pseudocode helps us gain insights into details that might have been missed in an initial design. It clearly shows many types of design errors. It also enables us to redesign before we start writing any actual code. This lowers the cost of producing software.

SUMMARY

When writing software, developers begin by stating the software's purpose. If they can write a short, clear statement of why they are writing the program and what need it will fill, they have a much better chance of being able to complete the program on time and within budget.

Before developers start writing the program, they create a program specification. The specification should list everything the program does. It often can be accomplished by designing the user interface.

Software designers and developers also must be able to describe the functionality of the program. Top-down design methods enable us to do this graphically.

After the program's functionality is defined, design the types and functions that will provide the functionality. Pseudocoding them helps clarify the implementation details.

In almost every professional situation, developers create a schedule for their project, or their parts of the project. They often use the bull's-eye approach to implement manageable portions of the program. This enables them to get important parts of the program written and debugged before they go on to the rest.

Remember that design is an iterative process. Developers often redesign parts of their software. Pseudocoding the functions for each program component helps find many details that were missed in the first design pass.

TECHNICAL NOTES

23.1   Designing a program's user interface may not tell us everything the program does. The software may also respond to events not generated by the user. For instance, a program may perform specific tasks at a certain day and time. In this case, it is responding to the system clock, not the user. This capability might not be reflected in the user interface.

23.2   Screen-oriented editors are also called full-screen editors because they allow the use of the full screen.

23.3   It is possible to implement a full-screen text editor that is also quite portable. However, it is very difficult. The information required to write such a program is beyond the scope of this book.

23.4   Literal values specified in the program's source are said to be **hard-coded** into the program.

23.5   Most software design methodologies will have you produce more design diagrams than we have using the generic methods shown in this chapter. They'll also require you to some sort of textual explanation (such as pseudocode) of the processes in your program.

TIPS

23.1   If you get into the habit of designing a message loop into your programs, programming for GUIs will be easier.

23.2   If there are few instances of a structure in a program, it may be a good idea for the structure to have an error status member.

23.3   As you gain experience in C programming, it is wise to become familiar with other styles of pseudocoding.

23.4   Experienced software developers often estimate their schedules and then double their original estimates. This practice helps them create realistic schedules for their projects.

23.5   If you are leading a team of programmers, doubling the team members' schedule estimates will help you produce a realistic schedule.

TRAPS

23.1   Putting an error status member into a structure can waste a lot of memory if there are many instances of the structure in the program.

23.2   Developers tend to be optimistic people. It is normal for developers to underestimate the amount of time required for a task. This can lead to schedule slips and unplanned delays.

REVIEW QUESTIONS

1. What problems can occur while writing the objectives of a program? What are some ways you can solve those problems?

2. Why is a program specification necessary? How would it affect the project if you just didn't write one?

3. What does it mean to design the functionality of a program? How does this help you implement it?

4. How does top-down design help you design the functionality of a program?

5. How do you go about picking types for a program?

6. What are some problems that can occur when you're designing types and functions for a program?

7. Why is a project schedule necessary? How does it help developers?

8. What is the bull's-eye approach to software development? Why is it useful?

9. What would happen if I wrote the software for the entire program I was working on and then did testing, integrating, and debugging?

10. Why is design an iterative process? What prevents you from doing it just once?

EXERCISES

1. Give five examples of poor purpose statements for programs. Explain why they are poor examples.

2. Give five examples of good program purpose statements. Explain why they are good.

3. Explain why designing a program's user interface helps create the program specification. Tell why designing the user interface may not be enough to provide a complete program specification. Give at least three examples.

4. Explain the process of top-down design. Give an example.

5. Explain why you must design a program's types and functions. Give an example of how to do it.

6. Describe how to make a project schedule. Explain the benefits of doing so. Give an example schedule.

For Exercises 7–10, assume that you are working as a software developer. Your boss has asked you to write a program that mimics a pocket calculator.

7. Design the user interface for the pocket calculator. Use that design to generate a program specification.

8. Create a top-down design of the calculator program's functionality.

9. Design the calculator program's types and functions.

10. Make a schedule for the calculator project. Tell which types and functions you would implement first and why.

In Exercises 11–15, suppose that you have been hired to write a full-featured programmer's text editor with a graphical user interface.

11. Write a statement of purpose for the GUI-based text editor.

12. Create a program specification and design the user interface (UI) for the GUI text editor. The UI must use horizontal and vertical menus, dialog boxes, scroll bars, and other interface elements commonly found in GUIs.

13. Create a top-down design of the GUI-based text editor.

14. Design the GUI text editor's types and functions.

15. Select one of the types you designed for Exercise 14. Pseudocode the functions for that type.

In Exercises 16–20, assume that you have decided to start a business writing computer games. Your first game is Space Attackers, which was introduced in Chapter 13.

16. Create a statement of purpose and a program specification for Space Attackers.

17. Design the user interface for Space Attackers.

18. Using the charts given in Chapter 13, create a detailed top-down design of the Space Attackers program.

19. Design the types and functions used in Space Attackers.

20. Select one of the types you designed in Exercise 19. Pseudocode all of the functions for that type.

GLOSSARY

Hard-Coded Logic or values that are specified in a program's source code.

Lazy Allocation Allocating memory only when data is actually stored.

Message Loop The primary loop that displays program output and reacts to the user's input.

Milestone A completed task in a software project.

24

Developing the
Text Editor: TEdit.c

OBJECTIVES

After reading this chapter, you should be able to:

- Implement the text editor source file TEdit.c.
- Debug and enhance the text editor program.

OUTLINE

PREVIEW

This chapter begins the implementation of the final text editor. It will follow the design in Chapter 23 as closely as possible. The file TEdit.c is discussed in this chapter. The remaining chapters in this book each present and discuss the other C source files for the text editor.

The source files presented in this and the remaining chapters are on the Examples CD. They can be found are in the Final directory, which is in the Examples directory on the CD.

24.1   A Quick Look at the Finished Program

Before looking at the C source code, it's helpful to compile the editor and run the program. When the program starts, it displays the screen shown in Figure 24.1.

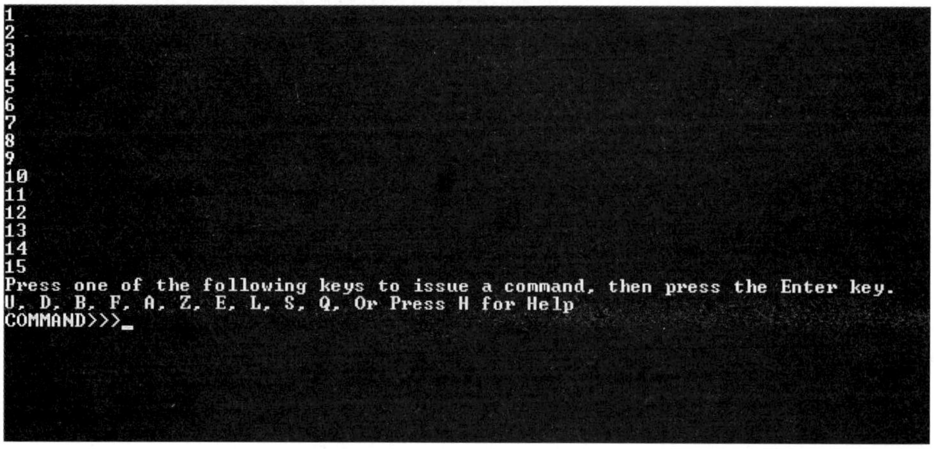

FIGURE 24.1   The Initial Screen of the Text Editor

```
1
2
3
4
5
6
7
8
9
10
11
12
13
14
15
Press one of the following keys to issue a command, then press the Enter key.
U, D, B, F, A, Z, E, L, S, Q, Or Press H for Help
COMMAND>>>_
```

The editor's text display area is fifteen lines long. It is followed by a line of instructions, the menu, and a prompt. At the prompt, users can type in single-character commands. If they enter the command to load a file, the editor will display a screen similar to Figure 24.2.

FIGURE 24.2   Loading a File
into the Editor

```
1   //----------------------------------------------------------------
2   /*
3   File Name: TEdit.c
4   Comments:  This file contains the functions which
5                          implement the text editor.
6   */
7   //----------------------------------------------------------------
8
9
10
11
12  //----------------------------------------------------------------
13  // Include files
14
15  #include <stdio.h>
Press one of the following keys to issue a command, then press the Enter key.
U, D, B, F, A, Z, E, L, S, Q, Or Press H for Help
COMMAND>>>
```

Notice that the text on line 5 of the screen shown in Figure 24.2 is indented differently than source code in this book. The indentation is caused by tab characters in the text file. This text editor program used the C Standard Library output functions to print the tab characters. Each type of computer has its own default tab size. Therefore, indentation often looks different when a file is displayed on various computer screens.

To solve this problem, most modern text editors implement their own tabbing. They enable the user to set the number of spaces for a tab character. Whenever they encounter a tab character in a text file, they will print that number of spaces on the screen rather than the tab character itself.

The source files for the editor are organized using the methods presented in Chapter 17. The file containing the main() function is TEdit.c. Text buffers are defined and implemented in TBuffer.h and TBuffer.c. TString.h and TString.c contain the definition and implementation of text strings. Instance lists are defined and implemented in InstList.h and InstList.c.

24.2   Writing TEdit.c

Because TEdit.c is somewhat long, its code is not printed in this chapter. To see the code, please see the TEdit.c on the Examples CD. TEdit.c contains the functions which form the high-level logic of the program.

After its comment banner, TEdit.c begins by including the header files it requires. On lines 27–49, it defines the constants it uses. These are followed by the definition of the enumerated type program_error. The constants defined with the program_error type are used as error status codes.

On lines 68–83, TEdit.c declares the prototypes of all the functions in the file except main(). Lines 88–108 contain the main() function itself.

As with most functions, main() begins by declaring the variables it uses. One of these is the text buffer. The other is an error status variable.

TECHNICAL NOTE 24.1
In programming books and magazines, input to which the program reacts is often referred to as messages.

Before the text buffer can be used, it must be initialized into a known state. The main() function accomplishes this by invoking TextBufferInitialize() and passing it the address of the text buffer. main() then calls the MessageLoop() function to process and react to input from the user. The message loop continues until the user wants to quit or until there is a fatal error.

If there was an error during the operation of the message loop, main() prints an error message for the user. On line 105 of TEdit.c, it frees the memory used by the text buffer. Lastly, it type casts the error status variable to an int and returns the current error status. It should type cast the error status variable because the main() function returns integers. Strictly speaking, it does not have to because enumerated values are really integers. However, it is good programming practice to do so.

The MessageLoop() function appears next in TEdit.c. Its only parameter is a pointer to the text buffer. It returns the program_error value. After it declares the variables it needs, MessageLoop() enters a for loop beginning on line 136. This is the program's message loop. It displays the current contents of the buffer by calling `ClearScreen()` and `DisplayText()`. Both of these functions are found in TEdit.c. Next, it invokes `Print-Menu()` to display the editor's main menu on the screen. It also calls `GetUserCommand()` to retrieve input messages from the user in the form of single-character commands.

On line 150, `MessageLoop()` enters a `switch` statement to react to the user's input. When the `switch` statement has processed the user's command, the `for` loop tests the variable `done` to see whether it is time to quit. The loop will continue for as long as the user does not want to exit the program and while there is no error. When the function does finally exit, it returns value in the error status variable.

The `ClearScreen()` function on lines 236–274 is different from previous versions. It uses conditional compilation to define program statements for specific operating systems. If the editor is running under MS DOS, or a DOS box under MS Windows, it will compile the statement on line 253. If the program is compiled to run on Unix or Linux, it uses the statement on line 257 to clear the screen. If it is intended for any other operating system, it compiles the statements on lines 261–268.

The `DisplayText()` function is largely unchanged from previous versions of the program. The primary difference is that it prints only the buffer line numbers. The display line numbers are omitted.

No changes were made to the `PrintMenu()` or `GetUserCommand()` functions. The `PrintHelp()` function is new. By calling the Standard Library output functions, it prints help information for the user.

24.3   Troubleshooting Guide

After reading this section, you should be able to:

* Become familiar with the basic kinds of software testing.
* Test the text editor.

24.3.1   The Need for Testing

Like all software, the text editor has to be tested before it can be used. Every software developer must have testing and debugging skills. Some developers choose to specialize in testing. They are extremely adept at finding problems in other peoples' code.

Testers should be looked upon as a developer's best friend. They find programmers' errors before the software is released. It is not at all helpful to programmers' careers if thousands of users find their mistakes after the software is on the market.

A great number of books are devoted to the subject of software testing. There are also specific software testing methodologies. A brief overview of software testing will be presented here. While it will not cover the subject completely, it gives an introduction to the testing process.

Generally speaking, there are three levels of testing, unit testing: integration testing, and functional testing.

24.3.2   Unit Testing

Testing each function by itself is usually referred to as **unit testing** in programming literature. During unit testing, each function in a file should be tested to its most extreme limits.

For example, unit testing of the `GetUserCommand()` function in TEdit.c would include:

1. Entering single, alphanumeric characters.
2. Entering no characters by just pressing the Enter key.
3. Entering single, non-alphanumeric characters like *, &, ~, and `.
4. Entering strings of alphanumeric characters.
5. Entering strings of nonalphanumeric characters.
6. Entering mixed strings of alphanumeric and nonalphanumeric characters.
7. Entering other characters from the ASCII set, such as the escape character (27) or the bell character (7).

8. Entering strings of other characters from the ASCII set.
9. Entering characters from the extended character set (characters whose values are greater than 127).
10. Entering strings of characters from the extended character set.

Every function in a program must be tested with at least the level of thoroughness indicated by this list.

During unit testing, all parameters to a function should be validated. The function needs to be tested with a variety of parameter values. Some of them should be the normal values the function was written to handle. Others must be extreme and unexpected values.

Unit testing starts as soon as functions in a program have been written.

24.3.3 Integration Testing

After all of the functions in a module of code have been tested individually, the must be integrated in to the program. Testing the functions together is called **integration testing**.

When writing the file TEdit.c, a good software engineer would test the function `GetUserCommand()` by itself. He would then do integration testing by calling `GetUserCommand()` from `MessageLoop()`. He would verify that `MessageLoop()` received input through `GetUserCommand()` and responded correctly to that input. As a minimum, the integration tests on `MessageLoop()` include:

1. Passing a valid pointer to a text buffer in the parameter `textBuffer`.
2. Passing the value `NULL` in the parameter `textBuffer`.
3. Checking that the screen is cleared on each pass through the message loop.
4. Validating that the current contents of the buffer are printed to the screen on every loop iteration.
5. Verifying that the menu is printed and that it is correct.
6. Ensuring that commands are properly read in from the keyboard.
7. Verifying that the correct `case` statement is executed when valid commands are entered.
8. Checking that incorrect user input causes the default case in the `switch` statement to be executed.
9. Validating the return values.

Integration testing can begin as soon as there is a group of functions written that call each other.

24.3.4 Functional Testing

Testing must also be performed from the user's point of view. Someone on the project runs the program and pretends to be a user. They verify that the program does not crash and does what it is supposed to. Every element of the user interface must be validated to be sure it is correct and that its appearance is attractive and appropriate. This is called **functional testing**.

For the text editor program, some of the functional tests which would be performed are:

1. Input each menu command one at a time, and ensure they work correctly.
2. Input invalid commands, and verify that they are handled gracefully by the software.
3. Load an empty file.
4. Load a file of moderate size.
5. Load a large file.
6. Load a file of an extremely large size, such as a file that is as large as the hard drive.
7. Save an empty file.
8. Save a file of moderate size.
9. Save a file of an extremely large size, such as one that is as large as or larger than the hard drive.
10. Input strings.
11. Input enough strings to use up all of the computer's memory.
12. Try to input more strings than memory will hold.
13. Edit existing strings.

These are only a few of the functional tests that would be required before software can be released professionally. Functional tests generally start when large parts of the program are completed.

SUMMARY

The file TEdit.c contains the text editor's `main()` function and those functions that form the high level logic of the program. It uses the text buffer and text string types, as well as their associated functions, to accomplish its tasks.

Like all functions, the functions in TEdit.c require testing. As a minimum, most software companies perform

unit testing, integration testing, and functional testing. Unit tests are tests on each function. Integration testing means performing tests on groups of functions. Testing the program from the user's point of view is called functional testing.

TECHNICAL NOTE

24.1 In programming books and magazines, input to which the program reacts is often referred to as messages.

REVIEW QUESTIONS

1. In previous versions of the text editor, the message loop was in `main()`. In the version presented in this chapter, it is in the `MessageLoop()` function. What are the advantages of this implementation? What are the disadvantages?

2. All of the constants in TEdit.c were created either as part of an enumerated type or with `#define` statements. Some or all of those created with `#define` statements could have been created with the keyword `const`. What are the advantages of using `const` rather than `#define`? What are the advantages of using `#define` rather than `const`?

3. The `DisplayText()` function prints the buffer line number for each line of text. Most text editors do not print this information. Do you think it is better to print it or leave it out? Give your reasons for thinking the way you do.

4. The `PrintMenu()` function prints the main menu as a collection of single characters. Each character indicates a command. This style of menu was common among early computer programs. What are its advantages? What are its disadvantages?

5. The `PrintHelp()` function is a first step toward a basic help system for a program. If programs have a good user interface, shouldn't users just be able to figure out how to use the programs by looking at them? Why do you think programs have help systems?

6. The `GetUserCommand()` function calls the C Standard Library `toupper()` function to convert all of its input to upper case. What are the advantages of this? What does `toupper()` return if the character that the user inputs is not a letter?

7. The `EditBuffer()` function uses a `do-while` loop to get valid user input. What are the advantages of using a `do-while` loop there? Would it be better to use a `while` loop or `for` loop? Why or why not?

8. After it attempts to load a text file, the `LoadFile()` function performs its error handling with a `switch` statement (lines 646–668 of TEdit.c). Are there any advantages to using a `switch` there rather than a series of chained `if-else` statements? The values `TBE_OUT_OF_MEMORY` and `TBE_CANT_ALLOCATE_BUFFER` both execute the same case. Is it a good idea to use `switch` statements in this way? Why or why not?

9. The `GetFileName()` function has a pointer to a `text_string` as its only parameter. Does this parameter need to be a pointer? Explain the reasons for your answer.

10. Is it necessary for the `GetFileName()` function to return the number of characters it reads? What are the advantages of having it return that value?

EXERCISES

1. Modify the `GetFileName()` function so that it does not use a pointer in its parameter list. Explain whether it works if the parameter is not a pointer.

2. The functions in TEdit.c do not all validate their parameters as they should. Modify the text editor so that all of

the functions validate their parameters with calls to `assert()` wherever appropriate.

3. For maintenance reasons, it is helpful to have all error messages in a program declared as string constants. Convert all of the error messages in TEdit.c to string constants.

Write a function called `PrintErrorMessage()` which prints nicely- formatted error messages. Pass all error messages as parameters to `PrintErrorMessage()`.

4. Create a function in TEdit.c called `Pause()`. It should print the message `"Press Enter to continue."` then call `getchar()` and `rewind()`. Use it wherever possible in the text editor.

5. Modify the text editor so that it allows the user to type a file name on the command line. If a file name appears as a command-line parameter when the program starts, have the editor load it.

6. Create an empty text file on your computer's disk. Load the file into the text editor. Describe how the editor reacted.

7. Perform the following tests on the text editor. For each test, write a description of the test and the results.
   a. At the main menu, enter single alphanumeric characters.
   b. At the main menu, enter no characters by pressing the Enter key.
   c. Enter no less than ten single nonalphanumeric characters such as *, &, ~, and `.

8. Perform the following tests on the text editor. For each test, write a description of the test and the results.
   a. At the main menu, enter single characters from the ASCII set whose values are less than 32.
   b. At the main menu, enter a string of characters from the ASCII set whose values are less than 32. Many types of computers enable you to enter extended characters by holding down the Alt key and typing the character's three digit extended ASCII value. For example, typing in the escape on an IBM compatible PC can be accomplished by holding down the Alt key and typing 027 on the number pad to the right of the typewriter key set.
   c. At the main menu, enter a string of characters. Have some of the ASCII values be less than 32 and some greater.

9. Perform the following tests on the text editor. For each test, write a description of the test and the results.
   a. At the main menu, enter strings of alphanumeric characters.
   b. At the main menu, enter strings of nonalphanumeric characters.
   c. At the main menu, enter mixed strings of alphanumeric and nonalphanumeric characters.

10. Perform the following tests on the text editor. For each test, write a description of the test and the results.
    a. At the main menu, input each menu command one at a time, and ensure they work.
    b. At the main menu, input invalid commands, and validate that they are handled gracefully by the software.
    c. At the main menu, enter characters from the extended character set (characters whose values are greater than 127). Many types of computers enable you to enter extended characters by holding down the Alt key and typing the character's three digit extended ASCII value. For example, a degree sign on an IBM-

compatible PC can be entered by holding down the Alt key and typing 248 on the number pad to the right of the typewriter key set.

11. Perform the following tests on the text editor. For each test, write a description of the test and the results.
    a. Type text into an empty text buffer. Scroll it up and down. Save the text.
    b. Load a file, edit it, and save it.
    c. Load a file, scroll past its end, enter additional text, and save it.

12. Perform the following tests on the text editor. For each test, write a description of the test and the results.
    a. Load a file, and then load the same file again.
    b. Load a file, and then load a different file.
    c. Load a file, save it without editing it, and then save it again.

13. Perform the following tests on the text editor. For each test, write a description of the test and the results.
    a. Load a fairly long text file. Scroll to the beginning and end using all of the different scroll commands.
    b. Type a line of text into the first row of an empty text buffer. Scroll to line 1,000. Save the file.
    c. Type a line of text into the first row of an empty text buffer. Scroll to line 10,000. Save the file.

14. Perform the following tests on the text editor. For each test, write a description of the test and the results.
    a. Attempt to load a file that does not exist.
    b. Attempt to load a file in another directory by specifying its path name.
    c. Attempt to load a file with an invalid file name.

15. Try entering characters from the extended ASCII set into an empty text buffer. Many types of computers enable you to enter extended characters by holding down the Alt key and typing the character's three digit extended ASCII value. For example, a degree sign on an IBM compatible PC can be entered by holding down the Alt key and typing 248 on the number pad to the right of the typewriter key set. Save the file with these characters. Exit the text editor and restart it. Load the file with the extended ASCII characters. Describe your results.

16. If a program is tested using functional testing, explain whether you think unit and integration testing are needed. Give the reasons for your opinion.

17. Assume that you have been asked to add features to the text editor. To do so, you need to reorganize the main menu such that it uses submenus. The new main menu will consist of the following:

F, E, U, D, B, F, A, Z, Or Press H for Help

The F stands for file, and, if selected, it will result in this submenu being displayed:

L, S, Q

where L causes the editor to load a file, S makes the program save a file, and Q ends the program.

In the main menu, pressing E displays an editing submenu. The editing submenu consists of:

E, C, T, P

where E stands for editing a line of text, C calls a function to copy a line of text, T calls a function to cut a line of text, and P calls a function to paste a line of text. At this point, you do not need the cut, copy, and paste functions work. Just write empty functions that the program can call.

The other choices in the main menu are the same as the commands in the editor presented in this chapter.

18. The text editor's `main()` function declares a text buffer, initializes it, and passes it to `MessageLoop()`. When `MessageLoop()` ends, it frees the buffer's memory. Explain whether you think the declaration, initialization, and deallocation of the buffer should be moved into the `MessageLoop()` function.

19. In addition to the tests presented in this chapter, create 5 other tests to perform on the text editor to see whether it works properly.

20. Perform the tests you wrote for Exercise 19 and report the results.

GLOSSARY

Functional Testing   Simulating the user's experience with the software testing the entire, integrated program.

Integration Testing   Testing functions that have been integrated into a program.

Unit Testing   Testing individual functions.

25

Developing the Text Editor: TBuffer.h, TBuffer.c, TString.h, and Tstring.c

OBJECTIVES

After reading this chapter, you should be able to:

- Implement the text editor files TBuffer.h and TBuffer.c.

- Implement the text editor files TString.h and TString.c.

- Perform automatic cleanup when the editor program exits.

OUTLINE

PREVIEW

This chapter implements the four files TBuffer.h, TBuffer.c, TString.h, and TString.c. As with previous versions of the text editor, TBuffer.h and TBuffer.c provide the definition and implementation of text buffers. TString.h and TString.c define and implement text strings. The code for these files is on the Examples CD included with this book. The code is in the Final subdirectory, which is in the Examples directory.

25.1   Writing TBuffer.h and TBuffer.c

A text buffer contains a collection of text strings. It provides functions for inserting strings into the buffer and operating on them in appropriate ways.

Lines 13–20 of TBuffer.h include the files required for implementing text buffers. Lines 24–37 create an enumerated type which defines the text buffer error codes. The prototypes for the text buffer functions appear on lines 60–102.

Like most C source files, TBuffer.c also begins by including the header files it needs. In addition, it declares the prototype of the `AllocateRows()` function. `AllocateRows()` is called exclusively by functions in the file TBuffer.c. Therefore, it is a `static` function.

The function `TextBufferInitialize()` appears on lines 36–63 of TBuffer.c. It sets a text buffer into a known state so that it can be used by the other text buffer functions.

Lines 67–137 show the function `TextBufferSetRow()`. It requires three parameters. The first is the text buffer whose row will be set. The second specifies the destination row number. The last parameter is the source string from which the characters will be copied.

If the parameter `rowNumber` specifies a row that has already been allocated, the function invokes `TextStringSetFromTextString()` to copy the characters into the text string associated with that row. If the array of text strings is not large enough to include the row number, that row has not been used previously to store characters. Therefore, a text string must be allocated for that row. This is accomplished by allocating a larger array of text strings.

In addition, the lines preceding the specified row may not have a text string associated with them. `TextBufferSetRow()` calls `AllocateRows()`. The `AllocateRows()` function not only allocates a text string for the specified row, but it also allocates text strings for all empty rows prior to the specified row. As a result, once the user types text into a row of the buffer, it and all the rows before it contain a text string.

If `AllocateRows()` is successful at allocating text strings, the `TextBuffer-SetRow()` function copies characters from the source text string into the destination row. Otherwise, an error condition is set. It can be checked by calling `TextBuffer-GetError()`.

Next, the `TextBufferGetRow()` function appears on lines 141–171 of TBuffer.c. It returns the text string contained in the row specified by its `rowNumber` parameter.

The code for the `TextBufferScrollUp()` function is given on lines 175–217. It scrolls the buffer up toward the beginning of the document by decrementing the `topLine` member. If `topLine` becomes less than zero, it is set to zero. Taking this action prevents the user from scrolling to a point before the beginning of the buffer.

The `TextBufferScrollDown()` function, which is on lines 221–257 of TBuffer.c, works in a somewhat similar fashion. It scrolls the buffer by incrementing the `topLine` member of a `text_buffer` structure by the number of rows specified in the `linesTo-Scroll` parameter. It does not prevent the user from scrolling beyond the end of the buffer. When users do, the buffer simply scrolls. If they attempt to enter text into a row beyond the end of the buffer, the `TextBufferSetRow()` function allocates text string for that row and every empty row before it.

The text editor program calls the `TextBufferScrollToBeginning()` and `TextBufferScrollToEnd()` functions, which appear on lines 261–282 and 286–317 respectively, to scroll rapidly to the top and bottom of a text buffer. The `TextBufferGetTo-pLine()` returns the current value of the `topLine` member of a `text_buffer` structure.

The `TextBufferSaveToFile()` function writes the contents of the buffer to a file. On line 385 of TBuffer.c, it tests to determine whether the buffer is dirty. If it is, `TextBufferSaveToFile()` attempts to write the buffer to the file. Otherwise, it does nothing.

To write the buffer to the specified file, `TextBufferSaveToFile()` calls `TextStringCopyAsCharArray()` to convert the file name to a character array. It must do this to be able to pass the file name to the `fopen()` function. The `TextStringCopy-AsCharArray()` allocates memory for the destination character array and copies characters from the text string into the array. It passes the address of the character array back to `TextBufferSaveToFile()` through its second parameter. The `TextBuffer-SaveToFile()` function then becomes responsible for managing that memory. When it no longer uses the character array, `TextBufferSaveToFile()` must delete the memory for it. This is done on line 394 of TBuffer.c.

If `TextBufferSaveToFile()` successfully converts the file name to a character array, it calls `fopen()` on line 392 to open the file. The function tests whether the file was opened on line 398. If the file was not opened, it sets an error status on line 429. There are many possible reasons why the file might not be opened. For example, the user might enter an invalid file name or try to save a file to a read-only drive such as a CD ROM drive.

If `TextBufferSaveToFile()` opened the file, it enters a new code block which begins on line 399 of TBuffer.c. Lines 400–401 declare two variables that are used only in this code block. Variables can be declared at the beginning of any block of code. So any time a program uses an opening brace ({), it is able to declare variables.

This raises a good design question. Should a function's variables be declared at the beginning of a function, or should they be declared only in the code block in which they are used?

The traditional answer to this question has been to declare all variables at the beginning of a function. Example 25.1 illustrates why.

EXAMPLE 25.1   A Potential Declaration Problem

```
1   void AFunction(void)
2   {
3        int i;
4
5        // Some code that uses the variable i goes here.
6
7        if (somethingHappend == TRUE)
8        {
```

```
 9              int i;
10
11              for (i=0;i<1000;i++)
12              {
13                      // Some code that uses the variable i goes here.
14              }
15        }
16  }
```

The function shown in Example 25.1 begins by declaring the variable i. The comment

```
// Some code that uses the variable i goes here.
```

marks the spot where there is some code that uses the variable i. Rather than write in actual code, the comment is used to keep the example uncluttered. The point is that on line 5 of AFunction() there is some code that uses the variable i.

AFunction() continues by entering an if statement on line 7. If the condition evaluates to true, the function begins a new code block. Inside that code block is another variable declaration. The name of the new variable is also i. This is allowed by the rules of the C language. The i inside the if statement on lines 7–15 is not the same i that is used in the rest of the function. This can become very confusing.

Some software designers teach that it is desirable to declare variables as close as possible to where they are used. In fact, it is the preferred practice in C++, C#, and Java. However, because of the possibility of declaring two variables in a function with the same name, this has not traditionally been done by C programmers. All variables have commonly been declared at the beginning of functions and not in any of their nested code blocks.

The style you use is primarily up to you. However, if you do declare variables that are not located at the beginning of functions, it is important to make sure you do not use the same name for two different variables in the same function.

On line 404 of TBuffer.c, the function TextBufferSaveToFile() enters a for loop which attempts to write each row of text in the buffer out to the file. It invokes TextBufferGetRow() to retrieve a row of the text buffer on line 411. This is not strictly necessary. Because this is a text buffer function, it could access the row directly. The advantage of using TextBufferGetRow() is that the TextBufferGetRow() function calls assert() to ensure the row number is valid. This validation comes at the cost of the overhead of a function call. When you are developing software, you often face tradeoffs of this type.

TextBufferSaveToFile() calls TextStringFPutString() to write the row to the specified file. If any of rows of the buffer could not be written to the buffer, TextBufferSaveToFile() sets an error status variable on line 420. It closes the output file on line 423.

The next function in TBuffer.c is TextBufferLoadFromFile(). After using some assertions to prevent programmer errors (lines 474–475), it tries to convert the file name to a character array. If it succeeds, it attempts to open the file. The function then frees the memory allocated for the character array.

If TextBufferLoadFromFile() is able to open the file, it enters a for loop to read each line of text from the file into the buffer. On each iteration of the for loop, TextBufferLoadFromFile() calls TextStringCreate() to allocate an instance of a text string. If the instance is allocated, the function reads a line of text from the text file. On line 514 of TBuffer.c, it calls TextBufferSetRow() to store the text string into the buffer.

Line 522 saves the number of rows of text that were read in from the text file. On line 523, TextBufferLoadFromFile() marks the buffer as dirty. It calls fclose() to close the text file on line 524.

The TextBufferGetBufferLength() and TextBufferGetError() functions simply return the values of the appropriate text_buffer structure members. TextBufferClearError() sets the errorStatus member of a text_buffer structure to TBE_NO_ERROR.

Lines 619–664 of TBuffer.c contain the TextBufferFree() function. The function enters a for loop on line 643. The statement in the loop frees the text string instance

TRAP 25.1
Declaring variables at the beginning of nested code blocks in a function enables programmers to declare two or more variables with the same name.

associated with each row of the buffer. After the loop completes, `TextBufferFree()` releases the memory used by the array of text strings and resets the buffer into its original state.

The final function in TBuffer.c is `AllocateRows()`. This is a `static` function that cannot be seen or called by functions outside TBuffer.c. It invokes the `realloc()` function to make the text buffer's array of text strings larger. If there is enough memory for the larger array, `AllocateRows()` enters a `for` loop on line 704. It uses the loop to create text string instances for each of the new rows of text. On lines 714–717, `AllocateRows()` saves the new array of text strings in the current text buffer. It also stores the new buffer length.

25.2   Writing TString.h and TString.c

As mentioned in Chapter 23, text strings have an internal and an external view. The external view of a text string is presented in TString.h.

After including the files it requires on lines 18–19, TString.h defines an enumerated type for error handling (lines 30–36). On line 47, it uses a `typedef` statement to create a type called `text_string`. The `text_string` type is an alias for the type `instance_identifier`. Variables of type `text_string` will contain the identifier of a text string instance.

TString.h also defines a macro used to determine whether a variable of type `text_string` contains a valid instance identifier. The prototypes for the text string functions appear on lines 66–110. Because a `text_string` is an identifier instead of an instance of a string, most of the `text_string` parameters to these functions are now input only. In most cases, the identifiers do not change even if the contents of the instances do. For this reason, they are input parameters.

TString.c defines the internal view of a text sting. It also contains the implementation of the text string functions. The internal definition of a text string occurs on lines 36–40. This structure contains a pointer to a dynamically allocated array of characters and an integer indicating how many characters have been allocated for the array (including the null character). The text string instance list will contain an array of pointers to `internal_text_string` structures.

On line 51, TString.c uses a macro named `DeclareInstanceList()` to declare an instance list called `stringList`. The macro both declares and initializes `stringList` as a `static` module global variable. It is accessible to all functions in the file TString.c.

TString.c next declares the prototype of the function `FreeCharacters()`. This is a `static` function used only by other functions in TString.c.

Programs call the `TextStringCreate()` function, on lines 68–135, to allocate and initialize an instance of a text string. The text string instance is allocated on lines 102–105. In cases where the user's computer is unable to allocate more memory, `TextStringCreate()` sets the parameter `errorStatus` to the value `TSE_CANT_ALLOCATE_STRING`. If the instance was allocated, `TextStringCreate()` invokes the `InstanceListAddItem()` function to store the text string in the instance list. The `InstanceListAddItem()` function returns the integer identifier of the instance. If, for some reason, `InstanceListAddItem()` was not able to add the text string to the instance list, the `TextStringCreate()` function stores an error value in the `errorStatus` parameter.

On lines 139–227, TString.c contains the function `TextStringSetFromCharArray()`. Programs call this function to copy characters from a character array into a text string. It does this by first retrieving a pointer to the text string instance specified by the parameter `destinationString`. An assertion is used to ensure the instance was retrieved. If it was not, it is a programmer error. Programmers using the text string functions should specify only text strings that are in the instance list. If they pass in an invalid text string identifier, it is a programmer error and not a runtime error. Therefore, it is handled with a call to `assert()`.

Whenever a programmer calls the `TextStringSetFromCharArray()` function, the intent is to store characters in a text string. If the text string already contains characters, they should be overwritten. The easiest way to do this is to free the memory that the characters occupy and reset the text string to an empty state. `TextStringSetFrom`-

CharArray() accomplishes with a call to the static function FreeCharacters(). This ensures that the destination text string is empty when TextStringSetFromCharArray() allocates characters for it.

On line 194 of TString.c, TextStringSetFromCharArray() determines whether the source array of characters is empty. If it is not, TextStringSetFromCharArray() invokes the C Standard Library function strlen() to get the length of the source character array. It then checks whether the length is greater than zero. The function must make this check because it is not safe to assume that the parameter charArray contains characters to copy. Programmers might call the TextStringSetFromCharArray() and pass it an empty string. They do this as a way of clearing characters out of a text string.

If the parameter charArray is an empty string and the text string instance contains characters, the statements on lines 185–191 make the instance empty. If the parameter charArray is an empty string and the text string instance is already empty, the TextStringSetFromCharArray() function does nothing.

If the programmer actually wants to copy characters from charArray into the text string, TextStringSetFromCharArray() allocates memory in the text string instance for the characters. After a successful allocation, TextStringSetFromCharArray() calls strcpy() to copy the characters from the array into the destination text string. It also saves the number of characters it allocates.

In the case of an unsuccessful allocation, TextStringSetFromCharArray() sets the variable errorStatus on line 218. It ends by returning the value in errorStatus.

The TextStringSetFromTextString(), which appears on lines 231–326 of TString.c, follows essentially the same algorithm as TextStringSetFromCharArray(). The primary difference between the two functions is that TextStringSetFromTextString() copies characters from a text string rather than a character array.

Applications use the TextStringSetCharacter() function to set individual characters in a string that has already been allocated. It cannot set characters in an empty string. Neither can it set characters beyond the null character, even if there is memory allocated. If the programmer using TextStringSetCharacter() attempts to set characters before the beginning or after the end of the string, the assert() statement on lines 380–381 of TString.c abort the program. Whenever the programmer specifies an invalid text string identifier, the calls to assert() on lines 370 and 376 abort the program.

To retrieve a character from a text string, programs invoke the TextStringGetCharacter() function. Like TextStringSetCharacter(), TextStringGetCharacter() uses assertions to ensure that the sourceString parameter specifies a valid text string and characterIndex specifies a valid character in the string.

Programmers call TextStringAppendCharacter() to append characters to the end of a text string. It does not matter whether the string is empty or already has characters stored in it. If there is unused space in the text string, TextStringAppendCharacter() puts the new character there. Otherwise, it allocates more memory for the string and store the character in the memory it allocates.

TextStringPrintString() provides programs with the ability to print text strings to stdout. TextStringScanString() reads a text string in from stdin. TextStringFGetString() reads text strings from text files, and TextStringFPutString() writes text strings to text files.

The TextStringGetLength() function calculates and returns the length of a text string. This is different than the number of characters allocated to a string. A text string can contain fewer characters than there are spaces allocated. In fact, it can even be empty and still have memory allocated to it. If the program stores eight characters into a text string (including the null character) and later sets the first character to '\0', then the string will have a length of zero but its charsAllocated member will be eight.

In addition, TString.c contains the TextStringCopyAsCharArray() function on lines 841–917. The purpose of this function is to convert text strings to character arrays. It does this by retrieving a pointer to the source text string from the instance list (lines 886–888), finding its length (line 893), and allocating a character array that is long enough to hold the characters and a null character (lines 896–897). If the memory is allocated, TextStringCopyAsCharArray() copies characters from the text string into the character array. Otherwise, it sets an error status variable.

The address of the character array is stored in the `destinationArray` parameter. Before a program calls `TextStringCopyAsCharArray()`, it declares a variable of type `char *`. When the program calls `TextStringCopyAsCharArray()`, it passes the address of the character pointer variable. Upon return, the character pointer variable will contains a pointer to the array allocated by `TextStringCopyAsCharArray()`. The calling program becomes responsible for that memory. If the program does not free it, there will be a memory leak.

Lines 921–965 of TString.c contain the `TextStringFree()` function. This function removes a text string instance from the instance list and frees the memory it occupies.

Unlike `TextStringFree()`, the `FreeCharacters()` function does not free a text string instance. This `static` function, which appears on lines 969–998, is only available to functions in TString.c. It frees the memory used for the instance's character array and sets the text string to an empty state.

25.3 Troubleshooting Guide

After reading this section, you should be able to:

- Perform automatic cleanup when the program ends.
- Recognize and limit dependencies between program modules.

25.3.1 Using `atexit()` for Automatic Program Cleanup

Whenever techniques involving dynamic memory allocation are used, it is possible for programs to leak memory. The text strings implemented TString.h and TString.c use instance lists containing pointers to dynamically allocated instances of the `internal_text_string` structure. If a program does not call `TextStringFree()` on a text string, there will be a memory leak. The text string instance will remain in the list, but the program may not be able to access it.

With a little extra effort, we can get text strings to clean up after themselves. The C Standard Library provides a function called `atexit()`. This function is called automatically when a program exits. The `atexit()` function calls other functions which perform program cleanup.

The `atexit()` function takes one parameter which is a pointer to a function. In C, it is possible for pointers to contain the addresses of functions. Pointers to functions can be used to call the function. This is a somewhat advanced topic, but one that is highly useful.

To see how this works, we must first create a function in TString.c that will clean up all text string instances in the instance list. The code for it is given in Example 25.2.

EXAMPLE 25.2   The Text String Cleanup Function

```
1    void TextStringCleanupInstanceList(void)
2    {
3          instance_list_size i;
4          internal_text_string *theString = NULL;
5
6          // For every item in the instance list...
7          for (i=0;i<InstanceListGetLength(&stringList);i++)
8          {
9                // Get the item.
10               theString = InstanceListGetItem(&stringList,i);
11
12               // If there was an item with that ID...
13               if ((theString != NULL) &&
14                     (InstanceListGetLastError(
15                           &stringList) == ILE_NO_ERROR))
16               {
17                     TextStringFree(i);
18               }
```

```
19              else
20              {
21                      InstanceListClearError(&stringList);
22              }
23          }
24  }
```

TECHNICAL NOTE 25.1
Because TextString-CleanupInstanceList() is not static, it is possible that functions outside of TString.c can call it using some rather tricky code. This is true even though its prototype is not declared in TString.h. The possibility that a programmer will actually go to that trouble is remote.

The TextStringCleanupInstanceList() function is not static. However, its prototype will go at the beginning of TString.c. This function must not be static, or atexit() will not be able to call it. Because its prototype is not in TString.h, it will not be visible in other files.

Notice that this function is called TextStringCleanupInstanceList(), rather than just CleanupInstanceList(). If text strings get used in another program, it is possible that there will be more than one data type using instance lists. Another programmer on the project might name her cleanup function CleanupInstanceList(). Even though functions outside TString.c may not be able to see TextStringCleanupInstanceList(), the linker can. Because TextStringCleanupInstanceList() is not static, its name must be unique throughout the entire program. To avoid possible name conflicts when linking, this function is named TextStringCleanupInstanceList() instead of CleanupInstanceList().

As Example 25.2 shows, TextStringCleanupInstanceList() uses a for loop to iterate through the instance list. If it finds any text string instances, it deletes them. Notice that it calls the InstanceListClearError() function. If TextString-CleanupInstanceList() calls InstanceListGetItem() and there is no text string at location i in the instance list, InstanceListGetItem() will set the instance list's error status to ILE_ITEM_NOT_FOUND. In this case, that is not an error. If there is no text string at location i, TextStringCleanupInstanceList() should just continue with the next iteration of the loop. Therefore, it clears the error status and continues.

To get the TextStringCleanupInstanceList() function called, the program must call the atexit() function from one of the text string functions. The most likely candidate is TextStringCreate(). The first time the program calls TextStringCreate(), the TextStringCreate() function can invoke atexit(). After it has been called once, atexit() should not be called again by TextStringCreate(). Example 25.3 contains a version of TextStringCreate() that fits these requirements.

EXAMPLE 25.3 Calling atexit()

```
1  text_string TextStringCreate(text_string_error *errorStatus)
2  {
3      text_string theString = -1;
4      internal_text_string *stringInstance = NULL;
5      static boolean beenCalled = FALSE;
6
7      assert(errorStatus);
8
9      // Allocate memory for an internal_text_string.
10     stringInstance =
11         (internal_text_string *)calloc(
12                                 1,
13                                 sizeof(internal_text_string));
14
15     // If the memory was allocated...
16     if (stringInstance != NULL)
17     {
18         // Add the internal_text_string to the instance list.
19         theString =
20             (text_string)InstanceListAddItem(
21                             &stringList,
```

```
22                                     (instance_list_item)stringInstance);
23
24                     // If it was not added...
25                     if ((theString < 0) ||
26                             (InstanceListGetLastError(&stringList) != ILE_NO_ERROR))
27                     {
28                             // Set an error condition.
29                             *errorStatus = TSE_CANT_ALLOCATE_STRING;
30                     }
31             }
32             // Else the memory was not allocated...
33             else
34             {
35                     // Set an error condition.
36                     *errorStatus = TSE_CANT_ALLOCATE_STRING;
37             }
38
39             // If this function has never been called...
40             if (!beenCalled)
41             {
42                     // Set the cleanup function.
43                     atexit(TextStringCleanupInstanceList);
44                     beenCalled = TRUE;
45             }
46
47             return (theString);
48     }
```

Lines 39–45 of Example 25.3 show an `if` statement which tests the variable `been-Called`. This is a `static` variable that is initialized the first time `TextStringCreate()` is called. On all other calls to `TextStringCreate()`, the initialization is not performed.

On the first invocation of `TextStringCreate()`, `beenCalled` is FALSE, so the body of the `if` statement is executed. The `if` statement calls the `atexit()` function. The parameter list of `atexit()` contains the name, `TextStringCleanupInstanceList` with no parentheses. This is how a program obtains the address of a function. That address is passed to `atexit()`, which calls the `TextStringCleanupInstanceList()` function just before the program ends.

The `atexit()` function requires that all cleanup functions it calls return no values. They are also not allowed to have any parameters.

Using this method of calling the `atexit()` function, text strings can protect against possible memory leaks that may occur during program execution.

TECHNICAL NOTE 25.2
Reminder: A .c file and its associated .h file are often referred to as a module of code or a code module.

25.3.2 Examining Program Module Dependencies

Because a text buffer is dependant on text strings, line 16 of TBuffer.h includes TString.h. If we ever decide to use text buffers in another program, we also must use text strings. Software designers say that these files, or code modules, have **high cohesion**.

Having high cohesion between code modules can be a real problem. If a developer writes a program in which most of the modules have high cohesion, it is unlikely that those modules will be reused in other programs. In general, developers try to have few dependancies between modules of source code.

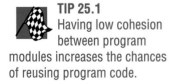

TIP 25.1
Having low cohesion between program modules increases the chances of reusing program code.

In the text editor, there is high cohesion between text buffers and text strings. There is also high cohesion between text strings and instance lists. As a result, any program which uses the files TBuffer.h and TBuffer.c also must use TString.h, TString.c, InstList.h, and InstList.c. This is not a large number of files and would generally not be considered a problem. Every program will contain some modules that are interdependent, causing cohesion.

Even though there is high cohesion between text buffers and text strings, the reverse is not true. Text strings can be included in any program without using text buffers. The same relationship exists between text strings and instance lists. To use text strings, instance lists also must be in the program. However, using instance lists does not require the use of text strings.

This relationship demonstrates that the text editor program is reasonably well designed. More complex types, such as text buffers, may depend on the presence of less complex types. The less complex types are the building blocks of the program. They do not depend on the presence of more complex types.

SUMMARY

Text buffers and text strings are two of the primary building blocks of the text editor program. As much as possible, they encapsulate their data and hide their implementations.

Using the `atexit()` function programs and program modules to perform cleanup tasks decreases the likelihood of errors such as memory leaks.

TECHNICAL NOTES

25.1   Because `TextStringCleanupInstanceList()` is not `static`, it is possible that functions outside of TString.c can call it using some rather tricky code. This is true even though its prototype is not declared in TString.h. The possi-

bility that a programmer will actually go to that trouble is remote.

25.2   Reminder: A .C file and its associated .H file are often referred to as a module of code or a code module.

TIP

25.1   Having low cohesion between program modules increases the chances of reusing program code.

TRAP

25.1   Declaring variables at the beginning of nested code blocks in a function enables programmers to declare two or more variables with the same name.

REVIEW QUESTIONS

1. In this chapter, text strings are implemented with an instance list, but the text buffer is not. Why do you think that is?

2. Is the list of text buffer functions both minimal and complete? What are the reasons for your opinion?

3. Is the list of text string functions both minimal and complete? What are the reasons for your opinion?

4. TString.h defines the `TextStringIsValid()` macro to validate text string identifiers. What other tests could be performed to validate text string identifiers?

5. If the function `TextStringCreate()` were to call the `atexit()` function, as suggested in Section 25.3.1, it would execute the `if` statement on line 40 of Example 25.3 every time it creates a text string. It would only execute the body of the `if` once. However, it would perform the test every time it was called. How do you think this would affect program performance? Is this effect significant enough to keep you from using the technique? Why or why not?

6. The `TextStringSetCharacter()` function stores a character into a text string. However, it will not assign characters to locations that are beyond the null character. The `TextStringAppendCharacter()` puts characters

onto the end of a string. Should there be a function in the text string interface that enables a programmer to set any character, anywhere in the string, regardless of the string's length? Why or why not?

7. What would happen if a program passed `stdin` as the second parameter to `TextStringFGetString()`? Would this work? Why or why not? What do you think this says about the function's design?

8. Another way to implement the `TextStringCopy-AsCharArray()` function is to have it return the address in the `charArray` member of the `internal_text_string` function. That way, no additional memory allocation need be done. Do you think this is a better approach to the task? Why or why not?

9. Should the `AllocateRows()` function in TBuffer.c be renamed to `TextBufferAllocateRows()` and be made available to functions outside of TBuffer.c? Why or why not?

10. Should the `FreeCharacters()` function in TString.c be renamed to `TextStringFreeCharacters()` and be made available to functions outside TString.c? Why or why not?

EXERCISES

1. Indicate which of the following are false and why.
   a. It is never good to have low cohesion between program modules.
   b. It is always good to have low cohesion between program modules.
   c. Cohesion between program modules is not important.
   d. Cohesion between unrelated program modules is never good.

2. Explain why dependencies between modules can decrease code reuse.

3. Type the following program into your program editor or IDE. Compile, link, and run it. Explain the results.

```
1   #include <stdio.h>
2   #include <stdlib.h>
3
4   void One(void);
5   void Two(void);
6   void Three(void);
7
8
9   int main()
10  {
11          printf("The order these functions are called ");
12          printf("in is:\n");
13          atexit(One);
14          atexit(Two);
15          atexit(Three);
16          return (0);
17  }
18
19
20  void One(void)
21  {
22          printf("One\n");
23  }
24
25
26  void Two(void)
27  {
28          printf("Two\n");
29  }
30
31
32  void Three(void)
33  {
34          printf("Three\n");
35  }
```

4. Make a list of at least five tests that should be performed on the `TextBufferSetRow()` function to ensure that it works correctly.

5. Make a list of at least five tests that should be performed on the `TextBufferGetRow()` function to ensure that it works correctly.

6. Make a list of at least five tests that should be performed on the `TextStringCopyAsCharArray()` function to ensure that it works correctly.

7. Make a list of at least five tests that should be performed on the `TextStringAppendCharacter()` function to ensure that it works correctly.

8. Most text editors have a File menu in which the user can save a file to the current file name or save it to another file name. Typically, these choices are called **Save** and **Save As**. Modify the text editor program to display a File menu in the main menu. It should contain the choices **Load**, **Save**, **Save As**, and **Quit**. Implement the **Save** and **Save As** options. When users select **Save**, and the file name is empty, prompt them for a file name. Add a new member to the `text_buffer`

structure called `fileName`. Once the file name is obtained, store it in `fileName`. If the user selects **Save** again, save the buffer to the same file name. If they choose **Save As**, prompt for and retrieve a new file name. Save the new file name in `fileName` and use it as the destination file name for any further saves.

9. In TBuffer.c, the funciton `TextBufferSetRow()` doesn't validate its `text_string` parameter. Modify the program so that it does this. Explain whether you think this test is important, and why.

10. TString.c contains a magic number. The value –1 appears on line 96. Tell whether you think this value should be replaced with a constant or left as it is. Give your reasons. If you were to replace it with a constant, explain where in the program you would define the constant.

11. Whenever a text buffer is altered, it should be marked as dirty. However, the `TextBufferSetRow()` function in TBuffer.c does not mark the buffer as dirty after it changes the buffer's contents. Modify the program so that it does.

12. The `TextBufferLoadFromFile()` in TBuffer.c does not check to see if the buffer is dirty. Modify the program so that it does. If buffer is dirty, ask the user if it should be saved before the file is loaded. If the answer is yes, save the contents of the buffer.

13. The `TextBufferSaveToFile()` function saves the buffer to a file even if the file already exists. With this implementation, it is easy for a user to accidentally overwrite a file. Modify `TextBufferSaveToFile()` so that it checks whether the file already exists. If so, have the function ask whether the user wants to overwrite the existing text or append to the end of it and overwrite or append as the user instructs.

14. Most text editors have an Edit menu containing the choices **Copy**, **Cut**, and **Paste**. The **Copy** selection copies a line of text into a what is called a *scrap buffer*. Modify the text editor to display an Edit menu in the main menu. When **Edit** is chosen from the main menu, have the program display a menu with the **Copy**, **Cut**, and **Paste** selections. Add a member of type `text_string` to the `text_buffer` structure called `scrapBuffer`. When the user selects **Copy** from the **Edit** menu, have the program ask for the number of the row to copy. If the row number is valid, copy that row of text into the scrap buffer.

15. Most text editors have an Edit menu containing the choices **Copy**, **Cut**, and **Paste**. The **Copy** selection copies a line of text into a what is called a *scrap buffer*. Modify the text editor to display an Edit menu in the main menu. When **Edit** is chosen from the main menu, have the program display a menu with the **Copy**, **Cut**, and **Paste** selections. Add a member of type `text_string` to the `text_buffer` structure called `scrapBuffer`. When the user selects **Cut** from the **Edit** menu, have the program ask for the number of the row to cut. If the row number is valid, copy that row of text into the scrap buffer and remove it from the text buffer.

16. Most text editors have an Edit menu containing the choices **Copy**, **Cut**, and **Paste**. The **Copy** selection copies a line of text into a what is called a *scrap buffer*. Modify the text editor to display an Edit menu in the main menu. When **Edit** is chosen from the main menu, have the program display a menu with the **Copy**, **Cut**, and **Paste** selections. Add a member of type `text_string` to the `text_buffer` structure called `scrapBuffer`. When the user selects **Paste** from the **Edit** menu, have the ask for the number of the row to paste. If the row number is valid, begin at the specified row and move all of the text strings in the buffer down one row. Copy the text string from the scrap buffer into the specified row.

17. There are at least two other checks that the `TextStringIsValid()` function in TString.c should perform to determine whether the text string instance identifier is valid. Make `TextStringIsValid()` a function rather than a macro and perform these additional checks.

18. Explain whether you think the use of `atexit()` as presented in Section 25.3.1 in this chapter is worthwhile. Give detailed reasons for your thinking.

19. The functions in the files TBuffer.c and TString.c do not contain enough error checking. Add any error checking you think is missing. Hint: `TextBufferSaveToFile()` and `TextBufferLoadFromFile()` do not assert that their `fileName` parameters are valid text strings. Look for other errors of this type.

20. There is a mistake in the function `TextBufferScrollDown()` in TBuffer.c. Explain what the mistake is and fix the function.

GLOSSARY

High Cohesion   Program modules with high cohesion must be used together. They are dependant on one another.

26

Developing the Text Editor: InstList.h, InstList.c, MiscType.h, and Platform.h

OBJECTIVES

After reading this chapter, you should be able to:

- Implement the text editor files InstList.h and InstList.c.

- Implement the text editor files MiscType.h and Platform.h.

- Summarize and explain the programming skills you've acquired through the text editor project.

OUTLINE

PREVIEW

This chapter wraps up the development of the text editor and provides an opportunity to summarize the skills and techniques presented in this book. To aid in that summary, the final section contains a project post-mortem rather than a Summary section and a Troubleshooting Guide.

26.1   Writing InstList.h and InstList.c

The file InstList.h, which is on the Examples CD, contains the definition of the instance_list type, as well as other types, constants, and prototypes needed for use with instance lists.

As with the other primary programmer-defined types in the text editor program, the instance_list type includes an enumerated type containing the error codes for instance lists. This enumeration appears on lines 17–23 of InstList.h. The file also provides the definitions of the types instance_list_size, instance_identifier, and instance_list_item. The actual definition of the instance_list type is on lines 39–44. Its itemArray member is used to point at a dynamically allocated array of items in the list. The listLength member specifies the number of items allocated for itemArray. The errorStatus member stores the list's current error status.

InstList.h defines the macro DeclareInstanceList() on lines 56–60. This macro was used in TString.c to declare and initialize the text string instance list. On lines 68–93, InstList.h provides the prototypes for the instance list functions. The code for the instance list functions can be found in InstList.c.

Lines 28–112 of InstList.c define the InstanceListAddItem() function. On lines 64–73, InstanceListAddItem() scans for an empty spot in the list. If it finds an unused location in the array, it adds the item in that location on line 105. If the list has not yet been allocated, or the list is full, the for loop will not find an empty spot in the array. In that case, it calculates the new size of the list and allocates an array of that size (lines 78–81). If the program is able to allocate memory for the list, it saves the new list in the itemArray of the instance_list structure on line 86. It adds the new item to the list on line 89. On line 90 of InstList.c, InstanceListAddItem() saves the identifier of the item. When InstanceListAddItem() ends, it returns this value. InstanceListAddItem() grows the list one item at a time. As a result, the size of the list is always incremented by one (line 92).

The next function in InstList.c is `InstanceListGetItem()`. This function retrieves the specified list item. As the definition of the type `instance_list_item` shows, all list items are really pointers of type `void *`. The `InstanceListGetItem()` function returns the specified item's pointer without removing it from the list. This enables programs to perform operations on items in the list. If there is not an item in the array location specified by the `itemID` parameter, `InstanceListGetItem()` sets the `errorStatus` member of the instance list to `ILE_ITEM_NOT_FOUND`.

Programs call the `InstanceListGetLength()` function, which is shown on lines 175–197 of InstList.c, to retrieve the number of items allocated for the instance list.

The `InstanceListRemoveItem()` function appears on lines 201–249. It retrieves an item from the list and returns it to the program. The function also sets the array location occupied by the item to `NULL`, removing it from the list.

`InstanceListGetLastError()`, on lines 253–276 of InstList.c, returns the value in an instance list's `errorStatus` member. The `InstanceListClearError()` function clears the error status by setting `errorStatus` to `ILE_NO_ERROR`.

26.2   Writing Platform.h and MiscType.h

Both Platform.h and MiscType.h are extremely short files. Platform.h defines constants which indicate the type of computer and operating system for which the text editor is being compiled. The code given in Chapters 24–26 works on IBM-compatible PCs under MS DOS, or in a DOS box under Windows. It also runs on most versions of Unix, including Linux. In addition, it will work in a console window on a Unix- or Linux-based GUI.

MiscType.h defines the type `boolean`, as well as the constants `TRUE` and `FALSE`.

26.3   Project Post-Mortem

Whenever we as developers end a project, it's good to look back and determine what we've learned through writing the program we've just completed.

Writing the text editor gave experience in writing a complete program, rather than just a series of small examples. While building the various components of the editor, you've had the opportunity to declare variables of atomic data types. You've also declared used variables of programmer-defined types. The editor required the use of many of the flow control statements C provides.

The text editor project provided the opportunity to become proficient with arrays, strings, and string-handling functions. It gave the chance to use various techniques to encapsulate data and hide the implementation of data types. The methods of encapsulation and implementation hiding presented in this book lead very naturally to those used in object-oriented programming. Learning languages such as C++, C#, and Java should be very straightforward as a result of becoming conversant in these techniques.

In addition, you've seen some of the power and flexibility of the C preprocessor, as well as the benefits of using it. In implementing the editor, you've used both static and dynamic memory allocation. You've had practice with pointers, which are often a source of problems for even experienced C programmers. The editor also provided a chance to practice with the C Standard Library file input and output functions.

The text editor project demonstrated structured design and programming techniques. Every programmer-defined type was planned using top-down design. The functions required for these types were determined and implemented. Each of the primary programmer-defined types were organized into a pair of .h and .c files, as they should be in professional programs. The highest-level logic of the program appeared in the file containing the `main()` function.

The questions and exercises at the end of the chapters in this book gave an opportunity to analyze the implementation of the text editor. You've had a chance to look closely at the strengths and weaknesses of the code presented here. The mistakes you've seen in the program were included intentionally. They are representative of the mistakes we all make as software developers.

In addition to learning C programming, the text editor project provided the opportunity to design, develop, test, and debug software. You now should be familiar enough with the basics of software design to create robust software in C. It takes much more than just an understanding of the C programming language. You should also be familiar with the essentials of software testing.

During each phase of creating the text editor, there were choices to be made. Some techniques are simpler to write and debug but require more memory or are slower than others. Others are more complex but result in faster or smaller software. Some methods, such as instance lists, require more effort to implement but provide greater type safety and integrity of data. Often, you will have to decide which is more important, program size or speed. Professional programmers are constantly faced with these types of decisions. As professional developers, we need to understand as many techniques and methods for writing software as possible. We also must be able to state clear reasons for using the ones we choose in a particular program. This ability makes you valuable to an employer. It is easier to find people who have C language skills than it is to find people who understand software implementation issues and can make sound decisions about them. Looking for opportunities to acquire that understanding will help propel your software development career forward.

This book stressed that much of programming style is a matter of convention. There are reasons for following conventions and reasons for breaking them. Whichever we do when we write software, we should do it with some forethought and not offhandedly.

There are far more tools available to you as a developer than can be presented in one book. The more tools and techniques that you can use and use well, the more likely you are to be successful in your job. To be true masters the art of software development, you and I need to always be studying our craft. The software industry never stays still, and neither must we.

On a personal level, it is my hope as the author that this book will help you on your way to a successful career as a software engineer.

REVIEW QUESTIONS

1. What do you think of the user interface of the text editor? How could it be improved?

2. Do you think that text strings should be implemented with an instance list? Why or why not?

3. Should the text buffer be implemented using an instance list? Why or why not?

4. What are some of the advantages of using instance lists?

5. What are some of the disadvantages of using instance lists?

6. What are the advantages of having the portability constants defined in Platform.h rather than somewhere else in the program? What are the disadvantages?

7. Should MistType.h and Platform.h be combined into one file? Why or why not?

8. In addition to C language proficiency, what other skills do programmers need in order to be hired as a professional developer?

9. The text editor program contains extensive comments. What are some reasons comments might be important in a program? What does the presence of these comments indicate to you about developing good writing skills?

10. What skills do you think are important for testing and debugging software?

EXERCISES

1. In InstList.c, the `InstanceListAddItem()` function doesn't validate the parameter `theItem`. Modify this function so that the parameter is validated.

2. The `InstanceListGetItem()` and `InstanceListRemoveItem()` functions in InstList.c both use `if` statements to validate their parameters called `itemID`. Explain whether you think this implementation is correct. Specifically, discuss whether you think this should be handled as a programmer error or a runtime error. Give precise reasons for your thinking.

3. In the function `InstanceListRemoveItem()`, it is possible that a programmer may pass in through the `itemID` parameter the identifier of an empty location in the list. As a result, it is possible to call `InstanceListRemoveItem()` and get back a NULL pointer as the return value. Fix this error in the way you think most appropriate. Explain why you chose the implementation you did.

4. Examine each of the instance list functions. Find any that do not validate their parameters as they should. Modify the functions so that the validations are performed.

5. Implement the `text_buffer` type using an instance list. Enable the editor to declare an array of buffers. Modify the user interface so that the user is able to edit more than one document at a time and switch between buffers.

6. Explain how you can tell the difference between programmer errors and runtime errors.

7. Design five tests that you think should be performed on the `InstanceListAddItem()` function in InstList.c. Write a program to perform these tests. Describe the results.

8. Design five tests that you think should be performed on the `InstanceListGetItem()` function in InstList.c. Write a program to perform these tests. Describe the results.

9. Design five tests that you think should be performed on the `InstanceListRemoveItem()` function in InstList.c. Write a program to perform these tests. Describe the results.

10. Design fifteen functional tests that you think should be performed on the text editor program. Perform the tests and explain your results.

11. Explain at least two techniques for preventing memory leaks in C programs that use dynamic allocation.

12. Out of all of the C language skills that you learned from this book, describe the ones that you think are the most important. Give the reasons for their importance.

13. Out of all of the C language skills that you learned from this book, describe the ones that you think are the most difficult. Explain how you can make these tasks more manageable.

14. Out of all of the software design skills that you learned from this book, describe the ones that you think are the most important. Give the reasons for their importance.

15. Out of all of the software testing skills that you learned from this book, describe the ones that you think are the most important. Give the reasons for their importance.

16. Out of all of the error handling skills that you learned from this book, describe the ones that you think are the most important. Give the reasons for their importance.

17. Out of all of the data encapsulation and implementation hiding skills that you learned from this book, describe the ones that you think are the most important. Give the reasons for their importance.

18. Explain some of the stylistic techniques use in programming that were discussed in this book. Present both the most common style and at least one alternative. Tell which you prefer and why.

19. Make a list of techniques presented in this book that were specifically mentioned as helping prepare you for programming with object oriented languages and GUIs.

20. Go to your school or local library, and make a list of at least five good sources of information on software design. Also make a list of at least five good sources of information on software testing. Finally, make a list of five periodicals devoted to programming in C, C++, C#, or Java.

27

Moving to C++, C#, and Java

OBJECTIVES

After reading this chapter, you should be able to:

- Name and explain the most fundamental concepts associated with object-oriented programming.

- Evaluate when it is appropriate to use C++, C#, or Java for a programming project.

OUTLINE

PREVIEW

One of the greatest legacies of the C programming language is the fact that it is the basis for other popular languages. This chapter provides an overview of three such languages: C++, Java, and C#.

27.1   C as the Basis for Other Languages

There was a time when most new programs were being written in C. That is no longer the case. These days, C is used primarily by those programming hardware.

However, C is such a solid programming language that it is the direct ancestor of the most popular programming languages in use today. At the time this writing, most new programs are being written in C++, Java, and C# (pronounced "C sharp"). We'll take a brief look at each of these languages in turn. All three of these programming languages are derived directly from C. Each adds its own unique and powerful ideas to the foundation provided by the C programming language. This enduring foundation is a tribute to those who originally created C.

27.2   C++

Like C, the C++ programming language came out of Bell Labs. It was originally written by Bjarne Stroustrup in the early 1980s. C++ shares the same essential language syntax as C. In fact, C programs can be compiled with any C++ compiler.

The C++ language extends C by adding **object-oriented programming language** features. The development style used in this book demonstrates many object-oriented principles. Recall that past chapters demonstrated how to create new types with member data. They showed how to create an API for each type and completely encapsulate the type's data through the use of instance lists.

C++ provides these same capabilities and more. In C++, they are easier to use because they are built right into the language. Through the use of **classes**, C++ enables developers to create data types that are **software objects**. These software objects have both member data *and member functions*. The member functions form the object's API, and they provide the means for operating on the data in the object. For the most part, only the member functions can directly access the member data. This helps maintain the consistency and validity of the data in the object.

Example 27.1 illustrates C++ objects through the use of classes. As the example shows, defining a class is very much like defining a C structure. The primary difference is that C++ classes enable you to use the keywords `public` and `private` to specify the scope of the members of the class. Members declared `public` can be accessed by any part of the program. Only member functions can access data members that are declared as `private`. Like most C++ classes, the `point_2d` class declares its member data as `private`. The member functions are `public`.

EXAMPLE 27.1   A C++ Class Definition

```
1   typedef int point_component;
2   class point_2d
3   {
4       public:
5               point_2d();
6               point_d2(point_component xValue, point_component yValue);
7
8               void X(point_component xValue);
9               point_component X();
10
11              void Y(point_component yValue);
12              point_component Y();
13
14      private:
15              point_component x,y;
16  };
```

This sample class demonstrates several important features of C++. As previously mentioned, it combines member data an API of functions into a single software object. Access to each is clearly specified.

In addition, the class demonstrates the use of **constructors**. A constructor is a function that initializes an object into a known state whenever the program creates the object. As you can see, there are prototypes for two constructors for the `point_2d` class. The two constructors have different prototypes. The first takes no parameters, and the second takes two. The ability to have two functions with the same name in a class is called **overloading**. Almost all functions can be overloaded in C++. The `point_2d` class overloads the constructors and the member functions.

At first, features such as overloading may seem somewhat confusing. For instance, it may be unclear why there are two functions called X() and two called Y(). Looking at their prototypes helps clear things up. The first X() function returns `void` and takes an x value as a parameter. Because it takes a parameter and returns nothing, its purpose is to copy the x value passed into the member function into the class's data member called x. The second X() function takes no parameters and returns a value. Its purpose is to retrieve an x value from the class's data member called x. This same pattern is used for the data member called y.

In addition to encapsulation and overloading, C++ provides a method of extending and reusing programmer-defined types called **inheritance**. Example 27.2 provides an illustration of inheritance.

EXAMPLE 27.2   Using Inheritance

```
1   class point_3d : public class_2d
2   {
3       public:
4               point_3d();
5               point_3d(point_component xValue,
6                        point_component yValue,
7                        point_component zValue);
8
9               void Z(point_component zValue);
```

```
10            point_component Z(void);
11
12       private:
13            point_component z;
14  };
```

The `point_3d` class in Example 27.2 inherits all of the member data and functions of the `point_2d` class from Example 27.1. Therefore, it is not necessary to declare the x and y data members in the `point_3d` class. They are already there. Likewise, the `point_3d` class inherits the X() and Y() functions. The only additions to be made are those that extend the class for the z direction.

Although this is just a small sampling of the features of C++, it demonstrates some of its power and extensibility. In fact, experience with C++ has shown that it is more powerful and extensible than almost any other object-oriented language. However, of all of the derivatives of C, it is probably the most complex to learn and use. In addition, it can be extremely difficult to debug in some circumstances. In spite of these drawbacks, it is the language of choice for developers of high performance applications.

27.3   Java

The Java programming language was invented at Sun Microsystems in 1991. It rapidly became the language of preference for Internet application development. Java eliminates some of the complexities of C++. Developers generally find it easier to debug. To date, however, it has not been demonstrated that Java is as flexible and efficient as C or C++.

TECHNICAL NOTE 27.1
Java was originally developed with portability in mind. It was often touted as a way to "write a program once, and run it anywhere." Although that was a great goal, it proved harder to achieve than originally thought. Even so, Java is far more portable than any of the C language derivatives that came before it.

One of the great things about Java is that it is far more portable than C or C++. Java programs can often run on many different types of computers and operating systems *without being changed in any way*. This cannot be said for *all* Java programs, but it is true for many of them.

Java gets its portability from the fact that it does not compile its programs to executable code. Instead, it compiles to **bytecode**. Bytecode is a machine-independent format. It cannot be executed directly on any computer. Bytecode programs run on the Java Virtual Machine (JVM). The JVM interprets each line of bytecode and executes it, line by line. Hardware and operating systems manufacturers implement the JVM for their particular types of computers or operating systems. To Java programs, virtually all JVMs look exactly alike. As a result, a single Java program can run on most JVMs.

Java shares much of the syntax of C and C++. Programmers who know C and C++ generally find it easy to learn Java. The Java language provides greater object orientation than C++ by emphasizing the notion of a class. In Java, virtually everything is a class, including the program itself.

One of the strengths of Java is that it does not suffer from the memory management headaches that are common in C and C++. Java handles most memory management tasks for you. However, it does so at a price. Java programs are seldom as fast or as efficient as C++ programs.

27.4   C#

A recent addition to the C family of languages is C#, invented and published by the Microsoft Corporation. The Java programming language was invented at Sun Microsystems, and to a great degree, Sun still controls the language specifications. C# is Microsoft's response. Microsoft hopes that C# will become the dominant language for web development. Whether it does or not, it will undoubtedly be an important development language.

Like Java, C# programs are not compiled to an executable format. They are compiled to Microsoft Intermediate Language (MSIL). Programs in MSIL are interpreted on a virtual machine called the Common Language Runtime (CLR).

C# contains most of the same features as Java. In addition, it is compatible with Microsoft's new .NET (pronounced "dot net") Framework. The .NET Framework is intended to

TECHNICAL NOTE 27.2 Developers often call the familiar problems associated with program components "DLL hell." DLL stands for dynamic link library. DLLs are intended to be highly reusable program modules that can be shared by many programs. Unfortunately, when one program upgrades a DLL, it often breaks other programs that share the same DLL. C# is designed to reduce such problems.

enable developers to rapidly create and deploy applications. Its features should help decrease or completely solve problems associated with upgrading the components of a program.

In C#, absolutely everything is an object. If developers do not declare their data as objects, C# uses a technique called **boxing** to silently package it as one or more objects. Fortunately, this is invisible to you and I. When we need our atomic data types to be objects, they are. When we need them to be an atomic data type again, C# uses **unboxing** to convert it back.

To enable components written in C# to access existing program components, C# adds the concepts of **managed** and **unmanaged code**. Managed code is executed securely by the CLR. The CLR passes unmanaged code directly to the computer for executing. This means older program components can be run from a C# program as unmanaged code. However, doing so sacrifices all of the security features built into C#.

Although it is not as fast or flexible as C or C++, C# is at least as efficient and flexible as Java. Like Java, it is well suited to programs for the World Wide Web. It is also extremely good for developing programs that access databases.

SUMMARY

Because of its efficiency and flexibility, the C programming language is the basis of other popular computer languages. In particular, C++, Java, and C# are all derived from C. All three of these languages support object-oriented extensions to C. Each has its own advantages and disadvantages.

TECHNICAL NOTES

27.1 Java was originally developed with portability in mind. It was often touted as a way to "write a program once, and run it anywhere." Although that was a great goal, it proved harder to achieve than originally thought. Even so, Java is far more portable than any of the C language derivatives that came before it.

27.2 Java was originally developed with portability in mind. It was often touted as a way to "write a program once, and run it anywhere." Although that was a great goal, it proved harder to achieve than originally thought. Even so, Java is far more portable than any of the C language derivatives that came before it.

GLOSSARY

Boxing   A method of packaging atomic data types as objects.

Bytecode   A set of platform-independent instructions into which programs can be compiled. They must be executed by a virtual machine designed for the particular hardware and operating system.

Class   A way of defining types that creates software objects. Classes support encapsulation, polymorphism (overloading), and inheritance. They define class data and an interface of class member functions (often called methods).

Constructor   A special type of member function that initializes an object into a known state.

Inheritance   A method of reusing objects by deriving a new class from an existing class.

Managed Code   Code that is executed by the Common Language Runtime, and therefore takes advantage of its security and memory management features.

Object-Oriented Programming Language   Languages that support object oriented programming concepts such as encapsulation, polymorphism (overloading), and inheritance.

Overloading   Creating two or more functions that share the same name but have different prototypes.

Software Objects   Reusable software components that contain data and define an interface of member functions that perform operations on the data.

Unboxing   A method of converting boxed data back into its atomic type.

Unmanaged Code   Program instructions that are not executed by the Common Language Runtime. Instead, they are passed onto the computer and operating system to be executed directly.

Appendix A

Installing and Using Visual C++

Visual C++ Special Edition

This book ships with two CD ROMs. One of them is a special edition of the Visual C++ 6.0 by Microsoft Corporation. This compiler has all of the functionality you would normally expect with a full-featured C/C++ compiler. You can use it to develop programs for non-commercial use.

Like all ANSI-compatible C++ compilers, Visual C++ compiles C programs. All of the programs in this book have been tested with this compiler.

Installing VC++

Installing Visual C++ is straightforward. Insert the VC++ CD into your CD ROM drive. If the installation program does not execute automatically, use the following procedure.

1. Click your **Start** menu and choose **Run**.
2. In the dialog box that appears, type
   ```
   <d>:\Setup
   ```
   where <d> represents the letter of your CD ROM drive.
3. Press Enter. The setup program should begin.

Using VC++

Before you can write a C program in Visual C++, you must create a project. To do so, use the following steps.

1. From the main menu of the Visual C++ program, select **File**.
2. Choose **New** from the **File** menu.
3. In the dialog box that appears, you will see a tabbed page. If the **Projects** tab is not uppermost, click on the **Projects** tab.
4. In the list of project types, select **Win32 Console Application**.

5. Type the name of the project in the **Project Name** box.
6. Select the directory for the project in the **Location** box. Click the **OK** button.
7. In the dialog box that appears, select **An empty project**, and click **Finish**.

At this point, you must create a new file and add it to your project. To create a new file, do the following.

1. From the Visual C++ **File** menu, select **New**.
2. In the dialog box that appears, click **C/C++ header file** to create a header (.h) file. Alternatively, select C++ source file to create a C source (.c) file.
3. Type the name and extension of the .h or .c file into the box labeled **File Name**. Click **OK**.

Now that you have a project and a file, you must insert the file into the project. To accomplish this task, use the following steps.

1. From the Visual C++ **Project** menu, select **Add to Project**.
2. Choose **File**.
3. Use the **Insert Files into Project** dialog box to find and select the name of the file to add. Click **OK**.

Compiling with VC++

To compile your C program in Visual C++, press the F5 key. Alternatively, select **Build** in the Visual C++ **Build** menu.

Other Compilers

You should be able to use any ANSI-compatible C compiler to compile the programs in this book. For example, you can use the C/C++ compiler from the Gnu Compiler Collection. You can find more information about the Gnu GCC project at the GCC home page on the World Wide Web, which is http://www.gcc.gnu.org/.

The Open Source community has created a special version of GCC that compiles programs for DOS and Windows. To find out more about it see

http://www.nanotech. wisc.edu/~khan/software/gnu-win32/index.html.

In addition, you can download and install GUI-based IDEs and debuggers from the Internet. You'll find a list of them at

http://www.nanotech.wisc.edu/~khan/software/gnu-win32/ide-and-gui.html.

Appendix B

The ASCII Character Set

Character	Decimal Value	Hexadecimal Value	Represents
NUL	0	0x00	Null character
SOH	1	0x01	^A
STX	2	0x02	^B
ETX	3	0x03	^C
EOT	4	0x04	^D
ENQ	5	0x05	^E
ACK	6	0x06	^F
BEL	7	0x07	^G, Rings bell or beeps speaker
BS	8	0x08	^H, Backspace
HT	9	0x09	^I, Tab
LF	10	0x0A	^J, Linefeed
VT	11	0x0B	^K, Vertical tab
FF	12	0x0C	^L. Form feed
CR	13	0x0D	^M, Carriage Return
SO	14	0x0E	^N
SI	15	0x0F	^O
DLE	16	0x10	^P
DC1	17	0x11	^Q
DC2	18	0x12	^R
DC3	19	0x13	^S
DC4	20	0x14	^T
NAK	21	0x15	^U
SYN	22	0x16	^V
ETB	23	0x17	^W
CAN	24	0x18	^X
EM	25	0x19	^Y
SUB	26	0x1A	^Z
ESC	27	0x1B	Escape
FS	28	0x1C	^/
GS	29	0x1D	^]
RS	30	0x1E	^=
US	31	0x1F	^-

Character	Decimal Value	Hexadecimal Value	Represents
SP	32	0x20	Spacebar
!	33	0x21	!
"	34	0x22	"
#	35	0x23	#
$	36	0x24	$
%	37	0x25	%
&	38	0x26	&
'	39	0x27	'
(	40	0x28	(
)	41	0x29	)
*	42	0x2A	*
+	43	0x2B	+
,	44	0x2C	,
-	45	0x2D	-
	46	0x2E	.
/	47	0x2F	/
0	48	0x30	0
1	49	0x31	1
2	50	0x32	2
3	51	0x33	3
4	52	0x34	4
5	53	0x35	5
6	54	0x36	6
7	55	0x37	7
8	56	0x38	8
9	57	0x39	9
:	58	0x3A	:
;	59	0x3B	;
<	60	0x3C	<
=	61	0x3D	=
>	62	0x3E	>
?	63	0x3F	?
@	64	0x40	@
A	65	0x41	A
B	66	0x42	B
C	67	0x43	C
D	68	0x44	D
E	69	0x45	E
F	70	0x46	F
G	71	0x47	G
H	72	0x48	H
I	73	0x49	I
J	74	0x4A	J
K	75	0x4B	K
L	76	0x4C	L
M	77	0x4D	M
N	78	0x4E	N
O	79	0x4F	O
P	80	0x50	P
Q	81	0x51	Q
R	82	0x52	R
S	83	0x53	S
T	84	0x54	T
U	85	0x55	U
V	86	0x56	V
W	87	0x57	W
X	88	0x58	X
Y	89	0x59	Y
Z	90	0x5A	Z

(continued on next page)

Character	Decimal Value	Hexadecimal Value	Represents
[	91	0x5B	[
\	92	0x5C	\
]	93	0x5D	]
^	94	0x5E	^
_	95	0x5F	_
`	96	0x60	`
a	97	0x61	a
b	98	0x62	b
c	99	0x63	c
d	100	0x64	d
e	101	0x65	e
f	102	0x66	f
g	103	0x67	g
h	104	0x68	h
i	105	0x69	i
j	106	0x6A	j
k	107	0x6B	k
l	108	0x6C	l
m	109	0x6D	m
n	110	0x6E	n
o	111	0x6F	o
p	112	0x70	p
q	113	0x71	q
r	114	0x72	r
s	115	0x73	s
t	116	0x74	t
u	117	0x75	u
v	118	0x76	v
w	119	0x77	w
x	120	0x78	x
y	121	0x79	y
z	122	0x7A	z
{	123	0x7B	}
		124	0x7C		
}	125	0x7D	}
~	126	0x7E	~
DEL	127	0x7F	Delete

Appendix C

Operator Precedence in C

Level	Operator	Associativity	Operation
1	()	L-R*	Call function or force precedence.
	[ ]	L-R	Array subscript.
	->	L-R	Indirection membership (pointer).
	.	L-R	Direct membership.
2	+	R-L	Unary plus (positive sign).
	-	R-L	Unary minus (negative sign).
	~	R-L	Negate bits (one's complement).
	!	R-L	Logical negation (logical not).
	++	R-L	Increment (pre- and post-).
	--	R-L	Decrement (pre- and post-).
	&	R-L	Address of (pointer).
	*	R-L	Dereference (pointer).
	sizeof	R-L	Size (in bytes).
3	*.	L-R	C dereference.
	->	L-R	C dereference.
4	*	L-R	Multiplication.
	/	L-R	Division.
	%	L-R	Modulus.
5	+	L-R	Addition.
	-	L-R	Subtraction.
6	>>	L-R	Right shift.
	<<	L-R	Left shift.
7	>	L-R	Greater than.
	>=	L-R	Greater than or equal to.
	<	L-R	Less than.
	<=	L-R	Less than or equal to.
8	==	L-R	Equal to.
	!=	L-R	Not equal to.
9	&	L-R	Bitwise AND.

Note: L-R indicates left to right associativity. R-L indicates right to left associativity.

Level	Operator	Associativity	Operation
10	|	L-R	Bitwise OR.
11	&&	L-R	Logical AND.
12	||	L-R	Logical OR.
13	?:	R-L	Conditional.
14	=	R-L	Assignment.
	+=	R-L	Assign sum.
	-=	R-L	Assign difference.
	*=	R-L	Assign product.
	/=	R-L	Assign quotient.
	%=	R-L	Assign modulus.
	&=	R-L	Assign bitwise AND.
	|=	R-L	Assign bitwise OR.
	>>=	R-L	Assign right shift.
	<<=	R-L	Assign left shift.

Appendix D

Binary, Decimal, and Hexadecimal Numbers

Number Bases

Our system of counting is based on the number 10. The most likely reason for that is that we have 10 fingers and 10 toes. In a base-10 number system, which is also called a decimal number system, we count

$$0\ 1\ 2\ 3\ 4\ 5\ 6\ 7\ 8\ 9$$

From there we start over. The number ten is represented by

$$10$$

which is one ten and no ones. The number eleven is

$$11$$

which means one ten plus one one. Twelve is one ten and two ones. We continue counting in this manner until we reach 99, which is nine tens and nine ones. Then we write

$$100$$

which is equal to one hundred, zero tens, and zero ones. So the number 256 is two hundreds, five tens, and six ones. Another way to write this is

$$2 \times 100 + 5 \times 10 + 6 \times 1$$

or

$$2 \times 10^2 + 5 \times 10^1 + 6 \times 10^0$$

Any number to the zero power is always equal to one.

The binary number system, which is based on the number 2 instead of 10, works the same way. In fact, all number systems of any base work in this manner. In binary, we count

$$0\ 1$$

That's all the digits that are available in base 2. To represent the number two, we write

$$10$$

which is one two and no ones. The other way to write it is

$$1 \times 2^1 + 0 \times 2^0$$

To represent three, we use

$$11$$

which equals

$$1 \times 2^1 + 1 \times 2^0$$

In this way, any number we can represent with base 10 can be represented in base 2. Table D.1 shows the numbers 0 through 20 in binary and decimal.

TABLE D.1 Binary and Decimal Numbers

Binary	Decimal
0	0
1	1
10	2
11	3
100	4
101	5
110	6
111	7
1000	8
1001	9
1010	10
1011	11
1100	12
1101	13
1110	14
1111	15
10000	16
10001	17
10010	18
10011	19
10100	20

Base 16, which is also called hexadecimal, requires more digits than base 10. We use the symbols 0–9 to represent the numbers zero through nine. However, in base 16, the number 10 represents sixteen, not ten. Therefore, we must have a way to represent the numbers ten through fifteen. To do this, we use the letters A through F. So the number twenty-six in base 16 is written as 1A. Another way to write the value 1A is

$$1 \times 16^1 + 10 \times 16^0$$

which is the same as 16 + 10, or twenty-six. Table D.2 contains the numbers 0 through 32 in hexadecimal and decimal.

TABLE D.2 Hexadecimal and Decimal Numbers

Hexadecimal	Decimal
0	0
1	1
2	2
3	3
4	4
5	5
6	6
7	7

(continued on next page)

Hexadecimal	Decimal
8	8
9	9
A	10
B	11
C	12
D	13
E	14
F	15
10	16
11	17
12	18
13	19
14	20
15	21
16	22
17	23
18	24
19	25
1A	26
1B	27
1C	28
1D	29
1E	30
1F	31
20	32

Converting Between Bases

Because the binary, hexadecimal, and decimal number systems are commonly used in C programs, C programmers must be able to convert numbers from any of these number systems to any of the others.

Converting Any Base to Decimal

Because we're so used to base 10, converting binary or hexadecimal numbers to decimal is straightforward. We've already seen how it's done.

Suppose we want to convert the binary number 10011 to its decimal equivalent. The conversion is performed by writing the number as

$$1 \times 2^4 + 0 \times 2^3 + 0 \times 2^2 + 1 \times 2^1 + 1 \times 2^0$$

which gives

$$16 + 0 + 0 + 2 + 1$$

or 19. If we think our reader might be unsure about which base a number is in, we write the base number as a subscript. So 19 in base 10 is like this

$$19_{10}$$

This same method of conversion works for any number base. For example, to convert the hexadecimal number A23B1 to decimal, we write it as

$$A \times 16^4 + 2 \times 16^3 + 3 \times 16^2 + B \times 16^1 + 1 \times 16^0$$

Because the hexadecimal numbers A and B are 10 and 11 in decimal, we can rewrite this as

$$10 \times 16^4 + 2 \times 16^3 + 3 \times 16^2 + 11 \times 16^1 + 1 \times 16^0$$

If we work out the powers of 16, the result is

$$10 \times 65{,}536 + 2 \times 4{,}096 + 3 \times 256 + 11 \times 16 + 1 \times 1$$

or

$$655{,}360 + 8{,}192 + 768 + 176 + 1$$

This equals 664,497 in base 10.

Converting Decimal to Binary

Converting decimal numbers to binary or hexadecimal takes a bit more work, but there's a handy shortcut for doing it. I call this method "upside down division."

To demonstrate this technique, we'll convert the number 55 into binary. The first step is to write the 55 inside an upside-down division sign, like this

$$\underline{|55}$$

Next, divide the 55 by 2 and put the answer underneath the upside-down division symbol. The remainder goes off to the right, in this manner

```
2 |55
  27   1
```

The largest integer number of times that 55 can be divided by 2 is 27, so that's what we write under the upside-down division symbol. However, 2 x 27 is 54. So when we divide 55 by 2, we get 27 with a remainder of 1. The 1 is written to the right of the 27.

To finish the conversion, just keep going. Divide 27 by 2, and write both the answer and remainder. This continues until we reach zero, as shown here.

```
2 |55
 2|27   1
 2|13   1
 2|6    1
 2|3    0
 2|1    1
   0    1
```

The answer is read in the remainder column from bottom to top. The number 55 in base 10 is 110111 in base 2. This can be confirmed by converting 110111 back to base 10, which gives

$$1 \times 2^5 + 1 \times 2^4 + 0 \times 2^3 + 1 \times 2^2 + 1 \times 2^1 + 1 \times 2^0$$

The result of this equation is

$$1 \times 32 + 1 \times 16 + 0 \times 8 + 1 \times 4 + 1 \times 2 + 1 \times 1$$

which equals 55 in base 10.

Converting Decimal to Hexadecimal

The upside-down division method can also be used to convert decimal numbers to other bases, such as base 16. However, instead of dividing by 2, divide by the base number.

For instance, when converting the decimal number 55 to base 16, the process looks like this

```
16|55
 16|3   7
    0   3
```

The number 55 in base 10 is 37 in base 16. Here's a longer example of converting decimal to hexadecimal.

```
16 | 48,265
   16 | 3,016   9
      16 | 188   8
         16 | 11   C
              0   B
```

48,265 divided by 16 is 3,016 with a remainder of 9. 3,016 divided by 16 is 188 with a remainder of 8. 188 divided by 16 is 11 with a remainder of 12. However, because we want the answer in hexadecimal, we write 12 as C. 11 divided by 16 is 0 with a remainder of 11. As with the 12, we want the 11 in hexadecimal, so we write the hexadecimal digit B. The decimal number 48,265 in hexadecimal is BC89.

Converting Binary to Hexadecimal

Converting binary numbers to hexadecimal is very straightforward. It takes four binary digits to make one hexadecimal digit. Table D.3 illustrates this relationship.

TABLE D.3 Binary and Hexadecimal Numbers

Binary	Hexadecimal
0000	0
0001	1
0010	2
0011	3
0100	4
0101	5
0110	6
0111	7
1000	8
1001	9
1010	A
1011	B
1100	C
1101	D
1110	E
1111	F

Table D.3 counts from 0 to 15 in both binary and hexadecimal. All of the binary numbers are in groups of four digits. They contain leading zeros where needed. The leading zeros do not change the value of the number.

When converting the binary number 110001010101001 to hexadecimal, begin by collecting the binary digits into groups of four from right to left. This gives

110 0010 1010 1001

Notice that the leftmost group only has three digits. To fix that, we just add a leading zero to make it four. When we do, we get

0110 0010 1010 1001

The next step is to loop up each individual digit in Table D.3. It is a good idea to memorize this table as rapidly as possible. Developers do these conversions throughout their careers.

As Table D.3 shows, the binary digits 0110 is 6 in hexadecimal. If we loop up each digit, the complete conversion will be

```
0110 0010 1010 1001
  6    2    A    9
```

Therefore, the binary number 110001010101001 in hexadecimal is 62A9.

Converting Hexadecimal to Binary

Changing numbers from hexadecimal to binary is even easier. This is esp‹
have memorized Table D.3. Suppose you want to convert the hexadecimal n‹
binary. The digit A is 1010 in binary. The hexadecimal digit 4 is 0100. B is 1‹
0101. Put them together for the final result of 1010010010110101. That's all the‹

EXERCISES

1. Convert the decimal number 10 to binary and hexadecimal.

2. Convert the binary number 100000001001 to decimal and hexadecimal.

3. Convert the hexadecimal number ABCDEF to binary and decimal.

4. Convert the decimal number 2048 to binary and hexadecimal.

5. Convert the binary number 1111111101 to decimal and hexadecimal.

6. Convert the hexadecimal number 10AF22 to binary and decimal.

7. Convert the decimal number 88 to binary and hexadecimal.

8. Convert the binary number 1010101010101010 to decimal and hexadecimal.

9. Convert the hexadecimal number 1F01 to binary and decimal.

10. Convert the decimal number 332,299 to binary and hexadecimal.

11. Convert the hexadecimal number 30AE20C to binary and decimal.

12. Convert the binary number 111001101 to decimal and hexadecimal.

13. Convert the decimal number 4,096 to binary and hexadecimal.

14. Convert the hexadecimal number 1000 to binary and decimal.

15. Convert the decimal number 1,000 to binary and hexadecimal.

16. Convert the binary number 1000 to decimal and hexadecimal.

17. Convert the hexadecimal number 512 to decimal and binary.

18. Convert the binary number 1101000100101110111110010111 to decimal and hexadecimal.

19. Convert the decimal number 64 to binary and hexadecimal.

20. Convert the hexadecimal number 2048 to binary and decimal.